Adobe® InDesign® cs
Bible

Adobe® InDesign® CS Bible

Galen Gruman

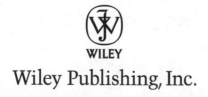

WILEY

Wiley Publishing, Inc.

Adobe® InDesign® CS Bible

Published by
Wiley Publishing, Inc.
10475 Crosspoint Boulevard
Indianapolis, IN 46256
www.wiley.com

Copyright © 2004 by Wiley Publishing, Inc., Indianapolis, Indiana

Published simultaneously in Canada

Library of Congress Control Number is available from the publisher.

ISBN: 0-7645-4227-3

Manufactured in the United States of America

10 9 8 7 6 5 4 3 2 1

1O/QT/RR/QT/IN

About the Author

Galen Gruman is principal at The Zango Group, an editorial and marketing consulting firm, and senior editorial associate at BayCreative, a creative consultancy, as well as editorial director at EmergeMedia, publisher of *IT Wireless*. He has also been editor of *Macworld* and *M-Business*, executive editor of *Upside*, West Coast bureau chief of *Computerworld*, and vice president of content for ThirdAge.com. He is coauthor of 13 other books on desktop publishing. Gruman led one of the first successful conversions of a national magazine to desktop publishing in 1986 and has covered publishing technology since then for several publications, including the trade weekly *InfoWorld*, for which he began writing in 1986, and *Macworld*, whose staff he joined in 1991. Originally a newspaper reporter in Los Angeles, Gruman got bit by the production-technology bug in 1979 and hasn't recovered.

Credits

Acquisitions Editor
Mike Roney

Project Editor
Elizabeth Kuball

Technical Editor
Jonathan Woolson

Editorial Manager
Rev Mengle

Vice President & Executive Group Publisher
Richard Swadley

Vice President and Executive Publisher
Bob Ipsen

Vice President and Publisher
Joseph B. Wikert

Executive Editorial Director
Mary Bednarek

Project Coordinator
Regina Snyder

Graphics and Production Specialists
Amanda Carter
Jennifer Click
Joyce Haughey
Michael Kruzil
Clint Lahnen
Kristin McMullan
Barry Offringa
Lynsey Osborn

Quality Control Technicians
Andy Hollandbeck
Brian H. Walls

Proofreading and Indexing
TECHBOOKS Production Services

To my brothers, Darius and Stephen, who doggedly pursue their goals.

Foreword: InDesign's Impact

When Adobe came up with the beta code name K2 for the very first version of InDesign, I was intrigued by the choice. You see K2 is also the name of the second highest mountain range in the world and is considered by many climbers to be the ultimate climb of a lifetime. So how do these two entities relate? Well, when K2 evolved into Adobe InDesign, which made a slow but persistent entry into the marketplace, many concerns were raised. Version 1.0 was considered too risky and unstable to use, just as the K2 mountain peak was once considered too risky to climb. Flash-forward to 2003 — as K2 is well-noted as the ultimate mountain climb, InDesign CS has been penned as the ultimate page-layout application.

The original marketing campaign for Adobe InDesign was "Innovative, Interesting, Inspirational, Insightful, Incredible, Ineffable, and Ingenious." And then when Adobe asked "Are you *in?*" I responded, "Indubitably."

Not only has the release of Adobe InDesign made a major impact on the publishing industry, it has also made a huge impact on my life. If it weren't for Adobe's development of a new page-layout application, I never would have gotten the opportunity to develop and moderate the "Page Layout in Transition" session held at the Seybold SF conference in 1999. This session led to the "The Seybold Shootout: QuarkXPress versus Adobe InDesign" session, which I have developed and moderated every year since the release of InDesign.

I have been involved in many aspects of the print and publishing industry over the last 20 years. I started out as a typographer, which in 1984 was a fancy word for *typesetter*. I loved the typographic control I could exercise within my compositions. Today, I consult with publishers throughout the country to help them solve production challenges, train their staffs, and stay current in publishing technology. After the demise of photo-typesetting, I thought I would never have the true pleasure of setting type again. Adobe InDesign has given me back the typographic control that I so desire. Thank you, Adobe, for reincarnating the typographer in me.

The publishing industry, just as every other industry, deserves a choice in the production tools that we use to build and complete our projects. InDesign gives you that choice with a robust and complete desktop publishing application. Adobe has listened to its customers just as Kevin Costner listened to the voice in *Field of*

Dreams. The voice told Kevin Costner's character to "Build it, and they will come." We said to Adobe, "Build it, and we will buy it." Well, Adobe built it and I, along with many others, bought it. It was the best software purchase I ever made, no doubt about it. You will feel the same way.

When author Galen Gruman asked me to write a foreword for this book, I did not hesitate a single moment before agreeing. Galen's industry experience has made him a reliable source of information, and he's well respected and trusted. I have read several of his books and magazine articles, which are lively, fun, and educational to the reader. Congratulations, Galen!

Shellie L. Hall
Principal
DuckType

Foreword: The InDesign Mission

In the foreword to Galen Gruman's original *Adobe InDesign Bible,* Adobe InDesign engineering manager Stacy Molitor talked about the InDesign mission in terms of its modern architecture and code base. Four years later, our direction for developing the product remains the same: Develop an application that is responsive to customers' needs, that is extensible for external developers, and that can serve as a foundation for future development. InDesign CS is all that and so much more. Today, the engineering magic that is InDesign translates into new opportunities of creativity, design, and innovation for the InDesign user.

Having said that, the test of a professional tool is how dependable is it when crunch time comes and the final product needs to be delivered to the client or print-service provider. InDesign delivers as a workhorse tool that won't let you down when minutes count. Usability, dependability, and innovation — these are words that have driven the development mission of InDesign.

Now let's talk about what makes the latest release of InDesign so special. In response to customer requests to have InDesign let them work faster and smarter, Adobe has enhanced InDesign's operational ease and flexibility: Set up your workspace to maximize efficiency for different design tasks and then save those palette locations as named workspaces that you can switch to at any moment. Dock palettes in collapsible bays along the window edge, so critical tools are instantly available when you need them and out of the way when you don't.

For QuarkXPress users coming to InDesign for the first time: Welcome. Our goal is to make your transition as smooth as possible. InDesign CS opens QuarkXPress 3.3–4 documents directly, so you can bring your valuable legacy documents with you. You can also select the QuarkXPress-compatible set of keyboard shortcuts, so InDesign will work with the shortcuts you're accustomed to using. Add these to InDesign's integration with your other Adobe tools: How much easier could we make it?

For print-service providers, we know you work in competitive businesses on the front lines of design. The success of your shop depends on having efficient workflows that consistently deliver what customers need no matter how much they're pushing the limits. InDesign is built to be a precise, reliable production workhorse that outputs pages beautifully, day in and day out. Every aspect of the printing interface incorporates the real-world knowledge and experience shared with us by thousands of printers worldwide. InDesign even exceeds your expectations with features like the Separations Preview and Transparency Flattener palettes, designed specifically to help print-service providers prevent costly mistakes before they appear on film or press.

For our PageMaker users, InDesign is packed with innovative features that top your wish list, including multiple undo/redo, outstanding typography controls, character styles, easy-to-edit drop shadows and other transparency effects, flexible table creation, editable gradients, custom corner styles, arrowheads, and direct export of Adobe PDF files. It's packed with familiar PageMaker features that are notably enhanced. Yes, InDesign has a story editor. Yes, InDesign generates tables of contents, indexes, and other elements of long documents. And yes, you'll even find your old friend, the Control palette.

No matter who you are or what part of the publishing industry you work in, InDesign CS is a solid choice. And you are not alone in this transition. Since the inception of InDesign 1.0 in 1999, there are thousands of service providers around the world supporting InDesign files. And every day, more and more publishers, large and small alike, are making the switch to an InDesign-based workflow. You can feel comfortable knowing that you are using a widely accepted tool from a company you can trust.

Best of all, Adobe InDesign integrates tightly with the applications you already use for your design work. Adobe Photoshop, Illustrator, and Acrobat files can be placed into your documents without any need to flatten, resave, or convert them. Talk about productivity and time savings. And now, InDesign is part of the larger Adobe Creative Suite, which brings the ultimate in integration and productivity to Adobe creative products. This Bible works for InDesign whether used by itself or within the Creative Suite.

Adobe has a long track record of listening to our customers and incorporating what you need into our software. As a professional design and layout application, we know Adobe InDesign demonstrates this commitment in every way. Each version has incorporated input from thousands worldwide, and each version has leapfrogged the competition with its innovation, power, and responsiveness — whether to new operating systems or new design requirements. We hope you enjoy using InDesign CS.

B. Mark Hilton
Director, Product Management
Creative Professional Products
Adobe Systems, Inc.

Preface

I've spent nearly 20 years working with page-layout software, heading one of the first efforts by a national magazine to go from traditional tools to electronic ones in 1986. Over the years, I've also reviewed all the page-layout tools for various magazines, including *InfoWorld* and *Macworld*. For the first five years, I felt that Ventura Publisher was the best page-layout program available, and in the 1990s, I judged QuarkXPress to be the best. During that time, I saw PageMaker sink into irrelevance because of neglect by Adobe and, more recently, I saw QuarkXPress follow a similar path of complacency. So I was excited in 1999 by the first version of InDesign but disappointed that it had several drawbacks that could have been avoided considering it came so many years after Ventura Publisher, PageMaker, and QuarkXPress had addressed most users' needs. The promise was strong, but the product was still very rough around the edges. Users saw that and didn't widely adopt InDesign. Version 2 corrected many of the deficiencies, and user adoption of InDesign accordingly skyrocketed in 2002.

Four years after that first version of InDesign was released, my disappointment is gone. Adobe has made InDesign CS — version 3 of the program — as strong as — and in many cases stronger than — QuarkXPress. Although QuarkXPress does a few things that InDesign does not, there are more things that InDesign does that QuarkXPress does not.

It's been a good decade — there has been serious competition in the desktop publishing world, and InDesign is clearly the ascending tool for publishers today. Whether InDesign supplants QuarkXPress is irrelevant — what matters is that layout artists have an incredibly powerful tool in the form of InDesign to let them deliver on their creative aspirations and vision. I can only hope that this book helps you achieve those ambitions.

Acknowledgments

Freelance writers and layout artists John Cruise and Kelly Kordes Anton contributed significantly to the previous edition of this book, and this edition incorporates many of those contributions.

Thanks to the development and product marketing staff at Adobe for providing early versions of the InDesign CS software and listening to suggestions on making it even better. And thanks to the editors and production staff at Wiley Publishing for their efforts in making this book possible, especially to project editor Elizabeth Kuball and technical reviewer Jonathan Woolson for their improvements to the book's content and clarity.

The www.INDDcentral.com Web site and its contents are copyrighted by The Zango Group.

The Adobe Open Options user guides and FAQs were designed by BayCreative LLC and copyrighted by Adobe Systems Inc. The *II Wireless Essential Products Guides* was designed by Galen Gruman and copyrighted by EmergeMedia Inc. The YMCA of Oakville brochure examples were designed by Branimir Zlamalik of Gb.com and copyrighted by the YMCA of Oakville, Ontario. The Jackson County (Ore.) Library Foundation brochure is designed and copyrighted by designer Shawn Busse of Kinesis. The *In the Footsteps of Paul* workbook is designed and copyrighted by Ronald Lanham. The Zango Group marketing collateral examples are copyrighted by The Zango Group. Original photographs are copyrighted by their photographers.

All materials are used by permission.

Contents at a Glance

Foreword: InDesign's Impact ix
Foreword: The InDesign Mission xi
Preface xiii
Acknowledgments xv
Introduction xxxix

InDesign QuickStart 1

Part I: Welcome to InDesign 21
Chapter 1: What InDesign Can Do for You 23
Chapter 2: A Tour of InDesign 31
Chapter 3: Getting InDesign Ready to Go 77

Part II: Document Fundamentals 119
Chapter 4: Creating, Opening, and Saving Documents 121
Chapter 5: Working with Pages 139
Chapter 6: Working with Layers 155
Chapter 7: Creating Layout Standards 169
Chapter 8: Defining Colors and Gradients 197
Chapter 9: Book Publishing 221

Part III: Object Fundamentals 243
Chapter 10: Adding Text Frames, Picture Frames, and Lines . . . 245
Chapter 11: Manipulating Frames and Lines 257
Chapter 12: Orchestrating Objects 285
Chapter 13: Timesaving Techniques 299

Part IV: Text Fundamentals 307
Chapter 14: Preparing Text Files for Import 309
Chapter 15: Working with Text 325
Chapter 16: Flowing Text through a Document 355
Chapter 17: Specifying Character Attributes 373
Chapter 18: Specifying Paragraph Attributes 393
Chapter 19: Creating Special Text Formatting 413
Chapter 20: Setting Up Style Sheets 441
Chapter 21: Setting Up Tabs and Tables 459

Part V: Graphics Fundamentals 481

Chapter 22: Preparing Picture Files for Import 483
Chapter 23: Importing Pictures 497
Chapter 24: Modifying Imported Pictures 507
Chapter 25: Special Effects for Pictures 525
Chapter 26: Drawing Free-Form Shapes and Curved Paths 547
Chapter 27: Modifying Shapes and Paths 563
Chapter 28: Treating Text as Artwork 581

Part VI: Output Fundamentals 591

Chapter 29: Preparing for Color Prepress 593
Chapter 30: Preparing for Printing 611
Chapter 31: Printing Techniques 627
Chapter 32: Creating Output Files 657

Part VII: Cross-Media Fundamentals 679

Chapter 33: Interactive Document Setup 681
Chapter 34: Working with XML 695

Part VIII: Going Beyond the Program 705

Chapter 35: Working with Others 707
Chapter 36: Using Plug-Ins 719
Chapter 37: Using Scripts 725

Part IX: Introduction to Publishing 739

Chapter 38: The Publishing Environment 741
Chapter 39: Layout Theory and Practice 759
Chapter 40: Typography Theory and Practice 783
Chapter 41: Using Special Characters 799
Chapter 42: Color Fundamentals 809

Part X: Appendixes **817**
Appendix A: Installing or Upgrading InDesign 819
Appendix B: What's New in InDesign CS 823
Appendix C: Switching from QuarkXPress 835
Appendix D: Switching from PageMaker 851
Appendix E: Switching to Mac OS X 859
Appendix F: Using Adobe InCopy 873
Appendix G: The InDesign Central Web Site 881
Appendix H: Shortcuts Cheat Sheet 883

Index 895

Contents

Foreword: InDesign's Impact ix

Foreword: The InDesign Mission xi

Preface xiii

Acknowledgments xv

Introduction xxxix

InDesign QuickStart 1

   Creating a New Document 2
   Working with Frames 4
   Working with Text 7
   Working with Lines 13
   Working with Pictures 14
   Creating Colors 16
   Applying Colors 18
   Printing a Composite 19

Part I: Welcome to InDesign   21

Chapter 1: What InDesign Can Do for You 23

   Discovering the InDesign Approach 26
      The frame-based metaphor 26
      The free-form metaphor 27
   Understanding Global and Local Control 27
      Knowing which tools to use 28
      Specifying measurement values 28
   Summary 30

Chapter 2: A Tour of InDesign 31

   The InDesign Application Folder 31
      The Presets folder 32
      The Plug-ins folder 32
      The Required folder 33
   Exploring the Document Window 33
      Title bar 33
      Zero point 36
      Scroll bars 37

Pasteboard, pages, and guides 37
Show/Hide Structure button 38
View Percentage field and pop-up menu 38
Page controls 38
Using Tools 40
Using Tool Tips and keyboard shortcuts 40
Opening and closing the Tools palette 42
Selecting tools 42
Tool definitions 43
Color buttons 52
View buttons 53
Working with Palettes and Panes 53
Panes versus palettes 54
Managing palettes 54
Using panes 57
Checking out the panes 58
Reviewing Menu Commands 66
InDesign menu 66
File menu 67
Edit menu 68
Layout menu 69
Type menu 69
Object menu 70
Table menu 71
View menu 72
Window menu 73
Help menu 74
Contextual menus 75
Summary 75

Chapter 3: Getting InDesign Ready to Go 77

Working with Preferences Files 77
InDesign Defaults file 77
Presets folder 78
Setting Preferences 78
General preferences 80
Text preferences 82
Composition preferences 85
Units & Increments preferences 87
Grids preferences 90
Guides & Pasteboard preferences 92
Dictionary preferences 94
Spelling preferences 96
Story Editor Display preferences 96
Display Performance preferences 98
Saved Files preferences 99
Updates preferences 100

Customizing Keyboard Shortcuts 100
    Using and modifying default shortcuts 103
    Using and modifying QuarkXPress shortcuts 104
    Viewing and printing shortcuts 105
Modifying Defaults for Documents, Text, and Objects 105
    Document defaults 105
    Text defaults 107
    Object defaults 108
Modifying Defaults for Views 109
Adding Default Colors and Styles 110
Reverting Preferences and Defaults 111
Changing Views 111
    Zooming and scrolling 112
    Object display options 116
Opening Multiple Document Windows 116
Summary 117

Part II: Document Fundamentals   119

Chapter 4: Creating, Opening, and Saving Documents 121

Before You Begin 121
Setting Up a New Publication 122
Opening Documents and Templates 127
    Opening documents versus opening templates 129
    Converting documents created with other programs 130
    Importing text files 132
    Recovering a document after a crash or power failure 132
Saving Documents and Templates 133
    Saving documents versus saving templates 134
    Knowing how to not save changes 135
    Saving files in other formats 136
Summary 136

Chapter 5: Working with Pages 139

Working with Multipage Documents 139
    Adding pages 140
    Copying pages 142
    Deleting pages 142
    Moving pages 142
    Creating island spreads 143
Working with Page Numbers 144
    Entering page references in text 144
    Dividing a document into sections 146
    Removing a section 148

Navigating Documents and Pages 148
    Navigating with the Pages pane 148
    Using the Navigator pane 149
Adjusting Page Layouts and Objects 150
Summary 153

Chapter 6: Working with Layers 155

Understanding Layers 155
Creating Layers 158
    Creating a layer 159
    Customizing layers 159
Working with Objects on Layers 161
    The active layer 161
    Selecting objects on layers 161
    Placing objects on layers 162
    Moving objects to different layers 163
Manipulating Layers 163
    Selecting layers 164
    Hiding layers 164
    Locking objects on layers 164
    Rearranging layers 165
    Combining layers 165
    Deleting layers 166
Summary 167

Chapter 7: Creating Layout Standards 169

Creating and Applying Master Pages 170
    The Pages pane 171
    Creating a new master page 174
    Laying out a master page 177
    Applying a master page to document pages 179
    Modifying master items on document pages 181
Using Templates 182
Storing Objects in Libraries 184
    Adding and deleting library objects 187
    Copying library objects onto document pages 190
Using Ruler Guides and Grids 190
    Ruler guides 191
    Working with the baseline grid 194
    Working with the document grid 195
Summary 196

Chapter 8: Defining Colors and Gradients 197

Defining Colors 198
    Creating colors 199
    Creating tints 203
    Creating mixed colors 204

Editing Colors and Tints 207
Deleting and Copying Swatches 208
    Deleting swatches 208
    Copying swatches 209
Spot Color versus Process Color 210
Working with Color Pictures 212
    Working with EPS files 212
    Working with TIFF files 213
    Working with PDF files 213
Working with Gradients 214
    Creating gradients 214
    Creating unnamed gradients 216
    Editing gradients 217
Applying Colors 219
Summary 220

Chapter 9: Book Publishing **221**
Managing Multiple Documents with Books 221
    Planning your book 222
    Creating and opening books 222
    Adding chapters to books 224
    Working with style sources 224
    Opening and editing chapters 225
    Understanding book pane status reports 225
    Synchronizing chapter formatting 226
    Printing chapters and books 227
    Handling chapters with sections 228
Creating Tables of Contents 229
    Planning a TOC 229
    Defining a TOC 230
    Generating a TOC 233
Indexing Documents and Books 234
    Choosing an indexing style 235
    Using the Index pane 235
Summary 242

Part III: Object Fundamentals   **243**

Chapter 10: Adding Text Frames, Picture Frames, and Lines **245**
Creating a Text Frame 246
Deleting Objects 249
Creating a Graphics Frame 249
Modifying a Frame's Shape 252
Drawing Straight Lines 254
Summary 256

Chapter 11: Manipulating Frames and Lines 257

Selecting Objects 258
   Selecting overlapping objects 259
   Selecting multiple objects 261
   Deselecting objects 262
Moving, Resizing, and Deleting Objects 262
   Moving objects 262
   Resizing objects 264
   Deleting objects 266
Adding Strokes, Fills, and Other Effects 266
   Adding strokes 267
   Creating custom strokes 272
   Adding fills 275
   Adding special effects to corners 275
   Performing other transformations on frames 276
Modifying Lines 283
Summary 283

Chapter 12: Orchestrating Objects 285

Stacking Objects 286
Combining Objects into a Group 289
   Groups within groups 290
   Selecting objects within groups 291
   Ungrouping 291
Nesting Objects within Frames 291
   Nesting frames within other frames 292
Creating Inline Frames 293
   Creating an inline frame with the Paste command 294
   Creating an inline frame with the Place command 295
Locking Objects 296
Summary 297

Chapter 13: Timesaving Techniques 299

Creating Copies of Objects 299
Copying Objects between Documents 301
Aligning and Distributing Objects 302
Positioning Objects Precisely with Guides 304
Summary 306

Part IV: Text Fundamentals   307

Chapter 14: Preparing Text Files for Import 309

Determining Where to Format Documents 309
Importing Text Files 311
   Preserving special features in text files 312
   Avoiding text-file pitfalls 318

Using Tagged Text 319
    Working with exported Tagged Text files 319
    Using Tagged Text for database publishing 321
Summary 322

Chapter 15: Working with Text 325

Adding Text 325
    Typing text 325
    Pasting text 326
    Dragging and dropping text 327
    Importing text 328
    Exporting text 331
Editing Text 332
    Navigating text 332
    Highlighting text 333
    Cutting, copying, and pasting text 333
    Deleting and replacing text 334
    Undoing text edits 334
    Using the Story Editor 334
Searching and Replacing 335
    Searching and replacing text 335
    Finding special characters 337
    Searching and replacing formatting 340
Checking Spelling 342
    Specifying the text to check 342
    Using the Check Spelling dialog box 343
    Working with multiple languages 344
Customizing the Spelling and Hyphenation Dictionaries 345
    Customizing the spelling dictionary 346
    Customizing hyphenation points 347
    Setting spelling and hyphenation dictionary preferences 349
Adjusting Text Appearance in Text Frames 350
    Setting text frame options 350
    Scaling text with the mouse 353
Summary 354

Chapter 16: Flowing Text through a Document 355

Creating Text Frames 356
    Creating text frames on master pages 357
    Drawing additional text frames 359
Getting the Text 361
    Importing text files 361
    Handling word processor style sheets 362
Threading Text Frames 364
    Threading frames manually 364
    Threading frames semi-automatically 366
    Threading frames and adding pages automatically 367
    Breaking and rerouting threads 368

Adjusting Columns 368
    Specifying columns in master frames 369
    Adjusting columns in text frames 369
    Placing rules between columns 370
Summary 371

Chapter 17: Specifying Character Attributes **373**

Working with Character Formats 374
Changing Font Family, Type Style, and Size 376
    Changing font family and type style 377
    Changing font size 379
Applying Other Character Formats 380
    Horizontal Scale and Vertical Scale 381
    Baseline Shift 382
    Skew (false italic) 382
    Language 383
    All Caps and Small Caps 384
    Superscript and Subscript 384
    Underline and Strikethrough 385
    Ligatures 385
    OpenType options 386
    No Break 388
Leaving Space between Characters and Lines 389
    Kerning 390
    Tracking 391
    Leading 391
Summary 392

Chapter 18: Specifying Paragraph Attributes **393**

Leading 396
Controlling Alignment and Indents 396
    Alignment 396
    Indents 398
    Lock to Baseline Grid 398
Adding Space between Paragraphs 399
Adding Drop Caps 400
Controlling Hyphenation and Justification 401
    Manual hyphenation 402
    Automatic hyphenation 402
    Justifications controls 404
    Composing text 407
Setting Other Paragraph Formats 408
    Keep Options 408
    Paragraph Rules 409
Summary 411

Chapter 19: Creating Special Text Formatting 413

Indenting Text 413
    First-line indents 415
    Hanging indents 415
    Block indents 415
Adding Bullets and Formatting Lists 416
    Adding bullets or numerals 416
    Deciding on initial formatting for bullets and numerals 417
    Adding space between bullets or numerals 118
    Applying style sheets for numbered and bulleted lists 419
Adding Initial Caps 420
    Creating automatic drop caps 420
    Creating raised initial caps 422
    Converting text to outlines for initial caps 423
    Using graphics as initial caps 423
Labeling Paragraphs 423
Adding Professional Touches 426
    Reversing type out of its background 426
    Creating sidebars and pull quotes 428
    Formatting fractions 428
    Hanging punctuation 430
    Choosing and placing end-of-story markers 431
Applying Color to Text 432
Rotating Text 433
    Using the Rotation Angle field 434
    Using the Rotate tool 434
Scaling Text 435
Underline and Strikethrough Options 435
Drop Shadows and Feathering 437
    Drop shadows 437
    Feathering 438
Summary 439

Chapter 20: Setting Up Style Sheets 441

Creating and Applying Style Sheets 442
    Paragraph style sheets 442
    Character style sheets 447
Working with Nested Styles 449
Changing Style Sheets 452
    Modifying style sheets 452
    Modifying text that's been styled with a style sheet 453
    Unapplying style sheets 453
Importing Style Sheets 454
    Importing style sheets from InDesign documents 454
    Working with style sheets in imported text files 455
Summary 457

Chapter 21: Setting Up Tabs and Tables 459

Using the Tabs Pane 460
   Tab style buttons 462
   X (position) field 463
   Leader field 463
   Align On field 464
   Tab ruler 464
   Magnet icon 465
   Tabs pane menu 465
Creating Tables 465
   Creating a table 467
   Working with rows and columns 471
   Working with cells 472
Converting Tabs to Tables 478
Summary 479

Part V: Graphics Fundamentals   481

Chapter 22: Preparing Picture Files for Import 483

Determining Where to Format Documents 483
Preparing Graphics Files 484
   Graphics embedded in text files 484
   Issues with vector files 486
   Issues with bitmap formats 489
Identifying Color Issues 494
   Color systems 495
   Calibrated color 495
Summary 496

Chapter 23: Importing Pictures 497

Using the Place Command 498
Specifying Import Options 500
   Import options for bitmap pictures 501
   Import options for vector file formats 503
Knowing Other Ways to Import Pictures 504
   Copy and Paste 505
   Drag and Drop 505
   Adobe Illustrator files 505
Summary 506

Chapter 24: Modifying Imported Pictures 507

Making Basic Picture Modifications 507
   Cropping pictures 508
   Rotating, scaling, and shearing pictures 510

Using the Control Palette and the Transform Pane 512
    Changing an object's point of origin 514
    Repositioning a picture within its frame 514
    Scaling a picture 515
    Rotating a picture 515
    Skewing a picture 516
    Flipping a picture 516
Figuring Out the Fitting Commands 517
Modifying Bitmap Graphics versus Vector Graphics 518
    Applying color and tint to bitmap pictures 518
    Applying a tint to a picture 519
Managing Links to Imported Pictures 519
Summary 524

Chapter 25: Special Effects for Pictures **525**

Wrapping Text around Pictures 525
    The Text Wrap pane 526
    Changing the shape of a text wrap 532
Working with Clipping Paths 532
    Using a free-form shape to clip a picture 534
    Using InDesign's Clipping Path command 535
Using Transparency 537
Trying Other Special Effects 540
    Using text characters as graphics frames 541
    Using compound shapes as graphics frames 542
    Creating inline frames 542
    Slicing a picture with the Scissors tool 543
Applying Lighting Effects 544
    Drop shadows 544
    Feathering 545
Summary 546

Chapter 26: Drawing Free-Form Shapes and Curved Paths **547**

Finding Out All about Paths 548
    The properties of a path 548
    The anatomy of a path 551
Drawing Lines with the Pen Tool 553
    Straight and zigzag lines 553
    Curved lines 554
    Combining straight and curved segments 558
Drawing Free-Form Shapes 560
Summary 562

Chapter 27: Modifying Shapes and Paths **563**

Adding and Deleting Anchor Points 564
Modifying Segments 566
    Moving anchor points 566

Converting anchor points 567
Manipulating direction handles 569
Working with Open and Closed Paths 570
Extending an open path and connecting open paths 570
Closing an open path 571
Using the Scissors tool 572
Working with Compound Paths 573
Creating compound paths 575
Editing compound paths 575
Changing a subpath's direction 576
Splitting a compound path 577
Using the Pathfinder 577
Adding Corner Effects to Paths 578
Summary 579

Chapter 28: Treating Text as Artwork **581**

Applying Strokes to Type 581
Applying Color to Type 587
Converting Text into Graphics 588
Summary 590

Part VI: Output Fundamentals **591**

Chapter 29: Preparing for Color Prepress **593**

Calibrating Color 594
Setting up your system 595
Adjusting on-screen display 597
Using calibrations from other programs 599
Calibrating imported colors 600
Saving color-management preferences 601
Changing document color settings 601
Calibrating output 603
Working with Color Traps 603
Using choking versus spreading 603
Specifying trapping presets 606
Specifying trapping to pages 609
Summary 610

Chapter 30: Preparing for Printing **611**

Making Initial Preparations 611
Setting up Macintosh printers 612
Setting up Windows printers 613
Preflighting Your Document 615
Creating a Document Package 619

Dealing with Service Bureaus 622
    Sending documents versus output files 622
    Determining output settings 623
    Ensuring correct bleeds 624
    Sending oversized pages 625
Summary 625

Chapter 31: Printing Techniques 627

Selecting InDesign Printing Options 627
    General options 628
    The General pane 631
    The Setup pane 632
    The Marks and Bleeds pane 634
    The Output pane 637
    The Graphics pane 641
    The Color Management pane 643
    The Advanced pane 644
    The Summary pane 646
Printing to File 646
Working with Spot Colors and Separations 647
    The Ink Manager dialog box 647
    Process colors 649
    Color and separations preview 650
    Screen angles 651
Working with Transparency 652
Summary 655

Chapter 32: Creating Output Files 657

Selecting the Best Output Option 657
    Exporting to PDF 658
    Exporting to EPS 658
    Exporting to PostScript prepress 659
Creating PDF Files 661
    Exporting PDF files 661
    Using the Summary pane 671
    Printing to PDF format 672
Creating EPS Files 673
    The General pane 673
    The Advanced pane 676
Creating PostScript Prepress Files 677
Summary 678

Part VII: Cross-Media Fundamentals   679

Chapter 33: Interactive Document Setup 681

Using Hyperlinks in PDF and eBook Files 682
    Creating hyperlinks 682
    Modifying and deleting hyperlinks 685
Creating Bookmarks 686
Creating Page Actions 688
Playing Movies and Sound 691
    Move Options 692
    Sound Options 693
Summary 694

Chapter 34: Working with XML 695

Importing and Creating XML Tags 696
    Importing tags 696
    Creating tags 697
    Mapping tags and styles 697
Applying Tags 698
Taking Advantage of Other XML Options 700
Exporting XML Files 701
Summary 703

Part VIII: Going Beyond the Program   705

Chapter 35: Working with Others 707

Sharing with Other Users 708
    Where InDesign stores what 708
    Preference files 709
    Color definitions 709
    Style sheets 710
    Spelling dictionaries 710
    Graphics and text files 711
    Libraries 711
    Templates 711
    Master pages 712
Mixing Mac/Windows Environments 713
    InDesign differences 713
    Platform differences 715
    Transfer methods 717
Summary 718

Chapter 36: Using Plug-Ins 719

Using the Default Plug-Ins 719
Purchasing Special-Purpose Plug-ins 720

Knowing How Plug-Ins Work within InDesign 721
Setting Plug-In Preferences 722
Summary 724

Chapter 37: Using Scripts 725

Using Scripts 726
Exploring JavaScript 728
Exploring AppleScript 729
Learning the language 729
What you need to write and run scripts 730
Locating more AppleScript tools 731
Exploring VBA 731
Learning the language 732
What you need to write and run scripts 733
Creating and Running Scripts 734
Writing simple scripts 734
Labeling items 736
Writing conditional scripts 736
Summary 738

Part IX: Introduction to Publishing 739

Chapter 38: The Publishing Environment 741

Choosing the Right Hardware 741
The computer 741
Storage capacity 742
Connectivity 744
The Mac/PC connection 744
The network connection 745
The Internet connection 746
Input and output devices 747
Getting the Essential Software 749
Working with Fonts 750
Procuring fonts 750
Installing fonts through the operating system 753
Using a font manager and font utilities 755
Summary 757

Chapter 39: Layout Theory and Practice 759

Layout Terms 759
Layout tools 759
Design elements 761
Image manipulation 762
Seven Basic Rules of Good Design 762
Rule #1: Keep an idea file 763
Rule #2: Plan your document 763
Rule #3: Keep it simple 764

Rule #4: Leave some white space 764
Rule #5: Don't use every bell and whistle 764
Rule #6: Make it look like what it is 765
Rule #7: Don't break Rule #6 765
Getting Started 765
Visualizing your layout 766
Sketching your layout on paper 766
Sketching your layout in InDesign 768
Imitating and Creating Good Designs 769
Avoiding formulas 769
Laying out ads and circulars 771
Creating newsletters 774
Working with magazines 777
Doing other cool stuff 779
Looking at common threads 780
Summary 781

Chapter 40: Typography Theory and Practice **783**

Identifying Terms 783
Characters 784
Typographic measurement units 786
Spacing 786
Paragraphs 788
Hyphenation 789
Using Typographic Color and Typefaces 790
Typographic color 790
The influence of typeface 790
Learning about Typefaces 791
Typeface variations 791
What's in a face? 793
A font is a typeface by any other name 793
Selecting the Right Typefaces 794
Defining a standard set 794
Some basic guidelines 794
Summary 797

Chapter 41: Using Special Characters **799**

Shortcuts for Symbols 801
Shortcuts for Foreign Characters 803
Summary 808

Chapter 42: Color Fundamentals **809**

Defining Color Terms 809
Understanding Process and Spot Color 811
Identifying methods of color printing 811
Mixing spot and process colors 811
Converting spot color to process color 812

Working with Color Models 812
Paper Variation Models 814
Summary 815

Part X: Appendixes   817

Appendix A: Installing or Upgrading InDesign 819

InDesign CS System Requirements 819
Installing InDesign CS 820
Upgrading from Prior Versions of InDesign 821

Appendix B: What's New in InDesign CS 823

InDesign Interface 823
   Operating-system interaction 823
   Presets and shortcuts 823
   Palettes and panes 824
   Preferences 825
Document and Object Functions 825
   Document settings 825
   Page actions 826
   Libraries and books 826
   File exchange 826
   Object selection 827
Text Functions 827
   Text editing and import 827
   Text frame modifications 827
   Text wrap 827
   Paragraph and character formatting 828
   Tables 828
   Glyphs and fonts 829
Color and Gradient Functions 829
   Colors 829
   Gradients 830
Graphics Functions 830
   Image editing 830
   Strokes and paths 830
Output Functions 831
   Presets 831
   Page options 831
   PDF export 831
   Color and image handling 831
   Font handling 832
Other Functions 832
   PDF and eBooks creation 832
   XML files 833
   Scripting 833

Appendix C: Switching from QuarkXPress 835

Opening QuarkXPress Documents 835
Switching from QuarkXPress 837
Converting Keyboard Shortcuts 839
    Document differences 841
    Working with objects rather than items 842
    Flowing text 843
    Editing text 843
    Formatting text 844
    Working with tables 845
    Working with graphics 846
    Manipulating pages 847
    Working with color 848
    Printing and output 849

Appendix D: Switching from PageMaker 851

Opening PageMaker Documents 851
Differences from PageMaker 852
    Using tools and setting preferences 853
    Working with objects rather than elements 853
    Working with text 854
    Working with graphics 856
    Manipulating pages 856
    Working with color 857

Appendix E: Switching to Mac OS X 859

Interface Issues 859
    Dock 860
    Common menus 861
    Folder views and navigation 862
Where Is Everything? 864
    Network connections and file sharing 865
    Printers 865
    Applications 866
    Fonts 866
Running Mac OS 9 Applications 867
Customizing Mac OS X 869
    Classic 870
    Dock 871
    Login Items 871
    My Account and Accounts 871
    Network and Sharing 871

Appendix F: Using Adobe InCopy **873**

   Using InCopy in InDesign 873
      Working with notes 874
      Working with other users 875
   Using InCopy Alone 877
      Story views 877
      Story checkout, check in, and saving 878
      Revisions tracking 879
      Special features 880

Appendix G: The InDesign Central Web Site **881**

Appendix H: Shortcuts Cheat Sheet **883**

Index 895

Introduction

Welcome to the *Adobe InDesign CS Bible* — your personal guide to a powerful, full-featured publishing program that offers precise but flexible control over all aspects of page design. My goal is to guide you each step of the way through the publishing process, showing you how to make Adobe's InDesign CS — also known as InDesign 3 — work for you. You'll also learn tips and tricks about publishing design that you can use in any document, whether it was created in InDesign or not.

Taking the best from the two schools of thought on desktop publishing, InDesign merges the highly structured approach of programs such as QuarkXPress and Corel Ventura Publisher with the more naturalistic approach of Adobe PageMaker, which InDesign all but replaced in 1999. Thus, InDesign offers a wide range of desktop-publishing capabilities for sophisticated designers who develop magazines, books, ads, and product brochures. It also gives the power of the press to individuals and groups who use the program's impressive set of publishing tools to communicate their thoughts, dreams, and philosophies.

Version CS of InDesign takes that strong basis and makes it even better, often in subtle ways meant to make the workflow process easier and more intuitive. InDesign was chock-full of features in its previous version, but the features could be hard to find and awkward to use because of a slavish mirroring of the Adobe Photoshop and Illustrator user interfaces. Although InDesign adheres strongly to that core Adobe interface, it's been tweaked to work more naturally for a layout artist's needs.

InDesign also lets you take advantage of electronic publishing. Not only can you produce high-quality, lively flyers, newsletters, magazines, and similar publications in InDesign, you can also create rich, colorful documents that can be viewed on the Web, distributed by CD, or sent directly to a printing press for faithful print reproduction.

In a nutshell, InDesign is meant to help those who educate, inform, and document the world in which we live. Join me in learning how to use this powerful program.

What This Book Offers

So, since InDesign comes with good documentation that is full of examples, why do you need this book? To see the bigger picture. Publishing design involves much more than understanding a particular program's tools — it involves knowing when, how, and, most important, *why* to use them. In this book, I help you realize the potential of InDesign by applying its tools to real-world publishing-design needs. I also identify any weaknesses and explain how to overcome them — something that vendor manuals rarely do.

Some desktop publishers have years of high-end creative, design-intensive experience. Others are just getting started in publishing, perhaps by producing simple newsletters or flyers to advertise a community event. Not a few are exploring the brave new world of Web publishing.

Desktop publishers fall into several classes:

✦ Designers new to InDesign but familiar with other desktop publishing software

✦ Designers familiar with print publishing but new to electronic publishing

✦ Experienced designers new to desktop technologies

✦ Novice designers new to desktop technologies

No matter which class you're in, you'll find that this book addresses your needs. You don't need a degree in design or ten years' experience producing national ad campaigns — you can use this book if you're responsible for developing and implementing the look of documents, whether a four-page company newsletter or a four-color billboard ad. The basic techniques and issues are the same for both ends of the spectrum. And this book, of course, covers in detail the specialized needs — such as table creation, image control, color output, and electronic publishing — of specialty designers. (If you're just learning such advanced techniques, be sure to read the sidebars that explain the underlying issues.) Regardless of your level of experience with desktop publishing, this book will help you use InDesign.

What distinguishes this book from the rest is that it does not attempt to substitute for the documentation that accompanies InDesign. Instead, it guides you through the *process* of publishing a document, regardless of whether that document is your first or your thousandth.

How to Read This Book

The *Adobe InDesign CS Bible* is made up of 42 chapters and 8 appendixes divided into 10 parts, in addition to the QuickStart that appears just before Part I begins. If you're a novice InDesign user but familiar with desktop publishing, I suggest you read the book in order, because the process of page design is presented in the typical publishing workflow. You first learn how (and why) to create basic pages, containers, placeholders, and templates; then you learn how to work with specific elements (such as text and graphics); and finally, you learn how to use special effects and deal with prepress issues (such as output control, image manipulation, trapping, and printing).

If you're experienced with InDesign, read the book in any order you want — pick those sections or chapters that cover the InDesign implementation issues you want to know more about. You should also find the exhaustive index a real aid in finding what you're looking for.

If you're new to publishing, be sure to start with Part IX: "Introduction to Publishing," which teaches novice publishers the basics. And experienced publishers should at least skim this part as well — you're likely to find new ideas and perspectives on how you approach your work.

Whether you're reading the book sequentially or nonsequentially, you'll find the many cross-references helpful. Publication design is ultimately successful because the result is more than the sum of its parts — and the tools used to create and implement your designs cannot be used in isolation. Because this is true, having one "right" order or grouping of content is impossible. The cross-references let you know where to get additional information when what you're seeking to understand or learn doesn't fit the way I've organized this book.

Following is a brief description of the parts you will find in the *Adobe InDesign CS Bible*.

InDesign QuickStart

This guide walks you through the creation of a document to give you a quick tour of the program, from creation to printing. It's a convenient way to see the main InDesign features in action and quickly get a sense of how they work.

Part I: Welcome to InDesign

This part walks you through the initial steps of using InDesign to create your publications. I give you a basic introduction to InDesign itself, explaining the concepts it uses in its layout approach. I also highlight what's special about InDesign.

Part II: Document Fundamentals

This part explains how to create the basic containers — documents, pages, and layers — of a publishing project and how to set the standards for your documents, from master pages, libraries, and templates to guides and colors. InDesign comes with a set of tools that lets you automate repetitive work, apply common elements to a range of pages, and customize page settings, among other capabilities. This part walks you through the ins and outs of all of them. You'll also learn how to use the book-publishing features meant to standardize the production of multichapter projects.

Part III: Object Fundamentals

This part explains how InDesign's frame and line tools work so you can create and manipulate layout objects. With these building blocks, you construct almost all the components in a layout, from the frame containers that hold text and pictures to original artwork you create in InDesign. You'll also learn how to move, group, copy, and lock such objects and how to automate repetitive object actions to save time.

Part IV: Text Fundamentals

This part shows you how to import and work with text files, including the application of typographic features to really jazz up your layout. You'll also learn how to create tables and how to set up style sheets to automate the application of typography to document text.

Part V: Graphics Fundamentals

This part discusses how to use InDesign to manipulate and work with pictures and images in your layout, whether imported from another program or created within InDesign. Although text carries the message, a picture is what gets your attention — and often can say more than any collection of words. This part helps you get the most out of your images in InDesign. It also shows you how you can use the tools in InDesign to create a variety of shapes that can be used as original artwork or as specialty containers for text and images.

Part VI: Output Fundamentals

This part walks you through the output steps of publishing. This part shows you what you need to be aware of as well as showing you how to output your documents for printing or for use in the Adobe Portable Document Format (PDF), which is often used for network- and CD-based documents, as well as for Web-based documents.

Part VII: Cross-Media Fundamentals

This part discusses how InDesign can help you create interactive documents — those that take advantage of multimedia files, page actions, and forms — that are distributed via the PDF format or as an eBook. You'll also learn the basics of working with XML, the structured content system widely used by Web-oriented content engines. InDesign can both create XML files and use XML files to turn templates into completed InDesign documents for automated publishing systems.

Part VIII: Going Beyond the Program

This part expands your horizons. Very few publishers work by themselves, and most have a whole raft of tools to work their miracles. The chapters in this part expose you to key insights in working beyond InDesign, covering workgroup issues, the use of plug-ins to add new capabilities, and the use of scripts to automate your work.

Part IX: Introduction to Publishing

This part is a quick tour of publishing fundamentals for new and experienced users alike. I cover the essential tools for a complete publishing environment, show you how to use special characters in your documents, define the terms used in publishing, and explain the basic principles to good layout, typography, and color usage.

Part X: Appendixes

The appendixes in this book take you through the ins and outs of how to install Adobe InDesign, what is new in version CS, how QuarkXPress and PageMaker users can more easily make the switch to InDesign, how to switch to Mac OS X (InDesign CS does not support Mac OS 9), and how to use the optional InCopy group-editing tools. You'll also find an appendix with all the shortcuts in one place, and another that previews the companion Web site www.INDDcentral.com.

Conventions Used in This Book

Before I begin showing you the ins and outs of InDesign, I need to spend a few minutes reviewing the terms and conventions used in this book.

InDesign commands

The InDesign commands that you select by using the program menus appear in this book in normal typeface. When you choose some menu commands, a related pull-down menu or a pop-up menu appears. If I describe a situation in which you need to select one menu and then choose a command from a secondary menu or list box, I use an arrow symbol. For example, "Choose Layout ⇨ Margins and Columns" means that you should choose the Margins and Columns command from the Layout menu.

Like most modern programs, InDesign has an interface feature that has proved to be quite popular called *tabbed panes*. This is a method of stuffing several dialog boxes into one dialog box. You see tabs, like those in file folders, and by clicking a tab, the pane of options for that tab comes to the front of the dialog box. You can even move tabs from one dialog box to another to create the arrangement that best suits your work style. In this book, I will tell you to go to the pane, which you do by clicking on the tab where the name of the pane is to display the pane. For example, "Go to the General pane" means click the General tab in the current dialog box.

Mouse conventions

Because you use a mouse to perform many functions in InDesign, you need to be familiar with the following terms and instructions. And, yes, when I say *mouse*, I also mean other pointing devices, such as trackballs and pen tablets.

✦ **Pointer:** The small graphic icon that moves on the screen as you move your mouse is a pointer (also called a *cursor*). The pointer takes on different shapes depending on the tool you select, the current location of the mouse, and the function you're performing.

✦ **Click:** Most Mac mice have only one button, but some have two or more; all PC mice have at least two buttons. If you have a multibutton mouse, quickly press and release the leftmost mouse button once when I say to click the mouse. (If your mouse has only one button — you guessed it — just press and release the button you have.)

✦ **Double-click:** When I say to double-click, quickly press and release the left-most mouse button twice (if your mouse has only one button, just press and release twice the button you have). On some multibutton mice, one of the buttons can function as a double-click (you click it once, the mouse clicks twice); if your mouse has this feature, use it — it saves strain on your hand.

✦ **Right-click:** A Windows feature since Windows 95, right-clicking means clicking the right-hand mouse button. On a Mac's one-button mouse, hold the Control key when clicking the mouse button to achieve the right-click effect. On multibutton Mac mice, assign one of the buttons to the Control+click combination. (Mac OS X automatically assigns the right-hand button to Control+click.)

✦ **Drag:** Dragging is used for moving and sizing items in an InDesign document. To drag an item, position the mouse pointer on it. Press and hold down the mouse button, and then slide the mouse across a flat surface to drag the item. Release the mouse button to drop the dragged item in its new location.

Dealing with computer-platform appearance issues

InDesign runs on Mac OS X 10.2 (Jaguar), Windows 2000 with Service Pack 2 or later installed, and Windows XP, as well as later versions of these operating systems. Most desktop publishers use Apple Computer's Macintosh, and thus most readers of this book will likely be Mac-based. That's why I use Mac screenshots in the illustrations throughout this book. (Plus, Adobe uses Windows screenshots in its documentation.) But the minority in publishing who use Microsoft's Windows continues to grow, especially for business-oriented and personal publishing, so I do show Windows screenshots when notable differences exist. Adobe has done a good job of ensuring that the interface for InDesign is almost identical — within the natural differences between Mac and Windows — on the two platforms.

Keyboard conventions

This book provides both the Macintosh and Windows shortcuts throughout, with the Mac shortcut first. In most cases, the Mac and Windows shortcuts are the same, except for the names of the keys, as follows:

✦ The Mac's Command key (⌘) is the most-used shortcut key. Its Windows equivalent is Ctrl.

✦ Shift is the same on the Mac and Windows. In many Mac program menus — including InDesign — Shift is displayed by the symbol ⇧.

✦ The Option key on the Mac is usually the same as the Alt key in Windows. In many Mac program menus — including InDesign — you'll see the symbol ⌥ used.

✦ The Control key on the Mac has no Windows equivalent (it is *not* the same as the Windows Ctrl key). Many Mac programs indicate it with the symbol ∧ in their menus.

If you're supposed to press several keys at the same time, I indicate that by placing plus signs (+) between them. Thus, Shift+⌘+A means press and hold the Shift and ⌘ keys, then press A. After you've pressed the A key, let go of all three keys. (You don't need to hold down the last letter in the sequence.)

I also use the plus sign (+) to join keys to mouse movements. For example, Option+drag means to hold the Option key while dragging the mouse on the Mac, and Alt+drag means to hold the Alt key while dragging the mouse in Windows.

Also note that InDesign lets you change the shortcuts associated with menu and other commands (by choosing Edit ⇨ Keyboard Shortcuts). Throughout the book, I assume the shortcuts in use are the default ones and that you haven't altered them.

Icons

You'll notice special graphic symbols, or *icons,* used throughout this book. I use these icons to call your attention to points that are particularly important or worth noting:

The New Feature icon indicates a technique or action that is new to InDesign CS.

The Tip icon indicates a technique or action in InDesign that will save you time or effort.

The Note icon indicates information that you should remember for future use—something that may seem minor or inconsequential but will, in reality, resurface.

The Caution icon is used to warn you of potential hang-ups or pitfalls you may encounter while using InDesign (and how to avoid them).

The Cross-Reference icon points you to different parts of the book that contain related or expanded information on a particular topic.

The Platform Difference icon alerts you to differences using InDesign on the Macintosh versus in Windows.

The QuarkXPress User icon alerts QuarkXPress users who are switching to InDesign to significant differences in function and approach between the two programs.

InDesign QuickStart

In This QuickStart

Creating a new document

Working with frames

Working with lines

Working with text and pictures

Creating and applying colors

Printing a composite

Although InDesign is a complex program that lets you do everything from designing a fashion magazine to indexing a book to generating separation plates for professional printing, you can get started building documents with just a few simple skills. If you're in a hurry to get started on a document — or you have a job interview tomorrow based on your "proficiency" in InDesign — work through the steps in this section. You'll learn the basic building blocks of documents (frames and lines) and the two primary tools (Selection and Direct Selection).

By all means, do not assume that these steps provide all you need to know about InDesign. From here, head to related sections of the book and explore the full functionality of the program. If you're not sure where to start, figure out what you'll be doing the most. For example, if you'll be flowing text into a newsletter template, head to Part IV: Text Fundamentals.

To create the sample document shown in Figure QS-1 — an annual compendium of case studies from a publication called *IT Wireless* — you'll need InDesign, a text file from a program such as Microsoft Word, a graphic file such as a TIFF file, and a laser or ink-jet printer. You can follow the steps exactly (substituting your own text, graphic, and fonts), or you can vary the design as much as you want.

Figure QS-1: Combining formatted text and several graphics with a few simple frames and lines produces a completely designed magazine article.

Creating a New Document

When you create a new document in InDesign, you're actually specifying the final size and setup of the pages in the document.

1. **Start InDesign.**

2. **Choose File ➪ New ➪ Document, or press ⌘+N or Ctrl+N.**

   The New Document dialog box appears (see Figure QS-2).

3. **In the Page Size pop-up menu, choose Letter.**

4. **Check Facing Pages, because this is a magazine printed on two sides, thus needing both left- and right-page versions.**

5. **Check Master Text Frame.**

6. **Set the number of columns to 2, with a gutter width of 1p6 (0.25 in).**

Figure QS-2: Set up the page size and other attributes for your document in the New Document dialog box.

7. **Set the margin guides at 4p6 (0.75 in) for the top and inside, 3p6 (0.583 in) for the bottom, and 3p (0.5 in) for the outside.**

   Note that this copy of InDesign has been set with picas as the default measurement for vertical and horizontal measurement, one of two typical settings for publications. (The other is to set horizontal at picas and vertical measurements at inches.)

8. **Click the Save Preset button, and give these specifications a name.**

   The example uses *ITW Case Studies*. Assigning a name to these specifications lets you select these exact settings for future documents for this publication by choosing the preset name from the Document preset pop-up menu.

9. **Click OK to create the new document's new layout.**

   InDesign creates one 8½-by-11-inch page.

10. **Choose File ⇨ Save As, or press Shift+⌘+S or Ctrl+Shift+S.**

11. **In the Save As field, type** ITW Case Studies 2003.indd, **as shown in Figure QS-3; choose a location for the file, then click Save.**

Cross-Reference

For more information about creating a new document, see Chapter 4.

Figure QS-3: Use the Save As dialog box to name a new document.

Working with Frames

By using the automatic text frame, you've already created the frame for the article text. But the article has colored frames at top for the story title that need to be created via frames.

1. **Select the Rectangle Frame tool.**

   To see the names of tools, point at them until a Tool Tip displays.

2. **Click and drag to create a frame that is approximately 21p (3.5 in) wide and 4p (0.667 in) tall, as shown in Figure QS-4.**

   You'll fine-tune the size and placement in the next steps. The new frame is selected, as indicated by the white handles. If the frame becomes deselected in the following steps, click on it to select it.

3. **Highlight the X: field in the Control palette (Window ⇨ Control, or Option+⌘+6 or Ctrl+Alt+6), which specifies the item's origin across (placement from the left edge of the page); type 4p6 in this field.**

Figure QS-4. Use any of the frame tools to create background shapes into which you will import a picture.

4. Tab to the **Y: field, which specifies the item's origin down (placement from the top of the page)**; type 4p6 **in this field.**

5. **Tab to the W: field, which specifies the item's width;** type 21p **in this field.**

6. **Tab to the H: field, which specifies the item's height;** type 4p **in this field.**

7. **Press Return or Enter to reposition and resize the frame according to the values shown in Figure QS-5.**

8. **Choose Item ⇨ Duplicate, or press Option+Shift+⌘+D or Ctrl+Alt+Shift+D.**

   If necessary, first click on the new frame to select it.

Figure QS-5: The Control palette lets you precisely size items.

9. **Highlight the X: field in the Control palette, then type** 25p6.

10. **Tab to the Y: field, then type** 4p6.

11. **Tab to the W: field, then type** 22p6.

12. **If the H: field is not already set to 4p, enter** 4p **in its field.**

13. **Press Return to reposition and resize the second frame, as shown in Figure QS-6.**

    Later, you will add color to this frame.

Cross-Reference

For more information about working with frames, see Chapters 10 and 11.

Figure QS-6: Resizing and repositioning the second frame with the Control palette.

Working with Text

In InDesign, text goes inside a text frame. You can type text into the frame or import a text file in various formats. Once text is inside the frame, you can change the font, size, color, and many more options. First, you'll create text frames and type text into them.

1. **Select the Rectangle Frame tool.**

2. **Click and drag to create a frame that is approximately 45p (7.5 in) wide and 4p tall, as shown in Figure QS-7.**

   The new frame is selected, as indicated by the white handles. If the frame becomes deselected in the following steps, click on it to select it.

Figure QS-7: Use the Rectangle Text Frame tool to create a container for text.

3. **To size and place the frame precisely, type the following values in the Control palette: X: 4p6, Y: 9p6, W: 43p6, H: 5p0.**

4. **Select the Content tool (the hand), then click in the new frame to hold the story's headline.**

5. **Type the words** Public Safety's Second Wireless Wave **in the frame.**

6. **Highlight the entire phrase and choose a different font from the Control palette's Font menu (the example uses Frutiger).**

7. **Choose a type style from the Style menu (the example uses 65 Bold).**

8. **Choose 28 pt from the Size menu, as shown in Figure QS-8.**

9. **In the frame at upper-right, enter two paragraph returns and the phrase CASE STUDY (in all caps).**

10. **Highlight the text *CASE STUDY* and apply the font Frutiger 76 Black Italic to it; make the point size 12 pt.**

Figure QS-8: When text is highlighted, you can format it using controls on the right side of the Measurements palette.

Now you'll put text in the text frame that was created through the Automatic Text Frame feature earlier:

1. **Choose File ➪ Place, or press ⌘+D or Ctrl+D.**

   The Place dialog box (shown in Figure QS-9) appears.

2. **Locate a text file in a format such as Microsoft Word.**

3. **Check Show Import Options.**

   The file used in the example has just two style sheets in use: Normal and Headline 2.

4. **Click to select the text file, then click Open.**

   The Microsoft Word Import Options dialog box appears.

Figure QS-9: Choose File ➪ Place, or press
⌘+D or Ctrl+D, to import text from a word
processor.

5. **Be sure that Use Typographer's Quotes is checked, then click OK to import the file.**

   InDesign will show the loaded-text icon (it looks like a tiny paragraph) that indicates a file ready to be placed into a frame.

Note

If the text file you import does not fit in the frame, a red square in the lower-right corner indicates that text is overflowing. There is no need to worry about that for these purposes. If you do not have a text file, simply type another sentence in the frame.

6. **Click the two-column master text frame to pour the text into it.**

   Figure QS-10 shows the result.

7. **Because the first page of the article has the two empty frames at top as well as the headline frame, you'll want to resize the master text frame for this page so the story text doesn't overprint the other frames**. (You can also set text wrap for each of those frames using the Text Wrap pane, covered later in this QuickStart.) To resize, drag the middle frame handle at the top of the frame, and drag the frame's top below the three other frames.

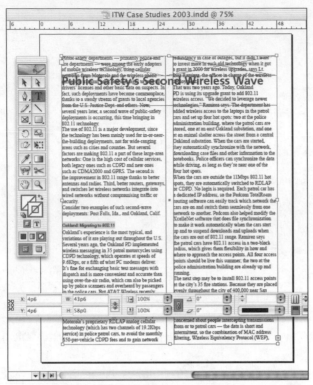

Figure QS-10: When text is placed into the automatic text frame, it overprints other frames that overlap it.

With the text placed, you now need to format it:

1. **With the Text tool, click anywhere in the text and highlight all the text using ⌘+A or Ctrl+A.**

2. **Choose Type ➪ Character, or press ⌘+T or Ctrl+T, to open the Character pane and select a font (the example uses ITC Veljovic), select a type style (Book, here), set the point size to 9.5 pt, and set the leading to 11 pt.**

   You could also use the Control palette to set these settings. Figure QS-11 shows the pane and the results.

3. **Make sure all the text is still selected, and choose Type ➪ Paragraph, or press Option+⌘+T or Ctrl+Alt+T, to open the Paragraph pane.**

4. **Make sure the alignment is set to Justified, the first line indent to 0p10, and the Hyphenate option is checked, as shown in Figure QS-12.**

   You could also use the Control palette.

Figure QS-11: Use the Character pane or Control palette to set the font, type style, point size, and leading.

5. For the first paragraph, add a drop cap by clicking the paragraph with the Text tool and choosing Drop Caps & Nested Styles from the Paragraph Pane's palette menu. Enter 4 in the Lines field and 1 in the Characters field. Click OK. Highlight the first letter in this paragraph, then go to the Character pane and change the font to Frutiger and the Type Style to 65 Bold.

6. Find the internal section headlines in the story and format them to be left-aligned, hyphenation turned off, the first-line indent set to 0p, space above to 1p, space after to 0p3, the point size to 11 pt, and the font to Frutiger 65 Bold using the Paragraph and Character panes, or by using the Control palette.

Figure QS-12: Use the Paragraph pane or Control palette to set the justification.

7. Find the paragraphs that immediately follow the internal headlines and change the first-line indent to 0p **using the Paragraph pane.**

Figure QS-13 shows the results of all this text formatting.

Figure QS-13: Your document should look something like this.

8. If you'll create pages with the same type specifications, create style sheets from the formatted text:

a. Start with the drop cap: Highlight the text, then choose New Character Style from the Character Style pane's palette menu. (Choose Type ⇨ Character Styles or press Shift+F11.) Provide a name at the top of the New Character Styles dialog box, verify the attributes in the Basic Character Formats pane, then click OK.

b. Now, click anywhere in the regular story text with the Text tool, then choose New Paragraph Style from the Paragraph Styles pane's palette menu. (Choose Type ⇨ Paragraph Styles, or press F11, to open the pane.) Provide a name at the top of the New Paragraph Style dialog box, then verify the attributes in the Basic Character Formats, Indents and

Spacing, Hyphenation, and Justification panes. (For the drop cap paragraph style, you'll also use the Drop Caps and Nested Styles pane; select the drop cap character style you created earlier in the Character Style pop-up menu.) Click OK when done. You should end up with one character style (it could be called Drop Cap) and five paragraph styles (they could be called Main Headline, Internal Headline, Body Text, Drop Cap Body Text, and First Body Text).

    c. Apply these styles to your text by clicking anywhere in a paragraph, then clicking the appropriate name in the Paragraph Styles pane. To apply a character style (such as to the drop cap), select the appropriate text, then click on the appropriate name in the Character Styles pane.

9. Choose File ⇨ Save, or press ⌘+S or Ctrl+S to save your work.

Cross-Reference For more information about entering, importing, and formatting text, see Part IV: Text Fundamentals.

Working with Lines

You can create lines of any shape and size, then change the style, width, and color. Here, I'm adding a line to the document's master page, so it appears on all pages. To work on a master page, double-click a master page icon in the Pages pane (Window ⇨ Pages, or F12). Figure QS-14 shows the pane.

Figure QS-14: The Pages pane lets you work on master pages, as well as create new pages.

1. Select the Line tool.

2. Be sure the Stroke icon in the Tools palette is set to black — click the icon, then click the small black icon in the row below.

3. Position the mouse where you want to draw the line (here, below the master text frame), then click and drag to create a line, as shown in Figure QS-15.

Press the Shift key while you drag to constrain the tool to drawing a horizontal or vertical line. The new line is selected, as indicated by the white handles. If the line becomes deselected in the following steps, click on it to select it.

Figure QS-15: Use the Line tool to create lines at any angle.

4. **Precisely place and size the line using the Control palette, as follows: for the left page: X: 55p6, Y: 63p9, L: 43p6; for the right page: X: 3p, Y: 63p9, L: 43p6.**

5. **Make the stroke 1 pt, also in the Control palette.**

6. **Return to the story page you worked on previously by double-clicking its icon in the Pages pane.**

7. **Choose File ⇨ Save, or press ⌘+S or Ctrl+S, to save your work.**

Cross-Reference

For more information about working with lines, see Chapter 11.

Working with Pictures

In InDesign, any image that you import into a layout — whether it's a digital photograph, chart, or line drawing — is referred to as a picture. Pictures go inside picture frames — either one you create before you place a picture, or one that InDesign creates automatically when you import a picture but have no frame selected. Once a picture is inside a frame, you can change its size and placement.

1. **Click and hold on the Rectangle Frame tool.**

2. **Position the pointer on the page, then click and drag to create a rectangular picture frame of any shape.**

   The new frame is selected, as indicated by the white handles. If the frame becomes deselected in the following steps, click on it to select it.

3. **To size the frame precisely, type the following values in the Control palette: X: 22p8, Y: 30p8, W: 25p4, H: 25p4.**

4. **To import a picture, choose File ⇨ Place, or press ⌘+D or Ctrl+D.**

5. **Locate a graphic file such as a TIFF, JPEG, GIF, or EPS as shown in Figure QS-16; select it and click Open.**

Figure QS-16: Choose File ➪ Place, or press
⌘+D or Ctrl+D, to import graphics into frames.

6. **If necessary, highlight the Scale X Percentage field in the Control palette. Type a new scale such as 80%.**

The Scale Y Percentage field should change to the same value as long as the two fields are locked (a chain icon appears to their right; if the chain is open, click the icon to lock the two fields).

You can also resize the image to fit the frame by choosing Object ➪ Fitting ➪ Fit Content Proportionally (Option+Shift+⌘+E or Ctrl+Alt+Shift+E).

7. **Add a runaround to the image so text does not run to the image: Choose Window ➪ Type & Tables ➪ Text Wrap, or press Option+⌘+W or Ctrl+Alt+W, to get the pane shown in Figure QS-17. Select the Wrap Around Bounding Box icon (the second from the left), and set the wrap margins in the four fields (there's one for each side) to 0p6.**

8. **Import a logo graphic for the first frame you created and size it to fit, as shown in Figure QS-17.**

It doesn't have to fill the whole width of that frame.

Figure QS-17: Set text wrap with the Text Wrap pane.

Cross-Reference For more information about working with pictures, see Part V: Graphics Fundamentals.

Creating Colors

To apply the color you want to an item or text, first you need to create that color. By default, InDesign provides a few colors: cyan, magenta, yellow, [Black], red, blue, green, [Paper] (white), [None], and [Registration]. (The names that InDesign puts in brackets are colors that cannot be deleted or modified.) In most cases, you'll be creating additional colors to suit your documents.

1. **To open the Swatches pane, where you create, modify, and apply colors, choose Window ⇨ Swatches, or press F5.**

   Here, you'll be creating a color based on a color in our imported logo.

2. Select the Eyedropper tool and then click on the background color in that logo.

For the *IT Wireless* Magazine logo shown in Figure QS-17, the color is a dark blue.

3. Choose New Color Swatch from the pane's palette menu.

4. From the Color Mode pop-up menu, choose CMYK.

This will create a color based on the four process colors widely used in commercial printing: cyan, magenta, yellow, and black.

Because you selected a color with the Eyedropper tool, the New Color Swatch dialog box shows the values, as Figure QS-18 shows. If you had not first selected a color with the Eyedropper tool, you would enter values or slide the four sliders to select a desired color. If the Name with Color Value option is checked, InDesign will name the color automatically; if it is unchecked, you can give it a more memorable name such as Bright Navy.

Figure QS-18: Create a CMYK color by first selecting a color from an object in the layout with the Eyedropper tool, or by selecting the proportions of the constituent colors in the New Color Swatch dialog box.

5. Click OK to create the color and close the dialog box.

If you wanted to create more colors, click Add instead. Click OK only when you want to close the dialog box.

Cross-Reference

For more information about creating colors, see Chapter 8.

Applying Colors

InDesign's Swatches palette, combined with the Tools palette, makes it easy to experiment with different colors. You can apply colors to frame backgrounds, lines, strokes, some imported images, and text.

1. **Be sure the Swatches pane is open (Window ⇨ Swatches, or F5).**

2. **Click on the two frames at the top of the page with the Selection tool.**

   To select both, click one, then Shift+Click the other.

3. **Make sure the Fill icon is selected in the Tools palette, as it is in Figure QS-19.**

   This tells InDesign what you want to color the object, not any strokes it may have.

4. **Click the name of the color you created in the previous section.**

   The selected frames will now fill with the color.

Figure QS-19: Click a color to apply it to the background of a frame.

5. Highlight the text *CASE STUDY* in the upper-left frame.

6. Again ensuring the Fill icon is selected in the Tools palette, click the [Paper] color in the Swatches pane.

   This makes the text white.

7. Choose File ➪ Save, or press ⌘+S or Ctrl+S, to save your work.

For more information about applying colors, see Chapters 11 and 28.

Printing a Composite

Whether you're designing a document for black-and-white photocopying, color printing, professional printing, or even for PDF, you'll need to review drafts. By default, InDesign is set up to your system's default printer with just a few clicks.

1. Choose File ➪ Print, or press ⌘+P or Ctrl+P.

If you press Return or Enter as soon as the Print dialog box displays, chances are that InDesign will print a usable draft on your laser printer. However, if you've selected a different page size, orientation, or other option, you may want to confirm the other settings.

2. At the top of the dialog box, the Printer pop-up menu is usually set to your system's default printer.

   You can leave this setting or locate and select the printer you're actually using. It's best to select your actual printer.

3. Go to the Output pane and make sure the Color pop-up menu is set to Composite Grayscale if you're printing to a black-and-white laser printer and to Composite CMYK if you're printing to a color ink-jet or laser printer.

4. Look at the page preview at the lower-left of the dialog box and make sure the page (indicated by the light-gray rectangle) fits within the printer paper (indicated by the blue line), as shown in Figure QS-20.

5. Click Print.

For more information about printing, see Part VI: Output Fundamentals.

Figure QS-20: The Print dialog box lets you confirm that your document fits on the paper in the selected printer, as well as set the appropriate print settings for your document and target printer.

✦　　✦　　✦

Welcome to InDesign

P A R T

]

♦   ♦   ♦   ♦

Chapter 1
What InDesign
Can Do for You

Chapter 2
A Tour of InDesign

Chapter 3
Getting InDesign
Ready to Go

You're ready to go — you've bought InDesign, installed it, even launched it. But now what? It's a new program for you, and while the program has a certain familiarity by virtue of looking like most other Macintosh or Windows programs, it is a new program, so you're not really sure what to do next. The answer is simple: Read on. The chapters in Part I walk you through the initial steps of using InDesign to create your publications.

First, in Chapter 1, I give you a basic introduction to InDesign itself, explaining the concepts it uses in its layout approach. I also highlight what's so special about InDesign and define a whole passel of publishing and InDesign terms to make sure that we're working from the same page, and so you're not confused when you see new terms in this book, in InDesign's menus and help system, or from colleagues.

With the basic context out of the way, Chapter 2 gives you a tour through InDesign's interface — its array of tools, menus, palettes, panes, dialog boxes — and covers what components come with the program. You also learn what's new in InDesign CS (also known as version 3).

That sets the stage for Chapter 3, which shows you how to adjust the InDesign interface by setting global preferences, changing view zooms for your documents, and setting your own keyboard shortcuts.

What InDesign Can Do for You

◆ ◆ ◆ ◆

In This Chapter

Learning what
InDesign can do

Discovering the
InDesign approaches
to layout

Understanding global
and local control

Identifying InDesign
terminology

◆ ◆ ◆ ◆

Although Adobe InDesign is a relatively new desktop-publishing program, its history actually spans more than 15 years; it succeeds the venerable Adobe PageMaker, the first popular desktop-publishing program. InDesign *is* an all-new program — make no mistake about that — but it draws on the experience and design of PageMaker, which Adobe Systems acquired in 1994 and significantly modified in the intervening years. As Adobe's entry into the professional, more-creative publishing space that has been dominated by QuarkXPress, the developers of InDesign also learned a lot of lessons from QuarkXPress, offering many comparable features in a way that fits the InDesign publishing workflow model.

Why does this history matter? Because chances are you already use PageMaker or, more likely, QuarkXPress and are switching to InDesign or adding InDesign to your software toolkit. You'll find a lot of familiar things in InDesign, but InDesign is a new product that borrows from PageMaker and other Adobe products, as well as from its chief rival, QuarkXPress. It also adds new components of its own. So draw upon your experience with PageMaker, QuarkXPress, or other Adobe software, but don't let that experience fool you into thinking you can run InDesign on autopilot. Instead, be sure to really learn InDesign's approaches.

Cross-Reference If you're switching to InDesign from QuarkXPress or PageMaker, be sure to check out Appendix C or Appendix D. These appendixes will help you translate your QuarkXPress and PageMaker expertise into InDesign's frame of reference.

What makes InDesign special

The release of PageMaker in 1986 launched the desktop publishing revolution, and in the following years, PageMaker and its competitors added tons of cool features. It may be hard to imagine that there's anything new to add to this publishing toolkit.

Well, InDesign's creators have managed to add a few new features. Following are the significant additions to the desktop publishing toolkit, courtesy of InDesign (note that this list doesn't include enhanced versions of features found in competitors such as QuarkXPress and Ventura Publisher, or in PageMaker):

✦ **Multiline composer,** which lets InDesign adjust the spacing and hyphenation over several lines of text at once — rather than the typical one-line-in-isolation of other programs — to achieve the best possible spacing and hyphenation. (See Chapter 18.)

✦ **Optical margin alignment,** which actually moves some characters past the margin of your columns to create the optical illusion that all the characters line up. This works because some characters' shapes fool the eye into thinking they begin before or after where they really do, so although technically aligned, they appear not to be. Optical margin alignment fixes that. (See Chapter 18.)

✦ **Optical kerning**, which adjusts the spacing between characters based on their shapes, for the most natural look possible without resorting to hand-tuning their spacing. (See Chapter 18.)

✦ **A menu for inserting special characters,** so you no longer have to remember codes or use separate programs like the Mac's Key Caps or the Windows Character Map to add special symbols like bullets (•) and section indicators (§). Your word processor has likely had this feature for a few years, but this is a first in desktop publishing. (See Chapter 15.)

✦ **Glyph scaling,** which lets InDesign stretch or compress characters to make them fit better on a line. (A *glyph* is a character.) This works in addition to tracking and kerning, which adjust the spacing between characters to make them fit better on a line. (See Chapter 18.)

✦ **Custom strokes for characters,** which let you change the look of characters by making their outlines thicker or thinner. You can also give the part of the characters inside the outlines a different color, to create an outline effect. (Normally, the part inside the stroke is the same color as the stroke, so the reader sees a normal, solid character.) (See Chapter 18.)

✦ **EPS display,** so you can now see the detailed contents of an EPS file rather than rely on a poor-quality preview image or, worse, see an X or gray box in place of the image. (See Chapter 22.)

✦ **Illustrator and Photoshop file import,** so you can place these graphics files directly in your layout. (See Chapter 23.)

✦ **Multiple views of the document,** so you can have several windows open for the same document, letting you see different sections at the same time. (See Chapter 3.)

✦ **Custom drop-shadow creation,** so you can create exactly the kind of drop-shadow effect you want and not be stuck with a canned option. (See Chapter 11.)

So what can InDesign do for you? A lot. For years, layout designers had to choose between a free-form but manual approach to layout (PageMaker) and a structured but easily revised approach (QuarkXPress). Most chose the latter. With InDesign, you can choose both. That's important for both novice and experienced users, because it isn't a one-size-fits-all answer. Sometimes (for example, if your project is a one-time publication or an experimental effort), creating a layout from scratch—almost as if you were doing it by hand on paper—is the best approach. And sometimes using a highly formatted template that you can modify as needed is the best approach, because there's no need to reinvent the wheel for common documents.

InDesign can handle sophisticated tasks like magazine and newspaper page layout, but its simple approach to publishing also makes it a good choice for smaller projects like flyers and newsletters. InDesign is also a good choice for corporate publishing tasks such as proposals and annual reports. Plug-in software from other vendors adds extra capabilities; for example, Virginia Systems offers several plug-ins that make InDesign a good tool for books and academic papers.

Cross-Reference   For more on plug-in software, see Chapter 36.

But that's not all. InDesign is not merely a merger of QuarkXPress and PageMaker—though it will seem that way to experienced users. It is designed from the ground up as an *electronic* publishing tool. That means documents can easily be sent to service bureaus and printing presses for direct output, saving you lots of time and money. It also means you can create documents for electronic distribution, particularly using the Adobe Acrobat Portable Document Format (PDF). These electronic files can include interactive features such as forms and sounds.

Cross-Reference   See Part VI and Part VII for more in-depth coverage of output and interactive-document fundamentals.

This chapter details the wide range of uses and features of InDesign, points out the ways in which InDesign can be useful to you, and describes the basic metaphor on which the program is based. I also provide a comprehensive list of the terms—clearly and concisely defined—that I use throughout the book. So whether you're an expert or novice, read on and prepare yourself for a great InDesign adventure.

Discovering the InDesign Approach

Publishing programs, although similar in many ways, differ in their approach to the publishing task. One way to describe a program's approach to publishing is to talk about its *metaphor,* or the overall way that it handles publishing tasks. Some programs use a *free-form metaphor,* which means that the method used to assemble a document is based on assembling page elements as you would if they were placed on a pasteboard until ready for use (this is also called the *pasteboard metaphor,* although that's a less precise term because software using other metaphors can still include a pasteboard). Other programs approach page layout using a *frame-based metaphor,* in which frames (or boxes) hold both the page elements and the attributes that control the appearance of those elements. InDesign uses both the free-form metaphor and the frame-based metaphor.

The frame-based metaphor

Under a frame-based metaphor, you build pages by assembling a variety of frames that will contain your text and graphics. First, you set up the basic framework of the document — the page size and orientation, margins, number of columns, and so on. You then fill that framework with text, pictures, and lines.

Note These frames and lines need not be straight or square. With InDesign, you can create frames that are shaped by Bézier curves. (In the 1970s, French engineer Pierre Bézier created the mathematics that make these adjustable curves work.)

There are several reasons to use frames:

✦ **To create a template for documents like newsletters and magazines that use the same basic elements for many articles.** You create the frames and then add the text and graphics appropriate for each specific article — modifying, adding, and deleting frames as necessary for each article.

✦ **To get a sense of how you want your elements to be placed and sized before you start working with the actual elements.** This is similar to creating a pencil sketch on paper before doing a formal layout.

✦ **To ensure specific size and placement of elements up front — in this case, you're often working with a template or guidelines that limit size and placement of elements.** In many cases, you can copy an existing frame, because its size is one you're using in several locations of your layout. For structured or partly structured documents like newsletters and magazines, I find setting up my documents up front so elements are sized and placed correctly easier than resizing elements one at a time later.

Note Bear in mind that whether you start by creating frames in which you will later place graphics or text or you simply place the text and graphics directly on your page, you're using frames. In the case of direct placement of elements on the page, InDesign creates a frame automatically for each element. The difference is that the frame InDesign creates is based on the amount of text or the size of the graphic, rather than on your specific specifications. Of course, in either case, you can modify the frames and the elements within them.

The free-form metaphor

Under a free-form (pasteboard) metaphor, you draw the pages' content as if you're working on paper. Depending on how long you've been in this business, you may well remember having paste-up boards with strips of type, camera-ready line drawings, halftone pictures strewn about, sticking to pasteboard thanks to the wax on their backs. You would then assemble all those pieces until you got the combination that looked right to you. The free-form metaphor encourages an experimental approach, which is particularly well suited to one-of-a-kind documents such as ads, brochures, annual reports, and marketing materials.

 In a frame-based approach, you can certainly experiment by using the frames as placeholders for actual text and graphics. But visual thinkers like to work with actual objects, and that's why the free-form metaphor works much better for them. With InDesign, you pick the metaphor that works for your style, your current situation, and your mood. After all, both approaches can lead to the same design.

Understanding Global and Local Control

The power of desktop publishing in general, and InDesign in particular, is that it lets you automate time-consuming layout and typesetting tasks while letting you customize each step of the process according to your needs. This duality of structure and flexibility—implemented via the dual use of the frame-based and free-form layout metaphors—carries over to all operations, from typography to color: You can use *global* controls to establish general settings for layout elements and then use *local* controls to modify those elements to meet specific publishing requirements. The key to using global and local tools effectively is to know when each is appropriate.

Global tools include

> ✦ General preferences and application preferences (see Chapter 3)
>
> ✦ Master pages (see Chapter 7)
>
> ✦ Style sheets (see Chapter 20)
>
> ✦ Sections of page numbers (see Chapter 5)
>
> ✦ Color definitions (see Chapter 8)
>
> ✦ Hyphenation and justification (see Chapter 18)
>
> ✦ Libraries (see Chapter 7)

Note   Styles and master pages are the two main global settings that you can expect to override locally throughout a document. You shouldn't be surprised to make such changes often because, although the layout and typographic functions that style sheets and master pages automate are the fundamental components of any document's look, they don't always work for all a publication's specific content.

Local tools include

✦ Frame tools (see Chapter 10, Chapter 11, Chapter 12, Chapter 21, and Chapter 25)

✦ Character and paragraph tools (see Chapter 17, Chapter 18, Chapter 19, and Chapter 20)

✦ Graphics tools (see Part V)

Knowing which tools to use

In many cases, it's obvious which tool to use. If, for example, you maintain certain layout standards throughout a document, then using master pages is the obvious way to keep your work in order. Using styles is the best solution if you want to apply standard character and paragraph formatting throughout a document. When you work with special-case documents, such as a single-page display ad, it doesn't make much sense to spend time designing master pages and styles — it's easier just to format one-of-a-kind elements on the fly.

In other cases, deciding which tool is appropriate is more difficult. For example, you can create *drop caps* (large initial letters set into a paragraph of type, like the drop cap that starts each chapter in this book) as a character option in the Character pane, or you can create a *character style* (formatting that you can apply to any selected text, ensuring the same formatting is applied each time) that contains the drop-cap settings and apply that style to the drop cap. Which method you choose will depend on the complexity of your document and how often you'll need to perform the action. The more often you find yourself doing something, the more often you should use a global tool (like character styles).

Fortunately, you don't have to decide between global and local tools right away while designing a document. You can always create styles from existing formatting later or add elements to a master page if you find you need them to appear on every page.

Specifying measurement values

Another situation in which you can choose between local or global controls is specifying measurement values. Regardless of the default measurement unit you set (and that appears in all dialog boxes, panes, and palettes), you can use any unit when entering measurements in an InDesign dialog box. If, for example, the default measurement is picas, but you're accustomed to working with inches, go ahead and enter measurements in inches.

InDesign Vocabulary 101

InDesign comes with its own terminology, much of it adopted from other Adobe products. The general ones (not covered elsewhere in this book) include the following:

✦ **Link:** The connection that InDesign makes to an imported file; the link contains the file's location, last modification date, and last modification time. A link can reference any image or text file that you have imported into a layout. InDesign can notify you when a source text or graphics file has changed, so you can choose whether to update the version in your layout. (A *hyperlink,* often also abbreviated to *link* in casual conversation, connects elements in a Web page to other Web pages.)

✦ **Package:** The collecting of all files needed to deliver a layout for printing or Web posting.

✦ **PDF:** The Adobe Portable Document Format is the standard for electronic documents. No matter what kind of computer it is viewed on (Windows, Macintosh, or Unix), a PDF document retains high fidelity to the original in typography, graphics representation, and layout. InDesign can both place PDF files as if they were graphics and export its own pages to PDF format.

✦ **Place:** To import a picture or text file.

✦ **Plug-in:** A piece of software that loads into InDesign and becomes part of InDesign, to add more capabilities.

Not too long ago, only a few publishing professionals knew—or cared about—what the words *pica, kerning, crop,* or *color model* meant. Today, these words are becoming commonplace, because almost everyone who wants to produce a nice-looking report, a simple newsletter, or a magazine encounters these terms in the menus and manuals of their layout programs. Occasionally, the terms are used incorrectly or are replaced with general terms to make nonprofessional users feel less threatened, but that substitution ends up confusing professional printers, people who work in service bureaus, and Internet service providers. For a primer on publishing terms, see Chapter 39, Chapter 40, and Chapter 42.

InDesign accepts any of the following codes for measurement units:

✦ x", xi, x in, or x inch (for inches)

✦ xp (for picas)

✦ $x$pt or 0px (for points)

✦ xc (for ciceros)

✦ $x$cm (for centimeters)

✦ $x$mm (for millimeters)

Tip

Note that the x above indicates where you specify the value, such as 1i for 1 inch). It doesn't matter whether you put a space between the value and the code: *1inch* and *1 inch* are the same as far as InDesign is concerned.

You can enter fractional picas in two ways: in decimal format (as in *8.5p*) and in picas and points (as in *8p6*). Either of these settings results in a measurement of 8½ picas (there are 12 points in a pica).

Summary

InDesign offers a strong set of features for professional publishers working on brochures, magazines, advertisements, and similar publications. Although it lacks specialized tools for database publishing (such as for catalogs), it offers many unique features such as a multilane composer, glyph scaling, and customer character strokes.

InDesign's use of both the free-form and structured layout metaphors makes it very flexible, letting you pick the layout style that works best for you and for your document's specific needs.

✦　　✦　　✦

A Tour of InDesign

In This Chapter

Discovering what's inside the application folder

Exploring the document window

Using tools, panes, and palettes

Reviewing menu commands

The first time you use a program, it can be overwhelming. You're not sure what you can actually do with the program, and each program has its own idiosyncrasies. InDesign is no different. If you're familiar with other Adobe applications, such as PageMaker or Photoshop, the InDesign software interface will be familiar to you. Even if you've been using QuarkXPress, you'll be able to translate much of what you see in InDesign to QuarkXPress terms.

But because every program is unique, each has its own style and approaches. So now that you're ready to start using InDesign, follow through this chapter to find out where InDesign puts its capabilities and how to access them. When you first launch InDesign, you'll see a Tools palette on the left, and you may see several other palettes on the right. InDesign is ready and waiting for you to open a document and start working.

However, taking a few minutes to familiarize yourself with the interface is invaluable to learning new software. After all, without a basic understanding of what you're looking at on-screen, it's difficult to begin working in InDesign.

> **Note**   InDesign CS lets you change the shortcuts associated with menu and other commands. (Chapter 3 covers this feature in more detail.) Throughout the book, I assume the shortcuts in use are the default ones.

The InDesign Application Folder

Often, users simply launch an application from an alias or shortcut and never even look in the application folder. This is just fine, until it comes time to install a new plug-in or share important information with other users. Familiarizing yourself with the basic contents helps you be sure you're not throwing away anything important and that you're working with the correct files and folders.

If you locate the InDesign application folder on your hard drive and open it, you'll see it's chock-full of stuff you may not even recognize. The three things you need to know about in this folder are the Presets folder, the Plug-ins folder, and the Required folder.

The Presets folder

The Presets folder contains three kinds of standards: shortcut sets, color swatch libraries, and workspaces. InDesign lets you create shortcut sets, so different users can have their own shortcut definitions; these preferences are stored in the InDesign Shortcut Sets folder in the Presets folder. The Swatch Libraries folder contains color-swatch libraries — both those that come with InDesign and any you might add yourself. Finally, the Workspaces folder contains workspace definitions; a *workspace* is a set of palettes and palette positions that you can save (for example, you can have all text-editing palettes appear when you're working on text).

Cross-Reference

I cover shortcut sets and workspaces in Chapter 3. I cover swatch libraries in Chapter 8.

The Plug-ins folder

The Plug-ins folder in the InDesign folder contains small software modules, called *plug-ins,* that add both core features and additional, optional features to InDesign. The Plug-ins folder contains a variety of subfolders such as Dictionaries, Filters, and Graphics, which make locating files easy.

To install additional plug-ins from Adobe or other companies, add them to the Plug-ins folder. Follow the instructions provided by each vendor — some have an installation program, while others have you copy the plug-in file to the Plug-ins folder.

To remove a plug-in, simply drag it out of the subfolder of the Plug-ins folder and store it someplace else or delete it.

Tip

To keep track of required files and plug-ins versus optional ones, you may want to create an Optional Plug-ins folder and install any optional plug-ins there rather than in the existing folders in the Plug-ins folder.

You also use the Plug-ins folder to get access to any customizations you make to the spelling or hyphenation dictionaries in InDesign. These custom settings are saved in the files inside the Dictionaries folder. If you're in a workgroup, the only way to ensure that everyone is working with the same spelling and hyphenation standards — so that text flows the same way on everyone's computer — is to share the dictionary files.

Cross-Reference See Chapter 35 for more information on maintaining standards across workgroups. See Chapter 36 for details on managing plug-ins.

The Required folder

The Required folder is similar to the Plug-ins folder in that it contains components of InDesign. The difference is that the components in the Required folder are necessary for InDesign to function, so you should not modify this folder or its contents.

Exploring the Document Window

When you're running InDesign, the first thing to do is create a new, empty document by choosing File ➪ New, or ⌘+N or Ctrl+N, and clicking OK immediately. This gives you a document window so you can start exploring the application. (Never mind the settings for now — you're just exploring.)

No matter what size document you're dealing with or how many pages it has, all documents are contained within a standard window. The window provides controls that help in creating and placing objects, changing the view scale, and navigating between pages. Figure 2-1 shows all the standard elements of a new document window.

Title bar

The bar across the top of the window is known as the *title bar*. InDesign's title bar not only reports the name of the document, but also the magnification at which you're viewing it. For example, the words *Herb Article @ 68%* centered in the title bar mean that you're looking at an InDesign document file called Herb Article and you're viewing it at 68 percent — a typical percent value you'll land at when choosing View ➪ Fit Page in Window (⌘+0 [zero] or Ctrl+0 [zero]) on a 17-inch monitor. The title bar also includes three boxes for manipulating the document window, as shown in Figure 2-1.

 Tip Double-clicking the document title bar on the Mac minimizes the window. In Windows, it maximizes the window (or restores the window if it is already maximized).

 Platform Difference Slight differences exist between the Macintosh and Windows interfaces for document windows. The Windows controls for window sizing appear in the upper-right corner rather than in the upper-left corner. In Windows, the Maximize box performs the same role as the Mac's Zoom box. Note that the Maximize box becomes the Restore box when the document window is *maximized* (made to fill the screen); the Restore box returns the window to its previous size. Also, in Windows, you can resize a window by dragging any side or corner, not just the Size box at the lower right. Figure 2-2 shows the Windows window-sizing controls.

Zero point (ruler origin)

Close box

Minimize box   Title bar   Page margins   Pane   Palette menu

Zoom box   Rulers   Page boundary   Palettes   Pane tabs

Page field   Page pop-up menu   Scroll button

Page-turning buttons   Page-turning buttons   Scroll bar

View Percentage pop-up menu   Scroll arrows

View Percentage field   Pasteboard Size box

Show/Hide Structure button

Figure 2-1: The standard document window provides controls for managing documents on-screen, changing the view scale, displaying different pages, and placing objects on pages.

Figure 2-2: The Windows window-sizing controls.

New document windows always display a horizontal ruler across the top and a vertical ruler down the left side. The horizontal ruler measures from the top left corner of the page across the entire spread; the vertical ruler measures from the top to the bottom of the current page.

You can use these rulers to judge the size and placement of frames and lines on your page. Although InDesign provides more-precise methods for placing objects — such as the Transform and Control panes, in which you can enter exact values — designers often use the rulers for rough placement while they experiment with a design, as shown in Figure 2-3.

Figure 2-3: This box's top is aligned with the 8-pica mark on the vertical ruler.

By default, both rulers display increments in picas, but you can change the measurement system for each ruler in the Units & Increments pane of the Preferences dialog box (choose InDesign ⇨ Preferences on the Mac or Edit ⇨ Preferences in Windows, or press ⌘+K or Ctrl+K). If you do this while no documents are open, the rulers in all new documents will display in your preferred measurement systems. If a document is open, the rulers are changed only in that document.

Chapter 3 explains ruler increments in more detail.

If you need more space on-screen or want to preview a design without all the layout tools, you can hide the rulers by choosing View ⇨ Hide Rulers, or by pressing ⌘+R or Ctrl+R. Most users show the rulers all the time out of habit, but the rulers aren't really necessary in template-driven documents such as magazines where all the placement decisions are indicated by guides and master pages. If you're editing text on a smaller monitor, you might appreciate the space gain of not having rulers, minimal though it might be.

Zero point

The intersection of the rulers in the upper-left corner of the page is called the *zero point*. Known as the *ruler origin* in other applications, this is the starting place for all horizontal and vertical measurements. If you need to place items in relation to another spot on the page (for example, from the center of a spread rather than from the left-hand page), you can move the zero point by clicking and dragging it to a new location. The X and Y values in the Transform pane and Control palette update as you drag the zero point so you can place it precisely. The zero point is document-wide, so it changes for all pages or spreads in the document. To restore the zero point to the upper-left corner of the left-most page, double-click the intersection of the rulers in the upper-left corner.

After the zero point is moved, all the objects on the page display new X and Y values even though they haven't moved. Objects above or to the left of the zero point will have negative X and Y values, and the X and Y values of other objects will not relate to their actual position on the page or spread.

All this can be potentially confusing, especially in a workgroup when other users may change the zero point and forget to restore it to the upper-left corner. To solve this problem, you can lock the ruler origin, making it more difficult for users to change it. Control+click or right-click the ruler origin and choose Lock Zero Point from the contextual menu. Granted, the Unlock Zero Point command is right there as well, so users can just as easily unlock it. But even though unlocking it is easy to undo, it's still worth using this feature, because some users won't know how to unlock it and others will be reminded that you don't want them messing with the zero point.

Scroll bars

Standard scroll bars run down the right side and across the bottom of the document window. As in most applications, you can either drag the scroll boxes or click the scroll arrows to move around on a page or move to other pages in the document.

Pasteboard, pages, and guides

Inside the rulers, you'll see a white area surrounding the black, drop-shadowed outlines of your pages (refer to Figure 2-1). The work area surrounding the page is called the *pasteboard,* and it's designed as a workspace for creating, experimenting with, and temporarily storing objects. You can also use the pasteboard to bleed objects off a page so they'll print to the edge of a trimmed page. Unlike PageMaker (and like QuarkXPress), each page or spread in InDesign has its own pasteboard. There's 1 inch of pasteboard above and below each page, and a space equal to the page width to the left and right of each page or spread. For example, a spread consisting of two 4-inch pages will have 4 inches of pasteboard to the left and 4 inches of pasteboard to the right.

Pages, drawn with black outlines, reflect the page size you set up in the New Document dialog box (File ➪ New, or ⌘+N or Ctrl+N). If it looks like two pages are touching, you're looking at a multipage spread. By default, you'll see magenta lines across the top and bottom of each page showing the top and bottom margins you specified when you created the document. Violet-colored lines indicate the left and right margins (for single-page documents) or inside and outside margins (for facing-page documents). These lines are nonprinting guides that can help you position objects.

You can change the placement of these guides choosing Layout ➪ Margins and Columns, and you can create additional guides by dragging them off the horizontal and vertical ruler.

Cross-Reference   I cover guides in detail in Chapter 4.

If you can't see the guide colors well, you can change them for all new documents. When no documents are open, choose new colors in the Guides pane of the Preferences dialog box (choose InDesign ➪ Preferences on the Mac or Edit ➪ Preferences in Windows, or press ⌘+K or Ctrl+K). The Margins color changes the horizontal guides and the Columns color affects the vertical guides.

Show/Hide Structure button

The dual-arrow button at the bottom of the document window (refer to Figure 2-1), called the Show/Hide Structure button, opens and closes the XML Structure window, which is used in Web-oriented documents based on the Extensible Markup Language (XML).

Cross-Reference   I cover XML in Chapter 34.

View Percentage field and pop-up menu

The lower-left corner of the document window contains the View Percentage field and pop-up menu that lets you change the document's view percent. The view scale can be as small as 5 percent and as large as 4,000 percent, and you can modify it in 0.01 percent increments. You have three options for using the View Percentage field and pop-up menu:

✦ To change the view to a preset value, click the arrow on the field and choose an option from the pop-up menu, as shown in Figure 2-4.

✦ To change the view to a specific value, highlight the value in the field, enter a new value, and press Return or Enter.

✦ To jump into the field quickly and enter a specific value, press Option+⌘+5 or Ctrl+Alt+5, enter a new value, and press Return or Enter. (This method lets you change the view without taking your hands off the keyboard.)

Figure 2-4: You can choose from a list of preset view percentages using the list in the View Percentage pop-up menu.

Page controls

InDesign has several controls for maneuvering through pages: Page-turning buttons, and the Page field and pop-up menu. There are also controls for entering prefixes for sections' page numbers and for indicating absolute page numbers in a document that contains multiple sections.

Page-turning buttons

Next to the View Percentage pop-up menu, you'll find a combined page-number field and pop-up menu encased by two sets of arrows, shown in Figure 2-5. These arrows are page-turning buttons, which let you turn pages sequentially or jump to the first or last page in the document. From left to right, clicking these arrows takes you to the first page, the previous page, the next page, and the last page.

Figure 2-5: Buttons on the bottom of the document window (at right) let you flip from page to page.

Page field and pop-up menu

The document window also provides a control for jumping to a specific page or master page in a document. To jump to a specific page number, highlight the current number in the page-number field, enter a new page number, and press Return or Enter. A shortcut to highlighting the field is ⌘+J or Ctrl+J.

To jump to a master page, enter the first few characters of the master page's name in the field. Jumping to document pages can be a little more complicated. Because the page number that displays and prints on the document page does not have to match the position of the page in the document — for example, the third page might be labeled "iii" instead of "3" — there are two methods for entering the page number you want to jump to: section page numbers and absolute page numbers.

You can also use the pop-up menu to the right of the page-number field to get a list of available pages, including master pages.

Section page numbers

A *section page number,* specified through the Numbering & Section Options dialog box (in the Pages pane's palette menu), is a customized page number. You use section numbers if your document needs to start on a page other than 1 — for example, if you're working on a magazine and each article is saved in a different document. You can also split a single document into separate sections of page numbers, and use section page numbers to change the format of numbers to Roman numerals, letters, and so on.

To jump to or print a page with a section page number, you need to indicate which section it is and what page number is displayed on the page. InDesign provides a default name for sections, starting at Sec1. When you enter a section page number, you must separate the section name and the page number with a colon. For example, if you start the page numbering on page 51, you'll need to enter Sec1:51 in the page-number field to jump to that page. Having to include this undisplayed section information makes this option fairly unappealing, so you may prefer to use absolute page numbers (see the following section).

Absolute page numbers

An *absolute page number* indicates a page's position in the document, such as 1 for the first page, 2 for the second page, and so on. To specify an absolute page number in the page-number field or other dialog box (such as Print) that involves selecting pages, you enter a plus sign before the number that represents the page's position. For example, the first page in the document is always +1, the second page is always +2, and so on. If you don't enter a plus sign, the first page with the number 1 is what InDesign will assume you mean—this may not be the first page in the document. For example, perhaps you have a five-page section with Roman numerals followed by a 30-page section with Arabic numerals; entering just **1** will go to the first page in the Arabic-numbered section, while entering +**1** will go to the first page in the document (*i*, in this case).

Using Tools

InDesign always displays a floating palette called the Tools palette (also sometimes referred to as the Toolbox by InDesign documentation), which contains 30 tools plus 13 other functions. It displays by default at the upper-left of the screen (refer to Figure 2-1). The tools let you create and manipulate the objects that make up your pages. The tools work similarly to those in other Adobe products (such as Photoshop, Illustrator, and PageMaker), and they work somewhat like the tools in QuarkXPress. But the tools do not work like the toolbars in your word processor, which are more like macros that make something happen. With InDesign's tools, for the most part, you select the tool and do something with it—draw a new frame, rotate a line, crop an image, and so on.

With so many tools, all of which perform limited functions, understanding what each tool does is imperative. When it comes to tools, InDesign has little intuition— it requires you to select the precise tool for the action you want to complete. The software is unable to predict that you might want to make a box slightly larger while you're editing text, or that you might want to reshape a frame at the same time you're resizing it. You need to learn which tool to use and get used to switching tools—a lot.

QuarkXPress User The limited functionality of each tool may be familiar to PageMaker users but is likely to drive a QuarkXPress convert crazy. In recent years QuarkXPress has made tools more flexible, so users don't have to switch as often when they go from, for example, editing content to resizing the frame to better fit that content. If you're a QuarkXPress user, pay special attention to the tool definitions that follow so you can translate the InDesign tools to tools that you understand.

Using Tool Tips and keyboard shortcuts

To start getting familiar with the tools, first make sure Show Tool Tips is checked in the General pane of the Preferences dialog box (choose InDesign ➪ Preferences on the Mac or Edit ➪ Preferences in Windows, or press ⌘+K or Ctrl+K). Point at each tool to learn its official name, as shown in Figure 2-6; let the pointer rest on the tool for a few seconds and a Tool Tip will display, telling you the name and shortcut key of that tool. Knowing the actual name is the key to learning about any tool — after all, neither the InDesign documentation's index nor this book's index lists tools by the way they look (for example, "little black pointer" or "empty square"); instead, if you want to look up a tool, you need to know the tool's name ("Selection tool" or "Rectangle tool," for example).

While you're learning the tool names, you'll notice a single letter in parentheses next to each tool name. This is the shortcut key to selecting that tool. For example, the (T) next to the Type tool indicates that pressing T selects the Type tool. The Tools palette's shortcuts don't use modifier keys like ⌘ and Ctrl. If you're editing text or otherwise have the Type tool selected — or if you're in a text-entry field in a pane or dialog box — entering these shortcuts will simply insert the text where your cursor is.

Figure 2-6: Tool Tips provide the names of tools along with the shortcut key (in parentheses) that you can use to select that tool.

Caution   If you're not careful, you can enter nonsense text in your articles because of the way the Tools palette's shortcuts work (without having to press ⌘ or Ctrl). This shortcut makes no sense in a program that includes significant text-handling functionality. Adobe's graphics programs, such a Photoshop and Illustrator, use such single-letter shortcuts, which does make sense because artists rarely used text in them. Adobe has decided to standardize the interface across all its products, which in this case results in an unintuitive and potentially damaging approach.

After you learn all the keyboard commands, you can create and refine a layout without ever reaching for the Tools palette. In no time, you'll be switching from the Scale tool to the Rotate tool with a quick punch of the R key, then hitting T to add a text frame. Now, obviously, you can't use the keyboard commands for selecting tools while typing or editing text, but they are worth remembering for switching tools while designing a layout. In many production environments, copy editors handle text changes, while layout artists handle design issues — in such environments, the layout artists would learn these shortcuts, while the copy editors would avoid them.

Opening and closing the Tools palette

Opening and closing the Tools palette is easy. One method of opening (or closing) the Tools palette is to choose Window ➪ Tools. The other method of opening (or closing) the Tools palette is more obscure: Pressing the Tab key (with any tool but the Type tool selected) closes all open palettes, including the Tools palette. To reopen those palettes, press Tab again. To reopen just the Tools palette, choose Window ➪ Tools.

You can reposition the Tools palette by dragging it to a new location on-screen — make sure you drag it by its title bar. You can also change its orientation and appearance by double-clicking the title bar. The first double-click converts the Tools palette to be one icon wide rather than the default two icons wide. The second double-click rotates the Tools palette to horizontal orientation. A third double-click restores it to the standard two-icon-wide vertical orientation. Figure 2-7 shows the three options.

Selecting tools

To select a tool and start using it, click it in the Tools palette. As long as you're not using the Type tool, you can also press a keyboard shortcut displayed in parentheses in the Tool Tips.

In addition to the tools you can see, the Tools palette contains a few hidden tools that are consolidated into little pop-out menus. Any tool with a small arrow in its lower-right corner is hiding one or more similar tools, as shown in Figure 2-8. To access hidden tools, click and hold on a tool with a pop-out indicator. When the pop-out displays, click one of the new tools to replace the standard tool with the pop-out tool.

Note   Many of the pop-out tools also have keyboard shortcuts, as Figure 2-8 shows.

Figure 2-7. By clicking on the Tools palette's title bar (in which there is no title, just the bar), you can change its appearance and orientation.

Tool definitions

In real life you can often get by using the wrong tool for a job—using a flat screw-driver instead of a Phillips, or a shoe instead of a flyswatter. This won't work in InDesign. Whether you're typing, reshaping an object, or applying a color, there's one—and only one tool—for the job. Loosely organized with the most commonly used tools at the top, the Tools palette includes tools for creating and manipulating frames and lines—the objects that make up your designs (refer to Figure 2-8).

Note

Frames are shapes and containers that you can size, position, and reshape with precision. InDesign has three types of frames: empty (unassigned) frames for blocks of color, text frames for type, and graphics frames for imported images. By default, most frames are empty but can be easily converted to text or graphics frames. Other frames are created specifically as text or graphics frames.

New Feature

The InDesign CS Tools palette adds the Measure and Push Button tools, as well as the Bleed Mode and Slug Mode buttons in the Preview Mode button's new pop-up menu. Also, the Scissors tool now occupies its own place in the Tools palette, no longer stored in the Gradient tool's pop-up menu (that pop-up menu no longer exists in version CS).

Figure 2-8: The Tools palette. If a small triangle displays in the lower-right corner of a tool, you can click and hold on it to display pop-out tools. Pop-outs are shown for all tools that have them, with the tool at the top the one that is the default tool for the Tools palette.

Adobe tool

In the Adobe world of software, the first item of the Tools palette is actually a big button that takes you to the Adobe Web site. A fairly large, prominent tool for something you can do just as easily many other ways, the Adobe tool does show the product icon so you always know from the Tools palette that InDesign is active.

Selection tool

The Selection tool (shortcut V) lets you select objects on the page and move or resize them. You might want to rename this tool in your mind to the Mover tool because it's the only tool that lets you drag objects around on-screen.

QuarkXPress User   Think of the Selection tool as half your Item tool.

Tip

If you're working with text and have the Type tool selected, you can switch to the Selection tool by holding down ⌘ or Ctrl, instead of using the Tools palette.

Here's how the Selection tool works:

✦ **To select any object on a document page,** click on it. If you can't seem to click on it, it might be an object placed by a *master page* (a preformatted page used to format pages automatically) or it might be behind another object.

✦ **To select an object placed by a master page,** press Shift+⌘ or Ctrl+Shift while you click.

✦ **To select an object that is completely behind another object,** ⌘+click it or Ctrl+click it.

✦ **To select multiple objects,** click and drag around the objects or Shift+click them individually. Because you need to press the Shift key anyway while selecting objects placed by master pages, you can always multiple-select those objects.

✦ **To move selected objects,** click somewhere within the objects and drag the mouse.

✦ **To resize a selected object,** drag any handle. Press Shift+⌘ or Ctrl+Shift while you drag to maintain the proportions of the object.

✦ **To resize both a selected frame and its graphic,** press ⌘ or Ctrl while you drag. Press Shift+⌘ or Ctrl+Shift to keep things proportional.

Tip

To resize multiple objects simultaneously, you must first group them (choose Object ⇨ Group, or press ⌘+G or Ctrl+G). Otherwise, only the object whose handle is being dragged will resize. Ungroup via Object ⇨ Ungroup, or Shift+⌘+G or Ctrl+Shift+G.

Direct Selection tool

The Direct Selection tool (shortcut A) lets you select individual handles on objects to reshape them, and it lets you move graphics independently of their frames.

QuarkXPress User

Think of the Direct Selection tool as the other half of your Item tool and also as the Content tool for pictures.

Here's how the Direct Selection tool works:

✦ **To select an object to reshape it,** click it to display anchor points on the edges (the anchor points are hollow handles that you can select individually, as shown in Figure 2-9). You can drag the anchor points to reshape the object.

✦ **To select objects placed by a master page,** Shift+⌘+click or Ctrl+Shift+click, as with the Selection tool. The Direct Selection tool lets you easily select objects behind other objects and to select items within groups.

✦ **To select multiple objects,** click and drag around the objects or Shift+click them. Because you need to press the Shift key anyway while selecting objects placed by master pages, you can always multiple-select those objects.

✦ **To move a graphic within its frame,** click inside the frame and drag the graphic.

✦ **To move a frame leaving the graphic in place,** click an edge of the frame and drag it.

In addition to using the Selection tool for *threading* (linking) text frames (see Chapter 16), you can use the Direct Selection tool. This is one of the few cases where you have more than one tool to handle a task.

Figure 2-9: Clicking and dragging a hollow anchor point with the Direct Selection tool lets you reshape items.

Pen tool

The Pen tool (shortcut P) lets you create paths consisting of straight and curved segments. Modeled after the pen tools in Illustrator and Photoshop, this is the tool for creating simple illustrations within InDesign.

If a path you create with the Pen tool is left open, the object is essentially a line that you can color or adjust stroke settings for. If the path is closed, the object is basically an empty frame. You can import text or graphics into the paths using the Place command (choose File ➪ Place, or press ⌘+D or Ctrl+D) or you can type into the path using the Type tool. If you decide to place text or graphics in an open path, the path closes automatically and becomes a frame. (To place text on a path, first choose the Type on a Path tool (shortcut Shift+T), then click the path.)

Here's how the Pen tool works:

✦ **To create straight segments of a path,** click to establish an anchor point, then move the mouse to the next location, click again, and so on. To move an anchor point after clicking, press the spacebar and drag the segment.

✦ **To create curved segments of a path,** click and drag, then release the mouse button to end the segment.

✦ **To close a path and create a frame,** click over the first anchor point created (the hollow one).

✦ **To leave a path open and create a line,** ⌘+click or Ctrl+click away from the path or select another tool.

The Pen tool includes a pop-out containing three additional tools for reshaping lines and frames: Add Anchor Point (shortcut =), Delete Anchor Point (shortcut - [hyphen]), and Convert Direction Point (shortcut Shift+C).

Cross-Reference For more information about using these tools, see Chapter 26 and Chapter 27.

Type tool

The Type tool (shortcut T) lets you enter, edit, and format text. The Type tool also lets you create rectangular text frames as you need them.

QuarkXPress User Think of the Type tool as a combination of the Rectangle Text Box tool and the Content tool for text — except remember that it doesn't let you do anything else such as resizing a frame when working as the Content tool equivalent.

Here's how the Type tool works:

✦ **To create a rectangular text frame,** click and drag; hold the Shift key to create a perfect square.

✦ **To begin typing or editing text,** click in a text frame or in any empty frame.

✦ **To highlight text so you can format it,** cut and paste it, drag-move it, and so on.

✦ **To select a word,** double-click anywhere in the word.

✦ **To select a paragraph,** triple-click anywhere in the paragraph.

✦ **To select all the text in a *story* (a series of threaded text frames),** choose Edit ➪ Select All or press ⌘+A or Ctrl+A.

You can place or drag-and-drop text files, and you can *thread* (link) text frames with either of the selection tools, but they won't let you touch the text.

The Type tool has a pop-out menu to select the Type on a Path tool (shortcut Shift+T), which lets you select a path or frame and enter text onto it so it follows the path or frame's outline.

Line tool

The Line tool (shortcut E) lets you draw freestanding lines (rules) on your page. To use this tool, simply click and drag it. You can use the rulers, the new Control palette, or the Transform pane to size and position the line precisely. Pressing the Shift key while you click and drag constrains the line angle to 45-degree increments, which is useful for creating straight horizontal and vertical lines.

Frame tools

There are three frame tools — Rectangle Frame (shortcut F), Ellipse Frame, and Polygon Frame — in InDesign. Their icons are distinguished by a large X inside. The latter two tools, which have no shortcuts, are available from the Rectangle Frame tool's pop-up menu. The frames created via these tools are meant to hold either pictures or text. To create frames with these tools, click and drag using the rulers or information in the Transform pane or Control palette to judge the size and placement. To create a perfect circle with the Ellipse Frame tool or a perfect square with the Rectangle Frame tool, press the Shift key while you click and drag.

You can fill and stroke the empty frames for use as design elements or you can import text and graphics into them using the Place command (File ➪ Place, or ⌘+D or Ctrl+D). You can also click in an empty frame with the Type tool to begin typing in it.

QuarkXPress User

The InDesign frame tools are the same as picture- and text-box tools in QuarkXPress, except that InDesign's boxes can hold either type of content, so there are not two variants of these tools in InDesign as there are in QuarkXPress.

To create a rectangle or ellipse, you click somewhere in the document window and drag the mouse to another location. The rectangle or ellipse fills the area. But creating a polygon frame works differently:

1. **Double-click the Polygon tool to display the Polygon Settings dialog box**, shown in Figure 2-10.

2. **Enter a value between 3 and 100 in the Number of Sides field to specify how many sides you want on your polygon.**

3. **If you want to create a star shape, use the Star Inset field to specify the size of the spikes.**

   The percent value specifies the distance between the polygon's bounding box and the insides of the spikes (for example, 50% creates spikes that are halfway between the bounding box and the center of the polygon).

4. **Click OK to close the Polygon Settings dialog box.**

   The settings are saved with the active document for the next time you use the Polygon tool.

5. **Click and drag to create the polygon, using the rulers or the Transform pane or Control palette to judge the size and placement.**

Figure 2-10: Double-clicking the Polygon tool displays the Polygon Settings dialog box, which you can use to specify the number of sides on a polygon, as well as any starburst spike settings.

To create a symmetrical polygon, in which all the sides are the same size, press the Shift key while you click and drag the Polygon tool.

Graphics tools

If you'd rather create actual graphics frames, use the Rectangle (shortcut M), Ellipse (shortcut L), or Polygon tools. (The Ellipse and Polygon tools are pop-out tools available from the Rectangle tool.) The tools are meant to create shapes that you will use as artwork, rather than as containers. But you can place text or graphics into one of these shapes the same way as you would a frame. Essentially, the graphics tools are superfluous and can be ignored.

Rotate tool

The Rotate tool (shortcut R) lets you change the angle of selected items visually. To use the Rotate tool, first select an item with the Selection tool or the Direct Selection tool, then select the Rotate tool. Or ⌘+click or Ctrl+click an object with the Rotate tool. Click and drag in any direction. The object rotates from the default location of the anchor point, which is the center of the selected object. You can drag the anchor point to a new location, as shown in Figure 2-11. To rotate an object in 45-degree increments, press the Shift key while you click and drag.

Scale tool

The Scale tool (shortcut S) lets you grab any object and resize it horizontally, vertically, or proportionally. When you scale text or graphics frames, the size of the text and image are resized as well. As with the Rotate tool, the Scale tool doesn't let you select items to scale. You either need to select an object first with a selection tool, or ⌘+click or Ctrl+click it with the Scale tool.

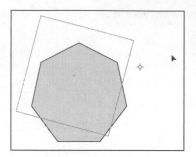

Figure 2-11: You can drag the anchor point for rotating items from the center of an object to a different location.

The Scale tool works as follows:

✦ **To make an object wider,** drag to the left.

✦ **To make an object narrower,** drag to the right.

✦ **To make an object taller,** drag down.

✦ **To make an object shorter,** drag up.

✦ **To resize an object both horizontally and vertically,** drag up or down diagonally.

✦ **To resize an object proportionally,** press the Shift key while you drag.

Shear tool

The Shear tool (shortcut O) works much the same as the Scale tool. Instead of resizing the object and contents, the Shear tool slants selected objects in the direction you drag.

Free Transform tool

The Free Transform tool (shortcut E) is handy because it lets you move, rotate, and reshape objects all with one tool. If you click and hold the mouse within the object, you can drag it. If you click any of the handles on the object frame, you can resize it. If you click and hold on any edge (except where there is a handle) or anywhere outside the object, you can rotate the object.

Measure tool

The Measure tool, which has no shortcut, opens the new Info pane and lets you draw a line whose dimensions show up in that pane so you can measure an arbitrary distance. You can see objects' dimensions in the Control palette and in the Transform and Info panes, but the value of the Measure tool is in determining the distance between objects rather than the dimensions of objects. It can also come in handy when measuring the distance across multiple objects.

New Feature   The Measure tool is new to InDesign CS.

Scissors tool

The Scissors tool (shortcut C) lets you cut paths into separate paths. When you cut an open path (a line), you get two separate lines. When you cut a closed path in one place, you get an open path. When you cut a closed path (a frame) in two places, you get two closed paths containing the same contents. Note that you cannot cut paths containing text.

To use the Scissors tool, ⌘+click or Ctrl+click an object to select it. Then do the following:

✦ **To cut a path,** click anywhere on the path. The path will not appear to be cut until you drag an anchor point with either the Selection tool or the Direct Selection tool.

✦ **To divide a frame into two separate frames,** click at two different locations on a path.

Eyedropper tool

The Eyedropper tool (shortcut I) displays the color settings for the object location clicked with it. This is handy way to find out the color makeup of imported graphics so you can then create a color swatch that matches it exactly.

 Cross-Reference I cover color and gradients in Chapter 8.

Gradient tool

The Gradient tool (shortcut G) lets you change the direction of existing gradient fills or strokes applied to objects. To apply gradients to objects, you use the Gradient pane (accessible via Window ➪ Gradient) as discussed in Chapter 8.

To change the gradient direction, follow these steps:

1. **Select an object.**

2. **Click either the Fill button or the Stroke button (immediately below the Gradient tool) to indicate where the gradient you want to change is.**

3. **Select the Gradient tool.**

4. **Click within the object at the start point, then drag to the end point.**

   You can drag from the inside out, from top to bottom, from left to right, and so on, depending on the effect you want to achieve.

Push Button tool

The new Push Button tool, which has no shortcut, creates rectangular frames that are used as buttons in Acrobat forms, which you can create in InDesign.

Hand tool

The Hand tool (shortcut H) lets you scoot pages around to view a different portion of a page or another page entirely. The Hand tool is an entirely visual method of scrolling, allowing you to see the page contents at all times. To use the Hand tool, click and drag in any direction. You can access the Hand tool temporarily without actually switching tools by pressing Option+spacebar or Alt+Spacebar.

New Feature

The Option+spacebar and Alt+spacebar shortcuts for temporary Hand tool access replace the shortcuts previously used — spacebar when not using the Text tool and Shift+spacebar when using the Text tool. This eliminates the confusion caused by having different shortcuts for the same action depending on what tool is selected.

Zoom tool

The Zoom tool (shortcut Z) lets you increase and decrease the document view scale. You can highlight a specific area on a page to change its view or you can click on-screen to change the view scale within InDesign's preset increments (shown in the View Percentage field and pop-up menu in the lower-left corner of the document window).

The Zoom tool works as follows:

✦ **To increase the view scale by a preset increment,** click on-screen.

✦ **To increase the view scale of an area,** click and drag around it.

✦ **To decrease the view scale by a preset increment,** Option+click or Alt+click on-screen.

✦ **To decrease the view scale of an area,** press Option or Alt while you click and drag around it.

Tip

You can access the Zoom tool temporarily without actually switching tools by pressing ⌘+spacebar or Ctrl+spacebar to zoom in and Option+⌘+spacebar or Ctrl+Alt+spacebar to zoom out.

You can also use ⌘++ (plus) or Ctrl++ (plus) to zoom in and ⌘+- (hyphen) or Ctrl+- (hyphen) to zoom out, or choose View ⇨ Zoom In or View ⇨ Zoom Out.

Color buttons

The bottom portion of the Tools palette contains buttons for applying colors to the edges of objects (strokes) and the insides of objects (fills). You use these buttons with the Stroke, Color, Gradient, and Swatches panes to apply and experiment with the colors applied to objects. Refer to Figure 2-8 for an illustration of these buttons.

Here's how the color buttons work:

✦ **To modify the fill (or background) of the selected object,** click the Fill button.

✦ **To modify the stroke (or outside edges) of the selected object,** click the Stroke button. (The shortcut X toggles between the Fill and Stroke buttons.)

✦ **Once you've clicked the Stroke or Fill button, use the Color, Swatches, or Gradient panes to apply a new color or gradient.**

✦ **To switch the color and/or gradient of the stroke and fill,** click the Swap Fill Stroke button or use the shortcut Shift+X.

✦ To revert the selected object to InDesign's default of a white fill and a black stroke, click the Default Fill/Stroke button or use the shortcut D.

✦ **To apply the last color used in the Swatches or Color pane,** click the Color button or use the shortcut <.

✦ **To apply the last gradient pattern used in the Swatches or Gradient pane,** click the Gradient button or use the shortcut . (period).

✦ **To remove the stroke or fill from an object,** click None or use the shortcut /.

View buttons

At the very bottom of the Tools palette are the two view buttons: Normal View Mode and Preview Mode. The first shows the pasteboard, margins, and guidelines, while the second hides those to give an unadorned preview of the final document.

New Feature

InDesign CS adds two new preview options via a pop-up menu in the Preview Mode button: Bleed mode and Slug mode. Bleed mode shows any objects that bleed beyond the page boundaries, while Slug mode shows the space reserved for information such as crop marks and color separation names used in final output. You set these up when you create new documents or by choosing File ⬧ Document Setup.

Working with Palettes and Panes

Initially, software developers used floating palettes to provide convenient access to commonly used options such as colors, fonts, and style sheets. Palettes provide a more interactive method of working with features, because the screen is not obscured by a large dialog box and you can access the controls quickly. Eventually, palettes started to move away from serving as a convenient alternative to commands and became the primary method — often the *only* method — for performing many tasks.

Panes versus palettes

Using an approach pioneered by Photoshop, InDesign's palettes are often composed of multiple panes. Each pane has a tab (like a file folder does) that you click to switch to that pane. InDesign lets you drag panes from one palette to another, as well as to anywhere on-screen (creating a new palette with just the one pane). That makes the distinction between a palette and a pane somewhat artificial. In this book, I use *palette* to refer to the entity that holds one or more panes, or for entities like the Tools and Control palettes that are self-contained floating objects containing commands. I refer to *panes* as anything that can be made a pane, even if you might have made it into its own palette (for example, I still call the Transform pane *the Transform* pane, even if I move it into its own palette).

Almost every palette (whether it contains one pane or many panes) has a palette menu, which provides a pop-up menu of options specific to that pane. (It is much like a contextual menu.) The palette menu's options are specific to the current pane.

Note The word *pane* has another use in InDesign. A pane is also a specific area in a dialog box. Such multipane dialog boxes also have tabs (and in some cases, option lists) that let you switch among the panes. Having multiple panes in a dialog box lets Adobe fit more functionality into the same space on-screen.

There are so many panes in InDesign—even more than in previous versions—that you might want to consider hooking up a second monitor for displaying them. And break out the computer glasses and your decoder ring, because the panes are small and laden with mysterious icons.

As with the tools, if you make sure Show Tool Tips is checked in the General pane of the Preferences dialog box (choose InDesign ➪ Preferences on the Mac or Edit ➪ Preferences in Windows, or press ⌘+K or Ctrl+K), you'll get some pretty good hints as to what the pane icons and fields do.

Managing palettes

Because there are so many panes in InDesign—22 standard palettes including the Tools palette (as shown in Figure 2-12) and *not* including any libraries or any of the 13 panes you might make into their own palettes—you're not going to want them all open all the time. In fact, as Figure 2-12 shows, they palettes would fill an entire screen if they were all open. Therefore, you might have some palettes you leave open all the time, some you open only while formatting text, and some that you open and close for one-time uses. As you become familiar with the palettes, you'll discover which ones you want to keep open.

Many palettes actually consist of multiple panes, such as the default combination of the Transform, Character, and Paragraph panes. You can create different combinations of panes to customize the palettes.

Figure 2-12: With all the palettes in InDesign open, working on a document is impossible.

New Feature

To try to gain some control over InDesign's palette profligacy, you can create *workspaces,* which are essentially memorized palette collections. Display the palettes you want, where you want them, and create a new workspace by choosing Window ➪ Workspace ➪ Save Workspace. Give it a name that makes sense, such as Text Palettes. That workspace is now available via Window ➪ Workspace ➪ [Workspace Name], automatically displaying just those saved palettes in their saved locations. By having several such workspaces, you can quickly switch among collections of palettes based on the tasks you're focused on.

Here's how panes work in InDesign:

✦ **To open a pane,** choose its menu command (such as Window ➪ Color). Some panes have keyboard shortcuts, as indicated in the menu. Opening a pane will open a palette, which might contain other panes.

✦ **To close a palette,** click its Close box in the upper-left corner (Macintosh) or upper-right corner (Windows). This will close all the panes in the palette. (You can't close a pane that's part of a palette with other panes. To get rid of such a pane, you either close the palette and all its panes, or you drag the pane to its own palette and then close that new palette.)

✦ **To shrink a palette down to the names of the panes within it,** click its Zoom box (Macintosh) or Minimize box (Windows).

✦ **To move a palette,** drag its title bar.

✦ **To select a different pane in a palette,** click its tab.

✦ **To combine the panes of different palettes,** drag and drop a pane's tab into another palette.

✦ **To pull a pane out of a palette into its own,** drag and drop its tab out of the palette into its own palette.

Note

A few palettes contain arrows in the lower-right corner that you can drag to resize the palette, and some palette menus let you change the orientation of the palette from horizontal to vertical.

A few palettes also use a double-arrow character next to the pane name to indicate that there is more to the pane than may be displayed; click the pane title to expand or collapse those extra options.

New Feature

You can collapse panes to tabs on the side of the screen and open them by clicking the pane's tab. (Figure 2-13 shows these side tabs in use.) To collapse a pane into a side tab, click on the palette's tab and drag it to the left or right side of your screen. To open the pane, click its tab. To collapse the pane, double-click its tab. To separate a pane from the screen edge, drag the tab out from the side of your screen or move it into a palette.

When you install InDesign, three palettes are placed along the right side of your screen by default; they contain the Pages, Layers, and Info panes; the Swatches, Character Styles, and Paragraph Styles panes; and the Stroke, Color, Transparency, and Gradient panes. If you open other panes, they will open as floating panes rather than be aligned to the side of the screen, but you can always move them to a screen edge if you prefer that placement.

Figure 2-13: The new side-tabs feature lets you dock pane tabs at the side of the monitor window and click the tab names to open them when needed.

Marrying and divorcing palette panes

Although it may seem as if combining and splitting panes is the antidote to InDesign's palette-itis, the resulting palettes can be difficult to work with. Combined panes can become cumbersome: If you combine panes that have different default sizes or orientations, each time you click a different pane the palette changes its size — this can be fairly disorienting. Plus, you can't see and reach for different types of options as easily, because you have to activate different panes. On the other hand, splitting panes into too many separate palettes can leave you with an overwhelming number of palettes.

In general, you'll want to split palettes that you use often and combine or close panes that you use rarely. And you might change the palette configuration based on the type of document. If you're working on a movie poster, you'll definitely want the Navigator pane but might have little use for the Pages pane. Or if you're laying out a newsletter that is formatted exclusively with style sheets, you might as well close the Character and Paragraph panes.

Use the new workspaces feature to save different pane and palette configurations for different points in the workflow or for different kinds of documents.

Also use the new Control palette instead of panes, since it provides access to most common functions. Even better, the Control palette adjusts its display based on what the current object is, so you get just the relevant options. For example, when you select a text frame, the Control palette provides the most of functions of the Transform, Character Style, Character, Paragraph, Paragraph Styles, and Stroke panes.

Using panes

To use a pane, first you need to activate it. You can do this by clicking its tab (if the palette containing it is open) or by choosing its menu command in the Window menu (if the pane is not open or if another pane in that palette is active). You'll need to be on the lookout here — If a menu command brings a pane forward in a palette, you might not even notice.

When a pane is active, controls in panes have the following characteristics:

✦ Click a pop-up menu to display and select an option; the changes take effect immediately.

✦ Highlight a value in a field to enter a new value. To implement the value, press Shift+Return or Shift+Enter. Or you can Tab to the next field or Shift+Tab to the previous field. Or just click in a different field or elsewhere in the document. To get out of a field you've modified, leaving the object unscathed, press Esc.

✦ Some fields include up and down arrows that you can click to increase or decrease the value in the field.

✦ Fields accept values in all different measurement systems. (I discuss this in detail in Chapter 3.)

✦ In addition to entering values in fields, you can enter calculations. You can add to, subtract from, multiply, and divide values in fields using the following operators: +, –, * (multiply), and / (divide). For example, to reduce the width of a frame by half, you might type **/2** next to the current value of 4.5 inches in the Width field. Or, to increase the length of a line by 6 points, you can type **+6** next to the current value in the Length field.

New to InDesign CS, you can also use percentages in fields, such as 50%, which adjusts the current value by that percentage.

✦ Most panes provide a full menu that you can display by clicking the arrow in the upper-right corner. The *palette menu* provides commands related to the current pane's contents (for example, the Character Styles pane provides a command for creating a New Style, as shown in Figure 2-14).

Figure 2-14: Most panes include palette menus that provide access to related features.

Checking out the panes

Like the tools in InDesign, each pane has a distinct function. The use of each pane is covered in detail in the appropriate chapters throughout this book (for example, the Layers pane is covered in Chapter 6). But with the help of Tool Tips and a quick introduction to their primary purpose, you can start using many of the panes to start performing basic functions.

InDesign CS adds seven new panes. The most useful is the Control palette, which combines many attributes in one location. Other new panes include the Bookmarks, Flattener Preview, Info, Pathfinder, Separations Preview, and States panes.

Here is a quick summary of the InDesign panes (all available via the Window menu unless otherwise indicated). Note that in the figures of the various panes, the full pane is shown for any that have the option of showing just some options; these panes have a double-arrow to the right of the pane name.

✦ **Tools palette:** As covered earlier in this chapter, this palette is the mechanism by which you select the appropriate tool to accomplish various layouts tasks.

✦ **Control palette (shortcut Option+⌘+6 or Ctrl+Alt+6):** This is one of the most useful features in InDesign. It combines many attributes about the currently selected object so you can minimize the use of other panes and menu items. The palette changes based on what is selected, as Figure 2-15 shows.

QuarkXPress User

The Control palette by default is docked to the top of the screen. QuarkXPress users might want to float it at the bottom to mimic QuarkXPress's interface.

Figure 2-15: The Control palette for frames with pictures (top), frames with text (middle), and frames with lines (bottom).

✦ **Links pane (shortcut Shift+⌘+D or Ctrl+Shift+D):** The Links pane shows the original location of imported graphics and text files (see Figure 2-16).

Figure 2-16: The Links pane.

✦ **Character pane (choose Window ➪ Type & Tables ➪ Character, or press ⌘+T or Ctrl+T):** Use this pane (shown in Figure 2-17) to change common attributes of highlighted text such as the font, size, leading, kerning, tracking, and scaling.

✦ **Paragraph pane (choose Window ⇨ Type & Tables ⇨ Paragraph, or press Option+⌘+T or Ctrl+Option+T):** Use this pane (shown in Figure 2-17) to change common attributes of selected paragraphs such as the alignment, indents, space before and after, and hyphenation.

Figure 2-17: The Character pane (left) and the Paragraph pane (right).

✦ **Character Styles pane (choose Window ⇨ Type & Tables ⇨ Character Styles, or press Shift+F11):** Use this pane (shown in Figure 2-18) to create and apply style sheets consisting of character-level formats.

✦ **Paragraph Styles pane (choose Window ⇨ Type & Tables ⇨ Paragraph Styles, or press F11):** Use this pane (shown in Figure 2-18) to create and apply style sheets consisting of paragraph-level formats.

Figure 2-18: The Character Styles pane (left) and the Paragraph Styles pane (right).

✦ **Tabs pane (choose Window ⇨ Type & Tables ⇨ Tabs, or press Shift+⌘+T or Ctrl+Shift+T):** This pane (shown in Figure 2-19) lets you create tab stops for selected paragraphs; you can also specify alignment, position, and leader characters for the tabs.

✦ **Story pane (choose Window ⇨ Type & Tables ⇨ Story):** It's small but important — the Story pane (shown in Figure 2-19) lets you specify hanging punctuation for all the frames in a story by checking Optical Margin Alignment. You can also change the type size if the need arises.

Figure 2-19: The Tabs pane (left) and the Story pane (right).

✦ **Glyphs pane (choose Window ⇨ Type & Tables ⇨ Glyphs):** The Glyphs pane lets you access special characters within a font. Figure 2-20 shows the Glyphs pane.

Several of the text-oriented panes are available from the Type menu: Character, Paragraph, Tabs, Glyphs, Story, Character Styles, and Paragraph Styles. This provides faster access than accessing them through the Window ⇨ Type & Tables submenu.

Figure 2-20: The Glyphs pane

✦ **Text Wrap pane (choose Window ⇨ Type & Tables ⇨ Text Wrap or press Option+⌘+W or Ctrl+Alt+W):** The Text Wrap pane (shown in Figure 2-21) provides intuitive buttons for controlling how text runs around selected objects.

✦ **Transform pane (shortcut F9):** This pane (shown in Figure 2-21) lets you specify size, placement, scale, rotation, and shear of selected objects with the Transform pane.

✦ **Align pane (shortcut F8):** The Align pane (shown in Figure 2-21) provides buttons that let you evenly distribute or realign multiple-selected objects with one click.

Figure 2-21: The Text Wrap pane (left), the Transform pane (center), and the Align pane (right).

✦ **Pages pane (shortcut F12):** Use this pane (shown in Figure 2-22) to create master pages and to add, rearrange, and delete document pages. You can also create sections of page numbers using the Pages pane's palette menu.

✦ **Layers pane (shortcut F7):** The Layers pane (shown in Figure 2-22) provides access to vertical slices of a document that you can use to control the stacking order of objects, to isolate specific portions of a design, or to store revisions of the same document.

✦ **Navigator pane:** The Navigator pane (shown in Figure 2-22) shows a color proxy version of pages and lets you isolate a portion of any page to display in the document window.

Figure 2-22: The Pages pane (left), the Layers pane (center), and the Navigator pane (right).

✦ **Swatches pane (shortcut F5):** The Swatches pane (shown in Figure 2-23) lets you create named colors such as those using Pantone, Focoltone, and Toyo inks, and apply the colors to text, strokes, and fills.

✦ **Stroke pane (shortcut F10):** Use the Stroke pane (shown in Figure 2-23) to outline the edges of frames and lines; you have control over the thickness and the pattern of the outlines.

✦ **Color pane (shortcut F6):** The Color pane (shown in Figure 2-23) lets you create LAB, CMYK, and RGB colors, and apply the colors to text, strokes, and fills. (LAB, CMYK, and RGB are all composite color models, in which all colors are made by mixing a small number of primary colors. Chapters 8 and 42 describe these models in detail.)

✦ **Gradient pane:** Use the Gradient pane (shown in Figure 2-23) to create a stroke or fill consisting of a graduated blend between two colors.

✦ **Attributes pane:** The Attributes pane (shown in Figure 2-23) lets you specify that the stroke or fill in selected objects overprints the background.

✦ **Table pane:** The Table pane (shown in Figure 2-24) lets you adjust table settings.

✦ **Index pane:** The Index pane (shown in Figure 2-24) lets you add and manage index and table-of-contents entries.

Figure 2-23: Clockwise from upper left:
The Swatches, Stroke, Color, Attributes,
and Gradient panes.

Figure 2-24: The Table pane (left) and the
Index pane (right).

✦ **Scripts pane:** The Scripts pane (shown in Figure 2-25) shows available AppleScripts, Visual Basic scripts, and Java scripts in the Scripts folder in the InDesign folder.

✦ **Script Label pane:** The Script Label'pane (shown in Figure 2-25) lets you change the label of the selected script.

Figure 2-25: The Scripts pane (left) and the
Script Label pane (right).

✦ **Pathfinder pane:** This new pane (shown in Figure 2-26) lets you manipulate paths, such as combining, separating, and otherwise working with open and closed paths.

Figure 2-26: The Pathfinder pane.

✦ **Transparency pane:** The Transparency pane (shown in Figure 2-27) lets you adjust the solidity of images to create fading and overlap effects.

✦ **Flattener Preview pane:** This new pane (shown in Figure 2-27) lets you see what page items (typically those with transparency) are *flattened* (made solid) during printing or exporting to Encapsulated PostScript (EPS), Scalable Vector Graphics (SVG, an Adobe vector format for the Web), or Portable Document Format (PDF) 1.3 formats. Flattening occurs for printing devices and graphics export formats that don't support transparency.

Figure 2-27: The Transparency pane (left)
and the Flattener Preview pane (right).

✦ **Separations Preview pane:** This new pane (shown in Figure 2-28) lets you see page items with various color plates enabled, as well as preview the effects of different ink densities.

✦ **Trap Presets pane:** The Trap Presets pane (shown in Figure 2-28) lets you set and apply different trapping settings to objects, which controls how abutting and overlapping objects print to avoid gaps caused by paper-feed variations during printing.

Figure 2-28: The Separations Preview pane (left) and the Trap Presets pane (right).

✦ **Info pane:** This new pane (shown in Figure 2-29) shows some of the characteristics — such as size, position, and cropping — of selected objects.

Figure 2-29: The Info pane.

✦ **States pane:** This new pane shown in Figure 2-30) sets button actions for both Web pages and PDF files.

✦ **Tags pane:** The Tags pane (shown in Figure 2-30) lets you add XML tags and map them to paragraph and character styles. XML tags determine the formatting for XML data sources used in XML documents.

✦ **Bookmarks pane:** This new pane (shown in Figure 2-30) creates the bookmarks used in PDF files to create clickable indexes and tables of contents.

✦ **Hyperlinks pane:** The Hyperlinks pane (shown in Figure 2-30) lets you set up hyperlinks from and to document objects and pages, as well as to World Wide Web locations.

Figure 2-30: Clockwise from upper left: The States, Tags, Bookmarks, and Hyperlinks panes.

Reviewing Menu Commands

With so many palettes and panes, menu commands take on a more secondary function in InDesign. Many menu commands do nothing but display a palette or bring a pane of a palette forward. But to get comfortable in InDesign, you do need to know the basic function of each menu.

QuarkXPress User

If you're switching from QuarkXPress, you might get lost in the menus, so charts in Appendixes C and D of this book — which cover how to make the move from QuarkXPress or PageMaker to InDesign — show the equivalent menus.

InDesign menu

The InDesign menu, shown in Figure 2-31 contains preference and plug-in settings, as well as the command to exit the program and to hide it. The Services menu option contains Mac OS X functions, not any InDesign-specific options.

The InDesign menu is available only on the Mac. In Windows, the About InDesign and Configure Plug-ins menu options reside in the Help menu, the Preferences menu option resides in the Edit menu, and the Quit InDesign menu option resides in the File menu. The other InDesign menu options are Mac OS X–specific.

Figure 2-31: The InDesign menu.

File menu

The File menu (shown in Figure 2-32) lets you perform actions on entire documents, libraries, and books, including creating, opening, saving, closing, and printing. The Place command lets you import graphics and text files, and the Export command lets you save documents in different formats such as EPS, HTML, and PDF. The Windows version also includes the Quit menu option.

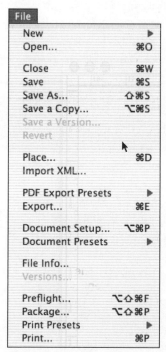

Figure 2-32: The File menu.

Edit menu

InDesign's Edit menu (shown in Figure 2-33) provides access to its invaluable multiple undo and redo features, as well as the standard Cut, Copy, Paste, and Clear commands. You'll find Duplicate and Step and Repeat here, even though you might be searching the Object menu for them. The Edit menu also provides commands for searching and replacing text and formats, checking spelling, and editing spelling and hyphenation dictionaries, as well as for opening the new Story Editor text-editing feature. It also provides access to color settings and keyboard shortcut preferences. The Windows version also contains the Preferences menu option.

Figure 2-33: The Edit menu.

Layout menu

With the Layout menu (shown in Figure 2-34), you can change the position of the column and margin guides you established in the New Document dialog box, create guides at specific locations, and resize an entire document proportionally. You can also turn pages in a document and insert automatic page numbers using Layout menu commands. Finally, this menu contains the commands for setting up tables of contents.

Figure 2-34: The Layout menu.

Type menu

The Type menu (shown in Figure 2-35) provides all your controls for formatting text — character formats, paragraph formats, tabs, and style sheets. The Story command lets you specify hanging punctuation for all the frames in a story. You can also convert text to a frame and insert special characters using a dialog box rather than keyboard shortcuts.

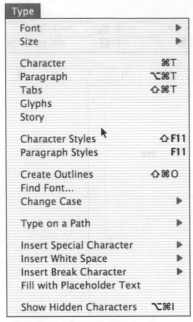

Figure 2-35: The Type menu.

Object menu

Use the Object menu (shown in Figure 2-36) for layout functions such as controlling the stacking order of lines and frames, grouping objects together, locking objects to the page, and wrapping text around objects. You can manipulate objects, such as changing the number of columns and text inset in the Text Frame Options dialog box or fine-tuning the corners of a frame using the Corner Effects dialog box. For working with graphics, the Object menu lets you fit graphics to frames and frames to graphics, create clipping paths, merge and separate paths, apply colors to some types of images, and create drop shadows. It also lets you insert movies and audio files for interactive PDF documents.

Figure 2-36: The Object menu.

Table menu

The Table menu (shown in Figure 2-37) contains the controls to create and edit tables. Here you create tables, modify them, convert text into tables and vice versa, manage table cells, and control row and column spacing.

Figure 2-37: The Table menu.

View menu

With the View menu (shown in Figure 2-38), you can change the view scale of the document, choose whether objects placed by master pages display, and specify which layout tools display: *threads* (links between text frames), the edges of frames, rulers, guides, the baseline grid, and the document grid. You can also specify whether guides are locked, and whether items snap to guides and the document grid.

Tip   If you're expecting to use the View menu to show and hide invisible characters such as spaces and tabs, look in the Type menu instead.

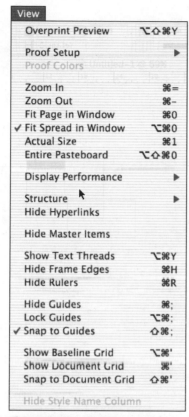

Figure 2-38: The View menu.

Window menu

For the most part, the Window menu (shown in Figure 2-39) opens palettes or brings panes of palettes forward. Other commands let you manage document windows, opening additional windows for the same document and redistributing document windows on-screen. Currently open documents are listed at the bottom the menu.

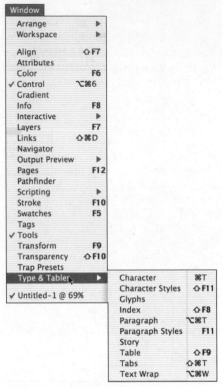

Figure 2-39: The Window menu.

Help menu

The Help menu (shown in Figure 2-40) contains links to Adobe's HTML help files, as well as to Adobe's program-update function. The Windows version also contains the Configure Plug-ins menu option.

Figure 2-40: The Help menu.

Contextual menus

The last interface element you'll find useful in InDesign is the contextual menu. By Control+clicking or right-clicking the document, an object, the rulers, and so on, you can display a menu of options for modifying whatever it is you're clicking on. See Figure 2-41 for an example of several contextual menus.

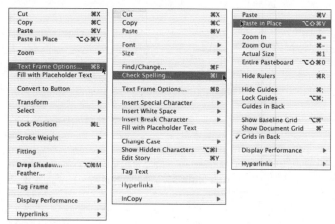

Figure 2-41: The contextual menu for a text frame (left), for highlighted text (center), and for the document (right).

Summary

InDesign stored its preferences in a file that you can copy to other users, to ensure standard interface in workgroups. It offers its functionality through a variety of interface methods: palettes, menu options, and contextual menus, as well as through some navigation controls in the document window. Panes are the primary vehicle for accessing InDesign features.

The variety of panes can be overwhelming, so InDesign lets you save different workspace sets that let you specify which panes to display and where in each set. You can move pane tabs to the side of your monitor screen to keep them accessible but less distracting. You can also move, separate, and combine panes into palette groups of your choice. Among new panes are the Bookmarks, Flattener Preview, Info, Pathfinder, Separations Preview, and States panes. The new Control palette is a great time-saver, grouping many functions into one palette, showing only the relevant options for different kinds of objects.

✦   ✦   ✦

Getting InDesign Ready to Go

In This Chapter

Knowing where preferences are stored

Setting preferences for documents and the application

Customizing keyboard shortcuts

Setting defaults for documents, text, and objects

Creating default colors and style sheets

Changing the view scale

Although you may not realize it, Adobe has made a variety of educated guesses about the way you work. For example, it assumes you work in picas, that you prefer low-resolution previews of images, and that you use typographers' quotes. Adobe has also made decisions about the default properties of text, the default color swatches included with documents, and the default attributes of some objects. In all cases, Adobe tried to make the defaults appropriate for most publishers.

But no matter how much thought Adobe put into making these educated guesses, they won't work for everybody. In fact, it's unlikely that every single setting will work for you. So no matter how tempted you are to jump in and start working, take a minute to prepare InDesign for the way you actually work. Otherwise, you'll end up conforming the way you work to InDesign's decisions, making it more difficult to learn the program and get your work done; or you'll end up making the same changes to document after document, wasting time in the process.

Working with Preferences Files

InDesign stores preferences in several places. Some are stored in the documents themselves, so they work as expected as they are moved from user to user. Others are stored in files on your computer and affect only you.

InDesign Defaults file

The preferences you set in InDesign, from measurement units to color-calibration settings, are all stored in the InDesign Defaults file. On the Mac, this file is in the InDesign 3.0 folder in the Adobe InDesign folder in the Preferences folder in the current user's Library folder. In Windows, it is in the \Document and Settings\[Current User]\Application Data\Adobe\InDesign\Version 3.0 folder on the drive that contains Windows.

To specify these defaults, you modify settings in the Preferences dialog box when no documents are open. All new documents you create are based on these settings.

Because some of the information affects how text flows and how documents look, you may want to standardize it for a workgroup by setting preferences once and sharing the InDesign Defaults file. (Sharing the file is a simple matter of giving copies of the file to other InDesign users to place in the appropriate system folder.)

New Feature   InDesign CS adds the option of deleting the InDesign Defaults preference files when opening InDesign: Press Control+Option+Shift+⌘ or Ctrl+Alt+Shift when launching InDesign.

Note   If you make changes to preferences while a document is open, the change is saved with that document and not in the InDesign Defaults file. The document remembers its own preference settings so it will look the same when it's opened on other computers running InDesign.

Presets folder

The Presets folder in your InDesign application folder contains three kinds of standards: shortcut sets, color-swatch libraries, and workspaces. InDesign lets you create shortcut sets, so different users can have their own shortcut definitions; these preferences are stored in the InDesign Shortcut Sets folder in the Presets folder. The Swatch Libraries folder contains color-swatch libraries, both those that come with InDesign and any you might add yourself. Finally, the Workspaces folder contains workspace definitions; a *workspace* is a set of palettes and palette positions that you can save so, for example, you can have all text editing palettes appear when you're working on text.

Setting Preferences

Preferences are settings that affect an entire document — such as what measurement system you're using on rulers, what color the guides are, and whether substituted fonts are highlighted. In InDesign, you access these settings through the Preferences dialog box (choose InDesign ⇨ Preferences on the Mac or Edit ⇨ Preferences in Windows, or press ⌘+K or Ctrl+K). They are stored in the InDesign Defaults files in your InDesign application folder.

InDesign has two methods for changing preferences: You can change preferences when no documents are open to create new settings for all future documents, or you can change preferences for the active document, which affects only that document. Your strategy for changing preferences depends on the way you work and the needs of specific documents. For example, if you generally prefer to work in points, you might change the default measurement system to points with no documents open. However, you might have a design such as an envelope that makes more sense in inches, so you can change the measurement system for that specific document.

The Preferences dialog box provides ten types of settings divided into panes: General, Text, Composition, Units & Increments, Grids, Guides, Dictionary, Spelling, Story Editor Display, and Display Performance. The steps for setting preferences stay the same, regardless of the changes you need to make.

New Feature

The Workgroup preferences pane no longer exists in InDesign CS. Its functions — which involve managing documents in a workgroup environment — are now part of the Open and Save dialog boxes. The new Updates pane is essentially the same as the old Online Settings pane; you use it to set how often InDesign automatically connects to Adobe's servers to get product updates. Finally, the Spelling and Story Editor Display preference panes are new.

When using the Preferences dialog box:

1. Determine whether the change is for a specific document or for all future documents, then open or close documents accordingly. If no documents are open, the changes are stored in your preferences file and will be remembered for all new documents. If a document is open, the changes are in effect for that document only.

2. Choose InDesign ➪ Preferences on the Mac or Edit ➪ Preferences in Windows, or press ⌘+K or Ctrl+K, to open the General pane. Alternately, you can choose a specific command from the Preferences submenu of the File menu. For example, you might choose File ➪ Preferences ➪ Composition. (There are no shortcuts for these submenus.)

3. To switch to a specific pane, choose an option from the list at the left of the dialog box, as shown in Figure 3-1.

4. Change any settings in any of the panes, and then click OK. The changes are saved with the active document or in the InDesign Defaults file.

Note

This section takes a comprehensive look at all the preferences in InDesign. Preferences that affect specific features are often discussed again in the relevant chapters. For example, Dictionary preferences are covered in the section on spell-checking in Chapter 15.

Caution

Unlike most actions you perform in InDesign, you cannot reverse changes to preferences using the Undo command (Edit ➪ Undo, or ⌘+Z or Ctrl+Z). If you change your mind about a preference setting, open the Preferences dialog box and change the setting again.

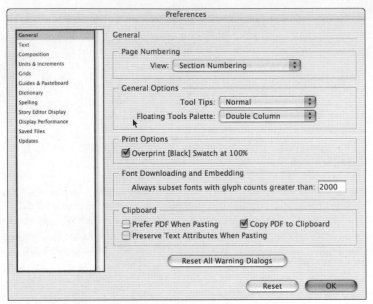

Figure 3-1: The General pane of the Preferences dialog box.

General preferences

Options in the General pane (refer to Figure 3-1) affect the way several features in InDesign work.

Page Numbering area

In the Page Numbering area of the Preferences dialog box, the View pop-up menu controls how page numbers display in the fields such as the page-number field on the document window. (See Chapter 2 for information about the difference between section page numbers and absolute page numbers.) Here are the controls:

✦ The default setting, Section Numbering, means that InDesign shows the page numbers according to the information in the Section Options dialog box accessed via the Pages pane's palette menu. When Section Numbering is selected, by default you need to enter section page numbers, such as "Sec2:3," in fields.

✦ The Absolute Numbering option, which I prefer, shows page numbers according to each page's position in the document. For example, the first page is 1, the second page is 2, and the third page is 3, even if the pages display the Roman numerals i, ii, and iii. When this option is selected, you can always jump to the first page in a document by entering **1** in the Page Number box.

General Options area

InDesign has two options in the General Options section over tool display. The Tool Tips pop-up menu has three options: Normal, Fast, and None. None turns off *tool tips,* the labels that pop up when the mouse hovers over a pane's icons. Fast makes the labels appear faster, which is best for new users learning the interface. Normal is the default setting and is the best for experienced users, since it waits a bit before displaying the label so they don't pop up if you're just moving the mouse slowly.

The second option is the Tools Palette pop-up menu, which lets you set the Tools palette as single-column width or the default double-column width. This is a matter of personal preference.

Print Options area

By default, Overprint Black is checked so that any black text, strokes, or fills overprint. This usually results in clearer text and lines. (This option applies to the Black color in the Swatches pane, rather than say a black swatch that you create.) If you uncheck Overprint Black, all black text, strokes, and fills knock out of their backgrounds, which results in a lighter black and could cause some misregistration when printing. (See Chapters 8 and 29 for more details on creating colors and trapping colors, respectively.)

Font Downloading and Embedding area

The Always Subset Fonts with Glyph Counts Greater Than field is used for OpenType fonts that have many special characters, such as accented letters, symbols, and diacritical marks. To prevent output files from getting clogged up with very large font files, this option lets you set the maximum number of characters (glyphs) that can be downloaded from a font file into an output file. Any characters actually used are always downloaded; the reason you might want to download an entire font is so someone could edit the file as a PDF or EPS file and have access to all characters in the proper fonts for such editing.

 New Feature The Always Subset Fonts with Glyph Counts Greater Than field is new to InDesign CS.

Clipboard area

The Clipboard area controls how image and text formatting are handled when copying elements to the Clipboard (through Edit ➪ Copy, or ⌘+C or Ctrl+C, and Edit ➪ Cut, or ⌘+X or Ctrl+X). There are three options:

✦ The Prefer PDF When Pasting check box converts items copied from Adobe Illustrator into PDF format so that transparency objects, blends, and patterns are preserved during the paste operation into InDesign.

✦ The Copy PDF to Clipboard check box creates a temporary PDF file when you copy items from InDesign for pasting into applications such as Illustrator.

✦ The new Preserve Text Attributes When Pasting check box preserves formatting such as italics and bold when text is copied. This can be helpful or a pain,
depending on whether you want copied text to preserve its formatting or you
prefer copied text to take on the formatting of the destination location's text.
The right answer will depend on your specific layouts.

 New Feature   The Preserve Text Attributes When Pasting option is new to InDesign CS.

Reset All Warning Dialogs button

Use this button to turn on warning dialogs you may have turned off. Most warning
dialog boxes have an option to turn off future warnings, and this resets them so
they all display again.

Text preferences

Options in the Text pane of the Preferences dialog box, shown in Figure 3-2, affect
how several character formats work, whether you use typographer's quotes, and
how text displays on-screen.

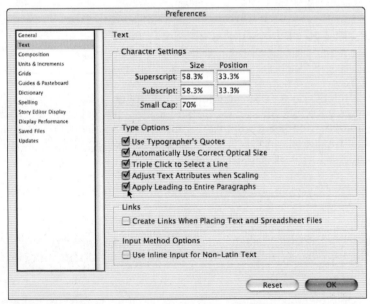

Figure 3-2: The Text pane of the Preferences dialog box.

Character Settings area

The palette menu on the Character pane (Window ⇨ Type & Tables ⇨ Character, or ⌘+T or Ctrl+T) lets you format highlighted characters as Superscript (reduced and raised above the baseline), Subscript (reduced and dropped below the baseline), or Small Caps (reduced versions of capital letters). Note that Superscript, Subscript, and Small Caps characters do not need to be reduced — they can actually be enlarged instead. The controls in the Character Settings area govern precisely how these characters are placed and resized.

✦ The Size fields in the Superscript and Subscript areas let you specify how much to scale these characters. The default is 58.3 percent, but you can enter a value between 1 and 200 percent. I prefer 60 or 65 percent, depending on the type size and font.

✦ The Position fields let you specify how much to shift Superscript characters up and Subscript characters down. The default is 33.3 percent, but you can enter a value between –500 and 500 percent. I prefer 30 percent for subscripts and 35 percent for superscripts.

✦ The Small Cap field lets you specify the scale of Small Caps characters in relation to the actual capital letters in the font. The default is 70 percent, but you can enter a value between 1 and 200 percent.

See Chapter 40 for information about using the "true small caps" variation of a typeface, when available, rather than the Small Cap character format.

Type Options area

The first four of the five Type Options, which control different aspects of InDesign's character handling, are all checked by default.

✦ When you press the quote key on the keyboard with Use Typographer's Quotes checked, InDesign inserts the correct typographer's quotes (often called *curly quotes*) for the current language in use. For example, for U.S. English, InDesign inserts typographic single quotes (' ') or double quotes (" ") rather than straight quotes. For French, InDesign inserts double angle brackets (« »). InDesign knows what language's characters to use based on the Language pop-up menu in the Character pane (Window ⇨ Type & Tables ⇨ Character, or ⌘+T or Ctrl+T) or in the Paragraph Style and Character Style dialog boxes' Advanced Character Formats pane (Window ⇨ Type & Tables ⇨ Paragraph Styles, or F11, and Window ⇨ Type & Tables ⇨ Character Styles, or Shift+F11, respectively).

✦ Automatically Use Correct Optical Size, when checked, automatically accesses OpenType and PostScript fonts that include an optimal size axis, which ensures optimal readability at any size.

✦ Triple Click to Select a Line, if checked, lets you triple-click anywhere in a line to select the whole line. This used to be a standard shortcut in Mac applications but had fallen into disuse recently.

✦ Adjust Text Attributes When Scaling, if checked, lets InDesign change text size and proportional scaling when you resize the text box or path that contains the text. Unchecked, the text formatting is untouched. It makes sense to check this option if you're working on display ads and other materials where you are sizing text visually and interactively; it does not make sense in magazines, books, and other more-structured projects where the text attributes are standardized and changes to objects' size are meant to change the containers' size, not the text's size.

✦ Apply Leading to Entire Paragraph, if checked, applies leading changes to the entire paragraph as opposed to the current line. In most cases, you want the leading to be applied to all paragraphs, so I recommend that this box be checked (it is *not* checked by default in InDesign).

QuarkXPress User

Like other layout programs, QuarkXPress rightfully treats leading as a paragraph attribute, so be sure to check the Apply Leading to Entire Paragraph option in InDesign to make it work like it should. But note that InDesign does not support QuarkXPress's additive leading capability (where you enter **+2 pt** to make the leading two points more than whatever the current point size is), so leading in InDesign will never exactly match the QuarkXPress approach.

Links area

The Create Links When Placing Text and Spreadsheet Files creates links to your source text files, so InDesign can alert you when those files change so you can reimport them if desired. (InDesign always does this for graphics files.) Check the box if you want InDesign to track such links.

New Feature The Create Links check box is new to InDesign CS.

Input Method Options area

The Use Inline Input for Non-Latin Text check box enables input method editors (IMEs) from Microsoft, Apple, or other companies, if installed on your computer, for entering Asian language characters on a non-Asian operating system. It's meant for the occasional use of Chinese, Japanese, or Korean characters. If you publish regularly in these languages, you should use the appropriate Asian version of InDesign instead.

New Feature The Use Inline Input for Non-Latin Text check box is new to InDesign CS.

Composition preferences

In general, preferences in the Composition pane, shown in Figure 3-3, affect entire paragraphs rather than individual characters.

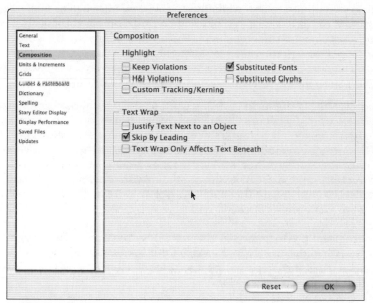

Figure 3-3: The Composition pane of the Preferences dialog box.

Highlight area

The Highlight check boxes control whether InDesign calls attention to possible typesetting problems by drawing a highlighter pen effect behind the text.

✦ Keep Violations, which is unchecked by default, highlights the last line in a text frame when it cannot follow the rules specified in the Keep Options dialog box in the Paragraph pane's palette menu (Window ⇨ Type & Tables ⇨ Paragraph, or Option+⌘+T or Ctrl+Alt+T). For example, if the Keep Options settings require more lines to stay together than fit in the text frame and thus bump all the text in a frame to the next text frame in the chain, the Keep Options rules are violated and the last line of text is highlighted so you know to change the frame size or the Keep Options rules for that text.

✦ When checked, H&J Violations uses three shades of yellow to mark lines that might be too loose or too tight due to the combination of spacing and hyphenation settings. The darker the shade, the worse InDesign considers the problem to be. H&J Violations is unchecked by default; you might want to check it while fine-tuning type, then uncheck it when you're finished.

✦ Custom Tracking/Kerning, if checked, highlights custom tracking and kerning (essentially, anywhere you overrode the defaults) in a bluish green. It's handy for copy editors to quickly find such overrides to make sure they're not too tight or loose for readability reasons.

✦ Substituted Fonts is checked by default and uses pink highlight to indicate characters in fonts that are not available to InDesign. InDesign actually uses Adobe Sans MM or Adobe Serif MM to create a replacement for missing fonts, so the text looks close to the actual font. For editing purposes, the substituted fonts work fine, although the pink highlight can be distracting. But for output purposes, it's important that you have the correct fonts, so you may want to live with the irritation and have InDesign highlight substituted fonts for you.

✦ Substituted Glyphs highlights in pink any glyphs (special characters) that were substituted. This usually occurs when you have multiple versions of the same font, with different special characters in each version. For example, a file using the euro (€) currency symbol might have been created in the newest version of, say, Syntax. But a copy editor working on the same file may have an older version of Syntax that doesn't have the euro symbol in it. Having Substituted Glyphs checked would ensure that such a problem were highlighted. I recommend you have this option checked.

Note   InDesign is hypersensitive to fonts (see Chapter 15), so you'll get such highlighting even when you have the correct font installed but the wrong face applied to it (such as Normal rather than Regular); in these cases, the font style will have brackets ([ ]) around it in the Character pane.

Text Wrap area

As the label makes clear, the three options here affect how text wraps:

✦ Justify Text Next to an Object, if checked, overrides any local justification settings to make text wrapping around an object be justified. That means the text will smoothly follow the object's shape, rather than keep any ragged margins that can make the wrap look strange. This option comes into play when you wrap ragged (left-aligned or right-aligned) text around objects; I recommend that you avoid wrapping text on its ragged side, because it looks awkward. Although this option eliminates the awkwardness of ragged text that wraps around an object, it presents a different awkwardness: having some text ragged (that which is not wrapping) and some text justified (that which is wrapping).

✦ Skip by Leading, if checked, uses the text's leading to determine how much space follows an object that it is wrapping. This has an effect only if you choose the Jump Object text-wrap option in the Text Wrap pane. (See Chapter 25 for more on text wrap.)

✦ Text Wrap Only Affects Text Beneath, if checked, has only text below an object wrap around that object. This lets you have some text overlap an image and some text overwrap it, depending on the text's location in the stacking order.

The Skip by Leading and Text Wrap Only Affects Text Beneath check boxes are new to InDesign CS.

Units & Increments preferences

The measurement systems you use for positioning items and the way the arrows on the keyboard increase or decrease settings are controlled by settings in the Units & Increments pane shown in Figure 3-4.

Figure 3-4: The Units & Increments pane of the Preferences dialog box.

Ruler Units area

The Ruler Units area affects three things: the origin point (by page, by spread, or by the spine) and the measurement system displayed on the horizontal and vertical ruler on the document window and the default values in fields used for positioning objects.

The Origin pop-up menu determines the zero point (typically, the upper-left corner of the page) for object positions. If you choose Page, objects' positions are relative to each page's upper-left corner. If you choose Spread, objects' positions are relative to the current spread's upper-left corner. If you choose Spine, objects' positions are relative to the binding spine of each spread—the very top and center of where the two pages meet.

With the Vertical and Horizontal pop-up menus, you can specify one measurement system for the horizontal ruler and measurements, and specify another measurement system for the vertical ruler and measurements. For example, you might use points for horizontal measurements so you can use the rulers to gauge tab and indent settings, while using inches for vertical measurements. For example, if you choose Inches for both the Horizontal and Vertical Ruler Units, not only will the rulers display inches, but the X, Y, W, and H fields on the Transform pane (Window ➪ Transform or F9) display values in inches as well.

Note   To display the document ruler, choose View ➪ Show Ruler, or press ⌘+R or Ctrl+R.

Tip   The default horizontal and vertical measurement system is picas. If you aren't accustomed to working in picas, be sure to change the default Horizontal and Vertical Ruler Units when no documents are open. This ensures that all future documents use your preferred measurement system. (If you make the change with a document open, the change will only apply to the open document.)

To specify the measurement systems you want to use, choose an option from the Horizontal pop-up menu and from the Vertical pop-up menu. You have the following options:

✦ **Points:** A typesetting measurement equal to $\frac{1}{72}$ of an inch. To enter values in points, type a *p* before the value or *pt* after the value (p6 or 6 pt, for example).

Tip   InDesign doesn't care if you put spaces between numbers and the abbreviations in your measurements — **3 p** is read the same as **3p**, and **0.4 inch** is read the same as **0.4inch**, for example.

✦ **Picas:** A typesetting measurement equal to $\frac{1}{6}$ of an inch. To enter values in picas, type a **p** after the value (for example, 6p).

✦ **Inches:** An English measurement system, which is divided into 16ths. To enter values in inches, type **i in**, **inch**, *or* " after the value. For example, 3i, 3in, 3 inch, and 3" are all read by InDesign as "3 inches."

New Feature   The use of QuarkXPress's " to indicate inches is new to InDesign CS.

✦ **Inches decimal:** Inches divided into 10ths on the ruler rather than 16ths. To enter values in inches decimal, include a decimal point as appropriate and type **i**, **in**, **inch**, or " after the value.

✦ **Millimeters:** A metric measurement that is $\frac{1}{10}$ of a centimeter. To enter values in millimeters, type **mm** after the value. For example, 14mm.

✦ **Centimeters:** A metric measurement that is about $\frac{1}{3}$ of an inch. To enter values in centimeters, type **cm** after the value. For example, 2.3cm.

✦ **Ciceros:** A European typesetting measurement that is slightly larger than a pica. To enter values in ciceros, type **c** after the value. For example, 2c.

✦ **Custom:** This option lets you set a customer number of points as your measurement unit, placing a labeled tick mark at every point increment you specify. You get to customize the number of tick marks between the labeled marks by entering a value in the Points field. For example, if you enter *12* in the field, you'll get a tick mark at each pica, because there are 12 points in a pica.

Tip

Despite the Ruler Units you specify, you can enter values in any fields using any supported measurement system. For example, if you're working in picas, you can enter an inch value in the Width field by typing **1 in** InDesign will automatically convert the value to picas for you. You can enter values in picas and points by placing a *p* between the two values. For example, entering **1p2** indicates 1 pica and 2 points.

Keyboard Increments area

The arrow keys on the keyboard let you move selected objects right, left, up, or down. You can also use the arrow keys and other keyboard shortcuts to change some text formatting. You can customize the way these shortcuts work, for example by specifying how far each click of an arrow key moves an item.

Note

These preferences are not used consistently to modify the arrow keys or keyboard shortcuts. Basically, the Cursor Key field works with all four arrow keys. The Size/Leading value works with the up and down arrow keys for leading, while the Kerning field works with the left and right arrows. Meanwhile, the Size/Leading value works with a regular keyboard shortcut, and the Baseline Shift field works only while clicking the arrow keys when the Baseline Shift field is highlighted on the Character pane.

The options are

✦ **Cursor Key field:** When you select an object with the Selection tool or the Direct Selection tool, you can move it up, down, left, or right using the arrow keys on the keyboard. By default, the item moves 1 point. You can change the increment to a value between 0 (which would be useless) and 8p4 (1.3888 inches). For example, if you're using a document grid, you might change the increment to match the grid lines.

Tip

If you press the Shift key while you press an arrow key, the object moves ten times the amount specified in the Cursor Key field. Holding the Option or Alt key while you press an arrow key creates a copy of the selected object at the distance specified in the Cursor Key field. Holding the Shift key with the Option or Alt key while you press an arrow key creates a copy of the selected object at ten times the amount specified in the Cursor Key field. This last combination is a very simple and quick way to create a grid of text or image boxes with equal spacing between them.

✦ **Size/Leading field:** The value you enter in this field, which is 2 points by default, specifies how much point size or leading is increased or decreased when implemented with keyboard commands. You can enter a value between 1 and 100.

Tip

To increase the point size of selected text, press Shift+⌘+> or Ctrl+Shift+>; to decrease the point size, press Shift+⌘+< or Ctrl+Shift+<. Add Option or Alt to the combination to multiply the increment by five. To modify leading for selected text, Option+click or Alt+click the up or down arrow on the keyboard.

✦ **Baseline Shift field:** You can shift the baseline of highlighted text up or down by clicking in the Baseline Shift field on the Character pane, then clicking the up or down arrow on the keyboard. You can change the default value of 2 points to any value between 1 and 100. If you press the Shift key while clicking, the increment is multiplied by five.

✦ **Kerning field:** To kern text with keyboard commands, you position the cursor between two letters, then Option+click or Alt+click the right arrow button to increase kerning or the left arrow to decrease kerning. By default, each click changes kerning by $^{20}/_{1000}$ of an em. You can change this value to anything between 1 and 100. Hold the ⌘ or Ctrl key to multiply the increment by five.

Grids preferences

Grids preferences let you set up a baseline grid, commonly used to space text evenly across columns, and a document-wide grid, which you can use for positioning or drawing objects. If you're planning a structured design that will use a grid, you'll want to set it up before you start working in the document. It's likely that each design you create will have different grid settings based on its individual content, so you probably won't change Grids preferences with no documents open. The Grids pane is shown in Figure 3-5.

Note

By default, both the baseline grid and the document grid display on every spread behind all objects; the document grid displays on the pasteboard as well. Both grids cover the entire document and cannot be associated with a specific master page or layer. You can have grids display in front by unchecking the Grids in Back check box.

Baseline Grid area

You can specify the color of the baseline grid, where it starts, how far apart each grid line is, and when it displays. To display the baseline grid for a document, choose View ➪ Show Baseline Grid, or press Option+⌘+' (apostrophe) or Ctrl+Alt+' (apostrophe). You have the following options:

✦ **Color pop-up menu:** The default color of the baseline grid is Light Blue. If this color is difficult for you to see, or if you're accustomed to the pink lines in QuarkXPress, you can choose a different color from the Color pop-up menu. Choose Other to access the system color picker and create your own color.

✦ **Start field:** This value specifies how far down from the top of the page the grid starts. The Start value, which defaults to 3p0, usually matches your top margin.

✦ **Increment Every field:** The amount of space between grid lines is specified in the Increment Every field. The default value of 1p0 is usually changed to match the leading of your body text so text aligns with the grid.

✦ **View Threshold field:** You can prevent the baseline grid from displaying when you decrease the view percentage. If you're using the default setting, the baseline grid will not display at views below 75 percent. You can enter a value between 5 and 4,000 percent.

Tip

You might want to change the View Threshold to match the document's most common Fit in Window view. For example, a magazine page on a 15-inch monitor in a full window might display at around 65 percent when you choose View ⇨ Fit in Window. Usually you use Fit in Window to get an overall look at the page, and the baseline grid would simply be in the way.

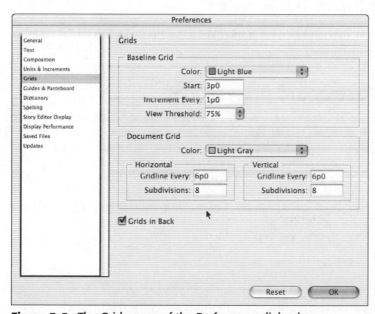

Figure 3-5: The Grids pane of the Preferences dialog box.

Document Grid area

The document grid consists of intersecting horizontal and vertical gridlines, forming a pattern of small squares that you can use for object placement and for drawing symmetrical objects. You can customize the color and spacing of the grid lines. To display the document grid, choose View ➪ Show Document Grid, or press ⌘+' (apostrophe) or Ctrl+' (apostrophe). You have the following options:

✦ **Color pop-up menu:** The default color of the document grid is Light Gray. Although this light shade is unobtrusive, you might want to change it to something brighter or darker so you can see it better. You can choose a different color from the Color pop-up menu or choose Other to create your own.

✦ **Gridline Every field:** The major grid lines, which are slightly darker, are positioned according to this value. The default value is 6p0; in general, you'll want to specify a value within the measurement system you're using. For example, if you're working in inches, you might enter **1 inch** in the Gridline Every field. That way, the gridlines match up with the major tick marks on the ruler. You set the horizontal and vertical settings separately.

✦ **Subdivisions field:** Although this is a number and not a measurement, it ends up specifying the amount of space between grid lines. The major grid lines established in the Gridline Every field are divided according to the value you enter here. For example, if you entered **1 inch** in the Gridline Every field, and you enter **4** in the Subdivisions field, you will get a gridline at each quarter-inch. The default number of subdivisions is 8. You set the horizontal and vertical settings separately.

Guides & Pasteboard preferences

When you create a new document, you set up margins in the New Document dialog box (File ➪ New, or ⌘+N or Ctrl+N). For more alignment options within a document, you can create guidelines by dragging them off the rulers or using the Layout ➪ Create Guides command. Settings in the Guides & Pasteboard pane, shown in Figure 3-6, controls the color and other attributes of the margins and guides.

New Feature   This pane had been called simply Guides in previous versions of InDesign. InDesign CS also adds the new Pasteboard Options section, as well as more guides for which you can select the colors.

Color area

In the Color area, the Color pop-up menus for Margins, Columns, Bleed, Slug, and Pasteboard let you choose a color other than the defaults. If you want to make your own color, choose Custom to access the system color picker. The Margins color, Magenta by default, displays on all horizontal guides; the Columns color, Violet by default, displays on all vertical guides. To display guides in a document, choose View ➪ Show Guides, or press ⌘+R or Ctrl+R.

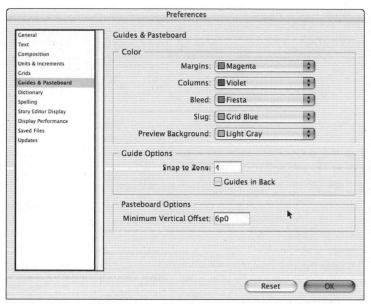

Figure 3-6: The Guides & Pasteboard pane of the Preferences dialog box.

Guide Options area

Although this is a new area in the InDesign CS Guides & Pasteboard dialog box, its options are the same as in the InDesign 2 Guides pane:

✦ The Snap to Zone field value specifies how close you need to drag an object to a grid line or guide line to make it snap (think of it as the line's magnetic field). The default Snap to Zone value is 4 pixels, but you can enter a value between 1 and 36. You enable snapping to the grid via the Snap to Document Grid and Snap to Guides commands in the View menu.

✦ By default, margins and guides display in front of all objects. If you prefer to have objects obscure margins and guides, check Guides in Back in the Guide Options area. Note that baseline grids and document grids always display behind all objects, regardless of this setting.

QuarkXPress User

This Guides in Back feature is for those QuarkXPress 3.3 users who never figured out how to change the unfortunate default of placing guides in back, and are therefore accustomed to working with guides this way.

Pasteboard Options area

The new Pasteboard Options area has the new Minimum Vertical Offset field, where you specify the amount of pasteboard to display above and below your pages. The default is 6p0 (1 inch).

Dictionary preferences

The Dictionary pane, shown in Figure 3-7, sets options related to hyphenation and spelling dictionaries, as well as to quotation marks.

Cross-Reference   See Chapter 15 for more information about the default dictionaries that ship with InDesign.

Figure 3-7: The Dictionary pane of the Preferences dialog box.

Language area

The Language area begins with a pop-up menu that lets you choose a language for which you want to choose a different hyphenation or spelling dictionary:

✦ The Hyphenation pop-up menu lets you choose from any hyphenation dictionaries installed for the selected language. Typically, there is only the default dictionary, such as Proximity, in this pop-up menu.

✦ The Spelling pop-up menu lets you choose from any spelling dictionaries installed for the selected language. Typically, there is only the default dictionary, such as Proximity, in this pop-up menu.

Note   To install different dictionaries, place them in the Dictionaries folder inside the Plug-ins folder (inside your InDesign folder). Press Option+⌘+/ or Ctrl+Alt+/ to update the pop-up menus in the Dictionary pane without restarting InDesign. (In a workgroup, it's important that everyone use the same dictionary.) Eventually, you may be able to purchase third-party spelling or hyphenation dictionaries for InDesign — although no third-party commercial dictionaries have been released since InDesign was created in 1999. For example, you might be able to purchase a different Traditional German dictionary with more words than the one InDesign has. In that case, when you check the spelling of a word with Traditional German as its language format, InDesign would consult the third-party dictionary rather than the default.

The Language area also lets you set the quotation marks you want use. Different languages use different quotation marks, and InDesign adjusts the quotation marks automatically when you switch the language. However, there may be some cases where you might want to override the languages' default quotation-mark settings, which you can do in the Double Quotes and Single Quotes pop-up menus.

Note that changing the quotation-mark options for one language does not affect the settings for others. Each language can have independent settings for the quotation marks used.

 Caution   After you change a language's quotation-mark settings, there's no way to reset them to the language defaults except to choose the proper options from the pop-up menus. That means you need to remember what the original, correct setting was.

Hyphenation Exceptions area

The Compose Using pop-up menu has three options that specify what to use for hyphenation exceptions, which are overrides to the language dictionary's hyphenation rules. For example, you may choose not to hyphenate a short word like *preset* that has a legitimate hyphenation *(pre-set)*. And you may correct the hyphenation of specialized terms not in the language's dictionary.

The options here dictate how you manage those exceptions. By default, InDesign stores hyphenation exceptions in an outside file, so multiple users can standardize on the same exceptions list. But you can also store exceptions in a document, perhaps for unique needs. The Compose Using pop-up menu lets you select from Document, User Dictionary, and User Dictionary and Document options. Choose User Dictionary if you want to override any exceptions stored in the document — perhaps they're wrong or the copy editors want to rely only on a standard exception list. Choose Document if you want to ignore exceptions stored in an outside file. Choose User Dictionary and Document if you want to use both.

User Dictionary area

This area has two options that are checked by default and should stay that way:

✦ Merge User Dictionary into Document, if checked, copies the user dictionary file into the document, so if the file is sent to someone else who doesn't have access to that dictionary, the hyphenation in the document will be preserved.

The main reason *not* to check this box is if you need to keep your files to a minimum size; otherwise, checking this box prevents reflow when you pass a document to a service bureau or another designer, especially if you have *any* custom hyphenations.

✦ Recompose All Stories When Modified, if checked, redoes the document's hyphenation to reflect the changed user dictionary.

Spelling preferences

The Spelling pane, shown in Figure 3-8, lets you control what the InDesign spell checker examines when it checks spelling in a document. There's little reason not to check all four options — Misspelled Words, Repeated Words, Uncapitalized Words, and Uncapitalized Sentences. Note that Uncapitalized Words checks for known proper nouns that aren't capitalized.

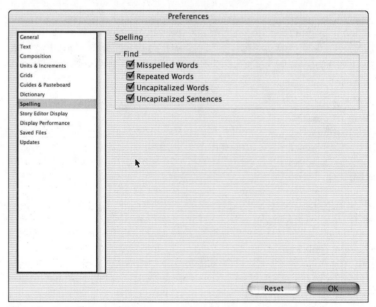

Figure 3-8: The Spelling pane of the Preferences dialog box.

Story Editor Display preferences

The Story Editor Display pane controls how the Story Editor displays text and the text cursor. Figure 3-9 shows the pane.

New Feature   The Story Editor Display pane is new to InDesign CS, as is the Story Editor, a mini word processor that Adobe has long had in its PageMaker product. Chapter 15 covers the Story Editor in detail.

Figure 3-9: The Story Editor Display pane of the Preferences dialog box.

Text Display Options area

The Text Display Options area determines how text displays in the Story Editor. All are meant to make it easy to edit text on-screen.

Two pop-up menus control the basic display: Text Color and Background. You'll rarely want to change either of these from the default of black for the text color and white for the background. (You might want to choose a light yellow or green as a background color to be a bit easier on the eye.) The Theme pop-up menu has four predefined text color/background combinations that will override any changes you make to the Text Color and Background pop-up menus. Of those four themes, you'll want to keep Ink on Paper, which is simply black text on a white background. The other three options provide hard-to-read displays modeled after the very first computer displays in the 1970s and early 1980s.

The next set of options let you customize the text itself in the Story Editor. The Display Font pop-up menu lets you choose a font that is easy to read — you can use any active font available on your computer — as well as a point size (the default of 12 points is usually quite readable, but you may want to enlarge or reduce that in specific cases). The Line Spacing pop-up menu lets you change the default of single-spaced presentation to 150%, Doublespace, and Triplespace. You may prefer 150% or Doublespace if you have a wide Story Editor window to help make reading the text easier. Finally, the Enable Anti-Aliasing check box lets you smooth on-screen font display, which can make text hard to read for some fonts, especially at small sizes, or make it easier to read for some fonts, especially at medium and large sizes.

Cursor Options area

InDesign gives you a choice of the text cursor that displays in the Story Editor. In the Cursor Options area, choose whichever looks best on-screen and is easy to find without obscuring the text under it. That will vary based on the font and point size chosen. If you want the text cursor to blink—that helps some people find it more easily—be sure to check the Blink check box.

Display Performance preferences

The Display Performance pane, shown in Figure 3-10, controls how images and text display on-screen.

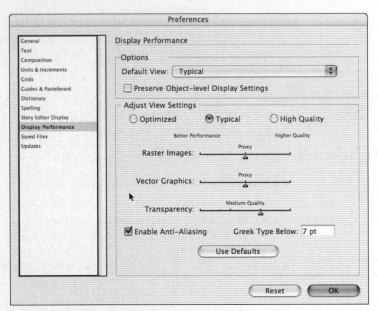

Figure 3-10: The Display Performance pane of the Preferences dialog box.

Default View Settings area

In the pop-up menu in the Default View Settings area, you can choose from three view settings: Typical, Optimized, and High Quality. These affect only what is displayed on-screen, not what is printed. The three options correspond to how you set the options in the Adjust View Settings area of this pane.

The Preserve Object-Level Display Settings check box overrides any view settings for specific images (which you set by choosing Object ⇨ Display Performance for a selected picture).

Adjust View Settings area

Use the sliders in the Adjust View Settings area to determine what Typical, Optimized, and High Quality should mean in your copy of InDesign. First, check the button for the quality level you want to set, then move the sliders for each of the three graphical aspects (Raster Images, Vector Images, and Transparency). Each slider bar has tick marks to show the available options. You have to move the slider all the way to a tick mark; you cannot choose a setting in between tick marks.

For raster (bitmap) images and vector images, you have three options: Gray Out, Proxy, and High Resolution. Proxy means a low-resolution version (72 dpi). For transparency, there are three quality levels available — Low, Medium, and High — as well as Off, which doesn't display objects behind transparent portions of an image.

The Adjust View Settings area also has two controls for text:

✦ The Enable Anti-Aliasing check box that, if checked, smoothes text display.

✦ The Greek Type Below field in which you set at what size text displays as gray lines rather than as actual characters.

Saved Files preferences

The Saved Files pane, shown in Figure 3-11, controls how recovery files and document previews are handled.

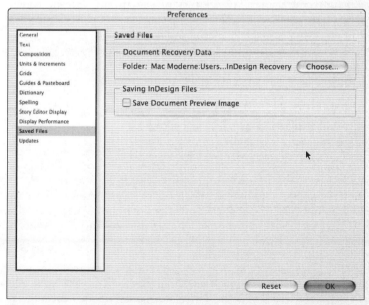

Figure 3-11: The Saved Files pane of the Preferences dialog box.

Document Recovery Data area

In this area, InDesign lets you specify the folder that contains autorecovery files, which lets you recover most or all of your work in case of a program or system crash. Click the Choose button to choose an alternate directory. There's really no reason to change the default, which places the recovery folder inside the current user's Documents folder (Mac) or My Documents folder (Windows).

Saving InDesign Files

The Save Document Preview Image check box, if checked, makes InDesign save a thumbnail view of the document's first page. That preview appears in the Open dialog box instead of the InDesign logo, when you select a file. It's handy when you've got a ton of files in a folder and can't remember which is which.

New Feature   The Saved File pane is new to InDesign CS, though the autorecovery option existed in InDesign 2's General pane. The document preview, though, is completely new in InDesign CS.

Updates preferences

The Updates pane, shown in Figure 3-12, lets you set how often InDesign connects to Adobe's servers over your Internet connection to download and install product updates. The Check for Updates pop-up menu's options are Never, Weekly, and Monthly.

The pane also has a button that displays Adobe's privacy policy (all the ways Adobe and its partner companies can use your customer registration information).

New Feature   The Updates pane is new to InDesign CS, replacing the previous version's Online Settings pane.

Customizing Keyboard Shortcuts

InDesign provides keyboard shortcuts for accessing most tools and menu commands, and for many pane options. For the most part, the keyboard shortcuts selected by Adobe either match platform standards — such as ⌘+X or Ctrl+X for Edit ⇨ Cut — or they're based on keyboard shortcuts in PageMaker, Photoshop, and Illustrator. Fortunately, you're not stuck with the keyboard shortcuts Adobe decided on — and I say "fortunately" because a few decisions and omissions are a little odd.

QuarkXPress User   You can choose to use shortcuts based on QuarkXPress 4.0 shortcuts, or you can modify a copy of the QuarkXPress set. Please note that the QuarkXPress 4.0 set is not a perfect match for *every* keyboard shortcut in QuarkXPress 4. I cover this topic in more depth later in this chapter.

Figure 3-12: The Updates pane of the Preferences dialog box.

The Keyboard Shortcuts dialog box (Edit ⇨ Keyboard Shortcuts), shown in Figure 3-13, provides all the tools you need for modifying keyboard shortcuts.

Figure 3-13: The Keyboard Shortcuts dialog box lets you create new sets of keyboard shortcuts.

To customize or not to customize

The ability to customize keyboard shortcuts, letting you work the way you want, is great — or is it? Maybe only if you work alone and never talk to anyone about your work or their work. Modified keyboard shortcuts can lead to confusion when discussing techniques, reading documentation, or sharing computers. While modifying keyboard shortcuts — or even while considering it — keep the following in mind:

✦ You can specify keyboard shortcuts for specific fonts and faces that you use frequently, such as a shortcut for Gill Sans Bold Italic. For the font to be listed in the Commands area, you'll need to make sure it's available to InDesign when you open the Keyboard Shortcuts dialog box.

✦ Don't change system-wide conventions such as the shortcuts for New, Open, Save, and Print.

✦ Don't change common keyboard commands to harmful shortcuts — for example, don't use ⌘+F or Ctrl+F for changing leading rather than invoking Find/Change.

✦ If you share computers in any way — even just another user reaching over your shoulder to provide assistance — adding keyboard shortcuts is safer than changing them. Your shortcuts will be slightly customized, but other users will be able to use your copy of InDesign without unexpected results.

✦ If you're at a 24-hour production shop in which two or three people share computers, each person can have his or her own set of named keyboard shortcuts. But this requires each user to remember to activate his or her own set.

✦ You can't export keyboard shortcuts to share with other users. If consistency is important, make sure everyone creates the same set.

✦ Don't modify keyboard shortcuts for computers in public places such as training centers or photocopy centers.

✦ QuarkXPress users coming to InDesign have to learn new software anyway, so they might benefit — in the long run — from learning new keyboard shortcuts as well. Even though using your old shortcuts will ease the initial transition, the frustration caused by missing or different shortcuts can be worse than learning new ones.

✦ When you're specifying keyboard shortcuts, remember to use a modifier key or keys: ⌘, Option, Shift, or Control on the Mac and Ctrl, Alt, or Shift on Windows. Single-letter or -number commands (which Adobe uses for selecting tools) obviously can't be used while you're editing text.

If all this makes me seem negative about customizing keyboard shortcuts, I'm really not. Just consider all the ramifications before you do any customizing.

Using and modifying default shortcuts

When you first launch InDesign, you're using the default set of shortcuts, which you can view in menus, in some tool tips, and in your documentation. (This book lists default shortcuts as well.) You cannot modify the default set, but you can create a new set based on it, then modify the shortcuts in that set.

The Keyboard Shortcuts dialog box (Edit ⇨ Keyboard Shortcuts), shown in Figure 3-13, provides all the tools you need for modifying keyboard shortcuts. To use the standard keyboard shortcuts after switching to another set, choose Default from the Set pop-up menu at the top of the dialog box, then click OK.

Here's how to create a new set:

1. **Choose Edit ⇨ Keyboard Shortcuts.**

2. **Click New Set.**

3. **In the New Set dialog box, choose Default from the Based On Set pop-up menu.**

4. **Enter a different name for the set in the Name field, then click OK to create the set.**

5. **To start modifying the commands, select a menu or type of shortcut to change from the Product Area pop-up menu.**

   For example, you can choose File Menu, Object Editing, or Typography.

6. **Scroll through the Commands area, and click to select a command so you can change its shortcut.**

   The Current Shortcuts area shows you the command's existing shortcut (if there is one).

7. **Click in the Press New Shortcut field. You have three options at this point:**

   • If a keyboard shortcut exists for this command, you can click Remove to delete it and free it up for another command.

   • If no keyboard shortcut exists for this command, you can press the actual modifier keys and command, then click Assign.

   • If a keyboard shortcut exists for this command, but you want to override it, you can press the actual modifier keys and command, then click Assign. (The shortcut you are overriding is shown below the Assign button.)

8. **Click Save after modifying a shortcut.**

9. When you're finished editing keyboard shortcuts, click OK to save them.

For the shortcuts that don't show in menus, you can print a list to use as a reference. See "Viewing and printing shortcuts" later in this chapter.

Tip

You might consider adding a keyboard shortcut for Layout ⇨ Create Guides, such as the unused Option+Shift+G or Alt+Shift+G. Another command sorely in need of a keyboard shortcut is Type ⇨ Insert Glyphs. Try the unused Option+Shift+I or Altl+Shift+I.

Using and modifying QuarkXPress shortcuts

If you're switching to InDesign from QuarkXPress — and are not accustomed to using Photoshop or Illustrator — the keyboard shortcuts in InDesign may seem odd. To ease the transition to InDesign, Adobe has provided a set of keyboard shortcuts based on those in QuarkXPress 4.0. I say "based on" because some QuarkXPress commands don't have equivalents and some work very differently, while other QuarkXPress shortcuts conflict with long-established Adobe shortcuts. And commands unique to InDesign still have their own keyboard shortcuts — for example, you can still select tools with the single letters shown in the tool tips.

Among the shortcuts you'll miss or be confused by are the following:

✦ Option or Alt for the Page Grabber Hand is missing (use the Navigator pane instead).

✦ ⌘+K or Ctrl+K for deleting selected objects is missing (you can always use the Delete key unless the Type tool is selected). (Even though InDesign's QuarkXPress 4.0 shortcut set maps the Preferences dialog box to QuarkXPress 4's ⌘+Y or Ctrl+Y shortcut, it also retains the standard Adobe shortcut of ⌘+K or Ctrl+K to open the Preferences dialog box.)

If you want to use the QuarkXPress set of keyboard shortcuts, choose Set for QuarkXPress 4.0 from the Set pop-up menu at the top of the Keyboard Shortcuts dialog box (Edit ⇨ Keyboard Shortcuts). You might want to print out the list of keyboard shortcuts and review them so you know what's available and what's different. (See "Viewing and printing shortcuts" later in this chapter.)

If you decide to use the QuarkXPress set of keyboard shortcuts, you might want to create a copy and modify some of them. For example, you can assign ⌘+K or Ctrl+K to Clear since you're used to it deleting items (rather than leave it set to open the Preferences dialog box). You can also repair the incorrect commands, although in many cases they're assigned to other commands and must be replaced.

Viewing and printing shortcuts

After you modify keyboard shortcuts, you may need a list for reference. (In addition, reviewing the entire QuarkXPress set before you start editing it is helpful.)

Click Show Set in the Keyboard Shortcuts dialog box (Edit ➪ Keyboard Shortcuts) to view a list of shortcuts for the currently selected set. The shortcuts are displayed in TextEdit (on the Macintosh) or in WordPad (in Windows). You can then print the list from that application.

Modifying Defaults for Documents, Text, and Objects

When you create a new document, start typing, or create a new object, it is based on default settings that you can change. For example, by default, a new document is always letter-sized, but if you design only CD covers, you can change the default.

You may need to work with InDesign for a while to determine which of these settings to change and what settings you prefer. When you identify a problem — for example, you realize that you always end up changing the inset for text frames — jot down a note about it or close all documents right then. When no documents are open, change the setting for all future documents.

Document defaults

You can modify the default size, margins, and columns in new documents; the default attributes of guides; and the way layouts are adjusted. To modify document defaults, choose the following with no documents open:

✦ **File ➪ Document Setup (Option+⌘+P or Ctrl+Alt+P).** The Document Setup dialog box, shown in Figure 3-14, lets you modify the default settings in the New Document dialog box for the Number of Pages, Page Size, Facing Pages, and Master Text Frame, as well as for bleeds and slugs if you click the More Options button.

✦ **Layout ➪ Margins and Columns.** The Margins and Columns dialog box, shown in Figure 3-15, lets you modify the default settings in the New Document dialog box for the Margins and Columns areas.

✦ **Layout ➪ Ruler Guides.** This adjusts the View Threshold and Color for all new guides. It opens the Ruler Guides dialog box, which is shown in Figure 3-16.

Figure 3-14: When no documents are open, the Document Setup dialog box lets you customize default settings in the New Document dialog box.

Figure 3-15: Use the Margins and Columns dialog box—when no documents are open—to establish default margins and columns.

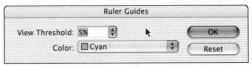

Figure 3-16: When no documents are open, the Ruler Guides dialog box lets you customize default settings for ruler display.

✦ **Layout ➪ Layout Adjustment.** The Layout Adjustment dialog box, shown in Figure 3-17, lets you resize entire layouts and customize how they are resized.

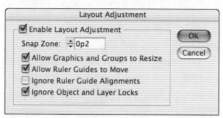

Figure 3-17: Use the Layout Adjustment dialog box—when no documents are open—to establish default layout-adjustment settings.

Text defaults

When you start typing in a new text frame, the text is formatted with default Character formats, Paragraph formats, and Story attributes. You can also choose to show invisible characters such as spaces and tabs by default; otherwise you'll need to activate it in each text-heavy document. To modify text defaults, choose

✦ **Window ➪ Type & Tables ➪ Character (⌘+T or Ctrl+T).** Choose default options for character formats such as Font, Size, and Leading from the Character pane.

✦ **Window ➪ Type & Tables ➪ Paragraph (Option+⌘+T or Ctrl+Alt+T).** Choose defaults for paragraph formats such as alignment, indents, spacing, and so on from the Paragraph pane.

✦ **Type ➪ Story.** This lets you activate Optical Margin Alignment by default. (Since Optical Margin Alignment works best for display type rather than body type, it's unlikely that you'll do this.)

✦ **Type ➪ Show Hidden Characters (⌘+Option+I or Ctrl+Alt+I).** Check this if you edit in InDesign a great deal and always end up turning on Show Hidden Characters.

You can also edit the spelling and hyphenation dictionaries while no documents are open by choosing Edit ➪ Dictionary. However, because all the edits are saved in the same file, it doesn't matter whether documents are open.

Object defaults

When you create new objects, they're based on some default settings. For example, you can specify how text wraps around objects. To modify object defaults, use the following commands:

✦ **Object ➪ Text Frame Options (⌘+B or Ctrl+B).** The Text Frame Options dialog box, shown in Figure 3-18, lets you specify the default Columns, Inset Spacing, First Baseline, and Ignore Text Wrap settings for new text frames.

✦ **Object ➪ Text Wrap (⌘+Option+W or Ctrl+Alt+W).** The Text Wrap pane lets you specify how text will wrap around all new objects.

✦ **Object ➪ Corner Effects (⌘+Option+R or Ctrl+Alt+R).** The Corner Effects dialog box lets you choose a style for the corners of all new frames except those created with the Type tool.

✦ **Object ➪ Clipping Path.** The Clipping Path dialog box lets you specify the default attributes of clipping paths imported into graphics frames.

✦ **Window ➪ Stroke (F10), Window ➪ Color, Window ➪ Gradient (F6), or Window ➪ Attributes.** These let you specify other default properties of objects. For example, if all objects you create are stroked (framed), specify a weight in the Stroke pane.

✦ **Double-click the Polygon tool to open the Polygon Settings dialog box (there is no menu command or keyboard shortcut),** which lets you specify the default number of sides and the inset for the first new polygon in a new document.

Figure 3-18: Use the Text Frame Options dialog box to specify default attributes of new text frames.

Modifying Defaults for Views

Another way to customize your copy of InDesign is to specify which layout tools display by default. The lower two-thirds of the View menu, shown in Figure 3-19, let you do this. If you'd prefer not to view the edges of frames, you can hide them by default. Or if you always want to start with a document-wide grid, you can show it by default. To modify viewing defaults, choose:

Figure 3-19: The View menu commands that are available when no documents are open.

✦ **View ➪ Show Text Threads (Option+⌘+Y or Ctrl+Alt+Y)** to show the links between text frames.

✦ **View ➪ Hide Frame Edges (⌘+H or Ctrl+H)** to hide the edges of frames.

✦ **View ➪ Hide Rulers (⌘+R or Ctrl+R)** to hide the horizontal and vertical ruler.

✦ **View ➪ Hide Guides (⌘+; [semicolon] or Ctrl+; [semicolon])** to hide margin, column, and layout guides.

✦ **View ➪ Show Baseline Grid (Option+⌘+' [apostrophe] or Ctrl+Alt+' [apostrophe])** to show the baseline grid established in the Grids pane of the Preferences dialog box (InDesign ➪ Preferences ➪ Grids on the Mac and Edit ➪ Preferences ➪ Grids in Windows).

✦ **View ➪ Show Document Grid (⌘+' [apostrophe] or Ctrl+' [apostrophe])** to show the document-wide grid established in the Grids pane of the Preferences dialog box.

In addition to changing which layout tools display by default, you can control some of their default behavior. Check or uncheck the following:

✦ **View ➪ Lock Guides (Option+⌘+; [semicolon] or Ctrl+Alt+; [semicolon]).** Unchecked by default, when you check this, all new guides are locked in place.

✦ **View ➪ Snap to Guides (Shift+⌘+; [semicolon] or Ctrl+Shift+; [semicolon]).** Checked by default, when you uncheck this, aligning objects with guides is more difficult, but positioning objects *near* guides is easier.

✦ **View ➪ Snap to Document Grid(no shortcut).** Unchecked by default, when you check this, objects are easy to align with document grid lines whether or not they're showing.

Although not specifically for viewing, you can also customize the way color management works. The Edit ➪ Color Settings options let you customize the default color transformations used for viewing and outputting colors (see Chapter 29).

Adding Default Colors and Styles

If you find yourself creating the same colors, paragraph style sheets, and character style sheets over and over again, create them with no documents open. They will be available to all future documents. To create these elements, use the New command in the palette menus for the following panes: Swatches (F5), Character Styles (Shift+F11), and Paragraph Styles (F11). You can also use the palette menus' Load commands to import colors and styles from existing documents instead of creating them from scratch. See the New Style and Load Paragraph Styles in Figure 3-20.

Figure 3-20: The Paragraph Styles pane's palette menu lets you create default character style sheets.

Reverting Preferences and Defaults

If you inherit a copy of InDesign from another user, or if you've been changing preferences and defaults at random and are unhappy with the results, you can revert InDesign to all its default settings. You will particularly want to do this if you're learning InDesign using tutorial files or in a class setting. Keep in mind that you will lose any keyboard shortcut sets you created.

To revert all preferences and defaults, deleting the InDesign Defaults preference files when opening InDesign, press Control+Option+Shift+⌘ or Ctrl+Alt+Shift when launching InDesign.

If you revert to the default preferences, you will not lose sets of keyboard shortcuts that you created. And since InDesign doesn't let you modify the default keyboard sets, you never have to revert to them.

Changing Views

Customizing also involves the way you look at your work. InDesign provides a variety of options for magnifying and displaying your work. Understanding these ahead of time and memorizing the ones that work best for your type of work, your eyesight, and your monitor will help you get started with InDesign.

Desktop publishing pioneers in the late 1980s often worked on publications using 9-inch black-and-white monitors, and they spent as much time zooming in, zooming out, and pushing oversized pages around on undersized screens as they did formatting text and modifying pictures. The best present you—or your employer—could give you is a large monitor (two large monitors aren't bad, either). In this era of pro-liferating panes, there's no such thing as too much screen space. But even if you have a huge monitor, you're going to find yourself zooming in and out and using InDesign's other display-related features to control what you see on-screen and help you work more efficiently.

Zooming and scrolling

When you begin building a page, it's often easiest to display the entire page (View ➪ Fit Page In Window; ⌘+0 [zero] or Ctrl+0 [zero]) or spread (View ➪ Fit Spread in Window) and work somewhat roughly—creating the required objects and position-ing them more or less where you want them. After you add text and pictures to your frames, you'll probably want to begin polishing the page by modifying individ-ual objects. At this point, seeing a reduced view of an entire page or spread isn't the best way to work. If you need to work on details, it's best to pull out a magnifying glass. With InDesign, this means tapping into the program's view-magnification capabilities.

You can zoom in to magnifications up to 4,000 percent and zoom out to magnifica-tions as small as 10 percent. Like many other features, you have several options for changing view magnification. You can zoom in and out using:

✦ The Zoom tool

✦ The zoom commands in the View menu

✦ The Zoom pop-up menu or the accompanying box at the bottom-left of the document window

The Zoom tool

If you're the type of designer who prefers the click-and-drag solution when it's avail-able, you'll probably use the Zoom tool to enlarge a portion of a page. Here's how it works:

1. **Select the Zoom tool or press Z if the Type tool is not selected.**

2. **At this point you have two options:**

   • You can move the Zoom pointer over the area you want to see and click the mouse. Each click enlarges the view to the next preset magnification percentage. (To display these percentages, click on the pop-up menu next to the Zoom field at the bottom-left corner of the document window.)

   • You can click and drag a rectangle that encloses the area you want to see. When you release the mouse, the area is centered in the document window. (When you hold down the Option or Alt key, the plus sign in the Zoom pointer changes to a minus sign. Clicking or clicking and dragging in this situation will zoom out instead of in.)

You never have to actually select the Zoom tool. Instead, use its keyboard shortcuts: ⌘+Spacebar or Ctrl+Spacebar (for zooming in) and Option+⌘+Spacebar or Ctrl+Alt+Spacebar (for zooming out).

Zoom options in the View menu

The third group of commands in the View menu, shown in Figure 3-21 let you change the view magnification. Here's a brief description of each command:

Figure 3-21: The zoom commands in the View menu.

✦ **Zoom In (⌘+= or Ctrl+=).** Enlarges the display magnification to the next highest percentage. (When no objects are active, the Zoom In command is available in the contextual menu.)

✦ **Zoom Out (⌘+- [hyphen] or Ctrl+- [hyphen]).** Reduces the display magnification to the next lowest percentage. (When no objects are active, the Zoom Out command is available in the contextual menu.)

Tip

If an object is active when you choose Zoom In or Zoom Out or use the Zoom field or pop-up menu, the object is centered in the document window after the view changes.

✦ **Fit Page in Window (⌘+0 [zero] or Ctrl+0 [zero]).** Reduces or enlarges the display magnification of the currently displayed page (the current page number is displayed in the page-number field at the lower-left of a document window) so that the entire page is visible (and centered) in the document window.

✦**Fit Spread in Window.** Similar to Fit Page In Window, except you use it if you're working on a facing-page document and want the entire spread to be on-screen.

✦ **Actual Size (⌘+1 or Ctrl+1).** Displays the document at 100 percent magnification. When you choose Actual Size, a pica is a pica and an inch is an inch—if your monitor is appropriately configured.

Tip

Double-clicking the Zoom tool is the same as choosing View ➪ Actual Size; it displays a document at 100 percent magnification.

✦ **Entire Pasteboard (Option+⌘+0 [zero] or Ctrl+Alt+0 [zero]).** Reduces the display magnification so that the current page or spread and its surrounding pasteboard are visible within the document window.

Tip

To switch back and forth between the last two magnification percentages, press Option+⌘+2 or Ctrl+Alt+2.

The Zoom box

The Zoom box in the bottom-left corner of the document window and its accompanying pop-up menu, shown in Figure 3-22, offer two additional methods for changing display magnification. To use the box, simply enter a value between 5 percent and 4,000 percent, then press Return or Enter. To use the pop-up menu, click on the arrow, and then choose one of the preset magnification values.

Tip

If an object is active when you choose Zoom In or Zoom Out (from the View menu) or use the Zoom box or pop-up menu, the object is centered in the document window after the view changes.

Pushing a page around with the Hand tool

Sometimes after you've zoomed in to work on a particular object, you'll want to work on a portion of the page that's not currently displayed. You can always zoom out, then use the Zoom tool or the zoom commands to zoom back in, or you can "push" the page around within the window until you can see the portion of the page you want to work on. To scroll, you can use the scroll bars and boxes on the right and bottom of the document window, or you can use the Hand tool (H). Simply select it, then click and drag to move the currently displayed page or spread around within the document window. When you can see what you want, release the mouse.

Figure 3-22: The Zoom box and its pop-up menu.

 Tip

To temporarily access the Hand tool when the Type tool is not selected, press the spacebar. The hand pointer is displayed. Click and drag to move the page within the document window. (This is one of InDesign's most useful keyboard shortcuts!)

Changing the view with the Navigator pane

The Navigator pane (Window ⬩ Navigator), shown in Figure 3-23, is the home of several display-related features, most of which are available elsewhere (and which I've already covered in this chapter).

Document window rectangle

Zoom slider

Zoom In button

Figure 3-23: The Navigator pane.

Tip

If you choose View All Spreads from the Navigator pane's pop-up menu, the page area at the top of the pane displays all of the document's spreads. The more spreads in a document, the smaller each one is displayed in the Navigator pane when View All Spreads is selected.

Object display options

Generally, you're going to want to display the objects you've placed on your pages. After all, what's displayed on-screen is what gets printed, right? Not exactly. For example, text and graphic frames are displayed on-screen with blue borders, even if they're empty, but the borders don't print. In addition to the six zoom commands (covered earlier in this chapter), the View menu includes two other commands that affect how objects are displayed:

✦ **View ➪ Display Master Items.** When this command is checked, any objects on the currently displayed document page's master page are displayed. When unchecked, master objects on the currently displayed page are hidden. This command is page-specific, which lets you show or hide master objects on a page-by-page basis.

✦ **View ➪ Show/Hide Frame Edges (⌘+H or Ctrl+H).** When you choose Hide Frame Edges, text and graphics frames are not displayed with a blue border. Additionally, an X is not displayed in empty graphics frames when frame edges are hidden. You might want to hide frame edges to see how a page will look when printed.

Tip

When you move an object by clicking and dragging, you have the choice of displaying the entire object (including the contents of a frame) or displaying only the bounding box. If you begin dragging immediately after clicking to select an object, only the bounding box is displayed as you drag. If you pause after clicking on an object until the stem of the arrow pointer disappears and then begin dragging, the entire object is displayed.

Opening Multiple Document Windows

Like most programs, InDesign lets you open several documents at once. It also takes this concept one step farther by letting you open multiple windows simultaneously for individual documents. Earlier in this chapter, I recommended using the largest monitor you can get your mitts on. A large monitor makes this feature even more useful. By opening multiple windows, you can

✦ **Display two (or more) different pages or spreads at once and work on them at the same time.** Well, you still have to work on them one at a time, but no navigation is required — you have only to click within the appropriate window.

✦ **Display multiple magnifications of the same page.** For example, you can work on a detail at high magnification in one window and display the entire page — and see the results of your detail work — at actual size in another window.

✦ **Display a master page in one window and a document page based on that master page in another window.** When you change the master page, the change is reflected in the window in which the associated document page is displayed.

To open a new window for the active document, choose Window ➪ Arrange ➪ New Window. The new window is displayed in front of the original window. To show both windows at once, choose Window ➪ Arrange ➪ Tile. When you choose the Tile command, all open windows are resized and displayed side by side. (If you choose Window ➪ Arrange ➪ Cascade, all open windows are displayed stacked and staggered on top of each other. The frontmost document window is visible; the title bars of the other windows are visible above the frontmost document.)

When multiple windows are open, clicking on a window's title bar or anywhere within the window activates it. Also, the names of all open documents are displayed at the bottom of the Window menu. Choosing a document name from the View menu brings that document to the front. If multiple windows are open for a particular document, each window is displayed (they're displayed in the order in which you created them) in the Window menu.

Tip When you open a document, it's displayed in the last window you used before you last saved it. Any other windows that were open when you saved the document are not saved.

Tip To close all windows for the currently displayed document, press Shift+⌘+W or Ctrl+Shift+W. To close all windows for all open documents, press Option+Shift+ ⌘+W or Ctrl+Alt+Shift+W.

Summary

InDesign provides extensive controls for setting preferences for everything from how objects appear on-screen and how text is managed for spelling and hyphenation to how keyboard shortcuts work and how color is handled. A new command lets you reset all preference changes to their defaults.

✦　　✦　　✦

Document Fundamentals

Chapter 4
Creating, Opening, and Saving Documents

Chapter 5
Working with Pages

Chapter 6
Working with Layers

Chapter 7
Creating Layout Standards

Chapter 8
Defining Colors and Gradients

Chapter 9
Book Publishing

Many InDesign users are tempted to launch right into the creation of new documents. And InDesign allows that, thanks to the freeform nature of many of its tools. You want to enter text? Just select the text tool and start typing, for example. But you'll get much more out of InDesign if you understand how to work with the underlying document structures. They're not as cool as adding text and graphics, but they'll let you create richer, more usable documents — and do so faster than the freeform approach for all but the one-of-a-kind documents that ad agencies might create.

Chapter 4 shows you the basics of the documents themselves: how to create, open, and save them, as well as how to change document views on-screen, so you can effectively adjust your view based on the level of detail you're working at.

Chapter 5 then shows you how to create pages — not just add them, but arrange them, set their dimensions and margins, and determine whether they'll be bound as facing pages (as in magazines and books) or as single-side pages (as in many reports). You'll also learn how to work with bleeds and slugs — items that extend beyond the page and are critical in many professionally printed documents.

With an understanding of the basic document and page structures, you're ready to take advantage of InDesign's layers feature, which lets you have multiple "sheets" in your document that you can show, hide, and arrange as needed. These are powerful for both multi-version documents and for faster layout operations within a document. Chapter 6 covers this topic.

Chapter 7 introduces you to the concept of layout standards — using templates, master pages, and libraries to save work in future documents that have similar elements. Sure, your first document will take longer to produce using these techniques, but you'll more than make up the time in future documents. They also help ensure consistency in multiuser environments.

Chapter 8 explains how to create colors, tints, and gradients in InDesign. Photoshop and Illustrator users will know the tools, but if you're not careful, you can use them to disastrous effect in InDesign. This chapter shows how to do colors right. A special eight-page Color Techniques insert shows the tools in action in full color.

Finally, Chapter 9 explains how to use long-document features — multichapter books, tables of contents, and indexes. Many layout artists never use these features, so you may skip this chapter initially, but understanding them can speed production of books, reports, and business documents.

Creating, Opening, and Saving Documents

✦ ✦ ✦ ✦

In This Chapter

Planning a publication

Creating a new document

Opening native and foreign documents

Saving and exporting documents

✦ ✦ ✦ ✦

Y ou're pumped up. You've purchased a copy of InDesign, installed it, checked out the interface, and now you're ready to put the program to work. So, what's next? Launch the application and start clicking? Hardly. Creating a publication with InDesign is much like going on a trip. You won't reach your destination unless you've prepared a plan for getting there. And you'll reach your destination more quickly and more easily if your plan is a sound one.

Remember, too, that most trips don't go exactly according to plan. InDesign is both versatile and forgiving. As you create a publication, you should feel free to change your mind, experiment, and let your creativity roam. As long as you reach your destination (on time!), taking a few detours is acceptable, and encountering a few roadblocks (small ones, you hope) is inevitable.

Before You Begin

Before you launch InDesign, open a new document, and begin working, you must answer several fundamental questions about the publication you'll be producing:

✦ What is the basic nature of the piece? Will it be printed, or will it be distributed over the Internet or an intranet? Is it going to be published as both a print and Web piece?

✦ If you're creating a printed publication, what are its dimensions?

✦ How many pages will it have? If it will be a multipage publication, will it have facing pages, like a book or a catalog, or will it be single-sided, like a flip chart?

✦ How many columns will each page have? How wide will the margins be?

✦ Does the budget allow for the use of color? If so, how many colors? What kind of paper will it be printed on? What kind of printer or printing press will be used?

✦ How will the publication be distributed? Under what circumstances will it be read? What's the life expectancy of the publication?

✦ If the publication is bound for the Internet, will you create an HTML file (which can be viewed by anybody with a Web browser) or a PDF file (which requires viewers to have the free Acrobat Reader application or browser plug-in)?

✦ And what about the content of your publication? What programs were used to create the text files and graphic files your publication will contain? Did you create the content yourself, or did others? What file formats were used for text and graphic files? What is the most effective way to present the content given the production requirements and budget?

As you answer these questions, a rough image of your publication will begin to take shape in your mind. When you're ready to begin turning your ideas into an actual publication, you have a couple of choices. Many designers whose skills date back to the days of traditional paste-up still prefer to use traditional tools — a drawing pad and colored markers or pencils in this case — to create rough sketches before they fire up their page-layout or illustration program. Other designers who were never exposed to such archaic tools are comfortable doing their brainstorming and sketching on the fly, using their favorite software. Whatever method suits you is fine. Keep in mind that, at this early stage, you shouldn't be spending much time fine-tuning details. You can do that later with InDesign.

An overly careful person can plan forever — in which case, nothing actually gets done. At some point, when the image you have of the publication you're creating is clear enough in your mind to begin work, it's time to create a new InDesign document.

Setting Up a New Publication

After you launch InDesign, you have two options: You can choose the Open command (File ➪ Open, or ⌘+O or Ctrl+O) to open a previously created document or template (more on opening documents and templates later in this chapter). Or you can choose File ➪ New, or ⌘+N or Ctrl+N, to create a new document.

When you create a new document, the New Document dialog box, shown in Figure 4-1, is displayed. It is here that you implement many of the decisions — including page size, number of pages, number of columns, and margin width — you arrived at during the planning stage. Although you're free to change your mind later, you'll save yourself time and potential headaches by sticking with the basic page parameters you establish in the New Document dialog box.

Figure 4-1: The settings you make in the New Document dialog box establish the basic framework for the pages in your publication. This example shows the settings used to create a standard 2-x-3½-inch business card. Notice that Facing Pages and Master Text Frame are not checked because they're not necessary for a one-page document.

Tip   To change the measurement units displayed in the New Document dialog box, choose InDesign ⇨ Preferences ⇨ Units & Increments on the Mac or Edit ⇨ Preferences ⇨ Units & Increments in Windows, or press ⌘+K or Ctrl+K, then choose the measurement system you want from the Horizontal and Vertical pop-up menus in the Ruler Units area. If you change preferences when no documents are open, your changes are applied to all subsequently created documents.

Here's how to create a new document:

1. **Choose File ⇨ New or press ⌘+N or Ctrl+N.**

2. **If you know exactly how many pages your publication will have, enter the number in the Number of Pages field.**

   If you don't know for sure, you can always add or delete pages later as needed.

3. **If you're creating a multipage publication that will have a spine, such as a book, catalog, or magazine, check Facing Pages. If you're creating a one-page document, such as a business card, an ad, or a poster, don't check Facing Pages.** Some publications, such as flip charts, presentations, and three-ring bound documents, have multiple pages but use only one side of the page. For such documents, don't check Facing Pages, either.

4. **If you want to flow text from page to page in a multipage document, such as a book or a catalog, check Master Text Frame.** (See Chapter 16 for more information about using master text frames.)

   If you check this box, InDesign automatically adds a text frame to the document's master page and to all document pages based on this master page. This saves you the work of creating a text box on each page and manually threading text through each frame.

5. **In the Page Size area, you can choose one of the predefined sizes from the pop-up menu.**

   Your options are Letter (8.5" by 11"), Legal (8.5" by 14"), Tabloid (11" by 17"), Letter Half (5.5" by 8.5"), Legal Half (7" by 8.5"), A4 (210mm by 297mm), A3 (297mm by 420mm), A5 (148mm by 210mm), B5 (176mm by 250mm), Compact Disc (4.7222" by 4.5"), or Custom. If you choose Custom, you can enter values in the Width and Height fields — and if you enter values in those fields, the Page Size automatically changes to Custom. The minimum height and width is 1 pica (0.1667"); the maximum is 216". Clicking the Portrait icon next to Orientation produces a vertical page (the larger of the Height and Width values is used in the Height field); clicking the Landscape icon produces a horizontal page (the larger of the Height and Width values is used in the Width field). You can also specify Height and Width values by clicking the up and down arrows associated with these fields.

Tip
When you specify page size, make sure the values you enter in the Height and Width fields are the size of the final printed piece — and not the size of the paper in your printer. For example, if you're creating a standard-sized business card, enter **3.5i** in the Width field and **2i** in the Height field. If you want to print *n-up* — meaning several "pages" on one sheet, such as several business cards on an 8½-x-11-inch sheet of paper — you can create a letter-sized document (8.5" by 11"), but you'll have to arrange the business cards within the page boundary and add your own crop marks for each card.

6. **Specify margin values in the Margins area.**

The *margin* is the white area around the outside of the page within which page elements — text and pictures — are placed. A document doesn't have to have margins (you can enter **0** into these fields), and if you want you can place text and pictures in the margin area. If Facing Pages is checked, Inside and Outside fields are available in the Margins area. Designers often specify larger inside margins for multipage publications to accommodate the fold at the spine. If Facing Pages is not checked, Left and Right fields replace the Inside and Outside fields. You can also specify margin values by clicking the up/down arrows associated with the fields.

7. **To specify how many columns your pages have, enter a value in the Columns field.**

You can also specify the number of columns by clicking the up/down arrows associated with the Column field.

8. **Specify a gutter distance (the gutter is the space between columns) in the Gutter field.**

You can also specify a gutter width value by clicking the up/down arrows associated with the Gutter field.

9. **If you click the More Options button, you'll get the Bleed and Slug area of the New Document dialog box (refer to Figure 4-1).**

The More Options button provides options to set bleed and slug areas. A *bleed area* is a margin on the outside of the page for objects you want to extend past the edge of the page — you want them to extend at least ⅛ inch so if there is any shifting of the paper during printing, there's no white space where the image should be (touching the edge of the page). The slug area is an area reserved for printing crop marks, color plate names, and other such printing information — some output devices will cut these off during printing unless a slug area is defined. For both bleed and slug areas, you can set the top, bottom, left, and right margins independently.

New Feature Bleed and slug areas are new to InDesign CS.

10. **Click OK to close the New Document dialog box.**

When you do, your new, blank document is displayed in a new document window. Figure 4-2 shows the window of a newly created document (a business card) that uses the settings shown in Figure 4-1.

New Feature InDesign CS lets you create predefined document types, called document presets, to supplement the standard ones such as Letter.

Figure 4-2: The business card settings in the New Document dialog box shown in Figure 4-1 resulted in the document you see here. The view percentage field in the lower-left corner of the document window shows that the business card is currently displayed at 352.38 percent of actual size.

There are three ways to create document presets:

✦ **You can save these new-document settings by clicking the Save Preset button in the New Document dialog box.** These saved settings will then appear in the Document Style pop-up menu in the future.

✦ **You can also add custom pages by editing the New Doc Sizes.txt file in the Presets folder (in the InDesign applications folder) and adding a new line for each document style as follows:** `name[tab]width[tab]height`. For example: `Business card[tab]3.5"[tab]2"`. This is a handy way to distribute document styles to multiple users. An example would be building a document style for every standard ad size for a magazine or newspaper to ensure correct dimensions on new ad documents.

✦ **You can choose File ⇨ Document Presets ⇨ Define to create (via the New button) a new document style or import (via the Load button) one from another document.** You can also edit and delete document presets via the dialog box shown in Figure 4-3.

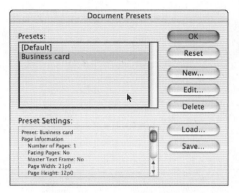

Figure 4-3: The new Document Presets dialog box lets you create, import, edit, and delete document styles.

Tip   You can bypass the New Document dialog box by pressing Shift+⌘+N or Ctrl+Shift+N. When you use this method, the most recent settings in the New Document dialog box are used for the new document.

Opening Documents and Templates

Opening documents with InDesign is pretty much the same as opening documents with any program. Simply choose File ⇨ Open or press ⌘+O or Ctrl+O, locate and click on the document you want to work on, then click the Open button. But InDesign offers a few options for opening documents you don't find in every program. For example, you can

- ✦ **Open more than one document at a time.**

- ✦ **Open a copy of a document instead of the original.** This keeps the original file from being overwritten accidentally — very helpful if you're making several variations of one document.

- ✦ **Open a template under its own name.** This makes editing templates easier than it is with other programs, specifically QuarkXPress.

- ✦ **Open documents created with PageMaker and QuarkXPress, as well as PDF files.**

Tip   InDesign's File menu displays the names of the five most recently saved documents in the Open Recent submenu that appears under the Open option in the File menu after you have opened a file.

To open a file:

1. **Choose File ▷ Open, or press ⌘+O or Ctrl+O.**

   The Open a File dialog box, shown in Figure 4-4, is displayed.

Figure 4-4: The Mac (left) and Windows (right) versions of the Open a File dialog box differ slightly. When you open a file, you have the option to open it normally (Open Normal), open the original copy of a template (Open Original), or open a copy of the file (Open Copy).

2. **Locate and open the folder that contains the document(s) you want to open. Click on a file name or hold down the ⌘ or Ctrl keys and click on multiple file names.**

   In Windows, the Files of Type pop-up menu offers the option to display: PageMaker 6.5–7.0 files, QuarkXPress 3.3–4.1 files, InDesign files, InDesign Interchange, and All Formats. Choose any of these options to display a specific file format in the file list. On a Mac, the Open a File dialog box will display any supported file formats that have a Mac icon, and the dialog box includes a Preview pane that displays a thumbnail version of the selected file or, more commonly, its icon.

Note   InDesign Interchange is a format that permits InDesign 2 to open the document. InDesign CS does not let you save its files to InDesign 2 format, so if you work with InDesign 2 users, they'll need to get the optional InDesign Interchange plug-in to save and open these files. InDesign CS will open InDesign 2 files without any additional software; the purpose of InDesign Interchange is to let InDesign 2 users work with InDesign 3 files and save them in a format that retains InDesign CS-specific features, which InDesign 2 otherwise would not support.

Tip

In Windows InDesign, use All Files InDesign in the Files of Type pop-up menu to display Mac files with no extensions. In Macintosh InDesign, use All Documents in the Show pop-up menus to display Windows files without the InDesign icons.

3. **If you want to open the original document (rather than a copy of the document), click Normal under Open As. To open a copy of a document, click Open Copy.**

   When you open a copy of a document, it's assigned a default name (Untitled-1, Untitled-2, and so on). If you want to use a template to create a new version of a publication, click Normal; InDesign will create a document based on the template. To open a template under its own name so that you can edit it, click Open Original. Templates are explained in the following section, "Opening documents versus opening templates."

4. **Click OK to close the dialog box.**

   Each document you opened is displayed in a separate document window. The page and view magnification displayed when a document was last saved is used when you open the document.

Tip

You can also open an InDesign document or template by double-clicking on its file icon. If InDesign is not running, double-clicking on a document or template file — as long as it has the proper icon on the Mac or file extension (.indd for documents and .indt for templates) in Windows — will launch the application and open the document/template. If InDesign is already running, the document is displayed in a new window.

Opening documents versus opening templates

Whenever you save a document, you have the option of saving a standard document file or a template (more on saving templates later in this chapter). A *template* is an InDesign file that's used to create multiple iterations of the same publication. For example, if you produce a monthly newsletter, you'll save gobs of time and ensure consistency from issue to issue by using a template as the starting point for each edition of the newsletter. A template is essentially the shell of a publication that contains the basic framework — page layout, master pages, style sheets, and so on — but doesn't contain any actual content.

Cross-Reference

For more information about creating templates, see Chapter 7.

When you open a template, you have two choices: You can either open a copy of the file and use it to create a new publication, or you can open the original file, make changes, and then save an updated version of the template. If you want to use a template as the starting point for a new publication, choose File ➪ Open or press ⌘+O or Ctrl+O, locate and select the template, and make sure Open Normal is selected in the Open a File dialog box (refer to Figure 4-4) before you click Open. If you want to modify a template, click Open Original. If Normal is selected, clicking OK opens a new document window and assigns the document a default name, Untitled-1, Untitled-2, and so on. If Open Original is selected, the original file is opened and the original name is displayed in the title bar.

Converting documents created with other programs

One of InDesign's hallmarks is its ability to open documents from other programs and convert them to InDesign documents. You can open PageMaker 6.5–7.0 and QuarkXPress 3.3–4.1*x* documents. (Adobe has no plans to support files in the version 5 or 6 formats of QuarkXPress.)

Well, *most* of the time you can open PageMaker and QuarkXPress documents. Because the other programs' formats are so different from InDesign's, and their capabilities differ as well, the chances of being able to import a foreign document and have it flawlessly convert to InDesign are small. So use this feature to do the first step in the conversion process, but expect to spend time cleaning up the converted files by hand. In some cases, you may see that the amount of cleanup work is more than simply re-creating the document in InDesign from scratch — don't panic when that's the case. And be happy when your documents convert effortlessly.

InDesign will alert you to any import issues of PageMaker and QuarkXPress files with a dialog box that appears after the import is complete, as Figure 4-5 shows.

InDesign cannot import PDF files so that the text and images are editable, but it can bring in PDF files as graphics for placement in your document. Chapter 23 covers this process in detail.

Figure 4-5: InDesign shows a Conversion Warnings dialog box if there are any issues in importing foreign file formats.

QuarkXPress

InDesign can read QuarkXPress files from version 3.3 through 4.1*x*. Because there are so many differences between QuarkXPress and InDesign, it's impossible to predict all the conversion issues that may arise. The good news is that a great many things work well, but some don't. Here are some common conversion issues to pay attention to:

✦ **If your QuarkXPress document relies on XTensions (a type of plug-in) to add capabilities (such as table creation), it will not convert correctly into InDesign and may not even import at all.** Examples include any documents built with QuarkXPress's indexing and book features.

✦ **QuarkXPress's leading model is different than InDesign's, so expect leading to sometimes vary significantly, especially if you use additive leading as the automatic leading method in QuarkXPress.**

✦ **InDesign won't retain kerning-table adjustments in QuarkXPress files.** (It does retain any kerning applied manually, which InDesign 2 did not.)

✦ **The customizable dashes in QuarkXPress are converted to solid and dashed lines — note that stripes do convert properly.**

✦ **Special gradient blends, such as the diamond-pattern, are converted to linear blends or circular blends.**

✦ **Text on a curved path is converted to regular text in a rectangular frame, even though InDesign supports text on paths.**

✦ **H&J sets don't have an equivalent in InDesign, so they do not convert, although any H&J settings are carried over into the converted paragraph styles.**

✦ **Libraries won't convert.**

✦ **Printer styles won't convert.**

 Appendix C covers other issues in moving from QuarkXPress to InDesign.

PageMaker

InDesign can read PageMaker 6.5 and 7.0 files. Because PageMaker and InDesign offer many of the same features, there are fewer translation issues between them. Some to take note of include the following:

✦ Fill patterns aren't supported.

✦ Libraries won't convert.

✦ Printer styles won't convert.

 Appendix D covers other issues in moving from PageMaker to InDesign.

Importing text files

In addition to letting you open InDesign, PageMaker, and QuarkXPress files, InDesign also lets you work with text files created with word processing programs. However, you can't open word processing files using the Open command (File ➪ Open, or ⌘+O or Ctrl+O). Instead, you must place, or import, text files using the Place command (File ➪ Place, or ⌘+D or Crtl+D).

You can use the Place command to import Rich Text Format (RTF), Microsoft Excel, Microsoft Word, and text-only (ASCII). For Word and Excel, InDesign supports all Mac versions since version 98 and all Windows versions since version 97.

InDesign also supports two proprietary text formats: Tagged Text, a way of coding text files with InDesign formatting information, and InDesign Interchange, a format that lets InDesign CS and InDesign 2 users work on the same files. (InDesign 2 users must buy the InDesign Interchange software, which includes the Scripting and XML Reader plug-ins, to use this format.)

Cross-Reference

For more information about importing text files, see Chapter 9. For more on Tagged Text, see Chapter 14.

In addition to letting you import text files, InDesign lets you export text files. See the "Saving files in other formats" section later in this chapter for more information.

Recovering a document after a crash or power failure

InDesign includes an automatic-recovery feature that protects your documents in the event of a power failure or a system crash. As you work on a document, any changes you make after saving it are stored in a separate, temporary file. Under normal circumstances, each time you choose Save, the information in the temporary file is applied to the document. The data in the temporary file is important only if you weren't able to save a document before crashing. A word of warning: Although InDesign's automatic recovery feature is a nice safety net, you should still be careful to save your work often. Here's how it works:

1. **Relaunch InDesign or, if necessary, restart your computer and then launch InDesign.**

2. **If automatic-recovery data is available, InDesign automatically opens the recovered document and displays the word "Recovered" in the document's title bar.**

   This lets you know that the document contains changes that were not included in the last saved version.

3. **If you want to save the recovered data, choose File ➪ Save; "Recovered" is removed as part of the filename, and InDesign will ask if you want to overwrite the old file.**

Overwriting the old file is easier than using File ➪ Save As and entering a name — unless you do want to save a copy of the file in case you want to go back to the old version later. If you want to use the last saved version of the document (and disregard the recovered data), close the file (File ➪ Close, or ⌘+W or Ctrl+W) without saving, then open the file (File ➪ Open, or ⌘+O or Ctrl+O).

Note

Sometimes, InDesign can't automatically recover the documents for you. Instead, it gives you the choice of recovering any files open during a crash or power outage, saving the recovery data for later, or deleting the recovery data. You'll typically want to recover the files immediately.

Saving Documents and Templates

When you open a new document, it's assigned a default name — Untitled-1, Untitled-2, and so on — and the first page is displayed in the document window. At this point, you're like a painter standing in front of a blank canvas. But painters don't have to worry about system crashes and power failures; you do. Make sure that when you work on InDesign documents, you follow the first rule of safe computing: Save early and often.

The second group of commands — Close, Save, Save As, Save a Copy As, and Revert — in InDesign's File menu provide options for saving the active/frontmost document. Here's a rundown of what each command does:

✦ **Close** (⌘+W, or Ctrl+W or Ctrl+F4) closes the active document. If the document has never been saved or if it's been changed since it was last saved, a dialog box lets you save, close without saving, or cancel and return to the document.

✦ **Save** (⌘+S or Ctrl+S) saves changes you've made to the active document since you last saved. If you choose Save for a document that hasn't yet been saved, the Save As dialog box is displayed. This dialog box lets you name and choose a storage folder for the document.

Tip

If you have more than one document open, you can save them all at once by pressing Option+Shift+⌘+S or Ctrl+Alt+Shift+S.

✦ **Save As** (Option+⌘+S or Ctrl+Alt+S) lets you save a copy of the active document in a different (or in the same) folder using a different (or the same) name. When you choose Save As — and when you choose Save for an unsaved document — the Save As dialog box, shown in Figure 4-6, appears.

✦ **Save a Copy As** lets you create a copy of the active document in a different (or in the same) folder using a different (or the same) name. When you use the Save a Copy As command, the original document remains open and retains its original name. It differs from Save As only in that it keeps the original document open.

✦ **Revert** undoes all changes you've made to a document since you last saved it. There is no way to undo this and reinstate all your changes after you revert, so be careful.

Figure 4-6: The Mac version of the Save As dialog box (left) and the Windows version (right) are slightly different.

Tip

InDesign's Save, Save As, and Save a Copy As commands let you save only InDesign documents and templates. If you want to save a document as an EPS, InDesign Interchange, XML, or PDF file, you should use the Export command (File ➪ Export), which is explained later in this chapter.

Saving documents versus saving templates

Whenever you save a document for the first time or you use the Save As or Save a Copy As command, the Save As dialog box lets you save a standard InDesign document file or a template.

In an ideal world, you would create a finished template, save it, and then open a copy of the template and use it to create an actual publication. In the real world, however, templates are often created by yanking the content out of a finished publication and then saving the gutted file as a template. Regardless of how you create your templates, make sure you remember to select the InDesign 3.0 Template option in the Save As dialog box. On the Mac, use the Format pop-up menu; in Windows, use the Save Type As pop-up menu.

If you forget to save a document as a template, it will open under its actual name. If you then make any changes and choose File ➪ Save (⌘+S or Ctrl+S), the changes are saved with the original document. If this happens, simply save the document again and choose the InDesign 3.0 Template option.

Choosing File ➪ Package lets you save a copy of a document along with all files — linked graphics, fonts, and ICC color profiles — required to print the document. This feature is particularly handy if you intend to send an InDesign document to an output provider. (See Chapter 30 for more information about the Package command.)

Choosing File ➪ Package for GoLive collects all the document's image files and creates an XML document for use in creating a Web version of your InDesign document in Adobe GoLive 7 or later — it does *not* create an HTML version of your InDesign document that can be used in any other Web-creation program.

Knowing how to not save changes

As mentioned earlier in this chapter, InDesign is a very forgiving program. If you make a mistake, change your mind, or work yourself into a complete mess, you don't have to remain in your predicament or save your work. InDesign offers several escape routes. You can:

✦ **Undo your last action by choosing Edit ➪ Undo or pressing ⌘+Z or Ctrl+Z.** (Some actions, particularly actions such as scrolling that do not affect any items or the underlying document structure, are not undoable.) You can undo multiple actions in the order they were done by choosing Edit ➪ Undo or pressing ⌘+Z or Ctrl+Z — each time you undo, the previous action is undone.

✦ **Redo an action you've undone by choosing Edit ➪ Redo or pressing Shift+⌘+Z or Ctrl+Shift+Z.** Alternately choosing Undo and Redo is a handy way of seeing a before/after view of a particular change. As with undo, you can redo multiple undone actions in the order in which they were undone.

✦ **To undo all changes you've made since last saving a document, choose File ➪ Revert.** There is no way to undo this and reinstate all your changes after you revert, so be careful.

If you perform an action and then change your mind while InDesign is completing the action, pressing Esc cancels the operation.

To undo any changes you've made after opening a dialog box, press Option or Alt, which changes the Cancel button into a Reset button, then click Reset. (This feature is not available in all dialog boxes.)

Saving files in other formats

InDesign's Save commands (File ➪ Save, File ➪ Save As, and File ➪ Save a Copy As) let you save documents and templates using InDesign's native file format. The Export command (File ➪ Export) lets you save the stories — and in some cases stories and whole layouts — in InDesign documents in several formats:

✦ **Word processing formats:** If you've placed the text cursor into a story, you can export its text (select a range of text if you want to export only that selection) into one of three formats: RTF for import into word processors with only basic formatting retained and Text Only for import into word processors that don't support RTF (no formatting is retained).

Note   You can save only one text file at a time. If you need to export several stories from the same document, you must do so one at a time.

✦ **InDesign workflow formats:** Whether text is selected via the Text tool or the Direct Selection tool, you can save the story in the InDesign Tagged Text format (for editing in a word processor and later reimport into InDesign with all InDesign formatting retained) or in the InDesign Interchange format (for import into InDesign 2).

New Feature   The new InDesign Interchange format lets users of InDesign 2 read InDesign CS files – if they acquire the Interchange software for InDesign 2. You cannot otherwise downsave to earlier versions of InDesign.

✦ **Production formats:** Whether text is selected via the Text tool or the Direct Selection tool, you can save the document — not just the story — in Encapsulated PostScript (EPS) or Adobe Portable Document Format (PDF) formats for use by prepress tools and service bureaus or for import into other applications as pictures.

✦ **Online formats:** Whether text is selected via the Text tool or the Direct Selection tool, you can save the document — not just the story — in Extensible Markup Language (XML) format for use in online database-oriented content-management systems, as well as a specific page, spread, or text selection into JPEG bitmap or Adobe SVG vector formats for use as online graphics.

When exporting a file, choose a format from the Formats pop-up menu (on the Mac) or from the Save as Type pop-up menu (in Windows) in the Export dialog box.

Summary

When you're ready to begin working on a new document, choose File ➪ New and then use the controls in the New Document dialog box to specify the page size, margins, column format, and any bleed and slug areas for the document. You can also save these settings for easy future use as document styles from the New Document dialog box.

After opening a new document, choose File ⇨ Save to save a standard InDesign document file or a template file. (A template is a preconstructed document that you use to create multiple versions of a publication.) You can choose File ⇨ Save As to save a copy of the current document, or you can choose File ⇨ Revert to discard your most recent round of changes. If you want to work on a document you've previously saved, choose File ⇨ Open.

In addition to opening InDesign documents and templates, you can open QuarkXPress 3.3 and 4.1x documents, as well as PageMaker 6.5 and 7.0 documents. Choosing File ⇨ Export lets you save InDesign documents as EPS, PDF, XML, JPEG, and SVG files, as well as save text in RTF, text-only, InDesign Tagged Text, and InDesign Interchange formats.

✦   ✦   ✦

Working with Pages

✦   ✦   ✦   ✦

In This Chapter

Adding, removing, and rearranging document pages

Adjusting page numbers and creating sections

Navigating through a document and scrolling in a page

Adjusting page layouts and objects

✦   ✦   ✦   ✦

It's a rare InDesign user who creates only one-page documents. Even if business cards, ads, and posters are your bread and butter, you'll probably produce at least a few multipage documents. If you'll be creating newsletters, newspapers, books, catalogs, or any other such multipage publications, you need to know how to add pages to your document, move pages around if you change your mind, and delete pages if necessary.

In addition to letting you create multipage documents — something that most illustration and image-editing programs don't — InDesign lets you divide multipage documents into independently numbered sections. As documents grow in size, your ability to navigate quickly to the page you want to work on becomes an important consideration. The longer you spend getting to the page you want, the less time you have to work on it. Fortunately, InDesign provides several navigation aids that make it easy to move around a page or a document.

Working with Multipage Documents

If you intend to create a multipage document, you should check the Facing Pages box in the New Document dialog box (File ⇨ New, or ⌘+N or Ctrl+N) when you create the document. You'll also want to display the Pages pane (Window ⇨ Pages or F12), shown in Figure 5-1, because it provides the controls that let you add pages (document and master), delete and move pages, apply master pages to document pages, and navigate through a document.

 Cross-Reference For more information about using the Pages pane to work on master pages, see Chapter 7.

Note The overwhelming majority of multipage documents are facing-page publications, such as books, catalogs, and magazines. Some exceptions are flip charts, Web pages, and three-hole-punched publications printed on only one side. In this chapter, the figures show examples of a facing-page document. If you're creating a single-sided multipage document, the techniques are the same as for facing-page documents, but the icons in the Pages pane will show only single-sided page icons (the icons aren't dog-eared).

Figure 5-1: The Pages pane and its palette menu. This is how the pane looks when you open a new, one-page, facing-page document.

Adding pages

A document can contain as many as 9,999 pages, though you'd never want to create a document nearly that long. In general, try to break up long publications into logical pieces. For example, if you're creating a book, it's a good idea to create separate documents for the front matter, each chapter, the index, and any other parts (appendices and so on). Also, if you're producing a long document, you'll want to take advantage of master pages (covered in Chapter 7), which save you the work of building each page from scratch.

When you create a multipage document, you're free to add however many pages you want. But be careful. Even though InDesign will let you create a seven-page newsletter, in real life, facing-page publications always have an even number of pages—usually a multiple of 4 and often a multiple of 16 because of the way printers arrange multiple pages on a single sheet of paper.

Here's how to add pages to a document:

1. **If it's not displayed, open the Pages pane by choosing Window ⇨ Pages or pressing F12.**

2. **From the Pages pane's palette menu, choose Insert Pages.**

   The Insert Pages dialog box, shown in Figure 5-2, is displayed.

Figure 5-2: The Insert Pages dialog box.

3. **In the Pages field, enter the number of pages you want to add.**

4. **Choose an option from the Insert pop-up menu: After Page, Before Page, At Start of Document, or At End of Document.**

   Be careful: If you've already started working on page 1, for example, make sure you add new pages after page 1. Otherwise, it won't be page 1 anymore and you'll have to move the objects you already created.

5. **Enter a page number in the field next to Insert or use the arrows to increase or decrease the value in one-page increments.**

6. **From the Master pop-up menu, choose the master page you want to apply to the new pages.**

7. **When you're finished, click OK to close the dialog box.**

You can also add new pages or spreads — spreads are added if a spread is selected in the Pages pane — one at a time at the end of a document, by clicking the Create New Page icon at the bottom of the Pages pane. When you use this method, the master page applied to the last document page is applied to each new page. Pages are added after the currently selected page in the pane.

You can also drag a master-page icon (or both pages in a facing-pages spread to add a spread) from the top of the Pages pane to add a page using a master page's settings (use the [None] page for a plain page) between any pair of document page spreads or to the right of the last document spread. If a vertical bar is displayed when you release the mouse button, the spread is placed between the spreads on either side of the bar. If a vertical bar is not displayed between document page spreads when you release the mouse button, the new spread is placed at the end of the document.

In previous versions of InDesign, if you added or removed an odd number of pages from a facing-pages document, all pages after the new or deleted pages changed sides: Even pages got bumped to become odd pages, and odd pages got bumped to become even pages. This wreaked havoc with page designs. For example, a two-page opening spread for a magazine article could get split so that the original left-hand page was on the right and the original right-hand page got bumped to the next (left-hand) page. But InDesign CS fixes that—pages are automatically changed from left-hand pages to right-hand pages, and vice versa, as needed when individual pages are added and removed in a facing-pages document.

Copying pages

You can copy pages from one document to another by dragging the page icon from the source document's Pages pane to the target document's Pages pane. Any master page(s) associated with the copied document pages(s) are copied as well.

The ability to drag-copy pages from one document to another is new to InDesign CS.

Deleting pages

InDesign offers a couple of choices for deleting pages from a document. You can

✦ **Select one or more page icons in the Pages pane and either drag them to the pane's Trash button or simply click the Trash button.** Click on a spread's page numbers to select both pages. You can click on a page icon or spread number and then Shift+click on another page icon or spread number to select a range of pages. Hold down the ⌘ or Ctrl key and click on page icons or spread numbers to select multiple, noncontiguous pages.

✦ **Select one or more page icons in the Pages pane and then choose Delete Page(s) or Delete Spread(s) from the pane's palette menu.**

Moving pages

Although you can move pages around in a document, this is something you should do with great care—if at all. Generally, if you want to move the objects on one page to another page, it's safer to cut or copy (Edit ➪ Cut, or ⌘+X or Ctrl+X, or Edit ➪ Copy, or ⌘+C or Ctrl+C) the objects than to move the page, which might cause subsequent pages to shuffle. If you absolutely need to move a single page, it's safer to move its spread. (Of course, if you're working on a single-sided facing-page document, shuffling is not an issue.)

To move a page, click on its icon, then drag the hand pointer between two spreads or between the pages of a spread. A vertical bar indicates where the selected page will be placed. Release the mouse button when the vertical bar is where you want to move the page. To move a spread, click on the page numbers beneath the icons (rather than on the page icons).

Creating island spreads

Have you ever seen a publication—a magazine, perhaps—that had a foldout page? Often such pages are ads (publishers love advertisers who buy multipage ads) or special sections. Or maybe you've seen a two-sided, multifold brochure with several panels, each the same size. A multipage spread of this type is often called a gatefold or accordion page, or an *island spread*.

When you designate a spread as an island spread, the spread's pages don't move if you add or delete any document pages in front of it. (Normally, when you add or delete pages, all subsequent pages are bumped backward or shuffled forward.)

When you create a island spread of three pages in a facing-page publication, you should always create them in pairs because, in an actual printed publication, if you add a third page to a two-page spread, the back side of the page becomes the third page in another three-page spread. Along the same lines, if you create a four-panel, trifold brochure, both the front and the back have four panels.

One last word about island spreads: They require special care throughout the production process, and they'll cost you extra at the printer and bindery. If you're creating a modest, black-and-white newsletter for a local nonprofit organization, throwing in a three-panel gatefold probably isn't an option. On the other hand, if you can find an advertiser with deep pockets, InDesign lets you create island spreads with up to ten pages.

To create an island spread, first select the pages in the existing spread that you want to make into an island spread, then choose Keep Spreads Together from the pane's palette menu. (When you designate a spread to be kept together, the page numbers below the spread in the Pages pane are displayed in brackets.) To add pages to an island spread, drag a document page icon (a master page icon won't work) next to or between the pages of an island spread. A vertical bar indicates where the page will be placed. When the bar is where you want to place the page, release the mouse button. To clear an island spread, select it in the Pages pane and then uncheck Keep Spreads Together in the pane's palette menu. Figure 5-3 shows a pair of three-page island spreads in a facing-page publication.

Tip You may want to create a section out of the extra pages in an island spread so that you can number them separately from the surrounding pages. Sections are covered later in this chapter.

Figure 5-3: In this example, pages 14, 15, and 16 are an island spread, as are pages 17, 18, and 19. The extra page in each spread is based on the A-Master master page.

Working with Page Numbers

Pages are numbered automatically starting at 1 based on the order in which they appear in the Pages pane. But you can change the page numbering from Arabic numerals to Roman numerals or letters, as well as change the start page to be something other than 1. To do so, select the first page in the document in the Pages pane and choose Layout ➪ Page Numbering & Sections or use the Numbering & Section Options Pages pane's palette menu. You'll get the dialog box shown in Figure 5-4. To change the initial page number, click the Start Page Numbering At radio button and enter a new starting page number in its field. To change the page numbering style from the default of Arabic numerals (1, 2, 3, 4, . . .), use the Style pop-up menu and choose from I, II, III, IV, . . . , i, ii, iii, iv, . . . , A, B, C, D, . . . , and a, b, c, d, ...

Figure 5-4: The Numbering and Section Options dialog box lets you change the starting page number and the types of numerals used.

Entering page references in text

You'll often want page references in text—the current page number in a folio, for example, or the target page number for a "continued on" reference. You could type in a page number manually on each page of a multipage document, but that can get old fast. As I mentioned earlier in this chapter, if you're working on a multipage document, you should be using master pages. And if you're using master pages, you should handle page numbers on document pages by placing page-number characters on their master pages.

If you want to add the current page number to a page, you can choose Type ⇨ Insert Special Character ⇨ Auto Page Number or press Option+⌘+N or Ctrl+Alt+N whenever the Type tool is active and the text cursor is flashing. If you move the page or the text frame, the page-number character is automatically updated to reflect the new page number.

Targeting versus selecting spreads

Depending on the task you're working on, you may want to use the Pages pane to *target* a spread or to *select* a spread. The choice you make determines the actions you can perform.

A target spread is the spread to which copied objects will be placed when you choose Paste, or to which library objects will be placed when you choose Place Items from a library pane's palette menu. The target spread is the one that's in the center of the document window and is indicated by the page number displayed in the page-number field at the lower-left corner of the document window. Only one spread can be the target spread at any one time. At reduced magnifications, it's possible to display several spreads in the document window. In this case, the number in the page-number field indicates the target spread.

When you select one or more spreads, you can then perform several page-level modifications, such as adjusting margin and column guides, applying a master page, or deleting the pages, in a single operation.

There are several ways to target a spread. You can

- ✦ Modify an object on the spread or its pasteboard.

- ✦ Click on a spread or its pasteboard.

- ✦ In the Pages pane, double-click the page numbers below the spread's page icons. (This also moves you to the document pages in the spread.)

You also have several options for selecting a page or spread:

- ✦ Click once on a page icon to select one page of a spread; click on the page numbers to select both pages. If you click twice, the page or spread is selected and targeted.

- ✦ Click on a page icon or spread number and then Shift+click on another page icon or spread number to select a range of pages.

- ✦ Hold down the ⌘ or Ctrl key and click on page icons or spread numbers to select multiple, noncontiguous pages.

In the Pages pane, the page numbers of the target spread are displayed reversed, white numbers in a black rectangle, while the page icons are highlighted in a light blue color.

To create "continued on" and "continued from" lines, you choose Type ➪ Insert Special Character ➪ Next Page Number, or use Option+Shift+⌘+] or Ctrl+Alt+Shift+], to have the next page's number inserted in your text, or choose Type ➪ Insert Special Character ➪ Previous Page Number, or press Option+Shift+⌘+[or Ctrl+Alt+Shift+[, to have the previous page's number inserted. That next or previous page will be the next or previous page in the story.

Tip   One flaw in InDesign's continued-line approach is that the text boxes must be linked, so you're likely to place your continued lines in the middle of your text. If the text reflows, so do the continued lines. Here's a way to avoid that: Create separate text boxes for your continued-on and continued-from text boxes. Now link those two boxes, not the story text. This way, the story text can reflow as needed without affecting your continued lines.

Dividing a document into sections

Some long documents are divided into parts that are numbered separately from the other parts. For example, the page numbers of the front matter of books often use Roman numerals, while standard Arabic numerals are used for the body of the book. If the book has appendices, a separate numbering scheme could be applied to these pages. In InDesign, such independently numbered parts are referred to as *sections*.

A multipage document can contain as many sections as you want (a section has to contain at least one page). If each section of a document will use a different page layout, you'll probably want to create a different master page for each section. Here's how to create a section:

1. **If it's not displayed, open the Pages pane by choosing Window ➪ Pages or pressing F12.**

2. **Click on the icon of the page you want to start a section.**

3. **Choose Numbering & Section Options from the pane's palette menu.**

   The New Section dialog box, shown in Figure 5-5, is displayed. (You can also create a section starting at the current page in your document by choosing Layout ➪ Numbering & Section Options.) By default, the Start Section box is checked. Leave it checked.

4. **In the Section Prefix field, enter up to five characters that will identify the section in the page-number box at the lower-left corner of the document window.**

   For example, if you enter Sec2, the first page of the section will be displayed as "Sec2:1" in the page-number box.

5. **From the Style menu, choose the Roman numeral, Arabic numeral, or alphabetic style you want to use for page numbers.**

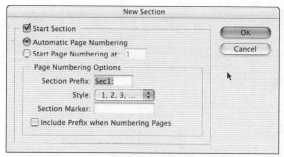

Figure 5-5: The New Section dialog box.

6. **For Page Numbering, choose Automatic Page Numbering if you want the first page of the section to be one number higher than the last page of the previous section. (The new section will use the specified style; the previous section may use this style or another style.) Choose Start Page Numbering At and enter a number in the accompanying field to specify a different starting number for the section.**

   For example, if a book begins with a section of front matter, you could begin the body section of a book on page 1 by choosing Start At and entering 1 in the field. If you choose Continue from Previous Section, the first page of the body section would begin one number higher than the Roman numeral on the last page of the front matter.

7. **In the Section Marker field, enter a text string that you can later automatically apply to pages in the section.**

   You might want to enter something straightforward like "Section 2" or, if the section is a chapter, the name of the chapter.

   Tip You can insert the section marker name in folios, chapter headings, and story text by choosing Type ⇨ Insert Special Character ⇨ Section Marker, or Option+Shift+⌘+N or Ctrl+Alt+Shift+N. This is a great way to get a chapter name (if you use it as the section marker) in your folio or to have cross-references in text to a section whose name might later change.

8. **Click OK to close the dialog box.**

When you create a section, it's indicated in the Pages pane by a small, black triangle over the icon of the first page in the section, as shown in Figure 5-6. (If you move the pointer over the black triangle, the name of the section is displayed.) The page-numbering scheme you've specified is reflected in the page numbers below the page icons. When you begin a section, it continues until the end of the document or until you begin a new section.

Tip By default, the Pages pane displays section numbers beneath the icons of document pages. If you want to display absolute page numbers—the first page is page 1 and all other pages are numbered sequentially—you can do so by choosing InDesign ➪ Preferences ➪ General on the Mac or Edit ➪ Preferences ➪ General in Windows, or by pressing ⌘+K or Ctrl+K, and choosing Absolute Numbering from the View pop-up menu.

Figure 5-6: The small triangle above a page icon represents a section start.

Removing a section

If you decide that you want to remove a section, navigate to the page that begins the section, choose Numbering & Section Options from the Pages pane's palette menu, and then uncheck the Section Start box.

Navigating Documents and Pages

Moving from page to page in a long document and scrolling around a large or magnified page are among the most common tasks you'll perform in InDesign. The more time you spend displaying the page or page area you want to work on, the less time you have to do the work you need to do. Like most trips, the less time you spend between destinations, the better.

For navigating through the pages of a document, the Pages pane (Window ➪ Pages or F12) offers the fastest ride. For navigating around in a page, you may want to switch to the Navigator pane (Window ➪ Navigator).

Navigating with the Pages pane

When the Pages pane is displayed, you can use it to quickly move from page to page in a multipage document and to switch between displaying master pages and document pages. To display a particular document page, double-click its icon. The selected page is centered in the document window. To display a master spread, double-click its icon in the lower half of the pane.

Tip

The Fit Page in Window command (View ⇨ Fit Page in Window, or ⌘+0 or Ctrl+0) and Fit Spread in Window command (View ⇨ Fit Page in Window, or Option+⌘+0 or Ctrl+Alt+0) let you enlarge or reduce the display magnification to fit the selected page or spread in the document window. (Note that the shortcuts use the numeral *0*, not the letter *O*.)

Using the Navigator pane

Although it's possible to use the Navigator pane (Window ⇨ Navigator) to move from page to page in a long document, the Pages pane is better for this task. The Navigator pane is more useful for scrolling within a page, particularly for doing detail work on a page that's displayed at a high magnification. If you're an Illustrator, PageMaker, or Photoshop user, you may already be familiar with the Navigator pane, which works the same in all three applications.

To display the Navigator pane, choose Window ⇨ Navigator. Figure 5-7 shows the Navigator pane and its palette menu.

Figure 5-7: The Navigator pane and its palette menu.

Changing view magnification

You can use the Navigator pane to zoom in or zoom out on the current spread. You have several options for zooming in and out:

✦ Click the handle on the zoom and drag left to zoom out, right to zoom in.

✦ Click the zoom-out icon to the left of the zoom slider to zoom out; click the zoom-in icon to the right of the zoom slider to zoom in.

✦ Enter a view percentage in the field at the bottom right of the Navigator pane. Enter a smaller value to zoom out; enter a larger value to zoom in. Enter 100% to display the page at actual size.

 Tip

You can also use the Zoom tool or its keyboard shortcuts to zoom in or out (⌘+ spacebar or Ctrl+spacebar to zoom in, Option+⌘+spacebar or Ctrl+Alt+spacebar to zoom out).

Scrolling with the Navigator pane

The rectangle displayed in the Navigator pane (on the actual screen it should show up red) indicates the area that's currently displayed in the document window. When you change the display magnification, the rectangle changes size (it gets larger as you zoom out and smaller as you zoom in). You can display a different area in the currently displayed spread by dragging the rectangle or by clicking outside it. If you click outside it, the point where you click is centered in the document window.

Other options in the Navigator pane

If red isn't your favorite color, you can change the color of the rectangle displayed in the Navigator pane by choosing Palette Options from its palette menu and then choosing a different color from the Color pop-up menu in the Palette Options dialog box.

If you choose Show All Spreads from the Navigator pane's palette menu, all the document's spreads are displayed in the pane. The more spreads you have, the smaller they're displayed and the smaller the rectangle becomes that indicates the area that's displayed in the document window. By dragging the rectangle from page to page you can navigate to a particular area on a page while remaining at the current display percentage. This can be a handy way of navigating, but if you're working on a document that has many pages, the page icons and rectangle can become too small to work with easily. Figure 5-8 shows the Navigator pane with the View All Spreads option selected.

Figure 5-8: The Navigator pane with View All Spreads selected.

Tip   You can also use the scroll bars at the right and bottom of the document window to move to different areas of a page or to a different page in a document or the keyboard shortcut (hold down the spacebar, then click and drag the hand pointer; the Type tool cannot be selected for this to work).

Adjusting Page Layouts and Objects

If you've ever created and worked with a document all the way to the finishing touches, and then discovered that the page size was wrong from the beginning, you know the meaning of frustration. Manually adjusting the size and placement of all the objects in a document is an ugly chore, one you want to avoid at all costs. However, should the unthinkable happen — you have to modify the size, orientation, or margins of a document that is partially or completely finished — InDesign will automatically resize and reposition objects when you change its basic layout.

For example, maybe you've created a magazine for an American audience that subsequently needs to be converted for publication in Europe. Most newsletters in the United States use letter-sized pages (8½ by 11 inches), while in Europe the standard page size for such publications is A4 (210 by 297 mm), which is slightly narrower and slightly taller than U.S. letter size. Of course, you'll have to change *color* to *colour, apartment* to *flat,* and so on. But you'll also have to both squeeze (horizontally) and stretch (vertically) every item on every page to accommodate the A4 page's dimensions. The Layout Adjustment command (Layout ➪ Layout Adjustment) gives you the option of turning this chore over to InDesign, which will automatically adjust object shape and position according to the new page size, column guides, and margins.

The Layout Adjustment dialog box lets you turn layout adjustment on or off and specify the rules used to adjust objects, when you change page size or orientation (via the Document Setup dialog box; File ➪ Document Setup or Option+⌘+P or Ctrl+Alt+P) or margins or columns (via the Margin and Columns dialog box, accessed via Layout ➪ Margins and Columns). To adjust a layout:

1. **Choose Layout ➪ Layout Adjustment to display the Layout Adjustment dialog box, shown in Figure 5-9.**

2. **Check Enable Layout Adjustment to turn on the feature; uncheck it to turn it off.**

3. **In the Snap Zone field, enter the distance within which an object edge will automatically snap to a guideline when layout adjustment is performed.**

4. **Check Allow Graphics and Groups to Resize if you want InDesign to resize objects when layout adjustment is performed.**

   If you don't check this box, InDesign will move objects but not resize them (the preferred option).

5. **Check Allow Ruler Guides to Move if you want InDesign to adjust the position of ruler guides proportionally according to a new page size.**

   Generally, ruler guides are placed relative to the margins and page edges, so you'll probably want to check this box.

6. **Check Ignore Ruler Guide Alignments if you want InDesign to ignore ruler guides when adjusting the position of objects during layout adjustment.**

   If you think that objects may snap to ruler guides that you don't want them to snap to during layout adjustment, check this box. If it's checked, InDesign will still snap object edges to other margin and column guides.

7. **Check Ignore Object and Layer Locks to let InDesign move locked objects (either objects locked directly via Object ➪ Lock Position, or via ⌘+L or Ctrl+L, or objects that reside on a locked layer).**

   Otherwise, locked objects will not be adjusted.

8. **When you're done, click OK to close the dialog box.**

Figure 5-9: The Layout Adjustment dialog box.

The Layout Adjustment feature works best when there's not much work for it to do. But if you radically change a document that you've already done considerable work on, the Layout Adjustment feature usually creates more work than it saves. For example, the switch from a U.S. letter-sized page to an A4-sized page is a relatively minor change and the layout adjustments will probably be barely noticeable. But if you decide to change a tabloid-sized poster into a business card in midstream, well, you're probably better off starting over.

Here are a few things to keep in mind if you decide to use InDesign's Layout Adjustment feature:

✦ If you change page size, the margin widths (the distance between the left and right margins and the page edges) remain the same.

✦ If you change page size, column guides and ruler guides are repositioned proportionally to the new size.

✦ If you change the number of columns, column guides are added or removed accordingly.

✦ If an object edge is aligned with a guideline before layout adjustment, it remains aligned with the guideline after adjustment. If two or more edges of an object are aligned with guidelines, the object is resized so that the edges remain aligned with the guidelines after layout adjustment.

✦ If you change the page size, objects are moved so that they're in the same relative position on the new page.

✦ If you've used margin, column, and ruler guides to place objects on pages, layout adjustment will be more effective than if you've placed objects or ruler guides randomly on pages.

✦ Check for text reflow when you modify a document's page size, margins, or column guides. Decreasing a document's page size can cause text to overflow a text frame whose dimensions have been reduced.

✦ Check *everything* in your document after the adjustment is complete. Take the time to look over every page of your document. You never know what InDesign has actually done until you see it with your own eyes.

Tip If you decide to enable layout adjustment for a particular publication, you may want to begin by using the Save As command (File⇨Save As or Shift+⌘+S or Ctrl+Shift+S) to create a copy. That way, if you ever need to revert back to the original version, you can simply open the original document.

Summary

If you're working on a multipage document, you'll want to display the Pages pane. It lets you add, move, and delete document pages and create multipage spreads called *island spreads*.

If you're working on a long document with multiple parts, and you want to number each part separately, you can create sections to manage these multiple page-numbering schemes within the document. You can also have InDesign automatically add the correct page numbers for folios and continued lines, as well as section names in folios and other text.

As you work on a long document, you can use the Pages pane to target a specific page or spread in the document window, to select multiple pages or spreads so that you can move, modify, or delete them collectively, and to navigate from page to page in a multipage document. If you're doing detail work or working on a large page, you can use the Navigator pane to scroll around the page and to change the view magnification.

If you decide to change the layout of a publication after you've started work, you can use the Layout Adjustment feature to automatically adjust the size and position of objects and guidelines when you change the document's page size, margins, or columns.

✦　　✦　　✦

Working with Layers

✦ ✦ ✦ ✦

In This Chapter

Understanding the purpose and use of layers

Creating layers

Working with objects on layers

Manipulating layers

✦ ✦ ✦ ✦

Publishers seem to spend a lot of time doing the same things: creating several different versions of the same ad for different markets or flowing text in another language into a design. The goal of software is to automate the predictable so you have more time for creativity. Toward this goal, InDesign provides a method for preserving the time you put into creating and editing a layout that is used for more than one purpose: *layers.*

If you've ever seen a series of clear plastic overlays in presentations, understanding layers is easy. In one of those old overhead presentations, the teacher might have started with one overlay containing a graphic, then added another overlay with descriptive text, then added a third overlay containing a chart. Each overlay contained distinct content, but you could see through each one to the others to get the entire message. InDesign's layers are somewhat like this, letting you isolate content on slices of a document. You can then show and hide layers, lock objects on layers, rearrange layers, and more.

Understanding Layers

Each document contains a default layer, Layer 1, which contains all your objects until you create and select a new layer. Objects on the default layer — and any other layer for that matter — follow the standard *stacking order* of InDesign. (The first object you create is the backmost, the last one you create is the frontmost, and all the other objects fall somewhere in between. See Chapter 12 for complete information about stacking order.)

Like the clear plastic overlays, the order of the layers also affects the stacking order of the objects. Objects on the bottom layer are behind other objects, and objects on the top layer are in front of other objects. In Figure 6-1, the "Background Images" layer toward the bottom of the list contains the business card's standard graphics and the main text. Two additional layers contain different sets of contact information, in separate text frames, for different people.

Figure 6-1: A business card with different layers for each person's card. The graphics common to all cards are on their own layer.

Although layers are often compared to plastic overlays, there's one big difference: Layers are not specific to individual pages. Each layer encompasses the entire document, which doesn't make much difference when you're working on a 1-page ad but makes a significant difference when it comes to a 16-page newsletter. When you create layers and place objects on them, it's important that your strategy considers all the pages in the document.

The Layers pane (Window ➪ Layers, or F7) is your gateway to creating and manipulating layers (see Figure 6-2). As with other panes, when Show Tool Tips is checked in the General pane of the Preferences dialog box (choose InDesign ➪ Preferences on the Mac or Edit ➪ Preferences in Windows, or press ⌘+K or Ctrl+K), you can learn what controls do by pointing at them. If you know what the controls do, you can intuit a great deal of how to work with layers.

Active object box indicating layer of selected object

Pen icon indicating the active layer

Pencil icon indicating a locked layer

Eye icon indicating
a visible layer

Palette menu for
manipulating layers

New Layer button for creating layers

Trash Can button for deleting layers

Figure 6-2: The Layers pane.

When, where, and why to use layers

The layers feature is one that you can honestly ignore. If you never looked at the Layers pane, you could continue to do your work in InDesign. But take a look at the possibilities and see if they fit into your workflow. In the long run, if you use layers you'll save time and prevent mistakes that can result when you need to track changes across multiple documents.

Say you've created an ad with the same copy in it but a different headline and image for each city the ad runs in. You can place the boilerplate information on one layer and the information that changes on other layers. If any of the boilerplate information changes, you only need to change it once. To print different versions of the ad, you control which layers print.

You might use layers in the following situations:

✦ **A project with a high-resolution background image, such as a texture, that takes a long time to redraw.** You can hide that layer while designing other elements, then show it occasionally to see how it works with the rest of the design.

✦ **A document that you need to produce in several versions — for example, a produce ad with different prices for different cities or a clothing catalog featuring different coats depending on the area's climate.** You can place the content that changes on separate layers, then print the layers you need.

Continued

Continued

✦ **A project that includes objects you don't want to print.** If you want to suppress printout of objects for any reason, the only way you can do this is to place them on a layer and hide it. You might have a layer that's used for nothing but adding editorial and design comments, which is deleted when the document is final.

✦ **A publication that is translated into several languages.** Depending on the layout, you can place all the common objects on one layer, then create a different layer for each language's text. Changes to the common objects only need to happen once — unlike if you created copies of the original document and flowed the translated text into the copies.

✦ **To experiment with different layouts of the same document.** You can show and hide layers to present different options to your supervisor or client. This strategy lets you use common elements, such as the logo and legal information, in several versions of the same design.

✦ **A complex design that contains many overlapping objects, text wraps, and grouped objects.** Say the background of a page consists of a checkerboard pattern made up of filled, rectangular frames. You don't want to accidentally select the blocks while you're working with other objects. If you isolate complex objects on their own layer, you can show only that layer to work on it, hide that layer to concentrate on other layers, lock the layer so objects can't be selected, and otherwise manipulate the layer.

✦ **To create bulletproof templates.** Locked layers are a great way to decrease the possibility of items in a template being moved or deleted. Move all the objects you don't want moved or deleted on a layer and lock it. Although a layer can be unlocked, it will keep the people who use the template from accidentally moving or removing anything too quickly.

When determining whether objects should go on a layer, remember that layers are document-wide and not page-specific.

Creating Layers

Each document contains a default layer, Layer 1, which contains all the objects you place on master pages and document pages — until you create and activate new layers. You can create as many layers as you need; the number of layers in a document is limited only by the RAM available to InDesign. Once you create a new layer, it's activated automatically so you can begin working on it.

Creating a layer

The Layers pane (Window ⇨ Layers or F7) provides several methods for creating new layers. It doesn't matter which document page is displayed when you create a layer, because the layer will encompass all the pages in the document. To create a layer, do one of the following:

✦ **To create a new layer *on top of all existing layers,*** click the New Layer button on the Layers pane to get the New Layer dialog box. The layer will get the default name of "Layer *x.*"

✦ **To create a layer *above the selected layer,*** ⌘+click or Ctrl+click the New Layer button. The layer will get the default name of "Layer *x.*"

✦ **To create a new layer *on top of all existing layers but customize its name and identifying color,*** Option+click or Alt+click the New Layer button. Use the New Layer dialog box to specify options for the layer. (The New Layer dialog box — set with a custom name and color — is shown in Figure 6-3.)

Figure 6-3: The New Layer dialog box

Note   You can create a layer while a master page is displayed. Objects you create on a layer while a master page is displayed will be placed on all pages based on that master page. However, the layer is not specific to that master page. It is available for all document pages — even those based on other master pages — and you can place objects on it.

Customizing layers

A dialog box lets you customize the name, identifying color, guides, and lock status of objects on a new or existing layer. If you choose to customize the layer when you create it (by Option+clicking or Alt+clicking the New Layer button), the New Layer dialog box displays. If you choose to customize an existing layer, double-click on it to display the Layer Options dialog box. (You can also choose Layer Options for [Name of Layer] from the Layers pane's palette menu.)

Whether you're using the New Layer dialog box shown in Figure 6-3 or the nearly identical Layer Options dialog box, the options all work the same:

✦ **Name field:** Type a descriptive name for the layer. For example, if you're using layers for multilingual publishing, you might have a "U.S. English" layer, a "French" layer, and a "German" layer. If you're using layers so you can hide background objects while you're working, you might have a "Background Objects" layer.

✦ **Color pop-up menu and button:** A layer's color helps you identify which layer an object is on. The color displays to the left of the layer name in the Layers pane and displays on each object on that layer. The color is applied to frame edges, selection handles, bounding boxes, text ports, and text wraps. Note that the display of frame edges is controlled by the View/Hide ➪ Show Frame Edges command (also available through the shortcut Option+⌘+Y or Ctrl+Alt+Y). By default, InDesign applies a different color to each new layer, but you can customize it to something meaningful for your document and workflow. Choose a color from the list or double-click the color swatch to use from the operating system's color picker.

✦ **Show Layer check box:** Checked by default, this control lets you specify whether objects on a layer display and print. If you want to suppress printout of the objects on a layer (for example, to hide a different version of a document or to hide pictures while proofing), uncheck Show Layer. The Show Layer check box has the same effect as clicking the eye icon on the Layers pane.

✦ **Lock Layer check box:** Unchecked by default, this option lets you control whether objects on a layer can be edited. Check Lock Layer if you don't want to be able to select items and modify them. For example, in a document containing multiple versions of text on different layers, you might lock the layer containing background images and other objects that stay the same. The Lock Layer check box has the same effect as clicking the Pencil icon on the Layers pane.

✦ **Suppress Text Wrap When Layer Is Hidden check box:** Unchecked by default, this new option prevents text wrapping around the layer's objects when the layer is hidden. Be sure to check this check box when you use multiple layers for variations of the same content—such as multilingual text or different contacts for business cards—otherwise your layer's text could not display because it is wrapping around a hidden layer with an object of the same size in the same place.

New Feature   The Suppress Text Wrap When Layer Is Hidden check box is new to InDesign CS.

✦ **Show Guides check box:** This lets you control the display of guides that were created while the selected layer was active. When checked, as it is by default, you can create guides while any layer is active and view those guides on any layer. When unchecked, you cannot create guides. Any guides you created while that layer was active are not displayed, but you'll still be able to see guides created while other layers were active. Note that when guides are hidden entirely (View ⇨ Hide Guides, or ⌘+; [semicolon] or Ctrl+; [semicolon]), this command has no apparent effect.

✦ **Lock Guides check box:** This works similarly to Show Guides in that it only affects guides that were created while the layer was active. When unchecked, as it is by default, you can move guides on any layer for which Lock Guides is unchecked. When checked, you cannot move guides created while that layer was active. You can, however, move guides on other layers for which Lock Guides is unchecked. Note that when all guides are locked (View ⇨ Lock Guides, or Option+⌘+; [semicolon] or Ctrl+Alt+; [semicolon]) this command has no apparent effect.

Tip   You can multiple-select layers and customize them all at once. Since each layer must have a different name, the Name field is not available in the Layer Options dialog box when multiple layers are selected.

Working with Objects on Layers

Whether you're designing a magazine template from the ground up or modifying an existing ad, you can isolate specific types of objects on layers. You can create objects on a layer, move objects to a layer, or copy objects to a layer.

The active layer

The *active layer* is the one on which you're creating objects — whether you're using tools, importing text or graphics, dragging objects in from a library, or pasting objects from other layers or other documents. A pen icon to the right of a layer's name means it's the active one (refer to Figure 6-2). Although more than one layer can be selected at a time, only one can be active. To switch the active layer to another layer, click to the right of the layer name that you want to be active; the pen icon moves, making that the new active layer. Keep in mind that to activate a layer, it must be visible.

Regardless of which layer is the active layer, you can select, move, and modify objects on any visible, unlocked layer. (The display and locking of layers is controlled by the eye and pencil icons on the Layers pane, respectively, and by the Show Layer and Lock Layer check boxes in the Layer Options dialog box.)

Selecting objects on layers

Regardless of the active layer, you can select, move, and modify objects on any visible, unlocked layer. You can even select objects on different layers and manipulate them.

The Layers pane (Window ➭ Layers, or F7) helps you work with selected objects in the following ways:

✦ **To determine which layer an object belongs to,** match the color on its bounding box, handles, and so on, to a color to the left of a layer name.

✦ **To determine which layers contain active objects,** look to the right of the layer names. A small box next to a layer name (refer to Figure 6-2) indicates that it contains an active object.

✦ **To select all the objects on a layer,** Option+click or Alt+click the layer's name in the Layers pane. The layer must be active, unlocked, and visible.

Tip   To select master-page objects as well as document-page objects on a layer, you need to Option+Shift+click or Altl+Shift+click the layer name.

Placing objects on layers

To place objects on a layer, the layer must be active as indicated by the pen icon. To place objects on the layer, use any of these options:

✦ Use any tools to create paths and frames.

✦ Use the Place command (File ➭ Place, or ⌘+D or Ctrl+D) to import graphics or text.

✦ Use the Paste command (Edit ➭ Paste, or ⌘+V or Ctrl+V) to paste objects from the Clipboard onto the layer.

✦ Drag objects to the layer from a library or another document.

Note   When you create objects on master pages, they are placed on the default layer and are therefore behind other objects on document pages. To create objects on master pages that are in front of other objects, place the objects on a different layer while the master page is displayed.

Note   You can cut and paste objects from one page to another, but have the objects remain on their original layer — without concern about the active layer. To do this, use the Paste Remembers Layers command in the Layers pane's palette menu rather than Edit ➭ Paste, or ⌘+V or Ctrl+V. You might do this if you're moving the continuation of an article from one page to another but you want the text to remain on the same layer. (For example, if you're working on a multilingual document with separate layers for English, French, and Spanish text, using Paste Remembers Layer would ensure that text frames cut or copied from the French layer would be pasted onto the French layer on the new location.)

Moving objects to different layers

Once an object is on a layer, it isn't stuck there. You can copy and paste objects to selected layers, or you can move them using the Layers pane. When you move an object to a layer, it's placed in front of all other objects on a layer. To select multiple objects, remember to Shift+click them, then move them in one of the following ways:

✦ **To paste objects on a different layer,** first cut or copy objects to the Clipboard. Activate the layer you want to put the objects on, then use the Paste command (Edit ⇨ Paste, or ⌘+V or Ctrl+V). This method works well for moving objects that are currently on different layers.

✦ **To move objects to a different layer,** drag the active object box (to the right of a layer's name) to another layer. When you use this method, it doesn't matter which layer is active. However, you can't move objects from different layers to the same layer using this method. (If you select multiple objects that reside on different layers, dragging the box moves only objects that reside on the first layer on which you selected an object.)

✦ **To move objects to a hidden or locked layer,** press ⌘ or Ctrl while you drag the active object box.

✦ **To copy rather than move objects to a different layer,** press Option or Alt while you drag the active object box.

✦ **To copy objects to a hidden or locked layer,** press Option+⌘ or Ctrl+Alt while you drag the active object box.

Tip

After designing a new template, you might realize that working with it would be easier if you had isolated certain objects on layers. You can create new layers, then move objects to them at this point. Just make sure the layers are in the same stacking order as the original objects.

Manipulating Layers

Using the Layers pane, you can select and manipulate entire layers. These changes affect all the objects on the layer — for example, if you hide a layer, all its objects are hidden; if you move a layer up, all its objects display in front of objects on lower layers. Functions that affect an entire layer include hiding, locking, rearranging, merging, and deleting.

Selecting layers

The active layer, containing the pen icon, is always selected. You can extend the selection to include other layers the same way you multiple-select objects: Shift+ click for a continuous selection and ⌘+click or Ctrl+click for a noncontiguous selection. When layers are selected, you can move them within the stacking order of layers, modify attributes in the Layer Options dialog box, merge them, or delete them.

Hiding layers

When you hide a layer, none of the objects on that layer displays or prints. You might hide layers for a variety of reasons, including to speed screen redraw by hiding layers containing high-resolution graphics, to control which version of a publication prints, and to simply focus on one area of a design without the distraction of other areas. To show or hide layers using the Layers pane, do one of the following:

✦ **Click the eye icon in the first column to the left of a layer's name.** When the eye's column is blank, the layer is hidden. Click in the column again to show the layer. You can also double-click a layer and check or uncheck Show Layer in the Layer Options dialog box.

✦ **If no layers are hidden, you can show only the active layer by choosing Hide Others from the palette menu.**

✦ **Regardless of the state of other layers, you can show only one layer by Option+clicking or Alt+clicking in the first column next to its name.** All other layers will be hidden.

✦ **If any layers are hidden, you can show all layers by choosing Show All Layers from the palette menu.** You can also Option+click or Alt+click twice in the first column to show all layers.

Note   When you use the Package command (File ➪ Package, or Option+Shift+⌘+P or Ctrl+Alt+Shift+P) to prepare a document for a service bureau, InDesign includes only visible layers. This lets you hide the layers containing different versions of the document and be sure that they aren't accidentally printed.

QuarkXPress User   You cannot print hidden layers in InDesign CS as you can in QuarkXPress 6. You must make them visible before printing.

Locking objects on layers

When you lock a layer, you cannot select or modify objects on it — even if the locked layer is active. You might lock a layer containing boilerplate text or a layer containing a complex drawing that you don't want altered. Locking and unlocking layers is easy, so you might lock one layer while focusing on another, then unlock it. To lock or unlock layers using the Layers pane, do one of the following:

✦ **Click the blank box in the second column to the left of a layer's name.**
When the pencil icon is displayed, the layer is locked. Click the pencil icon to unlock the layer. You can also double-click a layer and check or uncheck Lock Layer in the Layer Options dialog box.

✦ **If no layers are locked, you can lock all but the active layer by choosing Lock Others from the palette menu.**

✦ **If any layers are locked, you can unlock all layers by choosing Unlock All Layers from the palette menu.**

✦ **You can toggle between Lock Others and Unlock All Layers by Option+ clicking or Alt+clicking the blank box or the pencil icon.**

 When you lock an object to a page (Object ➪ Lock Object, or ⌘+L or Ctrl+L), the object stays locked regardless of its layer's lock status.

Rearranging layers

Each layer has its own front-to-back stacking order, with the first object you create on the layer being its backmost object. You can modify the stacking order of objects on a single layer using the Arrange commands in the Object menu. Objects are further stacked according to the order in which the layers are listed in the Layers pane. The layer at the top of the list contains the frontmost objects and the layer at the bottom of the list contains the backmost objects.

If you find that all the objects on one layer need to be in front of all the objects on another layer, you can move that layer up or down in the list. In fact, you can move multiple-selected layers up or down, even if the selection is noncontiguous. To move layers, click on the selection and drag it up or down. When you move layers, remember that layers are document-wide so you're actually changing the stacking order of objects on all the pages.

 You might be accustomed to moving objects to the front of the stacking order to make them easily editable. Working this way, you might be tempted to bring a layer up to the top of the layer stacking order so you can edit it easily, then move it back to its original location. Try to get out of that habit, though, and into the habit of simply showing the layer you need to work on and hiding the others.

Combining layers

If you decide that all the objects on one layer belong on a different layer — throughout the document — you can merge the layers. When you're learning about the power of layers, it's easy to create a document that is unnecessarily complex (for example, you might have put each object on a different layer and realized that the document has become difficult to work with). The good news is that you can also merge all the layers in a document to *flatten* it to a single layer. To flatten all layers:

1. **Select the *target layer* (where you want all the objects to end up) by clicking on it.**

2. **Select the *source layers* (which contain the objects you want to move) in addition to the target layer.**

   Shift+click, or ⌘+click or Ctrl+click, to add the source layers to the selection.

3. **Make sure the target layer contains the pen icon and that the target and source layers are all selected.**

4. **Choose Merge Layers from the Layers pane's palette menu.**

   All objects on the source layers are moved to the target layer, and the source layers are deleted.

Note

When you merge layers, the stacking order of objects does not change, so the design looks the same — with one notable exception: If you created objects on a layer while a master page was displayed, those objects go to the *back* of the stacking order with the regular master-page objects.

Deleting layers

If you've carefully isolated portions of a document on different layers, then find that you won't need that portion of the document, you can delete the layer. For example, if you have a U.S. English and an International English layer, and you decide that you can't afford to print the two different versions and one dialect's readers will simply have to suffer, you can delete the unneeded layer. You might also delete layers that you don't end up using to simplify a document.

When you delete layers, all the objects on the layer throughout the document are deleted. To ensure that you don't need any of the objects before deleting a layer, you can hide all other layers, then look at the remaining objects on each page. If you think you might need them later for this or another document, you can drag them to the pasteboard or place them in a library.

Using the Layers pane, you can delete selected layers in the following ways:

✦ Drag the selection to the Trash button.

✦ Click the Trash button. (The current layer — the one with the pen icon — will be deleted.)

✦ Choose Delete Layer from the Layers pane's palette menu.

If any of the layers contain objects, a warning reminds you that they will be deleted. And of course the ubiquitous Undo command (Edit ➪ Undo, or ⌘+Z or Ctrl+Z) lets you recover from accidental deletions.

 Tip To remove all layers that do not contain objects, choose Delete Unused Layers from the Layers palette.

Summary

If you take the time to integrate layers into your workflow, you can save time and effort in creating multilingual publications, produce multiple versions of a document, and benefit from greater flexibility with objects. Until you create new layers, all the objects are placed on the default layers. Although each layer has its own stacking order, the order of layers also affects stacking order.

You can create objects on the active layer, and you can move objects to different layers. Even though objects are on layers, you can continue to select and modify them as you normally would — provided that the layers are visible and unlocked. Hiding layers suppresses the printout of objects, in addition to preventing their display. To streamline a document, you can merge and delete layers.

✦　　✦　　✦

Creating Layout Standards

In This Chapter

Automating repetitive
tasks

Working with master
pages

Creating templates

Using libraries

Working with other
page-layout tools

Think for a moment about the publications you produce. Chances are that most of your work involves creating multiple iterations of a basic set of publications, and each publication looks more or less the same from issue to issue. For example, periodicals such as newsletters, magazines, and newspapers don't change much from one issue to the next (disregarding the occasional redesigns that all publications undergo). The ongoing uniformity of such things as page size, margins, page layouts, text formats, even the tone of the writing, gives each publication a unique look and feel.

If you had to start from scratch every time you created a publication, you'd spend the bulk of your time setting up your documents and have little time left to attend to the appearance of the content (you'd probably get terribly bored, too). Few things are less rewarding than doing the same job over and over. Fortunately, InDesign includes several extremely useful features that let you automate repetitive tasks. This chapter focuses on three of them — master pages, templates, and libraries:

   ✦ A *master page* is a preconstructed page layout that you can use when adding pages to a multipage document. With master pages, you can design a single "background" page and then use it as the basis for as many document pages as you want. Without master pages, you would have to create every page from scratch.

   ✦ A *template* is a preconstructed document that's used to create multiple iterations of the same design or publication. A template is a shell of a document that contains everything in a publication — except content. Each time you need to create a new version of a repeatedly produced publication, you open its template, add the content (text and pictures), tweak as desired, and then print. Next issue, same thing.

✦ As its name suggests, a *library* is a place where you store things. Specifically, InDesign libraries are files for storing objects that you've created in InDesign and that you intend to use repeatedly in multiple documents.

When you combine master pages, templates, and libraries with the ability to create character and paragraph style sheets (covered in Chapter 20), you have a powerful set of automation tools. Style sheets automate text formatting; libraries automate object creation; master pages automate page construction; and templates automate document construction.

How and to what extent you use these features depends on your personal preferences and the publications you produce. You might think that something as small as a business card wouldn't benefit from any of these features, but if it's a business card for a corporate employee, the chances are that, other than the personal information, it's exactly the same as business cards of every other employee. By creating and saving a business-card template, you could quickly build cards for several or several hundred new employees. All you have to do is open the template; add the name, title, and phone number of the new employee; and then print.

For other publications, you might use several — perhaps all — of the aforementioned timesaving features. A good newsletter template, for example, would contain a set of style sheets for formatting text, probably a master spread or two (depending on whether all pages shared exactly the same design), and perhaps an associated library of frequently used objects — house ads, corporate logos, boilerplate text, and so on.

Tip   Although this chapter begins with master pages, this doesn't mean that you should begin work on a publication by creating master pages. You may prefer to work on text formatting tasks first and build style sheets before turning your attention to page-layout and document-construction tasks. One of the best things about InDesign is that it lets you perform tasks in whatever order makes most sense to you. Over time, you'll develop a personal modus operandi for creating publications. Whatever style you develop, make sure that you make full use of style sheets, libraries, master pages, and templates.

Note   In this chapter, the terms *master page* and *master spread* are used interchangeably. If you're working on a facing-page document, you'll use facing-page masters that have both left- and right-hand pages. These are master spreads. For single-sided documents, a master page has only a single page.

Creating and Applying Master Pages

Before the arrival of personal computers, publications were created by graphic designers who leaned over light tables and — armed with matte knives and waxing machines — stuck galleys of type, halftones, and plastic overlays onto paste-up boards. The paste-up boards were usually oversized sheets of white card paper on which was printed a grid of light blue lines. The blue guidelines indicated such things as the edge of the final, trimmed page, the margins in which text and pictures were placed, column boundaries, and so on. These guidelines helped the designer position elements on a page and also helped ensure consistent placement of repeating page elements, such as page numbers.

Although there are no paste-up boards in the electronic publishing world, the concept has survived in the form of *master pages*. A master page is a nonprinting page that you can use as the background (that is, as the starting point) for document pages. Typically, master pages contain text and graphic elements that appear on all pages of a publication, such as page numbers, headers, footers, folios, and so on. And like their paste-up board ancestors, master pages also include guidelines that indicate page edges, column boundaries, and margins, as well as other manually created guidelines to aid page designers in placing objects. By placing items on master pages, you save yourself the repetitive work of placing the same items one by one on each and every document page.

By default, every InDesign document you create contains a master page. Whether you use the master page or create and use additional master pages depends on the kind of publication you're creating. If it's a single-page document, such as a business card, or an advertisement, you don't need to worry about master pages at all. (Generally, master pages are of little use for one-page documents.) However, if you're creating a multipage document like a newsletter, a book, or a catalog, using master pages will save you time and help ensure design consistency. It's impossible to overstate the importance of master pages. They're one of InDesign's most powerful features.

The Pages pane

When you work on multipage documents, you'll probably want to display the Pages pane (Window ➪ Pages or F12), shown in Figure 7-1. The Pages pane displays an icon-based view of document pages (bottom) and master pages (top) in the current document. The controls in the Pages pane and its accompanying pop-up menu let you perform several master page–related tasks, including creating and deleting master pages, applying master pages to document pages, and creating master pages out of document pages. The Pages pane also lets you add and remove document pages.

Cross-Reference See Chapter 5 for more information about adding and removing document pages.

Figure 7-1: The Pages pane. The document page icons at the bottom of the pane show that the publication has eight pages. The master-page icons at the top show the default masters: None and A-Master.

Here's a quick rundown of the controls available in the Pages pane and the commands in its pop-up menu:

✦ The page icons at the top of the pane represent master pages. Every document includes a master page called [None], which includes only margin guidelines, and A-Master, which reflects the margin and column settings you specified in the New Document dialog box when you created the document. If a letter is displayed on a master page icon, it indicates that the master spread is based on another (parent) master page; for example, if you have a master page named C-Master and the icons for C-Master have the letter *A,* then C-Master is based on A-Master. A master page's name is displayed below its icon. If a master page and its name are highlighted, it means that master page is displayed in the document window. If a master page name is displayed in reverse type, it's currently displayed in the document window.

✦ The page icons at the bottom of the pane represent document pages. Dog-eared icons represent left and right pages in a facing-page document. The letter displayed on a page icon indicates the master page it's based on. (If no letter is displayed, the page is based on the blank master page.) The numbers below the page icons indicate the page numbers, including section numbering, if any (sections are covered in Chapter 5). If a page and its number are highlighted, it means that page is currently displayed in the document window. If a page number is displayed in reverse type (that is, white characters on a black background), it means that it's currently displayed in the document window.

✦ The Create New Page button (notepad icon) at the bottom of the pane lets you add a new page with a mouse click.

✦ The Delete Selected Pages button (trash can icon) lets you delete document and master pages.

✦ The Insert Pages palette menu command lets you add pages to a document and specify the master page on which they're based.

✦ The New Master palette menu command lets you add a new master page.

✦ The Duplicate Spread and Duplicate Page palette menu commands do exactly what the names say. They let you duplicate a page or a facing-page spread. The name of the command depends on whether a page or spread is highlighted in the pane.

✦ The Delete Page, Delete Spread, Delete Master Page, and Delete Master Spread palette menu commands let you delete single pages and facing-page spreads (both document pages and master pages). Again, the menu name will change based on what is selected in the pane.

✦ The Select Unused Masters palette menu command selects all unused master pages and spreads, so you can easily identify and perhaps delete them.

✦ The Master Options palette menu command is used for changing master-page attributes, including name and parent master page (if you want to base a master page on another master page).

✦ The Apply Master to Pages palette menu command is used for applying a master-page layout to one or more document pages.

✦ The Save As Master palette menu command lets you convert a document page into a master page.

✦ The Override All Master Page Items palette menu command lets you have any local changes to the selected pages override the master-page settings. This command moves all master items to the document page on the selected pages.

New Feature

The Override All Master Pages function is new to InDesign CS.

✦ The Remove All Local Overrides and the Remove Selected Local Overrides palette menu commands returns master objects that you've modified on specific document pages to their original condition. If no object is selected, the menu command is Remove All Local Overrides; if one or more objects are selected, the menu command is Remove Selected Local Overrides.

✦ The Detach Selection from Master palette menu command removes any master page items that had been modified on the selected pages from the master page *for those selected document pages* only. Essentially, this command prevents you from using the Remove All Local Overrides or Remove Selected

Local Overrides commands for these document pages, permanently changing the master pages for them.

✦ The Keep Spread Together palette menu command ensures that the pages will not be split apart as you add pages. Normally, adding a single page shuffles all subsequent pages so they form new spreads. With this command, existing spreads are maintained, so adding an odd number of pages will not cause them to be reshuffled.

✦ The Palette Options palette menu command controls icon size, position, and other Pages pane display settings.

✦ The Numbering & Section Options palette menu command lets you establish independently numbered sections in a single document. For example, you could create a section if you wanted to use a different numbering scheme (Roman numerals, perhaps) for the front matter of a book than for the body. (See Chapter 5 for more information about sections.)

✦ The Spread Flattening palette menu command lets you control image flattening for specific spreads. *Flattening* is InDesign's term for reducing the resolution of graphics to save disk space and speed output time. Typically, you'd flatten images for Web-oriented documents, since the Web displays images at the relatively low resolution of 72 dpi. You might also flatten high-resolution graphics when printing a draft version, to speed up printing.

Chapter 31 covers flattening in more detail.

Creating a new master page

If all the pages in the publication you're creating share essentially the same page design, you don't need to create a new master page. Instead, you can simply use the default master page called A-Master that every document has. But if you intend to use more than one page layout in your document — maybe you're building a magazine and you want some pages to use a three-column format and others to use a two-column format — you'll need to create additional master pages.

Before you create a new master page, you should have a general idea of how you want it to look. In particular, you should know where you want to place margins, column boundaries, and repeating elements, such as page numbers. (Laying out master pages is covered later in this section.) When you're ready to create a new master page, here's what you do:

1. **If the Pages pane is not displayed, choose Windows ⇨ Pages or press F12.**

2. **From the Pages pane's palette menu, choose New Master.**

You can also press Option+⌘ or Ctrl+Alt and click the Create New Page button at the bottom of the pane. The New Master dialog box, shown in Figure 7-2, is displayed.

Figure 7-2: The New Master dialog box.

3. **In the Prefix field, specify a one-character prefix that's attached to the front of the master page name and displayed on associated document page icons in the Pages pane.**

The default will be a letter, such as B, C, or D.

4. **In the Name field, enter a name for the master page.**

Use something descriptive, like "3-column Layout," "Front Matter Layout," or "Chapter Title Pages."

5. **If you want to base the master page on another master page you've already created, choose the parent master page from the Based on Master pop-up menu.**

Basing a master page on another master page is covered in more detail later in this section.

6. **In the Number of Pages field, enter the number of pages you want to include in the master spread.**

Typically, you'll enter **2** for a facing-page document and **1** for a single-page document.

7. **After you've finished specifying the attributes of the new master page, click OK to close the dialog box.**

After you create a new master page, it's displayed in the document window. (When a master page is displayed, its name is displayed in the Page Number field in the bottom-left corner of the document window.) You can modify any of a master page's attributes at any time by clicking on its icon at the top of the Pages pane, choosing Master Options from the pane's palette menu, and then changing any of the settings in the Master Options dialog box, which is identical to the New Master dialog box.

Basing a master page on another master page

If you find that a particular publication requires more than one master page, you may want to first lay out a base master page (you could use the default A-Master) and then create additional master pages that share the same basic layout but are slightly different. For example, if the magazine you're working on uses two-, three-, and four-column page layouts, you could create the two-column master spread first and include all repeating page elements. You could then create two additional master page spreads, base them on the two-column master, and specify different column formats. The two "children" masters would be identical to the parent except for the number of columns. If you subsequently decide to modify, move, or delete a repeating page element, such as the issue date in the folio, you could make the change on the parent master and it will automatically be applied to the children masters.

When you create a new master page, the New Master dialog box provides the option to base it on an existing master page. You can also choose or change a master spread's parent by:

✦ Choosing Master Options in the Pages pane's palette menu and then choosing a master page from the Based on Master pop-up menu.

✦ Dragging and dropping the icon of a master spread (the parent) onto the icon of another master spread (the child). Be careful if you use this method. It's possible to base only one page of a master spread on another, but in most cases you'll want to base both pages of the child master on both pages of the parent master. To do so, make sure that when you release the mouse button both pages of the child are highlighted.

✦ Clicking on the master spread you want to be the child, then pressing Option or Alt and clicking on the master spread you want to be the parent.

When you base a master page on another master page, the prefix of the parent is displayed on the page icon of the child.

Tip   If you base a master spread on another master spread, you can still modify the master objects (that is, the objects inherited from the parent master) on the child master page. As with regular document pages, you have to Shift+⌘+click or Ctrl+Shift+click on the object inherited from a parent master to release it before you can edit it on a child master.

QuarkXPress User   QuarkXPress cannot base a master page on another, so InDesign users who are used to QuarkXPress may ignore this feature. But they shouldn't — it has the same power that based-on formatting provides style sheets in QuarkXPress and InDesign.

Creating a master spread from a document spread

Generally, if you need a new master spread, you'll begin by choosing New Master from the Pages pane's palette menu. But you can also create a master spread from a spread of document pages. To do so, highlight the spread of document pages by clicking on the page numbers below the page icons in the Pages pane, then choose Save as Master from the Pages pane's palette menu. The new master is assigned a default name and prefix. If you want to modify any of its attributes, click on its name in the Pages pane, then choose Master Options from the pop-up menu.

Duplicating a master

You can create a copy of a master spread by clicking on its icon and then choosing Duplicate Master Spread from the Pages pane's palette menu or by clicking on its icon, dragging it onto the Create new page button, and releasing the mouse. If you duplicate a master spread, there is not a parent/child relationship between the original master and the copy (as there is when you base a master on another master).

Deleting a master

To delete a master page, click on its name and then choose Delete Master Page from the Pages pane's palette menu. You can also click on the master icon, then click the Trash icon in the Pages pane or drag the icon directly to the Trash.

Laying out a master page

Because a master page is similar to a document page, you can use the same approach for building both master and document pages. Some designers prefer to do a preliminary sketch on paper and then re-create the design in InDesign. You may like to do your creative brainstorming at your computer, in which case you can use InDesign as your sketchpad. The main difference between document pages and master pages is that master pages don't contain any content (other than elements that appear on every page). So, when you're building a master page, you should be thinking more about the page's overall infrastructure than about details.

Here are a few things to keep in mind when designing master pages:

✦ **If you're working on a facing-page document (most multipage publications have facing-pages), you'll create facing-page master spreads.** The left-hand page (used for even-numbered document pages) and right-hand page (used for odd-numbered document pages) of the master spreads you create will be — more or less — mirror opposites of each other. For example, page numbers are generally placed near the outside edge of facing pages so that they're visible when a reader thumbs through the pages. Or you may decide to place the publication name on one side of a spread and balance it by placing the date of publication in the same position on the other side.

✦ **If you want to automatically place page numbers on document pages, you should add a page number character on each page of your master spreads.** To add a page number character, draw a text frame with the Type tool, then choose Type ⇨ Insert Special Character ⇨ Auto Page Number or press Option+⌘+N or Ctrl+Alt+N. The prefix of the master page (A, B, C, and so on) is displayed on the master page, but on document pages, the actual page number is used. When you add a page number to a master page, make sure to format it as you want the actual page numbers to look on document pages.

✦ **Perhaps the most important elements of a master page are the margins and column guides.** To specify margins and columns for a master page, make sure the page is displayed in the document window, then choose Layout ⇨ Margins and Columns. The Margins and Columns dialog box, shown in Figure 7-3, is displayed. The controls in this dialog box let you specify the position of the margins, the number of columns, and the gutter width (space between columns).

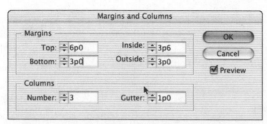

Figure 7-3: The Margins and Columns dialog box.

When placing text elements on master pages, you may want to use placeholder text instead of actual text. For example, if you produce a monthly magazine and you want to include the name of the month on each spread (perhaps opposite the name of the newsletter on the facing page), you could use placeholder text like "[Name of month]" or "[Add month here]." If you use placeholder text, format it as you want the actual text to look on document pages. Of course, be sure to replace the placeholder text with the actual text in your final document.

✦ If you want to place additional guidelines on a master page, you can add as many custom guidelines as you want. (Guidelines are covered later in this chapter.)

✦ Like objects on document pages, the objects you place on master pages have a stacking order. On document pages, all master objects remain beneath any objects you add to the page.

Figure 7-4 shows a typical master page spread for a newsletter. Whenever you want to make a change to a master page, double-click on its icon in the Pages pane to display it in the document window.

To copy a master page from one document to another, display the source document, click on the master's name in the Pages pane, drag it to the window of the target document, and then release the mouse button.

QuarkXPress User

The ability to move master pages from one document to another, or even from one layout to another in a QuarkXPress 6 project, does not exist in QuarkXPress. So QuarkXPress users may be in the habit of using libraries to transfer master-page items from one document to another. In InDesign, you don't need to take this circuitous route.

Figure 7-4: A typical three-column master layout for a newsletter. The footer at the bottom of the left- and right-hand pages includes a page-number character (B) on the outside.

Applying a master page to document pages

After you've built a master page, you can apply it to new document pages as you add them or to existing pages. (See Chapter 5 for information about adding and removing document pages.) For facing-page documents, you can apply both pages of a master spread to both pages of a document spread, or you can apply one page of a master spread to one page of a document spread. For example, you could apply a master page with a two-column format to the left-hand page of a document spread and apply a master page with a three-column format to the right-hand page.

To apply only one page of a master spread to a document page, click on the icon of the master spread and then drag it onto the icon of the document page you want to format. When the target document page is highlighted (framed in a black rectangle, as shown in the left side of Figure 7-5), release the mouse button. If both document pages are highlighted, both sides of the master spread are applied to the document spread.

To apply both pages of a master spread to both pages of a document spread, drag the master spread's icon onto the document spread's page numbers (under its page icon). When both pages of the target document spread are highlighted, as shown in the right side of Figure 7-5, release the mouse button.

Figure 7-5: Left: Applying a single page of a master spread to a document page. Right: Applying both pages of a master spread to a document spread.

InDesign also lets you apply a master page to multiple document pages in a single operation. You can

✦ **Select the document pages to which you want to apply a master.** You can click on a page then Shift+click on another page to select a range of pages, or you can hold down the ⌘ or Ctrl keys and click on pages to select nonconsecutive pages. After you've selected the document pages, press Option or Alt and click on the master page you want to apply.

✦ **Choose Apply Master to Pages from the Pages pane's palette menu.** The Apply Master dialog box, shown in Figure 7-6, is displayed. Choose the master page you want to apply from the Apply Master pop-up menu and specify the pages to which you want to apply it in the To Pages field. Use commas to separate page numbers; use a hyphen to specify a range of pages. For example, you could enter **2, 4-6, 8** to apply the selected master to pages 2, 4, 5, 6, and 8.

Figure 7-6: The Apply Master dialog box.

You can also use these techniques to apply a different master page to a document page. If you want to disassociate a document page from its applied master page, you can apply the default None master page the same way you apply any other master page.

Modifying master items on document pages

As you work on a document page that's based on a master, you may find that you need to modify, move, or delete a master object. For example, you might apply a master to the first page of a newsletter and then decide that the page number you've placed on the master page isn't necessary for page 1. In this case, you'd select the master object on the document page and delete it. Any change you make to a master object on a local page is referred to as a *local override*.

If you remove a master object from a document page, you sever the object's relationship to the master-page object for that document page only. If you subsequently move or modify the object on the master page, it won't affect the deleted object on the document page—it remains deleted on that particular document page.

However, you can modify a master object on a document page without completely breaking its relationship to the corresponding object on the master page. For example, if you change the size, position, or content of a master object on a document page, any subsequent size, position, or content change you make to the object on the master page does not affect the object you modified. But any changes you make to the stroke or fill of the object on the master page are applied to the overridden master object on the document page. Similarly, if you use any of the transformation tools or the corresponding controls in the Transform pane to modify a master object on a document page, any similar transformations applied to the corresponding object on the master page are not applied to the overridden object.

In other words, any type of attribute applied to the item on a particular document page prevents any changes to the same attribute on the master page from affecting that document page.

Tip   The Display Master Items command (View ➪ Display Master Items) lets you show or hide master objects on document pages. When a checkmark is displayed next to the name of the command, master objects are displayed.

To modify a master object on a document page, you must select it. However, master objects behave slightly differently than other objects on document pages. Specifically, to select a master object on a document page, you must hold down Shift+⌘ or Ctrl+Shift when you click on the object with one of the selection tools. After you select a master object on a document page, you can modify it in the same manner as you modify non-master objects.

If you modify one or more master objects on a document page and then decide you want to revert back to using the original master objects, you can remove the local overrides. To do so, display the document page that contains the master

objects you've modified, select the objects, and then choose Remove Selected
Local Overrides from the Pages pane's palette menu. If no objects are selected, the
command name changes to Remove All Local Overrides (if the selected spread
doesn't have any modified master objects, the command is not available).

Using Templates

A template is a preconstructed InDesign document that you use as the starting
point for creating multiple versions of the same design or publication. For example,
if you were assigned the task of creating ten testimonial ads that share the same
layout but use different pictures and text, you would begin by creating a template
that contains all the elements that are the same in every ad — placeholder frames
for the pictures and text, guidelines, and so on. Along the same lines, if you produce
periodicals like a newsletter or a magazine, you should create a template for
each one.

The process of creating a template is much the same as creating a document. You
create the required character and paragraph style sheets, master pages, repeating
elements (for example, the nameplate on the first page and mailing information on
the back page), and so on. The only thing you don't add to a template is actual
content.

It would be nice if designers had the luxury of creating a template for each new
publication they produced. But in the real world, templates are often created by
gutting an existing document. The first time you create a publication such as a
newsletter, the main goal during production is getting a finished document to the
printer — hopefully on time. After you've finished the first issue of a publication
(or a prototype), you can open the file, remove all objects and content that aren't
repeated in every issue, and then save the gutted file as a template. This is probably how you'll wind up building many of your templates.

Here are the steps in creating a template:

1. **Choose File ⇨ Save As or press Shift+⌘+S or Ctrl+Shift+S to display the Save
   As dialog box, shown in Figure 7-7.**

2. **Choose a storage folder and specify a name for the file.**

   It's not a bad idea to add "Template" to the filename, if possible. It lets whoever uses the file know its purpose.

3. **On a Mac, choose InDesign 3.0 Template in the Format pop-up menu. On a
   PC, choose InDesign 3.0 Template from the Save As Type pop-up menu.**

4. **Click OK to close the Save As dialog box and save the template.**

Tip   If you're designing a template that will be used by others, you might want to add a layer of instructions. When it's time to print a document based on the template, simply hide the annotation layer. (See Chapter 6 for more information about working with layers.)

Figure 7-7: Saving templates is slightly different on a Mac (top) from saving templates in Windows (bottom).

A template is almost exactly the same as a standard InDesign document with one major exception: A template is slightly protected from being overridden. When you open a template, it's assigned a default name (Untitled-1, Untitled-2, and so on). The first time you choose File ➪ Save, or press ⌘+S or Ctrl+S, the Save As dialog box is displayed.

Note   As you use a template over time, you're likely to discover that you forgot to include something—perhaps a style sheet, a repeating element on a particular master page, or an entire master page. To modify a template, you must open it, make your changes, and then use the Save or Save As command to save the file in the same place and with the same name as the original.

Storing Objects in Libraries

If you're a savvy InDesign user, you'll never build the same document twice. After all, that's what templates are for. Along the same lines, you never have to create the same object twice; that's what libraries are for. An InDesign library is a file—similar in some ways to a document file—in which you can store individual objects, groups and nested objects, ruler guides, and grids (ruler guides and grids are covered in the next section). For example, if you've created a logo in InDesign and you want to use it in other documents, you could place it in a library. Once you've saved an object in a library, it's as though you have an endless supply of copies. Every time you need a copy, all you have to do is drag one out of the library.

Creating a library is easy: Choose File ➪ New ➪ Library, choose a location to save the library in, give the library a name, and click OK. Figure 7-8 shows the dialog box.

Figure 7-8: The dialog box in which you save a new library.

You can create as many libraries as you want and store them wherever is most convenient, including on a networked server so other InDesign users can share them. When it comes to naming and organizing libraries, the choice is yours. If you work for an advertising agency, for example, you may decide to create a separate library for each client; each library could contain logos, images, boilerplate text (disclaimers, copyright information, legal blurbs), and so on. If you work for an in-house art department, you could create separate libraries for corporate logos (black-and-white, grayscale, and two-color/four-color variations), house ads, frequently used pictures, and standing art.

Tip   InDesign libraries are cross-platform. That is, you can open libraries created on a Mac using a PC and vice versa. On the PC, libraries have the filename extension .indl, while on the Mac they don't have to have a filename extension. In a cross-platform environment, add the PC filename extensions even to Mac files so Windows InDesign will recognize the file as a library.

After you create a new library, an empty library pane is displayed, as shown in Figure 7-9. The name you assigned is displayed in its title bar. You add items by dragging them to the pane. You can group the pane with other panes (by dragging its tab onto another pane) or close it by clicking its close box or choosing Close Library from its pop-up menu.

Figure 7-9: A new (empty) library and its accompanying pop-up menu.

At this point, you're ready to begin placing objects into the library, after which, you can begin copying the objects into other documents. Before we look at moving items into and out of libraries, here's a brief description of the controls in a library pane and the commands in the accompanying pop-up menu (refer to Figure 7-9):

✦ The numbers in the lower-left corner of the pane indicate the number of objects currently displayed in the pane (though not necessarily visible depending on the size of the pane) and the number of objects in the library. Search capabilities let you display a subset of the entire library.

✦ Clicking the Library Item Information button displays the Item Information dialog box, shown in Figure 7-10. Here you can assign a name, type, and description to a library object. (You can search for library objects based on these attributes.)

✦ The Show Library Subset button displays a dialog box that lets you locate and display objects that meet certain search criteria.

Figure 7-10: The Item Information dialog box.

✦ The New Library Item lets you add a selected object on a document page to a library.

✦ The Delete Library Item button lets you delete highlighted objects in the library.

✦ The Close Library palette menu command does the same thing as clicking a library pane's close box.

Note   If a library pane is part of another palette, if it is the frontmost palette, and if you close that palette, the library pane is closed as well. But if the library pane is not the frontmost pane in the palette, the library remains open when you close the palette.

✦ The Add Item and Add All Items on Page commands let you add a selected item or all items on a document page to a library. You can also simply drag items into the pane.

✦ The Place Item(s) command lets you place copies of selected library objects into a document.

✦ The Delete Item(s) command lets you remove selected library objects from the library.

✦ The Item Information command displays the Item Information dialog box (refer to Figure 7-10).

✦ The Show Subset command opens the same dialog box that's displayed if you click the Show Library Subset button. The dialog box lets you locate and display objects that meet certain search criteria.

✦ The Show All command displays all library objects (rather than a subset identified by a previous search).

✦ When the List View option is checked, library objects are displayed in a list rather than as Thumbnails.

✦ When the Thumbnails View option is checked, each library object is displayed in its own thumbnail window.

✦ The Sort Items command lets you sort library items by name, type, and date.

To open an existing library, choose File ➪ Open or press ⌘+O or Ctrl+O.

Note   Multiple users can share a library, but only if it's locked (meaning people can use items in the library but not add new ones). To lock a library on the Mac, locate the library file in the Finder, select it, choose File ➪ Get Info, and select the Locked option. In Windows, locate the library file in its current folder, right-click the file-name or icon, then select Read-Only from the Properties contextual menu's General pane.

To delete a library, you must delete the file. Either drag the file icon to the Trash (Mac) or move the file icon to the Recycle Bin (Windows).

Adding and deleting library objects

In addition to placing individual objects, such as text and graphics frames, into a library, you can also place multiple-selected objects, groups, nested frames, ruler guides, guidelines, and all objects on a page.

There are several ways to add objects to a library. You can

✦ Select one or more objects and then drag and drop them into an open library pane.

✦ Select one or more objects and then click the New Library Item button at the bottom of an open library pane.

✦ Select one or more objects and then choose Add Item from the pop-up menu of an open library pane.

✦ Choose Add All Items on Page from the pop-up menu of an open library pane to add all objects on the current page or spread.

Tip   If you hold down the Option or Alt key when adding an object to a library using any of the preceding methods, the Item Information dialog box is displayed. This dialog box lets you add searchable attributes to the object.

To delete a library object, drag its icon to the Trash icon at the bottom of the pane or click on the object once and then choose Delete Item(s) from the library pane's palette menu. You can select a range of objects by clicking on the first one and then Shift+clicking on the last one. You can select multiple, noncontinuous objects by holding down the ⌘ or Ctrl key and clicking on their icon.

Library caveats

Because the attributes of the original object are retained when you place a copy in a library, there are some pitfalls you have to watch out for:

✦ **If you move, modify, or delete the original graphic files associated with a picture you've placed in a library and then copy the library object into a document, the Links pane will report that the graphics file is modified or missing (just as it would if you imported the picture then moved, modified, or deleted the original).** It's a good idea to store graphics files used in libraries in a common location, such as in a Standards folder on the network, so the graphics files aren't accidentally moved or deleted when you delete or archive a set of project files that happen to contain objects placed in libraries.

✦ **If you copy a text frame from a library onto a document page, any character style sheets, paragraph style sheets, or colors in the library object that have the same name as character style sheets, paragraph style sheets, or colors in the target document are replaced by those in the target document.** If the target document does not contain character style sheets, paragraph style sheets, or colors in the placed text, they're added to the document.

✦ **If you copy a text frame from a library onto a document page, make sure that the fonts are available.** If they're not available, you'll have to choose alternate fonts.

When you place an object into a library, all its attributes are saved. For example, if you import a picture into a document and then place a copy of the picture into a library, the path to the original picture file is saved, as are any transformations you've applied to the picture or its frame (scale, rotation, shear, and so on). If you save text in a library, all formats, including style sheets, are retained.

Cataloging library objects

If your libraries contain only a few objects, finding the one you're looking for won't be very hard. But a library can hold as many objects as you want, and as a library becomes bigger, locating a particular object gets increasingly difficult. To make library objects easier to find, InDesign lets you tag them with several searchable attributes.

To tag a library element, select it and then choose Item Information from the library pane's palette menu. You can also display the Item Information dialog box by double-clicking on a library object or by clicking once on a library object and then clicking the Library Item Information icon at the bottom of the library pane. (Figure 7-10 shows the Item Information dialog box.) Now specify a Name, Object Type, and/or Description. In the Description field, it's a good idea to enter one or more keywords that describe the object so that you can easily find it later. Click OK to close the dialog box and return to the document.

InDesign lets you search for library objects based on the information specified in the Item Information dialog box. For example, if you've placed several different corporate logos into a library that includes many other objects, you could search for the term *logo* in the Name or Description field. If you used the word *logo* in either of these fields for your logos, a search of these fields for the word *logo* will identify and display your logos. The ability to search for library objects based on name and description is a good reason to name your library objects carefully and consistently and to specify keywords in the Description field of the Item Information dialog box. Follow these steps:

1. **Choose Show Subset from a library pane's palette menu or click on the Show Library Subset icon at the bottom of the pane.**

   The Subset dialog box, shown in Figure 7-11, is displayed.

Figure 7-11: The Subset dialog box.

2. **To search the entire library, click Search Entire Library; to search only the objects currently displayed in the page, click Search Currently Shown Items.**

3. **From the leftmost pop-up menu in the Parameters area, choose the Item Information category you want to search: Item Name, Creation Date, Object Type, or Description.**

4. **From the next pop-up menu choose Contains if you intend to search for text contained in the chosen category; choose Doesn't Contain if you want to exclude objects that contain the text you specify.**

5. **In the rightmost field, type the word or phrase you want to search for (if Contains is selected) or exclude (if Doesn't Contain is selected).**

6. **To add more search criteria, click More Choices; to reduce the number of search criteria, click Fewer Choices.**

   You can add up to five levels of search criteria.

7. **To display objects that match all search criteria, select Match All; to display objects that match any of the search criteria, select Match Any One.**

   These options are available only if two or more levels of search criteria are displayed.

8. **Click OK to conduct the search and close the dialog box.**

All the objects that match the search criteria are displayed in the pane. The pane is empty if no objects matched the search criteria. If you want to display all objects after conducting a search, choose Show All from the library pane's palette menu.

Tip   The Sort Items command in a library pane's palette menu lets you sort objects by Name, Oldest, Newest, and Type. If you sort by Oldest or Newest, items are arranged based on the order in which they were placed into the library.

Copying library objects onto document pages

Once you've placed an object into a library and, optionally, specified item information for the object, you can place copies of the library object into any document or into another library. To place a copy of a library object onto the currently displayed document page, click on the object's icon in the library pane and drag it onto the page. As you drag, the outline of the library object is displayed. Release the mouse button when the outline is positioned where you want to place the object. You can also place a library object onto a document by clicking on its icon and then choosing Place Item(s).

Tip   You can copy an object from one library to another by dragging its icon from the source library pane and dropping it onto the target library pane. If you hold down the Option or Alt key when dragging and dropping an object between libraries, the original object is removed from the source library (in effect moving it from one library to the other).

Using Ruler Guides and Grids

If you've every seen a carpenter use a chalked string to "snap" a temporary line to use as an aid for aligning objects, you understand the concept behind guidelines. They're not structurally necessary and they don't show in the final product, yet they can still make your work easier. InDesign lets you create and display three types of nonprinting guidelines:

✦ *Ruler guides* are moveable guidelines that you can create by hand or automatically. They're helpful for placing items precisely and aligning multiple items.

✦ A *baseline grid* is a series of horizontal lines that help in aligning lines of text and objects across a multicolumn page. When displayed, a baseline grid makes a page look like a sheet of lined paper.

✦ A *document grid* is a crisscross of horizontal and vertical lines that aid in object alignment and placement.

InDesign's grids and guides capabilities verge on overkill. Chances are you'll end up using a combination of ruler guides and the baseline or ruler guides and the document grid, but using all three is more complicated than necessary.

Ruler guides

InDesign lets you create individual ruler guides manually or a set of ruler guides automatically with the Create Guides command (Layout ⇨ Create Guides).

Creating ruler guides manually

To create manual ruler guides, go to the page or spread onto which you want to place ruler guides. (If the rulers are not displayed at the top and left of the document window, choose View ⇨ Show Rulers or press ⌘+R or Ctrl+R.) Now click on the horizontal ruler or vertical ruler, and drag the pointer onto a page or the pasteboard. Release the mouse button when the guideline is positioned where you want it. If you release the mouse when the pointer is over a page, the ruler guide extends from one edge of the page to the other (but not across a spread). If you release the mouse button when the pointer is over the pasteboard, the ruler guide extends across both pages of a spread and the pasteboard. If you want a guide to extend across a spread and the pasteboard, you can also hold down the ⌘ or Ctrl key as you drag and release the mouse when the pointer is over a page.

Tip You can place both a horizontal and vertical guide at the same time by pressing ⌘ or Ctrl and dragging the ruler intersection point onto a page.

Ruler guides are cyan in color (unless you change the color using Layout ⇨ Ruler Guides) and are associated with the layer onto which they're placed. You can show and hide ruler guides by showing and hiding the layers that contain them. You can even create layers that contain nothing but ruler guides and then show and hide them as you wish. (See Chapter 6 for more information about layers.)

Tip You can also place a guide that extends across the page or spread and pasteboard by double-clicking on the vertical or horizontal ruler.

Tip If you want to create ruler guides for several document pages, create a master page, add the guides to the master page, and then apply the master to the appropriate document pages.

Creating a set of guides automatically

Follow these steps to create a set of ruler guides:

1. **If the documents contains multiple layers, display the Layers pane (Window ⇨ Layers or F7) and click the name of the layer to which you want to add guides.**

See Chapter 6 for more information about layers.

2. **Choose Layout ⇨ Create Guides.**

   The Create Guides dialog box, shown in Figure 7-12, is displayed. Check Preview if you want to see the guides on the current document page as you create them.

Figure 7-12: The Create Guides dialog box, along with the guides it created.

3. **In the Rows and Columns areas specify the number of guides you want to add in the Number fields and, optionally, specify a Gutter width between horizontal (Rows) and vertical (Columns) guides.**

   Enter 0 in the Gutter fields if you don't want gutters between guides.

4. **In the Options area, click Margins to fit the guides in the margin boundaries; click Page to fit the guides within the page boundary.**

5. **Check Remove Existing Ruler Guides to remove any previously placed ruler guides.**

6. **When you're done specifying the attributes of the ruler guides, click OK to close the dialog box.**

Working with ruler guides

Once you've created ruler guides, you can show or hide them, lock or unlock them, and select and move, copy and paste, or delete one or more guides at a time. Here are a few pointers for working with ruler guides:

✦ To display or hide ruler guides, choose View ➪ Show/Hide Guides or press ⌘+; (semicolon) or Ctrl+; (semicolon).

✦ To lock or unlock all ruler guides, choose View ➪ Lock Guides or press Option+⌘+; (semicolon) or Ctrl+Alt+; (semicolon). (If Lock Guides is checked, ruler guides are locked.)

✦ To select a ruler guide, click on it with a selection tool. To select multiple guides, hold down the Shift key and click on them. The color of a selected guide changes from blue to the color of its layer. To select all ruler guides on a page or spread, press Option+⌘+G or Ctrl+Alt+G.

✦ To move a guide, click and drag it as you would any object. To move multiple guides, select them and then drag them. To move guides to another page, select them, choose Edit ➪ Cut, or ⌘+X or Ctrl+X, or Edit ➪ Copy, or ⌘+C or Ctrl+C, display the target page, then choose Edit ➪ Paste, or ⌘+V or Ctrl+V. If the target page is the same shape as the source page, the guides are placed in their original position.

✦ To delete ruler guides, select them and then press Delete or Backspace.

✦ To change the color of the ruler guides and the view percentage above which they're displayed (the default view threshold is 5 percent), choose Layout ➪ Ruler Guides. The Ruler Guides dialog box, shown in Figure 7-13, is displayed. Modify the View Threshold value and choose a different color from the Color pop-up menu, and then click OK. If you change the settings in the Ruler Guides dialog box when no documents are open, the new settings become defaults and are applied to all subsequently created documents.

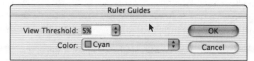

Figure 7-13: The Ruler Guides dialog box.

✦ To display ruler guides behind objects instead of in front, choose InDesign ➪ Preferences ➪ Guides & Pasteboard on the Mac or Edit ➪ Preferences ➪ Guides & Pasteboard in Windows, or press ⌘+K or Ctrl+K, and check Guides in Back in the Guide Options section of the dialog box.

✦ If the Snap to Guides command (View ➪ Snap to Guides, or Shift+⌘+; [semi-colon] or Ctrl+Shift+; [semicolon]) is checked, objects edges will snap to ruler guides when you drag them in the snap zone. To specify the *snap zone* (the distance — in pixels — at which an object will snap to a guide), choose InDesign ➪ Preferences ➪ Guides & Pasteboard on the Mac or Edit ➪ Preferences ➪ Guides & Pasteboard in Windows, or press ⌘+K or Ctrl+K, and enter a value in the Snap to Zone field in the Guide Options section of the dialog box.

Working with the baseline grid

Every new document you create includes a baseline grid. If the document you're working on uses a multicolumn page layout, a baseline grid can be helpful for aligning text baselines across columns and for ensuring that object edges align with text baselines. Baseline grids aren't much use for small documents — business cards, ads, and so on — and one-column designs. Here's how to create them:

1. **Choose InDesign ➪ Preferences ➪ Grids on the Mac or Edit ➪ Preferences ➪ Grids in Windows, or press ⌘+K or Ctrl+K and choose the Grids pane.**

   The Grids pane, shown in Figure 7-14, is displayed.

Figure 7-14: The Grids pane of the Preferences dialog box.

2. **Choose a color from the Color pop-up menu in the Baseline Grid area.**

3. **In the Start field, enter the distance between the top of the page and the first grid line.**

   If you enter **0**, the Increment Every value determines the distance between the top of the page and the first grid line.

4. **Enter the distance between grid lines in the Increment Every field.**

   Generally, the value you enter in this field will be the same as the leading value you use for the publication's body text.

5. **Choose a View Threshold percentage from the pop-up menu or enter a value in the field.**

   Generally, you don't want to display the baseline grid at reduced view percentages because grid lines become tightly spaced.

6. **Click OK to close the dialog box and return to the document.**

A baseline grid is document-wide (that is, you can't change it from page to page), and grid lines are displayed behind all objects, layers, and ruler guides. The default baseline grid begins a ½ inch from the top of a document page, the grid lines are light blue lines and placed 1 pica apart; and grid lines are displayed at view percentages above 75 percent. If you change any of these settings when no documents are open, the changes are applied to all subsequently created documents; if a document is open, changes apply only to that document.

Tip   The Show/Hide Baseline Grid command (View ⇨ Show/Hide Baseline Grid, or Option+⌘+' [apostrophe] or Ctrl+Alt+' [apostrophe]) lets you display and hide a document's baseline grid.

Working with the document grid

Like the baseline grid, every document includes a default *document grid,* which is a set of horizontal and vertical lines. And like baseline grids, you may or may not find the document grid to be a useful aid for laying out pages. If you like working on graph paper in the real world, the document guide may be just your cup of tea. On the other hand, you may find document grids to be too constricting and opt not to use them. If you want to use document grids, follow these steps:

1. **Choose InDesign ⇨ Preferences ⇨ Grids on the Mac or Edit ⇨ Preferences ⇨ Grids in Windows, or press ⌘+K or Ctrl+K.**

   The Grids pane displays (refer to Figure 7-14).

2. **Choose a color from the Color pop-up menu in the Document Grid area.**

3. **Enter the distance between grid lines in the Gridline Every field.**

   If your basic measurement unit is an inch, you'll probably want to use the default value of 1 inch.

4. **Enter the number of divisions between grid lines in the Subdivisions field.**

If your basic measurement unit is an inch, you can specify a value of 6 to subdivide the grid into 1-pica squares. Or, if you prefer, you can enter a value of 4, 8, 16, and so on to subdivide the grid into standard divisions of an inch.

5. **Click OK to close the dialog box and return to the document.**

Tip

The Show/Hide Document Grid command (View ➪ Show/Hide Document Grid or ⌘+' [apostrophe] or Ctrl+' [apostrophe]) lets you display and hide the document grid.

Summary

If you want to be a true InDesign expert, you must take advantage of three of its most powerful features: master pages, templates, and libraries. All these features save time and ensure design consistency across documents. A master page is a preformatted page design that you can apply to document pages in a multipage publication; a template is a preconstructed document that serves as the starting point when you need to create multiple versions of the same publication; and a library is a storage file in which you can save any object you've created with InDesign for use in other publications.

To help you place and align objects, InDesign lets you create three types of guidelines: ruler guides, the baseline grid, and the document grid. You can show or hide guidelines, and you have the option to snap object edges to guidelines when you drag them in the specified snap zone.

✦   ✦   ✦

Defining Colors and Gradients

Although color is most widely used by high-end publishers — people producing magazines and catalogs — color is becoming more accessible to all publishers, thanks to the recent emergence of inexpensive color printers, color copiers, and leading-edge desktop-publishing programs. Whether you want to produce limited-run documents on a color printer, create newsletters using spot colors, or publish magazines and catalogs using process colors and special inks, InDesign offers the tools that you need to do the job well.

You can use color in your graphics or apply colors to text and layout elements (such as bars along the edge of a page). Or you can use color in both ways. To a great extent, where you define and apply color determines what you can do with it.

 Chapter 29 covers color matching and other high-end color output issues in depth. This chapter concentrates on how to create and apply colors within InDesign.

In This Chapter

Defining colors and tints

Mixing colors

Editing colors and tints

Copying and deleting swatches

Understanding process color versus spot color

Simulating other color models

Understanding color issues in imported graphics

Working with gradients

Defining Colors

InDesign comes with a few predefined colors: black, registration (black on each negative for the printing press), paper (white), none (transparent), cyan, magenta, yellow, red, green, and blue. So you'll likely want to add a few of your own.

Before you can apply any colors — whether to bitmap images or to layout elements such as strokes, text, frames, and shapes — you must first define the colors. But before you can define colors, you have a couple decisions to make first:

✦ Do you want to create your own color by mixing basic colors like red, green, and blue (called RGB and typically used for screen display), or cyan, yellow, magenta, and black (called CMYK or process colors, and typically used for printing presses)?

✦ Do you want to use a color from an ink maker like Pantone or Toyo? These colors — called *spot colors* — are typically used as an extra ink on your document but can also be converted to the standard four colors and so are handy when you'll know the color you want when you see it.

The answer will tell you where you need to go to create your new color. Figure 8-1 shows the two panes for creating and choosing colors: the Colors pane and the Swatches pane, accessible for future use.

 Note If no document is open when you create, edit, or delete colors, the new color palette becomes the default for all future documents.

You can change the appearance of the entries in the Swatches pane by using the three options in the Swatches pane's palette menu: Name (the default), Small Name (a tighter list view), Small Swatch (no names, just small icons), and Large Swatch (no names, just larger icons). Also, use the Hide Options menu to suppress display of the Stroke, Fill, Formatting Affects Container, and Formatting Affects Text buttons and the Tint field and pop-up menu; Show Options brings them back.

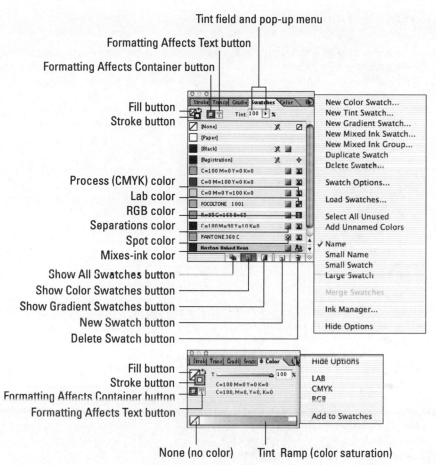

Figure 8-1: The two panes for creating and selecting colors: the Swatches pane (top) and the Color pane (bottom).

Creating colors

To create your own color, go to the Swatches pane (Window ➪ Swatches or F5) and select New Color Swatch from the palette menu. You'll get the New Color Swatch dialog box shown in Figure 8-2. Now follow these steps:

Figure 8-2: The New Color Swatch dialog box lets you define colors. (At top is the dialog box for CMYK color mixing; at bottom is the dialog box for the swatch-based Pantone colors.) An identical dialog box named Swatch Options lets you edit them.

1. **In the Swatch Name field, give your color a name that describes it, such as Lime Green or Bright Purple.**

   You can also check Name with Color Value, which uses the color values to make up the color name, as done for the first three colors under [Registration] in Figure 8-1. But this option is available only for CMYK, RGB, and LAB colors, not for swatch-based colors such as Pantone.

Tip   You can name a CMYK, RGB, or LAB color anything you want. To make it easier to remember what a defined color looks like, either use descriptive names (such as Grass Green) or use names based on the color settings (InDesign will do this for you automatically if you select the Name with Color Value check box and have chosen Process as the Color Type). For example, if you create a color in the CMYK model, give it a name based on its mix, such as *55C 0M 91Y 0K* for that grass-green color—composed of 55 percent cyan, 0 percent magenta, 91 percent yellow, and 0 percent black. (Believe it or not, this naming convention is how professionals specify colors on paste-up boards.) InDesign's Name with Color Value option would name this color *C=55 M=0 Y=91 K=0*. The same system applies to the RGB, HSB, and LAB models. That way, you can look at the Swatches pane and immediately tell what color you'll get.

2. **In the Color Type pop-up menu, choose from Process or Spot.**

   These are covered later in this chapter—leave the color type at Process if you're not sure.

3. **In the Color Mode pop-up menu, choose the mixing system or swatch library (both are considered to be *color models*) you will use:**

   - **CMYK:** Cyan, magenta, yellow, and black, the colors used in professional printing presses and many color printers.

   - **RGB:** Red, green, and blue, the colors used on a computer monitor, for CD-based or Web-based documents or for some color printers.

   - **LAB:** Luminosity, *A* axis, *B* axis, a way of defining colors created by the international standards group Commission Internationale d'Éclairage (the CIE, which translates to International Commission on Illumination in English).

   - **A swatch-based model:** Sets of premixed colors from various vendors, including DIC, Focoltone, HKS, Pantone, Toyo Ink, and Trumatch for print documents, as well as a Web-specific set and sets specific to Windows and the Mac OS for on-screen documents. InDesign also has the Other Library from which you can select any swatch library file in Adobe Illustrator format.

4. **For the CMYK, RGB, and LAB models, use the sliders to create your new color.**

   A preview will display in the box at left. For the swatch-based models, scroll through the lists of colors and select one.

5. **If you want to create multiple colors, click Add after each color definition and then click Done when done.**

   To create just one color, click OK instead of Add. You can also Cancel to abort the current color definition.

New Feature   The Add button in the New Color Swatch, New Tint Swatch, and New Gradient Swatch dialog boxes is new to InDesign CS.

Tip

Because regular black can appear weak when it's overprinted by other colors, many designers create what printers call *superblack* (also called *rich* black) by combining 100 percent black and 100 percent magenta. (Some use cyan instead of magenta.) You can define superblack as a separate color or redefine the registration color as 100 percent of all four process colors, and use that as a superblack. Note that superblack should be used only in large areas — using it on type or small objects will increase the chances of registration problems for those items.

The most popular swatch libraries used by professional publishers are those from Pantone, whose Pantone Matching System (PMS) is the de facto standard for most publishers in specifying spot-color inks. The Pantone swatch libraries come in several variations, of which InDesign includes four:

✦ **Pantone Process Coated:** Use this when you color-separate Pantone colors and your printer uses the standard Pantone-brand process-color inks. (These colors will reproduce reliably when color-separated, while the other Pantone swatch libraries' colors often will not.) Colors in this variant will automatically have the code *DS* (digital SWOP, or standard web offset printing) prefixed to their names and *C* (coated) appended.

✦ **Pantone Solid Coated:** Use this when your printer will use actual Pantone inks (as spot colors) when printing to coated paper stock. Colors in this variant will have the code *C* (coated) appended to their names.

✦ **Pantone Solid Matte:** Use this when your printer will use actual Pantone inks (as spot colors) when printing to matte-finished paper stock. Colors in this variant will have the code *M* (matte) appended to their names.

✦ **Pantone Solid Uncoated:** Use this when your printer will use actual Pantone inks (as spot colors) when printing to uncoated paper stock. Colors in this variant will have the code *U* (uncoated) appended to their names.

Note

Unlike InDesign, both PageMaker and QuarkXPress support more Pantone color swatches — such as metallics and pastels — and QuarkXPress also supports the high-fidelity Pantone Hexachrome colors. Check out www.INDDcentral.com for Pantone library sources for InDesign.

Tip

When printing on uncoated paper stock with any colors designed for use on coated stock (which is glossier and shinier), you will usually get weaker, less-saturated color reproduction. That's because the colors designed for uncoated stock are a little richer to make up for the fact that some of the ink gets absorbed into the paper. In uncoated stock, there is much less absorption because the coating acts as a barrier. A matte finish is not as glossy as coated stock but more glossy than uncoated paper.

The other swatch libraries available in InDesign are

✦ **DIC Color:** The Dainippon Ink & Chemical library, used mainly in Japan.

✦ **Focoltone:** A CMYK-based library from Focoltone, used mainly in Asia.

✦ **HKS:** Used in mainly Germany and other European countries, with variants for industrial printing such as on plastics, it uses various combinations of cyan, magenta, and yellow with black overlays to achieve different shades.

✦ **System:** InDesign has two system libraries, one for Macs and one for Windows. Both are sets of RGB colors available on all Macs or PCs, for on-screen publications such as CD-based presentations.

✦ **Toyo:** A spot-color model from Toyo Ink, used mainly in Japan.

✦ **Trumatch:** A CMYK-based library from Trumatch, used mainly in Europe.

✦ **Web:** A set of RGB colors that all Mac and PC browsers display consistently, for use in Web documents.

Note   Several of the swatch library names are in all uppercase in InDesign's menus and dialog boxes. That's because they're trademarked names, which some people (such as those at Adobe) like to indicate by using all caps. That's just a convention and means nothing per se.

Tip   Color swatches based on the CMYK colors — such as Focoltone, Pantone Process, and Trumatch — will accurately color-separate and, thus, print accurately on a printing press, since a printing press uses the CMYK colors. Other swatches' colors often do not color-separate accurately, because they are supposed to represent special inks that may have elements like metals and clays designed to give metallic or pastel appearances that simply can't be replicated by combining cyan, magenta, yellow, and black. Similarly, some colors (like several hues of orange and green) can't be accurately created using the CMYK colors.

Creating tints

A *tint* is a shade of a color. InDesign lets you create such tints as separate color swatches, so they're easy to use for multiple items. The process is easy:

1. **In the Swatches pane, just select a color you want to create a tint from.**

2. **Using the palette menu, select New Tint Swatch.**

   You'll get the New Tint Swatch dialog box shown in Figure 8-3.

Figure 8-3: The New Tint Swatch dialog box lets you define colors. A nearly identical dialog box named Swatch Options lets you edit them—the difference is that, when editing, you can change all the other color values, not just the degree of tint.

3. **Use the slider to adjust the tint, or enter a value in the field at right.**

4. **Click Add to create another tint from the same base color, then click Done when you're done (or just click OK if you're adding a single tint).**

   Click Cancel to abort the current tint. Any new tint will have the same name as the original color and the percentage of shading, such as Leaf Green 66%.

You can create a tint from a tint, which can be confusing. Fortunately, InDesign goes back to the original color when letting you create the new tint. Thus, if you select Leaf Green 66% and move the slider to 33%, you'll get a 33 percent tint of the original Leaf Green, not a 33 percent tint of the Leaf Green 66% (which would be equivalent to a 22 percent tint of the original Leaf Green).

Creating mixed colors

InDesign CS offers another type of color: mixed-ink color. Essentially, a mixed-ink color combines a spot color with the default process colors (cyan, magenta, yellow, and black) to create new color swatches. For example, you could combine 38 percent black with 100 percent Pantone 130C to get a darker version of Pantone 130C (called a *duotone*, though InDesign doesn't limit you to mixing spot colors with just black, as traditional duotones do).

Mixed-ink colors are new to InDesign CS.

The evils of the Color pane's colors

Many people will try to use the Color pane (Window ➪ Color or F6) to define colors, but that's a mistake.

At first, you may not realize you can create colors from the Color pane. It shows a gradation of the last color used and lets you change the tint for that color on the current object. But if you go to the palette menu and choose a color model (RGB, CMYK, or LAB), you'll get a set of mixing controls (refer to Figure 8-1).

So what's the problem? Colors created via the Color pane won't appear in your Swatches pane and so can't be used for other objects. Called *unnamed colors* because they don't appear anywhere, these can be dangerous for publishers to use. (Adobe added them to InDesign to be consistent with how Illustrator defines colors — a foolish consistency.)

First, you can't modify them later in the Swatches pane if you want to adjust the color for all objects using them.

Second, you can't specify the color to print as a spot color, which you might later decide is how you want to print a particular color. They will print only as process colors and will not show up in the list of colors in the Color pane of the Print dialog box (see Chapter 31 for more details on this).

Fortunately, there is a way to prevent unnamed colors: If you go to the Color pane and modify a color without thinking about it, choose Add to Swatches from the palette menu to add the modified color to the Swatches pane. Of course, if you forget to do this, you'll have an unnamed color, so it's best to think "Swatches pane" when you think about adding or editing colors instead of the more obvious "Color pane." If you do forget, you can use the Add Unnamed Colors menu item in the Swatches pane's palette menu to add the colors to the Swatches pane.

To create a mixed-ink swatch, select the spot color you want to begin with and then choose New Mixed Ink Swatch from the Swatches pane's palette menu. You get the dialog box shown in Figure 8-4, in which you select the percentages of the spot color and any or all of the default process colors you want to mix. You also give the new color a name. Click Add to add another mixed-ink swatch based on the current spot color, then click Done when you're done. If you're creating just one color, click OK instead of Add. You can click Cancel to abort the current mixed-ink color definition.

Tip   Be sure to test such mixes by creating a color proof first — they may not look as you expect when actually printed because of how printing presses handle a color overlapping other colors.

Figure 8-4: The New Mixed Ink Swatch dialog box lets you mix a selected spot color with any or all of the default process colors to create new shades and variations.

There's more to mixed-ink colors than creating them one by one. InDesign lets you create mixed-ink groups, which are a series of colors based on a spot color and one or more default process colors. Figure 8-5 shows the New Mixed Ink Group dialog box, in which you select the colors to mix as you do in the New Mixed Ink Swatch dialog box. This feature is handy to create a palette of colors within a color range.

But you do more than simply mix the colors. In this dialog box, you specify an initial tint for each color you want to mix, then how many times you want to create a color using it, as well as the increment of color for each creation. This can be confusing, so let's walk through the options in Figure 8-5.

Process Cyan is chosen with an Initial value of 34%, a Repeat setting of 2, and an Increment of 46%. Also chosen is the spot color HKS 03 E, with an Initial value of 67%, a Repeat setting of 3, and an Increment of 10%. This combination will create 12 mixed-ink swatches, as shown in the Swatch Preview section (click Preview Swatches to display the preview colors).

InDesign uses the settings and first mixes 67 percent of HKS 03 E with 34 percent of process cyan. That's one swatch. Then it mixes 67 percent of HKS 03 E with 80 percent of cyan (adding the increment of 46%). It does so one more time, for 100 percent cyan, since there was a Repeat setting of 2 — note that InDesign stops at 100 percent saturation even if the Increment results in a higher number.

So that's three mixed-ink swatches based on 67 percent of HKS 03 E. InDesign now repeats this mixing with the next increment of HKS 03 E (77 percent, based on the Increment value of 10% for that color). That's three more. The process is repeated two more times, one for 97 percent of HKS 03 E and one for 97 percent of HKS 03 E, to meet the Repeat setting of 3.

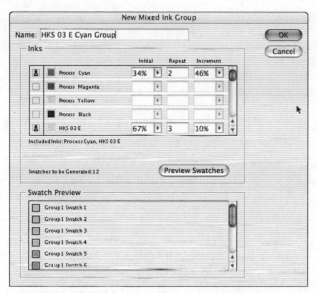

Figure 8-5: The New Mixed Ink Group dialog box lets you mix a selected spot color with any or all of the default process colors in user-defined increments to create a range of new shades and variations.

Tip   To figure out how many swatches will be created using this feature, add 1 to the number in each of the Repeat fields, then multiply the values. In the preceding example, you get $12 - (2+1) \times (3+1)$, or 3×4, or 12. That's because the Repeat setting indicates how many more variations to create *in addition to* those with the base (Initial) value.

Editing Colors and Tints

Editing colors is pretty easy in InDesign: For any color in the Swatches pane, just double-click the color or its name, and the Swatch Options dialog box (which is the same as the New Swatch dialog box shown previously in Figure 8-2) will display. Make any adjustments and click OK when you're done. Voilà! Your color is now changed.

Similarly, if you double-click a tint swatch, you get the Swatch Options dialog box, which lets you change the tint percentage.

Caution   When editing a tint, the Swatch Options dialog box also lets you change the other attributes of the color. It's key to remember that if you change those settings in the tint, all other tints based on the original color, as well as the original color, are changed accordingly. If you want to change a setting of just the tint — such as making it a spot color while leaving the original color a process color — you need to duplicate the original color and make a tint from that duplicate.

In addition to double-clicking a swatch to edit it, you can select Swatch Options from the palette menu, but why bother?

To help work with swatches, you can have InDesign show just color and tint swatches, just gradient swatches, or all swatches by using the icons at the bottom of the Swatches pane. Figure 8-1, shown earlier in the chapter, illustrates which icon does what.

InDesign also lets you merge swatches — select multiple swatches and then choose Merge Swatches from the Swatches pane's palette menu — but I suggest you avoid this. When InDesign merges swatches, it tries to calculate a new value based on the swatches' values, essentially weighting the CMYK values (RGB and other values are converted to CMYK first). But it's a crap shoot: You won't usually get the color you expect. If you want a shade between two colors, I recommend you create it as a new swatch, manually entering the desired CMYK (or RGB or LAB) values.

Deleting and Copying Swatches

When you create colors, tints, and gradients (described later in this chapter), you'll find it easy to go overboard and make too many. You'll also find that different documents have different colors, each created by different people, and you'll likely want to move colors from one document to another. InDesign provides basic tools for managing colors in and across documents.

Note   Remember that when selecting swatches for deletion or duplication, you can ⌘+click or Ctrl+click multiple swatches to work on all at once. Note that Shift+clicking selects all swatches between the first swatch clicked and the swatch that you Shift+click, whereas ⌘+click or Ctrl+click lets you select specific swatches in any order and in any location in the pane.

Deleting swatches

InDesign makes deleting swatches easy: Just select the color, tint, or gradient in the Swatches pane. Then choose Delete Swatch from the palette menu, or click the Trash Can icon on the Mac or the X icon in Windows (the Delete Swatch box) at the bottom of the Swatches pane.

Well, that's not quite it. You'll then get the dialog box shown in Figure 8-6, which lets you assign anything using the deleted swatch to a new color (the Defined Swatch option) or leave the color on any object that happens to be using it, but delete the swatch from the Swatches pane (the Unnamed Swatch option). (As explained in the sidebar "The evils of the Color pane's colors," unnamed colors should be avoided, so if your document is using a color, keep its swatch.)

Figure 8-6: The Delete Swatch dialog box lets you replace a deleted color with a new one, or leave the color applied to objects using it.

If you delete a tint and have it replaced with another color, any object using that tint will get the full-strength version of the new color, not a tint of it.

Likewise, if you delete a color swatch that you've based one or more tints on, those tints will also be deleted if you replace the deleted swatch with an unnamed swatch. However, if you delete a color swatch and replace it with a defined swatch, any tints of that deleted swatch will retain their tint percentages of the replacement defined swatch.

InDesign offers a nice option to quickly find all unused colors in the Swatches pane: the palette menu's Select All Unused option. Then you can just delete them in one fell swoop. Note that you don't get the option to assign each deleted color separately to another color in the Delete Swatch dialog box — they all are replaced with the color you select or are made into unnamed colors. Because no object uses these colors, choosing Unnamed Swatch in essence is the same as replacing them with a color using the Defined Swatch option.

If you delete a swatch and replace it with an unnamed swatch, you can recapture that deleted swatch later by choosing the Add Unnamed Colors menu item in the Swatches pane's palette menu.

Copying swatches

To duplicate a swatch, so you can create a new one based on it, use the Duplicate Swatch option in the Swatches pane. The word *copy* will be added to its name, and you edit it — including its name — as you would any swatch.

You can also import colors from other InDesign, Illustrator, and Illustrator EPS files by choosing Load Swatches from the Swatches pane's palette menu.

Tip   A quick way to import specific colors from another InDesign document or template is to drag the colors from that other file's Swatches pane into your current document or template.

Spot Color versus Process Color

Earlier in this chapter, I mentioned briefly that there are two types of colors that InDesign works with: spot and mixed. Understanding how these differ is key to using them effectively and saving hassles and money when printing your documents.

Several forms of color are used in printing, but the two basic ones are *process color* and *spot color.*

Process color refers to the use of four basic colors—cyan, magenta, yellow, and black (known as a group as *CMYK*)—that are mixed to reproduce most color tones the human eye can see. A separate negative is produced for each of the four process colors. This method, often called *four-color publishing,* is used for most color publishing.

Note   Like CMYK, RGB and LAB are also created by mixing colors, so InDesign refers to all such colors as *mixed colors,* leaving the term *process color* for CMYK, since that's an industry standard term for CMYK.

Spot color refers to any specific color ink—whether one of the process colors or some other hue—used for specific elements in a document. For example, if you print a document in black ink but print the company logo in red, the red is a spot color. A spot color is often called a *second color* even though you can use several spot colors in a document. Each spot color is output to its own negative (and not color-separated into CMYK).

Using spot color gives you access to special inks that are truer to the desired color than any mix of process colors can be. These inks come in several standards, with Pantone being the most popular. Trumatch, Focoltone, Toyo, and DIC are less popular but still common standards, with Trumatch used mainly in Asia, Focoltone in Europe, and Toyo and DIC in Japan. InDesign supports all five spot-color standards.

Spot-color inks can produce some colors that are impossible to achieve with process colors, such as metallics, neons, and milky pastels. You even can use varnishes as spot colors to give layout elements a different gleam from the rest of the page. Although experienced designers sometimes mix spot colors to produce special shades not otherwise available, it's unlikely that you will need to do so.

Tip

If you create spot colors, I suggest that you include the word *Spot* as part of the name, so you can quickly tell in a palette or menu whether a selected color will print on its own plate or be color-separated. InDesign does use an icon to tell you whether a color is process or spot, as well as what color model (CMYK, RGB, or LAB) it was defined in (refer to Figure 8-1), but using the word is often more visible than looking for a tiny icon.

Note

Adobe programs, including InDesign, show spot colors like Pantone, Toyo, and DIC as being based on the CMYK color model, even though they're not. It doesn't really matter, because if you print them as a spot color, they get their own plate and your printer will use the actual Pantone, Toyo, or DIC ink. And if you color-separate them into process colors, you'll get the CMYK values shown in the Swatch Options dialog box or by holding the mouse over the color name in the Swatches pane (if the Tool Tips option is enabled in the Preferences dialog box, as described in Chapter 3).

Some designers use both process and spot colors in a document — known as *using a fifth color.* Typically, the normal color images are color-separated and printed via the four process colors while a special element (such as a logo in metallic ink) is printed in a spot color. The process colors are output on the usual four negatives; the spot color is output on a separate, fifth negative and printed using a fifth plate, fifth ink roller, and fifth inkwell. You can use more than five colors; you're limited only by your budget and the capabilities of your printing plant.

No matter whether you set a color to be a spot color, you still have the option when you output to convert all spot colors to process (see Chapter 31). What you can't do when printing is select specific spot colors to be output as process colors (be color-separated) and let others remain spot colors. If you're going to color-separate some colors and have others print as spot colors, you must be sure to set them up properly in the Swatch Options dialog box.

InDesign can convert spot colors to process colors, and vice versa. This handy capability lets designers specify the colors they want through a system they're familiar with, such as Pantone, without the added expense of special spot-color inks and extra negatives.

You can convert a color defined in any model to the CMYK, RGB, or LAB models simply by selecting one of those models when editing the color: Just use the Color Mode pop-up menu in the Swatch Options dialog box.

Caution

Colors defined in one model and converted to another may not reproduce exactly the same because the physics underlying each color model differ slightly. Each model was designed for use in a different medium such as paper or a video monitor.

Although conversions are almost never an exact match, there are guidebooks that can show you in advance the color that will be created. With Pantone Process variation (which InDesign supports), designers can pick a Pantone color that will color-separate predictably. And the Focoltone and Trumatch colors were created by mixing process colors, so all can reliably be color-separated into CMYK.

Tip   If you use Pantone colors, I suggest that you get a copy of the *Pantone Process Color Imaging Guide: CMYK Edition* swatchbook, available from several sources, including art and printing supply stores, mail-order catalogs, and Pantone itself. This swatchbook shows each Pantone color and the CMYK equivalent so that you can see how accurate the conversion will be and, thus, whether you want to use the actual Pantone ink on its own negative or convert to CMYK.

Working with Color Pictures

When you work with imported graphics, whether they are illustrations or scanned photographs, color is part of the graphic file. So the responsibility for color controls lies primarily with the creator of the picture. It is best to use color files in CMYK EPS or DCS format (for illustrations) or CMYK TIFF format (for scans and bitmaps). These standards are de facto for color publishing, so InDesign is particularly adept at working with them. (See Chapter 22 for details on preparing graphics files for import.)

Note   RGB is the standard color model used by scanners and graphics software because monitors use red, green, and blue electron guns to display images. The dilemma most designers face is that an RGB image displays properly on-screen but may appear with slightly adjusted hues in print, while a CMYK image may print correctly but appear incorrectly on-screen. Most designers get good at mentally shifting the colors from one model to another, as they see the results of their work in print over time. Until that happens, rely on color proofs from your printer to see what your images actually look like when printed.

Caution   Color files pasted via the clipboard should print properly after they're pasted into an InDesign picture box. But problems do sometimes occur, such as dropped colors or altered colors, depending on the applications involved and the amount of memory available. If you drag files from Photoshop or Illustrator directly into InDesign, rather than use copy and paste, you should have no such problems.

Working with EPS files

InDesign automatically imports color definitions from EPS files, so you'll see any spot colors in them show up in your Color pane and in menus and dialog boxes that display color lists.

Note If you create files in EPS format, do any required color trapping in the source application — InDesign offers only basic trapping capabilities (see Chapter 29).

Not all programs encode color information the same way. If you create EPS files in some illustration programs, colors may not print as expected. One of three things can happen:

✦ Each color prints on its own plate (as if it were a spot color), even if you defined it as a process color.

✦ A spot color is color-separated into CMYK even when you define it as a spot color in both the source program and in InDesign.

✦ A color prints as black.

There is no easy solution, since the problem is in how the illustration program manages color internally. The only safe bet is to use a program that uses standard color-definition methods; these include the latest versions of Adobe Illustrator, CorelDraw, and Macromedia FreeHand.

Working with TIFF files

Color TIFF files do not cause such peculiarities, since they don't use spot colors — by their very nature, they are broken down into RGB or CMYK when they are created.

InDesign can color-separate RGB TIFF files, as well as CMYK TIFF files. You may notice a color shift for color-separated RGB images, or for RGB images printed on a CMYK proofing printer. The degree of shift will depend on the device and whether any color-management system (CMS) plug-ins were used in creating the image, and whether the same one is active in InDesign for printing. Chapter 29 covers this in more detail.

Working with PDF files

InDesign will accurately import any colors used in a PDF file.

Caution Even though InDesign doesn't support Hexachrome colors, it does retain any Hexachrome colors in the PDF file and will retain them for output *only* if you export the InDesign file to PDF format. Otherwise, the Hexachrome colors are converted to CMYK when you print or generate a PostScript file from InDesign. Many Hexachrome colors do not print properly when converted to CMYK, so you should always export InDesign files using Hexachrome PDF images to PDF for output. If that's not possible, edit the original image in the program that generated the PDF, or in a program like Illustrator that can edit PDF files, and choose CMYK colors instead, and then reexport the PDF image.

Working with Gradients

A technique that has increased in popularity is the gradient, which blends two or more colors in a sequence, going from, say, green to blue to yellow to orange. InDesign has a powerful gradient creation feature that lets you define and apply gradients to pretty much any object you create in InDesign: text, lines, frames, shapes, and their outlines (strokes).

Note   Gradients go by several names among artists. Others include *blends* and *graduated fills.*

Creating gradients

In the Swatches pane, where you define colors and tints you can also define gradients: Just use the New Gradient Swatch option in the palette menu. You'll get the dialog box shown in Figure 8-7. The first two options are straightforward:

✦ Enter a name for the gradient in the Swatch Name field. Picking a name is a bit more difficult than for a color, but use something like "Blue to Red" or "Bright Multihue" or "Logo Gradient" that has a meaning specific to the colors used or to its role in your document.

✦ In the Type pop-up menu, choose Linear or Radial. A linear blend goes in one direction, while a radial blend radiates out in a circle from a central point. (Later in this section, Figure 8-10 shows some example gradients.)

Figure 8-7: The New Gradient Swatch dialog box.

Now it gets a little tricky. Follow these steps:

1. **Select a stop point — one of the squares at the bottom of the dialog box, on either side of the gradient ramp that shows the gradient as you define it.**

   The stop points are essentially the "from" and "to" colors, with the "from" being the stop point at left and the "to" being the stop point at right. With a stop point selected, you can now define its color.

2. **Choose what color model you want to define the color in — select from CMYK, RGB, LAB, and Swatches in the Stop color pop-up menu.**

   The area directly beneath the pop-up menu will change accordingly, displaying sliders for CMYK, RGB, and LAB, as well as a list of all colors from the Swatches pane for Swatches.

3. **Now create or select the color you want for that stop point.**

New Feature

In InDesign CS, you can now select the [Paper] swatch — essentially, transparency or no color — as a stop point in a gradient. Now you can also drag swatches from the Swatches pane to the gradient ramp.

4. **Repeat Steps 1 and 2 for the other stop point.**

   Note that the color model for the two stop points don't have to be the same — you can blend from a Pantone spot color to a CMYK color, for example.

You now have a simple gradient. But you don't have to stop there. Here are your options:

✦ **You can change the rate at which the colors transition by sliding the diamond icon at the top of the gradient ramp.**

✦ **You can create additional stop points by clicking right below the gradient ramp.** By having several stop points, you can have multiple color transitions in a gradient. (Think of them like tab stops in text — you can define as many as you need.) You delete unwanted stop points by dragging them to the bottom of the dialog box.

Notice that there's a diamond icon between each pair of stop points — that means each can have its own transition rate. Figure 8-8 shows a complex gradient being defined.

Tip

When you create a new gradient, InDesign will use the settings from the last one you created. If you want to create a gradient similar to an existing one, click on that existing gradient before selecting New Gradient Swatch from the palette menu. InDesign will copy the selected gradient's settings to the new one, which you can then edit. One reason to use this is to create, say, a radial version of an existing linear gradient.

Figure 8-8: A complex, multihued gradient being defined.

The Swatches pane will show the actual gradient next to its name. You'll also see the pattern in the Fill box or Stroke box in the Tools palette if that gradient is currently selected as a fill or stroke, as well as in the Gradient box in that palette, whether or not it's currently applied as a fill or stroke.

Note   If a gradient mixes spot colors and process colors, InDesign will convert the spot colors to process colors.

Tip   If you want to share your settings with others, you can give them the color definitions for each stop point, as well as the exact location of each stop point and transition control — notice the Location field at the bottom of the dialog box. As you click each control and stop point, it shows the current setting. You can also adjust the settings for the select control or stop point by changing the value in the field, rather than sliding the control or point.

Creating unnamed gradients

Just as it does with colors, InDesign lets you create *unnamed gradients* — gradients that have no swatches. My caution on using this feature for colors applies less for gradients, since all colors in a gradient are converted to process colors and/or use defined spot-color swatches — so there are no unnamed colors in their output. Here's how it works:

1. **Select the object you want to apply the gradient to.**

   Make sure the stroke or fill, as appropriate, is active in the Toolbox.

2. **Go to the Gradient pane (Window ⇨ Gradient), shown in Figure 8-9.**

3. **Select a stop point.**

4. **Now go to the Color pane.**

   It's usually in the same palette as the Gradient pane, but use Window ⇨ Color or F6 to display it if not.

5. **Create a color using the CMYK, RGB, or LAB models.**

   Use the palette menu to choose the model.

6. **Repeat Steps 2 through 5 for the other stop point.**

7. **Create any additional stop points by clicking below the gradient ramp, and adjust the transition controls as desired.**

Figure 8-9: The Gradient pane, for creating unnamed gradients and for adjusting linear gradients' angles.

Editing gradients

Editing a gradient is as simple as double-clicking its name in the Swatches menu or selecting it and choosing Edit Gradient Swatch. You'll get the Gradient Options dialog box, which is nearly identical to the New Gradient Swatch dialog box in Figures 8-7 and 8-8.

What's different in the Gradient Options dialog box is the Preview check box, which lets you see a gradient change in a selected object (if it's visible on-screen, of course) as you make changes in the Gradient Options dialog box.

The Gradient pane used to create unnamed gradients also has a use for gradient swatches. After you've applied a linear gradient — whether via a gradient swatch or as an unnamed gradient — you can change the angle of the gradient, as done with the bottom middle gradient in Figure 8-10 (compare it to the otherwise identical object at the bottom right). Just enter a value in the Angle field to rotate the gradient's direction.

Figure 8-10: Examples of gradients.

You can't rotate a radial gradient, because it's circular and, thus, any rotation will have no effect. That's why InDesign grays out the Angle field for radial gradients. But you still can adjust the location of a radial gradient — as well as that of a linear gradient — using the Gradient tool in the Tools palette (shown at left). After applying a gradient to an object, select the Gradient tool and draw a line in the object, as shown in Figure 8-11:

Figure 8-11: The Gradient tool lets you set the offset, adjust the gradient length, and (for gradient blends) adjust the gradient angle.

✦ For a linear gradient, the start point will correspond to where you want the first stop point of the gradient to be, while the end point will correspond to the last point. This lets you stretch or compress the gradient, as well as offset the gradient within the object. Also, the angle at which you draw the line becomes the angle for the gradient.

✦ For a radial gradient, the line becomes the start and end point for the gradient, in effect offsetting it, as done in the upper-left gradient in Figure 8-10 (compare it to the standard gradient setting for the same object at upper-right).

InDesign Color Techniques

Adobe InDesign offers a strong set of tools for color creation and control, as Chapters 8 and 29 show in detail. This special eight-page color section shows some of these tools in action, using InDesign's actual capabilities. Most images in this section are color photographs scanned in at 24-bit RGB files at 600 dpi and converted to CMYK TIFF images in Adobe Photoshop. I also adjusted brightness, sharpness, and color balance as needed.

Color Models

Color is made up of light, but the printing model and computer-monitor models act very differently. Color printing is based on how light reflects off paper through inks — the standard inks in printing are cyan, magenta, yellow, and black (CMYK), although there are specialty inks such as Pantone, Toyo, and Trumatch. The ink absorbs all colors but the one you see; for example, your eyes can see cyan because the ink has absorbed all the other colors that light would normally pick up. That's why mixing several inks produces a dark brown or gray — most of the light is absorbed by the multiple inks. By contrast, computer monitors use a model based on how the three colors of light — red, green, and blue (RGB) — combine. All three combine to make white, while having none gives you black. Because the physics of the two models is different, what you see on-screen — or what your scanner or digital camera sees when capturing an image — won't necessarily match what is printed.

The CMYK model

The RGB model

CMYK color (far left) and RGB color (immediate left). For CMYK, the cube shows how cyan, magenta, and yellow combine in various percentages; the slider at the cube's right adds black, which has the effect of darkening the combination shown. In RGB, there's no slider since the three colors combine to produce all color shades (white is the absence of all colors). Below are example inks from specialty color libraries.

Pantone ink swatches

Pantone Process ink swatches

Pantone ink swatches

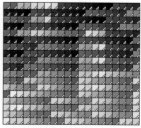

Pantone ink swatches

Colors on the Web

Although the Hypertext Markup Language (HTML) supports thousands of colors, you can count only on 216 colors to display properly on popular Macintosh and Windows Web browsers. That's because most browsers play it safe and assume that people have just the basic video support on their computers: 8-bit color depth, which permits 256 colors. Of those 256, Windows reserves 40 for its interface, leaving 216 for the browser to use. Understanding this, InDesign comes with a Web swatch library that has only the Web-safe colors.

The InDesign swatch library at right shows all Web-safe colors; compare that to the very partial (about 2 percent) listing of print-oriented colors shown in the swatches on the preceding page.

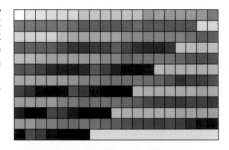

The examples below show how print-oriented colors are typically shifted when viewed in a Web browser.

Photo by Ken Marquis

Photograph in print

Photo by Ken Marquis

Photograph on the Web

Gradient in print

Gradient on the Web

Solid color in print

Solid color on the Web

Copying Colors from an Image

Even if you have an excellent sense of color, matching colors by eye can be difficult. Because you may want to use a color from an image in your document — as a text color or for lines or strokes — an accurate color matching tool is a necessity. Fortunately, InDesign has the Eyedropper tool to sample a color and add it to an object or to text.

Photo by Galen Gruman

The color-selection process is simple: Select the Eyedropper tool, then click on any colored object in your document. If another object is currently selected (via the Selection tool), that object will take on the clicked color. You can also Option+Shift+click or Alt+Shift+click an unselected object to apply the color to its background fill.

To add the color to your Swatches pane, select New Color Swatch from the Swatches pane's palette menu, then provide a name and choose Spot or Process from the Color Type menu, and click OK to save it.

After clicking a color with the Eyedropper tool, the Eyedropper tool changes to the Stroke Marker tool, which lets you change the color of text's stroke (outline) by highlighting the text with the Stroke Marker tool (click and drag over the text whose stroke you want to color). The Stroke Marker tool is shown at left.

Applying Color Tints

Adding color to an image, whether at full strength or as a lighter tint, can greatly change its character. The examples here show how you can apply color to an object to give your grayscale images a new look. To do more-complex colorizing, use an image editor like Adobe Photoshop or Corel Photo-Paint.

The original grayscale image is at upper left; the others all have a tint applied.

To change an image's foreground color (normally black), select the image with the Direct Selection tool and apply a color or tint swatch.

Note that you cannot change the background color (the white part) by applying a fill to the graphics frame — not even if your image has a transparent background.

Photo by Charlotte Walthert

Working with Gradients

Gradients (also called blends) add a sense of motion or depth to a background or image. An image editor or illustration program such as Photoshop, Photo-Paint, Illustrator, or CorelDraw gives you very fine control over gradients, letting you control their shape and pattern. InDesign approaches the ability of such programs, and in some cases surpasses them.

Two-color linear gradient

Even distribution, 0° angle

Even distribution, 30° angle

45% start, 0° angle

Even distribution, 90° angle

70% midpoint, –40° angle

Two-color radial gradient

Even distribution

Manual offset, 60% midpoint

45% start

20% midpoint

70% midpoint

Example gradients (at left), using various settings for the stop and start colors, as well as for the gradient midpoint and, for linear gradients, the angle. Below are examples of more-complex gradients. (Chapter 28 explains how to apply these settings.)

The Effects of Color Profiles

Like most professional design tools, InDesign uses color profiles to help ensure that your output will match as closely as possible the original image's colors (the capabilities and limits of your output device ultimately determine how close you can get). By applying color profiles and using InDesign's Rendering Intent color settings, you can change the output character of your images.

Photo by Galen Gruman

Compare the original image against the modified insets. The original uses the Generic CMYK color profile and is set with a Rendering Intent of Perceptual (Images), the default for photograph-like images.

In the top row, the insets all use the Generic CMYK profile but different Rendering Intent settings: from left to right, Saturation (Graphics), Relative Colorimetric, and Absolute Colorimetric.

The remainder of the inset images use the Rendering Intent setting of Perceptual (Images), but different profiles. In the second row, I applied the three Kodak SWOP Proofer CMYK profiles: from left to right, Coated, Uncoated, and Newspaper.

Finally, I applied the Color LW 12/600 PS profile (for an Apple color laser printer) in the third row and the 3M Color Matchprint Euro profile to the inset image in the final row.

Working with Traps

If you don't have your InDesign documents output to negatives or directly to plate and have them printed on a standard web offset press (SWOP), you don't need to worry about trapping. But if you do such professional output, trapping is an issue you should be aware of. InDesign lets you control trapping in some situations, based on what kind of output device you are using. These controls are global — affecting everything in the document — so if you want to set specific trapping settings for graphics, for example, you'll need to do so as part of creating the illustration in a program like Illustrator or CorelDraw. The one local control InDesign does offer is whether strokes and fills overprint or trap.

Photo by Galen Gruman

At right: The various trapping methods you can use in InDesign. Except for overprinting, each method is applied to every object in your document.

Knockout (no overlap of abutting colors)

Overprint

Centering (light color and dark color each move into each other)

Choke (dark color moves into light color)

Spread (light color moves into dark color)

InDesign lets you control on an object-by-object basis whether fills and strokes overprint or trap. In the images at left, I applied different settings. The text in the top image has the fill overprint and the stroke trap; the text in the middle image has the stroke overprint and the fill trap; the text in the bottom image has both traps (the default).

Working with Clipping Paths

InDesign can import clipping paths — invisible outlines — in images created in such programs as Photoshop. It can also create clipping paths from images placed in InDesign. However they are generated, the clipping paths become InDesign frame boundaries. Using clipping paths, you can create close-fitting text wraps or create masks in images through which other objects can appear.

Photo by Laura Antolovich

At top left is a picture imported with the clipping path ignored, while at top right is the same image with the path enabled. That let me put a gradient in the frame behind it to create a new background.

The set of bottom images is similar, except that in this case I created a clipping path that excluded the soccer ball so I could colorize it in InDesign by having a colored frame behind it.

InDesign can also create its own clipping paths by ignoring image areas that have less than a certain hue (see Chapter 25). This is less exact than in a program like Photoshop where you can specify the actual path, but it does work for simpler images.

Photo by Angela Burgess

Applying Colors

Applying colors, tints, and gradients to objects in InDesign is easy. Select the object, then click the Formatting Affects Text button or Formatting Affects Container button in the Swatches or Gradient pane as appropriate for what you want to apply the color to, then click the appropriate swatch.

Another way to apply colors, tints, and gradients is by selecting the object and using the Formatting Affects Text, Formatting Affects Content, Fill, or Stroke buttons in the Tools palette to determine what part of the object you want to color. You can use the Swatches or Gradients panes to select a swatch, or pick the last-used color and gradient from the Apply Color and Apply Gradient buttons on the Tools palette. Figure 8-12 shows the palette.

You can also apply colors and tints to gaps in strokes via the Stroke pane's palette options menu (select Show Options and select a gap color).

Figure 8-12: The Tools palette lets you choose what part of an object you want to color, as well as to apply the last-used color or gradient.

Summary

InDesign uses swatches to contain defined colors (including colors made up of other colors), tints, and gradient blends; the use of swatches lets you apply colors repeatedly with the assurance it's the same color each time, much as style sheets ensure consistent text formatting. Although you can also apply colors without using these swatches, doing so can cause output problems, especially when you're using color separations.

Key to defining colors is choosing the appropriate color model: spot or process. A spot color prints on its own plate, while a process color is separated into the four basic colors used in traditional color publishing. If you define too many colors as spot colors, you're likely to create an impossible-to-print or very-expensive-to-print document. InDesign lets you convert colors from spot to process and vice versa, so you can choose the right output options for each document. Similarly, it's best to create color images in the color model you intend to use for output: CMYK for traditional printing and RGB for on-screen display.

A powerful feature in InDesign is its ability to create gradient blends that can contain blends among multiple colors. No other layout program offers this level of control or flexibility on gradients, although image editors such as Photoshop go even further than InDesign does.

✦　　✦　　✦

Book Publishing

✦ ✦ ✦ ✦

In This Chapter

Managing multiple documents with books

Creating tables of contents and lists

Indexing documents and books

✦ ✦ ✦ ✦

When you're working on any type of longer document — a saddle-stitched booklet, a magazine, a perfect-bound textbook — you can easily spend more time on tracking project files, communicating with your workgroup, and manually creating tables of contents and indexes than you spend designing the publication. Longer projects such as these generally consist of multiple InDesign documents, which lets multiple users work on the project and creates smaller, more manageable documents. If you're working on this type of document, by yourself or in a workgroup, InDesign provides the Book feature for managing the document files, updating page numbers across documents, and ensuring consistency in the book.

For longer projects, InDesign also provides its Table of Contents feature, which lets you create and update automatically formatted tables of contents (TOCs). These TOCs are compiled from text formatted with specific paragraph style sheets (heads, subheads, and so on). If your publication needs an index, you can tag words throughout your text, then generate an automatically formatted index using the Index feature. The Table of Contents and Index features both work in single documents and for an entire book (and they both transfer to documents exported in PDF form).

Managing Multiple Documents with Books

In InDesign, a *book* is a special type of file that you create to track multiple documents for yourself or for a workgroup. A book file displays as a palette, and it lists each InDesign document — let's call them *chapters* to distinguish them from standalone documents — that you add to the book. Using the book palette, you can add, open and edit, rearrange, and print chapters of the book. Although the book feature is intended for workgroups — and indeed, multiple users can open the same book and access chapters — it also works well in a single-user environment. See the sidebar "The pros and cons of books" for more information.

Planning your book

If you decide that the book feature is appropriate and useful for a project, you'll want to do some planning before you even create a book. Use the following guidelines before you begin building your book in InDesign:

✦ **Organize your chapters in advance by deciding on the number, names, and order of the chapters.** You can make changes to a chapter's number, name, and order at any time, but figuring out these basics ahead of time will save you time in the long run.

✦ **Make decisions about the format of the book (style sheets, colors, pagination style, and so on) at the chapter level, beginning with the first chapter.**

✦ **Pay attention to formatting.** Formatting is important, because if your chapters use different color swatch names, style sheet names, and so on, synchronizing the formatting across the chapters will be difficult.

✦ **Use templates and style sheets to format the chapters uniformly.**

✦ **Decide where to store the book file itself (this must be a shared server for a workgroup); store the documents in this folder as well.** Set up the appropriate sharing through your operating system.

✦ **Make sure members of the workgroup have access to any templates, libraries, graphics, fonts, plug-ins, and so on necessary to work on the project.**

If you decide to use the book feature in a workgroup, be sure to review Chapter 36 for information about implementing standard preferences, templates, and more.

Creating and opening books

To create a new book, choose File ➪ New ➪ Book. The New Book dialog box, shown in Figure 9-1, lets you specify a location for the book and give it a name. If you're on a Mac and creating a book that may be used in Windows, you'll notice that InDesign automatically adds the .indb extension to the filename. Click OK to create and open the book.

To open an existing book, use the File ➪ Open command (⌘+O or Ctrl+O). The book will appear in its own pane in the palette (the palette has no title and will appear automatically if you open a book when no other books are open). If you're opening a book from a shared server, make sure to mount the server on your desktop first. You can also double-click a book's icon, which also shows the open book pane. To close a book pane, and any book panes that are in it, simply click its close box.

Multiple users on the same platform (Mac or PC) can open the same book palette at the same time. If another user makes changes to the book, those changes will show up in your copy of the book when you click on the palette.

The pros and cons of books

Although designed for workgroups, the implementation of the book feature in InDesign has some fatal flaws that may discourage you from using it that way. The problem is with how multiple users access book chapters:

✦ For a workgroup to access a book, the book itself must be stored on a shared server. Users can then open the book across the network and leave it open while they're working. To work on a document in the book, the user opens the document across the network as well. Not only can opening and saving the file be slow, but it leaves documents vulnerable to any instability in your network. (While you're working on the document, there is no local copy of it.)

✦ If multiple users are working on a book or its constituent documents, they might end up saving different versions, overwriting each other, since there is no built-in document-management system for multiuser access. However, InDesign will indicate in the book palette whether someone else has a document open, so you can at least monitor usage before saving changes.

Despite these drawbacks, the book feature does provide advantages in a workgroup situation that may outweigh any concerns you have. These include the abilities to:

✦ See who is working on each chapter and when.

✦ Update style sheets, colors, and TOC styles across documents for consistency.

✦ Update page numbers across multiple documents.

✦ Create a table of contents and an index for multiple documents. (In fact, using a book is the only way to generate a TOC and index for multiple documents.)

✦ Easily print all the chapters of a book with the same settings.

If you need some of the benefits of using a book (such as a table of contents for multiple documents), but you can't live with one of the drawbacks, you can start out with separate documents. Then, once the documents are in close-to-final form, you can combine them into a book on one computer and finish up the project in book form.

None of this is meant to discourage the single user from managing longer projects through the book feature. If you're producing a book by yourself, and it consists of multiple InDesign documents, by all means take advantage of the book feature. The only consideration is whether your output provider can handle the book file or will require you to combine the documents into a single document. (This may also be an issue if you're creating a PDF form of the document.)

Note   If you have multiple books open at the same time, each will appear in its own pane in the books palette.

Figure 9-1: To create a new book, choose
File ➪ New ➪ Book.

Adding chapters to books

New book panes are empty—you need to add your carefully prepared documents
to them. To do this, click the Add Document button, the + button on the bottom-
right of your book's pane (see Figure 9-2), or use the Add Document option in the
book pane's palette menu. Use the Add Chapter dialog box to locate and select the
first chapter you want to add. Click the Add button to make this the first chapter in
the book. Repeat this process to add to the book all the chapters you have ready
(you can also add more later).

Working with style sources

The first chapter you add to the book is, by default, the style source, as indicated
by the icon to the left of its filename. If the chapters of your book don't share common formatting, you don't need to worry about this feature. But with a book, that's
rarely the case—usually you want the text formatting, colors, and so on to remain
the same. The style source in an InDesign book defines the style sheets and
swatches that are common to all the chapters in the book. When you use the
Synchronize Styles and Swatches features, discussed in the "Synchronizing chapter
formatting section" later in this chapter, InDesign makes sure that the common
style sheets and swatches in each chapter in the book match those in the style
source.

If you decide to make a different chapter the style source, all you need to do is click
in the column to the left of that chapter's filename. This moves the icon indicating
the style source to that chapter (see Figure 9-2).

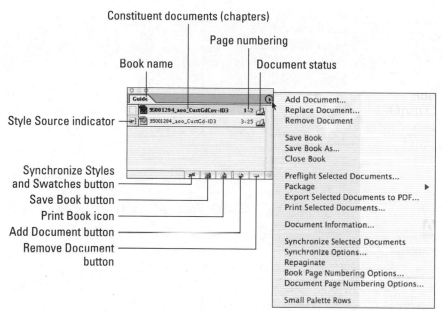

Figure 9-2: A book pane and its palette menu. The icon to the left of a chapter's filename indicates the style source. The status column shows which chapters are open on your computer, which are available to be opened, and which are missing (both are open here).

Opening and editing chapters

To work on a chapter in a book, first open the book. Then double-click the chapter name in the book pane. The chapter will open in InDesign just like any other InDesign document opens. Note that to open a chapter, it must be available, as discussed in the next section. When you're finished editing a chapter, save and close it as usual. (Any open chapter documents will remain open in InDesign even if you close the books palette.)

Note   If you need to take a chapter home and work on it, you can edit a chapter outside the book. To do this, first move the chapter's file to a different folder so the chapter displays as Missing in the book pane. This will keep other users from editing it while you have it. When you finish editing the file, place the edited file back in its original folder. The book pane will show this chapter as Modified.

Understanding book pane status reports

If you're using the book palette in a workgroup, it provides helpful status reports about each chapter, as shown in Figure 9-3. The statuses include

Figure 9-3: The status icons to the right of the filename. From top to bottom: Open, Available, Missing, Modified, and In Use.

✦ **Available:** The chapter can be opened, edited, or printed. Only one user at a time can open a chapter.

✦ **Open:** You have the chapter open and can edit it or print it. Nobody else can open the chapter at this time.

✦ **In Use:** Another user has the chapter open. In this case, you cannot edit or open the chapter.

✦ **Modified:** The chapter has been changed since the last time you opened the book palette. Simply click on the book pane to update it.

✦ **Missing:** The chapter's file has been moved since it was added to the book. Double-click the chapter name to open a Find File dialog box and locate it.

Synchronizing chapter formatting

To help you make sure that common formatting remains consistent across the document, the book pane provides a Synchronize Styles and Swatches button. Before you use the Synchronize Styles and Swatches button, be sure you're satisfied with the styles in the style source and that all chapters are available for editing. Then select the chapters you want to synchronize and click the Synchronize Styles and Swatches button. (You can also choose Synchronize Selected Documents from the palette menu.) InDesign will then:

✦ Compare the style sheets (character, paragraph, and TOC), swatches (color, tint, and gradient), and trap styles in the style source to those in each chapter.

✦ If anything is different, the information in each chapter will be updated to match the style source. This means that if someone changed the typeface in a style sheet in a chapter, it would revert to the typeface specified in the style source.

✦ If anything is missing from a chapter — for example, if you've just added a swatch to the style source — that information is added to each chapter.

If you click on Synchronize Styles and Swatches, each chapter will have the same basic set of style sheets, swatches, and trap styles as the style source. I say "basic set" because you can still add more of these specifications to each chapter. When using Synchronize Styles and Swatches, you need to keep in mind the following:

✦ Synchronize Styles and Swatches will *not* move additional style sheets, swatches, and trap styles with different names in chapters. Therefore, you can implement different formatting needs in a chapter by creating an additional style sheet in that chapter.

✦ Synchronize Styles and Swatches *cannot* solve any problems related to using the template or style sheets incorrectly, or change any local formatting applied to text (such as font changes or italics) or local changes to master page items.

Clearly, Synchronize Styles and Swatches is no cure-all for the renegade formatting that often occurs when multiple users work on the same project. Be sure everyone knows what the standards are for the design, how to implement the standards properly, and how to make local changes appropriately.

You can specify what is to be synchronized via the Synchronize Options option in a book pane's palette menu. You can choose any combination of TOC Styles, Character Styles, Paragraph Styles, Trap Styles, and Swatches.

Printing chapters and books

If you want to print multiple chapters in the book with the same settings, you can print through the book pane. You can print any chapters with the status of Available or Open. Here's how:

1. **To print the entire book, make sure no chapters are selected. To print a continuous range of chapters, Shift+click them. To print noncontinuous chapters, ⌘+click or Ctrl+click the chapters to select them.**

2. **Click the Print Book icon or choose Print Book or Print Selected Documents in the book pane's palette menu (the option will depend on whether chapters are selected in the book pane).**

   The standard InDesign Print dialog box opens. Note that the option to choose all pages or a range of pages is grayed out — you must print all chapters in the selected chapters.

3. **Make any adjustments in the Print dialog box.**

4. **Click Print to print the chapters.**

A related feature is the ability to output a book to PDF, using the Export Book to PDF or Export Selected Documents to PDF menu items in the palette menu. They work like their equivalent Print menus.

For more on printing and output settings, see Chapters 31 and 32.

Handling chapters with sections

When working with books, you have two choices for numbering pages: You can let the book palette number pages consecutively from one chapter to the next. Or you can add sections of page numbers, which carry through the book until you start a new section. In long documents, section page numbering is common because it lets you have page numbering such as 2.1–2.14 in, say, Chapter 2. (Plus, creating a section start is the only way to start a document on a left-facing page, which is often necessary in magazines.)

Numbering pages consecutively

If the chapters you add to a book have no sections in them, you end up with consecutive page numbering: The first page number of each chapter follows the last page number of the previous chapter (so if one chapter ends on page 16, the next chapter starts on page 17). If you open the Section dialog box (choose Numbering & Section Options in the Pages pane's palette menu), you'll see that Automatic Page Numbering is selected by default.

The consecutive page numbering works as follows:

✦ Whenever you add a chapter with no sections to a book, InDesign numbers pages consecutively throughout the book.

✦ As you add and delete pages from chapters, the page numbers are also updated.

✦ You can force repagination by choosing Repaginate from the book pane's palette menu.

✦ In facing-page documents, chapters always start on a right-facing page with an odd page number (even if the previous chapter ends on a right-facing page). In this case, InDesign "skips" the even page number (so one chapter might end on page 15 and the next chapter will start on page 17, leaving you to add a blank page 16 to the previous chapter for proper pagination).

Numbering pages with sections

If any chapters you add to books already contain sections of page numbers (implemented through the Section dialog box, which you access via the Numbering & Section Options menu option in the Pages pane's palette menu), the section page numbering overrides the book's consecutive page numbering. The section page numbering carries through chapters of the book until InDesign encounters a new section start. So if one chapter ends on page *iv,* the next page starts on page *v* unless you start a new section. Note that it's fairly typical in magazines to assign the page number in each article's document file, since there are usually ads between articles that are inserted later in the printing process.

 Cross-Reference   Using the options in the Section dialog box is covered in Chapter 5.

Creating Tables of Contents

Long documents such as books and catalogs lend themselves to tables of contents to give the reader a summary of the content and the locations for each section. In InDesign, a table of contents is simply a list of paragraphs that are formatted with the same style sheets. After you've created a book (or even a single document), InDesign can build a table of contents by scanning the chapters for the paragraph style sheets you specify. For example, if you create a book, you might have paragraph style sheets named Chapter Title, Section, and Subsection that you apply to chapter titles, chapter sections, and chapter subsections. Using the Table of Contents feature, InDesign can generate a table of contents that has all three levels.

Note   If you want to use the Table of Contents feature, you have to use style sheets. Not only do style sheets guarantee consistent formatting, but they tell InDesign what text you want to include in your table of contents (TOC). The other thing to keep in mind for TOCs: They are linear, either listing from top to bottom the text in the order it appears in a document or in alphabetical order.

Cross-Reference   Tables of contents rely on paragraph style sheets. For more on style sheets, see Chapters 17 and 18.

Planning a TOC

Before you start whipping up a TOC in InDesign, decide what the content of your TOC will be: All the text tagged with Head and Subhead paragraph style sheets? (Be sure style sheets are applied consistently to generate an accurate TOC, so if you're not sure about that, look through the documents or chapters.)

Creating other lists

Although InDesign calls its list-generation feature the Table of Contents feature, you can use it for other kinds of lists. Basically, anything that is tagged with a paragraph style can be used to create a list. For example, if your captions all have titles that use their own paragraph style, you can generate a list of figures by creating a TOC style that includes just, say, the Caption Title paragraph style. An InDesign document can have more than one "TOC," so you can have multiple lists in your document.

What InDesign cannot do is create a list based on *character* style sheets, so you can't create a list based on, say, names in a gossip column where the names use a character style sheet to make them bold and perhaps change font as well. Nor could you create a list based on caption titles that are part of a paragraph also containing the caption (you'd have a Caption Title character style to format the title within the complete paragraph) — and if you chose the Caption paragraph style to create a figures list in such a situation, your list would include the complete text of the captions as well as the embedded title.

You'll also need to create paragraph style sheets for the TOC itself—it's easy to forget that, because TOCs usually have several levels themselves (a title, as well as formatting specific to each level of listing), and each level should usually have its own paragraph style. You'll likely also need some character styles for your TOC—for example, you might want the page numbers to be bold, in which case you'd need a character style that applies boldface to them.

Tip   After you decide what will be in your TOC, use a little bit of dummy text to format a sample TOC *before* you create the style sheets to be used to format the TOC itself. Your formatting should include any indents for different levels in your list and it should include tabs and fill characters as necessary. When you're satisfied with the formatting of your sample TOC, create the TOC paragraph and character style sheets from it. Be sure to use clear names such as TOC-Level 1.

QuarkXPress User   InDesign can generate TOCs only based on paragraph style sheets, not on character style sheets. This means you can't create other kinds of lists, such as a list of companies in a magazine article or research report, based on the use of character style sheets. InDesign doesn't have a flexible Lists feature as QuarkXPress does, just the Table of Contents feature that is essentially a subset of QuarkXPress's Lists feature. However, as described in the "Creating other lists" sidebar, you can use the InDesign Table of Contents feature to create some lists in addition to TOCs.

Defining a TOC

InDesign uses TOC styles to manage the formatting of TOCs. A TOC style defines the text you want in a table of contents, what order it appears in, how page numbers are added, and how the various TOC elements are formatted. To create a TOC style, you choose the Layout ➪ Table of Contents Styles, which opens the dialog box shown in Figure 9-4.

Figure 9-4: The Table of Contents Styles dialog box.

In the Table of Contents Styles dialog box, choose New to create a new TOC style. You can also edit an existing style via the Edit button, delete one via the Delete button, and import one from another InDesign document via the Load button.

Here's how to create a TOC style after clicking the New button and getting the dialog box shown in Figure 9-5:

1. **Enter a name for the TOC style in the TOC Style field.**

   The default is TOC Style 1.

2. **In the Title field, enter a heading for the TOC.**

   This is the actual text that will appear in your table of contents.

Figure 9-5: The New Table of Contents Style dialog box.

3. **Use the Style pop-up menu to its right to choose the paragraph style that this title will have.**

   If you don't want a title, leave the Title field blank, but note that you'll still get an empty paragraph at the top of your TOC for this title. You can always delete that paragraph.

4. **In the Styles in Table of Contents section of the dialog box, click a paragraph style from the Other Styles list at right that you want to appear in your TOC.**

   For example, you might click Chapter Title in a book. Click <<Add to add it to the Include Paragraph Styles list at left. (Click Remove>> to remove any paragraph styles you don't want to be used in the TOC generation.)

5. **Now choose the formatting for the TOC entries that come from the selected paragraph style, using the Style section of the dialog box.**

   Here's where you apply the formatting to the text that appears in the TOC:

   - Use the Entry Style pop-up menu to select the paragraph style for the current TOC level.

   - Use the Page Number pop-up menu to determine how page numbers are handled: After Entry, Before Entry, and No Page Number (you might use this last option for alphabetically arranged categories in a catalog, where you want to list page numbers only for product classes and specific products). If you want the page numbers to have a character style applied, choose that style from the Style pop-up menu to the right of the Page Number pop-up menu. Use the Between Entry and Number field and pop-up menu to choose what appears between the TOC text and the page number. You can enter any characters you want, as well as have multiple characters; use the pop-up menu to select special characters such as bullets and tabs. In most cases, you would select a tab; the paragraph style selected earlier for the TOC entry would include leader information, such as having a series of periods between the text and the number. You can also apply a character style to the characters between the text and the page numbers via the Style pop-up menu at right.

   - If you want the entries at this level to be sorted alphabetically, such as for a list of companies in a magazine article, check the Sort Entries in Alphabetical Order check box.

   - If you want to change the level of the current TOC entry, use the Level pop-up menu. Note that you do not have to manually rearrange the order of items in the Include Paragraph Styles list by dragging them if you change the level of entries — InDesign will correctly sort them when it creates the TOC, even if the levels seem out of order in the Include Paragraph Styles list.

   - Choose the appropriate options from the Options section of the dialog box. Check Create PDF Bookmarks if you're exporting the document to PDF format and want the PDF file to have *bookmarks* (which are essentially a clickable set of TOC links). Check Run-in if you want all entries at the same level to be in one paragraph; this is not common for TOCs but is used in indexes and lists of figures. Check Replace Existing Table of Contents if you want InDesign to automatically replace an existing TOC if the TOC style is changed. Check Include Text on Hidden Layers if you want text on hidden layers to be included in the TOC. Finally, check Include Book Documents if you have a book open and want InDesign to generate a TOC based on all chapters in that book.

6. **Continue this process for each paragraph style whose text should be in the TOC, such as Section and Subsection in a book.**

Note that the order in which you add these styles determines the initial levels: The first paragraph style added is level 1, the second is level 2, and so on. But you can change the order by changing the Level setting, as described earlier.

QuarkXPress User

The level of formatting you can achieve over TOC entries in InDesign is greater than in QuarkXPress.

After you've defined a TOC style, you can go to the Edit TOC Style Sheet dialog box — it's identical to the New TOC style dialog box — and make any changes. Just choose Layout ⇨ Table of Contents Styles, select the TOC style to edit, and click Edit.

Generating a TOC

With a TOC style in place and your document properly formatted with the paragraph styles that the TOC style will look for when generating a TOC, you're ready to have InDesign create the actual TOC for you. But before you do this, make sure you've saved space in the document for the TOC. This could consist of a single text frame or a series of linked text frames, or simply an empty page or set of pages (depending on how long your TOC will be). When you're creating a table of contents for a book, it might be useful to flow the table of contents into its own chapter.

Tip

You might need to generate a TOC just to see how long it really is, then make the necessary space available in your document. It's imperative that you do this before generating a final TOC, because if you have to add or delete pages based on the TOC length, the TOC will have the old page numbers, not the current ones. If you do need to update page numbering after flowing a TOC, simply rebuild the TOC by selecting the text frame holding the TOC and then choosing Layout ⇨ Update Table of Contents.

To generate a TOC, choose Layout ⇨ Table of Contents. You'll get a dialog box that is identical to the New Table of Contents Style dialog box shown in Figure 9-5. If desired, you can make changes to the TOC style settings (if you want to save those changes for future TOCs generated by the TOC style, be sure to click the Save Style button). Then click OK to have InDesign generate the TOC. You may also get a dialog box asking if you want to include items in *overset text* (text that didn't fit in your document after you placed it); answer Yes or No as appropriate. It may take a minute or two for the program to generate the TOC.

If you've selected a text frame (with or without text in it), InDesign will place the TOC text in it. If no text frame is selected, InDesign will display the familiar text-insertion icon (the paragraph pointer) that it displays when you place a text file—either click a text frame to insert the TOC text in that frame or click on your document to have InDesign create a text frame in which to flow the TOC text.

Figure 9-6 shows a TOC generated by InDesign, in this case for a product catalog. Note how the section entries don't display page numbers—I chose No Page Numbers for this first level of TOC entry in my TOC style. (Figure 9-5 shows some of the body text for this document, so you can see some of the text that the TOC was generated from.)

Tip   To replace an existing TOC with an updated version, you can skip the Table of Contents dialog box altogether. Just select the current TOC's text frame and choose Layout ⇨ Update Table of Contents.

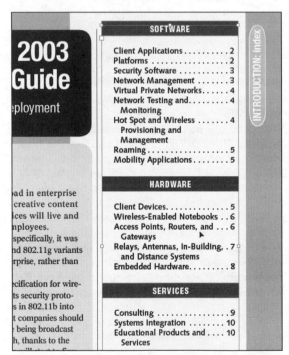

Figure 9-6: A sample TOC generated by InDesign.

Indexing Documents and Books

If you've ever been unable to find information in a book that you knew was there, you'll appreciate how important a good index can be. Short, simple documents can get by fine without indexes. But long books almost always need indexes to help the reader locate specific information. Indexing used to be a laborious process, involving lots of index cards. InDesign makes indexing much easier, while still relying on you to make key decisions about how the index will be formatted. The following sections show you how to do your part.

Cross-Reference After reading this chapter, you may find that you need a more sophisticated indexing tool than InDesign provides. Check out Sonar Bookends InDex Pro by Virginia Systems, to which I have a link on the companion Web site (`www.INDDcentral.com`). In addition, the company offers Sonar Bookends InXref for creating cross-references in text that update automatically and Sonar Bookends InFnote for creating footnotes in InDesign documents.

Choosing an indexing style

Your approach to developing an index depends on the indexing style you want to use. Large publishers usually have their own house style guides for indexes. If you don't have a style guide for indexes, I recommend that you read through the indexing guidelines in *The Chicago Manual of Style*. Another option is to use an index you like as a model and then take the steps necessary in InDesign to achieve that index style. Before you begin indexing your document, ask yourself the following questions:

✦ Do you want to capitalize all levels of all entries, or do you just want initial caps?

✦ Should headings appear in boldface?

✦ What type of punctuation will you use in your index?

✦ Will you capitalize secondary entries in the index?

✦ Should the index be nested or run-in style (see the sidebar "Nested or run-in index?")?

Once you make these decisions, it's a good idea to make a small dummy of your index. From the dummy, create a master page for index pages, paragraph style sheets for letter headings (A, B, C, and so on in the index), paragraph style sheets for each level of the index (including indents as appropriate), and character style sheets for any special formatting you want on page numbers or cross-reference text. InDesign doesn't do any of this for you — if you don't set up style sheets for your index, your multilevel index will simply look linear when it's built.

Using the Index pane

When a chapter or document is ready to be indexed, open the Index pane (Window ➪ Type & Tables ➪ Index, or Shift+F8). You use this pane to add words to the index in up to four indent levels, edit or delete index entries, or create cross-references. The Index pane appears in Figure 9-7.

Figure 9-7: The Index pane.

Understanding Reference and Topic modes

The Index pane has two modes, indicated by the radio buttons at the top: Reference and Topic. Reference mode is the mode you should be in when adding and editing entries from selected text. If you're creating an index in a book, be sure to click the Book check box as well in the Index pane.

The Topic mode is meant to give you a clean environment in which to enter the topic names and levels that you want your index to have. Then, when an indexer adds an index entry, she can use the topics that appear in the bottom of the New Page Reference and double-click the topic to use that topic definition rather than whatever she might enter herself in the dialog box. You don't have to use Topic mode if you don't want to — all index entries create *topics* (InDesign-speak for the entry text). Although a well-intentioned feature meant to help standardize index entries, the Topic mode's use is not intuitive, and most indexers will simply ignore it, adding entries manually from selected text or by typing phrases into the Index pane when in Reference mode.

Note that only topics have actual references (where text occurs on actual pages, not in the pasteboard, on a master page, or in overset text) or cross-references. So don't worry about unused topic text appearing in your index.

Entering index items

To add entries to your index, choose New Page Reference from the Index pane's palette menu to get the dialog box shown in Figure 9-8. Here's how the controls work:

✦ If you selected text first in your document, the text is entered automatically into Topic Level 1. Otherwise, type in the text that you want to add to the index. The text will be added to the Topic list and, if it is in the document, also to the list of index entries.

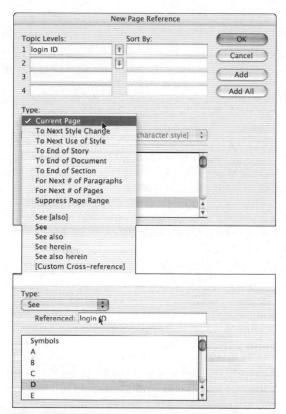

Figure 9-8: The New Page Reference dialog box. The bottom portion changes if you select one of the cross-reference options in the Type pop-up menu, as shown in the dialog box portion at the bottom of the figure.

✦ You can enter text that controls how the entry is sorted in the Sort By column. For example, if the highlighted text is *The Zango Group,* but you wanted it sorted as if it were *Zango Group, The* (so it appears with the *Z* entries in the index), enter *Zango Group, The* in the Sorted By column. Similarly, you might have the movie title *2001: A Space Odyssey* sorted as *Two Thousand and One: A Space Odyssey* so the listing appears properly with the *T* entries in the index.

✦ More complex indexes will take advantage of the four possible entry levels. You may want an index entry to appear under a higher-level topic. For example, you may want *2001: A Space Odyssey* to appear in the index under *Classic Science Fiction,* in which case you would enter *Classic Science Fiction* in the Topic Level 1 field and *2001: A Space Odyssey* in the Topic Level 2 field.

✦ Use the Type pop-up menu to determine the page entries for the index entry. The pop-up menu has two basic sections.

- One section covers the entry's range — typically, you just want the current page number the text appears on, but in some cases, you might want to indicate that a topic spans a number of pages, a document section, all text with a specific style, or one of the other options. For example, if you have a section about France in a world-history book, you might want the main entry to indicate the whole section — such as *France, 167-203,* while leaving references in other sections (such as references in a section on Germany) to be for just the page it appears on. If you choose For Next # of Pages or For Next # of Paragraphs, the dialog box will display the Number field for you to enter how many paragraphs or pages you want the index entry's range to span. Note that you can apply a character style to the page number generated in the index by checking Number Style Override and choosing a character style in the pop-up menu to its right.

- The other section covers cross-references, letting you choose from several types. The dialog box changes slightly, as shown in Figure 9-8, if you choose a cross-reference entry. It adds the Reference text field for you to enter the text that the index will contain after the cross-reference. For example, in the figure, the entry *secure login* will display in the index as *Secure login: See login ID.* You can create your own custom cross-references by choosing [Custom Cross-reference]; InDesign will display the Custom text field and pop-up menu in which you enter (or select from previously entered) text that you want InDesign to use. For example, you might want the cross-reference to say *Go to* rather than one of the defaults like *See.*

Note Use *See* to point readers to the appropriate index entry; use *See Also* to point the readers to additional useful information elsewhere in the index; use *See Herein* to point readers to a subentry for this index entry; and use *See Also Herein* to point readers to additional useful information in a subentry to this index entry.

✦ To add text within the range specified, click Add. (If the text entered is not in the specified range, the text will be added to the Topic list, but no index entry will appear for the text.) To add all occurrences of the text in the document (or book), click Add All.

✦ To change previously defined index entries, choose Page Reference Options in the Index pane's palette menu.

Note At the bottom of the New Page Reference dialog box is a list of letters as well as the entry Symbols. You can scroll through this list of headings to see what is already in the index under each letter. Although you might think clicking a letter would force the current index entry to appear in that letter's section of the index, it does not.

Nested or run-in index?

There is no right way to index, but common sense should be a guide. Determine which index format you use by the number of levels in the index's hierarchy. If the index has only two levels, a run-in format works well, but an index with three or more levels requires a nested format for the sake of clarity.

Nested indexes look like this:

Kitchen Hardware
　　Buying, 191
　　Cost estimates, 242–248
　　Design guidelines 92–94, 96, 99–101
　　Hiring contractors, 275–284
　　Installation, 180–195
　　Sizing, 91–99
　　Standards, 24–28, 98, 133
　　Tools, 199–203, 224, 282–283

Run-in indexes look like this:

Kitchen Hardware: Buying, 191; Cost estimates, 242–248; Design guidelines 92–94, 96, 99–101; Hiring contractors, 275–284; Installation, 180–195; Sizing, 91–99; Standards, 24–28, 98, 133; Tools, 199–203, 224, 282–283

Although InDesign doesn't force you to make this decision until you actually build the index, you really need to make it before you get started. If you tag words for a four-level nested index, but then build a run-in index, your index will have some logic problems.

Working with the index

The Index pane's palette menu has several options useful in fine-tuning and generating the index:

✦ **Duplicate Topic** lets you duplicate a topic entry so you use the settings in one entry without having to reselect them all.

✦ **Delete Topic** removes a topic (and any associated entries) from the index.

✦ **Import Topics** lets you import topic lists from other InDesign documents.

✦ **Go to Selected Marker** causes InDesign to jump to the text that contains the selected index entry in the Index pane. This is a handy way of seeing if the reference in the text truly merits being listed in the index.

✦ **Topic Options** lets you edit the Level and Sort By settings for topic entries; these affect all index entries that use them.

✦ **Capitalize** lets you standardize the capitalization of topic entries — you can choose Selected Topic, Selected Topic and All Subtopics, All Level 1 Topics, and All Topics.

✦ **Update Preview** updates the index entries in the Index pane to reflect page-number changes, new occurrences of index text occurrences, and deleted occurrences of indexed text. It does not change the actual index.

✦ **Generate Index** creates the actual index in your document, via the dialog box shown in Figure 9-9. Here, you specify the title for the Index, the paragraph style sheet for that title, whether a selected index is replaced with the new one, whether an entire book is indexed, whether layers on hidden layers are indexed, whether the index is nested or run-in (see the sidebar "Nested or run-in index?"), whether empty index headings and sections are included, what paragraph styles are applied to each level of index entry and what character styles are applied to different portions of index entries, and finally the characters used as separators within index entries. (Click the More Options button to see the nested/run-in and later options.) After you generate an index, you will get the standard InDesign text-insertion pointer (the paragraph symbol); click an existing text frame into which you want to flow the index, or click anywhere in a document to have InDesign create the text frame for you and flow the index text into it.

✦ **Find** lets you find text within the entries and topics in the Index pane — it adds a Find field and ↓ (Search Forward) and ↑ (Search Backward) buttons to the Index pane.

Figure 9-9: The Generate Index dialog box, with all options displayed.

✦ **Show Unused Topics** highlights topics for which there are no index entries, so you can easily delete them.

Tip

Each time you edit text in a document or book chapter, it's a good idea to rebuild the index so the page numbers in it are updated. There is no dynamic link between a flowed and formatted index and the index markers in text.

QuarkXPress User

The InDesign index features are similar to those in QuarkXPress, though the InDesign Index pane and QuarkXPress Index palette are organized differently. (Furthermore, InDesign puts all its controls in the Index pane; there are no preferences to set in the Preferences dialog box as there are in QuarkXPress.)

Among the differences in functionality: QuarkXPress lets you automatically reverse the text in the Text field as you add it to the index. (For example, you can change *Classic Science Fiction* to *Science Fiction, Classic.*) InDesign does not have this feature, nor does it have a shortcut command for quick index-entry additions as QuarkXPress does.

But InDesign has the ability to generate custom cross-reference text and to specify the capitalization for topics. InDesign can also show index entries for all chapters in a book, not just for the current chapter. (Although QuarkXPress can index an entire book, its Index palette can only show entries for the current chapter, which may lead to different index formatting and word choices from chapter to chapter.) InDesign also has more formatting options for index-entry text elements and separators.

Incorporating indexing into a workflow

If you're working on a document by yourself, or you're creating a fairly simple index in a workgroup, you can pretty much index as you go. Or you can plan some time at the end of the editorial cycle to go through a document or chapters to index them. But if your publication requires professional indexing — as would be the case for the multilevel index of a long book such as this one — deciding when to send your original InDesign files out for indexing is difficult. You might do it one chapter at a time, right after editorial approval and right before the file goes to production. Or you might send each chapter out for indexing before the last round of edits. What you can't do is continue working on one copy of your InDesign documents while another copy is being indexed — there is no way to move the index tags to another file.

On a tight schedule, you may be tempted to move your InDesign documents into production while another copy of your files is indexed. You then generate the index, send that file to production, then send the whole thing to print. The index is trapped in InDesign documents that aren't final — unfortunate, because the next time you edit the document, you would like to have the index tags in it. If you have to work this way, you'll need to decide whether to reindex the publication or redo the production work.

Summary

The book, TOC, and indexing features of InDesign can significantly streamline longer projects, especially those consisting of multiple documents. Although the book feature can be used in a workgroup, it's also ideal for a single user to combine multiple documents into a single publication. In fact, the only way to create a table of contents (or other list) or an index for multiple documents is to combine the documents into a book.

The TOC feature makes it easy to generate tables of contents, and it can also be used for some other kinds of lists, as long as the source text is tagged with consistent paragraph styles. The indexing feature, on the other hand, can only be considered easy by people with knowledge of the indexing process. Although most users can make use of the simpler features — such as adding a First Level entry that consists of text highlighted in the document — the more complicated your index, the more you may need a professional indexer. If you do need a professional, be sure your schedule allows time for the indexer to take possession of your InDesign files.

✦   ✦   ✦

Object Fundamentals

Chapter 10
Adding Text Frames,
Picture Frames,
and Lines

Chapter 11
Manipulating Lines
and Frames

Chapter 12
Orchestrating
Objects

Chapter 13
Timesaving
Techniques

The basic objects in InDesign are frames and lines. With these building blocks, you construct almost all the components in a layout — from the frame containers that hold text and pictures to original artwork you create in InDesign. The chapters in this part explain how the frame and line tools work, so you can create and manipulate layout objects.

First, Chapter 10 explains how to create frames and lines using the various shapes available in InDesign, from rectangles to curved lines. This chapter also explains how to convert a frame into one that can contain text or pictures, even if it wasn't designed to in the first place.

Once you've created frames and lines, you'll need to modify and embellish them. Chapter 11 explains how to reshape, resize, color, rotate, shear (skew), and do other manipulations to your frames and lines. This chapter gives you the knowledge you need to creatively apply and modify objects.

With your frames created to your liking, you'll find that you'll want to act on them even further, using InDesign's orchestration tools. For example, you may want to change the position of an object relative to another, to create a layered effect or have something appear on top of something else. You'll also want to group objects, so you can work on them all at once, such as moving a group all at once to ensure all objects in the group retain their positions relative to each other. Finally, you'll want to take advantage of InDesign's lock feature, which prevents you or someone else working on your document from inadvertently moving, adjusting, or deleting specific objects. Chapter 12 shows you how to do all this.

As you get more proficient in creating and modifying objects, you'll find yourself copying existing objects to reuse previous work. InDesign's step-and-repeat and other copy tools will help you do that, whether it's repeating an object within a page or reusing it in another document. Also, as you work with multiple objects, you'll find InDesign's alignment tools to be very handy to let you position both individual objects and groups of objects easily and accurately. Chapter 13 shows you how to copy and precisely position objects.

Adding Text Frames, Picture Frames, and Lines

In This Chapter

Knowing how and
when to create
frames for text and
pictures

Creating text frames

Creating graphics
frames

Modifying a frame's
shape

Drawing straight lines

When you create a new InDesign document, you make
several important decisions — including the page
size, number of columns, and gutter width — that determine
the basic structure of your publication. After you click OK in
the New Document dialog box (File ➪ New, or ⌘+N or Ctrl+N),
you're greeted with a blank first page. Much like an artist con-
fronting an empty canvas, it's now time for you to add the
text, pictures, and graphic elements (shapes and lines) that
will make up the final piece.

InDesign uses *objects* as the building blocks you manipulate to
create finished pages. An object is a container that can (but
doesn't have to) hold text or graphics, as well as attributes
such as color, strokes, and gradients; when an object contains
an imported graphic or text; if an object was created as a
placeholder for a graphic or text, it's referred to as a *frame*. A
frame looks and behaves much the same as an object but has
some additional properties:

   ✦ If you change the size or shape of a frame that contains
     text, you affect the flow of text in the frame and in any
     subsequent frames of a multiframe story.

   ✦ If you change the size or shape of a frame that contains
     an imported graphic, you also change the portion of the
     graphic that's visible.

Designing pages in InDesign is largely a matter of creating and
modifying frames and modifying the text and graphics the
frames contain. If, for example, you're creating a simple, one-
page publication such as a business card, an advertisement,

or a poster, you'll likely add several text frames to the page; each text frame will hold a different piece of textual information. In the case of a business card, text frames would contain the company name, the name and title of the cardholder, the company address and phone numbers, and so on. If you want to include pictures or computer-generated illustrations in your piece—maybe you want to add an EPS version of a corporate logo to your business card or a scanned image to an ad—you must also add graphics frames. A graphics frame serves as the cropping shape for the image within.

In this chapter, I show you how to create and modify basic text frames, graphics frames, and straight lines. After you create a text frame, you can enter text directly into it or you can place a text file from a word processing program. (For information about importing, formatting, and flowing text through a document, see Part IV.) After you create a graphics frame, you can import a graphic into it and then crop, scale, or apply other effects to the graphic. (For more information about importing and modifying graphics, see Part V.)

New Feature

InDesign adds the Control palette in version CS, taken from PageMaker (which took it from QuarkXPress). It provides the basic controls for objects all in one place. Chapter 11 covers this versatile palette in more depth, though you can get a glimpse of it in several figures in this chapter.

Cross-Reference

This chapter focuses on creating simple frames and straight lines. You can also create complex shapes and convert them to frames for holding text and pictures. For more information about using InDesign's Pen tool to create freeform shapes and curved lines, see Part V.

Creating a Text Frame

All the text blocks in an InDesign document are contained in text frames. Unlike a word processing program, which doesn't let you do anything but enter text, InDesign requires you to create a text frame before you can add text to a page using the keyboard. If you want to import the text from a word processing file onto a page, you don't have to create a text frame before you import. After you create a new text frame, you can enter and format text, move or resize the frame, and add graphic effects to the frame edge and the frame background.

Cross-Reference

For information about importing text, see Chapters 14 and 15.

The Tools palette contains several tools for creating both shapes and graphics frames, and because any shape or graphics frame can be converted into a text frame, you can use any of these tools to create a container that you intend to fill with text. However, in most cases, your text will be contained within simple, rectangular text frames, and the quickest and easiest way to create such a frame is with the Type tool (it's the tool with a big T on it).

Tip

If you want to place a particular piece of text on every page in a multipage publication (for example, the title of a book or the name of a magazine), you should place the text frame on a master page.

Cross-Reference

For more information about placing text frames on master pages, see Chapter 7.

Here's how to create a text frame:

1. **Select the Type tool by clicking on it or by pressing T.**

2. **Move the I-beam pointer anywhere within the currently displayed page or on the pasteboard.**

3. **Click and hold the mouse button, and while holding down the mouse button, drag in any direction.**

   As you drag, a crosshair pointer is displayed in the corner opposite your starting point, and a blue rectangle indicates the boundary of the frame, as shown in Figure 10-1. You can look at the width and height values displayed in the Control palette or the Transform pane as you drag to help you get the size you want. Holding down the Shift key as you drag creates a square.

4. **When the frame is the size and shape you want, release the mouse button.**

   The flashing cursor is displayed in the finished frame, indicating that you can enter new text via the keyboard. Don't worry too much about being precise when you create a text frame: You can always go back later and fine-tune its size and position.

Tip

When you create a text frame with the Type tool, you can align the frame edge with a guideline by clicking within the number of pixels specified in the Snap to Zone in the Guides & Pasteboard pane of the Preferences dialog box (File ➪ Preferences on the Mac or Edit ➪ Preferences in Windows, or ⌘+K or Ctrl+K).

At this point, you can begin typing, or you can click and drag elsewhere on the page or pasteboard to create another text frame. To add text to the frame, you can also:

✦ Choose File ➪ Place to import a word processing file. (If no text frame is selected, InDesign will create a text frame for you.)

✦ Paste in text that you've copied from another InDesign document or from a document created with another program.

Note

If you paste text that's been copied from another program, you'll lose any formatting applied to the text. If you paste text copied from within InDesign, formatting is retained, unless you deselect the Preserve Text Attributes When Pasting check box in the General pane of the Preferences dialog box — a new option in InDesign CS.

✦ Drag and drop text highlighted from text from another document.

Figure 10-1: Creating a text frame with the Type tool is a simple matter of clicking and dragging until the rectangle that's displayed as you drag is approximately the size and shape of the intended text block.

Tip   There are a couple of other ways to place text on a page: (1) You can drag the icon of a text file or a supported word processing file directly from the Windows Explorer (desktop or folder) or from the Mac Finder (desktop or folder) onto an InDesign page. (2) You can use your operating system's drag-and-drop text feature to drag highlighted text from a document created with another program (Microsoft Word, for example) into an InDesign document window. In both cases, a new text frame is created.

Whenever the Text tool is selected, you can create as many new text frames as you want. Just make sure not to click in an existing text frame when your intention is to create a new one. If you click within an existing frame when the Type tool is selected, the flashing cursor is displayed and InDesign thinks you want to enter text.

In addition to adding text to a newly created text frame, you can also move, resize, delete, or add a border (called a *stroke*) or a colored background. But you can't do any of these things when the Type tool is selected. You have to switch to the Selection tool or the Direct Selection tool. (See Chapter 11 for more about modifying frames and Chapter 8 for more on creating colors.)

If you accidentally use the Type tool to create a frame that you want to use as a container for a graphic, you can change it to a graphics frame by choosing Object ➪ Content ➪ Graphic.

Because InDesign lets you convert any empty shape into a text frame or a graphics frame and convert any text or graphics frame into an empty shape, it doesn't really matter what tool you use to create a particular shape. However, you have to be careful when working with shapes and frames. For example, using the Place command (File ➪ Place, or ⌘+D or Ctrl+D) to place an imported image into a text frame produces different results (placing an image in a text frame creates an anchored graphic within text, which limits your ability to size, position, and otherwise modify it) than placing an image within a graphics frame (you have nearly unlimited control over its attributes).

Deleting Objects

There are several ways to delete objects in InDesign. Most people either have favorites or use a method that's easiest to adopt in their current state (such as using a mouse action to delete a frame when they're using the mouse already to size frames). Be sure you select an object with the Selection tool. The methods are

+ Use the keyboard shortcuts ⌘+X or Ctrl+X to cut objects; use ⌘-Delete or Backspace to delete (clear) the object. (Cleared objects are not placed into the Mac clipboard and thus cannot be pasted back.)
+ Use the menu commands Edit ➪ Cut or Edit ➪ Clear.
+ Use the Cut command in the contextual menu you get when Control+clicking or right-clicking an object.
+ Drag the object to the Mac's Trash Can or the Windows Recycle Bin.

The ability to delete objects by dragging them to the trash is new in InDesign CS.

Creating a Graphics Frame

Although you can use InDesign's illustration features to create the kind of vector graphics that can be created with dedicated illustration programs such as Illustrator, FreeHand, and CorelDraw, you may find yourself needing to import an illustration that you or somebody else created using another program. You may also want to add other kinds of digital images to a publication, such as a scanned photograph, a piece of clip art stored on a CD-ROM, or a stock photograph that you've downloaded from the Internet.

In InDesign, all imported images are contained within graphics frames. The Tools palette contains three tools for drawing graphics frames:

✦ The Ellipse Frame tool lets you create oval and round frames.

✦ The Rectangle Frame tool lets you create rectangular and square frames.

✦ The Polygon Frame tool lets you create equilateral polygons and starburst-shaped frames.

The first time you use InDesign, the Rectangle Frame tool is displayed in the Tools palette, as is the Rectangle tool for creating boxes that hold neither text nor graphics. (The frame tools have an X through their icons.) To access the other frame tools, click and hold on the Rectangle Frame tool to display a pop-up menu with the Ellipse Frame and Polygon Frame tools. Drag and release to select a different frame tool. When you do, it replaces the Rectangle Frame tool in the Toolbox until the next time you change the tool.

Tip   If you accidentally use the Ellipse, Rectangle, or Polygon tool (instead of the frame version of these tools) to create an object that you subsequently want to use as a graphics frame (or a text frame for that matter), you can change the frame's contents via Object ➪ Content.

You can create a graphics frame using any of the frame tools, and then use the Place commands (File ➪ Place, or ⌘+D or Ctrl+D) to import an image into the selected frame, or you can use the Place command to import an image directly onto a page without first creating a graphics frame. In this chapter, you'll learn how to create basic graphics frames into which you can then import an image. (See Part V for more information about importing images using the Place command and modifying images.)

Tip   Whether you use the Place command to import an image into a selected frame or you place an image directly onto a page, the results are similar: A frame surrounds the picture and also serves as the picture's cropping shape.

Here's how to add a new graphics frame:

1. **Select the Ellipse Frame tool, the Rectangle Frame tool (or press F), or the Polygon Frame tool.**

2. **Move the crosshair pointer anywhere within the currently displayed page or on the pasteboard.**

3. **Click and hold the mouse button, and while holding down the mouse button, drag in any direction.**

   As you drag, the crosshair pointer is displayed in the corner opposite your starting point and a blue shape indicates the boundary of the frame. You can look at the width and height values displayed in the Control palette or Transform pane as you drag to help you get the size you want. Holding down the Shift key as you drag creates a circle if the Ellipse Frame tool is selected, a square if the Rectangle Frame tool is selected, and an equilateral polygon or starburst if the Polygon Frame tool is selected.

4. **When the frame is the size and shape you want, release the mouse button.**

Don't worry too much about being precise when you create a graphics frame. You can always go back later and fine-tune it. Figure 10-2 shows an oval graphics frame.

Figure 10-2: Creating a graphics frame with any of the frame-creation tools is the same as creating a text frame with the Type tool. Choose the appropriate frame tool, then click, drag, and release. In this example, an elliptical graphics frame has just been created; its bounding box is displayed with resizing handles.

Note

When you release the mouse button after creating a graphics frame, the frame you created is active. If the Selection tool was previously selected, the frame is displayed within its bounding box, which contains eight resizing handles. If the Direct Selection tool was previously selected, moveable anchor points are displayed at each vertex of the frame. In both cases, you have to change tools if you want to change the shape or size of the bounding box or the frame. The Selection tool lets you change the shape of the frame's bounding box by dragging any of the resizing handles; the Direct Selection tool lets you change the shape of the frame itself by moving the frame's anchor points. Chapter 11 explains how to resize a frame with the Selection tool; see Part V for information about modifying the shape of a frame using the Direct Selection tool.

When you create a graphics frame with any of the frame tools, you can align the frame edge with a guideline by clicking within the number of pixels specified in the Snap to Zone in the Guides & Pasteboard pane of the Preferences dialog box (choose File ➪ Preferences on the Mac or Edit ➪ Preferences in Windows, or press ⌘+K or Ctrl+K). When the crosshair pointer is near a guideline, a small, hollow arrowhead is displayed below and to the right of the crosshair.

If you've gone to the trouble of creating a graphics frame, chances are that sooner or later you'll want to place an image within it. To add a picture to a graphics frame, you can

✦ Use the Place command (File ➪ Place, or ⌘+D or Ctrl+D) to import a graphic file in any supported format.

✦ Paste in a graphic that you've copied from within InDesign.

You can also place an image on a page — and automatically create a new graphics frame — by dragging a supported graphic file directly from Windows Explorer (desktop or folder) or the Mac Finder (desktop or folder) onto an InDesign page.

See Part V for more information about importing images and modifying imported images.

Modifying a Frame's Shape

When a frame is active, you can modify it — by adding a stroke to its edges or a background color, by rotating, skewing, or shearing it, and so on.

A word of warning: Don't try to click on a frame handle when a frame-creation tool is selected. Instead of moving the handle you click on, you'll end up creating a new frame. You have to switch to one of the Selection tools to move or resize a graphics frame.

You can configure the Polygon tool and the Polygon Frame tool to create either regular polygons or starburst shapes. Double-click on either of the Polygon tools to display the Polygon Settings dialog box, shown in Figure 10-3. The value in the Number of Sides field determines how many sides your polygons will have. If you want to create a starburst shape, specify a value in the Star Inset field. As you increase the percentage value, the spikes become longer and pointier. When you change the values in the Polygon Settings dialog box, the new values are used for both versions of the polygon tool.

Figure 10-3: The Polygon Settings dialog box lets you specify the number of sides your polygons will have and, optionally, create starburst shapes by specifying a Star Inset value. Shown above the dialog box is a starburst created with the settings shown in the dialog box.

You cannot modify an existing polygon's attributes by selecting the polygon and then opening the Polygon Settings dialog box—you must either edit its shape via the Direct Selection tool, as covered in Chapter 26, or change attributes in the Polygon Settings dialog box and create a new polygon.

When any of the frame-creation tools is selected, you can create as many new frames as you want. Simply keep clicking, dragging, and releasing. After you create a graphics frame, you can modify it (without changing tools) by adding a border or a colored background or by applying any of the effects—such as rotation, shear, and scale—in the Control palette or Transform pane. You can also move or resize a graphics frame, but you have to switch to the Selection tool or the Direct Selection tool to do so.

The difference between the Selection tool and the Direct Selection tool takes some getting used to for QuarkXPress users. In terms of working with content, the Direct Selection tool is much like QuarkXPress's Content tool, but it also lets you edit the frame as if it were a Bézier object. For example, if the Direct Selection tool is selected and you drag a point on the frame, you'll move that point and thus change the shape of the object—a rectangle would be converted into a polygon, since the lines immediately adjacent to the moved point will move with the point, while the rest of the frame will not be affected. In QuarkXPress, if the Content tool is selected and you drag a point on the frame, you'll resize the frame (perhaps nonproportionally) but the entire side(s) adjacent to the point will move with the point, so a rectangle would still be a rectangle. To change a frame in the way that QuarkXPress does with both the Content and Item tools, use the Selection tool in InDesign.

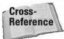

See Chapter 11 for more about modifying frames and Chapters 26 and 27 for sophisticated shape creation and manipulation techniques.

Drawing Straight Lines

Although they're not as flashy or versatile as graphic shapes and frames, lines can serve many useful purposes in well-designed pages. For example, plain ol' vertical rules can be used to separate columns of text in a multicolumn page or the rows and columns of data in a table. Dashed lines are useful for indicating folds and cut lines on brochures and coupons. And lines with arrowheads are handy if you have to create a map or a technical illustration.

InDesign lets you create straight lines with the Line tool and zigzag lines, curved lines, and freeform shapes with the Pen tool. In this chapter, I keep things simple and limit the discussion to the Line tool.

Cross-Reference   For information about using the Pen tool, see Chapter 26.

To draw a straight line:

1. **Select the Line tool (or press \).**

2. **Move the I-beam pointer anywhere within the currently displayed page or on the pasteboard.**

3. **Click and hold the mouse button, and while holding down the mouse button, drag in any direction.**

   As you drag, a thin, blue line is displayed from the point where you first clicked to the current position of the crosshair pointer. Holding down the Shift key as you drag constrains the line to horizontal, vertical or a 45-degree diagonal.

Tip   To create such constrained lines without holding the Shift key, you can also use the Orthogonal Line tool, which you access by holding on the Line tool and dragging the pointer to the crosshair icon that represents the Orthogonal Line tool in the pop-up menu.

4. **When the line is the length and angle you want, release the mouse button.**

   Don't worry too much about being precise when you create a line: You can always go back later and fine-tune it. Figure 10-4 shows a new line.

Note   When you release the mouse button after creating a line, the line is active. If the Selection tool was previously selected, the line is displayed within a rectangular bounding box, which contains eight resizing handles. If the Direct Selection tool was previously selected, moveable anchor points are displayed at the end of the line. In both cases, you have to change tools if you want to change the shape or size of the bounding box or the line. The Selection tool lets you change the shape of the line's bounding box (which also changes the angle and length of the line)

by dragging any of the resizing handles. The Direct Selection tool lets you change the length and angle of the line itself by moving anchor points on the frame. Chapter 11 explains how to resize lines with the Selection tool; see Part V for information about modifying shapes using the Direct Selection tool.

Figure 10-4: After you create a line with the Line tool, the active line is displayed either within a rectangular bounding box that has eight resizing handles (if the Selection tool was previously selected; left) or with anchor points at both ends (if the Direct Selection tool was previously selected; right).

Tip

When you create a line, it takes on the characteristics specified in the Stroke pane (Window ⇨ Stroke, or F10). When you first open a document, the default line width is 1 point. If you want to change the appearance of your lines, double-click the Line tool and adjust the Weight in the Stroke pane that will appear. If you make this adjustment when no document is open, all new documents will use the new line settings.

When the Line tool is selected, you can create as many new lines as you want. Simply keep clicking, dragging, and releasing. After you create a line, you can modify it (without changing tools) by changing any of the attributes—including weight, style, and start/end shapes—in the Stroke pane.

Cross-Reference

See Chapter 11 for more about modifying lines.

Summary

Empty objects, frames that hold text and pictures, and lines are the fundamental building blocks of pages. InDesign's Tools palette contains several tools for creating these objects. The easiest way to create a text frame is by clicking and dragging a rectangle with the Type tool. After you create a text frame, you can enter text directly into it or import a text file, then modify the appearance of the frame or the text within. Similarly, after you create a graphics frame, you can import a picture into it and then crop, scale, or apply other effects to the graphic or modify the frame. The Line tool lets you draw straight lines, which you can modify by changing color, width, and style.

✦   ✦   ✦

Manipulating Frames and Lines

✦ ✦ ✦ ✦

In This Chapter

Selecting, moving, resizing, and deleting objects

Adding strokes and fills to frames

Applying other graphic effects to frames

Changing the appearance of lines

✦ ✦ ✦ ✦

The primary purpose of the text frames and picture frames that you add to the pages of your InDesign documents is to hold text and pictures, and much of the time you spend using InDesign will involve modifying the appearance of the text and pictures you put in your frames. However, like real-world containers — bags, boxes, cartons, and cans — text frames and picture frames exist independently of their contents (they don't even have to have any contents), and you can modify the position, shape, and appearance of frames without affecting the text and pictures within.

In this chapter, you'll learn how to manipulate the frames and lines that you add to your pages. If you've ever worked with a page-layout or illustration program, many of the basic techniques for manipulating objects will seem very familiar:

✦ **If you want to move or modify an object, you must first select it.**

✦ **If you want to select an object, you must first choose a selection tool.** InDesign offers two tools for selecting objects — the Selection tool (the solid arrow pointer; shortcut V) and the Direct Selection tool (the hollow arrow pointer; shortcut A). These tools are explained in the "Selecting Objects" section later in this chapter.

✦ **When an object is selected, commands and controls for changing its position and appearance become available.**

Cross-Reference For information on working with the text within a frame, see Part IV; for information on working with imported pictures, see Part V.

New Feature   InDesign CS includes a feature long available in QuarkXPress and PageMaker. The new Control palette (like the QuarkXPress Measurements palette and the PageMaker Control palette) provides a whole range of controls for selected objects. The options change based on what is selected, which reduces on-screen palette clutter. Among the most commonly used options in the Control palette are the ones to move and resize objects.

Selecting Objects

All InDesign objects — unassigned shapes, text and picture frames, and straight and curved lines — have at least two levels of selection. You can select the object itself, or you can select the rectangular bounding box that encloses the object. (For rectangular objects, the bounding box and the shape are the same.) The tool that you choose — either the Direct Selection tool or the Selection tool — determines what you can do to the object you select:

✦ **The Direct Selection tool lets you select any of the individual anchor points (and direction handles of freeform shapes and curved lines) on an object.** If you click with the Direct Selection tool on an object that has a bounding box, the shape within is selected; the bounding box is not selected. You can also move an object with the Direct Selection tool by clicking within the object and dragging.

✦ **The Selection tool lets you select an entire object by clicking anywhere in the object.** This is the best tool to use if you want to move or resize an object. (You can also move objects with the Direct Selection tool.) When you click on an object with the Selection tool, the object's bounding box is selected.

QuarkXPress User   The difference between the Selection tool and the Direct Selection tool takes some getting used to for QuarkXPress users. In terms of working with content, the Direct Selection tool is much like QuarkXPress's Content tool, but it also lets you edit frames as if they were Bézier objects. For example, if the Direct Selection tool is selected and you drag a point on the frame, you'll move that point and, thus, change the shape of the object — a rectangle would be converted into a polygon, since the lines immediately adjacent to the moved point will move with the point, while the rest of the frame will not be affected. In QuarkXPress, if the Content tool is selected and you drag a point on the frame, you'll resize the frame (perhaps nonproportionally) but the entire side(s) adjacent to the point will move with the point, so a rectangle would still be a rectangle. To change a frame in the way that QuarkXPress does with both the Content and Item tools, use the Selection tool in InDesign.

Cross-Reference   You'll find more information about using the Direct Selection tool to select and change the shape of objects by dragging anchor points and direction handles in Chapter 27.

Here's how to select a frame or line with the Selection tool:

1. **Select the Selection tool by clicking on it or, if the Type tool is not selected, by pressing V.**

2. **Move the pointer anywhere within an object, then click and release.**

   To select an unassigned shape with no background color, you must click on its edge. If you click within the shape, the object is not selected.

When you release the mouse button, the object you clicked on — or the object's bounding box if it has one — is displayed with a blue outline and eight resizing handles (four on the corners and four on the midpoints of the sides), as shown in Figure 11-1. Figure 11-2 shows the same text frame selected via the Direct Selection tool, with one of the points being dragged to reshape the frame.

Figure 11-1: When you select a frame with the Selection tool, in this case an oval text frame, the bounding box is displayed with eight resizing handles.

Figure 11-2: When you select a frame with the Direct Selection tool, in this case an oval text frame, the frame's control points, or nodes, are displayed. Here, I am moving one of those points. Note how it reshapes — not resizes — the frame.

Tip

You can also select an object with the Selection tool by clicking and dragging a rectangle. Simply click on an empty portion of the page or pasteboard near the object you want to select and drag out a rectangle that intersects the object (you don't have to enclose the entire object). Clicking and dragging is a handy way to select multiple objects.

Selecting overlapping objects

You'll often have multiple objects overlapping in your layout, with some objects completely obscured by others. So how do you select them? By using the new Select menu option in the Object menu. Figure 11-3 shows the Select submenu and its options.

Figure 11-3: The new Select submenu in the
Object menu.

InDesign CS adds the Select submenu, which provides new controls for object
selection, to the Object menu.

The first four options let you select another object relative to the currently selected
object:

✦ **First Object Above** (Option+Shift+⌘+] or Ctrl+Alt+Shift+]) selects the topmost
object.

✦ **Next Object Above** (Option+⌘+] or Ctrl+Alt+]) selects the object immediately
on top of the current object.

✦ **Next Object Below** (Option+⌘+[or Ctrl+Alt+[) selects the object immediately
under the current object.

✦ **Last Object Below** (Option+Shift+⌘+[or Ctrl+Alt+Shift+[) selects the bottommost object.

If no objects are selected, InDesign will base its selection on the creation order.

You can also access these four selection options by Control+clicking or right-
clicking an object and choosing the Select menu from the contextual menu.

The Select submenu has four other options:

✦ If an object has content (text or picture) and you've selected its frame, choose Object ➪ Select ➪ Select Content to choose the content within the object.

✦ If an object has content (text or picture) and you've selected its content, choose Object ➪ Select ➪ Select Container to choose the frame.

✦ If you have selected an object in a group of objects, using the Direct Selection tool, choose Object ➪ Select ➪ Previous Item to navigate to the previous object in the group.

✦ Similarly, If you have selected an object in a group of objects, using the Direct Selection tool, choose Object ➪ Select ➪ Next Item to navigate to the previous object in the group.

Note   Object creation order determines what is "previous" or "next" in a group.

Selecting multiple objects

When an object is selected, you can move or modify it. When several objects are selected, you can move or modify all the objects at once, saving you the time and drudgery of selecting and performing the same modification to several objects one at a time. You have several options for selecting multiple objects. You can

✦ **Choose the Selection tool and hold down the Shift key while clicking in succession on the objects you want to select.**

✦ **Choose either the Selection tool or the Direct Selection tool, then click on an empty portion of the page and drag a rectangle around any portion of each object you want to select.** Make sure you don't click on an item or you'll move it when you drag.

   • If you use the Selection tool, the bounding box of each item is selected. You can resize any of the bounding boxes, but the anchor points and direction lines of the shapes within are not selected and cannot be moved.

   • If you use the Direct Selection tool, the anchor points and direction handles of the shapes in the bounding boxes are selected. You can change the shape of any of the objects by dragging an anchor point or direction handle.

✦ **If you want to select all items on a page or spread, choose Edit ➪ Select All or press ⌘+A or Ctrl+A.** (If the Type tool is selected and a text frame is active when you choose Select All, you'll highlight all the text, if any, in the frame.)

If the Direct Selection tool is selected when you choose Select All, the anchor points and direction handles of the shapes in the selected objects' bounding boxes are selected. If any other tool is selected when you choose Select All, the bounding boxes of the objects are selected.

Tip   To select a master item on a document page, you must hold down Shift+⌘ or Ctrl+Shift as you click on it. For more information about using master pages, see Chapter 7.

Deselecting objects

A selected object will remain selected until you cause it to become deselected, and there are many reasons you might want to deselect an item. For example, you might want to deselect a text frame if you want to see how it looks when displayed without the frame's in and out ports visible. Or you might want to simply "let go" of an object you just finished working on. There are several ways to deselect a selected object. You can

✦ Click on an empty portion of the page with either of the selection tools selected.

✦ Hold down the Shift key with either of the selection tools selected and click on the object you want to deselect.

✦ Choose any of the object-creation tools (the Pen tool, the Line tool, or any of the shape- and frame-creation tools), then click and drag to create a new object.

✦ If you want to deselect all items on a page or spread, choose Edit ➪ Deselect All or press Shift+⌘+A or Ctrl+Shift+A. (If the Type tool is selected and a text frame is active when you choose Deselect All, you'll deselect any text that's highlighted in the frame.)

Moving, Resizing, and Deleting Objects

One of the great things about using computers to create publications is that it's easy to change your mind. For example, if you don't like where you've placed an object, it's easy to move it or remove it altogether. When you combine this flexibility with InDesign's option to undo as many previous actions as you want, you're free to experiment to your heart's content.

Moving objects

Before you can move an object, you must first select it. Once an object is selected, InDesign provides several methods for moving it. You can move a selected object by:

✦ **Clicking and dragging it to a different location.** When you drag an object, you can move it anywhere within the current page or spread, into an open library (see Chapter 7 for more information about libraries), or into another document (if another document is open and its window is visible). If you drag an object from one document to another, a copy of the object is placed in the target document and the original object remains unchanged in the source document.

Hold down the Shift key as you drag to restrict the angle of movement to multiples of 45 degrees.

You can create a *clone* (that is, an exact duplicate) of an object when you move it by pressing the Option or Alt key as you drag with a selection tool. Not only is this a handy way to create a duplicate, it's also a great way to experiment: You can practice on a clone without jeopardizing the original.

✦ **Pressing any of the arrow keys.** Each time you press an arrow key, the object is nudged by the distance specified in the Cursor Key field in the Units & Increments pane of the Preferences dialog box (choose File ➪ Preferences on the Mac or Edit ➪ Preferences in Windows, or press ⌘+K or Ctrl+K). The default nudge value is 1 point. If you hold down the Shift key when using arrow keys, the nudge increment is 10 points.

If you hold down the Option or Alt key as you nudge an object with the arrow keys, a clone of the selected object is created.

✦ **Changing the X and Y values in the new Control palette or in the Transform pane.** These values determine the distance between an object's point of origin and the ruler origin, where the horizontal and vertical rulers intersect (usually the upper-left corner of a page or spread). (If the Control palette is not displayed, activate it by choosing Window ➪ Control or pressing Option+⌘+6 or Ctrl+Alt+6. If the Transform pane is not displayed, activate it by choosing Windows ➪ Transform or pressing F9.) Figure 11-4 shows the Control palette and Transform pane and their controls. If you want, change the object's point of origin — where the X and Y coordinates refer to.

The grid of small, white squares in the far left of the Control palette and in the upper-left corner of the Transform pane let you specify the point on the object used to position the object relative to the page origin. If a shape or curved line is selected, all nine squares are selectable for the point of origin; if a straight line is selected, six of the small squares are grayed out and only three squares are selectable for the point of origin. Click on a white square to change the point of origin. (The current point of origin is indicated by a square displaying as black rather than as white.)

To create a clone of an object, press Option+Return or Alt+Enter after changing the X and/or Y value in the Control palette or Transform pane.

Figure 11-4: If you prefer modifying values precisely to clicking and dragging, use the Control palette or Transform pane to move objects and perform other modifications. The Control palette is more flexible, providing different options based on what is selected. In this figure, the six horizontal panes are, from top to bottom, the Control palette for a text frame, text in a text frame or on a text path, a graphics frame, an image in a graphics frame, a line, and multiple objects. At bottom is the Transform pane.

Each of the preceding methods for moving objects has its merits. The method you choose will depend on how you prefer to work.

Resizing objects

After you create a shape, frame, or line, you may find that it's too big or too small for your design. No problem. Resizing objects is as easy as moving them. And as is the case with repositioning objects, you have multiple options for resizing. You can

✦ **Click and drag an object's bounding box using the Selection tool.** To change the width and height, drag a corner handle. To change only the width or height, drag a midpoint handle. If you hold the Shift key as you drag, the object's original proportions are retained.

More about scaling frames

You can also resize an object by selecting it and then changing the values in the Scale X percentage and Scale Y percentage fields in the Control palette or Transform pane. If you scale a picture frame with the Selection tool, both the frame and the picture within are scaled. If you scale a picture frame with the Direct Selection tool, only the frame size changes. If you scale a text frame with either selection tool, both the frame and its text are scaled. (By the way, if you resize an object by scaling it, you can return to its original size by choosing 100% from the Scale X percentage and Scale Y percentage pop-up menus.)

The distinction in InDesign between a frame and its contents and between the Selection and Direct Selection tools can be a little confusing. The option to resize an object by changing its scale only adds to the confusion. The simplest method is to resize an object by dragging bounding box handles or changing width and height values in the Transform pane.

Also, note that you can flip the contents of a picture frame or text frame by dragging a bounding box handle across and beyond the opposite corner or edge. Although this isn't a scaling operation, you accomplish it by dragging a handle as if you were resizing.

Tip

When you resize a picture frame by clicking and dragging a handle, the picture within isn't affected unless you hold down ⌘ or Ctrl as you drag. Holding down ⌘ or Ctrl and dragging changes the picture's scale as well as the size of the frame.

Tip

If you drag immediately after clicking on a handle, only a frame's bounding box is displayed as you drag. If you click and then pause until the pointer changes, the contents within are displayed as you drag.

✦ **After selecting the object with either selection tool, modify the horizontal and/or vertical scaling by changing the width and/or height values in the Control palette or Transform pane.** If you want, change the object's point of origin. The grid of small, white squares in the far left of the Control palette or in the upper-left corner of the Transform pane lets you specify the point on the object used to position the object relative to the page origin. If a shape or curved line is selected, all nine squares are selectable for the point of origin; if a straight line is selected, six of the small squares are grayed out and only three squares are selectable for the point of origin. Click on a white square to change the point of origin. (The current point of origin is indicated by a square displaying as black rather than as white.)

Note

If the Direct Selection tool is selected when you click on an object, the object's anchor points and direction handles are displayed. Clicking and dragging a point or a handle changes the shape of the object. For more information about changing the shape of objects, see Chapter 27.

Deleting objects

Alas, not all the objects you create will survive all the way to the final version of your publication. Some will wind up on the cutting room floor, so to speak. You can always move an object to the pasteboard if you're not sure whether you want to get rid of it altogether (objects on the pasteboard won't print). But when it's time to ax an object, oblivion is just a keystroke or two away. If you delete a text or picture frame, the contents are removed as well as the frame.

Here's how to delete objects: Using either selection tool, click on the object you want to delete, then press the Delete key or Backspace key. You can also delete a selected item by choosing Edit ➪ Clear.

QuarkXPress User   If you're a QuarkXPress user, you may find yourself instinctively pressing ⌘+K or Ctrl+K to delete an object. In InDesign, this shortcut displays the Preferences dialog box. Even if you use Edit ➪ Keyboard Shortcuts to switch to InDesign's built-in QuarkXPress shortcuts, the ⌘+K or Ctrl+K shortcut won't work to delete items. However, you can create a new set of shortcuts (by making a copy of the QuarkXPress set if you want) and assigning ⌘+K or Ctrl+K to the Clear command.

Tip   Choosing Edit ➪ Cut, or ⌘+X or Ctrl+X, also removes a selected object. However, in this case a copy of the object is saved to the Clipboard (and can be pasted elsewhere with Edit ➪ Paste, or ⌘+P or Ctrl+P) until you cut or copy something else or you shut down your computer.

Adding Strokes, Fills, and Other Effects

When you create a new frame, there's not much to it. It has no content, no color (it's transparent — or *none-colored* in InDesign's vocabulary), and no border. If you print a page with an empty frame, you'll get a blank page. Of course, when you place text or a picture into a frame, it springs to life. But whether a frame is empty or filled, InDesign lets you change its appearance in several ways. You can

   ✦ Add a border, or *stroke,* around a frame's perimeter and apply a solid color, a tint, or a gradient to the stroke.

   ✦ Add a solid color, a tint, or a gradient to the frame's background.

   ✦ Apply any of several corner effects.

   ✦ Scale, rotate, and/or *shear* (skew) the frame using tools or the Control palette or Transform pane.

Note   Choose View ➪ Show Frame Edges, or press ⌘+H or Ctrl+H, to see frame edges if they aren't already visible.

Adding strokes

In the old days of traditional paste-up, adding a simple, black border around a sidebar or a thin keyline around a picture was a tedious and time-consuming process of laying out adhesive tape and then hoping that your meticulously placed rules remained straight and your perfectly square corners remained tight long enough to make it to the printer. If you were unlucky, your rules wound up on the floor or stuck to somebody's elbows. Nowadays, computers make adding borders to shapes an easy task. InDesign lets you quickly apply strokes to the shapes you create and modify the thickness, color, and style of strokes.

To add a stroke to a frame:

1. **Select either of the selection tools and click on the frame to which you want to add a stroke, then click on the Stroke box in the Tools palette (see Figure 11-5).**

Fill box (shortcut X)
Default Fill and Stroke box (shortcut D)
Formatting Affects Container box
Apply Color (shortcut ,)
Apply Gradient (shortcut .)

Apply None box (shortcut /)
Formatting Affects Text box
Stroke box (shortcut X)
Swap Fill and Stroke box (shortcut Shift + X)

Figure 11-5: The color tools at the bottom of the Tools pane offer the quickest and easiest method of applying the last-used color or gradient to objects, or removing a color, tint, or gradient.

2. You now can click a color, tint, or gradient from the Swatches pane, or click on one of the three boxes at the bottom of the Tools palette, which (from left to right) let you use the last-selected color, last-selected gradient, or None (this removes the stroke's color, tint, or gradient).

 Cross-Reference   For information about adding colors to the Swatches pane, see Chapter 8.

When you add a stroke to a frame, it's assigned a width of 1 point. You can change the width and several other characteristics of a stroke using the controls in the Stroke pane. You can also change the stroke width and type in the Control palette. Figure 11-6 shows a graphics frame to which a 10-point dark orange stroke has been added, while Figure 11-7 shows a graphics frame whose stroke is a gradient.

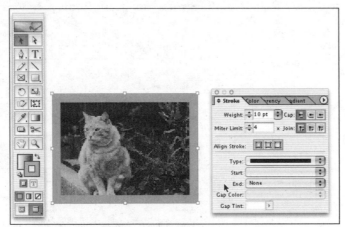

Figure 11-6: In this illustration, a 10-point orange stroke has been added to the graphics frame.

 New Feature   You can now enter percentages in pane fields for size- and scale-oriented items such as stroke widths. For example, to change a 1-point stroke to a hairline (0.25 points), you could enter **0.25 pt** or now enter **25%**.

Tip   The controls in the Color pane (Window ➪ Color or F6) let you change the tint of the color applied to a stroke, but I recommend you use the tint control on the Swatches pane (Window ➪ Swatches or F5) instead, so you don't accidentally use unnamed colors (see Chapter 8 for more information on this issue). The Gradient pane (Windows ➪ Gradient) gives you the option to apply either a linear or radial gradient. For linear gradients, you can specify the angle via the Angle field.

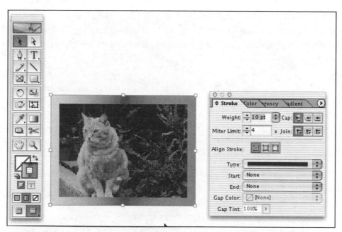

Figure 11-7: In this example, a gradient blend was applied to the frame's stroke; the blend was rotated 180 degrees.

When using the Stroke pane to modify a stroke:

1. **Select either of the selection tools and click on the object whose stroke you want to modify.**

2. **If the Stroke pane is not displayed, show it by choosing Window ✑ Stroke or pressing F10.**

3. **To change the width of stroke, enter a new value in the Weight field.**

   You can also change the Weight value by choosing a new value from the field's pop-up menu or by clicking the up and down arrows. (Each click increases or decreases the stroke by 1 point.)

4. **Set the Miter Limit.**

   The default of 4 is fine for almost all frames.

Note The value in the Stroke pane's Miter Limit field determines when a corner point switches from *mitered* (squared off) to beveled. You'll rarely use this feature; it's useful when you have thick lines joining at sharp angles. In such cases, the lines may extend farther than needed, and the miter value (1 to 500, with 1 being the most conservative setting and 500 the most forgiving) tells InDesign when to change the squared-off corner to a beveled one, which prevents the problem.

5. **Click on any of the three Cap icons to specify how dashes will look if you create a dashed stroke (covered in Step 9).**

   Figure 11-8 shows how each of the cap styles affect a dashed stroke.

Figure 11-8: The line in this illustration was selected with the Direct Selection tool. Each of the three available endcap styles — butt (left), round (center), and projecting (right) is shown.

6. **Click any of the three Join icons to specify how corners are handled.**

Figure 11-9 shows how each of the join styles affects a corner.

Figure 11-9: The Stroke pane lets you apply mitered (left), rounded (center), and beveled (right) corners to shapes.

7. **Choose an Align Stroke option.**

The default is the first button, Align Stroke to Center, which has the stroke straddle the frame. In the 10-point stroke in Figures 11-6 and 11-7, 5 points of that stroke width are on the outside of the frame boundary, and 5 points of it are inside the frame boundary. You can also choose Align Stroke to Inside, which places the entire thickness inside the frame boundary, or Align Stroke to Outside, which places the entire thickness outside the frame boundary.

8. **You can also choose end points for your strokes (this only affects lines, not rectangles, ellipses, and other closed-loop shapes) using the Start and End pop-up menus.**

Figure 11-10 shows the options.

Figure 11-10: The Start options in the Stroke pane. The End options are identical.

9. **To create a dashed line instead of a solid line, choose an option from the Type pop-up menu.** (These are also available from the Control palette.)

You'll see 16 types of predefined dashes and stripes, as shown in Figure 11-11. The Gap Color and Gap Tint fields at the bottom of the Stroke pane become active as well, to let you choose a specific color and tint for the gaps in dashes and stripes.

Figure 11-11: The predefined dash and stripe options in the Stroke pane's Type pop-up menu.

New Feature   Several Stroke pane options are new to InDesign CS: the Gap Color and Gap Tint fields and the Align Stroke options.

 Tip   To see the full Stroke pane, double-click the icon to the left of the Stroke pane's label. By default, the pane shows only the Weight, Cap, Miter Limit, and Join options.

Creating custom strokes

InDesign CS lets you create custom strokes: dashed, dotted, and striped lines. To create custom dashes or stripes, choose the Stroke Styles option in the Stroke pane's palette menu. Figure 11-12 shows the Stroke Styles dialog box from which you can create new strokes, edit or delete existing ones, and import (load) strokes from a stroke styles file which you create by saving a document's strokes as a separate file for import into other documents via the Save button; stroke style files have the filename extension .inst.

Figure 11-12: The Stroke Styles dialog box.

 New Feature   New to InDesign CS is the ability to create your own custom dashes, dotted lines, and stripes.

 QuarkXPress User   The InDesign Stroke Styles feature looks and works very much like the QuarkXPress Dashes & Stripes feature. The major difference is that InDesign has a separate option for dotted lines.

Note that you cannot edit or delete the seven default stripe patterns shown in the figure, nor can you edit or delete the default dash patterns — they're not even available in the dialog box. When you edit or create a stroke pattern, you get the New Stroke Style dialog box, shown in Figure 11-13. In the Name field, enter a name for your stroke. In the Type pop-up menu, you can choose to create (or convert a stripe you are editing to) a dashed, dotted, or striped stroke.

Figure 11-13: The dashes version of the New Stroke Style dialog box.

For dashes, you can resize the dash component by dragging the down-pointing tri-angle at the end of the dash in the ruler section. You can add dash segments by sim-ply clicking on the ruler and dragging a segment to the desired width. Or you can use the Start and Length fields to manually specify them. The Pattern Length field is where you indicate the length of the segment you're defining; this is then repeated to fill the frame or line the stroke is applied to. In the Corners pop-up menu, you tell InDesign whether to adjust how the dashes and gaps are handled at corners; the default is Adjust Dashes and gaps, a setting you should keep — it will make sure your corners have dash segments that extend along both sides of the corner, which looks neater. (Your other options are Adjust Dashes, Adjust Gaps, and None.) You can also choose a cap style and the stroke weight. The preview section of the pane lets you see your dash as you create or edit it.

For dots, you get a similar dialog box as for dashes, as Figure 11-14 shows. The Start and Length fields disappear, replaced with the Center field that determines where any added dots are placed on the ruler. (The initial dot, shown as a half-circle, starts at 0 and cannot be moved or deleted.) The Caps field is also gone.

Tip To delete a dash or dot segment, just drag it to the left, off the ruler.

For stripes, you get the dialog box shown in Figure 11-15. The principle is the same as for dashes: You create segments (in this case vertical, not horizontal) for the stripes by dragging on the ruler. However, the stripes version of the dialog box expresses its values in percentages because the actual thickness of each stripe is determined by the stroke weight — the thicker the stroke, the thicker each stripe is in the overall stroke.

Figure 11-14: The dotted-line version of the New Stroke Style dialog box.

Note   In all three versions of the New Stroke Style dialog box, you click Add to add the stroke to your document. When you're done creating strokes, click Done. (When editing a stroke, you won't have the Add button available.)

Figure 11-15: The stripe version of the New Stroke Style dialog box.

Adding fills

The option to add a stroke to any shape becomes even more powerful when combined with the option to fill any shape with a color or tint. For example, adding a stroke around a text frame is an effective way to draw attention to a sidebar. Adding a fill to a shape is much like adding a stroke, and the options available for specifying color and tint are identical. The only difference is that you click the Fill box in the Toolbox palette rather than the Stroke box.

Tip

If you really want to turn eyes, you can create reversed text within the frame by adding a fill color and lightening the text. But remember: Reversed text is harder to read, so keep the text size on the large side, and use this effect sparingly. You'll often want to make the reversed-out text boldface to aid in its readability.

Adding special effects to corners

Anytime you're working on an object that has any sharp corners, you have the option to add a little pizzazz to the corners via InDesign's Corner Effects feature (Object ➪ Corner Effects). Five built-in corner styles, shown in Figure 11-16, are available. Note that if the shape contains only smooth points, any corner effect you apply won't be noticeable.

Figure 11-16: The Corner Effects dialog box lets you apply any of five effects to frame corners.

Caution

A word of caution about adding fancy corners: These effects are handy for such things as certificates and coupons, but don't get carried away and use them for everyday tasks such as frames for pictures and text unless you have a good reason. Few things kill a design like too much graphic embellishment.

QuarkXPress User The corner-style feature in InDesign is similar to the text-box and picture-box variants in QuarkXPress, which offer the same corners except for the Fancy option. In QuarkXPress, you create, or convert, a box to a variant that has one of these corner effects, while in InDesign, you apply the corner effect to a frame.

To add a corner effect:

1. **Select either of the selection tools and click on the shape to which you want to add a corner effect, then choose Object ⇨ Corner Effects to display the Corner Effects dialog box.**

2. **Choose an option from the Effect pop-up menu.**

3. **Enter a distance in the Size field.**

   The Size value determines the length that the effect extends from the corner.

4. **Click OK to close the dialog box and apply your changes.**

Tip Click the Preview button to view changes as you make them.

Tip If you can't see a corner effect after applying one, make sure that a color is applied to the stroke or try making the object's stroke thicker. Increasing the Size value in the Corner Effects dialog box can also make a corner effect more visible.

Performing other transformations on frames

Earlier in this chapter, I explained how to change the size of an item by clicking and dragging bounding box handles with the selection tools and by changing the values in the Control palette's or Transform pane's width and height fields. InDesign also provides some tools and several controls in the Control palette and Transform pane that let you perform more-dramatic effects on objects, such as rotation, mirroring, and *shearing* (which distorts a shape by applying a combination of rotation and slant). Keep in mind that if you press Option or Alt as you drag, you'll work on a copy of the object. To get finer control as you drag, click farther from the active object's point of origin.

How you use these special effects is up to you and is limited only by your imagination. As always, discretion is advised. Just because InDesign has some pretty cool features doesn't mean that you should use them in every publication you create.

Tip If you drag immediately after clicking on an object, the object is displayed in its original location and the object's bounding box moves as you drag. If you click and then pause until the crosshair changes to an arrowhead, the object is displayed as you drag.

Using the Rotation tool

If you need to rotate an object, and you prefer to accomplish such tasks by clicking and dragging rather than by entering values in fields, you'll want to use the Rotation tool. Here's how:

1. **Select the Rotation tool.**

   If the Type tool isn't selected, you can also press R to select the Rotation tool.

2. **If it's not already selected, click on the object you want to rotate.**

   If you want, you can drag the point of origin from its default location in the upper-left-hand corner of the bounding box to a different location. The object rotates around the point of origin. Figure 11-17 shows a text frame being rotated around the default point of origin (the upper-left corner).

3. **Move the pointer away from the point of origin, then click and drag with a circular motion, clockwise or counterclockwise.**

   Hold the Shift key as you drag to constrain rotation increments to 45 degrees.

4. **Release the mouse button when the object is at the angle you want.**

Figure 11-17: When you rotate an object with the Rotation tool, a moving bounding box is displayed along with the original object if you drag immediately after clicking, as in this example. If you pause before dragging, the moving object and its contents are displayed as you drag.

Using the Scale tool

The easiest way to scale an object is to drag a bounding box handle, as described earlier in this chapter.

To scale an object manually:

1. **Select the Scale tool.**

   If the Type tool isn't selected, you can also press S to select the Scale tool.

2. **If it's not already selected, click on the object you want to scale.**

   If you want, you can drag the point of origin from its default location in the upper-left-hand corner of the bounding box to a different location. When the object grows or shrinks, the point of origin doesn't move.

3. **Move the pointer away from the point of origin, then click and drag.**

   Hold the Shift key and drag horizontally to apply only horizontal scale, vertically to apply only vertical scale, and diagonally to apply horizontal and vertical and keep the object's original proportions.

4. **Release the mouse button when the object is the size you want.**

   Figure 11-18 shows an object that's being scaled with the scale tool.

Figure 11-18: Clicking and dragging with the Scale tool enlarges or reduces a frame. In this example, the Scale tool is being used to enlarge a frame.

Caution If you use the Scale tool on a text frame, the text within is scaled as well. However, if you use the Scale tool on a picture frame, the picture is not scaled. You can prevent InDesign from scaling text in a scaled frame by deselecting the Adjust Text Attributes When Scaling check box in the Text pane of the Preferences dialog box (choose InDesign ➪ Preferences on the Mac or Edit ➪ Preferences in Windows, or press ⌘+K or Ctrl+K).

Using the Shear tool

When you shear an object with the Shear tool, you actually perform two transformations at once: rotation and slant. Because the contents within text frames and picture frames are distorted along with the frames when you shear an object, you'll probably use this tool only for special effects.

QuarkXPress User The InDesign Shear tool is not the same as the QuarkXPress Skew tool — Shear both slants and rotates an object, while Skew just slants it. To simulate the QuarkXPress Skew tool, move the mouse horizontally when using the InDesign Shear tool — this ensures that there is no rotation. You can also use the Shear fields in the Control palette or Transform pane to only slant an object.

To shearing an object manually:

1. **Select the Shear tool.**

   If the Type tool isn't selected, you can also press O to select the Shear tool.

2. **If it's not selected, click on the object you want to shear.**

   If you want, you can drag the point of origin from its default location in the upper-left-hand corner of the bounding box to a different location. When you shear an object, the point of origin doesn't move.

3. **Move the pointer away from the point of origin, then click and drag.**

   Hold the Shift key and drag to constrain rotation increments to multiples of 45 degrees. Figure 11-19 shows a frame being sheared.

Modifying objects using the Transform pane

If you prefer to modify objects by specifying values in fields rather than by clicking and dragging, you can use the Transform pane (Window ➪ Transform or F9). Some designers prefer the click-and-drag approach when modifying objects because it more closely mimics traditional paste-up techniques: You put objects onto a page, then you move them around until you're satisfied. Others prefer the precision that entering transformation values into fields offers. Chances are, you'll do a little of both.

Figure 11-19: In this example, a frame is being sheared using the Shear tool.

For example, if you want to rotate a block of text exactly 45 degrees, entering a rotation value in the Transform pane is probably the quickest method. If you want to rotate a block of text to match the angle of a shape in an imported picture, you might decide that clicking and dragging is the best approach.

In the Transform pane, highlight the appropriate field in the Transform pane, enter a new value, then press Return or Enter. When an object is selected, you can also highlight fields in the pane by double-clicking on the corresponding transformation tools: Double-click the Rotation tool to highlight the Rotation field, the Scale tool to highlight the Horizontal scale field, and the Shear tool to highlight the Shear X angle field.

Tip   Press Shift+Return or Shift+Enter to apply changes without leaving the pane. Press Option+Return or Alt+Enter to apply a transformation value to a copy of the selected item.

Note   The Transform pane contains separate fields for horizontal scale (Scale X percentage) and vertical scale (Scale Y percentage). You can distort an object by applying different scale values. Applying equal horizontal and vertical scale values maintains an object's original proportions. Use the Constrain Proportions button (chain icon) to have changes in one scale field be automatically applied to the other.

Like almost all of InDesign panes, the Transform pane includes a palette menu, shown in Figure 11-20, that contains additional commands for modifying objects.

Before you try to apply any of the effects in the pop-up menu, make sure the object you want to change is selected.

Figure 11-20: The Transform pane's palette menu provides several commands for modifying objects.

Tip

If you select a text or picture frame with the Selection tool and then apply a transformation, both the contents and the frame are affected. If you select a frame with the Direct Selection tool and then apply a transformation, only the frame is affected.

Here's list of the commands and a brief description of what each one does:

✦ **Scale Text Attributes:** Select this option before changing a text frame's horizontal and/or vertical scale if you don't want to change the scale of the text within.

✦ **Rotate 180°, Rotate 90° CW, and Rotate 90° CCW:** These commands provide an alternative to the Rotation field. You can rotate an object 180 degrees, 90 degrees clockwise, or 90 degrees counterclockwise.

✦ **Flip Horizontal, Flip Vertical, and Flip Both:** These commands let you create a mirror version of the original.

✦ **Dimensions Include Stroke Weight:** Check this option if you want an object's height and width to be calculated from the outer edge of the object's stroke. Uncheck this option if you want to calculate an object's height and width from the center of the object's stroke. (In this case, a stroked object will actually be larger — by the width of the stroke — than the values in the width and height fields.)

✦ **Transform Content:** If checked, the frame's content (text or picture, plus fills and gradients) is transformed along with the frame. For example, if you rotate a frame, the text is rotated as well. If this option is unchecked, the text would not be rotated along with the frame.

✦ **Transform Group Content:** If you've selected multiple objects, this option becomes available, and it worked like Transform Content does.

✦ **Transformations Are Totals:** When this option is selected, the angle of rotation of a nested object is calculated relative to the horizontal/vertical orientation of the page. If Transformations Are Totals is checked, the angle of a nested object is calculated relative to the angle of the frame that contains it. For example, if Transformations Are Totals is selected and you paste an unrotated item into a frame that's been rotated 30 degrees, the angle of rotation for the nested item is 0 degrees; if you then uncheck Transformations Are Totals, the nested object's angle of rotation is –30 degrees.

✦ **Show Content Offset:** If checked, this option shows the position of the origin content (a picture) relative to the frame containing it in the X and Y fields in the Transform pane. If you move a picture within the frame, the offset will be positive as you move it to the right and/or down, and negative as you move it to the left and/or up. If unchecked, the Transform pane will instead show the absolute position on the page of the current reference point.

Modifying objects using the Control palette

I prefer using the new Control palette rather the Transform pane because the Control palette gives you more control over selected objects (refer to Figure 11-4).

For the operations such as scaling, shearing, rotating, and flipping, the Control palette works like the Transform pane described in the previous section. Its palette menu is also the same, with the following exception: There are three options that control its placement — Dock at Top, Dock at Bottom, and the default Float.

But the Control palette provides access to many options not available in the Transform pane for working with frames:

✦ You can set the frame stroke width and type.

✦ You can have content resized to fit the frame or have the frame resized to fit the content, as well as center the content in the frame.

✦ You can access the Select submenu options (covered earlier in this chapter).

✦ For text frames, you can set the number of columns in the frame and control the vertical justification of paragraphs.

✦ For text in a frame or on a path, you can set many character and paragraph attributes, such as font, size, leading, kerning, tracking, style (boldface, italics, strikethrough, and so on), vertical and horizontal scaling, skew, baseline shift, character style, language, ligatures, underline and strikethrough options, paragraph alignment (horizontal justification), indents, drop caps, baseline grid alignment, hyphenation, paragraph rules, keep options, and paragraph styles.

Modifying Lines

When you create a line with the Line tool, there's not much to it. It's plain, black, and 1-point wide. But, like a frame, you can modify the color, tint, and thickness of a line, and you can optionally apply a custom dashed style and endpoints. The process for modifying lines is the same as for modifying frames and for creating strokes in the first place, both of which are described earlier in this chapter.

Summary

After you create an object, you can move, modify, or delete it. If the object is a frame, you also have the option of modifying the text or picture within. Before you can modify an object, you must select it. When an object is selected, commands and controls for changing its position and appearance become available. To select an object, you must first choose either the Selection tool or the Direct Selection tool. If a frame is selected, you can add a stroke around its border, add a color to its background, or change its shape using the Rotate, Scale, or Shear tools or the corresponding fields in the Control palette or Transform pane. If a line is selected, you can change its width, color, and style.

✦　　✦　　✦

Orchestrating Objects

In This Chapter

Changing the
stacking order of
objects

Working with groups

Nesting objects

Inserting objects
within a text thread

Locking objects

Text frames, picture frames, graphic shapes, and lines are the building blocks with which you construct InDesign pages. Becoming familiar with creating and modifying individual objects, which is the focus of Chapters 10 and 11, is a key step in learning how to create publications with InDesign. The next step is to learn how to use several features that let you manipulate multiple objects at once and quickly adjust the relationships among the various objects that make up a page. A good InDesign user can handle individual objects one at a time with ease; a virtuoso user can simultaneously juggle several objects with equal ease.

Think of it this way: As an InDesign user, you're much like an architect. You begin with a blueprint — perhaps a rough, felt-tip pen sketch; maybe just a picture in your mind's eye — open a new document, and start construction. The settings you establish in the New Document dialog box (File ➪ New, or ⌘+N or Ctrl+N) — the page size, margin placement, column arrangement, and number of pages — serve as the foundation as you begin adding objects to your pages. You must then construct your building — or rather, your publication — using four basic components: text frames, picture frames, shapes, and lines. Each of those components can be tweaked and twisted in a nearly endless variety of ways while retaining basic properties. After all, a sheared (skewed) and mirrored text frame with a purple dashed stroke, a gradient background, and magenta text outlined in cyan is still just a text frame.

As a publication evolves, plans invariably change: An advertiser pulls out and a magazine article needs to be stretched an extra half-page by enlarging an InDesign-created illustration. A client loves his company's newsletter but wants the front-page picture cropped differently. A new product is added to a catalog and half the pages reflow. If you build your documents soundly from the ground up and use the features covered in this chapter, you'll be prepared to handle even the most challenging page building — and rebuilding — tasks.

Stacking Objects

Each time you begin work on a new page, you start with a clean slate (unless the page is based on a master page, in which case the master objects act as the page's background; see Chapter 7 for more on master pages). Every time you add an object to a page — either by using any of InDesign's object-creation tools or via the Place command (File ➪ Place, or ⌘+D or Ctrl+D) — the new object occupies a unique place in the page's object hierarchy, or *stacking order*.

The first object you place on a page is automatically positioned at the bottom of the stacking order; the next object is positioned one level higher than the first object (that is, on top of and in front of the backmost object); the next object is stacked one level higher; and so on for every object you add to the page. (It's not uncommon for a page to have several dozen or even several hundred objects.)

Tip   When building pages, always try to keep the number of objects to a minimum. For example, instead of putting a headline in one text frame and a subhead in a separate text frame directly below the one that contains the headline, use a single text frame. The leaner your pages, the leaner your documents. Lean documents save and print more quickly and are less problematic to modify than bloated documents.

Although each object occupies its own level, if the objects on a page don't overlap, then the stacking order is not an issue. But some of the most interesting graphic effects you can achieve with InDesign involve arranging several overlapping objects, so it's important to be aware of the three-dimensional nature of a page's stacking order.

Because objects are added in back-to-front order, it makes sense to build your pages from back to front. For example, if you want to use a lightly tinted version of a scanned image as the background for a page, you would first place the image on the page, then add other objects on top of or in front of the picture frame.

In an ideal world, the first object you placed on a page would remain forever the backmost, the last object would be the frontmost, and every object in between — created in perfect order from back to front — would relate correctly with every other object. In this perfect world, you would never have to worry about moving objects backward or forward.

But the world is not perfect, and you may change your mind about what you want to achieve in your layout after you've already placed objects in it. To change an object's position in a page's stacking order, use the Arrange command (Object ➪ Arrange), which offers four choices:

✦ Bring to Front (F5 or Ctrl+Shift+])

✦ Bring Forward (⌘+] or Ctrl+])

✦ Send to Back (Shift+F5 or Ctrl+Shift+[)

✦ Send Backward (⌘+[or Ctrl+[)

For example, you might want to see how a piece of text looks in front of an illustration. But if you created the text frame before you created or placed the illustration, you'll have to move the text frame forward (or the illustration backward) in the stacking order.

Cross-Reference   In addition to letting you change the stacking order of objects on a page, InDesign also lets you create document-wide layers. Each layer contains a separate collection of stacked objects. For more information about using layers, see Chapter 6.

To change the stacking order of objects:

1. **Use any of the object-creation tools to create four overlapping shapes, as shown in Figure 12-1.**

   The numbers in parentheses indicate the order in which you should create the shapes.

Figure 12-1: The first shape you create is the backmost, the second is one level above, and so on. In this example, the three smaller boxes partially overlap each other and they are all in front of the largest box.

2. **If it's not already displayed, open the Color pane by choosing Window ➪ Color or pressing F6.**

   You'll use this pane to change the shade of each object so you can easily tell them apart.

3. **Click on the Selection tool, click on the last object you created, then use the color tools in the Toolbox or the Color pane to fill the object with a color.**

Cross-Reference   See Chapter 11 for more information about applying strokes and fills to objects.

4. **Use the Color pane to fill each of the remaining boxes with a successively lighter tint of the color, as shown in Figure 12-2.**

In the example, the remaining shapes are tinted at 25%, 50%, and 75%, respectively.

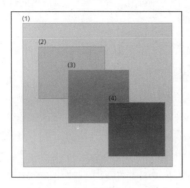

Figure 12-2: Applying tints to the shapes lets you see the stacking order of the four rectangles. Every InDesign object occupies one level in the stacking order.

5. **Click on the frontmost shape (the last one you created), then choose Object ⇨ Arrange ⇨ Send Backward or press ⌘+[or Ctrl+[.**

Notice that the Bring to Front and Bring Forward commands are not available. That's because you can't move the frontmost object any farther forward in the stacking order.

6. **Click on the backmost shape (the first one you created), then choose Object ⇨ Arrange ⇨ Bring Forward or press ⌘+] or Ctrl+].**

When you bring the object forward, one of the objects becomes obscured.

7. **Choose Object ⇨ Arrange ⇨ Bring to Front or press F5 or Ctrl+Shift+].**

The smaller shapes are now obscured by the largest one.

8. **Choose Object ⇨ Arrange ⇨ Send to Back or press Shift+F5 or Ctrl+Shift+[.**

The hidden objects are once again visible.

Tip

To select an object that's hidden behind one or more other objects, hold down the ⌘ or Ctrl key, then click anywhere within the area of the hidden object. The first click selects the topmost object; each successive click selects the next lowest object in the stacking order. When the bottom object is selected, the next click selects the top object. If you don't know where a hidden object is, you can simply click on the object or objects in front of it, then send the object(s) to the back.

New Feature

InDesign CS adds to the Object menu the Select submenu, which provides new controls for object selection. The first four options let you select another object relative to the currently selected object: First Object Above (Option+Shift+⌘+] or Ctrl+Alt+Shift+]) selects the topmost object, Next Object Above (Option+⌘+] or

Ctrl+Alt+]) selects the object immediately on top of the current object, Next Object Below (Option+⌘+[or Ctrl+Alt+[) selects the object immediately under the current object, and Last Object Below (Option+Shift+⌘+[or Ctrl+Alt+Shift+[) selects the bottommost object. If no objects are selected, InDesign will base its selection on the creation order. (Chapter 11 covers the Select submenu in more detail.) You can also access these four selection options by Control+clicking or right-clicking an object and choosing the Select menu from the contextual menu.

Combining Objects into a Group

InDesign lets you combine several objects into a group. A group of objects behaves like a single object, which means that you can cut, copy, move, or modify all the objects in a group in a single operation. Groups have many uses. For example, you might create a group to:

✦ Combine several objects that make up an illustration so that you can move, modify, copy, or scale all objects in a single operation.

✦ Keep a picture frame and its accompanying caption (text) frame together so that if you change your mind about their placement, you can reposition both objects at once.

✦ Combine several vertical lines that are used to separate the columns of a table so that you can quickly change the stroke, color, length, and position of all lines.

Tip

If you want to manipulate a group, choose the Selection tool, then click on any object in the group. The group's bounding box is displayed. Any transformation you perform is applied to all objects in the group. If you want to manipulate an object that's part of a group, select it using the Direct Selection tool.

To create a group:

1. **Select the Selection or Direct Selection tool.**

2. **Select all the objects you want to include in your group.**

3. **Choose Object ⇨ Group or press ⌘+G or Ctrl+G.**

Cross-Reference

See Chapter 11 for more information about selecting multiple objects.

That's all there is to it. When you create a group from objects that do not occupy successive levels in the stacking order, the objects are shuffled as necessary so that the grouped objects are stacked on adjacent layers directly below the topmost object. If you create a group from objects on different layers, all objects are moved to the top layer and stacked in succession beneath the topmost object. (See Chapter 6 for more about layers.)

Note You cannot create a group if some of the selected objects are locked and some are not locked. All selected objects must be locked or unlocked before you can group them. (Locking and unlocking objects is covered later in this chapter.)

Groups within groups

One nifty thing about groups is that you can include a group within a group. For example, all the objects in Figure 12-3 — five stars and two circles (a gray circle and a white circle form the moon) — have been grouped, making it easy to manipulate the whole illustration. But that's not all. The stars within the group are also a group. So are the two circles that make up the crescent moon. That is, first the stars were grouped together, then the two circles were grouped together, and finally then the group of stars was grouped with the group of circles that form the moon to create a larger group. Grouping the stars makes it easy to change all of them at once, as shown in Figure 12-4. And grouping the two circles that make up the crescent moon make it easy to move the moon.

Note A group can contain as many levels of subgroups, or *nested* groups, as you want, but it's best to keep things as simple as you can. The more levels of nested groups you have within a group, the more work it is to ungroup the objects.

Figure 12-3: The bounding box indicates that all the objects within have been grouped. What you can't tell from this illustration is that the five stars are a group within the larger group, which lets you move or modify all of them in a single operation, as shown in Figure 12-4.

Figure 12-4: The group selection tool (explained in the next section) lets you select a nested group. In this example, the nested group of stars was selected, then a radial blend was applied to all of them.

Selecting objects within groups

The main reason you create groups in the first place is so that you can delete, copy, move, or modify all the objects at once. But sometimes, you'll want to modify an object within a group. No problem. You don't have to ungroup objects to modify an individual object. InDesign offers several options for selecting objects — and nested groups — within groups. You can

✦ Select an individual object by clicking on it with the Direct Selection tool.

✦ Select the bounding box of an individual object by clicking on it with the Direct Selection tool, then switching to the Selection tool.

✦ Select multiple objects within a group by Shift+clicking each object with the Direct Selection tool.

✦ Select the bounding box of multiple objects within a group by Shift+clicking each object with the Direct Selection tool, then switching to the Selection tool.

✦ Select a nested group by clicking on any object within the nested group with the Direct Selection tool, then holding down the Option or Alt key and clicking again on the object. Holding down the Option or Alt key in this situation temporarily accesses the Group Selection tool, indicated by a small plus sign (+) below and to the right of the arrow pointer.

Ungrouping

After creating a group, you may eventually decide that you want to return the objects to their original, ungrouped state. To do so, simply click on any object in the group with the Selection tool, then choose Object ➪ Ungroup or press Shift+⌘+G or Ctrl+Shift+G. If you ungroup a group that contains a group, the contained group is not affected. To ungroup this subgroup, you must select it, then choose Ungroup again.

Nesting Objects within Frames

Not only does InDesign let you combine several objects into a group, you can also place an object within the boundaries of a frame. Just as a group that's embedded within a larger group is said to be a *nested* group, an object that's been placed within another frame is said to be a *nested* object. When you place an object within a frame, the containing frame acts as the cropping shape for the object within.

One of the more common uses of nested frames is for cropping imported graphics. When you place a graphic onto a page, the graphic is automatically placed within a frame. (You can also place a graphic within an existing frame.) You can reveal and hide different areas of the graphic by resizing or reshaping the container frame. Figure 12-5 shows an imported picture that's been placed within a circular frame.

Figure 12-5: In this example, the rectangle displayed with handles indicates the border of a picture that's been placed into a round frame. Clicking on the picture with the Direct Selection tool selects the picture rather than the round frame. To select the frame's bounding box instead of the picture, you would click on the picture with the Selection tool.

 For more information about importing and modifying pictures, see Part V.

Nesting frames within other frames

As you can with groups, you can place a frame within a frame within a frame and so on, to create as many nested levels as you want. The same caveat applies: Keep things as simple as possible to achieve the desired effect. To nest a frame within a frame:

1. **Use either the Selection tool or the Direct Selection tool to select the frame you want to nest within another frame**

2. **Choose Edit ➪ Copy or press ⌘+C or Ctrl+C.**

3. **Select the frame into which you want to place the copied object, then choose Edit ➪ Paste Into or press Option+⌘+V or Ctrl+Alt+V.**

Figure 12-6 shows a before/after example of a squiggly line that's been pasted into a circular frame, which serves as the masking shape for the line.

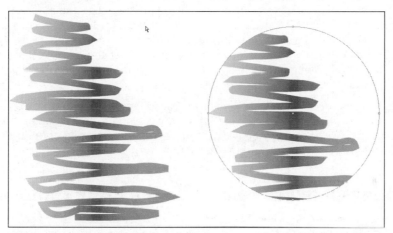

Figure 12-6: The squiggly line (left) was created with the Pen tool. It was then copied and pasted into (Edit ➪ Paste Into) a circular frame (right). Selecting the line with the Direct Selection tool would show the visible portion of the line within the oval cropping frame, as well as the parts of the line that are cropped.

Tip Selecting nested objects can be tricky. In general, the same selection techniques that work with groups work with nested frames. If you need to modify text within a nested — or grouped — text frame, simply click within the frame with the Type tool.

QuarkXPress User InDesign's nested frames are similar to QuarkXPress's constrained boxes.

Creating Inline Frames

In most cases, you'll want the objects you place on your pages to remain precisely where you put them. But sometimes, you'll want to place objects relative to related text in such a way that the objects move when the text is edited. For example, if you're creating a product catalog that's essentially a continuous list of product descriptions and you want to include a picture with each description, you can paste pictures within the text to create inline graphic frames.

An inline frame is treated like a single character. If you insert or delete text that precedes an inline frame, the frame moves forward or backward along with the rest of the text that follows the inserted/deleted text. There are two ways to create an inline frame: using the Paste command and using the Place command.

Caution

Inline graphics may interfere with line spacing in paragraphs with automatic leading. If the inline graphic is larger than the point size in use, the automatic leading value for that line is calculated from the graphic. This leads to inconsistent line spacing in the paragraph. To work around this, you can either apply a fixed amount of leading to all characters in the paragraph, adjust the size of inline graphics, place inline graphics at the beginning of a paragraph, or place inline graphics in their own paragraphs.

QuarkXPress User

InDesign's inline frames are similar to QuarkXPress's anchored boxes, with one important difference: If an inline frame is wider than the containing text frame, InDesign will hang the extra width of the inline frame outside of the width of the text frame, instead of causing a text overflow as it does in QuarkXPress.

Creating an inline frame with the Paste command

If you want to create an inline frame from an object you've already created, all you have to do is copy — or cut — the object and then paste it into text as you would a piece of highlighted text. Here's how:

1. **Use the Selection tool to select the object you want to paste within text.**

   Any type of object can be used: a line, an empty shape, a text or picture frame, even a group of objects.

2. **Choose Edit ➪ Copy or press ⌘+C or Ctrl+C.**

   If you don't need the original item, you can use the Cut command (Edit ➪ Cut; ⌘+X or Ctrl+X) instead of the Copy command. (An object that you cut or copy will remain on the Clipboard until you cut or copy something else or you turn off your computer. If you intend to use the original object elsewhere, it's better to use the Copy command when creating an inline frame.)

3. **Select the Type tool (or press T), then click within the text where you want to place the copied object.**

   Make sure the cursor is flashing where you intend to place the inline frame.

4. **Choose Edit ➪ Paste or press ⌘+V or Ctrl+V.**

   Figure 12-7 shows an example of an inline frame.

Tip

Inline graphics often work best when placed at the beginning of a paragraph. If you place an inline frame within text to which automatic leading has been applied, the resulting line spacing can be inconsistent. To fix this problem, you can resize the inline frame.

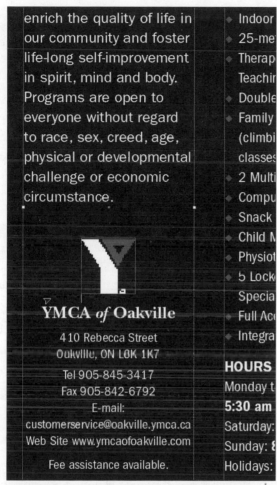

Figure 12-7: The YMCA logo is placed in the text as an inline frame so it will move up and down with the surrounding text.

Creating an inline frame with the Place command

In addition to using the Paste command to create an inline frame from an existing object, you can use the Place command to create an inline graphic from an external picture file. Here's how:

1. **Select the Type tool (or press T), then click within a text frame to establish the insertion point.**

2. **Choose File ⇨ Place or press ⌘+D or Ctrl+D.**

3. **Locate and select the graphic file you want to place within the text, then click Choose or Open.**

After you create an inline frame, you can adjust its position vertically or horizontally. To move an inline frame vertically:

1. **Use the Type tool to highlight the inline frame as you would highlight an individual text character.**

   In the Character pane, enter a positive value in the Baseline Shift field to move the inline frame up; enter a negative value to move the frame down.

2. **Use the Selection tool or Direct Selection tool to select the inline frame, then drag the frame up or down.**

To move an inline frame horizontally:

1. **With the Type tool selected, click between the inline frame and the character that precedes it.**

2. **Then use the kerning controls in the Character pane to enlarge or reduce the space between the inline frame and the preceding character.**

Tip   You can use the transform tools (Rotate, Scale, and Shear) and the Control palette or Transform pane to modify an inline frame as you modify any other frame.

Tip   To delete an inline frame, you can select it, then choose Edit ⇨ Clear or Edit ⇨ Cut, or you can position the cursor next to it and then press the Delete or Backspace key.

Locking Objects

If you're certain that you want a particular object to remain where it is, you can use Object ⇨ Lock Position, or ⌘+L or Ctrl+L, to prevent the object from being moved. Generally, you'll want to lock repeating elements such as headers, footers, folios, and page numbers so that they're not accidentally moved. (Such repeating elements are usually placed on a master page; you can lock objects on master pages, too.) A locked object can't be moved whether you click and drag it with the mouse or change the values in the X and Y fields in the Control palette or Transform pane. Not only can you *not* move a locked object, you can't delete one, either. However, you can change other attributes of a locked object, including its stroke and fill.

To unlock an object, use Object ⇨ Unlock Position, or Option+⌘+L or Ctrl+Alt+L.

Cross-Reference   You can also lock entire layers, as described in Chapter 6.

Summary

Most InDesign pages are made up of several objects. Each object occupies a separate level in a page's stacking order. The first object you place on a page occupies the bottom layer, and each new object you create or place occupies a new layer that's on top of all other layers. You can change a page's stacking order by moving individual items forward or backward in the stacking order. InDesign also provides several options for working with several objects at once. When multiple items are selected, you can combine them into a group that behaves like a single item. You can also place an object within a frame to create a nested object, and you can insert objects within a text thread to create inline frames that flow with the surrounding text.

✦   ✦   ✦

Timesaving Techniques

In This Chapter

Creating copies of objects

Aligning multiple objects

Using grid lines and guidelines when positioning objects

One of the advantages of using a computer for publishing is that it can do a lot of the work for you. That's particularly true of detail-oriented or repetitive work. InDesign has several features that let you save time by handling such repetitive, exacting chores for you. For example, if you're creating a checkerboard pattern as a page background, there's no need to create, modify, and place 20 or more frames by hand. You might start with one or two, then automatically duplicate and distribute the copies on your page.

Creating Copies of Objects

Once you've created something — a simple, rectangular frame or a complicated graphic made up of several dozen objects — InDesign makes it easy to reuse the original.

Here are your options:

✦ **Copy and Paste commands (Edit ⇨ Copy, or ⌘+C or Ctrl+C; Edit ⇨ Paste, or ⌘+V or Ctrl+V):** Using these commands is a good choice if you have to copy something from one page to another or from one document to another. But if you need a duplicate on the same page as the original, the Duplicate command is quicker. A great option is Paste in Place (Edit ⇨ Paste in Place, or Option+Shift+⌘+V or Ctrl+Alt+Shift+V) — this pastes an object in the same place as the original object. It's very handy when copying an element from one page to another, since it places the copy in the same location on the new page, saving you the effort of having to move it. (When copying among documents, Paste in Place may not be able to copy the object to the exact same location, since page dimensions may differ; in that case, Paste In Place will use the same X and Y coordinates as the original.)

✦ **Duplicate command (Edit ➪ Duplicate, or Option+Shift+⌘+D or Ctrl+Alt+Shift+D):** When you duplicate an object, the copy is placed 1 pica below and to the right of the original.

✦ **Manual cloning:** When you click and drag an object while holding down the Option or Alt key, a copy of the selected object is created. If you're a click-and-dragger, you may prefer this manual method to the Duplicate command.

✦ **Cloning with the Transform tools:** If you hold down the Option or Alt key while using any of the Transform tools (Rotate, Shear, and Scale), a copy of the selected object is transformed. The selected item remains unchanged.

✦ **Control palette and Transform pane cloning:** If you hold down the Option or Alt key when you exit the Control palette or Transform pane (by pressing Return or Enter or releasing the mouse after choosing an option from a menu), the transformation is applied to a copy of the selected item.

✦ **Step and Repeat command (Edit ➪ Step and Repeat, or Shift+⌘+V or Ctrl+Shift+V):** Think of the Step and Repeat dialog box (shown in Figure 13-1) as the Duplicate command on steroids. It lets you create multiple duplicates of selected objects and specify the horizontal and vertical offset of the duplicates. This command is handy if you have to create, for example, a vertical and/or horizontal grid of lines on a page. Simply draw a horizontal line at the top of the page or a vertical line along the left edge of the page. With the line selected, use the Step and Repeat command to place — and evenly space — as many additional lines as you need.

Figure 13-1: The Step and Repeat dialog box.

Figure 13-2 shows a typical task that's easily handled with the Step and Repeat command. First, the top row was built by creating three copies of the original with an inch of space between each duplicate; the second row was created by step-and-repeating three squares in the top row; and finally the bottom six rows were created by step-and-repeating the top two rows. Voilà!

Tip

If you need to use an object or a group of objects repeatedly, storing them in a library is a good idea. For example, if you've used InDesign to create a logo or a house ad, copy the objects into a library. Once you place something in a library, you can drag-copy as many clones as you want into any document. For more information about using libraries, see Chapter 7.

Figure 13-2: This checkerboard was created with three trips to the Step and Repeat dialog box.

Copying Objects between Documents

Occasionally, you'll want to use something you've created in one InDesign document in another document. For example, maybe an ad that ran in last month's newsletter is needed again for this month's edition. Or perhaps you created a small illustration for an ad that you want to use in a companion brochure. InDesign offers several options for moving objects between documents. You can

✦ Open the document that contains the objects you want to copy, select the objects, then copy them to the clipboard with Edit ➪ Copy, or ⌘+C or Ctrl+C. Open the target document and use Edit ➪ Paste, or ⌘+V or Ctrl+V, to place the copied objects. You can also use Edit ➪ Paste in Place, or Option+Shift+⌘+V or Ctrl+Alt+Shift+V, to paste the object at the same X and Y coordinates as the original.

✦ If you need to use the objects in more than one document, you can copy them into a library, which lets you place as many copies as you want in any document.

✦ You can open the source document (the one that contains the objects) and the target document and drag-copy the objects from the source document to the target document. (Choose Window ➪ Arrange ➪ Tile to display both document windows side by side.)

Aligning and Distributing Objects

InDesign lets you align and distribute objects, saving you the hassle of manually moving and placing each element, or figuring out the correct locations in the Control palette or Transform pane to do so. The Align pane is where InDesign offers these timesaving abilities.

New Feature InDesign CS adds the ability to create keyboard shortcuts for the Align and Distribute buttons. Although there are no default shortcuts, these buttons are now listed in the Object Editing commands in the Keyboard Shortcuts dialog box (Edit ➪ Keyboard Shortcuts) so you can create shortcuts for them. Chapter 3 covers keyboard shortcuts in more detail.

The Align pane (Window ➪ Align or Shift+F7), shown in Figure 13-3, has several buttons, described in the callouts, that let you manipulate the relative position of multiple objects in two ways. You can

Figure 13-3: The Align pane contains 14 buttons that let you control the alignment and space between selected objects. If the two Distribute Spacing buttons are not displayed at the bottom of the palette, choose Show Options from the palette menu.

✦ **Line up objects along a horizontal or vertical axis.** For example, if you've randomly placed several small graphic frames onto a page, you can use the alignment buttons in the Align pane to align them neatly—either horizontally or vertically. Figure 13-4 shows a before/after example of objects aligned with the Align pane.

Figure 13-4: The rectangles on the left were aligned along the left edge of the leftmost object by clicking the Horizontal Align Left button in the Align pane. The result of the alignment operation is shown on the right.

✦ **Distribute space evenly between objects along a horizontal or vertical axis.** Here's a typical problem that's easily solved by using this feature: You've carefully placed five small pictures on a page so that the top edges are aligned across the page and there is equal space between each picture. Then you find out one of the pictures needs to be cut. After deleting the unneeded picture, you could use the Align pane to redistribute the space between the remaining pictures so that they're again equally spaced. Figure 13-5 shows a before/after example of the Align pane's Distribute Spacing capability, here showing the feature to align a series of vertically arranged objects.

The Align buttons don't work with objects that have been locked with the Lock Position command (Object ➪ Lock Position, or ⌘+L or Ctrl+L). If you need to align a locked object, you must first unlock it (Object ➪ Unlock Position, or Option+⌘+ L or Ctrl+Alt+L). If the objects are on a locked layer, you'll need to unlock the layer.

The six alignment buttons are also available in the Control palette if you've selected multiple objects with the Selection tool (see Chapter 11 for more on the Control palette).

When you click on a button in the Align pane, selected objects are repositioned in the most logical manner. For example, if you click the Horizontal Align Left button, the selected objects are moved horizontally (to the left, in this case) so that the left edge of each object is aligned with the left edge of the leftmost object. Along the same lines, if you click the Vertical Distribute Center button, the selected objects are moved vertically so that there's an equal amount of space between the vertical center of each object.

Figure 13-5: The objects on the left are unequally spaced. Clicking the Vertical Distribute Space button in the Align pane repositions the objects so that the spaces between the objects are equal, as shown on the right.

Spacing can appear uneven if you click the Horizontal or Vertical Distribute buttons when objects of various sizes are selected. For objects of different sizes, you'll usually want to use the Distribute Spacing buttons (which make the space between objects even) rather than space objects based on their centers or sides (which is how the Distribute Object buttons work).

Note   If the two Distribute Spacing icons are not displayed at the bottom of the palette and you want to distribute objects, choose Show Options from the palette menu.

Tip   Sometimes the result of clicking a button in the Align pane isn't what you anticipate — or want. If this happens, simply choose Edit ➪ Undo or press ⌘+Z or Ctrl+Z and try another button.

Positioning Objects Precisely with Guides

Just as carpenters often use chalk lines to make sure things are straight when putting up the framework of a house, you can use guidelines and grid lines to help achieve precise object placement and alignment when building InDesign documents. InDesign lets you show or hide three kinds of guides: user-created vertical and horizontal guidelines, document grid lines, and baseline grid lines. You can tell InDesign to automatically snap object edges to guidelines and grid lines when you create, resize, or move an object within a user-specified distance.

Cross-Reference   For more about creating and using guidelines and grids, see Chapter 7.

You can create horizontal and vertical guidelines whenever you want by clicking on either the horizontal or vertical ruler and dragging the pointer onto the page or pasteboard. Choosing View ➪ Show Guides or ⌘+; (semicolon) or Ctrl+; (semicolon), turns guides on. The menu option name then changes to Hide Guides, so you can toggle guides on and off using the same shortcut.

When guidelines are displayed and Snap to Guides (View ➪ Snap to Guides, or Shift+⌘+; [semicolon] or Ctrl+Shift+; [semicolon]) is checked, an object edge will snap to a guideline when you create, resize, or move the object within the number of pixels specified in the Snap to Zone preference (choose InDesign ➪ Preferences on the Mac or Edit ➪ Preferences in Windows, or press ⌘+K or Ctrl+K, then go to the Guides & Pasteboard pane).

Note
When Snap to Guides is checked in the View menu, guidelines must be displayed (View ➪ Show Guides, or ⌘+; [semicolon] or Ctrl+; [semicolon]) for objects to snap to them. However, when Snap to Document Grid is checked, objects will snap to document grid lines and, when Snap to Guides is checked, objects will snap to baseline grid lines), regardless of whether the document grid or the baseline grid is displayed.

All documents include a document-wide grid of vertical and horizontal lines that you can use for creating, resizing, and positioning objects. The View ➪ Show Document Grid and Show ➪ Hide Document Grid commands, or ⌘+' (apostrophe) or Ctrl+' (apostrophe), toggle the document grid display on and off. When displayed, the document grid looks much like graph paper. When guidelines are displayed and View ➪ Snap to Document Grid, or Shift+⌘+' (apostrophe) or Ctrl+Shift+' (apostrophe), is checked, an object edge will snap to a document grid line when you create, resize, or move the object within the number of pixels specified in the Snap to Zone preference in the Preferences dialog box's Guides & Pasteboard pane.

Tip
If you want to align objects with text baselines and text baselines with the baseline grid, use the Grids pane preferences in the Preferences dialog box to specify the same vertical spacing for the Document Grid as for the Baseline Grid. For example, specify an Increment Every value of 1 pica in the Baseline Grid area, and specify a Subdivisions value of 6 in the Document Grid area.

In addition to the document grid, all documents have a built-in baseline grid that represents the leading increments of body text. The View ➪ Show Baseline Grid and View ➪ Hide Baseline Grid commands, or Option+⌘+' (apostrophe) or Ctrl+Alt+' (apostrophe), toggles baseline grid display on and off. When the baseline grid is displayed and Snap to Guides is checked, an object edge will snap to a baseline grid line when you create, resize, or move the object within the number of pixels specified in the Snap to Zone preference in the Guides & Pasteboard pane of the Preferences dialog box. You can use the Align to Baseline Grid option in a paragraph style or via the Paragraph pane (Type ➪ Paragraph) to lock the baselines of text in selected paragraphs to baseline grid lines, and you can modify a document's baseline grid via the Grids pane in the Preferences dialog box.

Tip

In addition to aligning objects with guides, you can also use the arrow keys to nudge items when precise positioning is required. This method works well when you're positioning an object relative to another object rather than aligning the object with a grid line. Each press of an arrow key moves the selected objects one point. If you hold down the Shift key when nudging, the increment is 10 points. You can set alternative nudge settings via the Cursor Key field in the Units & Increments pane of the Preferences dialog box. Holding the Shift key when nudging will move the selected objects 10 increments of whatever Cursor Key is set to.

Summary

When it comes to working with the objects you've placed on a page, InDesign provides several timesaving features. You can create a single copy of any object using the Copy and Paste commands (Edit menu), using the Duplicate command (Edit menu), or by Option+dragging or Alt+dragging a clone of the original. The Step and Repeat command (Edit menu) lets you create multiple copies of objects and position the copies relative to the originals. The Paste in Place command will paste an object at the same X and Y coordinates as the original object.

The Align pane (Window ⇨ Align or Shift+F7) lets you align multiple objects and control the amount of space between them, while vertical and horizontal ruler guides and snap-to-grid features help you accurately position and align items.

✦   ✦   ✦

Text Fundamentals

For many designers, text is the gray stuff that flows around pictures and headlines, but text is actually a key component of the layout and its design. It also involves much of the effort in creating a layout. The chapters in this part show you how to prepare, import, and format your text, including design-oriented text manipulation and table creation.

First, you need to understand how to prepare your text. Today's word processors are very powerful, and many people are tempted to use their many capabilities in files destined for InDesign. Don't be. Today's word processors do too much for files destined for a page-layout program, and the key to effective preparation is to do just the basics in your word processor, as Chapter 14 explains.

With your text ready to use, you need to bring it into InDesign, as well as enter some text directly into InDesign. Chapter 15 shows you how to do so, as well as how to edit text, spell-check it, and set its hyphenation rules. You'll also learn how to export text from InDesign into files usable by other programs.

It's rare that text all goes onto one page in a layout, which is why understanding text flow is so key. Chapter 16 explains how InDesign flows text from page to page and column to column, and how you can control how text flows as well as the appearance of the frames in which it is held.

With your text in place, you'll want to apply the appropriate formatting — fonts, size, justification, alignment, and so on — to it. Chapters 17 through 19 show how to format your text so it takes on the visual character you want in your layout. You'll want to automate your text formatting wherever possible. That's what style sheets do, and Chapter 20 explains how to create style sheets that let you apply consistent formatting to text throughout a document. Style sheets also let you change

Chapter 14
Preparing Text Files for Import

Chapter 15
Working with Text

Chapter 16
Flowing Text through a Document

Chapter 17
Specifying Character Attributes

Chapter 18
Specifying Paragraph Attributes

Chapter 19
Creating Special Text Formatting

Chapter 20
Setting Up Style Sheets

Chapter 21
Setting Up Tabs and Tables

text throughout a document with a few simple actions, rather than change everything by hand. The chapter also shows you how to work with the style sheets in your word processors to save even more layout time.

Finally, a special type of formatting involves tabs, which let you align text to specific locations. A more powerful variation is the ability to create and edit tables. Chapter 21 explains how to do both.

Preparing Text Files for Import

Y ou can import text into your InDesign documents in
several ways. InDesign is particularly adept at importing documents created in popular Macintosh and Windows
formats. And through the use of the Macintosh and Windows
clipboards (copy and paste), you can import file formats—
to a limited degree—that are not directly supported by
InDesign.

Determining Where to Format Documents

InDesign import capabilities may tempt you to do a lot of your
text formatting outside the program; however, it's not always
wise to do so. Here are some reasons why you *shouldn't* work
outside the program:

+ **Because a word processor's formatting capabilities
won't match all InDesign typographic features, it's often
not worthwhile to do extensive formatting in your
word processor.** This is particularly true of layout-
oriented formatting. Multiple columns and page numbers,
for example, will be of a much higher standard in your
final InDesign document than you could hope to create
in a word processor. After all, even the sophisticated formatting features in today's word processors don't begin
to approach those needed for true publishing.

+ **Similarly, formatting tables in your word processor or
spreadsheet is typically a wasted effort because you
have to re-create the tables using InDesign tab settings
(see Chapter 21).** If you turn your spreadsheet or chart
into a graphic before importing it, you cannot edit the
data. Nor can you resize the picture to fit a changing
layout without winding up with different-size numbers
among at least some charts—a definite no-no.

In This Chapter

Determining which
formatting tasks to do
in InDesign and
which to handle in
other programs

Working with files
across platforms

Preparing files for
import from word
processors and
spreadsheets

Working with special
file formats

Working with files across platforms

It's increasingly common for people in publishing to work in a cross-platform (Mac and Windows) environment. Even if you do all your InDesign work on one platform, chances are high that you'll receive files created on the other platform. (Most text editing is done on PCs, while most graphics and publishing work is done on the Mac, for example.)

Even with the improved compatibility between Mac and PC (mostly thanks to additions to the Mac OS that makes it easier to share files with PCs), you may still encounter some trip-ups dealing with something as simple as filenames when sharing files across platforms.

Both Windows and the Mac OS use icons to show you (and tell programs) what format a file is in. Windows and Mac OS X (but not earlier versions of the Mac OS) use filename extensions (often hidden from user view) to identify the file type. InDesign uses the file-name extension .INDD to denote InDesign documents. Without this filename extension, you won't be able to double-click a file icon to open it, although you can still open the file from InDesign's Open dialog box (File ⇨ Open, or ⌘+O or Ctrl+O), as long as you select All Documents from the Show pop-up menu (on the Mac) or All Files from the Files of Type pop-up menu (in Windows).

If filename extensions are hidden in Windows, choose Tools ⇨ Folder Options and then select the View tab to get the pane shown in the following figure. (You have to have a disk or folder open to have the View menu.) Uncheck the Hide Extensions for Known File Types item, then click OK.

If filename extensions are hidden in Mac OS X, use Finder ⇨ Preferences and then check the Always Show File Extensions option, as shown in the following figure, and close the dialog box. (You have to be using the Finder, not be in an application, to get this menu.)

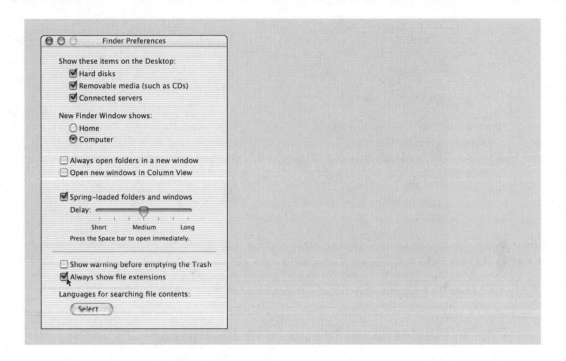

The bottom line is to use InDesign for your layout and complex text formatting (fonts, leading, and hyphenation), and use your word processor for basic text editing, style-sheet assignments (identifying headlines, body copy, and so forth), and basic character formatting (boldface, italics, and other meaning-oriented formatting).

Importing Text Files

What preparation do you possibly need to do for your word processor files? They should just load into InDesign as is, right? Not necessarily, even if your word processor supports one of the InDesign text-import formats. Actually, the key to preparing text files is to not *over* prepare them.

Most of today's major word processors include basic graphics and layout features to help users format single-document publications. Avoid using these features in files you intend to bring into InDesign. Do your sophisticated formatting in InDesign — that's one of the reasons you invested in such a powerful tool. This approach also enables you to do formatting in the context of your layout, rather than in a vacuum. Much of the graphics and layout formatting you do in a word processor is all for naught anyway because such nontextual formatting does not import into InDesign — you're importing text, not documents.

Tip   Limit your word processor formatting to the type of formatting that enhances reader understanding or conveys meaning. Such formatting may include using italic and boldface to emphasize a word, for example, or using style sheets to set headlines and bylines in different sizes and typefaces. (See Chapter 20 for tips on using style sheets in word processor text.) Let your editors focus on the words; leave presentation tasks to your layout artists.

One type of file preparation you may need to do is to translate text files into formats supported by InDesign. InDesign supports just Microsoft Word, Rich Text Format (RTF), and text-only (ASCII) formats. If you use Corel WordPerfect or AppleWorks, you'll need to save in one of those formats. Where possible, you should save in Microsoft Word format (up through the new Office 11 version), since InDesign supports more Word formatting capabilities than it does RTF capabilities, and the text-only format preserves no formatting.

Note   InDesign also imports InCopy files. InCopy is an Adobe text editor available only from publishing systems integrators who set up entire newsrooms, magazines, and other companies with large numbers of users to base their publication operations on InDesign. Appendix F covers InCopy in more detail.

Preserving special features in text files

Today's word processors let you do much more than enter and edit text. You also can create special characters, tables, headers and footers, and other document elements. Some of these features work when imported into a publishing program, but others don't. Table 14-1 shows which character formatting is preserved in Word.

Table 14-1 Imported Character Formatting		
	Macintosh Word 98 (8.0), 2001 (9.0), X (10.0)	*Windows Word 97 (8.0), 2000 (9.0), XP (10.0), 2003 (11.0)*
Character Formatting*		
All caps	Can import into InDesign.	Can import into InDesign.
Boldface	Can import into InDesign.	Can import into InDesign.
Color	Can import into InDesign.	Can import into InDesign.
Condense/ expand	Can import into InDesign.	Can import into InDesign.
Double strikethrough	Double strikethrough is converted to single strikethrough.	Double strikethrough is converted to single strikethrough.
Double underline	All underlining is converted to single underlines.	All underlining is converted to single underlines.

	Macintosh Word 98 (8.0), 2001 (9.0), X (10.0)	*Windows Word 97 (8.0), 2000 (9.0), XP (10.0), 2003 (11.0)*
Character Formatting*		
Emboss	Embossed text is made into paper color (usually white).	Embossed text is made into paper color (usually white).
Engrave	Engraved text is made into paper color (usually white).	Engraved text is made into paper color (usually white).
Font change	Can import into InDesign.	Can import into InDesign.
Hidden	Hidden text is deleted.	Hidden text is deleted.
Italics	Can import into InDesign.	Can import into InDesign.
Outline	Can import into InDesign.	Can import into InDesign.
Point size	Can import into InDesign.	Can import into InDesign.
Shadow	Imported as plain text.	Imported as plain text.
Small caps	Can import into InDesign.	Can import into InDesign.
Strikethrough	Can import into InDesign.	Can import into InDesign.
Subscript	Can import into InDesign.	Can import into InDesign.
Superscript	Can import into InDesign.	Can import into InDesign.
Underline	Can import into InDesign.	Can import into InDesign.
Word-only underline	All underlining is converted to single underlines.	All underlining is converted to single underlines.
Other Features		
Annotations/ comments	Cannot import into InDesign.	Cannot import into InDesign.
Bulleted lists	Can import into InDesign.	Can import into InDesign.
Drop caps	Can import into InDesign.	Can import into InDesign.
Footnotes	Footnote text is placed at end of text.	Footnote text is placed at end of text.
Indents	Can import into InDesign.	Can import into InDesign.
Numbered lists	Can import into InDesign.	Can import into InDesign.
Page breaks	Can import into InDesign.	Can import into InDesign.
Pictures	Can import into InDesign only if pictures are in an InDesign-supported format.	Can import into InDesign only if pictures are in an InDesign-supported format.

Continued

Table 14-1 *(continued)*		
	Macintosh Word 98 (8.0), 2001 (9.0), X (10.0)	**Windows Word 97 (8.0), 2000 (9.0), XP (10.0), 2003 (11.0)**
Other Features		
Redlining/ revisions	Revisions are converted to underline for additions and strikethrough for deletions.	Revisions are converted to underline for additions and strikethrough for deletions.
Section breaks	Ignored during import.	Ignored during import.
Special characters	Can import into InDesign.	Can import into InDesign.
Subscribed/ OLE items	Cannot import into InDesign.	Cannot import into InDesign.
Tables	Can import into InDesign. Borders are not converted.	Can import into InDesign. Borders are not converted.

*Note: Not all formatting listed may be available in every supported version of Word.

Tables

Word processors have developed very capable table editors, letting you format tabular information quickly and easily — and often rivaling dedicated spreadsheet programs. InDesign is rare in the world of page-layout programs in that it can import tables created in Word or Excel, as well as tables in RTF documents.

QuarkXPress User   InDesign does a good job of importing Word tables and Excel spreadsheets as tables, unlike QuarkXPress.

Headers and footers

Headers and footers are a layout issue, not a text issue, so there is no reason to include these elements in your word-processor document. Because page numbers will change based on your InDesign layout, there's no point in putting the headers and footers in your word processor document anyway. Note that if you do use them, they will not import into InDesign. Chapter 5 explains how to add these elements to your layout.

Footnotes and endnotes

If you use a word processor's footnote or endnote feature and import the text file, the notes are placed at the end of the imported text. The superscripted numerals or characters in the notes usually translate properly.

Hyperlinks

Modern word processors like Word let you include hyperlinks in their text, so when you export to HTML or PDF format, the reader can click the link and jump to a Web page or to another PDF file. When you import text files with such hyperlinks, InDesign will retain their visual formatting—hyperlinks usually display as blue underlined text—as well as the actual link.

Using special characters

The Mac and Windows both have built-in support for special characters, such as symbols, accented characters, and non-English letters. There are several ways to access these characters:

✦ **On both platforms, using keyboard shortcuts (see Chapter 41).**

✦ **On the Mac, using Apple's Key Caps program, which comes with the Mac OS and is located in the Applications\Utilities folder.** The following figure shows the program. The two sets of special characters are found by holding Option and Option+Shift (each results in a different set). Some fonts also have symbols accessible by using the Control key. Use the Fonts menu, as shown in the figure, to change fonts in Key Caps, in case a symbol you want is available in a font other than the one currently in use.

Continued

Continued

✦ **On the Mac, using a shareware utility like Günther Blaschek's PopChar X control panel.** The following figure shows PopChar X. Notice how the keyboard shortcut for each special character is shown at the bottom right as a character is highlighted. (The companion Web site, `www.INDDCentral.com`, has links to this and other utilities.)

✦ **On Windows, using the Character Map utility that comes with Windows.** The following figure shows the program. Just as Key Caps is usually installed in the Mac's Apple menu, Character Map is usually installed in the Windows equivalent Start menu (Start ➪ Programs ➪ Accessories ➪ System Tools ➪ Character Map).

On both platforms, you can use a word processor's own feature for special-character access. Microsoft Word, for example, has such an option (as the following figure shows) via Insert ⇨ Symbol or via the toolbar (if you added this command to your toolbar, look for the button with the Ω character). WordPerfect has a similar dialog box accessed via Insert ⇨ Symbols (Mac) or Insert ⇨ Character (Windows). (InDesign has its own dialog box like this for when you're adding symbols to your text from within your layout; access it via Type ⇨ Insert Glyphs.)

Not all fonts may have all special characters available. Typically, fonts from major type foundries like Adobe and Monotype have all the characters in each font, but custom-made fonts and those from other foundries may use different characters or have fewer. Also, fonts translated from Windows to the Mac, or vice versa, through a program like FontLab will likely have special characters in different locations than a native Mac or Windows font; Windows PostScript fonts generally have fewer special characters in the font than their Mac counterparts.

In-line graphics

Modern word processors typically support in-line graphics, enabling you to import a picture into your word-processor document and embed it in text. Word, for example, lets you import graphics, and InDesign, in turn, can import the graphics with your text — as long as they are in formats supported by InDesign. But graphics embedded in your word-processor document via Mac OS 9's Publish and Subscribe or via OLE (available in Windows and Mac OS 9) will *not* import into InDesign.

In-line graphics will import as their preview images, not as the original formats. This means that, in most cases, you'll get a lower-resolution version in your InDesign layout.

Tip

Despite their limitations, the use of in-line graphics in your word processor can be helpful when putting together an InDesign document: Use the in-line graphics whose previews are imported into InDesign as placeholders so that the layout artist knows you have embedded graphics. He or she can then replace the previews with the better-quality originals. If you find yourself using several graphics as characters (such as a company icon used as a bullet), use a font-creation program like FontLab to create a symbol typeface with those graphics. Then both your word-processor and layout documents can use the same, high-quality versions.

Avoiding text-file pitfalls

Sometimes, issues not related to the contents of a word-processor file can affect how files are imported into InDesign.

Fast save

Several programs (notably Microsoft Word) offer a fast-save feature, which adds information to the end of a word-processor document. The added information notes which text has been added and deleted and where the changes occurred. You can use this feature to save time because the program doesn't have to write the entire document to disk when you save the file. When you use the fast-save feature, however, text-import into publishing programs — including InDesign — becomes problematic. I suggest that you turn off fast save, at least for files you import into InDesign. With today's speedy hard drives, the time you gain by using fast save is barely noticeable, anyway. The vast majority of file corruption problems and bugs in Word are related to the fast-save feature and its use makes file recovery in the event of a crash problematic at best. To disable fast save, choose Tools ➪ Options, go to the Save pane, and deselect the Allow Fast Saves check box.

Fixing Microsoft Word's bad dashes

Most versions of Word have a default setting that converts two hyphens to an en dash (–) rather than an em dash (—), which is simply wrong typographically. (Word 98 for Mac and Word 2002/XP for Windows *don't* have this problem.)

To solve this problem, we recommend that you turn off Word's automatic conversion of two hyphens to a dash (Tools ➪ AutoCorrect ➪ AutoFormat as You Type). Instead, enter two hyphens in the Replace box in the AutoCorrect dialog box's AutoCorrect pane and put an em dash (shortcut Option+Shift+- [hyphen] on the Mac or Alt+0151 in Windows) in the With box, then click the Add button. This will make Word substitute the correct dash when you type in two consecutive hyphens.

Software versions

Pay attention to the version number of the word processor you use. This caution may seem obvious, but the issue still trips up a lot of people. Usually, old versions (two or more revisions old) or new versions (newer than the publishing or other importing program) cause import problems. The import filters either no longer recognize the old format (something has to go to make room for new formats) or were written before the new version of the word processor was released. InDesign supports Microsoft Word for Windows 97, 2000, XP, and 2003 and Word for Mac 98, 2001, and X, as well as the same-numbered versions of Excel.

Using Tagged Text

InDesign offers a file format of its own: Adobe InDesign Tagged Text. Tagged Text actually is ASCII (text-only) text that contains embedded codes to tell InDesign which formatting to apply. You embed these codes, which are similar to macros, as you create files in your word processor.

No matter what layout program they use, most people don't use the tagged-text option because the coding can be tortuous. Because you can't use tagged-text codes with your word processor's formatting, you must code everything with tagged text and save the document as an ASCII file. So why have Tagged Text at all? Because this format is the one format sure to support all the formatting you do in InDesign.

Working with exported Tagged Text files

The usefulness of Tagged Text is not in creating text for import, but in transferring files created in InDesign to another InDesign user (including someone working on another platform) or to a word processor for further work. You can export an InDesign story or piece of selected text in the Tagged Text format, and then transfer the exported file to another InDesign user or to a word processor for further editing.

Exporting a Tagged Text file into a word processor makes sense if you want to add or delete text without losing special formatting — such as fonts, kerning, or style tags — that your word processor doesn't support. After you edit the text, you can save the altered file (make sure that it is saved as ASCII text) and reimport it into your InDesign layout.

The best way to understand the Tagged Text format is to export some of your own documents to it, and open the resulting file in a word processor to see how InDesign coded the file. A warning: The Tagged Text format can be complex, especially because most codes have two forms, a short (abbreviated) one and a long (verbose) one — you choose which InDesign exports from the Export dialog box in InDesign (File ⇨ Export, then choose InDesign Tagged Text as the file format). Note that a Tagged Text file is simply an ASCII text file, so it will have the extension .TXT and use the standard text-only file icon in Windows and on the Mac.

Here's an example of verbose coding (because the code is so long, I had to add line breaks; slightly indented lines are actually part of the same code segment):

```
<ASCII-WIN>
<DefineParaStyle:Normal=<Nextstyle:Normal><cTypeface:Regular>
<cSize:10.000000><pHyphenationLadderLimit:0><pHyphenation:0>
<pHyphenationZone:18.000000><cFont:Times New Roman>
<cColorTint:100.000000>>
<DefineCharStyle:Default Paragraph Font=
<Nextstyle:Default Paragraph Font>>
<DefineCharStyle:Hyperlink=<BasedOn:Default Paragraph Font>
<Nextstyle:Hyperlink><cColor:Blue><cTypeface:Regular>
<cSize:10.000000><cHorizontalScale:1.000000>
<cBaselineShift:0.000000><cCase:Normal><cStrokeColor:>
<cUnderline:1><cFont:Times New Roman><cPosition:Normal>
<cStrikethru:0><cColorTint:100.000000>>
<ColorTable:=<Black:COLOR:CMYK:Process:0.000000,0.000000,
0.000000,1.000000><Blue:COLOR:RGB:Process:0.000000,0.000000,
1.000000>>
<ParaStyle:Normal><pHyphenation:1>
<CharStyle:Default Paragraph Font>
<CharStyle:><CharStyle:Hyperlink>www.adobe.com<CharStyle:>
<CharStyle:Default Paragraph Font>. <CharStyle:><pHyphenation:>
```

Here is the same text with abbreviated tags:

```
<ASCII-WIN>
<dps:Normal=<Nextstyle:Normal><ct:Regular><cs:10.000000>
<phll:0><ph:0><phz:18.000000><cf:Times New Roman>
<cct:100.000000>>
<dcs:Default Paragraph Font=<Nextstyle:Default Paragraph Font>>
<dcs:Hyperlink=<BasedOn:Default Paragraph Font>
<Nextstyle:Hyperlink><cc:Blue><ct:Regular><cs:10.000000>
<chs:1.000000><cbs:0.000000><ccase:Normal><csc:><cu:1>
<cf:Times New Roman><cp:Normal><cstrike:0><cct:100.000000>>
<ctable:=<Black:COLOR:CMYK:Process:0.000000,0.000000,0.000000,
1.000000><Blue:COLOR:RGB:Process:0.000000,0.000000,1.000000>>
<pstyle:Normal><ph:1><cstyle:Default Paragraph Font>
<cstyle:><cstyle:Hyperlink>www.adobe.com<cstyle:>
<cstyle:Default Paragraph Font>. <cstyle:><ph:>
```

What does all that coding mean? Well, that's for a one-page document with one frame that has simply one line of text:

```
This is a hyperlink to www.adobe.com.
```

The text is black, except for the Web address, which is in blue underline.

As you can see, there's a lot to Tagged Text codes. InDesign comes with a complete list of codes in a PDF file called Tagged Text.pdf that you'll find in the Tagged Text folder within the Adobe Technical Info folder on the InDesign CD-ROM.

In practical terms, you may not mind editing Tagged Text slightly or leaving them in a file when you alter its text. But you're not likely to forgo the friendly formatting available in your word processor and in InDesign to apply Tagged Text coding to everything in your text files.

Using Tagged Text for database publishing

Tagged Text format can be very handy as a start to database publishing. The codes in the preceding section define the formatting in a document. However, you don't need to go that far; you can simply *specify* paragraph tags using Tagged Text, so when text is imported into an InDesign document, InDesign knows what styles to apply. You would use this technique to import data gathered by, for example, a Web-based survey page or exported from a database. By placing the Tagged Text codes before each paragraph, you will save the effort of manually tagging every paragraph in InDesign.

For example, say you have a product director that lists the company name, URL, and product description. You'd have a text file with entries that look something like this:

```
<ASCII-WIN>
<pstyle:Company>Name 1
<pstyle:URL>Web address 1
<pstyle:Description>Descriptive text 1 goes here.
<pstyle:Company>Name 2
<pstyle:URL>Web address 2
<pstyle:Description>Descriptive text 2 goes here.
```

The <ASCII-WIN> (or <ASCII-MAC> if the file was created on a Mac) code appears only at the top of the file. The code <pstyle:*style name*> specifies the paragraph style to apply (for character styles, the code is <cstyle:*style name*>) — be sure that the name is an exact match, including any capitalization; otherwise, InDesign won't recognize the style you want to use.

To use text coded this way, you open an existing document that is already set up with text frames and text styles, then place the text file into the document. The tagged text will take on the designated styles, making it easy, for example, to flow an updated catalog into a template. Figure 14-1 shows a document created this way.

Figure 14-1: A catalog created by importing a Tagged Text file.

Summary

Because today's word processors are so powerful, there's a temptation to do a lot of sophisticated, layout-oriented formatting in them before bringing the files into a layout program like InDesign. But don't. No word processor has the typographic or layout ability of InDesign, and doing a lot of work in your word processing file is simply a waste of time—you'd need to do it over again in InDesign in the context of your layout anyhow.

Focus on the meaning-oriented formatting in your word processor: use of style sheets to indicate headlines, bylines, quotation blocks, and so on, as well as local formatting like italics, superscripts, and font changes.

When you're done preparing your text, be sure to save it in a format compatible with InDesign. Even if your word processor format is not compatible with InDesign, chances are it can save in one that is.

Finally, consider using the Tagged Text format to specify sophisticated formatting, such as defining paragraph and character styles in InDesign, in your word processor. This requires a familiarity with programming or coding in formats like HTML but can be a powerful way to add formatting for highly predictable, structured documents in your word processor before importing the file into InDesign. Using it just to specify paragraph and style sheets is a great way to bring database-oriented data, such as catalogs, into an InDesign template.

✦   ✦   ✦

Working with Text

In This Chapter

Adding text by typing, pasting, or importing

Editing text, including highlighting, cutting and pasting, and deleting

Exporting text for use in a word processor

Searching and replacing words and formats

Checking spelling

Customizing the spelling and hyphenation dictionaries

Adjusting text frames

Although you can use InDesign as your primary word processor, doing so is a little like buying an SUV for suburban errands — glamorous but unnecessary. In publishing, at least the first draft of text is generally written in Microsoft Word because this word processing program offers many editorial bells and whistles. Text is then imported into an InDesign publication. If you prefer to type in style, you can use InDesign's basic word processing features for entering text. After text is in a publication, you can use InDesign's editing, search and replace functions, and spell checker to refine your content.

Adding Text

No matter where your text originates — in your mind, in e-mail, on the Web, or in a word processor — you can add it to an InDesign publication easily. You can type text directly in InDesign, paste it, drag and drop it, or import it. InDesign works with text inside *frames* — holders for the copy — that you can create in advance or let InDesign create for you when you begin typing or when you import text.

Typing text

First, you can't do anything with text without the Type tool. Once the Type tool is selected, as shown in Figure 15-1, you can click in an existing block of text, or click and drag to create a new text frame. You can even click in any empty frame with the Type tool to convert it to a text frame.

Note What you can't do is simply click in your document and begin typing, as you can in PageMaker. InDesign is like other page-layout programs in that the text must be in a frame. Fortunately, you can create that frame just by clicking and dragging with the Type tool.

Figure 15-1: When the Type tool is selected, you can click in a text frame and start typing.

From this point, start typing to enter text.

Tip   You can't click in *master text frames* — text frames that are placed on the page by the master page in use — and simply start typing. To select a master text frame and add text to it, Shift+⌘+click or Ctrl+Shift+click it. (For more on master pages, see Chapter 7.)

Pasting text

When text is on the Mac or Windows Clipboard, you can paste it at the location of the cursor or replace highlighted text with it. If no text frame is active, InDesign creates a new rectangular text frame to contain the pasted text.

New Feature   Text that is cut or copied from InDesign retains its formatting, while text pasted from other programs normally loses its formatting. (Text pasted from other programs always retains its special characters such as curly quotes, em dashes, and accented characters.) In InDesign CS, you can now specify whether pasted text retains its formatting. Go to the General pane in the Preferences dialog box (choose InDesign ➪ Preferences on the Mac or Edit ➪ Preferences in Windows, or press ⌘+K or Ctrl+K) and select the Preserve Text Attributes When Pasting check box.

InDesign uses standard menu commands and keyboard commands for cutting/copying text to the Clipboard, and for pasting text. On the Mac, press ⌘+X to cut, ⌘+C to copy, and ⌘+V to paste. In Windows, press Ctrl+X to cut, Ctrl+C to copy, and Ctrl+V to paste.

Keep characters to a minimum

If you're new to professional publishing, you have a few things to learn about the difference between typing on a typewriter or into a word processor and entering text for a high-end publication:

✦ Remember that there's no need to type two spaces after a period or colon. In fact, it will cause awkward spacing and perhaps even text-flow issues.

✦ Don't enter extra paragraph returns for space between paragraphs and don't enter tabs to indent paragraphs — you'll accomplish both more consistently with paragraph attributes (Type ⇨ Paragraph, or Option+⌘+T or Ctrl+Alt+T).

✦ When you need to align text in columns, don't enter extra tabs; place the same amount of tabs between each column, then align the tabs (Type ⇨ Tabs, or Shift+⌘+T or Ctrl+Shift+T).

To see where you have tabs, paragraph breaks, spaces, and other such invisible characters, use the command Option+⌘+I or Ctrl+Alt+I, or choose Type ⇨ Show Hidden Characters, as the following figure shows.

Program Change Highlights for Adobe Open Options 3.0

• NEW! SPECIAL DISCOUNT FOR HIGH-VOLUME ORDERS OF ADOBE ACROBAT® SOFTWARE

• NEW! EXCLUSIVE AVAILABILITY OF ADOBE ACROBAT ELEMENTS SOFTWARE

• DISCONTINUED! ADOBE ACROBAT SITE LICENSE PROGRAM

Q. What are the benefits of Adobe Open Options 3.0?

A. Adobe Open Options® 3.0 volume software licensing programs streamline the procurement of licenses for the Adobe Acrobat product family. The new Adobe Acrobat Elements software is exclusively available through the Transactional License Program (TLP) and the Contractual License Program (CLP). These programs are the only venue for acquiring licenses of this new, essential PDF-creation tool for corporations and business users who do not need full Acrobat functionality. A minimum initial order of 1,000 licenses of Acrobat Elements is required. For Acrobat users who need more than PDF creation, Adobe Acrobat 6.0 Standard and Acrobat 6.0 Professional software will also be available under the TLP and CLP.

Adobe will offer corporate customers special high-volume discounts on orders of 1,000 or more units of new licenses and maintenance of Acrobat 6.0 Professional, Acrobat 6.0 Standard, or Acrobat Elements, when ordered in a single transaction under the CLP. This offer replaces the former Adobe Acrobat Site License Program (SLP) previously available to corporations and government entities; however, the SLP remains available to education customers. The order must be for one of the products in the Acrobat product family, on one line item in the order; different product titles and Maintenance Program orders cannot be combined to meet the 1,000-unit order minimum.

Q. How do I qualify for the Acrobat high-volume discounts?

Dragging and dropping text

If you're the kind of person who likes to juggle many open windows and applications, you can drag highlighted text from other programs — or even text files from the desktop or a folder — into an InDesign document. As with pasted text, text that you drag and drop is inserted at the location of the cursor, replaces highlighted text, or is placed in a new rectangular text frame.

Cross-Reference   Text files that are dragged in must be in a supported format: Microsoft Word 97/98 or later, Excel 97/98 or later, Rich Text Format (RTF), or text-only. Chapter 14 covers this in detail.

When you drag and drop a text selection, its formatting is lost (that's because InDesign assumes you want it to take on the attributes of the text you're inserting it into). However, when you drag and drop a text file, the process is treated more like a text import: The text retains its formatting and it brings its style sheets with it. Unlike using the Place command (File ➪ Place, or ⌘+D or Ctrl+D) to import text, drag and drop does not give you the option to specify how some of the formatting and styles in the text file are handled.

Importing text

If the text for your InDesign publication was written in a word processor, you can import it, with many styles intact, into a publication if it's in a supported version of Word or in the RTF format. You can also import ASCII text files and Tagged Text files. See Chapter 14 for more details.

When you import text using the Place dialog box, shown in Figure 15-2, it's placed according to your current selection:

Figure 15-2: The Place dialog box.

✦ If the cursor is within text in a text frame, the text is inserted at that location.

✦ If an empty text frame is selected, the text is imported into the frame.

✦ If no text frames are selected, a loaded-text icon (shown in Figure 15-3) lets you draw a rectangular text frame to contain the text or click in an existing empty frame or text frame.

Figure 15-3: The loaded-text icon (left). There are two variants—autoflow (center; hold the Shift key) and semi-autoflow (right; hold the Option or Alt key)—that let text flow to other frames during import.

To place text:

1. **Choose File ➪ Place, or press ⌘+D or Ctrl+D.**

2. **Locate the text file you want to import.**

3. **If you want to specify how to handle current formatting in the file, check the Show Import Options check box, shown in Figure 15-2, which opens the appropriate Import Options dialog box for the text file's format, as shown in Figure 15-4.**

   If you prefer memorizing keyboard commands to simply checking boxes, press Shift while you open the file to display the import options.

Tip

If you're importing a text-only file that contains paragraph returns at the end of each line, be sure to check Show Import Options as it will give you the option to remove them.

New Feature

InDesign CS now lets you import word processor and spreadsheet text as unformatted; select Remove Text and Table Formatting or Remove Text Formatting (depending on what kind of file is selected) in the Import Options dialog box.

4. **Check Retain Format to maintain paragraph and character attributes in the text and to import style sheets.**

   If the text contains style sheets with the same names but different attributes than style sheets already in the InDesign publication, the style sheets in the publication override those in the imported text.

Cross-Reference

See Chapter 20 for more on setting up style sheets, which save formatting so you can apply it to whole paragraphs or selections of text in one easy step.

5. **Check Convert Quotes to convert straight quotes (") to curly quotes (" ").**

Figure 15-4: The Import Options dialog box lets you select import options; the options will differ based on the type of file selected. Shown here are the options for a Tagged Text file (top) and a Word file (bottom).

6. **Click Open to import the text.**

7. **If you had not selected a frame before starting the text import, specify where to place the text by clicking and dragging the loaded-text icon to create a rectangular text frame, clicking in an existing frame, or clicking in any empty frame.**

   To cancel the text import, just select a different tool.

 If you click a frame that holds a graphic when importing text, the text will replace the graphic.

 If all the text you import doesn't fit in the selected text frame, see the "Threading text frames" section in Chapter 16 for more information on how to make it flow to other text frames.

 Unlike other layout programs, InDesign does *not* translate two consecutive hyphens (--) into em dashes (—), even if you check the Convert Quotes option. Fortunately, many modern word processors do this, so the chances of having two consecutive hyphens from recently created documents are slim. (In Word, use Tools ➪ AutoCorrect to enable this feature; in Word Perfect, use Tools ➪ QuickCorrect. Chapter 14 covers this in more detail.)

Handling import options

If you check Show Import Options in the Place dialog box, InDesign displays a set of options for handling formatting in the selected text file. These options vary based on the kind of file you are importing:

✦ **Text files:** You can choose a character set (ASCII or ANSI; ANSI supports different special symbols than the more common ASCII), the originating platform (which helps ensure paragraph returns are properly recognized, as well as some special symbols), and a language dictionary to associate with the text file, so InDesign will know how to spell-check and hyphenate it. In addition, you can specify how extraneous paragraph returns and spaces are handled, as well as convert keyboard quotes (") to typographic (curly) quotes (" ").

✦ **Tagged Text:** Options include converting keyboard quotes (") to typographic (curly) quotes (" "), as well as specifying whether to use style sheets in the tagged text or those in InDesign when style sheets conflict, and whether to preview problem tags.

✦ **Word and RTF:** You can import a table of contents and index as text; convert keyboard quotes (") to typographic (curly) quotes (" "); convert page breaks before paragraphs to column or page breaks; remove all text formatting; and convert tables to tabbed text.

✦ **Excel:** You can specify whether to import custom views, the worksheet you want to import, and a rectangular range of cells to import (separate the range with a colon, such as A1:C9 to import cells A1 through C9). Formatting options let you determine whether to use Excel's default spreadsheet styles or to specify the cell alignment and number of decimal places in a cell yourself. You can also specify whether cells expand to fit their contents and whether the spreadsheet should be converted to a table in InDesign. You can also convert keyboard quotes (") to typographic (curly) quotes (" ").

Exporting text

Unfortunately, you can't export text from InDesign into a word-processor format like Word; your options are RTF, InDesign Tagged Text, and text-only formats. (If you have the InCopy group editing tool covered in Appendix F, you can also export to the InCopy format.) The best option is RTF if you want to send the file to someone using a word processor, and it's Tagged Text if you want to send it to another InDesign user with all InDesign settings retained.

After you click in a text frame with the Type tool, you export text by choosing Edit ➪ Export, which provides a dialog box very much like the Save dialog box. Here, you choose the file format, filename, and file location. If you have selected text in a text frame, only that text will be exported; otherwise, the entire story will be exported.

Note   You can export only one story at a time. (A story is all text in linked text frames.)

Editing Text

When working in a layout, InDesign gives you the basic editing capabilities found in a word processor: cutting and pasting, deleting and inserting text, searching and replacing of text and text attributes, as well as help in spell-checking.

But before you begin to edit text, you need to see it. In many layout views, the text is too small to work with. Generally, you'll zoom in around the block of text using the Zoom tool. For quick access to the tool, press Z (except when the cursor is in a block of text!—in that case, you'll need to click the Zoom tool). Then click to zoom in. (To zoom out, hold the Option or Alt key when clicking.)

Another way to zoom in is to use the keyboard shortcut ⌘+= or Ctrl+=. Each time you use it, the magnification increases. (Zoom out via ⌘+- [hyphen] or Ctrl+- [hyphen].)

Tip   Choose the ⌘+= or Ctrl+= method when your text pointer is already on or near the text you want to zoom into—the pointer location is the centerpoint for the zoom. Use the Zoom tool when your pointer is not near the text you want to magnify; then move the Zoom pointer to the area you want to magnify, and click once for each level of desired magnification.

In addition to seeing the text larger, it also helps to see the spaces, tabs, and paragraph returns that exist in the text. Choose Type ➪ Show Hidden Characters or press Option+⌘+I or Ctrl+Alt+I (refer to Figure 15-1). In addition to seeing the text, you have to be able to access it, so choose the Type tool.

Navigating text

To work at a different text location, click in a different text frame or another location in the current text frame. You can also use the four arrow (cursor) keys on the keyboard to move one character to the right, one character to the left, one line up, or one line down. Add ⌘ or Ctrl to the arrow keys to jump one word to the right or left, or one paragraph up or down. The Home and End keys let you jump to the beginning or end of a line; add ⌘ or Ctrl to jump to the beginning or end of a story. (A *story* is text within a text frame or that is linked across several text frames, as described in Chapter 16.) Note that if your story begins or ends in a text frame on another page, InDesign will bring you to that page.

Tip As with most text editors, you can't enter text below the existing text in a frame. You'll need to click directly after the last character in the frame to start typing again.

New Feature If you double-click a text frame with any tool other than a drawing or frame tool, InDesign will automatically switch to the Text tool and place the insertion point where you double-clicked. (This also works for text paths and table cells.)

New Feature You can now resize text frames using the text tool. To do so, hold ⌘ or Ctrl, select a text frame handle, and resize the frame by dragging the mouse. Likewise, you can move a text frame by holding ⌘ or Ctrl, clicking in the frame, and dragging the mouse. When you release the mouse, you'll revert to the Text tool and your cursor will still be at the text-insertion point you last were at. So you can continue editing where you left off.

If you want to see how your text looks when you resize a text frame (whether you use the Text tool or not), hold the mouse button down for a second after selecting a handle; then when you resize the frame, you will see the text recompose as you move the mouse.

Highlighting text

To highlight text, you can always rely on the old click-and-drag method. Or, you can add the Shift key to the navigation commands in the previous section. For example, while ⌘+right arrow or Ctrl+right arrow moves the cursor one word to the right, Shift+⌘+right arrow or Ctrl+Shift+right arrow highlights the next word to the right. Likewise, Shift+⌘+End or Ctrl+Shift+End highlights all the text to the end of the story.

For precise text selections, double-click to select a word and its trailing space (this will not select its punctuation) and triple-click to select a paragraph. If you need the punctuation trailing a word, double-click, then press Shift+⌘+right arrow or Ctrl+Shift+right arrow to extend the selection. To select an entire story, choose Edit ⇨ Select All, or press ⌘+A or Ctrl+A.

To deselect text, choose Edit ⇨ Deselect All or press Shift+⌘+A or Ctrl+Shift+A. More simply, you can select another tool or click another area of the page.

Cutting, copying, and pasting text

After you've highlighted text, you can press ⌘+X or Ctrl+X to remove it from its story and place it on the Clipboard for later use. Use ⌘+C or Ctrl+C to leave the text in the story and place a copy on the Clipboard. Click anywhere else in text — within the same story, another story, or another publication — and press ⌘+V or Ctrl+V. If you're menu-driven, the Edit menu provides Cut, Copy, and Paste commands as well.

Deleting and replacing text

To remove text from a document, you can highlight it and choose Edit ➪ Clear or press Delete or Backspace on the keyboard. Or you can simply type over the highlighted text or paste new text on top of it.

QuarkXPress User

Don't use ⌘+K or Ctrl+K to clear text—while that works in QuarkXPress, this shortcut opens the Preferences dialog box in InDesign.

If text is not highlighted, you can delete text to the right or left of the cursor. On the Mac, press Delete to delete to the left and press Del (sometimes labeled Clear) to delete to the right. In Windows, press Backspace to delete to the left and Delete to delete to the right.

Undoing text edits

Remember to take advantage of InDesign's multiple undos while editing text. Choose Edit ➪ Undo and Edit ➪ Redo any time you change your mind about edits. The Undo and Redo keyboard commands are definitely worth remembering: ⌘+Z and Shift+⌘+Z or Ctrl+Z and Ctrl+Shift+Z.

Using the Story Editor

InDesign CS adds a feature long available in Adobe PageMaker: the Story Editor. This window, shown in Figure 15-5, lets you edit text without the distractions of your layout. It presents your text without line breaks or other nonessential formatting—you just see attributes like boldface and italics, as well as the names of the style sheets applied in a separate pane to the left. After clicking in a text frame, you open the Story Editor by choosing Edit ➪ Edit in Story Editor or pressing ⌘+Y or Ctrl+Y.

New Feature

The Story Editor is new to InDesign CS.

Cross-Reference

You set preferences for text size and font in the Story Editor Display pane of the Preferences dialog box (choose InDesign ➪ Preferences on the Mac or Edit ➪ Preferences in Windows, or press ⌘+K or Ctrl+K), as detailed in Chapter 3.

In the Story Editor, you use the same tools for selection, deletion, copying, pasting, and search and replace as you would in your layout. The Story Editor is not a separate word processor, simply a way to look at your text in a less-distracting environment for those times your mental focus is on the meaning and words, not the text appearance.

Figure 15-5: The Story Editor window.

Searching and Replacing

InDesign's Find/Change dialog (Edit ➪ Find/Change, or ⌘+F or Ctrl+F) lets you do everything from, for example, finding the next instance of *curry* in an article so you can insert *extra spicy* in red, to finding all instances of a deposed chef's name in six different documents. If you know how to use the search-and-replace feature in any word processor or page-layout application, you'll be comfortable with InDesign's Find/Change in no time.

Searching and replacing text

The Find/Change dialog box comes in two forms: reduced for finding and changing just text, and expanded for including attributes in a search. The More Options button expands the dialog box to include formatting options for your search and replace, and the Fewer Options button reduces it.

Before starting a Find/Change operation, determine the scope of your search:

✦ To search within a text selection, highlight it.

✦ To search from a certain location in a story to the end of it, click the cursor at that location.

✦ To search an entire story, select any frame or click at any point in a frame containing the story.

✦ To search an entire document, simply have that document open.

✦ To search multiple documents, open all of them (and close any that you don't want to search).

To search for text:

1. **Determine the scope of your search, as just described, open the needed documents, and insert the text cursor at the appropriate location.**

2. **Choose Edit ➪ Find/Change or press ⌘+F or Ctrl+F.**

3. **Use the Search pop-up menu, as shown in Figure 15-6, to specify the scope of your search: Document, All Documents, Story, To End of Story, or Selection.**

   Which options are available will be based on your current text selection in InDesign. Unavailable options are grayed out.

Figure 15-6: Use the Search pop-up menu in the Find/Change dialog box to specify the scope of the text to search.

Tip   As you're using the Find/Change dialog box to search and replace text, you can jump into a text frame (just click it with the Type pointer) and edit it as you please, then return to Find/Change by clicking the Find/Change dialog box.

4. **Type or paste the text you want to find in the Find What field.**

5. **Type or paste the replacement text into the Change To field.**

6. **Specify whether to find the word within other words (for example, *cafe* within *cafeteria* or just *cafe*) by checking or unchecking Whole Word.**

   When checked, Find/Change will only locate standalone instances of the Find What text.

7. **Specify whether to consider capitalization patterns in the Find/Change operation by checking or unchecking Case Sensitive.**

   When checked, Find/Change follows the capitalization of the text in the Find What and Change To fields exactly.

8. **Click Find Next to start the search.**

   Thereafter, click Find Next to skip instances of the Find What text, and click Change, Change All, or Change/Find to replace the Find What text with the Change To text. (Change simply changes the found text, Change All changes every instance of that found text in your selection or story, and Change/Find changes the current found text and moves on to the next occurrence of it — it basically does in one click the actions of clicking Change and then Find Next.)

Note   If you use the Change All feature, InDesign reports how many changes were made. If the number looks extraordinarily high and you suspect the Find/Change operation wasn't quite what you wanted, remember you can use InDesign's undo function (Edit ➪ Undo, or ⌘+Z or Ctrl+Z) to cancel the search and replace, and then try a different replace strategy.

9. **Click Done when you're all done.**

   Note that you can do several search-and-replace operations, which is why the dialog box stays open after completing a search — and that's why there is a Done button for you to tell InDesign to close the dialog box.

Tip   InDesign records your last 15 entries in the Find What and Change To fields, so you can repeat previous Find/Change operations. That's why each field is a pop-up menu. Click the menu to open it, and use the down-arrow key to scroll through those recorded operations.

Finding special characters

You're not limited to finding and changing words and phrases. You can search and replace spaces, tabs, paragraph returns, and other invisible characters along with special characters such as bullets, em dashes, and nonbreaking spaces. Searching and replacing these types of characters is often helpful for repair jobs: fixing imported text that contains double spaces after periods, extra returns between paragraphs, and hyphens instead of em dashes.

To enter invisible characters, special characters, or wild cards in the Find What or Change To fields, click the arrow buttons to the right of the fields. You'll get a menu that offers options such as Bullet Character, Hair Space, and Discretionary Hyphen, as shown in Figure 15-7. You can select any combination of these characters and combine them with other text and formatting attributes. Table 15-1 shows the text codes you can use in place of these menu items.

Figure 15-7: Click the right-facing arrow on the Find What and Change To fields to display a list of special characters.

Table 15-1
Text Codes for Search and Replace

Character	Code
Markers and Tabs	
Auto page numbering	^#
Section marker	^x
End of paragraph	^p
Forced line break	^n
Inline graphic marker*	^g
Tab	^t
Right-indent tab	^y
Indent to here	^i
Symbols	
Bullet (•)	^8
Caret (^)	^^
Copyright (©) symbol	^2
Paragraph (¶) symbol	^7
Registered trademark (®) symbol	^r
Section (§) symbol	^6
Punctuation	
Double left quotation mark (")	^{
Double right quotation mark (")	^}
Single left quotation mark (')	^[
Single right quotation mark (')	^]
Em dash (—)	^_
En dash (–)	^=
Discretionary hyphen	^-
Nonbreaking hyphen	^~

Continued

Table 15-1 *(continued)*	
Character	*Code*
Spaces	
Em space	^m
En space	^>
Flush space	^f
Hair space	^|
Nonbreaking space	^s
Thin space	^<
White space (any space or tab)*	^w
Wild Cards	
Any character*	^?
Any digit*	^9
Any letter*	^$

*Can be entered in the Find What box only.

Note   To search and replace regular spaces, type the number of spaces you want to find and change in the Find What and Change To fields — as if they were any other regular character.

If there are other characters not in InDesign's special-character menu that you want to search for or replace with, just enter their keyboard codes (see Chapter 41) or paste them into the field. (You can paste them by first copying them to the Clipboard from your document text, or from a utility like PopChar X or Key Caps on the Mac or Character Map in Windows, as Chapter 14 explains.)

InDesign also provides three wild cards, which let you search for unspecified characters, numbers, or letters in other text. For example, if you want to change all the numbered steps in a document to bulleted lists, you might search for Any Digit and replace it with a bullet. Or you can search for variations of a word to find, say, *cafe* and *café* at the same time.

Searching and replacing formatting

To find and change formatting or text with specific formatting, you can use the expanded Find/Change dialog box. For example, you might find all the blue words in 14-point Futura Extra Bold and change them to 12-point Mrs Eaves Bold. Or you might find all instances of the words *hot and spicy* in 15-point body text, then resize the text to 12 point and apply Red Litterbox.

To replace text formatting, follow these steps:

1. **To add formats to a Find/Change operation for text, click the More Options button in the Find/Change dialog box (if it was not clicked earlier).**

   The dialog box expands to include the Find Format Settings and Change Format Settings areas, as shown in Figure 15-8.

Figure 15-8: Clicking More Options in the Find/Change dialog box displays the Find Format Settings and Change Format Settings areas. Clicking Format opens the Find Format Settings or Change Format Settings dialog box.

2. **Use the Format buttons to display the Find Format Settings and Change Format Settings dialog boxes, which let you specify the formats you want to find.**

   The two dialog boxes are identical, except for their names; refer to Figure 15-8 for the Find Format Settings one.

3. **Use the menu at the top to specify the type of formatting: Style Options (style sheets), Basic Character Formats, Advanced Character Formats, Indents and Spacing, Keep Options, Character Color, OpenType Features, Underline Options, Strikethrough Options, and Drop Caps and Other.**

You can change multiple attributes at once by making selections from as many panes as needed.

Tip   To search and replace formatting only — regardless of the text to which it is applied — leave the Find What and Change To fields blank.

Locating and specifying all the formatting you want to find and change requires you to dig deeper and deeper into the Find Format Settings and Change Format Settings dialog boxes. Unfortunately, you can't really get a picture of all the formats you're selecting at once, and you have to keep jumping from one pane to the next. Fortunately, when you're finished selecting formats, the selected options are summarized in the Find Style Settings and Change Style Settings areas.

Checking Spelling

Search and replace can help fix mistakes in your text, but it's usually not enough. Another helpful tool is a spell checker, which reads through your text to look for misspelled words. Although you'll still want to proofread your documents, using the spell checker both in your word processor and in InDesign helps reduce the chances of errors in your final document.

InDesign's Check Spelling feature flags three types of possible editorial problems: repeated words such as *an an,* words with odd capitalization such as the internal capitalization (called *intercaps*) in software and company names (like *InDesign*), and words not found in the spelling dictionary that may be spelled wrong. You can customize the spelling dictionary, and you can purchase other companies' spelling dictionaries to add words from disciplines like law and medicine, as well as for other languages.

Specifying the text to check

InDesign lets you control which text is spell-checked so you can concentrate on a new story or paragraph added to a document, check all the text in a document toward the end of the publishing process, or check multiple documents at the same time on similar subject matter.

As with Find/Change, specifying the text to check is a two-step process: First set up the spell-check scope in the document, then specify the scope in the Search menu.

To set up the scope, highlight text, click in a story to check from the cursor forward, select a frame containing a story, or open multiple documents. Just as in search and replace, what you choose to open and select will determine what scope options InDesign has for spell-checking.

Then, open the Check Spelling dialog box (Edit ➪ Check Spelling, or ⌘+I or Ctrl+I) and choose an option from the Search pop-up menu: Document, All Documents, Story, To End of Story, and Selection. Figure 15-9 shows the dialog box. Depending on how you set up the scope, not all the options are available in the Search pop-up menu. For example, if you did not highlight text, the Selection option is not available. However, you can change the scope setup in the document while the Check Spelling dialog box is open — for example, you can open additional documents to check.

Figure 15-9: Use the Search pop-up menu in the Check Spelling dialog box to specify which text to spell-check.

Tip

To check the spelling of a single word, double-click to highlight it and then open the spell checker — the Check Spelling dialog box's Search pop-up menu is automatically set to Selection.

Tip

Control+click or right-click on a word or a point in a text frame (using the Type tool) to get the contextual menu from which you choose Check Spelling.

Using the Check Spelling dialog box

When you first open the Check Spelling dialog box, it displays "Ready to Spell Check" at the top. To begin checking the text scope you specified in the Search pop-up menu, click Start. When the spell checker encounters a word without a match in the dictionary or a possible capitalization problem, the dialog box displays "Not in Dictionary" at the top and shows the word. When the spell checker encounters repetition such as *me me,* the dialog box displays "Duplicate Word" and shows the repeated words. (Refer to Figure 15-9 for an illustration of the dialog box.) Use the buttons along the right side of the dialog box to handle flagged words as follows:

✦ To leave the current instance of a Not in Dictionary word or Duplicate Word unchanged, click Ignore. To leave all instances of the same problem unchanged, click Ignore All.

✦ To change the spelling of a Not in Dictionary word, click a word in the Suggested Corrections list or edit the spelling or capitalization in the Change To field. To make the change, click Change.

✦ To correct an instance of a Duplicate Word, edit the text in the Change To field, then click Change.

✦ To change all occurrences of a Not in Dictionary word or a Duplicate Word to the information in the Change To field, click Change All.

✦ To add a word flagged as incorrect — but that you know is correct — to InDesign's spelling dictionary, click Add.

✦ To close the Check Spelling dialog box after checking all the specified text, click Done.

While you're using Check Spelling, you can jump between the dialog box and the document at any time. This lets you edit a possibly misspelled word in context or to edit surrounding text as a result of changed spelling. So if you find an instance of *a a* in front of *apple,* you can change the entire phrase to *an apple* rather than just replace the duplicate *a a* with *a* in the dialog box and have to remember to later fix *a apple* to *an apple.*

Working with multiple languages

Each word in InDesign can have a distinct language assigned to it (English, French, Spanish, German, and so on). The word's language attribute tells InDesign which dictionary to consult when spell-checking or hyphenating the word. For example, if you have the word *français* in an English sentence, you can change the language of that word so it is no longer flagged by the English spell checker — the French spell checker would be used on it and recognize that the word is correctly spelled.

Note   Just because you have the ability to control language at the word level doesn't necessarily mean that you have to use it. In general, even when publishing to an international audience, full paragraphs or stories will be in the same language. For example, if you have the same packaging for a product sold in the United States and France, you might have one descriptive paragraph in English and the other in French. The English dictionary also contains many common words with foreign origins such as *jalapeño, mélange,* and *crêpe.*

To assign a language to text, highlight the text and choose an option from the Language pop-up menu on the Character pane, as shown in Figure 15-10. You can also set the language as part of a character or paragraph style (see Chapters 17 and 18 for more details). In the Check Spelling dialog box, a field above the Search menu shows the language of each word as it's checked. Unfortunately, you can't change the language in that dialog box.

Figure 15-10: The Language menu on the Character palette lets you choose a different language for hyphenating and spell-checking highlighted text.

Note There's a language option called [No Language]; selecting it prevents spell-checking and hyphenation.

Customizing the Spelling and Hyphenation Dictionaries

A spelling dictionary can never cover all the bases — you'll always have industry-specific words and proper nouns not found in the dictionary in use. In addition, copy editors tend to have their own preferences for how to hyphenate words. What they consider "correct" hyphenation may vary, and some word breaks are preferred over others. To solve both these problems, you can customize InDesign's dictionaries by adding words and specifying hyphenation. InDesign handles both spelling and hyphenation in one dictionary for each language, so you use the same controls to modify both spelling and hyphenation.

Changes made to a dictionary file are saved only in the dictionary file, not with an open document. So if you add words to the English: U.S.A. dictionary, the modified dictionary is used for spell-checking and hyphenating all text in documents that use the English: U.S.A. dictionary.

Tip   If you're in a workgroup, be sure to share the edited dictionary file so everyone is using the same spelling and hyphenation settings. (The file is located in the Dictionaries folder inside the Plug-ins folder inside your InDesign folder.) You can copy it for other users, who must then restart InDesign or press Option+⌘+/ or Ctrl+Alt+/ to reflow the text according to the new dictionary's hyphenation.

Customizing the spelling dictionary

While you're spell-checking, you'll often find words that don't match those in the dictionary. If you know the word is spelled correctly and likely to appear in your publications often, you can add it to the dictionary. In the future, this word will not be flagged and you won't have to click Ignore to skip it — and you can be sure that when it's used, it is spelled as it is in the dictionary.

While adding words to the dictionary, you can specify their capitalization. For example, InDesign's dictionary prefers *E-mail*. You can add *e-mail* if you prefer a lowercase *e* or *email* if you prefer to skip the hyphen. If you're adding a word that may have variations (such as *emailing*) be sure to add those variations separately.

To add words to the dictionary:

1. **Choose Edit ➪ Edit Dictionary.**

   The Dictionary dialog box, shown in Figure 15-11, appears.

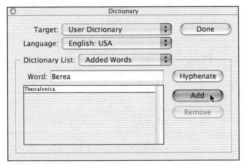

Figure 15-11: Enter new terms in the Word field, then click Add to include them in the spelling dictionary.

2. **Choose whether the addition to the dictionary affects just this document or all documents.**

   To do so, you use the Target pop-up menu, which will list the current document name as well as User Dictionary (to change the dictionary file). The advantage of making the spelling specific to the document is that all users, such as service bureaus, will have the same spellings; the disadvantage is that other documents won't share this spelling.

3. **Choose the dictionary that you want to edit from the Language menu.**

4. **Type or paste a word in the Word field.**

   The word can include special characters such as accents and hyphens, spaces, and a capitalization pattern to follow.

5. **If you want to edit the hyphenation, click Hyphenate.**

   You can add, remove, or modify the number of tildes to change the hyphenation rules for the word, as covered in the next section.

6. **Click Add.**

7. **Continue to add words and, when you're finished, click Done.**

Tip   When you're adding variations of words, you can double-click a word in the list to place it in the Word field as a starting place.

In addition to adding words through the Edit Dictionary dialog box, you can click Add in the Check Spelling dialog box when InDesign flags a word that you know is correct.

To delete a word that you added to the dictionary, select it in the list and click Remove. To change the spelling of a word you added, delete it then re-add it with the correct spelling. You can see all deleted words — just those deleted since you open the dialog box — by selecting Removed Words from the Dictionary List pop-up menu, so you can add back any deleted by error.

Customizing hyphenation points

Industries and publications usually have internal styles on how words hyphenate — especially if the text is justified. For example, a bridal magazine that uses the term *newlywed* often may prefer that it breaks at the end of a line as *newly-wed*. But if that hyphenation would cause poor spacing, the publisher might let it break at *new-lywed* as well. InDesign lets you modify the hyphenation dictionary by specifying new, hierarchical hyphenation points.

Note   When you customize the hyphenation points, be sure to add variations of words (such as the plural form *newlyweds*). InDesign sees each word as wholly unrelated, and, thus, won't apply the hyphenation of, say, *newlywed* to *newlyweds*.

To specifying hyphenation points:

1. **Choose Edit ➪ Edit Dictionary.**

2. **Choose from the Language menu the dictionary that you want to edit.**

3. **Type or paste the word in the Word field; you can also double-click a word in the list.**

4. **If you wish, click Hyphenate to see InDesign's suggestions for hyphenating the word.**

   You can then change the hyphenation according to Steps 5 and 6.

5. **Type a tilde (~, obtained by pressing Shift+`, the open single keyboard quote at the upper left of the keyboard) at your first preference for a hyphenation point.**

   If you don't want the word to hyphenate at all, type a tilde in front of it.

6. **Type tildes in other hyphenation points as well.**

   If you want to indicate a preference, use two tildes for your second choice, three tildes for your third choice, and so on. InDesign will first try to hyphenate your top preferences (single tildes), then it will try your second choices if the first ones don't work out, and so on. Figure 15-12 shows an example.

Figure 15-12: Enter hyphenation preferences in the Word field, using tildes (~) to indicate hyphenation points, then click Add to include them in the spelling dictionary.

7. **Click Add.**

8. **Continue to add words until you're finished, and then click Done.**

To revert a word to the default hyphenation, select it in the list and click Remove. To change the hyphenation, double-click a word in the list to enter it in the Word field, change the tildes, then click Add. When you're adding variations of words, you can double-click a word in the list to place it in the Word field as a starting place.

Tip
If a word actually includes a freestanding tilde (not as an accent, as in ñ), type \~ to indicate the character is part of the word. These are rare and happen mostly in World Wide Web addresses.

Setting spelling and hyphenation dictionary preferences

By default, when spell-checking and hyphenating text, InDesign consults dictionaries created by a company called Proximity. Because spelling and hyphenation points vary from dictionary to dictionary, and you may prefer one dictionary over another, you can purchase and install other companies' dictionaries to use instead of Proximity's. However, it's very hard to find commercial alternatives to the Proximity dictionaries, so most users will use the ones that come with InDesign and update them as needed.

The spelling and hyphenation in Proximity's dictionaries has the following origins: Catalan (Collins), Danish (IDE), Dutch (Van Dale), English: UK (Collins), English: USA (Franklin), English USA Legal (Merriam-Webster), English: USA Medical (Merriam-Webster), Finnish (IDE), French (Hachette), French: Canadian (Hachette), German: Traditional (Bertelsmann), German: Reformed (Bertelsmann), German: Swiss (Bertelsmann), Italian (Collins), Norwegian (IDE), Norwegian: Nynorsk (IDE), Portuguese (Collins), Portuguese: Brazilian (Collins), Spanish: Castilian (Collins), and Swedish (IDE).

To replace a dictionary:

1. **Place the dictionary file in the Dictionaries folder in the Plug-ins folder inside your InDesign folder.**

2. **Choose InDesign ⇨ Preferences on the Mac or Edit ⇨ Preferences in Windows, or press ⌘+K or Ctrl+K, and go to the Dictionary pane to get the dialog box shown in Figure 15-13.**

3. **In the Language pop-up menu, choose which language's dictionary you want to replace.**

4. **Choose the new dictionary from the Hyphenation Vendor and/or Spelling Vendor pop-up menu.**

5. **Click OK.**

Tip
If you change Dictionary Preferences with no documents open, the new dictionary becomes a program default and applies to all new documents. If a document is open, the change applies only to that document.

Figure 15-13: If you purchase and install different hyphenation and spelling dictionaries, you can select them in the Dictionary pane of the Preferences dialog box.

Adjusting Text Appearance in Text Frames

Although most adjustments to text frames — such as frame size, shape, and location — affect the layout, not the text, there are several text-frame attributes that *do* affect your text's appearance.

Setting text frame options

Most of these adjustments reside in the Text Frame Options dialog box, shown in Figure 15-14. You open the dialog box by selecting a frame and choosing Object ⇨ Text Frame Options, or pressing ⌘+B or Ctrl+B.

Cross-Reference

Chapter 10 covers the creation, modification, and deletion of text frames in more detail. Chapter 16 covers the Column settings in the Text Frame Options dialog box. The rest of Part IV covers formatting text.

Figure 15-14: The Text Frame Options dialog box.

These four sections of the Text Frame Options dialog box control text appearance:

✦ The Inset Spacing section creates an internal margin in the frame, putting space between the frame edge and the text. You can set the Top, Bottom, Left, and Right settings separately.

✦ The First Baseline section lets you determine where the baseline for the first line of text in the frame rests. (The baseline is the invisible line on which characters rest and through which descenders such as the lower portions of letters like *p* and *g* "poke through.") You have five options in the Offset pop-up menu, for which the use of each depends on your aesthetic goals:

• Ascent puts the baseline as close to the top of the frame as possible, so the tops of characters graze the text frame's top (or the margin you set in the Inset Spacing section). This is the default.

• Cap Height adjusts the baseline so that it is a cap height's distance from the frame top. The cap height is the height of a capital letter *C*, but some fonts have characters that extend above that location, and these fonts will have characters that rise above the top of the frame if you choose Cap Height here.

- Leading places the baseline from the frame's top in the same amount as the text's leading. If leading is set to 13 points, for example, the baseline will be 13 points from the top of the frame, no matter if that makes characters rise above the frame top (such as if the text size is set at 15 points) or causes a gap (such as if the text size is set at 9 points).

- x Height adjusts the baseline so that it is an x height's distance from the frame top. The x height is the height of a lowercase letter x. Selecting x Height ensures that capital letters and letters with ascenders (such as d and h) will poke through the top of the frame.

- Fixed uses the value in the Min. field to position the baseline. You would use this if you want the baseline for all text frames to be the same no matter what the text size and appearance is. That's pretty rare — standard practice is to have text positioned from the frame top relative to its size, which the other Offset options essentially do.

You can override any of the settings above by specifying an amount in the Min. field. The Min. field tells InDesign that the baseline must be at least a specific distance from the frame top. InDesign will first try to position the baseline based on the Offset amount, but if that is closer to the frame top than the Min. setting, the Min. setting will prevail.

✦ The Vertical Justification section controls the placement of text vertically in a text frame, similar right-, center-, or left-aligning a paragraph horizontally. The Top, Center, and Bottom options move the text to the top, the center, or bottom of the text frame. The Justify option is a bit different: It permits variable spacing between paragraphs, so the text fits the full depth of the frame. If you choose Justify, the leading within paragraphs is unaffected, but InDesign adds as much space as needed between each paragraph — up to the value set in the Paragraph Spacing Limit field — to ensure that the last line of text in the frame at the bottom of the frame. Because the default is 0p, text won't be vertically justified even if you choose Justify — you must also increase the Paragraph Spacing Limit value. Figure 15-15 shows some examples of this.

✦ The Ignore Text Wrap option, if checked, lets text in the text frame overprint another object, even if text wrap is set for that object. You would use this rarely, such as when you have a headline you want to overprint a graphic around which body text wraps.

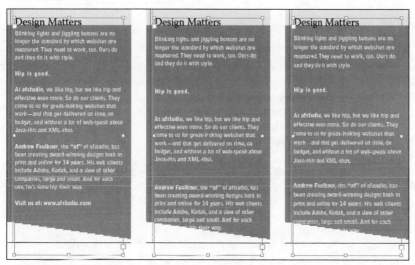

Figure 15-15: Examples of vertical justification, showing how the spacing changes as the number of lines changes. (Normal, top-aligned text is at left.)

Scaling text with the mouse

The other frame-oriented action you can take that affects text is resizing (scaling). Normally, when you resize a text frame, the text size is unaffected, and the text simply reflows in the new frame's dimensions. But you can also have the text resized along the same percentages as the frame itself. Here's how: Hold ⌘ or Ctrl when dragging a frame edge with the Selection tool. This will resize the text the same percentage horizontally or vertically as the frame is resized. (This also works for grouped text frames.)

The ability to resize text when resizing a text frame is new to InDesign CS.

Because these actions distort the text's appearance, you'll rarely use them. However, they can be useful when working on titles in creative materials such as ads where some distortion can bring an unusual but attractive look to text.

Summary

InDesign provides a variety of methods for getting text into your documents, including typing directly into a text frame, placing or dragging-and-dropping files generated in a word processor, and pasting text from other sources. You can also edit and enter text in the new Story Editor window.

You can export text from InDesign for use in a word processor or another InDesign user. Your options are RTF, InDesign Tagged Text, and text-only.

Once text is in InDesign, you can use the Find/Change feature to search and replace text and/or formatting in highlighted text, a whole story, a whole document, or a group of open documents. You have the same scope options when checking spelling.

You can customize the spelling and hyphenation dictionary to include industry-specific words or proper nouns, and to specify your preferences for how certain words are hyphenated. InDesign provides dictionaries for many languages to support international publishing.

The Text Frame Options dialog box lets you adjust the spacing of text within text frames. You can also resize text at the same percentages you resize its frame if you hold ⌘ or Ctrl when dragging a frame edge.

✦   ✦   ✦

Flowing Text through a Document

✦   ✦   ✦   ✦

In This Chapter

Creating text frames on master pages

Importing text to flow through frames

Linking frames and flowing text through them

Breaking and rerouting text flow

Specifying and adjusting columns

✦   ✦   ✦   ✦

It doesn't take much experience with InDesign to discover that all your text doesn't fit into the finite space provided by individual frames. Consider these scenarios:

✦ If you're laying out a newsletter, you might receive an article in the form of a Microsoft Word document that you need to flow into several columns across a spread.

✦ Or a magazine might have an article starting on page 20, then continuing on page 198, with the text originating from WordPerfect and saved as RTF for import into InDesign.

✦ And with catalogs, you might have a continuous file exported from a database that contains different product descriptions, which are positioned below the items' pictures.

✦ In book publishing, each chapter may be imported as a separate word processing file and flowed continuously through many pages.

✦ Even the text of a simple advertisement, delivered by a client via e-mail, might flow through several text frames.

In all these cases, the benefits of frames — the ability to size, resize, reshape, and place them with precision — seem limiting. When the text doesn't fit in a frame, what are you supposed to do? Well, don't resort to cutting and pasting text into different frames. You need to keep the imported text together and link the frames that will contain the text. InDesign refers to the process of linking frames as *threading* and considers linked frames to be *threaded.* You can link frames on a single page, link frames from one page to another no matter how many pages are in between, and link frames automatically to quickly flow text while adding new pages with frames.

The text flowing through a series of threaded frames is considered a *story*. When you edit text in a story, the text reflows throughout the columns and threaded frames. You can also spell-check and do search and replace for an entire story even though you have just one text frame active on-screen. Similarly, you can select all or some of the text in the story and change its formatting, copy it, or delete it.

Cross-Reference   Chapter 10 explains how to create frames, while Chapter 14 explains what kind of text can be imported. Chapter 13 explains how to select, spell-check, and search-and-replace text. Chapters 17, 18, 20, and 21 explain how to format text.

Creating Text Frames

On a simple layout such as a business card or advertisement, you might simply create text frames as you need them. In a newsletter scenario, you might drag text frames for an article in from a library. But with a book or even a text-heavy magazine, text frames are usually placed on master pages — a template for document pages — so they automatically appear on document pages. Many publications will combine master frames, individual frames, and threaded frames, as shown in Figure 16-1.

Figure 16-1: In this book spread, a text frame on a document page contains the headline "The Noble Bereans" and a text frame placed by the master page contains the folios at top. The body of the article is in a master text frame, which is threaded to other master text frames containing the body of the article on other pages.

For detailed information about using libraries and master pages, see Chapters 5 and 7.

Creating text frames on master pages

Master pages — predesigned pages that you can apply to other pages to automate layout and ensure consistency — can contain several types of text frames. You can have

- ✦ Text frames containing standing text such as a magazine's folio.
- ✦ Text frames containing placeholder text for elements such as figure captions or headlines.
- ✦ An automatically placed text frame for flowing text throughout pages. The automatically placed text frame is called the *master text frame* and is created in the New Document dialog box (File ➪ New, or ⌘+N or Ctrl+N).

Creating a master text frame

A master text frame is an empty text frame on the default master page that lets you automatically flow text through a document. When you create a new document, you can create a master text frame, which will fit within the margins and contain the number of columns you specify. Here's how it works:

1. **Choose File ➪ New or press ⌘ ɪ N or Ctrl+N.**

2. **Check Master Text Frame at the top of the New Document dialog box as shown in Figure 16-2.**

3. **Use the Page Size area to set up the size and orientation of the pages, and check Facing Pages if your pages will have a different inside and outside margin (as a book would).**

4. **Specify the size and placement of the master text frame by entering values in the Top, Bottom, Inside, and Outside (or Left and Right if Facing Pages is unchecked) fields.**

   InDesign will place guides according to these values and place a text frame within the guides. The text frame will fit within the boundaries of these values and the guides on the master page.

5. **Enter a value in the Number field in the Columns area to specify the number of columns in the master text frame.**

   To specify the amount of space between the columns, enter a value in the Gutter field. InDesign will place guides on the page to indicate the columns.

6. **Click OK to create a new document containing a master text frame.**

After you create a document with a master text frame, you'll see guides on the first document page indicating the placement of the frame.

Figure 16-2: Checking Master Text Frame in the New Document dialog box places a text frame on the default master page within the margins you specify.

Modifying master text frames

Although you set up the master text frame in the New Document dialog box, you're not confined to those settings. As you design a publication, you may need to change the size, shape, and/or number of columns in the master text frame. To display the master page, choose Window ➪ Pages or press F12. In the Pages pane, double-click the A-Master icon in the lower portion of the pane. Use the Selection tool to click the master text frame within the guides and modify it using the following options:

✦ The Control palette and Transform pane let you change the placement of a selected master text frame using the X and Y fields, the size using the W and H fields, the angle using the Rotation field, and the skew using the Shear field. You can also enter values in the Scale fields to increase or decrease the width and height of the text frame by percentages.

✦ The Text Frame Options dialog box (Object ➪ Text Frame Options, or ⌘+B or Ctrl+B), shown in Figure 16-3, lets you change the number of columns and the space between them, specify how far text is inset from each side of the frame, and specify the placement of the first baseline. If you don't want text within this box to wrap around any items in front of it, check Ignore Text Wrap at the bottom of the dialog box.

Cross-Reference

Chapter 15 covers all the options in this dialog box except for the Columns section. The Columns section is covered in the "Adjusting Columns" section later in this chapter.

Figure 16-3: To change the properties of a master text frame, select it on the master page and use the Text Frame Options dialog box.

✦ Style sheets, Story pane settings, and other text attributes are applied in the master text frame to the document text you flow into that frame. You can always override those attributes by applying other style sheets or formatting to the flowed text on your master text page.

Note

You can't edit the text settings in a master text frame when working on a document page unless you Shift+⌘+click or Ctrl+Shift+click it, so most designers only use the master text frame as a guide for placing text frames on their document pages.

✦ The Direct Selection tool lets you drag anchor points on the frame to change its shape.

QuarkXPress User

The InDesign master text frame is not the same as QuarkXPress's automatic text box on a master page. You cannot flow text into a QuarkXPress automatic text box while you're working on a master page — it is instead an empty text box that is placed on each of your layout pages for you automatically. Although you can have QuarkXPress flow text into automatic text boxes across pages as you add pages to your layout, you can also place text in these boxes individually, without them being linked. An InDesign master text frame is linked automatically from page to page and is not meant for holding text that does not flow from page to page.

Drawing additional text frames

The master text frame is helpful for containing body text that flows through a document. You're likely to need plenty of other text frames, on both master pages and document pages. Generally, these are smaller text frames intended to hold head-lines, captions, or short paragraphs of descriptive copy.

Creating text frames on master pages

If you're going to add text frames to a master page for repeating elements such as headers and footers, you need to display the master page. Choose Window ➪ Pages or press F12 to display the Pages pane. Then double-click the A-Master icon in the upper portion of the pane, as shown in Figure 16-4. Any text frames you add to mas-ter pages will display on document pages based on that master page. To switch back to the document and view the text frames, double-click a page icon in the upper portion of the Pages pane.

Figure 16-4: To access a master page so you can add or modify objects, double-click a master-page icon in the upper portion of the Pages pane.

Creating rectangular and variable-shaped text frames

To create rectangular text frames on document pages or master pages, select the Type tool. Click and drag to create text frames, and use the Control palette or Transform pane to fine-tune the placement and dimensions. Figure 16-5 shows a rectangular text frame used for a magazine folio.

For variable-shaped text frames such as circles or Bézier shapes, use the Pen tool, Ellipse tool, or Polygon tool to create an empty frame. Then convert the frame to a text frame by clicking it with a loaded text icon or choosing Object ➪ Content ➪ Text. (You get the loaded text icon when you place a text file or when you flow text from an existing frame, described later in this chapter.)

Tip   If you're working on a document page and want to type in a text frame placed on the page by a master page, select the Type tool and Shift+⌘+click or Ctrl+Shift+ click the frame.

Cross-Reference   You can also edit an existing rectangular text frame with the Direct Selection tool as if it were a freeform shape, as described in Chapters 11 and 27.

Getting the Text

Although you can type the text of a book or article directly into threaded text frames in InDesign, in most cases you will import text from a word processor. Most writers and copy editors will not have page-layout software and will, therefore, provide the story in an importable form such as Microsoft Word. Depending on your production workflow, they may have applied style sheets to the text in the word processor to indicate how the text should be formatted in InDesign.

Importing text files

The process of importing text files — and otherwise adding text to a document — is explained in full in Chapter 14. When working with documents that require threaded text frames, text is generally imported according to a few simple steps:

1. **Using the Type tool, select the first text frame that will contain the imported story.**

   If you need to select a master text frame, Shift+⌘+click it or Ctrl+Shift+click it.

2. **Choose File ➪ Place or press ⌘+D or Ctrl+D.**

3. **Use the controls at the top of the Place dialog box to locate the word processing file, then click on it.**

4. **Check Convert Quotes to convert any straight quotes to curly, typesetter's quotes; check Retain Format to import style sheets with the text; and check Show Import Options if the text contains any special elements such as tables that need to be converted.**

5. **Click Open to import the text into the selected text frame.**

   Text is likely to overflow the first frame, as shown in Figure 16-5.

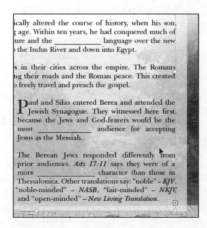

Figure 16-5: The plus sign in the lower-right corner of this text frame indicates there is more text than the frame can hold (called *overset text*).

Other text-importing techniques

InDesign lets you place text in several ways, not just by using the Place command:

✦ If your word processor supports drag and drop, you can drag a text selection directly from your word processor into an InDesign page. This creates a new text frame with the dragged text.

✦ You can copy and paste text from a word processor to an InDesign frame (note that the text's formatting will not be copied).

✦ Finally, you can drag a text file's icon from the desktop or folder into an InDesign page. This results in a loaded-text icon that you then use either to click the text frame you want to add it to or to click and drag to draw a new text frame in which to place the text.

Handling word processor style sheets

Whether writers are working on a 1,000-word story or a 40-page chapter of a book, chances are they're using some sort of formatting or style sheets in their word processing files. This might be as little as bold on headlines and space between paragraphs, or as sophisticated as different style sheets for each level of heading and type of paragraph in the manuscript.

When you import a word processing file into InDesign, you can bring the formatting and style sheets with it. (See Chapter 14 for a complete list of formatting options that will import from Microsoft Word.)

Isolated formatting might be used to indicate which style sheets should be applied in InDesign — for example, the writer might apply bold to one-line paragraphs that should be formatted as a subhead. However, if the writer applies appropriate paragraph style sheets to text in their word processor, much of the formatting in InDesign can be automated by importing the style sheets.

Note   Microsoft Word character style sheets are not imported into InDesign.

You can use these imported paragraph style sheets in two different ways, depending on whether style sheets with the same name already exist in the InDesign document. (To import style sheets with a word processing file, check Retain Format in the Place dialog box [File ⮕ Place, or ⌘+D or Ctrl+D].)

Editing imported paragraph style sheets

If you import paragraph style sheets with text, you can simply use the style sheets specified in the word processor to format the text. This method works well for designs that do not follow a template — for example, brochures or feature stories.

You might import the text, experiment with formatting it, then edit the imported style sheets in InDesign to reflect your design.

For example, say you import a magazine feature article that is formatted with three paragraph style sheets (Headline, Byline, and Body Copy) into an InDesign document that does not contain style sheets with those names. The three style sheets are added to InDesign's Paragraph Styles list and have similar specifications to what they had in the word processor. However, since InDesign offers more formatting options, you might edit those style sheets to fine-tune the text formatting. To edit a paragraph style sheet, select it in the Paragraph Styles pane, click the palette menu arrow, and choose Style Options as shown in Figure 16-6.

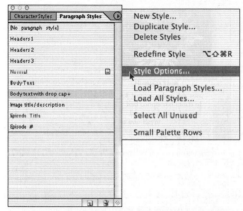

Figure 16-6: You can import simple style sheets from a word processor, then edit them in InDesign using the Style Options command in the Paragraph Styles pane.

Overriding imported paragraph style sheets

In documents that follow a template, you can provide writers with style sheet names that must be applied to their text. For example, say you're working on a tri-fold brochure that is part of an entire series of similar tri-folds. The writer might format the text with five paragraph style sheets that also exist in your InDesign document: Heads, Subheads, Body Copy, Bullets, and Quotes. The style sheet specifications in the word processor don't matter — only the name counts — because InDesign document style sheets override imported style sheets.

For example, the writer's style sheets use standard fonts such as Times and Helvetica along with bold and italic type styles to distinguish the types of text. But when the word processing file is imported into InDesign, the style sheets are overridden with InDesign style sheets that have the same name but specify the actual fonts used by the designer and the many formatting options available in InDesign.

You can supply writers either with actual style sheets or with only style sheet names:

✦ To supply style sheets, export text from a similar story in RTF format, which writers can open in their word processor; the word processor will add the style sheet names in the RTF file to its own style sheet list. The writers can then save these style sheet names to a template file and use that template for future documents. To export text, use the Export dialog box (File ⇨ Export, or ⌘+E or Ctrl+E) and choose Rich Text Format from the Format menu.

✦ Or you can simply give writers a list of style sheet names that they can create themselves to their own specifications. In this case, it's particularly important that the style sheets created in the word processor have exactly the same names as those in the InDesign document.

Threading Text Frames

InDesign provides three options for *threading* (or linking) text frames: manual, semi-autoflow, and autoflow. Each has its own icon, as shown in Figure 16-7. The method you choose depends on how much text you're dealing with and the size and quantity of your text frames:

Figure 16-7: The loaded-text icon (left). There are two variants — autoflow (center; hold the Shift key) and semi-autoflow (right; hold the Option or Alt key) — that let text flow to other frames during import.

✦ You might use the manual method, in which you click on the first text frame's out port and then on the second text frame, to link two text frames across several pages for an article continuation.

✦ The semi-autoflow method, which allows you to click on a series of text frames to flow text, works well for linking a succession of text frames in something like a catalog layout.

✦ The autoflow method adds text frames and pages as you import text and is intended for flowing long text files such as a book chapter or annual report.

Threading frames manually

To thread text frames manually, you simply use a selection tool to link out ports to in ports. You can pre-thread existing text frames by linking empty text frames, and add text later, or you can create threads from a text frame that contains text.

Tip　Linking manually from out port to in port works well for continuing a magazine article from one page to the next.

Note   Oddly, you cannot thread frames while the Type tool is selected, so remember to switch to a selection tool.

To thread text frames:

1. **Create a series of text frames through which you intend to flow text.**

   You can also create empty frames of other shapes, and the frames do not need to be on the same page.

2. **Click either the Selection tool or the Direction Selection tool.**

3. **Click the out port of the first text frame in the thread.**

   The pointer becomes the loaded text icon.

4. **Click the in port of the second text frame in the thread.**

   You can also click any empty frame or click and drag to draw a new text frame. How text flow behaves depends on the text frame's status:

   • If the first frame held no text, when text is later placed or typed into it, any text that does not fit that first text frame will flow into the second frame.

   • If the first frame held text but was not already linked to another text frame, any overset text will flow into the text frame.

   • If the first text frame was already linked to another text frame, the text will now be redirected to the text frame you just selected.

5. **Use the Pages pane to add or switch pages as necessary while you continue clicking out ports and in ports until your chain of threaded text frames is complete.**

6. **When you're finished threading text frames, select another object on the page or another tool.**

   When you import a story into any text frame in this chain, it will start in the upper-right corner of the first frame and flow through the frames in the same order as the threads.

 Tip   To see text threads easily while threading across pages, change the document view to 20 percent or so.

 Note   Text flows in the order in which you select frames. If you move a frame, its order in the text flow remains unchanged, so if you're not careful, you could, for example, accidentally have text flow from a frame at the top of the page to one at the bottom of a page and then to one in the middle of a page.

Threading frames semi-automatically

InDesign's semi-autoflow method of threading text frames varies only slightly from the manual method. Follow the same steps for threading text frames manually, except hold down the Option or Alt key each time you click in the next text frame. This lets you bypass the in ports and out ports and simply click from text frame to text frame to establish links. Note that if a text frame contains overset text, the text flows through the frames as you create the thread.

Tip   While first placing a word processing file, you can also Option+click or Alt+click in the first text frame to begin a semi-autoflow process.

Note   Remember to Option+click or Alt+click each text frame or you'll revert to manual threading.

Text frame anatomy

Before you start threading text frames, you need to understand what a text frame is trying to tell you about its text. To get the message, you need to select the text frames with one of the selection tools—when the Type tool is selected, all you can see is overset text. The text frame provides the following indicators, as shown in the figure.

✦ **In port (empty):** A small white square on the upper-left corner of a text frame is the in port, indicating where a story will enter the frame.

✦ **In port (with arrow):** Within a chain of threaded text frames, the in port might contain a right-facing arrow indicating that the story is continuing into this frame.

✦ **Out port (empty):** A small white square on the lower-right corner of a text frame is the out port, indicating that the story fits comfortably within the frame.

✦ **Out port (with arrow):** Within a chain of threaded text frames, the out port might contain a right-facing arrow indicating that the story is continuing into another frame.

✦ **Out port (with plus sign):** A small red plus sign in the out port indicates that more of the story exists than can fit in the text frame or chain of threaded text frames.

✦ **Threads:** When you choose View ⇨ Show Text Threads (or press Option+⌘+Y or Ctrl+Alt+Y), you can view threads, or lines, indicating the direction in which frames are threaded. (To see multiple text chains, Shift+click to select text frames from different threads.)

In the small text frame containing the byline, you can see an empty in port (upper-left corner) and an empty out port (lower-right corner), indicating that the text fits comfortably in the box. The lower-right corner of the first text frame on the page displays an out port with an arrow, indicating that text is flowing to another box. A thread shows exactly where the text enters the next text frame at its in port, which contains another arrow. The lower-right corner of the last text frame shows overset text, indicating that all the text still doesn't fit.

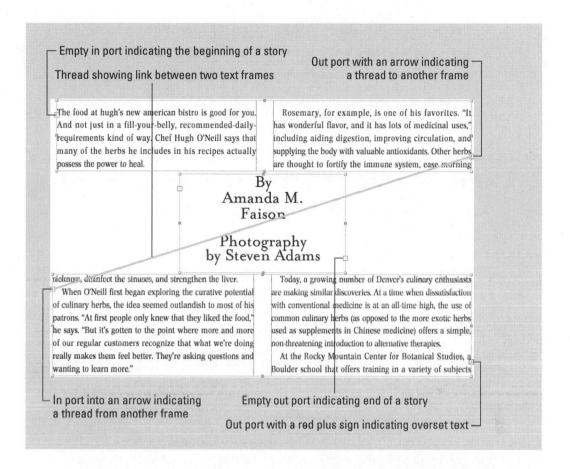

Threading frames and adding pages automatically

The autoflow method for threading frames is what lets you flow a lengthy story quickly through a document. You can either autoflow text into the master text frame or into automatically created text frames that fit within the column guides. InDesign flows the text into any existing pages, then adds new pages based on the current master page. You can initiate autoflow before or after placing a word processing file.

Placing text while autoflowing

If you haven't imported text yet, you can place a file and have it automatically flow through the document. This method works well for flowing text into pages that are all formatted the same way, such as a book. Here's how it works:

1. **Confirm that the master page in use has a master text frame or appropriate column guides.**

2. **With no text frames selected, choose File ➪ Place or press ⌘+D or Ctrl+D.**

3. **Locate and select a word processing file, then click Open.**

4. **When the loaded text icon displays, Shift+click in the first column that will contain the text.**

   InDesign adds all the necessary text frames and pages, and flows in the entire story.

Autoflowing after placing text

If you've already placed a text file into a single text frame or even a threaded chain of text frames, you can still autoflow text from the last text frame. To do this, click the overset icon in the out port, then Shift+click on any page to indicate where to start the autoflow.

Tip   You might use this method if you're placing the introduction to an article in a highly designed opener page, then flowing the rest of the article into standard pages.

Breaking and rerouting threads

After text frames are threaded, you have three options for changing the threads: You can break threads to stop text from flowing, insert a text frame into an existing chain of threaded text frames, and remove text frames from a thread.

✦ **To break the link between two text frames, double-click either an out port or an in port.** The thread between the two text frames is removed and all text that had flowed from that point is sucked out of the subsequent text frames and stored as overset text.

✦ **To insert a text frame after a specific text frame in a chain, click its out port.** Then, click and drag the loaded text icon to create a new text frame. That new frame is automatically threaded to the previous and next text frame.

✦ **To reroute text threads — for example to drop the middle text frame from a chain of three — click the text frame with the Selection tool and press Delete or Backspace.** The text frame is deleted and the threads are rerouted. You can Shift+click to multiple-select text frames to remove as well. Note that you cannot reroute text threads without removing the text frames.

Adjusting Columns

The placement of columns on the page and the amount of space between them has significant impact on readability. Column width, in general, works with type size and leading to create lines and rows of text that you can read easily. This means you're not getting lost from one line to the next, that you're not accidentally jumping across columns, and that you're not getting a headache while squinting at the page.

Tip

As a rule of thumb, as columns get wider, the type size and leading increase. For example, you might see 9-point text and 16-point leading in 2½-inch columns, while 16-point text and 13-point leading might work better in 3½-inch columns.

InDesign lets you place columns on the page automatically, create any number of columns within a text frame, and change columns at any time.

Specifying columns in master frames

If you choose to create a *master text frame*—an automatically placed text frame within the margin guides—when you create a new document, you can specify the number of columns in it at the same time.

In the Columns area in the New Document dialog box, shown in Figure 16-2, use the Number field to specify how many columns, and the Gutter field to specify how much space to place between the columns. (The gutter is the space between columns.) Whether or not you check Master Text Frame (which makes the frame appear on all pages), guides for these columns will still be placed on the page and can be used for placing text frames and other objects.

Adjusting columns in text frames

After you've created a text frame and even flowed text into it, you can change the number of columns in it. First, select the text frame with a selection tool or the Type tool (or Shift+click to select multiple text frames and change all their columns at once). Then choose Object ⇨ Text Frame Options or press ⌘+B or Ctrl+B. You can also use the Control palette to change the number of columns (see Chapter 10).

Tip

Although programs like InDesign and QuarkXPress have long offered multiple-column text frames, many designers still draw each column as a separate frame (a holdover from PageMaker's approach). Don't do that—it makes it easy to have columns of slightly different widths and slightly different positions, so text doesn't align properly. Use the columns feature in your text frames so you won't have to worry about sloppy layouts. Plus, using this feature makes it easy to change the number of columns—no need to resize existing text frames or relink them.

Note that the options in the Columns area work differently depending on whether Fixed Column Width is checked or unchecked:

✦ If it is unchecked, InDesign will subtract from the text frame's width the space specified for the gutters, then divide the remaining width by the number of columns to figure out how wide the columns can be. For example, a 10-inch-wide text frame with three columns and a gutter of ½ inch will end up with three 3-inch columns and two ½-inch gutters. The math is (10−[2 × 0.5]) ÷ 3.

✦ If it is checked, InDesign will resize the text frame to fit the number of columns you selected at the indicated size, as well as the gutters between them. For example, if in a 10-inch-wide text frame, you specify a column width of 5 inches and a gutter of ½ inch, and you choose three columns, you'll end up with a 16-inch-wide text frame containing three 5-inch columns and two ½-inch gutters. The math is $(3 \times 5) + (2 \times 0.5)$.

Check Preview to see the effects of your changes before finalizing them.

Placing rules between columns

The use of vertical rules (thin lines) between columns — called intercolumn rules — is an effective way to separate columns with small gutters (this is often done in newspapers, whose columns and gutters are usually thin). It can also add visual interest and a sense of old-fashioned authority — it was a common technique for newspapers early in this century and is still used by the august *Wall Street Journal*, for example.

Threading icons

While you're threading text, several icons provide visual cues as to the type of threading you're doing and what the results will be. (To view threads from a text frame selected with the Selection tool or Direct-Selection tool, choose View ➪ Show Text Threads or press Option+⌘+Y or Ctrl+Alt+Y.) The figure shows, from left to right, the loaded-text icon, the loaded-text frame-flow icon, the thread icon, the semi-autoflow text-flow icon, and the autoflow text-flow icon.

✦ The **loaded-text icon** contains text that needs to be placed or overset text that needs to be threaded into a new text frame.

✦ When the loaded-text icon is over a text frame, the icon changes so the icon is displayed in parentheses, becoming the **loaded-text frame-flow icon.** The same thing happens for the semi-autoflow icon.

✦ The **thread icon,** which looks like two links in a chain, displays while you're threading text frames manually. Specifically, the loaded-text icon changes to this icon when it's over an empty text frame that you can thread the current text frame to.

✦ The **semi-autoflow text-flow icon** displays when you Option+click or Alt+click text frames while threading a series of text frames.

✦ The **autoflow text-flow icon** displays when you Shift+click on a page to initiate the autoflow process, in which InDesign adds text frames and pages to contain the entire story.

Unfortunately, InDesign does not provide an automatic method for creating inter-column rules. To get around this lack, you need to draw lines on the page — in the center of the gutters — with the Line tool. Because you might resize text frames or change the number of columns while designing a document, you should add the vertical rules at the end of the process. In a document with a standard layout, such as a newspaper or magazine, you can place the rules between columns in text frames on the master page so they're automatically placed on every page. As always with such objects, you can modify them on individual document pages as needed (just be sure to Shift+⌘+click or Ctrl+Shift+click to select them when working in your document pages).

When drawing rules between columns, use the rulers to precisely position the lines. After you've drawn the lines, Shift+click to select all the lines and the text frames, then choose Object ➪ Group, or ⌘+G or Ctrl+G. When the lines are grouped to the text frame, you can move them all as a unit. This also prevents someone from accidentally moving a vertical rule later.

Tip Keep the width of intercolumn rules thin: usually a hairline (¼ point) or ½ point. Larger than that is usually too thick and can be confused with the border of a side-bar or other boxed element.

Summary

When text doesn't fit within a single text frame — the case in almost any multipage publication — you need to link (or *thread,* in InDesign lingo) the text frames. You can do this manually, threading one text frame to the next, or you can have InDesign automatically add pages containing threaded text frames. After frames are threaded, you can still reflow text by breaking text threads and rerouting the threads.

In addition to flowing text through the threaded frames, you can flow it through multiple columns within each frame. You can change the number of columns or their width within a frame at any time. To distinguish columns more visually, you can draw vertical lines between columns and group them with the text frames.

✦   ✦   ✦

Specifying Character Attributes

In This Chapter

Working with characters versus paragraphs

Changing font families, styles, and sizes

Applying other character formats

Controlling horizontal and vertical spacing

Type is the visual representation of the spoken word. A typographer is a person who designs with type. As a user of InDesign, chances are you're going to be making lots of decisions about the appearance of the text in the publications you produce. You are, whether you consider yourself one or not, a typographer. And not only are InDesign users typographers, they're typographers who have an extensive arsenal of text formatting tools that let them tweak and polish their type in a nearly infinite variety of ways.

Of all the decisions an InDesign user makes when designing a publication, decisions about type are arguably the most important. Why? Because a publication can't be effective if the text is hard to read. The difference between good typography and bad typography is the same as the difference between clear speaking and mumbling. The intent of a clear speaker and a mumbler may be the same, but the effect on the listener is quite different. In publishing, the printed words are the containers in which the writer's message is transported to the reader. As the caretaker of those words, you hold great power. Whether or not the message is successfully transported depends largely on your typographic decisions.

As you learn to use InDesign's powerful type formatting features, you should always remember the cardinal rule of typography: Type exists to honor content. By all means, you should take full advantage of the available tools, but sometimes knowing when not to use a fancy typographic feature is as important as knowing how to use the feature in the first place.

Cross-Reference This chapter focuses on modifying character-level typographic formats; Chapter 18 focuses on modifying paragraph-level formats. Chapter 28 offers a broader look at using InDesign to design with type.

Working with Character Formats

Before you begin looking at InDesign's character formatting features, you should be clear about a fundamental InDesign type-formatting concept: Using separate tools, InDesign lets you modify the appearance of highlighted characters *or* selected paragraphs:

✦ When characters are highlighted (or the text cursor is flashing), you can use the Character pane (Type ➪ Character, or ⌘+T or Ctrl+T), shown in Figure 17-1, to change their appearance in several ways. If you choose Hide Options from the palette menu, the Vertical Scale, Horizontal Scale, Baseline Shift, and Skew fields and the Language pop-up menu are not displayed.

✦ When paragraphs are selected, the Paragraph pane (Type ➪ Paragraph, or Option+⌘+T or Ctrl+Alt+T) lets you change how the paragraphs are constructed. (For more information about the Paragraph pane, see Chapter 18.)

The Character pane provides access to most of InDesign's character formatting options. Three of the options — Font Family, Type Style, and Size — are also available in the Type menu, and several options have keyboard shortcuts. The new Control palette offers all the formatting options of the Character pane plus others, as shown in Figure 17-2. (If the Control palette doesn't show the character formatting options shown in the figure, be sure to select text and click the A icon on the palette.)

Figure 17-1: The Character pane with all options shown.

Figure 17-2: The character formatting options in the new Control palette.

Note

In InDesign (like most programs), you can select only contiguous text. So if you have, for example, several subheads you want to apply a font to, you can't select them all and apply the formatting in one fell swoop. You'll have to do each text segment separately.

Tip

If the Type tool is selected and no objects are active, the controls in the Character pane are still available. In this situation, any changes you make in the Character pane become the default settings for the document and are automatically used when you create new text frames. If you change character formats when the cursor is flashing and no text is selected, your changes are applied at the insertion point. When you begin typing, you'll see the results of your changes.

InDesign lets you apply character formats to highlighted text in two ways: You can

✦ Use the controls in the Character pane or their keyboard shortcuts.

✦ Create and apply character-level style sheets.

Either way, you can apply the same formatting. The difference is that a character style sheet's settings are stored, so you can apply the exact same settings easily to other text. Plus, if you change a character style sheet's settings, any text based on it is automatically changed to reflect the new settings.

If you are working on a simple, one-page publication, such as a business card, a poster, or an ad, you'll probably use the Character pane to format the text elements. However, if you're producing a multipage publication — a newsletter, magazine, catalog, or newspaper, for example — you should take advantage of style sheets. Using them will save you time and make your job a whole lot easier.

Cross-Reference

For details about creating and applying character and paragraph style sheets, see Chapter 20.

Even if you do use style sheets for a particular publication, you'll probably also do some local formatting. For example, you would probably use the Character pane to format the type on the opening spread of a feature magazine article, and then use style sheets to quickly format the remainder of the article.

Cross-Reference   Some of the controls in the Transform pane let you change the appearance of all the text within a text frame. For more information about the Transform pane, see Chapter 11.

Tip   You can change the default character formats associated with the Type tool by making changes in the Character pane when no text is selected or the text-insertion cursor isn't flashing.

Changing Font Family, Type Style, and Size

These days, the terms *font, face, typeface, font family,* and *type style* are often used interchangeably. When you're talking with friends or colleagues about typography, it doesn't matter which term you use as long as you make yourself understood, but if you're going to be setting type with InDesign, you should be familiar with the font-related terms you'll find in the menus and panes.

The term *font,* or typeface, usually refers to a collection of characters — including letters, numbers, and special characters — that share the same overall appearance, including stroke width, weight, angle, and style. For example, Helvetica Plain, Arial Bold, Adobe Garamond Semibold Italic, and ITC New Baskerville Italic are well-known fonts. A *font family* is a collection of several fonts that share the same general appearance but differ in stroke width, weight, and/or stroke angle. Some examples of font families are Adobe Caslon, Berthold Baskerville, Times New Roman, and Tekton.

In InDesign each of the fonts that make up a font family is referred to as a *typestyle.* For example, the Times Europa font family is made up of four typestyles: Roman, Italic, Bold, and Bold Italic, as shown in Figure 17-3. When you choose a font family from the Character pane's Font menu, InDesign displays the family's typestyle variations in the accompanying Type Styles pop-up menu.

Figure 17-3: The Times Europa font family includes four typestyles — Roman, Italic, Bold, and Bold Italic — as shown here.

Unlike most word processing and desktop-publishing programs, InDesign doesn't include built-in shadow and outline styles. (These styles are available only if a font includes them.) Most programs create these stylistic variations artificially by modifying plain characters. If you want to create outline text, you can use the Stroke pane (Window ➪ Stroke, or F10) to apply a stroke. If you want to create a drop shadow for text, you can stack and offset two text frames.

Cross-Reference

For more on the Stroke pane and other text-as-art techniques, see Chapter 28. For more on creating special typographic effects, see Chapter 19.

Similarly, bold and italic variations are available only for font families that include these typestyles. This prevents you from applying, for example, italic to Trajan, a font family that doesn't include an italic variation. (InDesign does let you create false italics by skewing text, which is covered later in this chapter. However, you should avoid such heavy-handed shape twisting unless it's absolutely necessary.)

Changing font family and type style

When you change from one font to another in InDesign, you can choose a new font family and typestyle independently in the Character pane. For example, changing from Arial Bold to Times Bold or from Arial Regular to Berthold Baskerville Regular is a simple change of font family. However, if you switch from Bookman Light to Century Schoolbook Bold Italic, you're changing both family and typestyle.

New Feature

InDesign CS will sometimes display a font name multiple times in various panes and dialog boxes, such as the Character pane. This occurs if you have multiple versions of a font on your computer — say, both a TrueType and PostScript version of Helvetica. (Earlier versions of InDesign would show only one of these fonts, making the others inaccessible.) You can tell which is which by the code that InDesign appends to the font name: (TT) for TrueType, (T1) for PostScript Type 1, and (OTF) for OpenType. You really shouldn't have multiple versions of a font on your computer, since different versions can look and be spaced differently resulting in inconsistent appearance that's hard to fix. If you notice such multiple versions because InDesign calls them to your attention, delete or deactivate the unneeded fonts (typically, you would keep the PostScript version, or OpenType if supported by your service bureau).

Using the Character pane

The Character pane offers two methods for changing the font family applied to highlighted text. You can

✦ Click on the Font Family menu, then choose a name from the list of available font families.

✦ Click in front of or highlight the font name displayed in the Font Family field, type in the first few letters of the font family you want to apply, then click Return or Enter. For example, entering **Ari** will select Arial (if it's available on your computer).

When you change the font family applied to selected text, InDesign will try to maintain the applied typestyle. If, for example, you switch from Adobe Garamond Bold Italic to Adobe Caslon, InDesign will automatically use Adobe Caslon Bold Italic, which is one of several typestyles that make up this font family. But if you switch from Arial Bold Italic to Avant Garde, which doesn't include a bold italic variation, Avant Garde Book will be used instead.

Using the Control palette and Font submenu

If you use the Control palette, you first select the font family with the Font pop-up menu, then select a typestyle from a submenu, as Figure 17-4 shows. If a font family doesn't have typestyle variations, it will have no submenu. Similarly, you can also change the font family by choosing Type ➪ Font then selecting a name in the Font submenu.

Figure 17-4: To select a typestyle from the Control palette, first choose the font family from the Font pop-up menu, then choose a typestyle from the selected font's submenu.

In either case, if a particular font family includes a submenu with typestyle variations, you must also choose a type style. If you choose only a font family when typestyles are available in an accompanying submenu, no changes are applied to the selected text.

One advantage of using the Control palette or Font submenu instead of the Character pane is that you can reliably change the font family and the typestyle at the same time. If a corresponding typestyle does not exist when you change the font family via the Character pane, the base style (such as plain, book, or regular) of the new family is used. In this case, the Character pane's Type Style menu confusingly displays the name of the original typestyle in brackets.

Changing font size

InDesign lets you specify font sizes from 0.1 point to 1,296 points (108 inches) in increments as fine as 0.001 point. Of course, even if it were possible to clearly print type as small as a thousandth of a point (that is, $\frac{1}{2,000}$ of an inch), which is beyond the capabilities of most printers, nobody could read it without a microscope anyway.

Use good judgment when choosing font sizes. For example, headlines should be larger than subheads, which in turn are larger than body text, which is larger than photo credits, and so on.

InDesign offers several methods for changing the font size of highlighted text. You can

✦ Use one of several techniques in the Character pane and Control palette:

- Choose one of the predefined sizes from the Size menu in the Character pane or Control palette.

- Highlight the currently applied font size displayed in the accompanying editable field, enter a new size, then press Return or Enter.

- Use the up and down cursor keys to increase or decrease the size in 1-point increments. Holding Shift multiplies the increment to 10.

✦ Choose Type ⇨ Size, then choose one of the predefined sizes listed in the Size submenu. If you choose Other from the submenu, the Size field is highlighted in the Character pane. Enter a custom size, then press Return or Enter.

✦ Control+click or right-click a text selection, then choose a size from the Size submenu. If you choose Other from the submenu, the Font Size field is highlighted in the Character pane. Enter a custom size, then press Return or Enter.

✦ Use keyboard commands to adjust text size:

- Press Shift+⌘+> or Ctrl+Shift+> to enlarge highlighted text in 2-point increments. (You can set a different increment in the Units & Measurements pane in the Preferences dialog box, accessed by choosing InDesign ⇨ Preferences on the Mac or Edit ⇨ Preferences in Windows, or by pressing ⌘+K or Ctrl+K.)

- Press Shift+⌘+< or Ctrl+Shift+< to reduce highlighted text.

- Press Option+Shift+⌘+> or Ctrl+Alt+Shift+> to increase the text size in 10-point increments.

- Press Option+Shift+⌘+< or Ctrl+Alt+Shift+< to decrease the text size in 10-point increments.

InDesign CS fixes a flaw in earlier versions. Before, if you changed the size of a text box via the Transform pane, InDesign adjusted the text size accordingly on-screen but still reported the original text size in the Character pane and other character formatting tools. Now, InDesign changes the reported text size to match its new, actual size after the text box has been resized.

If text is highlighted and the Size field is empty, it means that more than one font size is used in the selected text.

Applying Other Character Formats

Font family, typestyle, and font size are the most commonly modified character formats, but the Character pane and Control palette contain several other controls for managing the appearance of type. Some of these controls are displayed in the pane window; others are available in the pane's pop-up menu. The Control palette offers more formatting options than the Character pane.

In the Control palette, you can adjust all caps, small caps, superscript, subscript, underline, strikethrough, kerning, tracking, horizontal and vertical scale, baseline shift, skew, character style, and language. Through the palette menu, you can also set ligatures, modify underline and strikethrough settings, control whether text may break (be hyphenated), and select OpenType features. Figure 17-5 shows the palette menu for the Control palette's character formatting.

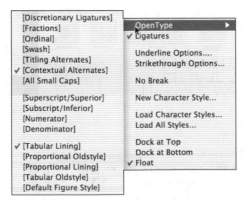

Figure 17-5: The palette menu for the Control palette's character formatting view.

In the Character pane, you can adjust kerning, tracking, horizontal and vertical scale, baseline shift, skew, and language. Through the palette menu, you can also set all caps, small caps, superscript, subscript, underline, strikethrough, ligatures, and underline and strikethrough settings, as well as control whether text may break (be hyphenated) and select OpenType features.

Note   You must choose Show Options from the Character pane's pop-up menu to display the Vertical Scale, Horizontal Scale, Baseline Shift, Skew, and Language options.

Figure 17-6 shows the various effects in action.

You can do ^{a}l$_l$ sorts^1$_b$ of *things with* text in InDesign

Figure 17-6: Various character formatting options applied to text. Top row: *can* has been scaled horizontally, and *do* vertically, while *all* has had each letter's baseline shifted by a different amount. Compare that to the true superscript and subscript following the word *sorts*. Middle row: The word *things* has been skewed, while the word *with* is in real italics; notice how different the letters *h, i,* and *t* differ.

Horizontal Scale and Vertical Scale

Some font families include condensed (that is, slightly squeezed) and/or expanded (slightly stretched) stylistic variations, but most don't. InDesign's Horizontal Scale option lets you create artificially condensed and expanded type by squeezing or stretching characters. Similarly, the Vertical Scale option lets you shrink or stretch type vertically.

Among typographers, there are two schools of thought about scaling type. One camp contends that such distortions of letterforms are taboo and should be avoided. The other side contends that a small amount of scaling doesn't adversely affect the original font and is acceptable. There's general agreement that overscaling should be avoided. For the most part, if you need to make text bigger or smaller, you should adjust font size; if you need to squeeze or stretch a range of text a bit, it's better to use InDesign's kerning and tracking controls (covered later in this chapter) because the letterforms are not affected. Only the space between letters changes when you kern or track text.

Unscaled text has a horizontal and vertical scale value of 100 percent. You can apply scaling values between 1 percent and 1,000 percent. If you apply equal horizontal and vertical scale values, you're making the original text proportionally larger or smaller. In this case, changing font size is a simpler solution. Keep in mind that when you scale text, you are not changing the font size. For example, 24-point type scaled vertically to 200 percent is 48 points tall, but its font size is still 24 points.

To change the scale of highlighted text, enter new values in the Horizontal and/or Vertical Scale fields in the Character pane or Control palette. If a value is highlighted in the Horizontal Scale or Vertical Scale field, you can also use the up and down cursor keys to increase and decrease the scaling in 1 percent increments; hold Shift to increase or decrease in 10 percent increments.

Baseline Shift

The baseline is an invisible horizontal line on which a line of characters rests. The bottom of each letter (except descenders, such as in *y, p, q, j,* and *g*) sits on the baseline. InDesign's Baseline Shift feature lets you move highlighted text above or below its baseline. This feature is useful for carefully placing such characters as trademark and copyright symbols and for creating custom fractions. (Unlike superscripts and subscripts, text whose baseline has shifted does not change size.)

To baseline-shift highlighted text, enter new values in the Baseline Shift field in the Character pane or Control palette. You can also use the up and down cursor keys to increase the baseline shift in 1-point increments, or hold Shift when using the cursor keys to increase or decrease it in 10-point increments.

Skew (false italic)

For fonts that don't have an italic typestyle, InDesign provides the option to *skew,* or slant, text to create an artificial italic variation of any font. (You can also use it with fonts that have a natural italic; refer to Figure 17-6.) Like horizontal and vertical text scaling, skewing is a clunky way of creating italic-looking text. Use this feature to create special typographic effects, such as the shadow text shown in Figure 17-7, or in situations where a true italic style is not available.

Skewed shadow

Figure 17-7: Skewing and shading a copy of the black text created the backlit shadow effect.

Note   Skewing as a form of italics typically works better for sans-serif typefaces than for serif typefaces, since the characters are simpler and have fewer embellishments that can get oddly distorted when skewed.

To skew highlighted text, you have two options:

✦ Enter an angle value between −85 and 85 in the Skew field in the Character pane or Control palette. Positive values slant text to the left; negative values slant text to the right.

✦ Click the accompanying up/down cursors when the cursor is in the Skew field to skew text in 1-degree increments. Holding down the Shift key while clicking the cursors changes the increment to 4 degrees.

Tip   You can also skew all the text in a text frame using the Shear tool or by changing the value in the Shear X angle field in the Transform pane. Slanting text by shearing a text frame does not affect the skew angle of the text. You can specify a skew angle for highlighted text independently from the frame's shear angle.

Language

The ability to correctly hyphenate and check the spelling of text in several languages is one of InDesign's most powerful features. The program uses dictionaries to accomplish these tasks. These dictionaries, each of which contains several hundred thousand words, also let you specify a different language for text on a character-by-character basis, although chances are that a single word will be the smallest text unit to which you will apply a separate language.

For example, an article about Spanish cooking might include the word *albòndigas* (the Spanish term for meatballs). By applying the Spanish: Castilian language to this word, as shown in Figure 17-8, InDesign will not flag it when you check spelling. However, if you were to apply U.S. English to *albòndigas*, it would show up as a misspelled word (unless you had added it to your dictionary; see the Tip that follows).

To assign a different language to highlighted text, choose the appropriate language from the Language menu in the Control palette or from the Character pane's palette menu, as shown in Figure 17-8.

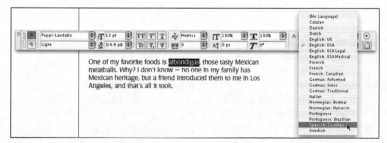

Figure 17-8: By applying the Spanish: Castilian language to *albòndigas*, as shown here, InDesign will use the associated dictionary when checking the spelling of this word.

Tip If you discover any correctly spelled words that are not included in a particular language dictionary, you can add the words to the dictionary. Choose Edit ➪ Dictionary and choose the appropriate dictionary in the Language pop-up menu to customize any dictionary.

QuarkXPress User The Passport edition of QuarkXPress has a similar feature to specify the hyphenation and spelling language, but not the standard version of QuarkXPress.

All Caps and Small Caps

When you choose All Caps, the uppercase version of all highlighted characters is used: Lowercase letters are converted to uppercase and uppercase letters remain unchanged.

Similarly, the Small Caps option affects just lowercase letters. When you choose Small Caps, InDesign will automatically use the Small Caps typestyle if one is available for the font family applied to the highlighted text (few font families include this style). If a Small Caps typestyle is not available, InDesign generates small caps from uppercase letters using the scale percentage specified in the Text pane of the Preferences dialog box (choose InDesign ➪ Preferences on the Mac or Edit ➪ Preferences in Windows, or press ⌘+K or Ctrl+K). The default scale value used to generate small caps text is 70% (of uppercase letters).

Tip You should never enter text in all capital letters, even if you think you want all caps. If you enter lowercase letters, you can easily change them to uppercase by applying the All Caps format, but if you enter uppercase letters, you can't change them to lowercase or to small caps without retyping them.

Superscript and Subscript

When you apply the Superscript and Subscript character formats to highlighted text, InDesign applies a baseline shift to the characters, lifting them above (for Superscript) or lowering them below (for Subscript) their baseline, *and* reduces their size.

The amount of baseline shift and scaling that's used for the Superscript and Subscript formats is determined by the Position and Size fields in the Text pane of the Preferences dialog box (choose InDesign ➪ Preferences on the Mac or Edit ➪ Preferences in Windows, or press ⌘+K or Ctrl+K). The default Position value for both formats is 33.3%, which means that characters are moved up or down by one-third of the applied leading value. The default Superscript and Subscript Size value is 58.3%, which means that superscripted and subscripted characters are reduced to 58.3% of the applied font size. The Text Preferences pane lets you specify separate default settings for Superscript and Subscript.

Tip
For most newspaper and magazine work, I prefer a size of 65% for superscripts and subscripts, as well as a position of 30% for subscripts and 35% for superscripts. These values work better than the InDesign defaults in the small text sizes and tight leading of such publications. If you change these settings when no document is open, they become the default for all future new documents.

You can use the Superscript and Subscript formats to create, for example, custom fractions or numbers for footnotes or to reposition special characters such as asterisks. To apply the Superscript or Subscript format to highlighted text, choose the appropriate option from the Character pane's pop-up menu. Figure 17-6 shows examples of text to which the default Superscript and Subscript settings have been applied.

Underline and Strikethrough

The Underline and Strikethrough formats are holdovers from the days of typewriters and are not typographically acceptable for indicating emphasis in text, which is better accomplished by using bold and/or italic typestyles.

Underlines can be useful in kickers and other text above a headline, as well as in documents formatted to look as if they are typewritten. Strikethrough is rarely useful in a document, though in textbooks and other educational materials, you may want to use it to indicate incorrect answers, eliminated choices, or deleted text (when showing how to edit).

If you do use underlines and strikethrough, InDesign lets you specify exactly how they look through the Underline Options and Strikethrough Options dialog boxes available in the palette menus of the Character pane and Control palette.

Cross-Reference
Chapter 19 covers these custom underline and strikethrough settings in detail.

Note
If you don't set a specific size for underlines and strikethroughs, the weight of an underline or strikethrough line is relative to the font size.

Ligatures

A ligature is a special character that combines two letters. Most early typefaces included five ligatures — ff, fi, fl, ffi, and ffl. These days, most fonts include just two ligatures — fi and fl. When you choose the Ligature option, InDesign automatically displays and prints a font's built-in ligatures — instead of the two component letters — if the font includes ligatures.

One nice thing about the Ligature option is that, even though a ligature looks like a single character on-screen, it's still fully editable. That is, you can click between the two-letter shapes and insert text if necessary. Also, a ligature created with the Ligatures option will not cause InDesign's spell checker to flag the word that contains it.

QuarkXPress User   Unlike Windows QuarkXPress, InDesign for Windows supports automatic ligatures in Windows fonts that have them.

To use ligatures within highlighted text, choose Ligatures from the Character pane's or Control palette's palette menu (Ligatures is set to On by default). Figure 17-9 shows a before-and-after example of text to which the Ligature option has been applied.

finally, I
can float!

finally, I
can float!

Figure 17-9: Ligatures are used in the top two lines but not in the bottom two. Notice the difference in space between the *fi* and *fl* letter pairs in *finally* and *float*.

For most Mac fonts that include ligatures, pressing Option+Shift+5 will insert the fi ligature, while Option+Shift+6 inserts the fl ligature. In Windows, you'll have to use the Alt code (hold the Alt key and press the character's four-digit code from the numeric keypad) or a program like Character Map that comes with Windows to access the ligature characters in fonts that support them. Either way, if you enter ligatures yourself, InDesign's spell checker will flag any words that contain them. For this reason, you may want to let the program handle the task of inserting ligatures.

OpenType options

The OpenType font standard developed by Adobe and Microsoft supports many more character variations than the ones most publishers use. In OpenType, many variations of a character exist in the same font, and you specify which variant you want for highlighted text in the Character pane's or Control palette's palette menu. For example:

✦ Perhaps the best known such variation involves numerals, of which there are titling and old-style forms.

✦ Another well-known character variant is small caps: Real small caps are designed to have the same weight as a lowercase character, so the strokes are actually thicker than the ones created by scaling down text, such as when you use InDesign's small caps feature.

✦ Many OpenType fonts include real fractions, not ones you generate by manipulating the size and position of numbers around a slash or *virgule* (the shorter version of a slash used in fractions).

Figure 17-10 shows examples of the two kinds of numerals, as well as the OpenType menu for an OpenType font that shows the kinds of variations available:

✦ **Titling figures,** also called modern figures, are much like uppercase letters in that they're all the same size and the bottom of each numeral rests on the baseline. Titling figures are often used within uppercase text.

✦ **Old-style figures,** also called text figures, hanging figures, and lowercase figures, are not uniform in size. In old-style figures, the numerals 3, 4, 5, 7, and 9 usually hang below the baseline like descenders in letters such as *g* and *y.* Similarly, the numerals 6 and 8 are taller than the others and rise above the x-height like ascenders in letters such as *b* and *l.*

For the vast majority of fonts in use today, applying an OpenType feature has no effect, since most fonts in use are standard Type 1 PostScript or TrueType. Among OpenType fonts, there is wide variation in what variations they support; InDesign indicates unavailable options by enclosing them in brackets in the menu, as shown in Figure 17-10.

Note

There is a type of font called an *expert font* that includes old-style numerals, fractions, true small caps, and other special characters. It is used as an adjunct to the regular version of the font, letting you manually apply the special characters. For example, if you used Garamond as your font, you could apply Garamond Expert to the numerals to get old-style numerals. This is a lot of work, so most people don't bother except for typographically sophisticated — and short — documents like ads. Unfortunately, InDesign doesn't detect the use of expert fonts and use them to apply OpenType-like attributes such as old-style numerals, true small caps, and true fractions when they are available. Instead, you have to apply them manually.

Figure 17-10: The top row of numbers uses typical titling figures—all are the same height. The bottom row uses old-style numerals. At right is the OpenType menu for the fonts used here.

No Break

InDesign lets you prevent individual words from being hyphenated or a string of words from being broken at the end of a line. For example, you may decide that you don't want to hyphenate software names, such as InDesign, CorelDraw, or FreeHand. Or perhaps you don't want to separate the *J* and the *P* in *J. P. Morgan.* The No Break option was created for situations such as these.

To prevent a word or a text string from being broken, highlight it, then choose No Break from the Character pane's or Control palette's palette menu.

Caution   If you apply the No Break option to a range of text that's longer than the width of the current column, InDesign will track the text so that it fits on a single line—squeezing it unacceptably.

Tip   You can also prevent a word from being hyphenated by placing a discretionary hyphen (Shift+⌘+- [hyphen] or Ctrl+Shift+- [hyphen]) in front of the first letter.

Leaving Space between Characters and Lines

Typographers often pay as much attention to the space between characters, words, and lines of text as they do to the appearance of the characters themselves. Their concern about space is well justified. The legibility of a block of text depends as much on the space around it — called *white space* — as it does on the readability of the font. InDesign offers two ways to adjust the space between characters:

✦ **Kerning:** *Kerning* is the adjustment of space between a pair of characters. Most fonts include built-in kerning tables that control the space between pesky character pairs, such as *LA*, *Yo*, and *WA*, that otherwise could appear to have a space between them even when there isn't one. Particularly at small font sizes, it's safe to use a font's built-in kerning information to control the space between letter pairs. But for large font sizes, for example the front-page nameplate of a newsletter or a magazine headline, you may want to manually adjust the space between certain character pairs to achieve consistent spacing.

✦ **Tracking:** *Tracking* is similar to kerning but applies to a range of highlighted text. Tracking is the process of adding or removing space among all letters in a range of text.

InDesign lets you apply kerning and/or tracking to highlighted text in $\frac{1}{1,000}$-em increments, called *units*. An em is as wide as the height of the current font size (that is, an em for 12-point text is 12 points wide), which means that kerning and tracking increments are relative to the applied font size.

InDesign's Leading (rhymes with *sledding*, not with *pleading*) feature lets you control the vertical space between lines of type. It's traditionally an attribute of paragraphs, but InDesign lets you apply it on a character-by-character basis. (To override the character-oriented approach, ensuring that leading changes affect entire paragraphs, check the Apply Leading to Entire Paragraphs option in the Text pane of the Preferences dialog box (choose InDesign ➪ Preferences on the Mac or Edit ➪ Preferences in Windows, or press ⌘+K or Ctrl+K).

Chapter 18 explains how to control the spacing between words, which is part of paragraph formatting.

InDesign users, especially QuarkXPress converts, may be surprised at the seemingly large kerning and tracking values produced by all the program's kerning and tracking methods. Keep in mind that InDesign lets you adjust space in 0.001-em units ($\frac{1}{1,000}$ of an em). In QuarkXPress, for example, the kerning unit is 0.005 em ($\frac{1}{200}$ of an em). So QuarkXPress users should not be surprised to see kerning and tracking values that are 10 to 20 times greater than you're used to — you're working with multiples of finer increments.

Kerning

The Kerning controls in the Character pane and Control palette provide three options for kerning letter pairs: Metrics kerning, Optical kerning, and manual kerning:

✦ **Metrics kerning** uses a font's built-in kerning pairs to control the space between character pairs in the highlighted text.

✦ **Optical kerning** has InDesign "look" at each letter pair in highlighted text and add or remove space between the letters based on the shapes of the characters.

✦ **Manual kerning** is adding or removing space between a specific letter pair in user-specified amounts.

The kerning method you use will depend on the circumstances. For example, some fonts include a large set of kerning pairs. Such fonts, especially at text font sizes (9 to 12 points) and lower, may look fine using the default Metrics kerning option, which uses built-in kerning pairs. On the other hand, if the font applied to high-lighted text has few or no built-in kerning pairs or if several different fonts are mixed together, the text may benefit from the Optical kerning method. At display type sizes (36 points and larger) you may want to manually kern individual letter pairs to suit your taste.

When the flashing text cursor is between a pair of characters, the Kerning field displays the pair's kerning value. If Metrics or Optical kerning is applied, the kerning value is displayed in parentheses.

To apply Metrics or Optical kerning to highlighted text, choose the appropriate option from the Kerning pop-up menu. To apply manual kerning, click between a pair of letters, then enter a value in the Kerning field or choose one of the predefined values. Negative values tighten; positive values loosen.

Tip　You can also use a keyboard shortcut to apply manual kerning. Press Option+left cursor or Alt+left cursor to decrease the kerning value in increments of 20 units; Press Option+right cursor or Alt+right cursor to increase the kerning value in increments of 20 units. If you add the ⌘ or Ctrl keys to these keyboard shortcuts, the increment is increased to 100 units. If you use the up and down cursor keys in the Kerning field in the Character pane or Control palette, you change the kerning in increments of 10, while holding the Shift key changes the increments to 25.

Caution　A warning about kerning and tracking: InDesign will happily let you tighten or loosen text to the point of illegibility. If this is the effect you're after, go for it. But as a general rule, when letter shapes start to collide, you've tightened too far.

Tracking

If you understand kerning, you can think of tracking as uniform kerning applied to a range of text. You might use tracking to tighten character spacing for a font that you think is too spacey or loosen spacing for a font that's too tight. Or you could track a paragraph tighter or looser to eliminate a short last line or a *widow* (the last line of a paragraph that falls at the top of a page or column).

To apply tracking to highlighted text, enter a value in the Character pane's Tracking field or choose one of the predefined values. Negative values tighten; positive values loosen (in 0.001-em increments). Use the same keyboard techniques as for kerning.

Leading

In the days of metal type, typesetters would insert thin strips of metal — specifically, lead — between rows of letters to aid legibility. In the world of digital typography, *leading* refers to the vertical space between lines of type as measured from baseline to baseline. Leading in InDesign is a character-level format, which means that you can apply different leading values within a single paragraph. InDesign looks separately at each line of text in a paragraph and uses the largest applied leading value within a line to determine the leading for that line.

Leading as a character format is a carryover from PageMaker (and not necessarily a good one). QuarkXPress users may find InDesign's leading method to be odd at first because leading is a paragraph-level format in that program. In most cases, you'll apply a single leading value to entire paragraphs, in which case leading behaves like a paragraph-level format.

By default, InDesign applies Auto Leading to text. When Auto Leading is applied, leading is equal to 120 percent of the font size. For example, if Auto Leading is applied to 10-point text, the leading value is 12 points; for 12-point text, Auto Leading is 14.4 points; and so on. As long as you don't change fonts or font sizes in a paragraph, Auto Leading works pretty well. But if you do change fonts or sizes, Auto Leading can result in inconsistent spacing between lines. For this reason, it's safer to specify an actual leading value.

Generally, it's a good idea to use a leading value that is slightly larger than the font size, which is why Auto Leading works in many cases. When the leading value equals the font size, text is said to be set *solid.* That's about as tight as you'll ever want to set leading, unless you're trying to achieve a special typographic effect or working with very large text sizes in ad-copy headlines. As is the case with kerning and tracking, when tight leading causes letters to collide — ascenders and descenders are the first to overlap — you've gone too far.

Tip

You can change InDesign's preset Auto Leading value of 120%. To do so, choose Type ➪ Paragraph, or Option+⌘+T or Ctrl+Alt+T, to display the Paragraph pane. Choose Justification in the palette menu, enter a new value in the Auto Leading field, and then click OK. (Why a character format setting is accessed via the Paragraph pane and what Auto Leading has to do with Justification are both mysteries.)

QuarkXPress User

Another mystery is why you cannot specify Auto Leading amounts in anything other than percentages. This will cause many QuarkXPress documents imported into InDesign to flow incorrectly, because QuarkXPress lets you set the Auto Leading to a specific value, such as +2 (which adds 2 points to the text size rather than use a percentage like 120 percent that results in awkward leading amounts like 14.4 points). Being able to specify a specific additive value like +2 makes sense for many kinds of layouts, so the inability to specify such values is an unfortunate continued omission in InDesign.

One thing QuarkXPress users can do to make InDesign work more like QuarkXPress's standard approach to leading is to ensure that Apply Leading to Entire Paragraphs is checked in the Text pane of the Preferences dialog box (InDesign ➪ Preferences on the Mac or Edit ➪ Preferences in Windows, or ⌘+K or Ctrl+K).

To modify the leading value applied to selected text, choose one of the predefined options from the Leading pop-up menu in the Character pane or Control palette, or enter a leading value in the field. You can enter values from 0 to 5,000 points in 0.001-point increments. You can also use the up and down cursor keys to change leading in 1-point increments.

Summary

As a user of InDesign, modifying the appearance of type is one of the more common tasks you'll perform. InDesign lets you modify the appearance of highlighted characters or selected paragraphs. When text is highlighted, you can use the controls in the Character pane or Control palette to change any of several character attributes: font family, size, typestyle, leading, kerning, tracking, vertical and horizontal scale, baseline shift, and skew. You can also set the hyphenation and spell-checking language, apply all caps or small caps, superscripts or subscripts, underline, strikethrough, ligatures, and OpenType variations. You also set line spacing (leading), something normally applied to entire paragraphs rather than InDesign's approach of applying it to selected text.

✦   ✦   ✦

Specifying Paragraph Attributes

◆ ◆ ◆ ◆

In This Chapter

Understanding
paragraph
fundamentals

Changing basic and
advanced paragraph
formats

Working with
hyphenation and
justification

Modifying other
paragraph formats

◆ ◆ ◆ ◆

Much like an individual character, a paragraph in InDesign is a basic typographic unit. When you create a new text frame and begin typing, you create a paragraph each time you press Return or Enter. A paragraph can be as short as one character or word on a single line or many words strung out over many lines. When you press Return or Enter, the paragraph formats of the preceding paragraph are automatically used for the subsequent paragraph (unless you've created style sheets that automatically change paragraph formats).

In general, paragraph formats control how the lines in the paragraph are constructed. Changing paragraph formats doesn't change the appearance of the individual characters within the paragraph. To do that, you must highlight the characters and modify character-level formats.

Cross-Reference This chapter focuses on modifying paragraph-level typographic formats; Chapter 17 focuses on modifying character-level formats. Chapter 20 covers the creation and use of style sheets for both characters and paragraphs.

To select a paragraph, simply click within it. Any change you make to a paragraph-level format will be applied to all the lines in the paragraph. (Unlike character-level formats, you don't have to highlight all the text in a paragraph to modify a paragraph-level format.) If you need to change the paragraph formats of several consecutive paragraphs, you can highlight all the text in all the paragraphs, or you can click anywhere in the first paragraph, drag anywhere within the last paragraph, then release the mouse button.

Just as you can't apply two different colors to a single character, you can't apply conflicting paragraph formats within a single paragraph. For example, you can't specify for one line in a paragraph to be left-aligned and the rest right-aligned. All lines in a paragraph must share the same alignment, indents, tab settings, and all other paragraph-level formats.

As is the case with character formats, there are two ways to apply paragraph formats:

✦ Use the controls in the Paragraph pane, shown in Figure 18-1, or their keyboard shortcuts.

✦ Create and apply paragraph-level style sheets.

A paragraph-level style sheet is essentially a text formatting macro that lets you apply several paragraph formats to selected paragraphs in a single operation. If you're working on a multipage publication such as a book, newspaper, magazine, or catalog that repeatedly uses the same basic text formats, you'll definitely want to use paragraph style sheets to handle the bulk of your formatting chores. But even if you use style sheets, you'll probably also use the Paragraph pane to do some manual paragraph formatting.

Tab settings are also a paragraph-level format. See Chapter 21 for a detailed explanation of InDesign's Tabs feature.

Figure 18-1 shows the Paragraph pane. It can have two appearances: If you choose Hide Options from the pop-up menu, the Space Before/After, Drop Cap, and Hyphenate controls are not displayed. You might want to combine the Character and Paragraph panes into a single text formatting pane, as shown here. You can also use the new Control palette's paragraph formatting options, shown in Figure 18-2.

If the Type tool is selected and no objects are active, any changes you make in the Paragraph pane become the default settings for the document and are automatically used when you create new text frames.

The Paragraph pane and Control palette provide access to most of InDesign's paragraph-formatting options. (To set tabs, you must open the Tabs pane by choosing Windows ➪ Type & Tables ➪ Tabs or by pressing Shift+⌘+T or Ctrl+Shift+T, as Chapter 21 covers.) Several of the options have keyboard shortcuts.

Figure 18-1: The Paragraph pane.

Figure 18-2: The Control palette's paragraph formatting options.

Leading

Leading, or the space between lines in a paragraph, is treated by InDesign as a character format via the Character pane or Control palette, even though it's traditionally an attribute of the paragraph. However, you can override InDesign's character-oriented approach so it works like all other layout programs. To ensure that leading changes affect entire paragraphs, check the Apply Leading to Entire Paragraphs option in the Text pane of the Preferences dialog box (choose InDesign ➪ Preferences on the Mac or Edit ➪ Preferences in Windows, or press ⌘+K or Ctrl+K).

For more details on how to apply leading, see Chapter 17.

Controlling Alignment and Indents

The seven alignment icons at the top of the Paragraph pane and the three fields and two icons just below are always displayed; the four additional fields and the Hyphenate check box are also displayed when you choose Show Options from the palette menu. InDesign refers to the top set of options as Basic Paragraph Formats; the additional five options are Advanced Paragraph Formats.

The top set lets you control a paragraph's alignment and indents (left, right, and first line) and lock text baselines to the document's baseline grid.

Alignment

The seven alignment icons at the top of the Paragraph pane control how line beginnings and endings in selected paragraphs are placed relative to the left and right margins. Here's a description of each alignment option (the icons do a pretty good job of showing what they do):

+ **Align Left (Shift+⌘+L or Ctrl+Shift+L):** Places the left edge of every line at the left margin (the margin can be the frame edge, frame inset, left indent, or column edge) and fits as many words (or syllables, if the hyphenation is turned on) on the line as possible. When a word (or syllable) won't fit at the end of a line, it's placed (flush left) on the next line. In left-aligned paragraphs, the right margin is said to be *ragged* because the leftover space at the right end of each line differs from line to line and produces a jagged edge.

Some designers prefer to use this alignment for columns of text because they like the irregular, somewhat organic shapes that result; others prefer to align both left and right edges (justify), which produces a more rigid, vertical look. Similarly, left-aligned text is sometimes hyphenated, sometimes not. (You'll find more about hyphenation and justification later in this chapter.)

✦ **Align Center (Shift+⌘+C or Ctrl+Shift+C):** To create centered text, the left-over space of each line is divided in half. One-half of the leftover space is placed on the left end of the line; the other half is placed on the right end. The result is that both the left and right edges of the paragraphs are ragged, and the text is balanced along a vertical axis.

✦ **Align Right (Shift+⌘+R or Ctrl+Shift+R):** This is a mirror opposite of Align Left. The right edge is straight; the left edge is ragged. Columns of text are seldom set flush right, because it's not as easy to read as flush left text. Right-aligned text is sometimes used for such things as captions placed to the left of a picture, blurbs on magazine covers, and advertising copy.

✦ **Left Justify (Shift+⌘+J or Ctrl+Shift+J):** In justified text, the left and right ends of each line are flush with the margins. The flush-left/flush-right results are produced by sprinkling the extra space of each line between characters and/or words or by reducing space between characters and/or words to accommodate additional characters (more about justification later in this chapter). Justified text is nearly always hyphenated (if you don't hyphenate justified text, spacing between letters and words is very inconsistent). Aligning the last line flush left is the traditional way of ending a paragraph.

✦ **Center Justify:** This is the same as Left Justify except that the last line is center-aligned.

✦ **Right Justify:** This is the same as Left Justify except that the last line is right-aligned.

✦ **Full Justify (Shift+⌘+F or Ctrl+Shift+F):** This is the same as Left Justify except that the last line is also forcibly justified. This option can produce very widely spaced last lines. The fewer the characters on the last line, the greater the spacing.

Note

These last three options are rarely used, and for good reason. People expect justified text to have the last line aligned left, and the space at the end of the line is a marker that the paragraph has ended. By changing the position of that last line, you can confuse your reader. So use Center Justify, Right Justify, and Full Justify options sparingly, in special situations where the reader won't be confused — typically in brief copy like ads and pull-quotes.

To apply a paragraph alignment to selected paragraphs, click on one of the icons. (The hand pointer is displayed when the pointer is over a pane button.) You can also use the keyboard shortcuts in the preceding list.

Note

Left-aligned paragraphs typically fit fewer characters per line than justified paragraphs. Most publications standardize on one of these two alignments for their body copy, and one factor in your decision may be how much copy you need to squeeze in.

Indents

You can move the edges of paragraphs away from the left and/or right margins and indent the first line using the indent controls in the Paragraph pane.

Left and right indents are often used for lengthy passages of quoted material within a column of text. Using indents is also a handy way of drawing attention to pull quotes and moving text away from a nearby picture.

The options are:

✦ **Left Indent:** Enter a value in this field to move the left edge of selected paragraphs away from the left margin. You can also use the up and down cursor keys. Each click increases the value by 1 point; holding down the Shift while clicking increases the increment to 1 pica.

✦ **Right Indent:** Enter a value in this field to move the right edge of selected paragraphs away from the right margin. You can also use the up and down cursor keys.

✦ **First-Line Indent:** Enter a value in this field to move the left edge of the first line of selected paragraphs away from the left margin. You can also click the up and down cursor keys. The value in the First-Line Indent field is added to any Left Indent value. For example, if you've specified a Left Indent value of 1 pica and you then specify a 1-pica First-Line Indent value, the first line of selected paragraphs will be indented 2 picas from the left margin. If you've specified a Left Indent value, you can specify a negative First-Line Indent value to create a *hanging indent* (also called an *outdent*). But you cannot specify a First-Line Indent value that would cause the first line to extend past the left edge of the text frame (that is, the First-Line Indent value can't exceed that of the Left Indent value).

Note   Using a tab or spaces to indent the first line of a paragraph, which is what was done in the age of typewriters, is usually not a good idea. You're better off specifying a First-Line Indent. Similarly, you can indent an entire paragraph by inserting a tab or multiple word spaces at the beginning of every line, but both are typographic no-nos. Use the indent controls instead.

Lock to Baseline Grid

Every document includes a grid of horizontal lines, called the *baseline grid,* that can be displayed or hidden (View ➪ Show/Hide Baseline Grid, or ⌘+Option+' or Ctrl+Alt+') and used to help position objects and text baselines. A document's baseline grid is established in the Grids pane of the Preferences dialog box (choose InDesign ➪ Preferences on the Mac or Edit ➪ Preferences in Windows, or press ⌘+K or Ctrl+K, then go to the Grids pane). Generally, a document's baseline grid interval is equal to the leading value applied to the body text. You can ensure that lines of text align across columns and pages by locking their baselines to the baseline grid.

Although you can use InDesign's Lock to Baseline Grid feature to align text baselines across columns and pages, you can produce the same results by combining uniform body text leading with other paragraph formats (Space Before and Space After). Some designers like the certainty and simplicity of the Lock to Baseline Grid feature; others prefer to control text alignment across columns themselves. Whichever works best for you is fine.

Note Keep in mind that when paragraphs are aligned to the baseline grid, the applied leading values are ignored.

To align the baselines of text in selected paragraphs with a document's baseline grid, click the Align to Baseline Grid button (it's the one on the right) in the Paragraph pane or Control palette. Click on the Do Not Align to Baseline Grid button if you don't want to align text baselines with baseline grid lines.

New Feature InDesign CS adds two new options to the Paragraph pane's palette menu and the Control palette's palette menu. One is Only Align First Line to Grid. The other is Balance Ragged Lines.

The Only Align First Line to Grid option, which aligns the first line of a paragraph to the baseline grid, is a handy way to align multiline subheads so the first line stays on the grid, but the extra lines can fall naturally. You can use this for any paragraph that you want to be the rest point if your text gets off the baseline grid, without forcing every line to align to the grid.

The other new option, Balance Ragged Lines, ensures that the rag is "balanced," that is to say where the lines alternate short and long (when possible), rather than fall in a seemingly random pattern. This is designed to make headlines and other large copy (such as in ads) be more visually pleasing. You wouldn't use this for body text, where the small text size and need to have efficient spacing would make this feature irrelevant. Unfortunately, this setting also will force hyphenation to achieve the "balanced" rag, which may be contrary to your intent.

Adding Space between Paragraphs

When you choose Show Options from the Paragraph pane's palette menu, four additional fields are displayed, as shown earlier in Figure 18-1. They're also always in the Control palette. Two of these fields let you insert space before and/or after paragraphs.

When you need to format a lengthy chunk of text with multiple paragraphs, there are two ways to indicate a new paragraph: You can

✦ Indent the paragraph's first line (by specifying a First-Line Indent value).

✦ Insert some extra space between the new paragraph and the preceding one.

Note   There's no rule that says you can't use both spacing methods, but generally you'll use one or the other. What you don't want to do is insert extra returns between a paragraph, which is what was done in the days of typewriters.

To insert space before selected paragraphs, enter a value in the Space Before field in the Paragraph pane. You can also use the up and down cursor keys; each click increases the value by 1 point, while holding down Shift increases the increment to 1 pica.

The Space After field works the same as the Space Before field but inserts space below selected paragraphs. Generally, you'll use Space Before or Space After to separate paragraphs. Combining both can be confusing.

Adding Drop Caps

A drop cap is created by "notching" a paragraph's first letter — or letters — into the upper-left corner of the paragraph. Drop caps are often used to embellish the first paragraph of a story, to draw attention to paragraphs, and to interrupt the grayness in columns of text. In the Paragraph pane or Control palette, InDesign lets you specify the number of letters you want to include in a drop cap and the number of lines you want to notch them.

To add one or more drop caps to selected paragraphs, enter a number in the Drop Cap Number field in the Paragraph pane or Control palette. That's how many characters will be made into drop caps. To specify the number of lines a drop cap will extend into a paragraph, enter a value in the Drop Cap Depth field.

After you've created a drop cap, you can modify it by highlighting it and then changing any of its character formats — font, size, color, and so on — using the Character pane or Control palette, as well as other panes (such as Stroke and Swatches). Figure 18-3 shows some examples of drop caps.

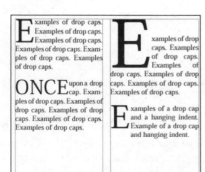

Figure 18-3: The drop cap in the top-left example has a one-character drop cap three lines deep. The bottom-left paragraph has a two-line, four-character drop cap. In the top-right example, the font size of a one-letter, four-line drop cap has been enlarged to raise it above the first line of text. In the bottom-left example, a Left Indent value combined with a negative First-Line Indent value produced the one-character, three-line drop cap's hanging indent.

A handy way to apply these settings is to use the Drop Cap & Nested Styles option in the Paragraph pane's or Control palette's palette menu. You can also use the shortcut Option+⌘+R or Ctrl+Alt+R. Figure 18-4 shows the dialog box.

Figure 18-4: The new Drop Caps & Nested Styles dialog box.

 New Feature   Nested styles are new to InDesign CS.

With this dialog box, you can set a character style that is applied to the paragraph. You can also use it to apply another character style to other text in the paragraph. To do so, click New Nested Style, then choose from the three pop-up menus to specify how the style is to be applied. The first pop-up menu lets you choose Through or Up To, the second the number of elements to apply the style through or up to, and the third pop-up menu lets you determine what elements you're using, as the figure shows.

 Cross-Reference   Because this feature is most useful when coupled with a paragraph style sheet (otherwise, it's easier to simply highlight some text in a paragraph and apply a character style to it), Chapter 20 covers nested styles in more detail.

Controlling Hyphenation and Justification

Hyphenation is the placement of hyphens between syllables in words that don't completely fit at the end of a line of text — a signal to the reader that the word continues on the next line. InDesign gives you the option to hyphenate or not hyphenate paragraphs, and if you choose to hyphenate, you can customize the settings that determine when and where hyphens are inserted.

Justification is the addition or removal of space between words and/or letters that produces the flush-left/flush-right appearance of justified paragraphs. InDesign's justification controls let you specify how space is added or removed when paragraphs are justified.

If your pages will contain columns of text, you'll have to decide whether to use left-aligned or justified paragraphs and whether you want to hyphenate words that don't entirely fit at the end of a line. As mentioned earlier, if you justify paragraphs, you'll almost certainly want to hyphenate them, too. If you opt for left-aligned paragraphs, whether to hyphenate is a personal choice.

InDesign offers two hyphenation methods: manual and automatic.

Manual hyphenation

If you want to break a particular word differently from the way InDesign would normally break the word, you can place a *discretionary hyphen* in the word. If the word falls at the end of a line in a hyphenated paragraph, InDesign will use the discretionary hyphen to split the word if the first syllable fits on the line. To insert a discretionary hyphen, use the shortcut Shift+⌘+- (hyphen) or Ctrl+Shift+- (hyphen) in the text where you want the hyphen to appear.

Tip   If you place a discretionary hyphen in a word, InDesign will break the word only at that point (or not break it at all). But you can place multiple discretionary hyphens within a single word; InDesign will use the one that produces the best results.

Note   InDesign uses discretionary hyphens only if you have checked the Hyphenate check box in the Paragraph pane or in the Control palette. If Hyphenate is not checked, neither manual nor automatic hyphenation is applied.

Automatic hyphenation

To automatically hyphenate selected paragraphs, all you have to do is check the Hyphenate check box in the Paragraph pane or Control palette. (The Hyphenate check box is displayed only if you choose Show Options from the palette menu.)

If you choose to hyphenate paragraphs, you can control how hyphenation is accomplished via the Hyphenation option in the palette menu. When you choose Hyphenation, the Hyphenation dialog box, shown in Figure 18-5, is displayed.

Figure 18-5: The Hyphenation dialog box.

Here's a brief description of each option:

✦ **Hyphenate check box:** This is a duplicate of the Hyphenate check box in the Paragraph pane and Control palette. If you didn't check it before opening the Hyphenation dialog box, you can check it here.

✦ **Words with at Least Letters:** Here, you specify the number of letters in the shortest word you want to hyphenate. For example, if you specify four letters, *mama* can be hyphenated, but *any* can't be.

✦ **After First Letters:** Here, you specify the minimum number of characters that can precede a hyphen. If you enter 2, for example, the word *atavistic* can be broken after *at*. If you specify 3, *atavistic* cannot be broken until after *ata*.

✦ **Before Last Letters:** This field is similar to After First Letters, but it determines the minimum number of characters that can follow a hyphen.

✦ **Hyphenation Limit:** Specify the number of consecutive lines that can be hyphenated in this field. Some designers limit the number of consecutive hyphens to two or three because they believe that too many consecutive hyphens produce an awkward, ladder-like look. If the Hyphenation Limit value you enter prevents hyphenation in a line that would otherwise be hyphenated, the line may look more spaced out than surrounding lines.

✦ **Hyphenation Zone:** This field applies only to nonjustified text and only when the Adobe Single-Line Composer option is selected (in the Paragraph pane's palette menu). A hyphenation point must fall within the distance specified in this field to be used. Otherwise-acceptable hyphenation points that do not fall within the specified hyphenation zone are ignored. You can also use the slider below the field to select a value rather than enter a value in this field.

✦ **Hyphenate Capitalized Words:** Select this option to break capitalized words, such as proper names and the first word of sentences. If you don't check this box, a capitalized word that would otherwise be hyphenated will get bumped to the next line, possibly producing excessive spacing in the previous line.

How many characters?

Consider changing the After First Letters hyphenation setting to 2 if you have narrow columns or large text. Although many typographers object to two-letter hyphenation — as in *ab-dicate* or *ra-dar* — it often looks better than text with large gaps caused by the reluctance to hyphenate such words. Hyphenation also makes sense for many words that use two-letter prefixes such as *in-*, *re-*, and *co-*.

Although I advocate two-letter hyphenation at the beginning of a word, I prefer three-letter hyphenation at the end (set via Before Last Letters). Except for words ending in *-ed* and sometimes *-al,* most words don't lend themselves to two-letter hyphenation at the end of the word. Part of this is functional — it's easy for readers to lose two letters beginning a line. I prefer two-letter hyphenations at the end of a word only when the alternative is awkward spacing. As with all typography, this ultimately is a personal or house style choice.

Regardless of the two- versus three-letter debate, words broken using minimum settings of 1 look awful. They also go against reader expectations, because the norm is to have several letters after a hyphen. Never use a minimum setting of 1 for After First Letters. If you do, you get hyphenations such as *A-sia*, *a-typical*, and *u-niform* that simply look terrible in print. They also don't provide enough context for the reader to anticipate the rest of the word. Likewise, never use a minimum of 1 for Before Last Letters because you get hyphenations such as *radi-o*.

When you're done specifying hyphenation settings in the Hyphenation dialog box, click OK to close the dialog box and return to your document.

Tip　You can prevent a particular word from being hyphenated by highlighting it and choosing No Break from the Control palette or from the palette menu of the Character pane (Window ⇨ Type & Tables ⇨ Character, or ⌘+T or Ctrl+T) or by placing a discretionary hyphen (Shift+⌘+- [hyphen] or Ctrl+Shift+- [hyphen]) in front of the first letter.

Justifications controls

InDesign provides three options for controlling how justification is achieved: You can

✦ Condense or expand the width of spaces, or *spacebands,* between words.

✦ Add or remove space between letters.

✦ Condense or expand the width of characters, or *glyphs.*

The options in the Justification dialog box, shown in Figure 18-6, let you specify the degree to which InDesign will adjust normal word spaces, character spacing, and character width to achieve justification. You access this dialog box via the palette menu in the Control palette or in the Paragraph pane, or by pressing Option+Shift+ ⌘+J or Ctrl+Alt+Shift+J. Although you can use the Justification controls on selected paragraphs, in most cases you will specify Justification settings when you create style sheets, particularly your body-text style sheets.

Figure 18-6: The Justification dialog box.

Here's a brief description of each option:

✦ **Word Spacing:** Enter the percentage of a spaceband character that you want to use whenever possible in the Desired field. (The default value is 100%, which uses a font's built-in width.) Enter the minimum acceptable percentage in the Minimum field; enter the maximum acceptable percentage in the Maximum field. The smallest value you can enter is 0%; the largest is 1000%. Some designers are adamant that only word spaces — not letter spaces — should be adjusted when justifying text. Others allow small adjustments to letter spacing as well.

✦ **Letter Spacing:** The default value of 0% in this field uses a font's built-in letter spacing. In the Desired field, enter a positive value to add space (in increments of 1% of an en space) between all letter pairs; enter a negative value to remove space. Enter the minimum acceptable percentage in the Minimum field; enter the maximum acceptable percentage in the Maximum field.

✦ **Glyph Scaling:** The default value of 100% uses a character's normal width. In the Desired field, enter a positive value to expand all character widths; enter a negative value to condense character widths. Enter the minimum acceptable percentage in the Minimum field; enter the maximum acceptable percentage in the Maximum field. Some designers adamantly contend that scaling characters is even more unacceptable than letter spacing, while others see no harm in scaling characters, as long as it's kept to a minimum. If you do apply glyph scaling, it's best to keep it to a range of 97 to 103 percent at most.

About word spacing

Word spacing — the space between words — is another important contributor to the aesthetics of a document. Think about it: If the words in a sentence are too close to one another, comprehension may be affected because of the difficulty in telling where one word ends and another begins. If the words are too far apart, the reader might have a difficult time following the thought that's being conveyed.

Here's a design rule I like to follow: The wider the column, the more space you can add between words. This is why books tend to have more word spacing than magazines. Like all other typographic issues, there's a subjective component to picking good word spacing. Experiment to see what works best in your documents.

Tip   I suggest 85 percent minimum, 100 percent optimum, and 150 percent maximum for word spacing; and −5 percent minimum, 0 percent optimum, and 10 percent maximum for letter spacing. I prefer minimum settings that are less than the optimum because they help text fit more easily in narrow columns. These settings work well for most newsletters and magazines output on an imagesetter. At the same time, I usually leave the maximum word spacing at 150 percent.

Note   When specifying values in the Justification dialog box, Minimum values must be smaller than Desired values, which in turn must be smaller than Maximum values.

If you use the Multi-Line Composer option (explained in the next section) for justified paragraphs, specifying a narrow range between minimum and maximum Word Spacing, Letter Spacing, and Glyph Scaling will generally produce good-looking results. However, if you choose the Single-Line Composer option, a broader range between Minimum and Maximum gives the composer more leeway in spacing words and letters and hyphenating words and can produce better-looking results. The best way to find out what values work best for you is to experiment with several settings. Print out hard copies and let your eyes decide which values produce the best results.

Note   A paragraph's justification settings are applied whether the paragraph is justified or not. However, for nonjustified paragraphs, only the Desired values for Word Spacing, Letter Spacing, and Glyph Scaling are used.

Note   The Auto Leading field in the Justification dialog box lets you specify a custom value for Auto Leading (covered in Chapter 17). In InDesign, this is a character-level format, even though it rightfully should be a paragraph format. Although it's great that InDesign also makes it available in this paragraph-oriented dialog box, it's a bit hidden here. Plus, it's too bad you can't specify an actual number of points (such as +2 to indicate 2 points of leading more than the text size), which is how leading is traditionally calculated.

Composing text

The Paragraph pane's palette menu offers two choices for implementing the hyphenation and justification settings you've established: the Adobe Single-Line Composer and the Adobe Multi-Line Composer. (These are also available in the Justification dialog box covered in the previous section.)

Adobe Single-Line Composer

In the past, programs like QuarkXPress and PageMaker have used single-line composition methods to flow text. This method marches line by line through a paragraph and sets each line as well as possible using the applied hyphenation and justification settings. The effect of modifying the spacing of one line on the lines above and below is not considered in single-line composition. If adjusting the space within a line causes poor spacing on the next line, tough luck. When you use the Adobe Single-Line Composer, the following rules apply:

✦ Adjusting word spacing is preferred over hyphenation.

✦ Hyphenation is preferred over glyph scaling.

✦ If spacing must be adjusted, removing space is preferred over adding space.

Adobe Multi-Line Composer

InDesign's Adobe Multi-Line Composer, which is selected by default, takes a broader approach to composition by looking at several lines at once. If a poorly spaced line can be fixed by adjusting the spacing of a previous line, the Multi-Line Composer will reflow the previous line. The Multi-Line Composer is governed by the following principles:

✦ The evenness of letter spacing and word spacing is the highest priority. The desirability of possible breakpoints is determined by how much they cause word and letter spacing to vary from the Desired settings.

✦ Uneven spacing is preferred to hyphenation. A breakpoint that does not require hyphenation is preferred over one that does.

✦ All possible breakpoints are ranked, and good breakpoints are preferred over bad ones.

The multiline composer is more sophisticated than the single-line option, offering generally better overall spacing since it will sacrifice optimal spacing a bit on one line to prevent really bad spacing on another, something the single-line method does not do.

However, there is one frustration dealing with the multiline composer: When you try to edit text or play with tracking to get rid of an orphan or widow, the multiline composer keeps adjusting the text across several lines, often counteracting your nips and tucks. The single-line composer doesn't do that.

Setting Other Paragraph Formats

The Paragraph pane's and Control palette's palette menu contains two additional paragraph-formatting options:

✦ **Keep Options** lets you determine how and when paragraphs can be split when they fall at the bottom of a column or page.

✦ **Paragraph Rules** lets you place a horizontal line in front of or after a paragraph. Lines placed using the Paragraph Rules feature become part of the text and move along with surrounding text when editing causes text reflow.

Keep Options

A widow is the last line of a paragraph that falls at the top of a column (the poor thing has been cut off from the rest of the family). An orphan is the first line of a paragraph that falls at the bottom of a column (it, too, has become separated from its family). InDesign's Keep Options feature lets you prevent widows and orphans; it also lets you keep paragraphs together when they would otherwise be broken at the bottom of a column.

When you choose Keep Options from the Paragraph pane's or Control palette's palette menu, the Keep Options dialog box, shown in Figure 18-7, is displayed.

Figure 18-7: The Keep Options dialog box.

The Keep Options dialog box provides several options for how paragraphs are managed as text breaks across columns and pages:

✦ **Keep with Next Lines:** This option applies to two consecutive paragraphs. Specify the number of lines of the second paragraph that must stay with the first paragraph if a column or page break occurs within the second paragraph.

This option is useful for preventing a subhead from being separated from the paragraph that follows.

✦ **Keep Lines Together:** Click this check box to prevent paragraphs from breaking and to control widows and orphans. When this box is checked, the two radio buttons below it become available. (The radio buttons present an either/or choice. One must be selected; At Start/End of Paragraph is selected by default.)

✦ **All Lines in Paragraph:** Select this option to prevent a paragraph from being broken at the end of a column or page. When a column or page break occurs within a paragraph to which this setting has been applied, the entire paragraph moves to the next column or page.

✦ **At Start/End of Paragraph:** Click this button to control widows and orphans. When this button is selected, the two fields below it become available:

- **Start Lines:** This field controls orphans. The value you enter is the minimum number of lines at the beginning of a paragraph that must be placed at the bottom of a column when a paragraph is split by a column ending.

- **End Lines:** This field controls widows. The value you enter is the minimum number of lines at the end of a paragraph that must be placed at the top of a column when a paragraph is split by a column ending.

Caution   Keep in mind that when you eliminate an orphan widow using Keep Options, the line that precedes the widow line is bumped to the next column or page, which can produce uneven column endings on multicolumn pages.

✦ **Start Paragraph:** From this pop-up menu, choose In Next Column to force a paragraph to begin in the next column or frame; choose On Next Page to force a paragraph to begin on the next page (such as for chapter headings). Your other choices are similar: On Next Odd Page and On Next Even Page. Choose Anywhere to let the paragraph begin where it would fall naturally in the sequence of text (no forced break).

Paragraph Rules

Usually, the easiest way to create a horizontal line is to use the Line Tool. But if you want to place a horizontal line within text so that the line moves with the text when editing causes the text to reflow, you need to create a paragraph rule. A paragraph rule looks much like a line created with the line tool but behaves like a text character. Paragraph rules have many uses. For example, you can place one above or below a subhead to make it more noticeable or to separate the subhead from the paragraph that precedes or follows it. Or you could place paragraph rules above and below a pull quote so that the rules and the pull quote text move if editing causes text reflow.

Here's how:

1. **Select the paragraph(s) to which you want to apply a rule above and/or a rule below, then choose Paragraph Rules from the Paragraph pane's or Control palette's palette menu, or use the shortcut Option+⌘+J or Ctrl+Alt+J.**

   You can also specify this as part of a paragraph style. The Paragraph Rules dialog box, shown in Figure 18-8, is displayed.

Figure 18-8: The Paragraph Rules dialog box.

2. **Choose Rule Above or Rule Below, then click Rule On.**

   You can add a rule above, below, or both. If you want to add rules above and below, you must click Rule On for both options and specify their settings separately. If you want to see the rule as you create it, click the Preview button.

3. **For Weight, choose a predefined thickness from the pop-up menu or enter a value in the field.**

4. **Choose a rule type from the Type pop-up menu.**

   Typically, you'd use just a simple line, but InDesign offers 17 types of lines, including dashed, striped, dotted, and wavy.

5. **Choose a color from the Color pop-up menu, which lists the colors displayed in the Swatches pane (Window ⇨ Swatches, or F5).**

   If you choose Text Color, InDesign automatically uses the color applied to the first character in the paragraph. If your ruling line is not a plain line, you can also choose the Gap Color to determine what color goes between dashes, stripes, dots, and so on in your line. For both the Color and Gap Color options, you can specify a corresponding tint (shade) with the Tint and Gap Tint pop-up menus, respectively.

6. **From the Width pop-up menu, choose Column if you want the rule to extend from the left edge of the column to the right edge of the column;**

choose Text if you want the rule to extend from the left edge of the frame or column to the line ending on the right.

7. **To indent the rule from the left and/or right edges, enter values in the Left Indent and/or Right Indent fields.**

8. **To control the vertical position of the rule, enter a value in the Offset field.**

   For a rule above, the offset value is measured upward from the baseline of the first line in a paragraph to the bottom of the rule; for a rule below, the offset is measured downward from the baseline of the last line in a paragraph to the top of the rule.

9. **Click the Overprint Stroke box if you want to print a rule on top of any underlying colors.**

   This ensures that any misregistration during printing will not result in white areas around the rule where the paper shows through. You typically use this for black or other dark colors. There's a similar Overprint Gap check box for lines that have a Gap Color.

10. **Click OK to close the dialog box, implement your changes, and return to your document.**

To remove a paragraph rule, click in the paragraph to which the rule is applied, choose Paragraph Rules from the Paragraph pane's pop-up menu, uncheck the Rule On box, then click OK.

Tip

You can use the Paragraph Rules feature to place a band of color behind text by specifying a line thickness at least 2 points larger than the text size and offsetting the rule so it moves up behind the text.

Summary

Much like character formats, InDesign's paragraph formats let you control the appearance of selected paragraphs. For example, you can control a paragraph's alignment and specify left, right, and/or first-line indents, and you can drop caps to and space between paragraphs. If you want to hyphenate a paragraph, you can add hyphenation points manually to individual words, or you can have InDesign automatically hyphenate words as appropriate.

If you choose to use InDesign's justification controls to specify how space is added or removed between characters and/or words to achieve justification, you also have two options for composing text (controlling the spacing approach): the multi-line composition method that looks at several lines of text at once, and the single-line method that looks at each line in isolation.

✦　　✦　　✦

Creating Special Text Formatting

In This Chapter

Indenting text, adding bullets, and formatting lists

Adding initial caps and run-in heads

Creating reverse type, sidebars, and pull quotes

Specifying hanging punctuation

Rotating and scaling text

Adding drop shadows and feathering

Once you learn the basics of typefaces, character formats, and paragraph formats, you can achieve just about any look with text. The trick is combining and applying the skills you've learned to produce special effects that not only look professional but also enhance the meaning of the text.

Glance at any professional publication — a national magazine, direct-mail catalog, cookbook, or product brochure — and you'll notice typographic techniques that set the publication apart from anything that can be easily produced in a word processor. (Even when word processors do offer a feature, they often lack the control necessary to really fine-tune an effect.) And skilled designers use these effects with a purpose — special bullet characters emphasize a theme, drop caps draw readers in, and pull quotes tantalize.

Throughout this chapter, you'll learn how standard InDesign features can produce typographic special effects, and more important, when to use them.

Indenting Text

InDesign lets you indent paragraphs from the left side, right side, or both sides of the column or text frame. You can also indent the first line of a paragraph independently of the rest of the paragraph. If Inset Spacing is specified in the Text Frame Options dialog box (Object ⇨ Text Frame Options, or ⌘+B or Ctrl+B), text is indented from the inset value. To apply indents, you use either the Control palette, the Paragraph pane (Window ⇨ Type & Tables ⇨ Paragraph, or Option+⌘+T or Ctrl+Alt+T).

Spacing guidelines for indents and bullets

The easy part of creating first-line indents, hanging indents, bulleted lists, and numbered lists in InDesign is using the software. The hard part can be deciding how much space to use. How do you decide how deep to make a first-line indent? How much space goes between a bullet and the text following it? Amateur publishers or designers, who are likely to be thinking in inches rather than points or picas, are likely to use too much space. They're tempted to use 0.25", 0.125", or another nice dividend of an inch for spacing rather than a more appropriate value such as 6 points. When deciding on spacing, consider the following:

✦ First-line indents that indicate new paragraphs should generally be one or two em spaces wide. The width of an em space is equal to the point size in use—so 10-point text should have a 10- or 20-point first-line indent. Opt for less space in narrower columns to avoid awkward space and more space in wider columns so the spacing is evident.

✦ As you remember from grade-school outlines, indents help organize information, with deeper indents indicating more detail about a topic. Professional publications, though, have many organizational options—such as headlines, subheads, and run-in heads—so they rarely have a need for more than two levels of indents. You might use indents on lengthy quotes, bulleted lists, numbered lists, kickers, and bylines. If you do, stick to the same amount of indent for each so the readers' eyes don't wander.

✦ In bulleted lists, use a hanging indent for a succession of two- or three-line bulleted paragraphs in wider columns. If your bulleted items are five or six lines long, especially in narrow columns, it might work better to use run-in heads to break up the information.

✦ Generally, the amount of space between a bullet and its text is equal to half the point size of the text. So if you're working with 11-point text, place 5.5 points between the bullet and text.

✦ When it comes to numbered lists, you need to decide whether you're going to include a period or other punctuation after the number and whether you'll ever have two-digit numbers. Numerals in most typefaces are the width of an en space, and they should be followed by the same amount of space the numbers and their punctuation take up. If you have a two-digit numeral, the numbers take up one em space and so should be followed by one em space.

While these values give you a good starting point, you might need to modify them based on the typeface, font size, column width, design, and overall goals of the publication.

Cross-Reference   For more on indenting and other paragraph settings, see Chapter 18. When you have a setting that works, create a paragraph style using it, as explained in Chapter 20.

First-line indents

To indicate a new paragraph, you might indent the first line or put a noticeable amount of space between paragraphs. If you opt to indent the first line, don't do it the typewriter way with tabs. Select the paragraphs, then enter a value in the First Line Left Indent field in the Paragraph pane or Control palette as shown in Figure 19-1. Press Shift+Return or Shift+Enter to see the results with the field still highlighted; press Return or Enter to get out of the pane and back into the document.

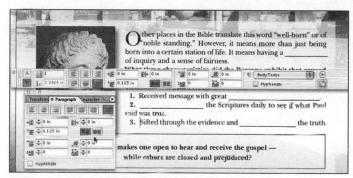

Figure 19-1: In this workbook, numbered paragraphs have a first-line indent of 0.125".

Hanging indents

In hanging indents, the first few characters of text (often a number or bullet) are aligned with the left margin while the remaining lines in the paragraph are indented. Notice the numbered items in Figure 19-2; the text that makes up the rest of the paragraphs "hangs" to the right of the numerals.

To create a hanging indent, first separate the textual items, bullets, or numbers from the text with a tab. Note the position of the tab, then specify a left indent for the paragraphs at the same location. Use the Left Indent field in the Control palette or Paragraph pane. Then enter the same value in the first-line indent field — except make the value negative to pull the first line back. For example, if you have a tab at 1.75", use a left indent of 1.75", and a first-line indent of –1.75". Figure 19-2 shows the same text as in Figure 19-1, formatted with an indent hang of 0.5".

Block indents

Publishers often offset quotes that are longer than a few lines by indenting the paragraph from both sides of the text frame or column. To do this, use the Left Indent and Right Indent fields in the Paragraph pane or Control palette. In general, use the same values you use for first-line indents, and indent both sides the same amount.

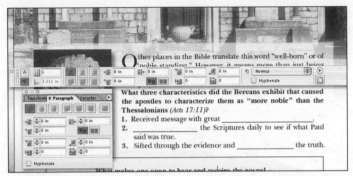

Figure 19-2: A hanging indent combines a tab and a left indent at the same value with a negative first-line indent.

Adding Bullets and Formatting Lists

Unlike many word processors, InDesign does not have a "bullet me" feature. You can't just highlight paragraphs and add bullets or numbers. You have to type a bullet character or numeral at the beginning of each paragraph and insert spaces or tabs to offset the text. The good thing about this is you have complete control over the bullet or numeral's font, color, size, and placement. And once you set up the formatting, you can automate it with both paragraph and character style sheets.

Note   You apply spacing to lists using tabs and indents — paragraph formats — so you'll want to make sure each bulleted or numbered item is followed by a paragraph return. (Choose Type ➪ Show Hidden Characters or press Option+⌘+I or Ctrl+Alt+I to confirm the existence of paragraph returns, which are indicated with the ¶ symbol.) If bullets or numerals exist in the text, look for a single tab character between the bullet or numeral and the following text. This lets you adjust only one tab stop. If you need to strip out extra tabs or change line breaks to paragraph returns, use the Find/Change dialog box (Edit ➪ Find/Change, or ⌘+F or Ctrl+F).

Adding bullets or numerals

Chances are, you're not writing in InDesign. The text was delivered in the form of a word processing file, and the writer or editor made some decisions about bullets or numerals. A lot of times, writers will simply enter an asterisk followed by a space to indicate a bullet. Or maybe an editor typed a numeral followed by a parenthesis in front of each step. Other times, writers or editors might use their word processor's automatic bullet or numbering feature. In many cases, you'll need to repair the bullets or numerals in the text using the Find/Change dialog box (Edit ⇨ Find/Change, or ⌘+F or Ctrl+F). The way you enter a bullet or numeral depends on what you started with:

✦ **If the writer or editor typed numerals or used an automatic numbering feature, the numbers and their punctuation arrive in InDesign intact.** However, you might want to change or even remove the punctuation following the numeral. The look of the numerals is more of a design decision than an editorial decision. If numerals are in a different typeface and/or in a different color, a period following the numeral might just look cluttered. Using Find/Change on a text selection, you can easily change or remove punctuation in numbered lists.

✦ **InDesign doesn't seem to like word processors' automatic bullets, converting them to characters in the current font, which will need to be changed to bullets.** Or, rather than using automatic bullets, the writer might have typed in asterisks, hyphens, or another character to indicate bullets. Once you determine what characters indicates bullets in your text, use Find/Change to change it to the bullet character you want. For example, you can search for an asterisk and change it to an *n* in the Zapf Dingbats font, which looks like a square ■.

✦ **If you're writing in InDesign, you can enter numerals and bullets as you type.** If you're editing and decide to add bullets or numerals to existing paragraphs, you can paste completely formatted bullets followed by tabs or spaces at the beginning of each paragraph. You can also paste a numeral, then edit the numeral's value as appropriate.

While you're adding bullet characters, decide on the font you're going to use. You can press Option+8 or Alt+8 for a simple, round en bullet (•) in the same typeface as the body text. You can choose a different character in the body text font, or pick a character in a symbol font such as Zapf Dingbats or Wingdings. Choose Type ⇨ Glyphs to see all the possibilities within a font, as explained in Chapter 41. For a list of common symbols, choose Type ⇨ Insert Special Character.

New Feature Choosing Type ⇨ Glyphs is a revised menu option for what had been Type ⇨ Insert Glyphs in the previous version of InDesign.

Deciding on initial formatting for bullets and numerals

Once your lists include bullets or numerals, use the Character pane (Window ⇨ Type & Tables ⇨ Character, or Option+⌘+T or Ctrl+Alt+T) to experiment with the formatting of a bullet or numeral. For example, change the typeface of a numeral and increase the size slightly or horizontally scale the symbol used for a bullet. You can also apply a color to the *stroke* (outlines) or *fill* (inside) of the bullets or numbers; see the "Applying Color to Text" section later in this chapter.

Adding space between bullets or numerals

In addition to the formatting of bullets and numerals, you need to decide how text will follow them. Figure 19-3 shows three different options for bullets. The first column shows an en bullet followed by a tab; the second column shows an en bullet followed by a tab and a hanging indent; the third column shows a Zapf Dingbats sideways heart used as a bullet followed by a tab and hanging indent. Figure 19-4 shows a typical example, from a brochure.

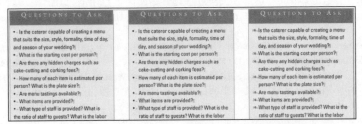

Figure 19-3: These three columns show the evolution of an en bullet to a fancy bullet followed by a hanging indent. In this case, the writer typed an en bullet followed by a tab in front of each paragraph in Microsoft Word (avoiding the Bullets and Numbering feature). The designer flowed in the text, formatted it, and repositioned the tab. In the second column, the designer specified a hanging indent. The designer then decided to choose a different character for the bullet, so she highlighted the text and used Find/Change to change en bullets to a sideways heart shape in Zapf Dingbats font.

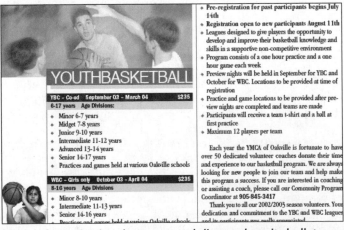

Figure 19-4: This brochure uses red diamonds as its bullets, separated from the text with a tab for consistent alignment.

Bullet character options

Although you may not know what they're called, you're used to seeing en bullets, the small round bullet (•) included in most typefaces. But you're not limited to using this character. You can use any character in the body text font, or you can switch to a symbol or pi font and choose a more decorative character.

Zapf Dingbats and Wingdings are the most common symbol fonts, offering an array of boxes, arrows, crosses, stars, and check marks. These can be cute and effective, but cute isn't always a good thing. If you opt for a different bullet character, make sure you have a reason and that it works well with the rest of the design. Check mark bullets in an election flyer might make sense; square bullets in a to-do list for a wedding caterer might not make sense.

Note that you might want to reduce the size of the symbol slightly and that you might need to use different spacing values than you would use with an en bullet.

Don't limit yourself to these two common fonts either. You can purchase many different symbol fonts to support different content. For example, you might see leaf-shaped bullets in an herb article and paw-print bullets in a pet training article. To use your own drawing or a logotype as a bullet, convert the drawing to a font using a utility such as Macromedia Fontographer and Pyrus FontLab (see the companion Web site `www.INDDcentral.com` for links to these and other font utilities).

The most consistent way to space a bulleted or numbered list is to separate the bullet or numeral from the text with a single tab as shown in Figure 19-4. You can then create a hanging indent as described earlier in this chapter, and you can indent the paragraphs from the left and/or right as you wish.

Applying style sheets for numbered and bulleted lists

The combination of paragraph and character formats necessary to produce numbered and bulleted lists can be tedious to apply. You'll want to save the basic formatting as a paragraph style sheet. If the bullets or numerals have different formatting, save that as a character style sheet. Make sure to specify keyboard commands for the style sheets so you can apply them quickly (see Chapter 20).

To apply the style sheets to existing text, first highlight all the paragraphs, then apply the paragraph style sheet. Then you can highlight each numeral or bullet and apply the character style sheet. With bullets, you can use Find/Change to locate all the bullets and apply the character style sheet.

New Feature The new Nested Styles feature lets you have the paragraph style automatically apply a character style to a user-specified range of text. Chapter 20 covers this in more depth.

With a nested style, you can automate this formatting. For example, you could have a paragraph style named Bullet that applies a character style named Bullet to the first character of the paragraph (for example, to apply the Zapf Dingbats font, which, if the first character in the paragraph is an *n*, results in a solid square bullet).

Caution   If you're not using nested styles, make sure to apply the paragraph style sheet first, and the character style sheet second, or the paragraph formatting will wipe out your special numeral or bullet formatting.

Adding Initial Caps

Nothing sets off a professional publication from an amateur or word-processed document like the use of initial caps. Decorative characters at the beginning of paragraphs serve both editorial and design purposes, drawing readers into the content with their size and position, while emphasizing a theme with their style.

You'll see initial caps ranging from a single four-line drop cap in the same typeface as the paragraph in a financial publication's letter from the editor to a 140-point word in a script face kicking off a feature article in a bridal magazine. Initial caps often use more decorative typefaces — you can even purchase fonts that consist only of ornate capital letters. A children's book might use a graphic of a letter formed from an animal's body, and a cooking magazine might use the outlines of a letter filled with an image of related foods. You can achieve all these effects with the typographic and layout features in InDesign.

Note   Don't forget that text is for reading. Heavily designed initial caps can become unrecognizable as text, leaving the reader with a disjointed word or sentence in the first paragraph of a story. No matter how gorgeous a 192-point *S* looks flowing behind a paragraph in rose-colored Kuenstler Script, if the readers don't recognize the *S*, he's left trying to make sense of the word *ensitivity.* You would have been better off leaving *Sensitivity* to start the paragraph and drawing a nice curly shape behind the text.

Creating automatic drop caps

A *drop cap* is an enlarged capital letter at the beginning of a paragraph that drops down several lines into the text. In daily newspapers and weekly magazines, which are likely to have limited production time, the most common effect you'll see is a simple drop cap in the paragraph's font. Simple drop caps such as these can be created automatically — in two simple steps — in InDesign. Even though drop caps look like character formatting, they're actually created through a paragraph format. This ensures that drop-cap formatting remains in the paragraph even if you edit or delete the original first characters.

To create a drop cap:

1. **Select the Type tool and click in the paragraph to select it.**

2. **Make sure either the Control palette or Paragraph pane is open.**

3. **Specify how many lines down the characters should drop into the paragraph by typing a number between 2 and 25 in the Drop Cap Number of Lines field.**

   Generally, you'll drop the characters three to five lines.

4. **Specify how many characters in the first line should be enlarged as drop caps by typing a number between 1 and 150 in the Drop Cap One or More Characters field.**

   Generally, it looks best to drop the first character or the first word in the story. If the columns are wide enough, you can drop the first phrase.

5. **Press Return or Enter to see the drop caps.**

Once you've created a drop cap with the InDesign feature, you can highlight the enlarged characters and change the font, color, or any other character formats. See Figure 19-5 for an example of a four-line drop in a different font and color.

> n two separate occasions, my wife and I stopped outside EG's Garden Grill in Grand Lake (near Winter Park). Both times we were with friends who balked at the menu prices posted in the window.

Figure 19-5: This drop cap has an entry of 4 in the Drop Cap Number of Lines field and 1 in the Drop Cap One or More Characters field. It also has the font changed to Univers Light Ultra Condensed and the color to brick red.

For different drop caps effects, try the following:

✦ Tab after the drop caps, then create a hanging indent so the text is aligned to the right of the characters.

✦ Kern between the drop caps and the paragraph text to tighten or expand the space.

✦ Baseline-shift the drop caps to move them up or down.

✦ Change the font size of the drop caps to enlarge them and raise them above the paragraph.

✦ Scale the drop caps to make them more dramatic.

Remember to save the drop caps' existence as a paragraph style sheet, and any modifications to the drop caps as a character style sheet.

Note   If you decide to drop the entire first word or phrase in a story, you'll have to count the number of characters and change the value in the Drop Cap One or More Characters field for each paragraph, since each paragraph's initial word or phrase will have a different number of characters. This means you can't apply the formatting automatically with a paragraph style sheet — you'll have to give each introductory paragraph individual attention.

Tip   If the first character in a paragraph is a quotation mark (" or '), it can look odd as a one-character drop cap. If you don't like this look, you have a couple options: You can either delete the opening quotation mark, an acceptable but potentially confusing practice, or you can use the first two characters in the paragraph as drop caps instead. Some publications simply prefer not to start paragraphs with quotes, preventing the problem from the editorial side.

Creating raised initial caps

Raised caps are another form of initial caps, enlarging and raising the first few characters of the paragraph above the first line in the paragraph. Creating raised caps is simple — highlight the characters you want to raise with the Type tool and enlarge them using the Font Size field on the Character pane (Window ➪ Type & Tables ➪ Character, or ⌘+T or Ctrl+T) or Control palette.

If you raise a word or phrase, you might need to track the raised words to tighten them. You also might need to kern between the raised text and the remainder of the line. Other options for raised caps include changing the font, color, and scale of the characters. See Figure 19-6 for an example of raised caps used in a subhead. If you plan to repeat the raised-cap formatting, save it as a character style sheet.

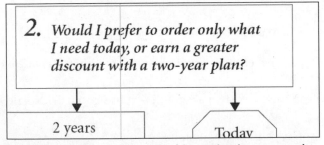

Figure 19-6: The number 2 in this caption is an example of a raised cap: It has a larger size than the text that follows to call attention to it, in this case as a step.

Converting text to outlines for initial caps

You can convert drop caps, raised initial caps, or any character in any font to a frame. You can then resize, scale, shear, fill, and stroke the character-shaped frame. To do this, highlight the characters with the Type tool, then choose Type ➪ Create Outlines, or press Shift+⌘+O or Ctrl+Shift+O. Frames are based on the size and outlines of the font in use and are automatically anchored in the paragraph so they flow with the text.

Note When you convert text to outlines, the characters no longer exist as text. If you converted part of a word, the remaining portions of the word may be flagged during a spelling check. If you need to edit the text, you will need to delete the outlines, retype the word, and convert the characters again.

Using graphics as initial caps

Rather than using text for initial caps, you can use graphics. You can purchase clip-art collections that consist of nothing but ornate capital letters to use as initial caps. To use a graphic as an initial cap, first delete the characters you will replace with graphics. Then, use the Place command (File ➪ Place, or ⌘+D or Ctrl+D) to import the graphic.

Size the graphic as appropriate, then place it behind the paragraph, next to the paragraph, or anchored in the text of the paragraph. To anchor a graphic in text, select it with the Selection tool and choose Edit ➪ Cut, or press ⌘+X or Ctrl+X. Select the Type tool and click at the beginning of the paragraph, then choose Edit ➪ Paste, or press ⌘+V or Ctrl+V. The graphic is now anchored to the text, so if text is reflowed, the graphical drop cap will flow with it.

In addition to importing graphics for use as initial caps, you can create your own graphics in InDesign. For example, you can place the initial cap character in its own text frame and create reverse type from it as discussed later in this chapter. Or you can shade the character and place it slightly behind the paragraph.

Labeling Paragraphs

Along with initial caps, changing the formatting of the first few words in a paragraph can indicate the beginning of a story or a new topic. This is commonly used for run-in heads, a short title usually in boldface or italic, and often in a contrasting font, that is on the same line as the rest of the paragraph.

The following descriptions show frequently used label formatting:

✦ **Boldface:** Bold speaks the loudest, and is generally used for subheads in magazines, newspapers, and reports. To apply boldface in InDesign, you must select the bold version of the typeface from the Style pop-up menu on the Character pane.

✦ *Italics:* If bold shouts, italics tends to whisper. It's a good choice for tertiary heads and to label bulleted items within a list. To apply italics in InDesign, you must select the oblique version of the typeface from the Style pop-up menu on the Character pane.

✦ <u>Underlines:</u> For a typewriter-effect, you might underline the text of a label. Use the Underline command available from the menu on the Character pane — you have no control over the style, thickness, or placement of the line.

✦ SMALL CAPS: For a subtle, classic look that blends well with the rest of the document, use small caps on labels. However, don't use small caps if you're using labels as subheads that allow readers to skim through a document and read only relevant portions. You have two choices for applying small caps from the Character pane: Choose a small-caps variation of a typeface from the Style pop-up menu or choose the Small Caps command from the palette menu.

✦ Typeface change: Rather than relying on different variations of a font, you can use a different font altogether, such as Futura Medium as used on this paragraph, for a label. To contrast with serif body text, you might choose a sans-serif typeface that complements the look of your publication. Often, this will be a variation of your headline font. To apply a typeface, use the Font pop-up menu in the Character pane or Control palette.

✦ Scaled text: Scaling text horizontally — up 10 or 20 percent — quietly differentiates it from the remainder of the paragraph. (More severe scaling will distort the typeface and could look unprofessional.) Unlike bold or underline, the text won't pop off the page at you, but it will be visually distinct. Scaling text vertically, however, can be too subtle unless combined with boldface or another style. Use the Horizontal Scale and Vertical Scale fields in the Character pane or Control palette to scale text.

✦ Size change: Creating a label by simply bumping the size up a point or two is another subtle design choice. The labels blend well with the body text, but they don't announce their presence enough to be used as subheads for scanning. To change the size of type, use the Font Size field in the Character pane or Control palette.

The label technique — whether implemented via local character formatting, a character style, or a nested style — can be used for any amount of text, from a single bullet to one or more sentences. For example, the guidebook shown in Figure 19-7 styles the first sentence in the introductory paragraph as italic. In many magazines, the first paragraph of a story often starts with a single drop cap, followed by the entire first line in small caps.

Figure 19-7: The use of nested styles in this paragraph automatically italicizes the first sentence in this intro paragraph.

The Nested Styles feature is flexible, letting you specify it to any number of characters, words, or sentences, as well as to specific locations such as the first tab. That lets you use it for numbered lists where the number of digits may change (such as a 15-item list that has both single-digit numbers like 9 and double-digit numbers like 10) — you'd have the nested style apply the appropriate character style through the first tab, so any numerals before the tab take on that character style. (For example, you might want to boldface the numbers in a list and change the font to a sans-serif one.) Figure 19-7 shows an example of this feature, where the intro paragraph uses a nested style to italicize the first sentence of the introductory paragraph. (The paragraph style also specifies the initial drop cap.)

Cross-Reference Chapter 20 covers nested styles in more detail.

To experiment with label formatting, use the attributes available via the Character pane or Control palette and their palette menus, such as font changes, horizontal scale, or small caps. Once you decide on the formatting for labels, you can apply it using character style sheets after paragraph style sheets are applied — and after the text is final. You may also be able to use the nested styles feature, if there is a consistent pattern to the label text, such as being a specific number of words or characters or being a sentence.

Note Depending on the formatting, applying a label style might reflow the text, causing a need for copyfitting.

Tip To provide a little more space between the label and the text, you might want to use an en space rather than a normal space.

Adding Professional Touches

With today's word processors and low-end page-layout programs offering pre-designed templates for birthday cards and reports, almost anyone can claim to be a designer. But a closer look reveals the difference — skilled graphic designers plan their typography and layout around the content, using typographic techniques to call attention to and refine content. The use of reverse type, sidebars, and pull quotes helps break up pages and organize text, while careful formatting of fractions, hanging punctuation, and end-of-story markers adds a professional touch.

Reversing type out of its background

This is the reverse of what you usually see — white type on a black background rather than black type on a white background. Of course, reverse type doesn't have to be white on black, but any lighter color on a darker color. You'll often see reverse type in table headings, *kickers* (explanatory blurbs above headlines), and decorative elements. Reverse type, which brightens text and pulls readers in, works best with larger type sizes and bold typefaces so the text isn't swallowed by the background.

InDesign doesn't have a reverse type command or typestyle — but using this effect involves just a simple combination of basic InDesign skills. To lighten the text, highlight it with the Type tool, click the Fill button on the Toolbox, and choose a light color from the Swatches pane (Window ➪ Swatches, or F5). For a dark background, you have three options: filling the text frame with a darker color, making the text frame transparent and placing it on top of darker objects, or using a ruling line behind the text.

For the first two options, select the text frame with the Selection tool or the Direct Selection tool, then click the Fill button on the Tools. To fill the text frame with a color, click a darker color on the Swatches pane. To make the text frame transparent, click the Apply None button on the Tools. Then place the text frame in front of a darker object or graphic.

For reverse-out type that is not in its own text frame, you use a ruling line of the appropriate width (at least a couple points larger than the text size) and move it into the text. If you use a Ruling Line Above, you would move the line down behind the text; if you use a Ruling Line Below, you'd move it up. Figure 19-8 shows reversed-out type used as description headings, as well as the Paragraph Rules dialog box and the settings used to create the effect. (To access this dialog box, choose Paragraph Rules from the palette menu of the Control palette or Paragraph pane, or press Option+⌘+J or Ctrl+Alt+J.)

Tip
When designing elements with reverse type, make sure the point size of the text is large enough to print clearly on the darker background. Consider the thinnest part of characters, especially in serif typefaces, when judging the size and thickness of reverse type. You'll often want to use a semibold or bolder version of a font so the text maintains its visual integrity.

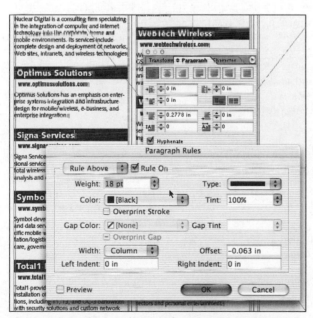

Figure 19-8: This product guide uses reversed-out text created via ruling lines for its description titles.

Creating sidebars and pull quotes

Pick up almost any publication, from *Time* magazine to your neighborhood newsletter, and you're almost guaranteed to see sidebars and pull quotes. So basic that you can even create them with a modern word processor, these treatments aren't really typographic treatments — they're just page-layout techniques involving text elements you create by applying simple InDesign skills.

A *sidebar* is supplemental text, formatted differently, and often placed within a shaded or outlined box. Sidebars help break up text-heavy pages and call attention to information that is often interesting but not essential to the main story. Even in technical publications, it's helpful to pull in-depth information or related text into sidebars to provide visual relief. To create a sidebar, you'll usually place the text in its own frame, then stroke the frame and optionally fill it with a tint. To inset the text from the edges of the frame, use the Text Frame Options dialog box (Object ⇨ Text Frame Options, or ⌘+B or Ctrl+B).

A *pull-quote* is a catchy one- or two-line excerpt from a publication that is enlarged and reformatted to achieve both editorial and design objectives. On the editorial side, pull quotes draw readers into articles with excerpts that do everything from summarize the content to provide shock value. On the design side, pull quotes break up staid columns and offer opportunities for typographic treatment that emphasize the content (such as colors and typefaces that reflect the mood of an article). Although the use of and length of pull quotes is often dictated by design, an editorial person should select the text and indicate it on hard copy or within text files. To create a pull quote, copy and paste the relevant text into its own text frame, then reformat the text and frame as you wish. Use the Text Wrap pane (Window ⇨ Type & Tables ⇨ Text Wrap, or Option+⌘+W or Ctrl+Alt+W) to control how text in columns wraps around the pull quote.

Formatting fractions

If you're in a big hurry, it's fine to type *1/3 cup* and get on with your life. It looks like a fraction, but it's kind of big and ugly, and it calls a little too much attention to itself. Compare the first line in Figure 19-9, which is formatted appropriately for a fraction, to the last two lines, which are not. InDesign doesn't provide an automatic fraction maker, but you can use expert typefaces or character formats to achieve professional-looking fractions.

QuarkXPress User   InDesign has no equivalent to QuarkXPress's fraction-building tool.

¹/3 espresso,
1/3 steamed milk,
1/3 cocoa

Figure 19-9: In the first line of text here, the "1/3" text is formatted manually to look like a true fraction.

Applying a fraction typeface

Some expert typefaces include a variation, appropriately called fractions, that include a number of common fractions such as ½, ⅓, ¼, and ¾. Adobe has so-called Expert Collections for many of its popular fonts; these collections include true small caps, true fractions, and other typographic characters. Many OpenType formats have these characters included as well. You can also use a symbol font, though the numerals may not exactly match the appearance of numerals in the rest of your text, since symbol fonts typically use plain fonts like Helvetica as their basis.

To use a true fraction from an Expert Collection, symbol, or OpenType font, choose Type ⇨ Glyph, then select the font and face from the pop-up menus at the bottom of the dialog box, then select the fraction you want.

Tip   If you're dealing with a wide range of fractions in something like a cookbook, you probably won't find all the fractions you need. Because it would be difficult to format fractions such as ⁵⁄₁₆ exactly the same as an expert font's ¼, you might opt for formatting all the fractions manually.

Formatting fractions manually

You'll notice that expert fractions are approximately the same size as a single character in that font. That's your eventual goal in formatting a fraction. Usually, you achieve this by decreasing the size of the two numerals, raising the numerator (the first, or top, number in the fraction), and kerning on either side of the slash as necessary.

For example, see the fraction in the first line of Figure 19-9. The rest of the text is set at 9 points, but the denominator (the number after the slash in a fraction, or *3* here) has been set to 6 points using the Font Size field in the Character pane. The *1* is set as a superscript using the Character pane. The *1/* and the */3* are both kerned by −50. (You can also use the Control palette to access these controls.) The font size and kerning that works for your font, size, and values will vary.

Macintosh fonts provide another option for refining fractions. It's a special kind of slash called a *virgule*, which is smaller and at more of an angle than a regular slash. Press Option+Shift+1 to enter a virgule, then kern around it as you would a slash. (The fraction in the first line of Figure 19-9 uses a virgule rather than a regular slash.)

Note InDesign's default superscript and subscript size is 58.3 percent of the character's size (this odd value actually equals 7⁄12, in keeping with typography's standard of using points, of which there are 12 in a pica, for text measurement). The numerator and denominator in a fraction should be the same size, so if you use InDesign's superscripts at its default settings, multiply the text's point size by 0.583 (just highlight the denominator text, go to the Size field in the Character pane or Control palette, and type ***0.583** in the Size field after the current point size). I recommend changing InDesign's superscript and subscript type styles to 65 percent to improve readability, especially at smaller sizes. You can change these default settings in the Text pane of the Preferences dialog box (choose InDesign ➪ Preferences on the Mac or Edit ➪ Preferences in Windows, or press ⌘+K or Ctrl+K).

Unless you're rarely confronted with fractions, by all means save your formatting as character style sheets. You'll be able to apply the formats with a keystroke or use Find/Change (Edit ➪ Find/Change, or ⌘+F or Ctrl+F) to locate numbers and selectively apply the appropriate character style sheet.

Hanging punctuation

When display type, such as a pull quote or headline type in ads, is left-aligned or justified, the edges can look uneven due to the gaps above, below, or next to quotation marks, punctuation, and some capital letters. See the text frame at right in Figure 19-10, which does not have hanging punctuation. To correct the unevenness, graphic designers use a technique called *hanging punctuation,* in which they extend the punctuation slightly beyond the edges of the rest of the text as shown in the text frame at left in Figure 19-10.

Note The "edge" of text is defined by the edges of the text frame or any Inset Spacing specified in the Text Frame Options dialog box (Object ➪ Text Frame Options, or ⌘+B or Ctrl+B).

InDesign's Optical Margin Alignment feature automates hanging punctuation, extending punctuation and the edges of some glyphs (such as a capital *T*) slightly outside the edges of the text. (Assume Adobe bills this feature as margin alignment rather than hanging punctuation because it also works with capital letters.)

Unfortunately, you can't control how much the characters "hang" outside the text boundaries — InDesign decides that for you. And Optical Margin Alignment applies to all the text frames in a story, rather than to highlighted text. This means you need to isolate into its own story any text for which you want hanging punctuation.

To specify Optical Margin Alignment, select any text frame in a story and choose Window ➪ Type & Tables ➪ Story. Check Optical Margin Alignment, as shown in Figure 19-10.

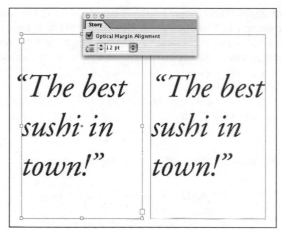

Figure 19-10: Notice the difference between the text frame at right, with standard alignment, and the text frame at left, with Optical Margin Alignment (otherwise known as *hanging punctuation*).

Note   In general, Optical Margin Alignment improves the look of display type whether it's left-aligned, centered, justified, or even right-aligned. However, Optical Margin Alignment will actually cause columns of body text to look uneven (as they are).

Choosing and placing end-of-story markers

In magazines, newsletters, and other publications with multiple stories, the text often continues from one page to the next. In newsmagazines, a story might meander from page to page, interrupted by sidebars and ads. In a fashion magazine, stories generally open on a splashy spread, then continue on text-heavy pages at the back of the magazine. In either case, readers can get confused about whether a story has ended. Designers solve this by placing a *dingbat* (a special character such as a square) at the end of each story.

You can use any dingbat character — in Zapf Dingbats, DF Organics, Woodtype, or Wingdings, for example — or an inline graphic to mark the end of a story. The end-of-story marker should reflect the overall design and feel of a publication, or emphasize the content. You might see a square used in a financial publication, a heart in a teen magazine, or a leaf in a gardening magazine. A derivative of the company's logo might even be used to mark the end of a story — you can easily envision the Nike swoosh used in this way.

To place a dingbat, first decide on the character and create a character style sheet for it. If you're using a graphic, you might consider converting it to a font with a utility such as Macromedia Fontographer or Pyrus FontLab so you can insert and format it automatically. If you're using an inline graphic, you might store it in an InDesign library (see Chapter 7) so it's easily accessible. Make sure everyone working on the publication knows the keystroke for entering the dingbat or the location of the graphic.

Once you have the character established, you need to decide where to place it. Generally, the dingbat will be flush with the right margin or right after the final punctuation in the last line:

✦ To place the dingbat flush with the right margin, there are two ways to set a right-aligned tab:

- One is to choose Type ➪ Insert Special Character ➪ Right Indent Tab or press Shift+Tab.

- The other way is to set a tab stop in the paragraph style sheet you use for final paragraphs (see Chapter 21 for more details on setting tabs). Because InDesign offers an easier method to right-indent a dingbat, you should use this method only if you want to right-align the dingbat to a place in the column other than at the right margin — essentially, if you want to have it indented a little from the right margin.

✦ To place the dingbat after the final punctuation, separate the two with an en space by typing Option+Spacebar or Ctrl+Shift+6, or with an em space by typing two en spaces.

Applying Color to Text

Just because you're printing on a four-color printing press or have a color printer doesn't mean you should be getting carried away with coloring text. You want to keep your content legible and unified, but that doesn't have to mean it's all black on white. You'll commonly see color in headlines, banners, subheads, and pull-quotes. However, you'll rarely see color applied to body text.

Colors applied to text are often derived from colors within related graphics or from a publication's traditional palette. In general, the smaller the type, the darker its color should be — with pastels reserved for large text, bright colors for bold text, and dark colors for body text. InDesign lets you make an entire character one color, or make the *fill* (inside) and *stroke* (outlines) of a character two different colors, as shown in Figure 19-11. You can even apply gradients to fills and strokes.

To color text:

1. **Click the Type tool in the Toolbox or press T.**

2. **Highlight the text you want to color.**

3. **Click the Fill button or the Stroke button on the Tools palette to specify whether you're coloring the character or its outlines.**

4. **If necessary, open the color Swatches pane by choosing Window ➪ Swatches or pressing F5.**

5. **Click a color swatch to apply it to the stroke or fill.**

6. **To specify the thickness of the stroke, use the Strokes pane (Window ➪ Stroke, or F10) and to apply a gradient to the stroke or fill, use the Gradient pane (Window ➪ Gradient).**

Cross-Reference For information about creating color swatches or working with gradients, see Chapters 8 and 28.

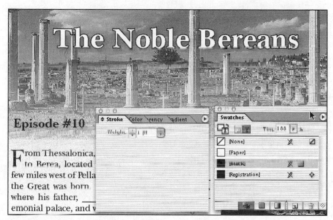

Figure 19-11: The episode headline has a 1-point black stroke and a fill color of white.

Rotating Text

You've seen newsletters with nameplates running horizontally down the first page and catalogs with *sale* splashed diagonally across pages. You do this by placing the text you want to rotate in its own frame, then rotating the entire frame. InDesign lets you rotate any object from 180 degrees to –180 degrees — basically, full circle. You can rotate in increments as small as 0.01 degree using the Rotate tool or 0.001 degree using the Rotation Angle field on the Transform pane or Control palette. (Figure 19-12 shows the icons.)

  Figure 19-12: The Rotate tool (left) from the Tools palette and the Rotation Angle field from the Transform pane and Control palette.

Using the Rotation Angle field

Use the Rotation Angle field on the Transform pane or Control palette if you know the angle you need. For example, to run text along the left side of a graphic like the photo credit in Figure 19-13, you rotate the frame 90 degrees. To use the Rotation Angle field, select the object with the Selection tool. Then choose an option from the pop-up menu, which offers 30-degree increments, or enter a value in the field. Hit Return or Enter to rotate the object.

Figure 19-13: The Rotation Angle field on the Transform pane or on the Control palette lets you rotate selected objects with 0.001 degree of precision. Entering a value in the field is ideal for turning a tab-like section head 90 degrees to place it within a frame shaped like a binder tab. You can also double-click the Rotation tool to get the Rotate dialog box shown at top to enter a precise rotation amount.

Using the Rotate tool

Use the Rotate tool to experiment with different angles while designing. To rotate items freehand, select the Rotate tool by clicking it in the Tools palette or pressing R (unless the Type tool is selected). If the object you want to rotate isn't selected, ⌘+click it or Ctrl+click it. Drag in any direction to rotate the object, releasing the mouse button as necessary to check the placement and any text wrap. To restrict the rotation to 45-degree increments, press the Shift key while you drag.

Tip

You can also double-click the Rotate tool to get a dialog box in which you enter a precise rotation value, as Figure 19-13 shows. Not only can you set the rotation amount, you can control whether the content rotates with the frame or whether the rotation will apply to a copy of the item.

Scaling Text

While you're roughing out a design, you'll probably find yourself changing type sizes, object placement, and colors as you go. Changing the size of text can get a little tedious — especially if the text is tucked into its own frame. You have to select the Type tool, highlight the text, enter a new size, then often switch to the Selection tool to resize the frame so the text doesn't overflow. For a more interactive method of resizing text, you can use the Scale tool to resize the text and its frame at the same time.

To use the Scale tool, click it in the Tools palette or press S (if the Type tool is not selected). If the text frame is not already selected it, you'll need to ⌘+click or Ctrl+click. Then simply drag any frame edge or handle in any direction. To scale proportionally so the text is not distorted, press the Shift key while you drag. The amount of scaling is reported in the Scale X Percentage and Scale Y Percentage fields in the Transform pane or in the Control palette.

Caution Be careful in scaling text frames and the text within them. If you modify multiple text frames that contain similar items (such as headlines), you'll end up with inconsistent text formatting for like items, which will look terrible. You should scale text only when It is a unique element, such as a headline in an ad, and thus not likely to create visual inconsistencies.

Underline and Strikethrough Options

InDesign lets you create custom underlines and strikethroughs. While you'll use these sparingly, they can be effective for design-oriented text presentation, such as shown in Figure 19-14.

New Feature The ability to create custom underlines and strikethroughs is new to InDesign CS.

The Character pane and Control palette's palette menus provide the Underline Options and Strikethrough Options menu items to create customer versions. The process for the two is similar:

Welcome to Las Vegas!

Rules of the Road

Figure 19-14: Examples of custom underlines and strikethroughs.

1. **Highlight the text to which you want the custom underline or strikethrough.**

2. **Specify the thickness, type, color, and other settings for the line that makes up the underline or the strikethrough line.**

   Note that if you choose a line type that has gaps — such as dashed, dotted, or striped lines — you can also choose a gap color, such as was done for the top example in Figure 19-14. Figure 19-15 shows the Underline Options and Strikethrough Options dialog boxes.

Figure 19-15: The Underline Options (top) and Strikethrough Options dialog boxes. At right is the list of line types available in both dialog boxes.

3. **Apply the underline or strikethrough style via the Control palette, Character pane, or keyboard shortcut (Shift+⌘+U and Shift+⌘+/, or Ctrl+Shift+U and Ctrl+Shift+/).**

Note that a custom underline or strikethrough created and applied this way is in effect only for the first text to which an underline or strikethrough is applied. InDesign reverts to the standard settings the next time you apply an underline or strikethrough. If you want to use a custom underline or strikethrough setting repeatedly, you should define the setting as part of a character style, as described in Chapter 20.

QuarkXPress User   InDesign has no equivalent to QuarkXPress's Underline Styles. Instead, specify custom underlines and strikethroughs as part of a character style sheet. To add stripes and dashed lines, open the Strokes pane (Window ⇨ Stroke, or F10) and select the Stroke Styles option from the palette menu, as described in Chapter 11.

Drop Shadows and Feathering

InDesign offers built-in drop shadow and feathering that let you create dimensional effects based on simulated lighting.

QuarkXPress User QuarkXPress does not offer drop shadow or feathering features, although there are third-party plug-ins to add these capabilities.

Drop shadows

The Drop Shadow dialog box is shown in Figure 19-16 and accessed by choosing Object ➪ Drop Shadow or pressing Option+⌘+M or Ctrl+Alt+M. To apply a drop shadow to an object, you select it with a selection tool — you cannot apply the shadow to just highlighted characters. In the dialog box, you set the following options:

✦ Check the Drop Shadow option to turn on the drop shadow function.

✦ Select a lighting type (technically, a blend mode) by choosing one of the 16 options in the Mode pop-up menu. (Chapter 25 covers these in detail.)

✦ Specify the opacity by entering a value in the Opacity field — 0% is invisible, while 100% is completely solid.

✦ Specify the shadow's position relative to the object using the X Offset and Y Offset fields. A positive X Offset moves the shadow to the right, while a positive Y Offset moves the shadow down. Negative values go in the other direction.

✦ Specify the shadow's size by entering a value in the Blur field — this blurs a copy of the text used in the drop shadow to make it look like it was created by shining light on solid letters.

✦ Choose a color source — Swatches, RGB, CMYK, and LAB — from the Color pop-up menu, then select a color from the sliders or swatches below. You'll get sliders for RGB, CMYK, and LAB with which to mix a color if you selected RGB, CMYK, or LAB in the Color pop-up menu, and a set of previously defined color swatches if you selected Swatches in the Color pop-up menu.

✦ To see the effects to your selected object as you experiment with various settings, check the Preview option.

Tip Although traditionally associated with text, you can apply drop shadows to any objects, such as frames and shapes.

Cross-Reference Chapter 25 covers transparency and opacity in more detail.

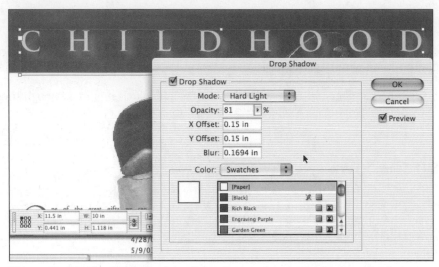

Figure 19-16: The Drop Shadow dialog box and an example drop shadow.

Feathering

A similar option to drop shadows is feathering, which essentially softens the edges of objects. Like drop shadows, feathering can be applied only to objects, not individual text, paths, or strokes. To feather an object, first select it and then choose Object ➪ Feather. You'll get the dialog box shown in Figure 19-17.

To apply feathering, check the Feather option. You then enter a value for the degree of feathering—smaller numbers have the least effect, larger numbers have the most effect. The featuring area starts at the outside edge of the object, so a larger number "eats into" the object, making it a wispier version of itself, as Figure 19-17 shows. The Corners pop-up menu gives you three options: Sharp, Rounded, and Diffused. The Sharp option retains the original shape as much as possible. The Rounded option rounds the corners of the object; it can distort the shape dramatically at larger Feather Width settings. The Diffused option creates a soft, almost smoky effect by making the object more translucent.

Figure 19-17: The Feather dialog box and an example feathering effect.

Summary

InDesign gives you the power to embellish and manipulate text in almost infinite ways. It's your responsibility to format text in ways that clarify and reinforce the content rather than simply decorate it. Bulleted lists — often created with special character bullets, tabs, and hanging indents — help break out information. Initial caps and run-in heads call attention to the beginning of a story or to topic shifts within a story. You can pull readers into a story with sidebars and pull quotes, which also break up text-heavy areas. For display type, InDesign provides an automatic method for hanging punctuation outside the margins, and it allows you to rotate and scale text. It also provides drop shadow and feathering tools that create dimensionality and lighting effects.

✦　　✦　　✦

Setting Up Style Sheets

✦ ✦ ✦ ✦

In This Chapter

Defining style sheets

Creating and applying paragraph and character style sheets

Working with nested styles

Modifying style sheet–formatted text

Modifying style sheets

Importing style sheets

✦ ✦ ✦ ✦

If you were assigned the task of making 500 star-shaped cookies, the first thing you'd do is find a star-shaped cookie cutter. Of course, you could shape each cookie by hand, but not only would this take considerably more time than using a cookie cutter, no two cookies would look exactly the same. Think of style sheets as cookie cutters for formatting text. They save you time and ensure consistency. If you'll be using InDesign to create long documents that require considerable text formatting, style sheets are indispensable.

InDesign lets you create two types of style sheets:

✦ A *character style sheet* is a set of character-level formats you can apply to a range of highlighted text in a single step.

✦ A *paragraph style sheet* is a set of both character- *and* paragraph-level formats you can apply to selected paragraphs in a single step.

In one respect, style sheets are far superior to cookie cutters. If you use a cookie cutter to create hundreds of cookies and then find out your cookies are the wrong shape, you're out of luck. But if you use a style sheet to format hundreds of pieces of text and then decide you don't like the look of the styled text, you can simply modify the style sheet. Any text you've formatted with a style sheet is automatically updated if you modify the style sheet.

Tip   When it comes to using style sheets, it's as important to know when **not** to use them as it is to know **when** to use them. For short documents — especially one-pagers such as business cards, ads, and posters — that contain relatively little text and don't use the same formats repeatedly, you're probably better off formatting the text by hand.

Tip

If you create multiple editions of a particular publication — for example, a form, a daily newspaper, a monthly magazine, or a corporate business card — you'll want to create a template. A template is a shell of a document that contains all the layout elements necessary to create the document — including style sheets if it's a multipage publication — but no content (except content that appears in every issue, such as copyright lines and mastheads). You use a template as the starting point each time you need to create a new version of a publication. For more information about templates, see Chapter 7.

Creating and Applying Style Sheets

Before you can use a style sheet to format text, you must create it. You can create style sheets whenever you want, but usually, creating style sheets is one of the first tasks you'll tackle when working on a long document. Also, you may want to create your paragraph style sheets first and then, if necessary, add character style sheets. In many cases, character style sheets are used to format text within paragraphs to which paragraph style sheets have already been applied.

Cross-Reference

See Chapter 17 for information about specifying character-level formats; see Chapter 18 for information about paragraph-level formats. Note that this chapter assumes you know how to use the character and paragraph formatting tools covered in those chapters.

Paragraph style sheets

Let's say you've been given the job of creating a newsletter. It will be several pages long and contain several stories. Each story will have the same text elements: a big headline, a smaller headline, an author byline, and body text. The stories will also include pictures, and each picture requires a caption and a credit line. Before you begin laying out pages and formatting text, you should create style sheets for all these repetitive text elements. The Paragraph Styles pane (Window ⇨ Type & Tables ⇨ Paragraph Styles, or F11), shown in Figure 20-1, is where you need to go for both creating and applying style sheets.

Tip

You may want to combine the Character Styles and Paragraph Styles panes into a single palette by click-dragging the tab of one pane on top of the other pane and then releasing the mouse. Similarly, you may want to combine the Character (Window ⇨ Type & Tables ⇨ Character, or ⌘+T or Ctrl+T) and Paragraph panes (Window ⇨ Type & Tables ⇨ Paragraph, or Option+⌘+T or Ctrl+Alt+T). If you're really into combining panes, you may want to combine all four panes into a single text formatting palette.

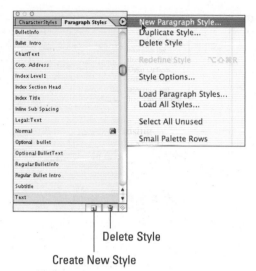

Delete Style

Create New Style

Figure 20-1: The Paragraph Styles pane and its palette menu.

Creating paragraph style sheets

The easiest way to create a paragraph style sheet is to manually apply character- and paragraph-level formats to a sample paragraph and then — with the sample paragraph selected — follow the steps below. If no text is selected when you create a style sheet, you'll have to specify character- and paragraph-level formats as you create the style sheet, which is more difficult than formatting a paragraph in advance. Here's how you create a paragraph style sheet from a preformatted paragraph:

1. **If it's not displayed, show the Paragraph Style pane by choosing Window ▷ Type & Tables ▷ Paragraph Styles or pressing F11.**

2. **Make sure you've highlighted a paragraph that's been styled with all the character and paragraph formats you want to include in your style sheet, then choose New Style from the Paragraph Styles pane's palette menu (refer to Figure 20-1).**

   The New Paragraph Style dialog box, shown in Figure 20-2, is displayed.

Tip   You can also create a new style by clicking the Create New Style button at the bottom of the pane. When you click this button, a new style sheet with a default name (Paragraph Style 1, Paragraph Style 2, and so on) is added to the list. The formats applied to the selected paragraph are included in the new style sheet; the New Paragraph Style dialog box is not displayed. If you want to modify any formats, double-click the new style sheet name in the pane; the Modify Paragraph Style Options dialog box is displayed. This dialog box is identical to the New Paragraph Style dialog box.

Figure 20-2: The New Paragraph Style dialog box.

3. **Enter a name for the style sheet in the Style Name field.**

Note

Assign your style sheet names with care; be descriptive. Imagine that somebody else will be using the document and assign a name that conveys the purpose of the style sheet. For example, anybody will know what a style sheet called Body Copy is used for, but a style sheet called Really Cool Style won't mean anything to anybody but you.

Tip

You may want to consider using a naming scheme that will display families of related style sheets together in the Paragraph Styles pane. (Step 5 below explains how to create a family of parent/children style sheets.) For example, you could use numbers (01, 02, 03, and so on) or letters (A. Body Copy/Base, A. Body Copy/Drop Cap, A. Body Copy/No Indent, and so on) in front of style sheet names to group style sheets.

4. **The scroll list to the left of the dialog box shows 14 options, as shown in Figure 20-2. If you want to change any character- or paragraph-level formats, choose the appropriate option, then make your changes.**

5. **The Based On pop-up menu displays the names of other paragraph style sheets. You can use this feature to create families of style sheets.**

   For example, you could create a style sheet called Body Copy/Base for the bulk of your body text, and then create variations such as Body Text/Drop Cap, Body Text/No Indent, and Body Text/Italic. If you used the Based On pop-up menu to base each of the variations on Body Text/Base and you then modified this "parent" style sheet, your changes are applied to all the variations.

6. **The Next Style pop-up menu also displays the names of other paragraph style sheets. If you want to automatically switch from the style sheet you're creating to another style sheet as you enter text, choose a style sheet name from the pop-up menu.**

If you specify a Next Style for a style sheet, it's automatically applied to a new paragraph when you press Return or Enter. If you choose Same Style (the default), the style sheet you're creating will continue to be applied to new paragraphs when you press Return or Enter while typing. Typically, you'd use Next Style for things like headlines that are always followed by a specific kind of paragraph (like a byline). And you'd typically use Same Style for body text, where the next paragraph usually has the same formatting.

7. **If you want (and you often should), you can assign a keyboard shortcut to a style sheet (Windows users must make sure Num Lock is on).**

   Hold down any combination of ⌘, Option, and Shift, or Ctrl, Alt, and Shift, and press any number on the keypad. (Letters and non-keypad numbers cannot be used for keyboard shortcuts.)

8. **When you're done specifying the attributes of your style sheet, click OK.**

Note

When you create a style sheet based on highlighted text, the new style sheet is automatically applied to the text.

Applying paragraph style sheets

After you've created a paragraph style sheet, applying it is easy. Just click within a paragraph or highlight text in a range of paragraphs, then click on the style sheet name in the Paragraph Styles pane or press its keyboard shortcut. (Windows users must make sure Num Lock is on when using shortcuts for styles.)

When you apply a style sheet to selected paragraphs, all local formats and applied character style sheets are retained. All other formats are replaced by those of the applied style sheet.

Tip

If you hold down Option or Alt when clicking on a name in the Paragraph Styles pane, any characters style sheets that have been applied within selected paragraphs are retained, as are the following character formats: Superscript, Subscript, Underline, Strikethrough, Language, and Baseline Shift. If you hold down Option+Shift or Alt+Shift when clicking on a style-sheet name, all local formatting within the selected paragraphs is removed.

Note

If a plus sign (+) is displayed to the right of a style-sheet name, it means that some of the text within the selected paragraphs has "local" formats that differ from those of the applied style sheet. This can occur if you apply a style sheet to text to which you've done some manual formatting or if you modify text formatting in a paragraph after applying a style sheet to it. (For example, you may have italicized the name of a book; that is a local change to the style sheet and will cause the + to appear.)

A few last words about paragraph style sheets. There are no hard-and-fast rules about how best to implement them. Like handwriting, you should develop your own style. How many style sheets you create, the names you use, whether you apply them with keyboard shortcuts or via the Paragraph Styles pane, and whether you use paragraph styles, character styles, or both are all matters of personal taste. One thing is indisputable: You should use style sheets whenever possible. They're a layout artist's best friend.

Managing paragraph style sheets

The Paragraph Style's pop-up menu, shown in Figure 20-1, displays nine options for managing style sheets; two buttons at the bottom of the pane let you create and delete paragraph styles. Here's a brief description of each option:

✦ **New Paragraph Style:** Creates a new paragraph style sheet. When you choose New Paragraph Style, the New Paragraph Style dialog box is displayed. The pane also has an iconic button to create a new style.

✦ **Duplicate Style:** Click on a style sheet name, and then click this button to create an exact copy. If you want to create a style sheet that's similar to one you've already created, you might want to choose New Style Sheet rather than Duplicate, and then use the Based On option to create a "child" of the original. If you choose Duplicate, the copy is identical to but not based on the original; if you modify the original, the copy is not affected. The pane also has an iconic button to create a new style.

✦ **Delete Style:** Choose this to delete highlighted style sheets. To select multiple styles, hold down the ⌘ or Ctrl keys as you click on their names. To select a range of styles, click on the first one, and then hold down the Shift key and click on the last one.

✦ **Redefine Style:** This option lets you modify an existing style sheet. Highlight text to which the style sheet you want to modify has been applied, change the formats as desired, then click Redefine Style. The newly applied formats are applied to the style sheet.

✦ **Style Options:** This option lets you modify an existing style sheet. When a style sheet is highlighted in the Paragraph Styles pane, choosing Style Options displays the Modify Paragraph Style Options dialog box, which is identical to the New Paragraph Style dialog box.

✦ **Load Paragraph Styles:** Choose this option if you want to import style sheets from another InDesign document. (Importing style sheets is discussed in detail later in this chapter.)

✦ **Load All Styles:** This option lets you import both paragraph and character style sheets from another InDesign document. Importing style sheets is discussed in detail later in this chapter.

✦ **Select All Unused:** Select this option to highlight the names of all paragraph style sheets that have not been applied to any paragraphs. This is a handy way of identifying unused styles in preparation for deleting them (by choosing the Delete Style option).

✦ **Small Palette Rows:** Click this option to reduce the text size in the Paragraph Styles pane. Although harder to read, a pane with this option set lets you access more styles without having to scroll. To return the pane to its normal text size, select this option again.

Character style sheets

Character style sheets are nearly identical in every respect to paragraph style sheets, but instead of using them to format selected paragraphs, you use character style sheets to apply character-level formats to a highlighted range of text. For example, you could use a character style sheet to:

✦ **Modify the appearance of the first several words in a paragraph.** For example, some publications — particularly magazines — will use a style variation such as small caps as a lead-in for a paragraph. You could use a character style sheet not only to switch the font style to small caps, but also to change size, color, font family, and so on.

✦ **Apply different formatting to such text elements as Web site, e-mail, and ftp addresses (URLs), within body text.**

✦ **Create other body text variations for such things as emphasis, book and movie titles, product and company names, and so on.**

Creating and applying character style sheets

Using character style sheets is much the same as using paragraph style sheets. First you create them; then you apply them. And you use the Character Styles pane (Window ➪ Type & Tables ➪ Character Styles, or Shift+F11), shown in Figure 20-3, to do both. As is the case with paragraph style sheets, the easiest way to create a character style sheet is to apply the character-level formats you want to use in the style sheet to some sample text, then follow the steps in this section. You can create a character style sheet from scratch (that is, without preformatting any text), but if you do, you'll have to set all the character formats when you create the style sheet.

Figure 20-3: The Character Styles pane and its palette menu.

To create a character style sheet from highlighted text:

1. **If it's not displayed, show the Character Style pane by choosing Type ⇨ Character Styles or pressing Shift+F11.**

2. **Make sure you've highlighted text that's been styled with all the character formats you want to include in your style sheet, then choose New Style from the Character Styles pane's pop-up menu.**

   The New Character Style dialog box, shown in Figure 20-4, is displayed.

Figure 20-4: The New Character Style dialog box.

Tip   You can also create a new style by clicking the Create New Style button at the bottom of the pane. When you click this button, a new style sheet with a default name (Character Style 1, Character Style 2, and so on) is added to the list. The formats applied to the selected text are included in the new style sheet; the New Character Style dialog box is not displayed. If you want to modify any formats, double-click the new style sheet name in the pane; the Modify Character Style Options dialog box is displayed. This dialog box is identical to the New Character Style dialog box.

3. **Enter a name for the style sheet in the Style Name field.**

4. **The scroll list to the left of the Style Name field displays seven options: General, Basic Character Formats, Advanced Character Formats, Character Color, OpenType Features, Underline Options, and Strikethrough Options. If you want to change any character-level formats, choose the appropriate option, then make your changes.**

5. **The Based On pop-up menu displays the names of other character style sheets. You can use this feature to create families of style sheets.**

For example, you could create a style sheet called "Body Copy/Base Character" that uses the same character attributes as your base Body Copy paragraph style sheet and then create variations such as "Body Text/Emphasis," "Body Text/URLs," and so on. If you used the Based On pop-up menu to base each of the variations on "Body Text/Base Character" and you then modified this "parent" style sheet, your changes would be applied to all the variations.

6. **If you want (and you should), you can assign a keyboard shortcut to a style sheet. (*Windows users:* Make sure Num Lock is on.)**

   Hold down any combination of ⌘, Option, and Shift, or Ctrl, Alt, and Shift, and press any number on the keypad. (Letters and non-keypad numbers cannot be used for keyboard shortcuts.)

7. **When you're done specifying the attributes of your style sheet, click OK.**

Managing character style sheets

The options displayed in the Character Styles pane's palette menu are the same as those for the Paragraph Styles palette menu, which are explained earlier in this chapter.

Working with Nested Styles

Often, you'll want to apply character formatting in a consistent manner to many paragraphs. For example, you may want to change the font for the first character in a bulleted list so that the correct symbol appears for the bullet. Or you might want to italicize the numerals in a numbered list. Or you might want to have the first four words of body text that appears after a headline be boldfaced and in small caps. Or you might want the first sentence in instructional paragraphs to be in italics. InDesign lets you automate such formatting via the Nested Styles feature.

New Feature The Nested Styles feature is new to InDesign CS.

Figure 20-5 shows an example of nested styles in use, along with the Drop Cap & Nested Styles dialog box in which you create them. Here, the first sentence of the introductory paragraph's text is set in italics.

Here's how the dialog box works:

1. **Define any character styles that you'll apply to text via a nested style.**

   Even if all you're doing is making text italic, you need to define a character style to do so. The nested Styles feature cannot apply any attributes other than those in a character style.

Figure 20-5: The use of a nested style is to have the first sentence in the introductory paragraph be set in italics.

2. **Go to the Paragraph Styles dialog box (Window ⇨ Type & Tables ⇨ Paragraph Styles, or F11) and select Drop Caps & Nested Styles.**

3. **Click the New Nested Style button.**

   An entry will appear under the Nested Styles label.

4. **The first column is where you choose from existing character styles.**

   This is what will be applied to text.

5. **The second column determines the scope end point: Through or Up To.**

   For example, if you choose Through for a nested style that is set for four words, all four words will get the nested style. If you choose Up To, the first three words will get the style and the fourth will not.

6. **The third column is where you specify how many items you want InDesign to count in determining the scope's end point.**

   For example, if you want to have the first seven characters have the style applied, choose 7. If you want to have the style applied up to the first tab, choose 1.

7. **The fourth column is where you specify the scope of text that you're applying the nested style to.**

Figure 20-6 shows the options. They break into two groups: a number of items (characters, words, and so on) and a specific character (tab, em space, and so on). Whatever you choose needs to be consistent in all your text, since InDesign will follow these rules slavishly.

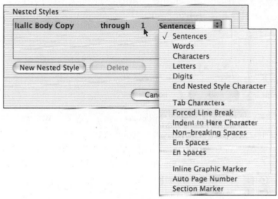

Figure 20-6: The scope options for a nested style determine what text receives the formatting.

8. **You can create multiple nested styles in one paragraph, with different rules for each. InDesign applies them in the order in which they appear in the dialog box, and each starts where the other ends. Use the up and down arrow buttons to change the order of nested styles.**

9. **You can preview the formatting if you had selected sample text before opening the dialog box by checking the Preview option.**

10. **Click OK when you're done.**

Note

The Nested Styles feature is included in the same dialog box as the Drop Caps feature. That's because a drop cap would be the first "nested style" in a paragraph and can never be anything but the first style. By combining the two into one dialog box, InDesign lets you treat a drop cap as part of a series of styles to be applied to a paragraph. If you want only a drop cap, you simply don't create a nested style.

Note

About the only thing missing from the Nested Styles feature is, unfortunately, an effect favored by many designers: applying a format to the first line in a paragraph, usually a paragraph that follows a headline. The most common version of this has the first line formatted in all small caps, then switching to normal capitalization for the rest of the paragraph.

InDesign CS's Nested Styles feature doesn't support this effect because it requires a specific stop point (number of characters, words, or sentences, or a specific character such as a tab, line break, indent-to-here, em space, en space, or the End Nested Style Character, which lets you set an arbitrary end). But there is no definite end point at the end of the line, as it depends on how InDesign flows and breaks the text, which will be different for each paragraph's first line.

The best you can do is highlight these manually and apply the small caps attribute yourself, or use the Nested Styles feature and manually insert the End Nested Style Character at the end of each line (choose Type ⇨ Insert Special Character ⇨ End Nested Style).

Changing Style Sheets

If you scratch your name into wet cement, you have only a few minutes to change your mind. After that, your formatting decisions are cast in stone, so to speak. Fortunately, style sheets are much more forgiving. Not only can you modify a style sheet whenever you want, you're free to manually modify text to which style sheets have been applied.

Modifying style sheets

The most important thing to know about modifying a style sheet is that all text to which a modified style sheet has been applied is automatically updated. Additionally, if you modify a "parent" style sheet, all "children" style sheets that were created by choosing Based On are also automatically updated.

There are two ways to modify an existing style sheet. You can

✦ **Click on the style sheet name in the Character Styles or Paragraph Styles pane, and then choose Style Options from the pane's palette menu.** The Modify Character Style Options or the Modify Paragraph Style Options dialog box is displayed. These dialog boxes are the same as the New Character Style and New Paragraph Style dialog boxes. Make whatever changes you want, then click OK.

✦ **Double-click on a style sheet name to display the Modify Character Style Options or Modify Paragraph Style Options dialog box.** If text is highlighted, the style sheet you double-click is applied to the text; if no text is selected, the style sheet you double-click becomes the default style and is automatically applied when you enter text in a newly created box. If you hold down Shift+⌘ or Ctrl+Shift when you double-click on a style sheet name, the style sheet is not applied to text.

Modifying text that's been styled with a style sheet

If you need to change the appearance of text that's been formatted using a style sheet, all you have to do is highlight the text — characters or paragraphs — and then use the Control palette, Character pane (Window ⇨ Type & Tables ⇨ Character, or ⌘+T or Ctrl+T), or the Paragraph pane (Window ⇨ Type & Tables ⇨ Character, or Option+⌘+T or Ctrl+Alt+T) to change the formats.

When you change any formats in text to which a style sheet has been applied, you are making "local" changes (to make "global" changes, you would modify the style sheet). When you change formatting in style-sheet formatted text, a plus sign (+) is displayed next to the style-sheet name in the Character Styles or Paragraph Styles pane, as shown in Figure 20-7.

Figure 20-7: A "local" format (the italic type style) has been applied to the highlighted text below, which was formatted with a style sheet. The + sign next to the style-sheet name in the Paragraph Styles pane indicates that local formatting has been applied within the paragraph.

Unapplying style sheets

If you want, you can remove the link between style sheet–formatted text and the assigned style sheet. All you have to do is highlight the text — a range of characters if you want to disassociate them from the applied character style sheet or one or more paragraphs if you want to disassociate it/them from the applied paragraph style sheet — then choose No Paragraph Style from the Paragraph Styles pane or No Character Style from the Character Styles pane. When you break the link between text and its applied style sheet, any local formatting is retained unless you hold down the Option or Alt key when you choose No Paragraph Style or No Character Style. If you hold down the Option or Alt key, local formatting is removed.

Along the same lines, if you delete a style sheet that's been applied to text, the formatting of that text remains unchanged, but if you click within or highlight the text, No Paragraph Style or No Character Style is displayed in the corresponding pane.

Importing Style Sheets

If you've created a style sheet, you never have to re-create it — assuming you've saved the document that contains the style sheet. InDesign lets you import character and paragraph style sheets from one document into another. Also, when you import text files from word processing programs that use style sheets, you can import the style sheets along with the text.

Importing style sheets from InDesign documents

The Paragraph Styles and Character Styles panes' palette menus contain commands that let you move style sheets between documents. The Paragraph Styles pane lets you import only paragraph style sheets or paragraph and character style sheets; the Character Styles pane lets you import only character style sheets or character and paragraph style sheets. Here's how you do it:

1. **If it's not displayed, show the Paragraph Styles pane by choosing Window ➪ Type & Tables ➪ Paragraph Styles or pressing F11, or show the Character Styles pane by choosing Window ➪ Type & Tables ➪ Character Styles or pressing Shift+F11.**

2. **Choose Load Paragraph Styles from the Paragraph Styles pane's palette menu if you want to import only paragraph styles; choose Load Character Styles from the Character Styles pane's palette menu if you want to import only character style sheets; or choose Load All Styles from either pane's palette menu if you want to import both character and paragraph style sheets.**

   Regardless of what kind of style sheets you choose to import, the Open a File dialog box, shown in Figure 20-8, is displayed.

3. **Use the controls in the Open a File dialog box to locate the InDesign document that contains the style sheets you want to import.**

4. **Double-click on the document name or click once on the document name, then click Open.**

If you import a style sheet that has the same name as an existing style sheet, the imported style sheet will replace the existing one. Any text formatted with the original style sheet will be reformatted using the imported style sheet.

Figure 20-8: The Open a File dialog box when loading style sheets from other documents.

QuarkXPress User

InDesign imports all style sheets when you use one of the Load commands. It does not let you select specific style sheets for import, as QuarkXPress does. That can add a lot of irrelevant style sheets to your InDesign document, unfortunately.

You can also use the Copy (Edit ➪ Copy, or ⌘+C or Ctrl+C) and Paste commands (Edit ➪ Paste, or ⌘+V or Ctrl +V) to move a style sheet from one document to another. Simply copy some text in the source document to which the style sheet you want to move has been applied. Then display the target document and use the Paste command to place the copied text into a text frame. The Character Styles and/or Paragraph Styles panes in the target document display the names of the new, "imported" styles.

Working with style sheets in imported text files

In most workgroup publishing environments, writers generate text using Microsoft Word, and InDesign users place the text in a layout and add other design elements—imported pictures, illustrations, lines, and so on—to create a finished publication. Whether writers are producing short magazine articles or lengthy book chapters, chances are they're doing some text formatting as they write—perhaps as little as applying occasional bold or italic styles or as much as using a complete set of style sheets, if their word processor supports them.

When you import a word processing file into InDesign, you can bring the formatting and style sheets along with the text. (See Chapter 4 for a complete list of formatting options that will import from Word.)

Isolated formatting might be used to indicate which style sheets should be applied in InDesign — for example, the writer might apply bold to one-line paragraphs that should be formatted as a subhead. However, if the writer applies appropriate paragraph style sheets to text in her word processor, much of the formatting in InDesign can be automated by importing the style sheets. (Note that word processors' character style sheets are not imported.)

You can use these imported paragraph style sheets in two different ways, depending on whether style sheets with the same name already exist in the InDesign document. To import style sheets with a word processing file, check Retain Format in the Place dialog box (File ⇨ Place, or ⌘+D or Ctrl+D).

Cross-Reference   For more information about using the Place command to import text files, see Chapter 16.

After you place a text file that contains style sheets, the Paragraph Styles pane displays the names of all the imported style sheets, and any text to which style sheets have been applied retains the style sheet's formats as well as a link to the style sheet.

Editing imported paragraph style sheets

If you import paragraph style sheets with text, you can simply use the style sheets specified in the word processor to format the text. This method works well for designs that do not follow a template — for example, brochures or feature stories. You might import the text, experiment with formatting it, then edit the imported style sheets in InDesign to reflect your design.

For example, say you import a magazine feature article that is formatted with three paragraph style sheets (Headline, Byline, and Body Copy) into an InDesign document that does not contain style sheets with those names. The three style sheets are added to InDesign's Paragraph Styles list and have similar specifications to what they had in the word processor. However, since InDesign offers more formatting options, you might modify those style sheets to fine-tune the text formatting. To edit a paragraph style sheet, select it in the Paragraph Styles pane, choose Style Options from the pane's palette menu, then make your changes in the Modify Paragraph Style Options dialog box.

Overriding imported paragraph style sheets

In documents that follow a template, you can provide writers with style-sheet names that must be applied to their text. For example, say you're working on a tri-fold brochure that is part of an entire series of similar tri-folds. The writer might format the text with five paragraph style sheets that also exist in your InDesign document: Heads, Subheads, Body Copy, Bullets, and Quotes. The style-sheet specifications in the word processor don't matter — only the name counts — because the style sheets in an InDesign document override style sheets in imported text files.

For example, the writer's style sheets use standard fonts such as Times and Helvetica along with bold and italic typestyles to distinguish the types of text. But when the word processing file is imported into InDesign, the style sheets are overridden with InDesign style sheets that have the same name but specify the actual fonts used by the designer and the many formatting options available in InDesign.

You can supply writers either with actual style sheets or with only style-sheet names:

✦ To supply style sheets, export text from a similar story in RTF format, which writers can open in their word processor; the word processor will add the style-sheet names in the RTF file to its own style sheet list. The writers can then save these style-sheet names to a template file and use that template for future documents. To export text, use the Export dialog box (File ⇨ Export, or ⌘+E or Ctrl+E) and choose Rich Text Format from the Formats pop-up menu.

✦ Or, you can simply give writers a list of style-sheet names that they can create themselves to their own specifications. In this case, it's particularly important that the style sheets created in the word processor have exactly the same names as those in the InDesign document.

Exporting style sheets

Although InDesign lets you export text (via the File ⇨ Export command), only a few file formats are supported: Text-only (ASCII), Rich Text Format (RTF), and InDesign Tagged Text.

An exported RTF file keeps the style-sheet names but not the actual formatting, which can make further editing difficult in a word processor. An InDesign Tagged Text file retains the style-sheet definitions, but it does so as codes, so again it's hard to deal with in a word processor.

Summary

If you're working on a document that uses the same text formats repeatedly, you can save time and ensure consistency by using style sheets. A style sheet is essentially a "macro" for formatting text. InDesign lets you create character-level style sheets and paragraph-level style sheets. Character style sheets let you apply

several character attributes — such as font, size, leading, kerning, and tracking —
to highlighted text at once. Similarly, you can use paragraph style sheets to apply
several paragraph formats — alignment, indents, drop caps, space before or after,
and so on — simultaneously to selected paragraphs. After you apply a style sheet
to text, you can still manually modify the text by highlighting it and overriding the
style sheet's formats. If you're importing a text file from Microsoft Word, you can
import any applied style sheets along with the text.

✦   ✦   ✦

Setting Up Tabs and Tables

♦ ♦ ♦ ♦

In This Chapter

Preparing tabbed text

Learning the Tabs pane

Creating tables

Formatting rows, columns, and cells

Converting text to tables

♦ ♦ ♦ ♦

If you ever used a typewriter, you may remember hitting the tab key to indent each paragraph. And you may have pounded on it repeatedly to align columns of data. In InDesign, you use first-line indents to distinguish the first line of a new paragraph, and you reserve tabs for separating columns of data. Although InDesign has a built-in table editor, you can create simple tables using regular tabs quickly with the tabs feature. For more sophisticated tables, use the table editor.

In InDesign, tabs are part of paragraph formats — meaning that, when you set them, they apply to all the text in selected paragraphs rather than to selected characters within a paragraph. By default, when you start typing in a paragraph or you create a new paragraph style sheet, there are invisible, automatic tab stops every half-inch. Regardless of the measurement system your rulers are set to use, when you hit tab you'll jump to the next 0.5-inch increment on the ruler.

As soon as you set a tab stop of your own, it overrides any of the automatic tab stops to its left. The automatic tab stops remain to the right until you override all of them.

Tip   Any tabs you set in the Tabs pane when no document is open are added to all future documents you create. Therefore, if tabs at every quarter-inch would be more useful to you, add them with no documents open.

InDesign provides four different types of tabs so you can

✦ Left-align text to the left at a tab stop (the default setting, and the one you'll use most often)

✦ Center text on either side of the tab stop (very useful in column headers)

✦ Right-align text at a tab stop (useful for columns of integers)

✦ Align a specific character in the text with the tab stop (such as a comma or period in a number)

Figure 21-1 shows examples of tabs.

Item			Ingredient		Amount		Price
»	Trifle	»	lemon juice	»	3/4 cup	»	$.89/20 oz.¶
»		»	eggs	»	4	»	$1.99/dozen¶
»		»	sugar	»	1 1/2 cups	»	$1.79/pound¶
»		»	heavy cream	»	1 cup	»	$.99/quart¶
»		»	strawberries	»	1 1/2 cups	»	$2.09/pound¶
»		»	pound cake	»	1	»	$2.75 each¶
»Whip Cream		»	heavy cream	»	1 1/2 cups	»	$.99/quart¶
»		»	sugar	»	1/4 cup	»	$1.79/pound¶
¶							
Item		»	Ingredient	»	Amount	»	Price¶
»	Trifle		lemon juice	»	3/4 cup		$.89/20 oz.¶
»		»	eggs	»	4	»	$1.99/dozen¶
»		»	sugar	»	1 1/2 cups		$1.79/pound¶
»		»	heavy cream	»	1 cup		$.99/quart¶
»		»	strawberries	»	1 1/2 cups	»	$2.09/pound¶
»		»	pound cake	»	1	»	$2.75 each¶
»Whip Cream		»	heavy cream	»	1 1/2 cups		$.99/quart¶

Figure 21-1: Under the Item column, Trifle and Whip Cream are positioned with right-aligned tabs. The three other column headings — Ingredient, Amount, and Price — are positioned with center tabs. In the chart, the ingredients are left-aligned, the amounts are center-aligned, and the prices are aligned on the dollar sign (top chart) and the decimal point (lower chart).

Using the Tabs Pane

To set tabs in InDesign you use the Tabs pane, which floats above your text so that you can keep it open until you're finished experimenting with tabs. To open the Tabs pane, choose Window ⇨ Type & Tables ⇨ Tabs or press Shift+⌘+T or

Ctrl+Shift+T. Figure 21-2 shows the Tabs pane along with a simple table created using two tab stops.

 Tip If you find yourself adjusting tab settings and indents at the same time, you might wish to combine the Tabs pane and the Paragraph pane. Simply drag the Tabs pane into the Paragraph pane or vice versa. Use the palette menu on the Paragraph pane to change its orientation to vertical so the palettes work together better. (By default, Adobe combines the Paragraph, Character, and Transform panes—we recommend you split the Paragraph and Character panes into separate palettes so you can see all your text formatting at once.)

Preparing text files for setting tabs

When importing text, the most common problem a designer encounters is that writers try to line up the text on their screen by using multiple tabs between columns, rather than setting appropriate tab stops in the first place and having one tab between each "cell." That's because word processors also have default tabs stops of 0.5", and most users use those defaults rather than figure out how to set tabs themselves. When you import the file with these tabs, the chances of items lining up in InDesign as they did in the word processor are pretty close to zero. That means a lot of cleanup work for the designer.

Before you start setting tabs in InDesign, take a look at the tabs already entered in the text. You can check this out in your word processor or in text that has been placed in InDesign. To view tab characters in InDesign, choose Type ⇨ Show Hidden Characters, or press Option+⌘+I or Ctrl+Alt+I. The light-blue double greater than symbols (>>) are tabs.

To set effective tabs for columns of data, each line or row of information should be its own paragraph, and each column of data should be separated by only one tab character. If there's only one tab between each column, you need to set only one tab stop per column and you can more carefully control a single tab stop rather than several.

Since the text is not in its final font or text frame, the current tab placement does not matter. But if necessary, the writer can change tab settings in Word to align the columns for proofreading or editing purposes.

As with multiple tabs stops, if there are extra paragraph returns between the rows or information or if each line ends in a soft return or line break (Shift+Return or Shift+Enter) rather than a paragraph return (Return or Enter), you should fix these with search and replace in your word processor or Find/Change (Edit ⇨ Find/Change, or ⌘+F or Ctrl+F) in InDesign.

It's best to insist that any word processor documents imported into InDesign be created so there is only one tab between each entry on a line, no matter how it looks in the word processor. Then you can set up the appropriate tab stops in InDesign.

Figure 21-2: The Tabs pane and a simple table created with two tab stops.

Tab style buttons

Four buttons on the Tabs pane let you control how the text aligns with the tab you're creating:

✦ **Left:** The default tab stops are left-aligned, which means that the left side of the text touches the tab stop as if it were a left margin. Most tabs you create for text will be left-aligned.

✦ **Center:** Centered tab stops are like the centered paragraph alignment, with text balanced evenly on either side of the tab stop. Center tabs are often used for table headings.

✦ **Right:** When you set right-aligned tabs, the right edge of text touches the tab stop. This is commonly used for aligning numbers that do not include decimals or for the last column in a table.

✦ **Align On:** By default, the last tab style button is for decimal tabs, which means that a period in the text aligns on the tab stop. If there's no period in the text, InDesign pretends that there is one after the last character. Instead of aligning on a period, you can specify a different character — such as a comma or dollar sign — for an Align On tab, and text will align to that character. You do this using the Align On field, covered later in this section.

Tip   If you need a tab flush with the right margin, for example to position a dingbat at the end of the story, click the Right Tab Style button and position it on the right side of the tab ruler. Then drag the right-aligned tab on top of the right indent arrow. (You can't actually click to place a tab on top of the arrow, but you can drag a tab on top of it.) An even faster way is to choose Type ➪ Special Characters ➪ Right Indent or press Shift+Tab.

X (position) field

The X field of the Tabs pane lets you specify a position for a new tab stop. You can enter a value in this field in 0.01-point increments, then press Shift+Enter or Shift+Return to create a tab. InDesign positions tabs relative to the left edge of the text frame or column. Or you can just click the mouse on the ruler where you want the tab to be, as described later.

Tip   Why enter numbers when you can just use the mouse? The reason is to get more accurate positioning than using the mouse usually allows, especially when you know exactly where the tab stop should be. Of course, you can add a tab via the mouse, then click it and enter a more precise value in the X field.

Note   If a text frame has Inset Spacing specified for its left edge in the Text Frame Options dialog box (Object ⇨ Text Frame Options, or ⌘+B or Ctrl+B), InDesign measures tabs from the text inset rather than from the frame.

As with other fields in InDesign, the X field can perform mathematical computations for you. So you can set a tab at half of 0.125 without figuring out that value, or you can move a tab by adding to or subtracting from its current value. It may seem unlikely that you would ever do this, but it's extremely handy for changing tab settings so they're, say, half as far apart as they used to be, or half as far apart plus 2 points to the right.

Note   The operands for performing math in fields are + (addition), – (subtraction), * (multiplication), and / (division). If you want to combine these operands — for example, add 5 then subtract 2 — you'll have to remember back to middle school and Algebra I to enter the operands in the correct order: multiply, divide, add, then subtract.

Leader field

A tab leader is a character or series of characters that fills the white space between tabs — like the periods you see between a table of contents entry and its page number. They got the name *leader* because they lead your eyes across the page. Figure 21-2 shows a dot leader in use between the donor's name and the donation amount.

InDesign lets you specify up to eight characters, including special characters, that will repeat to fill any white space. When you set a leader for a tab stop, the leaders actually fill any space prior to that tab stop (between the previous text and the tab location).

To spread out the leader characters, type spaces between the characters you enter. Don't enter spaces before and after a single character though, as that will result in two spaces between the character when the pattern repeats (unless that's the look you're going for). You can't enter special types of spaces — such as thin spaces or hair spaces — in the Leader field; you will always get em spaces.

Note   The reason to use tab leaders is to help the reader. Unless the design is more important than the content, you probably shouldn't use eight-character tab leaders even though you can. A cacophony of characters draws too much attention to itself and can be confusing. Because the pattern of leaders repeats, one space and a period are usually sufficient.

Note   To enter special characters in the Leader field, use keyboard commands, InDesign's Glyph pane, or a utility such as PopChar X or Character Map. If you use InDesign's Insert Special Character command (Type ➪ Insert Character) or the Glyph pane (Type ➪ Glyph), you'll insert a character into your text, which you'll have to cut and paste into the Leader field. It won't be inserted directly in the Leader field as you would expect.

Align On field

The Align On tab style defaults to a period, but you can replace the period with any character, including special characters. When that character is found in tabbed text, it will align on the tab stop. If that character is not found, InDesign pretends that it follows the last character in the tabbed string. The most common characters entered in the Align On field include a comma (,), dollar sign ($), cents symbol (¢), and opening or closing parentheses ((and)).

Tab ruler

Rather than entering values in the X field, you can position tabs by clicking on the ruler at the bottom of the Tabs pane. The Tab ruler has the following characteristics:

✦ **It displays in the same measurement system as the document, with 0 specifying the edges of the column.** If Inset Spacing is specified for the left edge of the text frame in the Text Frame Options dialog box (Object ➪ Text Frame Options, or ⌘+B or Ctrl+B), the ruler starts after the text inset in the first column.

✦ **The ruler provides arrows for controlling and displaying the selected paragraph's first-line, left, and right indents.** Dragging the two left arrows changes both the paragraph's first line and left indent, while dragging the top arrow changes only the first-line indent. Dragging the arrow at right changes the right indents. These arrows help you see indents in relation to tabs that you're setting.

✦ **Icons that match the tab styles display on the rulers to show you where and what type of tabs are already set.** You can drag these around to reposition existing tabs, and you can drag them off the ruler to delete tabs.

✦ **You can scroll through the ruler by clicking on it and dragging to the left or right.** This lets you set tabs beyond the current column or text box width, such as for text that flows into text boxes of different widths.

Magnet icon

Under the right circumstances, clicking the Magnet icon in the lower-left corner of the Tabs pane snaps the pane and the ruler to the selected text frame or column. The idea is to make it easier to see the tab stops in relation to an actual area of text.

For this to work, you need to make sure the top of the text frame is visible on-screen, the Type tool is selected, and you've placed the cursor in text or high-lighted text. If you don't meet all these prerequisites, nothing happens.

Once you manage to get the Tabs pane positioned correctly, it's quite useful. You can add and adjust tabs in relation to the text (provided that the text is at the top of the text frame!) and you can always see from where the tabs are measured. Even better, if you move the cursor to another column in the text frame, you can click the Magnet again to position the Tabs pane over that column.

Tabs pane menu

In addition to setting tabs in the Tabs pane, InDesign provides two additional options through the palette menu: Clear All and Repeat Tab:

✦ The Clear All command deletes any tabs you've created, and any text posi-tioned with tabs reverts to the position of the default tab stops. (You can delete an individual tab stop by dragging its icon off the ruler.)

✦ The Repeat Tab command lets you create a string of tabs across the ruler that are all the same distance apart. When you select a tab on the ruler and choose this command, InDesign measures the distance between the selected tab and the previous tab (or, if it's the first tab on the ruler, the distance between the selected tab and the left indent/text inset). The program then uses this dis-tance to place new tabs, with the same alignment, all the way across the ruler. InDesign repeats tabs only to the right of the selected tab, but it will insert tabs between other tab stops.

Creating Tables

Whether you're working on yesterday's box scores for the sports pages, an annual report, or a fun, little parenting magazine, you've got numbers. Numbers with dollar signs, numbers with decimals, numbers intermixed with text. You have to line the columns up correctly, not only so the information looks good but so it's easy to read as well. Then you often need to add ruling lines to help separate the material visually for the reader.

You could do all this with tab stops, ruling lines, and other InDesign tools. Or you could make your life easier and use InDesign's table editor, which lets you specify almost any attribute imaginable in a table through the Table pane and the Table menu.

Cross-Reference InDesign CS lets you import tables from Microsoft Word, RTF, and Microsoft Excel files, including some of their cell formatting. Likewise, you can convert their tables to tabbed text by using the options in the Import Options dialog box accessible when you place a file through the Place dialog box (File➪Place, or ⌘+D or Ctrl+D), as covered in Chapter 15.

Figure 21-3 shows the Table pane and Table menu, as well as a complex table used to display a YMCA activities schedule. You access the Table pane via Window➪ Type & Tables➪Table, or Shift+F9.

Figure 21-3: The Table pane and its palette menu, the Table menu, and a complex table created with them.

InDesign tables and QuarkXPress tables have several differences. Although both treat tables as collections of cells, InDesign offers more formatting options for cell strokes than QuarkXPress does. InDesign has more controls for text and row placement than QuarkXPress offers. InDesign also imports Word, Excel, and RTF tables, while QuarkXPress does not. But QuarkXPress offers more control over the flow of text among cells in a table — InDesign doesn't let you flow text from one cell to another, for example, much less control the order of that flow.

Creating a table

To create a table in InDesign, you first create or select a text frame with the text Tool and then choose Table ⇨ Insert Table or press Option+Shift+⌘+T or Ctrl+Alt+Shift+T. That produces the Insert Table dialog box, where you enter the number of body rows and columns and the number of header and footer rows. Click OK to have InDesign create the basic table, which will be set as wide as the text frame. The depth will be based on the number of rows, with each row defaulting to the height that will hold 12-point text.

With the basic table in place, you now format it using the Table pane and the Table menu. The pane contains cell formatting tools: You can increase or decrease the number of rows and columns, set the row and column height, set the text's vertical alignment within selected cells (top, middle, bottom, and justified), choose one of four text-rotation angles, and set the text margin within a cell separately for the top, bottom, left, and right. Note that all the Table pane's options affect only the currently selected cell(s), except for the Number of Rows and Number of Columns fields. Figure 21-4 shows the Table pane with its icons defined.

You set cell text's horizontal alignment using the paragraph formatting controls covered in Chapter 18. You can apply other paragraph and character formatting to cell text as described in Chapters 17 through 20. You can also apply tabs within cells using the Tabs pane covered earlier in this chapter.

For more sophisticated table attributes, use the Table Options dialog box and its five panes, as shown in Figures 21-5 through 21-8. You access this dialog box using the Table Options menu item in the Table pane's palette menu or by choosing Table ⇨ Table Options. In both menus, you can select a specific pane using a submenu from the Table Options menu item.

To add items to a table, you can type in text in any cell, paste text or graphics into a cell, or place text or graphics into a cell by choosing File ⇨ Place or pressing ⌘+D or Ctrl+D.

Figure 21-4: The Table pane.

Table Setup pane

The Table Setup pane (shown in Figure 21-5) lets you adjust the rows and columns, as you can do in the Table pane. It's also where you specify the table border's weight, line type, color, tint, gap color and tint (if you choose a dashed, dotted, or striped line for the border), the space before and after the table, and whether row lines (which InDesign calls *strokes*) are placed on top of column lines or vice versa. If your table has cells with different line settings that would be overridden by the table border, you can preserve those cell settings by checking the Preserve Local Formatting check box.

Figure 21-5: The Table Setup pane.

New Feature InDesign CS adds the ability to specify whether row lines overprint column lines or vice versa.

Tip You can open the Table Setup pane by pressing Option+Shift+⌘+B or Ctrl+Alt+ Shift+B.

Row Strokes and Column Strokes panes

InDesign lets you have the lines between columns and rows alternate color, thickness, and even type. Figure 21-6 shows the Row Strokes pane; the Column Strokes pane is identical, except that it applies to column (vertical) strokes rather than to row (horizontal) strokes.

Figure 21-6: The Row Strokes pane; the Column Strokes pane is identical.

You can choose a predefined alternation pattern using the Alternating Pattern pop-up menu, or simply enter a number in the First fields. The First field at the left of the pane specifies how many row strokes (or column strokes) get the formatting specified on the left side of the pane, while the First field at the right side specifies how many get the formatting specified at the right. InDesign will apply the formatting at left to the number of rows specified in its First field, then switch to the formatting at right for the number of rows specified in that First field. If there are still more rows, InDesign switches back to the left side's formatting, repeating the alternating pattern until it runs out of rows. The Column Strokes pane works the same way.

In addition to specifying the line attributes, you can also have InDesign skip a specified number of top and bottom rows (or columns) using the Skip First and

Skip Last fields. You would specify these so header and footer rows are excluded from the pattern.

Fills pane

The Fills pane, shown in Figure 21-7, is similar to the Row Strokes and Column Strokes panes. You set the color, tint, alternation pattern, and any skipped rows for fills you want applied to your table. The Alternating Pattern pop-up menu lets you pick from predefined numbers of columns or rows, depending on whether you want the fills to alternate from left to right or from top to bottom across the table.

Figure 21-7: The Fills pane.

If you choose Custom Row, InDesign will use the alternation settings in the Row Strokes pane; if you choose Custom Column, InDesign will use the alteration settings in the Column Strokes pane. That ensures the line color and other settings change with the fills.

Headers and Footers pane

The Headers and Footers pane, shown in Figure 21-8, lets you change the number of header and footer rows, as well as specify how often the header and footer repeats. (If your Word or RTF file's table used a heading row, InDesign will designate that as a reader row.) Your options are Every Text Column, Once per Frame, and Once per Page. You'll usually use one of the latter options, since it automatically repeats the header row for tables that break across text frames and/or pages.

Figure 21-8: The Headers and Footers pane.

Working with rows and columns

InDesign's table editing tools work very much like those in Microsoft Word. To select a row or column, click on an outside edge; you can also click in a cell with the Text tool and choose Table ➪ Select and then pick Row (⌘+3 or Ctrl+3) or Column (Option+⌘+3 or Ctrl+Alt+3). The same submenu also lets you pick all header rows, all footer rows, and all body (regular) rows.

To move to a specified row, you can choose Table ➪ Go to Row and enter the row's number, but it's usually easier to use your mouse to move to the desired row. After all, how often do you know the row's number?

To quickly select header rows or footer rows, choose Table ➪ Edit Header or Table ➪ Edit Footer.

Note　　Choose Table ➪ Select ➪ Table, or press Option+⌘+A or Ctrl+Alt+A, to select an entire table. Choose Table ➪ Delete ➪ Table to delete an entire table.

Adding and deleting

Insert or delete rows and columns using the Table menu or the Table pane's palette menu. Both have Insert and Delete menu options. Selected rows or columns will be deleted, while new rows or columns will be inserted before any selected row or column. You can also use the following shortcuts:

✦ **Delete Row:** ⌘+Backspace or Ctrl+Backspace

✦ **Delete Column:** Shift+Backspace

✦ **Insert Row:** ⌘+9 or Ctrl+9

✦ **Insert Column:** Option+⌘+9 or Ctrl+Alt+9

Manipulating rows and columns

You can make the space between rows or columns even by choosing Table ⇨ Distribute Rows Evenly or Table ⇨ Distribute Columns Evenly. But be careful: If you have merged several cells, that will increase the perceived column or row size and cause InDesign to excessively space rows or columns based on those merged cells' size.

You can also resize rows and columns by clicking on any of the cell boundaries and dragging them — similar to how you can resize columns and rows in Microsoft Word's table editor.

InDesign also lets you control how rows break across frames and pages, and whether rows must be kept together. But to do so it uses a dialog box oriented to cell formatting, covered later in this chapter.

New Feature   InDesign CS can now convert regular (body) rows to header and footer rows, or vice versa. Select the row(s) you want to convert, then choose Table ⇨ Convert Rows and then choose To Header, To Body, or To Footer as appropriate.

Note   All the row and column options are available in both the Table menu and the Table pane's palette menu, as well as via the contextual menu that appears if you have selected one or more cells and Control+click or right-click.

Working with cells

InDesign offers the Cell Options panes to manage the formatting of cells. It's accessible by choosing Cell Options from the Table menu or from the Table pane's palette menu. Four panes are available, as shown in Figures 21-9 through 21-12.

Text pane

The Text pane, accessible via the shortcut Option+⌘+B or Ctrl+Alt+B and shown in Figure 21-9, covers several options available in the Table pane covered earlier in this chapter, including the top, bottom, left, and right cell insets (margins), as well as vertical text alignment and text rotation. But it has several other options:

Figure 21-9: The Text pane

✦ **Paragraph Spacing Limit** determines the maximum space between paragraphs in a cell when you choose Justify from the Align Pop-up menu. This prevents there being too much space between paragraphs in a cell.

✦ **First Baseline** determines how the text baseline is positioned from the top of a cell. The options are Ascent, Cap Height, Leading, x Height, and Fixed.

Cross-Reference

Vertical alignment and baseline positioning work the same as they do for text frames, as covered in Chapter 15.

✦ **Clipping Contents to Cell** displays only the amount of text that fits in the cell's current size — it prevents the cell from expanding to accommodate the text.

Strokes and Fills pane

Shown in Figure 21-10, the Strokes and Fills pane lets you choose the weight, type, color, and tint of the strokes around a cell, as well as any gap color and tint (if you choose a striped, dashed, or dotted line as the stroke type).

At the top of the pane is the representation of the selected cell(s), depending on whether you had one or multiple cells highlighted before opening this pane. Figure 21-10 shows the representation when multiple cells are selected across more than one row and more than one column. (If you select multiple cells in one row, you'll get two cells shown side by side; if you select multiple cells in one column, you'll get two cells, one on top of the other.)

Figure 21-10: The Strokes and Fills pane.

You click on the cell boundary you want to apply the stroke formatting to and then choose the formatting you want. You could have different formatting for each of the left, right, top, and bottom outside cell boundaries, as well as different formatting for the horizontal boundary between selected cells and for the vertical formatting for the vertical boundary between selected cells. Usually, you'll select all outside boundaries and apply stroke formatting to all of them simultaneously, and you may do the same for the interior boundaries as well.

Note   InDesign does not show you the stroke formatting applied to the representation's segments, so you may not realize that different segments have different settings. Therefore, it's best to make sure the selected cells are visible and that you've checked the Preview option so you can see what you're actually applying to the cells.

In this pane, you can also select a fill color for the selected cells, based on existing color swatches, as well as a tint.

For both cell strokes and fills, you can set them as Overprint, which means the color will print on top of any underlying color, rather than knock out that color. Overprinting can change the color the reader sees, since it essentially mixes inks. Overprinting a blue fill on a yellow background, for example, would result in a green fill.

Rows and Columns pane

Shown in Figure 21-11, the Row and Columns pane sets row height and column width, as well as keep options for rows:

Figure 21-11: The Rows and Columns pane.

✦ With the Row Height pop-up menu, you specify the height as either Exactly or At Least the measurement to the right of the menu. This is the same as what you can specify in the Table pane.

✦ The Column Width field is also the same option you have in the Table pane to set the column width.

✦ The keep options control row placement. Use the Start Row pop-up menu to determine where the selected row starts: Anywhere, which means after the previous row (space permitting in the text frame, of course); In Next Text Column; In Next Frame; On Next Page; On Next Odd Page; or On Next Even Page. Check the Keep with Next Row check box to keep rows together.

Diagonal Lines pane

A unique InDesign feature is the ability to place diagonal lines in table cells. Figure 21-12 shows the Diagonal Lines pane. It's similar to other panes involving strokes but does have two specific options:

Figure 21-12: The Rows and Columns pane.

✦ You choose the type of diagonal line — top-left to bottom-right, bottom-left to top-right, or both — using the icons at the top of the pane.

✦ You determine whether the diagonal line appears on top of the cell contents or vice versa using the Draw pop-up menu.

Other cell options

Most of the work you'll do with cells involves entering and editing text (or graphics), applying fills and strokes, and setting margins (as covered earlier in this chapter), as well as formatting text (as covered in Chapters 17 through 20) and formatting frames (as covered in Chapters 10 and 11). After all, a cell is essentially just a text or graphics frame that's contained in a table with other frames. But there are a few other things to know about working with cells:

✦ You can merge and unmerge cells by highlighting the cell(s) and choosing Table ➪ Merge Cells or Table ➪ Unmerge Cells.

New Feature The ability to unmerge cells is new to InDesign CS.

✦ You can split cells by highlighting the cell(s) and choosing Table ➪ Split Cell Horizontally or Table ➪ Split Cell Vertically. To unsplit cells, you must merge them. (You could also choose Edit ➪ Undo, or press ⌘+Z or Ctrl+Z, before taking another action.) Split cells will take on the cell's current settings for text formatting, fill color, size, margins, and strokes.

✦ InDesign indicates text that does not fit in a cell with a large red dot in the cell, as Figure 21-13 shows.

Figure 21-13: InDesign indicates text that does not fit in a cell by displaying large red dots in the cell, as done at top here.

✦ You can apply colors and gradients to cells, as well as strokes, using the standard InDesign Swatches, Gradient, and Stroke panes (all accessible via the Window menu). These have the same effect as using the equivalent Table menu and Table pane options.

✦ The Control palette offers easy access to several cell and table features, as Figure 21-14 shows.

New Feature

The ability to apply stroke types, such as dashed and dotted lines, to cell edges is new to InDesign CS. You apply these strokes via the Stroke pane (Window⊳ Stroke, or F10). Use the palette menu to select the Stroke Styles menu option, which provides a list of styles and the ability to create your own, as Chapter 11 explains.

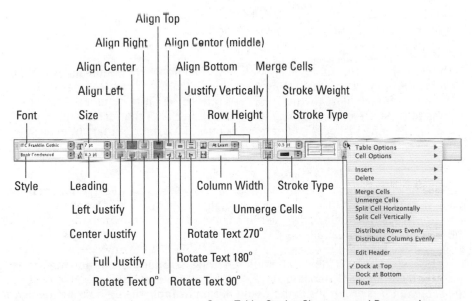

Figure 21-14: The Control palette when table cells are selected.

Converting Tabs to Tables

Often, you'll have a table done using tabs — whether imported from a word processor or originally created in InDesign with tabs — that you want to convert to a real
InDesign table. That's easy. Select the tabbed text you want to covert and choose
Table ➪ Convert Text to Table. You get the Convert Text to Table dialog box, shown
in Figure 21-15.

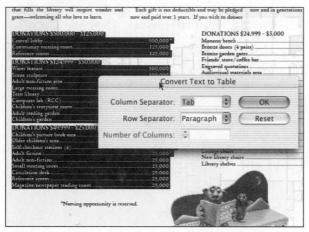

Figure 21-15: The Convert Text to Table dialog box.

In the Convert Text to Table dialog box, you can choose a Column Separator (Tab,
Comma, Paragraph, or a text string you enter in the field) or a Row Separator (same
options). Although most textual data uses tabs to separate columns and paragraphs to separate rows, you may encounter other data that uses something else.
For example, spreadsheets and databases often save data so that commas separate
columns rather than tabs. That's why InDesign lets you choose the separator characters before conversion.

During the conversion, InDesign will format the table using the standard settings,
using the current text formatting and the default cell insets and stroke types. You
can then adjust the table using the tools covered earlier in this chapter. Note that
the conversion will treat all rows as body rows.

You can also convert a table to text by selecting multiple cells or an entire table, as
described earlier, and choosing Table ➪ Convert Table to Text. InDesign presents
the same options as it does in the Convert Text to Table dialog box, so you again
can determine how the converted data appears.

In one way, InDesign is more savvy about text-to-table conversion than QuarkXPress is, since InDesign lets you choose any string as the column or row separator during conversion (just enter that string in the appropriate field). But in another way, InDesign is less savvy: QuarkXPress lets you "pivot" data during conversion, so you can swap columns and rows for a better fit.

Summary

Unlike the typewriter days, creating tabs in a page-layout application provides various options for aligning text with a tab and creating tab leaders. The Tabs pane (Window ➪ Type & Tables ➪ Tabs, or ⌘+Shift+T or Ctrl+Shift+T) provides an interactive ruler for positioning tabs along with all the other controls you need. Your ultimate success with using the Tabs feature depends on how well you prepared the text in the first place—the key is to position one tab correctly rather than entering several tabs to achieve the correct placement.

To create tables in InDesign, you use the Table pane (Window ➪ Type & Tables ➪ Table, or Shift+F9) to create the table outline, format cells, merge and split cells, apply colors and ruling lines, and do other complex table editing. You can also convert tabbed text into a table and vice versa.

✦　　✦　　✦

Graphics Fundamentals

Chapter 22
Preparing Picture
Files for Import

Chapter 23
Importing Pictures

Chapter 24
Modifying Imported
Pictures

Chapter 25
Special Effects for
Pictures

Chapter 26
Drawing Free-Form
Shapes and Curved
Paths

Chapter 27
Modifying Shapes
and Paths

Chapter 28
Treating Text
as Artwork

Although text carries the message, it's a picture that gets your attention and that often can say more than any collection of words. That's why working with pictures — photos, drawings, and other graphics — is so critical in layout. And that's why InDesign works closely with Adobe's image editing and illustration programs, Photoshop and Illustrator. But no matter what programs you use to create your images, you'll find InDesign able to work with all popular formats.

The first step is preparing your pictures for use in InDesign. Chapter 22 explains the do's, don'ts, and gotchas of all the image formats that InDesign can work with, showing you how to optimize the quality of your images and how to prevent font and color flaws when printing.

With your images ready to be used, the next step is actually importing them into InDesign. Chapter 23 explains how to bring pictures into your layout, including how to position them within frames.

Chapter 24 explains in depth how to work with your imported pictures. You'll learn how to change the size, crop, and other attributes of your pictures, as well as how to ensure that your layout uses the latest version of your pictures.

InDesign offers sophisticated controls for using your pictures for fancy layout techniques. For example, you can do curve-hugging text wraps around images and even create outlines from the picture contents that become frames in which to hold text or other elements. Chapter 25 explains these techniques.

But working with pictures involves more than importing them. InDesign also lets you create and edit them. Chapter 26 explains how to use InDesign's built-in drawing tools, while Chapter 27 explains how to edit, modify, and enhance those drawings.

Finally, text itself can be used as artwork, thanks to InDesign's ability to modify text attributes such as strokes and color. Chapter 28 covers a variety of text-as-art techniques.

Preparing Picture Files for Import

✦ ✦ ✦ ✦

In This Chapter

Determining which formatting tasks to do in InDesign and which to handle in other programs

Preparing files for import from graphics programs

Making special considerations for supported graphics formats

Working with files across platforms

Understanding color issues

✦ ✦ ✦ ✦

You can import graphics into your InDesign documents in several ways. InDesign is particularly adept at importing documents created in popular Macintosh and Windows formats. And through the Mac and Windows clipboards (copy and paste), you can import file formats — to a limited degree — that are not directly supported by InDesign.

Determining Where to Format Documents

Because InDesign has some built-in graphics features, as described in Chapters 26 through 28, you may be tempted to use InDesign as your graphics program. Don't. Its tools are fine for some work, such as creating shapes that text wraps around, borders, and gradations of color — but InDesign is not meant to be a professional graphics-creation tool. In fact, it's designed to work closely with such professional tools, especially Adobe's Illustrator and Photoshop.

Particularly for bitmap images such as scanned files and photographs, InDesign has few capabilities to apply special effects or otherwise manipulate the image's content, so you should do as much work as possible in your image editor, before bringing the file into InDesign. For example, you can resize, crop, rotate, and slant an imported image in InDesign, but you can't convert it from a full-color image into a duotone or change its line screen or brightness and contrast.

The bottom line is this: Use your graphics program for creating and editing original images and photos. Use InDesign's graphics features to embellish your layout, rather than create original artwork.

New Feature

InDesign CS lets you easily open a graphics program to edit placed images from within InDesign. Hold Option or Alt and then double-click the image. InDesign will then launch the program that created the graphic; if you don't own that program, InDesign will launch a compatible program if you have one. For example, if you Option+double-click or Alt+double-click an EPS file in your layout that was created in Adobe Illustrator, but you use Macromedia FreeHand instead, InDesign will launch FreeHand on your system.

Preparing Graphics Files

InDesign offers support for many major formats of graphics files. Some formats are more appropriate than others for certain kinds of tasks. The basic rules for creating your graphics files are as follows:

✦ **Save line art in a format such as EPS, PDF, Adobe Illustrator, Windows Metafile (WMF), Enhanced Metafile (EMF), or PICT.** (These object-oriented formats are called *vector* formats. Vector files are composed of instructions on how to draw various shapes.) InDesign works best with EPS, PDF, and Illustrator files.

✦ **Save bitmaps (photos and scans) in a format such as TIFF, Adobe Photoshop, PNG, JPEG, PCX, Windows Bitmap (BMP), GIF, Scitex Continuous Tone (SCT), or PICT.** (These pixel-oriented formats are called *raster* formats. Raster files are composed of a series of dots, or pixels, that make up the image.) InDesign works best with TIFF and Photoshop files.

Note

PICT files can be in vector or bitmap format depending on the original image and the program in which it was created or exported from. If you enlarge a PICT image and it begins to look blocky, it's a bitmap. Similarly, EPS and PDF files can contain bitmap images as well as vector ones.

Tip

If you output to high-end PostScript systems, make EPS and TIFF formats your standards, since these have become the standard graphics formats in publishing. If you're working almost exclusively with Adobe software, you can add the PDF, Illustrator, and Photoshop formats to this mix. (The Illustrator and PDF formats are variants of EPS.)

Graphics embedded in text files

Modern word processors typically support in-line graphics, letting you import a picture into your word-processor document and embed it in text. Word, for example, lets you import graphics, and InDesign, in turn, can import the graphics with your text. But graphics embedded in your word-processor document via Mac OS 8 and 9's Publish and Subscribe or via Windows's OLE will not import into InDesign.

In-line graphics will import as their preview images, not as the original formats. This means that in most cases, you'll get a *much* lower resolution version in your InDesign layout.

Tip   Despite their limitations, the use of in-line graphics in your word processor can be helpful when putting together an InDesign document: Use the in-line graphics whose previews are imported into InDesign as placeholders so that the layout artist knows you have embedded graphics. The artist can then replace the previews with the better-quality originals. If you find yourself using several graphics as characters (such as a company icon used as a bullet), use a font-creation program like Pyrus's FontLab or Macromedia's Fontographer to create a symbol typeface with those graphics. Then both your word processor and layout documents can use the same high-quality versions.

InDesign imports many file formats. If your graphics program's format is not one of the ones listed here, chances are it can save as or export to one. In the following list, the code in italics is the filename extension common for these files on PCs.

The file formats InDesign imports include

✦ **BMP:** The native Windows bitmap format. *.BMP, .DIB*

✦ **EPS:** The Encapsulated PostScript vector format favored by professional publishers. A variant is called DCS, a color-separated variant whose full name is Document Color Separation. *.EPS, .DCS*

✦ **GIF:** The Graphics Interchange Format common in Web documents. *.GIF*

✦ **JPEG:** The Joint Photographers Expert Group compressed bitmap format often used on the Web. *.JPG*

✦ **Illustrator:** The native format in Adobe Illustrator 5.5 through 10.0, is similar to EPS. *.AI*

✦ **PCX:** The PC Paintbrush format that was very popular in DOS programs and early version of Windows; it has now been largely supplanted by other formats. *.PCX, .RLE*

✦ **PDF:** The Portable Document Format that is a variant of EPS and is used for Web-, network-, and CD-based documents. *.PDF*

✦ **Photoshop:** The native format in Adobe Photoshop 5.0 through 7.0. *.PSD*

New Feature   Spot colors (called spot inks in Photoshop) are now imported into InDesign CS when you place Photoshop images into InDesign. They'll appear in the Swatches pane.

✦ **PICT:** Short for *Picture,* the Mac's native graphics format until Mac OS X (it can be bitmap or vector) that is little used in professional documents and is becoming less common even for inexpensive clip art. *.PCT*

✦ **PNG:** The Portable Network Graphics format that Adobe introduced several years ago as a more capable alternative to GIF. *.PNG*

✦ **QuickTime movie:** For use in interactive documents, InDesign supports this Apple-created, cross-platform format. *.MOV*

✦ **Scitex CT:** The continuous-tone bitmap format used on Scitex prepress systems. *.CT*

✦ **TIFF:** The Tagged Image File Format that is the bitmap standard for professional image editors and publishers. *.TIF*

✦ **Windows Metafile:** The format native to Windows but little used in professional documents. Since Office 2000, Microsoft applications create a new version called Enhanced Metafile. *.WMF, .EMF*

When importing any image, make sure Import Options is checked in the Place dialog box (File ⇨ Place, or ⌘+D or Ctrl+D). Even if you're happy with the default import options, it's good to see what the import options are so when a nondefault option does make sense, you're aware you have access to it.

InDesign does not support a few somewhat popular formats: AutoCAD Document Exchange Format (DXF), Computer Graphics Metafile (CGM), CorelDraw, and Eastman Kodak's Photo CD. DXF and CGM are vector formats used mainly in engineering and architecture, while CorelDraw is the native format of the leading consumer-oriented Windows illustration program, and Photo CD is a bitmap format meant for electronically distributed photographs.

Issues with vector files

Vector images are complex, since they can combine multiple elements — curves, lines, colors, fonts, bitmap images, and even other imported vector images. This means that you can unknowingly create a file that will cause problems when you try to output an InDesign layout file using it. Thus, when dealing with vector formats, there are several issues to keep in mind.

Embedded fonts

When you use fonts in text included in your graphics files, you usually have the option to convert the text to curves (graphics). This option ensures that your text will print on any printer.

If you don't use this conversion, make sure that your printer or service bureau has the fonts used in the graphic. Otherwise, the text does not print in the correct font (you will likely get Courier or Helvetica instead).

If your graphic has a lot of text, don't convert the text to curves — the image could get very complex and slow down printing. In this case, make sure that the output device has the same fonts as in the graphic.

PostScript files: EPS, DCS, Illustrator, and PDF

PostScript-based files come in several varieties — EPS, DCS, Illustrator, and PDF — and because the format is a complex one, there are more issues to be aware of up front.

EPS

The usual hang-up with EPS (Encapsulated PostScript) files is the preview header. The preview is a displayable copy of the EPS file. Because EPS files are actually made up of a series of commands that tell the printer how to draw the image, what you see on screen is not the actual graphic. Most programs create a preview image for EPS files, but many programs have trouble reading them, especially if the EPS file was generated on a different platform. In those cases, they display an X or a gray box in place of the image (the EPS file will print properly in such cases to a PostScript printer). That's why InDesign creates its own preview image when you import EPS files, lessening the chances of your seeing just an X or a gray box in place of the EPS preview.

When importing EPS files, InDesign lets you control some settings if you check Import Options in the Place dialog box. You can apply Photoshop clipping paths in the file, choose the preview format, convert the PostScript vector information into a bitmap (a process called *rasterization*), or embed links to OPI high-resolution source images (see Chapter 31 for details on OPI). Figure 22-1 shows the EPS Import Options dialog box.

Tip   In CorelDraw 6.0 and later, and in Adobe Illustrator 6.0 and later, be sure to set the EPS creation options to have no preview header — this keeps your files smaller. (In CorelDraw, export to EPS. In Illustrator 6.0 and later, save as Illustrator EPS. Note that Illustrator 5.x's native format is EPS, so don't look for an export or save-as option.)

DCS

The Document Color Separation (DCS) variant of EPS is a set of five files: an EPS preview file that links together four separation files (one each for cyan, magenta, yellow, and black). Use of this format ensures correct color separation when you output negatives for use in commercial printing. These files are often preferred over standard EPS files by service bureaus that do color correction. One variation of the DCS file format, DCS 2.0, also supports spot color plates in addition to the standard plates for cyan, magenta, yellow, and black.

Note   You should not use DCS files if you intend to create composite proof files or in-RIP separations from InDesign — InDesign will ignore the DCS separation files and just use the preview file for output. Only use DCS files if you're outputting separations (but not in-RIP separations). Chapter 31 covers this in detail.

Illustrator

Adobe Illustrator files are very similar to EPS, except they don't have a preview header. There are no special concerns to Illustrator files; just be sure to note the font and color issues noted previously in this section.

Figure 22-1: The EPS Import Options dialog box.

PDF

InDesign imports PDF files similar to how it imports EPS and other graphics files (File ➪ Place, or ⌘+D or Ctrl+D). To select a specific page for import, select the Import Options check box in the Place dialog box; you'll then get a new dialog box called Place PDF that lets you select which page to import, as Figure 22-2 shows. It also lets you determine how the file is cropped and whether InDesign places it on a transparent background (as opposed to the paper color).

When you import a PDF file, InDesign treats it as a graphic, placing just one user-selected page of the PDF file (if it has more than one page) into your document as an uneditable graphic. You can crop, resize, and do other such manipulations common to any graphic, but you can't work with the text or other imported PDF file's components.

Note   Special PDF features, like sounds, movies, hyperlinks, control buttons, and annotations, are ignored in the imported file.

Figure 22-2: The Place PDF dialog box.

Other vector formats

If you're outputting to negatives for professional printing, you should avoid non-PostScript vector formats. But they're fine for printing to inkjet and laser printers.

PICT

The standard Macintosh format for drawings, PICT (which stands for *Picture*) also supports bitmaps and is the standard format for Mac OS 8 and 9 screen-capture utilities. InDesign imports PICT files with no difficulty, but it cannot color-separate them for output to negatives. Because fonts in vector PICT graphics are automatically translated to curves, you need not worry about whether fonts used in your graphics are resident in your printer or available at your service bureau.

Windows Metafile

The standard Windows format for drawing, Windows Metafile is similar to PICT in that it can contain bitmap images as well as vector drawings. But InDesign will ignore any bitmap information in Windows Metafiles, stripping it out during import. Microsoft Office 2000 introduced a new version of this format, called Enhanced Metafile, which InDesign also supports.

Issues with bitmap formats

Bitmap (also called *raster*) formats are simpler than vector formats because they're made up of rows of dots *(pixels)*, not instructions on how to draw various shapes. But that doesn't mean that all bitmaps are alike.

Professional-level bitmap formats

Although InDesign supports a wide variety of bitmap formats, there is usually just one to worry about if you're producing professional documents for output on a printing press: TIFF. (You may also use the Scitex CT format if you're using Scitex output equipment to produce your negatives.) I suggest you convert other formats to TIFF, using your image editor (Corel Photo-Paint and Adobe Photoshop, the two top image editors, import and export most formats, as do other modern image editing programs) or a conversion program like the Mac shareware program GraphicConverter, Equilibrium's Debabelizer for Macintosh, or DataViz's Conversions Plus (for Windows) and MacLinkPlus (for Macintosh).

 For links to graphics conversion tools, go to this book's companion Web site, www.INDDcentral.com.

Photoshop

InDesign can import version 4.0 and later of this popular image editor's file format. When you place Photoshop files in InDesign, you can control how the alpha channel is imported — be sure to select Import Options in the Place dialog box to get this control. You also can apply any embedded clipping paths and import — or exclude — any embedded color profile.

Scitex CT

The continuous-tone Scitex CT format is used with Scitex output high-resolution devices, and is usually produced by Scitex scanners. If you're using this format, you should be outputting to a Scitex system. Otherwise, you're not going to get the advantage of its high resolution.

TIFF

The most popular bitmap format for publishers is TIFF, the *Tagged Image File Format* developed by Aldus (later bought by Adobe Systems) and Microsoft. TIFF supports color up to 24 bits (16.7 million colors) in both RGB and CMYK models, and every major photo-editing program supports TIFF on both the Macintosh and in Windows. TIFF also supports gray-scale and black-and-white files.

The biggest advantage to using TIFF files rather than other formats that also support color, such as PICT, is that InDesign is designed to take advantage of TIFF. For example, in an image editor, you can set clipping paths in a TIFF file, which act as a mask for the image. InDesign sees that path and uses it as the image boundary, making the area outside of it invisible. That in turn lets you have nonrectangular bitmap images in your layout — the clipping path becomes the visible boundary for your TIFF image. InDesign also supports embedded alpha channels and color profiles in TIFF files. Figure 22-3 shows the two Image Import Options panes — Image and Color — that apply to TIFF images, as well as to Photoshop and other formats.

Note While InDesign offers similar support for Adobe's own Photoshop program, the dominant professional image editor, I recommend sticking with a truly universal format such as TIFF.

The TIFF format has several variations, which InDesign supports. But because other programs aren't as forgiving, follow these guidelines to ensure smooth interaction with others:

✦ You should have no difficulty if you use the uncompressed and LZW-compressed TIFF formats supported by most Mac programs (and increasingly by most Windows programs). InDesign even supports the less-used Zip compression method for TIFF files. You should be safe using LZW-compressed TIFF files with any mainstream program, but if you do have difficulty, I recommend that you use uncompressed TIFF files.

✦ Use the byte order for the platform that the TIFF file is destined for. Macs and PCs use the opposite byte order — basically, the Mac reads the eight characters that comprise a byte in one direction and the PC reads it in another. Although InDesign reads both byte orders, other programs may not, so why invite confusion? Of course, if only InDesign and Photoshop users will work on your TIFF files, the byte order doesn't matter.

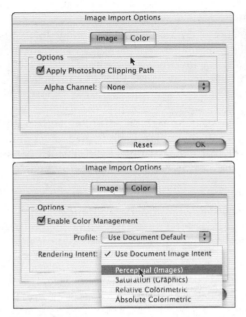

Figure 22-3: The two panes for TIFF, Photoshop, and most other bitmap images in the Image Import Options dialog box.

Web-oriented bitmap formats

In recent years, several formats have been developed for use on the Web, in the Hypertext Markup Language (HTML) documents found there. These formats — GIF, JPEG, and PNG — achieve small size (for faster downloading and display on your browser) by limiting image and color detail and richness.

Although you can use any supported graphics format for documents you expect to export to the Web's HTML format (InDesign will convert all images to GIF or JPEG when you export to HTML), if you know your document is bound for the Web, you might as well use a Web graphics format from the start.

Note   Because InDesign CS has dropped support for HTML export, there's little reason to use Web-oriented graphics in your InDesign files. If you're using InDesign to create PDF files for access via the Web, or if you're using InDesign to create XML files that will be presented on the Web, you might want to use these Web-oriented formats since they are more compact. Otherwise, stick with the print-oriented ones to get their better image quality.

GIF

The Graphics Interchange Format (GIF) is the oldest Web format. To help keep file size down, it is limited to 256 colors, reducing file size but also making it unsuitable for photographs and graphics with color blends. But its compression approach doesn't lose any image detail, so it works well for sketches, cartoons, and other simple images with sharp details.

JPEG

The Joint Photographers Expert Group (JPEG) compressed color-image format is used for very large images and the individual images comprising an animation or movie. Images compressed in this format may lose detail, which is why TIFF is preferred by publishers. But JPEG can be used effectively even on documents output to a printing press, since you can set the level of loss to none during export.

Still, JPEG is more useful on the Web, where the limited resolution of a computer monitor makes most of JPEG's detail loss hard to spot — giving you an acceptable trade-off of slightly blurry quality in return for a much smaller file size. It's particularly well-suited for photographs, since the lost detail is usually not noticeable because of all the other detail surrounding it.

If you do use JPEG for print work, note that you can provide a clipping path for it in programs like Photoshop. The clipping path lets the image have an irregular boundary (rendering the rest of its background transparent) so you can use InDesign effects such as text wrap.

PNG

A relatively new format, the Portable Network Graphics (PNG) format is meant to provide GIF's no-loss compression but support 24-bit color so it can be used for photography and subtly colored illustrations on the Web.

When importing PNG files, you can choose whether to retain the background color defined in the file or to substitute white — just be sure that Show Import Options is checked in the Place dialog box so that choice is presented. Similarly, you can also adjust the gamma value during import — the gamma is a setting that describes the color range of a device, and to ensure most accurate reproduction, you'd want the gamma setting for the PNG file to be the same as that of your output device (a printer or monitor). Figure 22-4 shows the PNG Settings pane in the Image Import Options dialog box.

Figure 22-4: The PNG Settings pane of the Image Import Options dialog box.

Working with files across platforms

It's increasingly common for people in publishing to work in a cross-platform (Mac and Windows) environment. Even if you do all your InDesign work on one platform, chances are good that you'll receive files created on the other platform. (Most text editing is done on PCs, while most graphics and publishing work is done on the Mac, for example.)

Even with the improved compatibility between Mac and PC (mostly thanks to additions to the Mac OS, which makes it easier to share files with PCs), there are still some trip-ups that you may encounter dealing with something as simple as filenames when sharing files across platforms.

Both Windows and the Mac use icons to show you (and tell programs) what format a file is in. Before Mac OS X, how those icons are created differ between the two platforms, and when you moved files from one platform to another, you could easily lose those icons. But Mac OS X, like Windows and Unix, relies on filename extensions – three or four letters after a period at the end of the filename – to identify the file type and thus display the correct icon. The default on both Windows and Mac OS X is to hide those filename extensions from display.

To see filename extensions in Windows, open any folder, choose Tools ➪ Folder Options, and then select the View tab to get the pane shown in the following figure. (You have to have a disk or folder open to have the View menu.) Uncheck the Hide Extensions for Known File Types option, then click OK. In Mac OS X, there's a similar control accessed from the Finder. Choose Finder ➪ Preferences, then check the Always Show File Extensions check box and close the dialog box.

Note that even though most OS X–native programs such as InDesign automatically add filename extensions when you save, older programs – especially those running in Classic Mode usually do not automatically add a filename extension. Be sure to add these extensions manually or configure the program to do so for you automatically if it has that option (Microsoft Office 2001 applications do, for example, in their Save dialog boxes).

Other bitmap formats

The other supported formats are ones that you should avoid, unless you're printing to inkjet or laser printers. If you have images in one of these formats and want to use it for professionally output documents, convert them to TIFF before using them in InDesign.

BMP

Like TIFF, the BMP Windows bitmap format supports color, gray-scale, and black-and-white images.

PCX

Like TIFF, PCX supports color, gray-scale, and black-and-white images.

PICT

PICT, the old standard Macintosh format for drawings, also supports bitmaps and is the standard format for Macintosh screen-capture utilities. InDesign imports PICT files with no difficulty.

Identifying Color Issues

It used to be that importing color from graphics files into publishing programs was an iffy proposition — colors would often not print properly even though they appeared correct on-screen. Those nightmares are largely a thing of the past, as modern page-layout software like InDesign can accurately detect color definitions in your source graphics, and modern illustration and image-editing programs are better at making that information accessible to programs like InDesign. So just note the following advice to ensure smooth color import.

If you create color images in an illustration or image-editing program, make sure that you create them using the CMYK color model or using a named spot color. If you use CMYK, the color is, in effect, pre-separated. With InDesign, any spot colors defined in an EPS file are automatically added to the Swatches pane for your document and set as a spot color.

Cross-Reference   See Chapter 8 for more on creating and editing colors.

If your program follows Adobe's EPS specifications (Adobe Illustrator, CorelDraw, and Macromedia FreeHand all do), InDesign will color-separate your EPS file, no matter whether it uses process or spot colors. Canvas automatically converts Pantone spot colors to process colors in your choice of RGB and CMYK models. For other programs, create your colors in the CMYK model to be sure they will print as color separations from InDesign.

Color systems

There are several color systems, or models, in use, and InDesign supports the common ones, including CMYK (process), RGB, Pantone, Focoltone, Dainippon Ink & Chemical (DIC), Toyo, Trumatch, and Web. A color system defines either a set of individual colors that have specially mixed inks (shown on swatchbooks, which have small samples of each color) or a range of colors that can be created by combining a limited number of inks (such as RGB—for red, green, and blue—and CMYK—for cyan, magenta, yellow, and black).

Chapter 8 describes the various color models, but for file import, it's best to use just three—CMYK (process), RGB, and the Pantone Matching System—since they're universally used and tend to be the most reliable when passing information from one system to another.

Note The advice on color systems applies to just vector images, since bitmap programs use CMYK or RGB as their actual color models, even if they offer swatchbooks of other models' colors.

Tip Most layout artists use Pantone to specify desired colors, so keep a Pantone swatchbook handy to see which CMYK values equal the desired Pantone color. (One of the available Pantone swatchbooks—*The Pantone Process Color Imaging Guide CMYK Edition*—shows each Pantone color next to the CMYK color build used to simulate it.) This book's companion Web site (www.INDDcentral.com) provides links to Pantone and other color swatchbooks.

Of course, you can simply pick a Pantone color from the electronic swatchbook in InDesign, and InDesign will convert it to CMYK if you specify it to be a process color (the default setting). Many high-end illustration programs, including Adobe Illustrator, support Pantone and can do this instant conversion as well. If available (as it is in InDesign), use the Pantone Process Coated color model because that is designed for output using CMYK printing presses. But remember: What you see on-screen won't match what you get on paper, so it's a good idea to have the printed Pantone swatchbook.

Calibrated color

With InDesign's Color Management System (CMS) feature enabled, the program will calibrate the output colors (whether printed to a color printer or color-separated for traditional printing) based on the source device and the target output device in an attempt to ensure that what you see on-screen comes close to what you'll see on the printed page. Although color calibration is a tricky science that rarely results in exact color latches across all input and output devices, it can help minimize differences as the image travels along the creation and production path.

Today, most image editing programs let you apply color profiles that conform with the International Color Committee (ICC) standards. If you're using color calibration, it's best to apply these ICC profiles in the images when you create them.

If you can't — or forget to — apply an ICC profile when creating your image, don't worry. You can add a profile (if you're creating images in a program that doesn't support ICC profiles) or apply a different one from InDesign.

 Cross-Reference   Chapter 29 covers color calibration in depth.

Summary

If you work with publishing-oriented graphics formats — EPS, PDF, Illustrator, TIFF, and Photoshop — created by mainstay programs like Adobe Photoshop, Adobe Illustrator, CorelDraw, Corel Photo-Paint, and Macromedia FreeHand, you'll likely have no difficulties importing graphics into or printing graphics from InDesign. But be sure to stick with common color models, particularly CMYK and Pantone.

And it's best to do any special effects in your graphics program — InDesign has limited abilities to manipulate graphics beyond layout-oriented functions like resizing, cropping, flipping, slanting, and text wrap. To ease access to your graphics programs, InDesign CS now lets you open them from within InDesign.

✦   ✦   ✦

Importing Pictures

In This Chapter

Using the Place command to import pictures

Specifying import options for various graphics formats

Figuring out other ways of importing pictures

Although InDesign's shape-creation tools, type-formatting options, and object-manipulation features provide great flexibility when it comes to designing pages, you're probably going to want to use other graphic elements — particularly scanned images and computer-generated illustrations — in your publications. InDesign lets you import graphics files in a variety of formats (see Chapter 22 for details about supported graphics file formats), and once you've imported a graphic, you have several options for modifying its appearance (see Chapter 24 for information about modifying imported pictures).

Note   The terms *graphic* and *picture* are interchangeable, referring to any type of graphic. An *image* is a bitmap graphic, such as that produced by an image editor or a scanner, while an *illustration* or *drawing* is a vector file produced by an Illustration program.

It's important to understand that when you import a picture into a document, InDesign establishes a link between the graphics file and the document file and then sends the original graphics file to the printer when the document is output. (There is one exception to this scenario — when you copy and paste a graphic into an InDesign document — that's explained later in this chapter.) InDesign links to graphics because a graphics file, particularly a high-resolution scanned picture, can be very large. If the entire graphics file were included in an InDesign document when you imported it, InDesign documents would quickly become prohibitively large. Instead, InDesign saves a low-resolution preview of an imported graphics file with the document, and it's this file that you see displayed on screen. InDesign remembers the location of the original file and uses this information when printing.

Note   If you place a graphic that's 48K or smaller, InDesign automatically embeds the full-resolution image rather than a low-resolution preview. See Chapter 24 for more information about embedding graphics and about managing links to graphics files.

When it's time to import a picture, you're responsible for knowing where the file is — whether it's stored on a floppy desk that your friend gave you, on your hard disk, on a networked file server, or on a local or networked CD-ROM.

Note   If you import a graphics file that's stored on any kind of removable media, such as a floppy disk, Zip disk, or CD, the link between the document and the graphics file will be broken when the media is removed. Generally, it's best to copy graphics files to your hard disk or to a networked file server before importing them into an InDesign document.

Using the Place Command

Although there are several ways to add a graphics file to an InDesign document (all of which are explained in this chapter), the Place command (File ➪ Place, or ⌘+D or Ctrl+D) is the method you should use most often. When you use the Place command, InDesign offers import options for various graphics file formats that are not available if you use other import methods.

Here's how to use the Place command to import a picture:

1. **If you want to import a picture into an existing frame, select the frame using either of the selection tools, then choose File ➪ Place or press ⌘+D or Ctrl+D.**

   The Place dialog box, shown in Figure 23-1, is displayed. If you want InDesign to create a new frame when you import the picture, make sure no object is selected when you choose Place.

Figure 23-1: The Place dialog box.

Note You can import a picture into any kind of frame or shape (including a curved line created with the Pen tool) except a straight line. Be careful: If the Type tool is selected when you use the Place command to import a picture into a selected text frame, you'll create an inline graphic at the text cursor's location (see Chapter 12 for information about creating inline graphics).

2. **Use the controls in the Place dialog box to locate and select the graphics file you want to import.**

3. **If you want to display import options that let you control how the selected graphics file is imported, either select Show Import Options, then click Choose or Open; or hold down the Shift key and double-click on the filename or Shift+click Choose or Open.**

If you choose to Show Import Options, the EPS Import Options, Place PDF, or Image Import Options dialog box, depending on what kind of picture you are importing, is displayed.

4. **Specify the desired import options, if any are applicable, then click OK.**

These options are covered later in this chapter.

5. **You can place the picture in an existing frame or in a new frame, as follows:**

   • If an empty frame is selected, the graphic is automatically placed in the frame. The upper-left corner of the picture is placed in the upper-left corner of the frame, and the frame acts as the cropping shape for the picture.

   • If a frame already holding a graphic is selected, InDesign will replace the existing graphic with the new one if you've checked Replace Selected Item in the Place dialog box. Otherwise, InDesign will assume you want to put the new graphic in a new frame.

   • To place the graphic into a new frame, click the loaded-graphic icon (shown in Figure 23-2) on an empty portion of a page or on the pasteboard. The point where you click establishes the upper-left corner of the resulting graphics frame, which is the same size as the imported picture and which acts as the picture's cropping shape.

   • To place the graphic in an existing, unselected frame, click in the frame with the loaded-graphic icon. The upper-left corner of the picture is placed in the upper-left corner of the frame, and the frame acts as a cropping shape.

 Figure 23-2: The loaded-graphic icon.

After you place a picture, it's displayed in the frame that contains it, and the frame is selected. If the Selection tool is selected, the eight handles of its bounding box are displayed; if the Direct Selection tool is selected, handles are displayed only in the corners. At this point, you can modify either the frame or the picture within, or you can move on to another task.

Tip

If you can store all your graphics files in a single location — not necessarily in a single folder, but perhaps within a folder hierarchy on your hard disk or a file server — you can minimize link problems. If you move, rename, or delete the original file after importing a graphic, you'll break the link, which will cause printing problems. Keeping all graphics files in a single, safe place — a place that's backed up regularly — is a good idea.

Specifying Import Options

If you've ever used a graphics application — for example, an image-editing program like Adobe Photoshop or an illustration program like Adobe Illustrator or Macromedia FreeHand — you're probably aware that when you save a graphics file, you have several options that control such things as file format, image size, color depth, preview quality, and so on. When you save a graphics file, the settings you specify are determined by the way in which the image will be used. For example, you could use Photoshop to save a high-resolution TIFF version of a scanned picture for use in a slick, four-color annual report or a low-resolution GIF version of the same picture for use on the company's Web page. Or you could use Illustrator or FreeHand to create a corporate logo that you'll use in various sizes in many of your printed publications.

If you choose to specify custom import settings when you import a graphics file, the choices you make will depend on the nature of the publication. For example, if it's bound for the Web, there's no need to work with or save pictures using resolutions that exceed a computer monitor's 72-dpi resolution. Along the same lines, if the publication will be printed, the image import settings you specify for a newspaper that will be printed on newsprint on a SWOP (standard web-offset printing) press will be different than those you specify for a four-color magazine printed on coated paper using a sheet-fed press.

If you choose Show Import Options when you place a picture, the options displayed in the resulting dialog boxes depend on the file format of the selected graphic. When you set options for a particular file, the options you specify remain in effect for that file format until you change them. If you don't choose Show Import Options when you place a picture, the most recent settings for the file format of the selected graphic are used.

Import options for bitmap pictures

InDesign gives you two sets of import options for the following types of bitmap images: TIFF, Photoshop, GIF, JPEG, Scitex CT, BMP, and PCX. You get three options for PNG files. There are no import options for PICT or QuickTime movie files. Figure 23-3 shows the three possible panes for bitmap images.

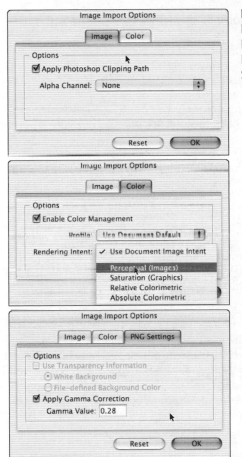

Figure 23-3: InDesign provides the Image and Color panes in the Image Import Options for most bitmap formats; PNG files have a third pane, PNG Settings.

Image pane

This pane lets you apply any embedded Photoshop clipping path and/or alpha channel to the image, for use to mask, or cut out, part of the image. Check the

Apply Photoshop Clipping Path option to import the clipping path along with the image; select an alpha channel from the Alpha Channel pop-up menu to import the alpha channel along with the image.

Chapter 25 covers clipping paths in more detail.

Color pane

In the Color pane, you can turn on color management for the image and control how the image is displayed.

Check the Enable Color Management option to enable color management. Using the Profile pop-up menu, choose a color-source profile that matches the color *gamut* (range) of the device (scanner, digital camera, and so on) or software used to create the file. InDesign will try to translate the colors in the file to the colors that the output device is capable of producing. (These profiles are installed in your operating system by other applications, not InDesign.)

See Chapter 29 for more information about using InDesign's color-management features.

Use the Rendering Intent pop-up menu to determine how InDesign translates the color in the selected graphics file with the gamut of the output device. If the picture is a scanned photograph, choose Perceptual (Images). The other options — Saturation (Graphics), Relative Colorimetric, and Absolute Colorimetric — are appropriate for images that contain mostly areas of solid color, such as Illustrator EPS files that have been opened in Photoshop and saved as TIFFs.

PNG Settings pane

Use this pane — available only if you place a PNG file — to use the transparency information in a PNG file, assuming it has a transparent background. You have two choices for controlling transparency handling: White Background and File-Defined Background. The former forces the transparent portion to display as white in InDesign; the latter uses whatever background color is specified in the PNG file itself.

This pane also lets you adjust the gamma value during import — the gamma is a setting that describes the color range of a device, and to ensure most accurate reproduction, you'd want the gamma setting for the PNG file to be the same as that of your output device (a printer or monitor). It is meant to correct for the file being created on a specific type of monitor. The reason is that Mac monitors tend to display colors more bluishly than Windows monitors, so colors created on each platform that look the same on-screen will differ slightly in print. However, to use this feature, you need to know the gamma setting for the final output device. Otherwise, leave it alone.

Import options for vector file formats

If you're importing vector files, the Import Options check box will result in one of
several dialog boxes appearing, depending on what the vector file type is. If you
import Illustrator or EPS files, you'll get the EPS Import Options dialog box; if you
import PDF files, you'll get the Place PDF dialog box. (Both are shown in Figure 23-4.)
There are no import options for Windows Metafile pictures.

Figure 23-4: The EPS Import Options and Place PDF dialog boxes.

EPS Import Options dialog box

If you use an Open Prepress Interface-based proxy workflow — that is, if an OPI-
based service provider supplies you with low-resolution versions of graphics files
that will eventually be replaced by high-resolution files during output — check
Read Embedded OPI Image Links if you want InDesign rather than your service
provider to perform image replacement during output. You should also check this
box if you import graphics files that contain OPI comments for other imported
graphics files; for example, an EPS file that contains OPI information for an embedded TIFF picture. Don't check this box if you don't use an OPI-based workflow or if
you want your service provider to handle image replacement during output. When
Read Embedded OPI Image Links is not checked, InDesign retains OPI comments
but doesn't use them. When you print (or export) the document, the proxy image
and the link information is sent.

Also use this pane to import any Photoshop clipping paths embedded in images
that are in the EPS file. Check the Apply Photoshop Clipping Path option to
enable this.

Finally, use this pane to control how the EPS file appears on-screen in InDesign. If you select Use TIFF or PICT Preview, InDesign will use the low-resolution proxy image embedded in the EPS file for display on-screen and print the picture using the embedded high-resolution PostScript instructions. If you select Rasterize the PostScript, InDesign will convert the PostScript file into a bitmap image during import. There's rarely a reason to rasterize an imported EPS file.

Place PDF dialog box

When you use the Place command to import a PDF file and you choose to Show Options, the Place PDF file dialog box, shown in Figure 23-4, is displayed. It provides several controls for specifying how the file is imported:

✦ Use the controls below the preview image to select the page you want to place (you can place only one page at a time). You can enter a page number in the field or use the arrows to scroll to page.

✦ Select one of the cropping options from the Crop To pop-up menu. If you choose Content, the page's bounding box or a rectangle that encloses all items, including page marks, is used to build the graphics frame. Choosing Art places the area defined by the file's creator, if any, as placeable artwork. For example, the person who created the file might have designated a particular graphic as placeable artwork. Choosing Crop places the area displayed and printed by Adobe Acrobat. Choosing Trim places the picture in an area equal to the final, trimmed piece. Choosing Bleed places the page area plus any specified bleed area. Choosing Media places an area defined by the paper size specified for the PDF document, including page marks.

✦ Click Transparent Background if you want the white areas of the PDF page to be transparent. Uncheck this option if you want to preserve the page's opaque white background.

Note   Some PDF files are protected with passwords or have printing, text editing, and other content-access functions disabled. If a PDF file is password-protected, you'll be prompted to enter the required password; do so and click OK. Note that some PDF files have a second password, called a Permissions Password, that you'll also need to open it.

If the selected file was saved with any security restrictions (no text editing, no printing, and so on), you can't place any pages of the file into InDesign. Ask the person who produced the file for an unrestricted copy.

Knowing Other Ways to Import Pictures

If you want to specify custom import options for an imported graphics file, you must use the Place command. However, if you don't need this level of control, InDesign offers three other options for importing pictures:

✦ You can also use your computer's Copy (File ➪ Copy, or ⌘+C or Ctrl+C) and Paste (File ➪ Paste, or ⌘+V or Ctrl+V) commands to move a graphics file between two InDesign documents or from a document created with another program into an InDesign document.

✦ You can drag and drop graphics file icons from your computer's desktop into InDesign documents.

✦ For Illustrator files, you can drag objects directly from Illustrator into InDesign.

If you use these methods to add a graphic to an InDesign document, some of the attributes of the original graphic may not survive the trip. The operating system, the file format, and the capabilities of the originating application all play roles in determining which attributes are preserved. If you want to be safe, use the Place command.

Copy and Paste

If you copy an object in an InDesign document and then paste it into a different InDesign document, the copy retains all the attributes of the original. In the case of a copied and pasted picture, all import settings, frame modifications, and picture modifications are retained, as is the link to the original graphics file.

When you copy and paste a graphic into an InDesign document, a link between the original graphics file and the InDesign document is *not* established. The graphic becomes part of the InDesign document, as though you created it using InDesign tools.

The Links pane (File ➪ Links, or Shift+⌘+D or Ctrl+Shift+D) helps you manage the links that are established between an InDesign document and a graphics file when you use the Place command. See Chapter 24 for more about managing links to graphics files.

Drag and Drop

When an InDesign document is open, you can import a graphics file in any supported file format by dragging the file's icon into the window of the InDesign document. When you drag and drop a graphics file into a document, a link between the original graphics file and the document is established, just as it would be if you had used the Place command.

Adobe Illustrator files

If you drag and drop an Illustrator file icon into an InDesign document window, the graphic behaves the same as it would if you had used the Place command. That is, individual elements within the graphic are not selectable or modifiable within InDesign. However, if you drag and drop Illustrator objects from an Illustrator document window into an InDesign document window, each object becomes a separate, editable InDesign object, as though you had created it in InDesign.

This is a handy way of moving objects that you may want to modify between Illustrator and InDesign. For example, you can create text along a path in an Illustrator document, then drag and drop the object into an InDesign document. Each character is converted into an editable shape, which you can stroke, fill, distort, and so on, using InDesign features. However, you cannot edit text along a path after you've dragged and dropped it into InDesign. (You'd have to go back to Illustrator, edit the original text, then drag and drop it again, then redo all your modifications.)

Using the Copy and Paste commands to add Illustrator objects to InDesign documents is the same as dragging and dropping objects between the programs. The copied objects behave the same as objects created in InDesign when you choose Paste, and no links are established.

New Feature   If you paste or drag and drop Illustrator objects into InDesign, any gradients are now editable in InDesign CS.

Summary

InDesign lets you import pictures in any of several supported graphics file formats. The preferred method for importing pictures is the Place command (File ⇨ Place, or ⌘+D or Ctrl+D) because it lets you customize various import settings that control how an imported picture is displayed and printed.

You can also import pictures into an InDesign document by dragging and dropping graphics file icons into a document window or by copying and pasting objects between InDesign documents or between documents created with other programs and InDesign documents.

If you need to use Illustrator-generated objects or graphics files in your InDesign documents, several options are available: the Place command, the Copy and Paste commands, file drag and drop, and interapplication drag and drop.

✦   ✦   ✦

Modifying Imported Pictures

✦ ✦ ✦ ✦

In This Chapter

Cropping and
scaling pictures

Rotating, scaling,
and skewing pictures
using transformation
tools

Modifying pictures
using the Transform
pane and Control
palette

Modifying vector
graphics versus
bitmap graphics

Applying colors and
tints to black-and-
white bitmaps

Managing links

✦ ✦ ✦ ✦

Getting a picture into your layout is one thing, but adjusting that graphic to make it really work in your layout is quite another. In almost every case, you'll want to manipulate the pictures you bring into your layout — change the size, crop out part of the image, wrap text around the image, and perhaps change the image color or distort its appearance.

The modifications you make will depend on your layout needs and the attributes of the pictures themselves. But no matter what modifications you end up making, you'll find yourself regularly using the techniques covered in this chapter.

Making Basic Picture Modifications

After you import a picture into an InDesign document, you can modify either the picture or the frame that contains it. The following options are available for modifying imported pictures:

✦ You can crop pictures in a rectangular or freeform frame.

✦ You can use tools, the Control palette, or the Transform pane to rotate, scale, and/or shear pictures.

✦ You can flip pictures horizontally and/or vertically via commands in the Control palette's palette menu or in the Transform pane's palette menu.

✦ You can apply color and tint to imported gray-scale and one-bit (black-and-white) bitmap pictures.

Cross-Reference For information about modifying frames, see Chapter 11.

Whether you want to modify a picture after importing it into a document or open the graphic file in its original program and modify it there is up to you.

InDesign lets you crop, rotate, scale, shear, and flip any imported picture regardless of format. Generally, you're safe applying any of these transformations on vector-based formats such as Illustrator-, FreeHand-, and CorelDraw-generated EPS graphics — but not Photoshop EPS files, which are pixel-based images in an EPS shell. Applying these transformations to DCS files is also safe. However, because EPS files are encased (thus, the term *encapsulated*) in a sort of protective shell, you can't select or modify any of the component pieces in InDesign — you must use a dedicated application to make such modifications.

For bitmapped images, such as TIFF, JPEG, GIF, and Photoshop-native files, all the aforementioned transformations except increasing horizontal and/or vertical scale are safe to perform in InDesign. But I recommend doing as much as possible in the original program, to minimize unexpected distortions in your final output. For example, if your imported images are more than twice as large as the size you need them to be in your layout, resize the images in an image editor, then reimport the resized image in InDesign. This speeds printing and prevents moiré patterns that could result when InDesign takes the reduced pixels of the original image and creates new pixels for output — resizing the image in an image editor usually resizes the pixels in a way that outputs well. Similarly, enlarging an image in InDesign can cause a blocky look, while an image editor might let you resize it in a way that preserves image detail.

Cropping pictures

Remember, when you import a picture using the Place command (File ➪ Place, or ⌘+D or Ctrl+D) or by dragging a graphics file into a document window, that the picture is contained in a graphics frame — either the frame that was selected when you placed the picture or the frame that was automatically created if a frame wasn't selected. The upper-left corner of an imported picture is automatically placed in the upper-left corner of its frame.

Resizing a picture's frame

The easiest way to crop a picture is to resize the frame that contains it. If you want to *mask out* (hide) portions of an imported picture, you have the option of using an irregular shape as the frame, a picture's built-in clipping path (if it has one), or a clipping path you generated in InDesign (by choosing Object ➪ Clipping Path or pressing Option+Shift+⌘+K or Ctrl+Alt+Shift+K).

Cross-Reference   Clipping paths are covered in Chapter 25.

To resize the frame, use the Selection tool to drag the frame's handles to reveal the portion of the picture you want to print (and to conceal the portion you don't want to print). Hold the Shift key as you drag to maintain the proportions of the frame.

Moving a picture in its frame

You can also click on a picture with the Direct Selection tool, and then drag the picture in its frame to reveal and conceal different parts of the picture. For example, you could crop the top and left edges of a picture by dragging the picture above and to the left of its original position (in the upper-left corner of the frame).

Of course, you could accomplish the same thing by selecting the frame with the Selection tool and dragging the upper-left corner down and to the right. The advantage of moving the image within the frame is that, when you've positioned the frame in the desired location in your layout, resizing the frame to crop the image then requires you to move the resized frame back to the desired location.

Using an irregular frame

If you want to use an irregular shape as the frame for a picture that's currently cropped by a rectangular frame, here's what you do:

1. **Click on the Direct Selection tool (or press A if the Type tool isn't selected).**

2. **Click on the picture you want to place in a freeform shape (don't click on its frame), then choose Edit ⇨ Copy or press ⌘+C or Ctrl+C.**

3. **Click on the shape (or create one if you haven't already) you want to use as a cropping frame.**

   It can be any kind of object except a straight line.

4. **Choose Edit ⇨ Paste Into or press Shift+⌘+V or Ctrl+Shift+V.**

   Figure 24-1 shows an example.

Figure 24-1: In this example, the coffee cup and saucer picture has been copied and pasted into a freeform frame that reveals only the cup. The shape was created by tracing the contour of the cup using the Pen tool.

For more information about creating and modifying freeform shapes, see Chapters 26 and 27.

Note   If you select a frame with the Direct Selection tool instead of the Selection tool, handles are displayed only at the frame corners rather than at the bounding-box corners and midpoints. When you select a frame with the Direct Selection tool, you can reshape the frame, and thus crop the picture differently, by dragging corner points, adding and deleting points, and so on.

Of course, you could also create the irregular shape first, and then use the Place command to place the graphic file directly into the shape. Using an irregular shape to crop a picture is similar to using a clipping path except that you create the irregular shape yourself using InDesign's object-creation tools while a clipping path is either built into a graphics file or generated by InDesign (via choosing Object ➪ Clipping Path or pressing Option+Shift+⌘+K or Ctrl+Alt+Shift+K).

Rotating, scaling, and shearing pictures

InDesign provides two methods for rotating, scaling, and shearing pictures: You can click and drag a picture using transformation tools, or you can use the Control palette or Transform pane, as explained in the next section, to enter numerical values into fields or to choose a preset value from a pop-up menu.

The method you use is up to you. If you're into the hands-on-mouse approach to object manipulation and page building, you'll probably prefer the click-and-drag method of modifying pictures. Others prefer the pane approach. You'll probably end up using both methods. Regardless of the tool you use, the steps for transforming a picture are pretty much the same:

1. **Click on the Direct Selection tool (or press A if the Type tool isn't selected).**

2. **Click on the picture you want to modify.**

3. **If you want, you can click and drag the object's point of origin (by default it's in the upper-left corner of a graphics frame).**

   All transformations applied to an object are applied relative to the point of origin. For example, when you rotate an item, it rotates around its point of origin.

4. **Click and drag to perform the transformation. Hold down the Shift key to constrain transformation increments to preset values.**

   For example, holding down the Shift key while rotating a picture limits rotation increments to multiples of 45 degrees. If you pause for a moment between clicking and dragging — long enough for the crosshair pointer to change to the arrowhead pointer — the transformed picture is displayed while you drag. If you don't pause, only the picture boundary is displayed while you drag. If the Transform pane is open, the value in the field that's associated with the selected tool changes as you drag.

5. **Release the mouse button when the picture looks the way you want it to look.**

Tip

If you hold down the Option or Alt key while using a transformation tool, the modification will be performed on a clone of the selected object.

Tip

If you double-click on a transformation tool, you'll get a dialog box that lets you select the appropriate settings for that tool.

Each transformation tool has a few idiosyncrasies (Figure 24-2 shows the tool icons):

Figure 24-2: The icons for the Rotation, Scale, Shear, and Free Transform tools in the Tools palette.

Rotation — Scale
Shear — Free Transform

✦ **Rotation tool:** You can select this tool by pressing R if the Type tool isn't selected. Holding down the Shift key while dragging limits rotation increments to multiples of 45 degrees.

✦ **Scale tool:** This tool shares a pop-up menu with the Shear tool. If you hold down the Shift key while dragging with the Scale tool, only the horizontal scale of the selected picture changes if you drag horizontally, only the vertical scale changes if you drag vertically, and the original proportions are maintained if you drag diagonally.

✦ **Shear tool:** This tool applies a combination of rotation and skew to a picture. (The Transform pane includes separate Rotation and Skew controls, but no Shear-specific controls. However, the Control palette has controls for all three.) Holding down the Shift key constrains the selected picture's rotation value to increments of 45 degrees.

✦ **Free Transform Tool:** Advanced users will like the Free Transform tool. When you select this tool, InDesign lets you scale, rotate, and resize — but not shear — selected objects. If you select within the frame, you can move the object by dragging it. If you select a frame handle (whether corner or mid-point), you can resize the object by dragging. Finally, if you move the mouse very close to a frame handle, you will see a curved arrow, which indicates you can rotate the object around that object's center point. Having a tool that does more than one thing can be confusing, but once you get the hang of it, it sure beats constantly changing tools!

Figure 24-3 shows the various dialog boxes that you get when double-clicking the Rotation, Scale, and Shear tools. These provide both numerical control over the operations but also let you choose to copy the transformed item.

Figure 24-3: The Rotation, Scale, and Shear dialog boxes.

Using the Control Palette and the Transform Pane

For more control than you get from the Rotation, Shear, and Scale tools, InDesign offers the Control palette and the Transform pane (Window ⇨ Transform, or F9), both shown in Figure 24-4, to perform several other modifications on a selected picture.

Figure 24-4: The Transform pane (top) and the Control palette for pictures (bottom), as well as their palette menus. Note that the Transform pane offers a subset of the Control palette's functions.

The Transform pane and Control palette have the following tools in common: Scale X Percentage, Scale Y Percentage, Rotation Angle, and Shear X Angle. Plus both let you choose a selection point (such as for rotation or shearing) and lock scaling to be proportional (making, for example, a 70 percent reduction in scale horizontally also reduce the picture 70 percent vertically).

The palette menus are almost identical, with both letting you rotate objects in pre-defined increments (90° clockwise, 90° counterclockwise, and 180°) and flipping objects vertically and/or horizontally. Both also let you control the degree of precision in transformations, as described later. The Control palette's palette menu offers access to the Stroke Styles dialog box (see Chapter 28), while the Transform pane's palette menu lets you select whether scaling a text frame also scales the text within it, plus whether just the currently selected object or the entire group it belongs to is affected by the transformation.

The Control palette offers several additional controls: specifying the stroke width and type, selecting the object or contents (the same as using the Selection tool or the Direction tool, respectively), fitting the content to the frame or fitting the frame to the content, centering the content, and selecting the previous or next object in a group.

Tip

If you hold down the Option or Alt key when you press Return or Enter to apply a value you've entered into a field in the Control palette or Transform pane, the modification is applied to a clone of the selected object.

Cross-Reference

Chapter 11 covers the Control palette's selection options, such as Next Object in Group. Chapter 12 covers group creation and modification.

Changing an object's point of origin

The nine small, white squares at the top-left corner of the Transform pane and far left of the Control palette let you specify the point of origin for the selected object. An object's point of origin is used to determine the values in the X Location (horizontal distance from left edge of page) and Y Location (vertical distance from top of page) fields. When you apply a transformation, it's applied to the selected object relative to the fixed point of origin. By default, the point of origin of a graphics frame is the center point.

A filled-in black square indicates the current point of origin. If no square is black, it means that a custom point of origin has been established by clicking and dragging the object's point of origin. In most cases, it's simplest to use the default point of origin, but you may want to click the middle square if, for example, you want to rotate a picture around its center, or you may use a different corner or midpoint in certain situations. To change the point of origin for a selected object, click on one of the small white squares.

Repositioning a picture within its frame

You can reposition a picture within its frame by changing the values in the Transform pane's or Control palette's X Location and/or Y Location fields. The values in these fields indicate the distance between the upper-left corner of the page and the selected object's point of origin.

QuarkXPress User

Users of QuarkXPress may find InDesign's location approach to be a little strange. In QuarkXPress, a picture's position is relative to the box that contains it; not the upper-left corner of the page. (I'm assuming here that you haven't moved the document's ruler origin, which by default is in the upper-left corner of a page or spread.)

Scaling a picture

You can scale a picture by changing the value in the Width and/or Height fields or by changing the value in the Horizontal Scale and/or Vertical Scale fields. Most graphics designers are familiar with the concept of scaling an object by specifying a percentage value. If you're one of them, you'll probably use the Scale fields. After all, horizontally scaling a 4-inch-wide picture to two-thirds of its original size by applying a Horizontal Scale value of 66.6% is easier than changing the picture's width to 2.667 inches.

You can enter scale values between 1% and 10000%. If you want to maintain a picture's original proportions, make sure the values in the Horizontal Scale and Vertical Scale fields are the same. If you want to return a picture to the size it was when you first imported it, specify Horizontal Scale and Vertical Scale values of 100%.

Tip

You can use math to figure out scale entries. For example, if you want the scale to be 30 percent larger, you could enter **+30%** rather than **130%**. Or you could enter **/6** to make the object one sixth of its current size. Other legitimate actions include subtraction (for example, **−29%**) and multiplication (for example, ***7**).

In addition to specifying a value in the Horizontal Scale or Vertical Scale field, you can choose one of the predefined values from the fields' pop-up menus, or you can highlight a value and press the up or down arrow keys on the keyboard. Each press of an arrow key changes the value by 1 percent. If you hold down the Shift key while clicking an arrow, the increment of change is 10 percent.

The Fitting options (Object ⇨ Fitting), which are explained later in this chapter, also let you change the scale of a picture relative to the size of its frame.

Rotating a picture

You can change the angle of a selected picture by entering a different value in the Rotation field, choosing one of the predefined angles from the field's pop-up menu, or by choosing any of the three rotation options — Rotate 180°, Rotate 90° CW, and Rotate 90° CCW — in the Transform pane's or Control palette's palette menu. If you choose one of these options, the current angle of the selected object is added to the applied angle. For example, if you choose Rotate 90° CCW (counterclockwise), an object that's currently rotated 12 degrees will end up with a rotation angle of 102 degrees. If you choose to enter a value in the Rotation field, positive values rotate the selected item counterclockwise; negative values rotate it clockwise.

Note The Transformations Are Totals option in the Transform pane's and Control palette's palette menu relates to the angle of rotation of a nested object. If Transformations Are Totals is checked, the Rotation angle displayed for a nested item is calculated by adding its angle to the angle of the containing frame. For example, if Transformations Are Totals is checked, a picture that's been rotated 30 degrees that's in a frame that's been rotated 30 degrees will display a Rotation value of 60°. If Transformations Are Totals were unchecked, the Rotation value would be 30°.

Skewing a picture

You can *skew*, or slant, a picture in its frame by applying a Skew value in the Transform pane or Control palette, or by choosing a predefined value from the field's pop-up menu. Positive skew values slant an object to the right (that is, the top edge of the object is moved to the right), while negative values slant an object to the left (the bottom edge is moved to the right). You can enter skew values between 1° and 89° (although values above 70° cause considerable distortion).

To "unskew" a picture, enter a Skew value of 0°. Figure 24-5 shows a picture that's been skewed.

Figure 24-5: The applied Skew value of –30° causes the picture to lean to the left.

Note When you use the Shear tool, you change the selected object's angle of rotation *and* skew angle simultaneously.

Flipping a picture

The three flipping commands — Flip Horizontal, Flip Vertical, and Flip Both — in the Transform pane's and Control palette's palette menu let you create a mirror image of a selected picture. If you choose Flip Horizontal, the picture is flipped along a vertical axis (that is, the right edge and left edge exchange places); if you choose Flip Vertical, the picture is flipped upside down; and if you choose Flip Both, the picture is flipped horizontally and vertically to produce an upside-down and backward version of the original.

Be careful when flipping pictures: Generally you'll want to flip both a picture and its frame. To do so, make sure you select the frame using the Selection tool (rather than the Direct Selection tool, which selects the picture itself). If you flip a picture that's been cropped in a frame, you'll probably have to recrop the picture.

 Note When you flip a picture, the axis around which the picture flips runs through the frame's point of origin.

Figuring Out the Fitting Commands

If you've placed a picture in a frame that's either larger or smaller than the picture, you can use the Fitting options (Object ➪ Fitting) to scale the picture to fit the frame proportionally or disproportionally or to scale the frame to fit the picture. Another option lets you center the picture in the frame.

The Fitting commands for pictures are available only if you've used the Selection tool to select a graphics frame. Here's a description of each of the four options:

✦ **Fit Content to Frame:** To resize a picture to fill the selected frame, choose Object ➪ Fitting ➪ Fit Content to Frame or press Option+⌘+E or Ctrl+Alt+E. If the frame is larger than the picture, the picture is enlarged; if the frame is smaller, the picture is reduced. If the picture and the frame have different proportions, the picture's proportions are changed so that the image completely fills the frame.

✦ **Fit Frame to Content:** To resize a frame so that it wraps snugly around a picture, choose Fit Frame to Content or press Option+⌘+C or Ctrl+Alt+C. The frame will be enlarged or reduced depending on the size of the picture, and the frame's proportions will be changed to match the proportions of the picture.

✦ **Center Content:** To center a picture in its frame, choose Center Content or press Shift+⌘+E or Ctrl+Shift+E. Neither the frame nor the picture are resized when you center a picture.

✦ **Fit Content Proportionally:** To resize a picture to fit in the selected frame while maintaining the picture's current proportions, choose Object ➪ Fitting ➪ Fit Content Proportionally or press Option+Shift+⌘+E or Ctrl+Alt+Shift+E. If the frame is larger than the picture, the picture is enlarged; if the frame is smaller, the picture is reduced. If the picture and the frame have different proportions, a portion of the frame background will show above and below or to the left and right of the picture. If you want, you can drag frame edges to make the frame shorter or narrower and eliminate any portions of the background that are visible.

Note For frames with strokes, the Fitting options align the outer edge of a picture with the center of the stroke. A stroke will obscure a strip along the picture's edge that's half the width of the stroke. The wider the stroke, the more of the picture that gets covered up.

Note All four of these options are available via icons in the Control palette.

Modifying Bitmap Graphics versus Vector Graphics

When it comes to working with bitmap and vector graphics in InDesign, there's not much difference. When you use the Place command, the import options for these two graphic formats are slightly different (see Chapter 23), but the transformation tools and the controls in the Transform pane and Control palette are available and work the same for all imported pictures regardless of their file format.

QuarkXPress User QuarkXPress provides limited features for modifying the appearance of bitmap pictures. InDesign does not. However, even in programs like InDesign, if you want to perform any serious pixel-level modifications to a bitmap graphic, you'll need to use a dedicated image-editing program such as Adobe Photoshop.

When it comes to performing picture modifications in InDesign, the only difference between bitmap graphics and vector-based graphics is that you can apply color and, optionally, tint to gray-scale and one-bit (black-and-white) bitmaps. These options are not available for vector-based images and color bitmaps.

Applying color and tint to bitmap pictures

You can apply color and tint only to gray-scale and black-and-white bitmap pictures. If you're unable to apply a color or tint to a bitmap picture that you think should be modifiable, check the picture's file type. To do so, open the Links pane (File ➪ Links, or Shift+⌘+D or Ctrl+Shift+D), then double-click the picture's name or click once on its name and choose Show Link Information from the pane's pop-up menu. The picture's color mode (CMYK, Grayscale, and so on) is displayed next to Color Space, and the picture's file format is displayed next to File Type.

To apply color to a picture:

1. **Click on the Direct Selection tool (or press A if the Type tool isn't selected).**

2. **Click in the picture's frame to select the picture.**

3. **Make sure the Fill icon is active in the Tool palette if you want to color the image's background. Make sure the Stroke icon is active if you want to color the frame's stroke (if any).**

4. **If it's not displayed, show the Swatches pane by choosing Windows ⇨ Swatches or pressing F5.**

5. **Click on a color in the scroll list.**

See Chapter 8 for information about defining colors.

You apply color to a selected picture's foreground by dragging a swatch from the Swatches pane and dropping it onto the picture.

Although InDesign doesn't have background, frame, and contents icons in its Swatches pane to let you select where color is applied, as QuarkXPress does, InDesign lets you determine what component of the image gets the color based on how you apply the color, as described earlier. Furthermore, you can use the Control palette's Select Container and Select Contents icons to choose whether the image background or contents, respectively, are colored when you click a swatch.

Note that InDesign does not have any options to change image contrast or line-screen element for gray-scale and black-and-white images, as QuarkXPress does. You'll need to apply such effects in an image editor.

Applying a tint to a picture

Applying a *color tint* — that is, a shade or a percentage of the applied color — to a picture is the same as applying a color. You must create a tint of an available color before you can apply the tint to a picture. To create a tint of a color, click the color in the Swatches pane, then choose New Tint Swatch from the Swatches pane's palette menu. Use the Tint controls in the New Swatch Tint dialog box to specify the percent of the color you want to use. After you create a tint, you apply it to a picture following the same steps you would use if you were applying color.

Managing Links to Imported Pictures

As Chapter 23 explained, when you place a graphic into an InDesign document — either via the Place command (File ⇨ Place, or ⌘+D or Ctrl+D) or by dragging and dropping a graphics file's icon directly into a document window — InDesign remembers the name and location of the original graphics file and uses this file when the document is printed.

If you always print your documents from your own computer, and your graphics never get modified, moved, renamed, or deleted, you won't have to worry much about managing the links between your InDesign documents and imported graphics files. But that scenario is the exception rather than the rule. Graphics files are often modified while the InDesign pages that contain them are under construction, and at many publishing sites, the computer used to create a document is seldom the computer from which it's printed.

Note If you import a graphics file that's 48K or smaller in size, the entire full-resolution image is automatically embedded in the InDesign document. The Links pane, explained later in this section, lets you manage links to these embedded graphic files and all other imported pictures.

Tip If you'll be taking your documents to a service provider for output, be sure to include all imported graphics files, as well. You can use InDesign's Preflight and Package features, which are covered in Chapter 30, to automatically collect graphics files in preparation for output.

The Links pane (File ➪ Links, or Shift+⌘+D or Ctrl+Shift+D), shown in Figure 24-6, displays link-related information about all imported graphics files, and the pane's accompanying pop-up menu provides tools for managing links. The scroll list displays the name of each imported graphic. A Missing Link icon is displayed for graphics that have been moved, renamed, or deleted since they were imported into the document. A Modified Link icon is displayed for graphics that have been modified since being imported.

Figure 24-6: The Links pane and its palette menu.

When you open a document that contains imported graphics files that have been modified, moved, renamed, or deleted since they were imported, the alert shown in Figure 24-7 is displayed. This alert tells you the number of files with *missing links* (that is, the original graphics file has been moved, renamed, or deleted) and with *modified links* (graphics files that have been opened and saved since they were imported). You don't have to update missing or modified links as soon as you open a document, but it's not a bad idea.

Figure 24-7: This alert is displayed when you open a document that contains imported pictures that have been modified, moved, renamed, or deleted. The Relink dialog box (bottom) is displayed if you click the Fix Links Automatically button.

To fix missing or modified links, click the Fix Links Automatically button, which will then open a Relink dialog box listing a missing link. That Relink dialog box has a Browse button for you to find the missing file. As you relink each missing file, InDesign will display the next missing file, until all are relinked. If you can't or don't want to relink a specific file, you can skip it by clicking the Skip button. When done, click OK.

If the status of a link to a particular graphics file changes while you're working on a document, a Missing Link or Modified Link icon is displayed in the Links pane. For example, if you import an illustration created with Illustrator or FreeHand into an InDesign document, then open, modify, and resave the illustration using its original program, the Links pane will display the Modified Link icon for that file.

Note Generally, you'll want to keep all links up to date. If you don't update the link for a modified graphic, it will still print correctly, but what you see on-screen may be quite different from what prints. Remember that when you import a graphics file, InDesign creates and saves a low-resolution screen preview for display. If the graphics file is then modified, InDesign will continue to use the old screen preview for screen display until you update the link.

If you try to print a document that contains a missing graphics file, the alert shown in Figure 24-7 is displayed. At this point, you can Cancel the print job and then use the Links pane to update the link, or you can click OK to print anyway. If you print anyway, InDesign will send the low-resolution screen preview to the printer instead of sending the original graphics file.

Note   If you import an EPS file that, in turn, contains OPI links to placed images in the file, the Links pane will display these links. You shouldn't change them. Doing so could cause printing problems.

The Links pane's palette menu has four groups of commands that let you manage links, embed the original graphics file of any imported graphic, display link information for individual graphics, and control how filenames are displayed in the pane. If you want to update, relink, or view information about a specific file, click on its name in the pane, then choose a command from the palette menu or click a button at the bottom of the pane, all of which are explained in the following sections.

Managing links

The first four command in the Links pane's palette menu let you reestablish links to missing and modified graphics files, display an imported graphic in the document window, and open the program used to create a graphic file:

✦ **Relink:** This command, and the Relink button (the leftmost at the bottom of the pane), lets you reestablish a missing link or replace the original file you imported with a different file. When you choose Relink or click the button, the Relink dialog box is displayed and shows the original path name and filename. You can enter a new path name and filename in the Location field, but it's easier to click Browse, which opens a standard Open dialog box. Use the controls to locate and select the original file or a different file, then click OK. (You can also drag and drop a file icon from the Mac OS Finder or Windows Explorer directly into the Relink dialog box.) If you want to restore broken links to multiple files, highlight their filenames in the scroll list, then choose Relink or click the Update Link button.

QuarkXPress User   InDesign's relink function is not as smart as QuarkXPress's equivalent Picture Usage. If you have multiple broken links to the same file in an InDesign document, you must relink each one manually from the Links pane. QuarkXPress will automatically fix all links to the same file as soon as you correct any link to it. That's another reason to use InDesign's automatic fix described earlier when you open a file with broken links.

✦ **Go To Link:** Choose this option, or click the Go to Link button (second from left) to display the highlighted graphics file in the document window. InDesign will, if necessary, navigate to the correct page and center the image in the document window. You can also display a particular graphic by double-clicking its name in the scroll list while holding down the Option or Alt key.

✦ **Edit Original:** If you want to modify an imported graphic, choose Edit Original from the palette menu or click the Edit Original button (far right). InDesign will try to locate and open the program used to create the file. This may or may not be possible, depending on the original program, the file format, and the programs available on your computer.

✦ **Update Link:** Choose this option or click the Update Link button (third from the left) to update the link to a modified graphic. Highlight multiple filenames, then choose Update Link or click the Update Link button to update all links at once.

Note

When you update missing and modified graphics, any transformations — rotation, shear, scale, and so on — that you've applied to the graphics or their frames are maintained.

Embedding imported pictures

The Links pane's Embed command lets you embed the complete file of any imported graphic. (Except for files that are 48K and smaller, you import only a low-resolution screen preview when you place a picture.) If you want to ensure that the graphics file will forever remain with a document, you can choose to embed it — however, by embedding graphics, you'll be producing larger document files, which means it will take you longer to open and save them.

To embed a picture, click on its name in the scroll list, then choose Embed from the Links pane's palette menu. An alert is displayed and informs you about the increased document size that will result. Click Yes to embed the file.

Caution

When you embed a file, the filename is no longer displayed in the Links pane, nor is an embedded file automatically updated if you modify the original. Generally, you should avoid embedding files, especially large ones, unless you're certain that they won't be modified.

Displaying link information

Choosing Link Information from the Links pane's palette menu displays the Link Information dialog box, shown in Figure 24-8. This dialog box doesn't let you do much (the Previous and Next buttons let you display information about the previous and next files in the list, but that's about it), but it does display 11 sometimes useful bits of information about the highlighted graphics file, including its name, status, creation date, file type, and location.

Figure 24-8: The Link Information dialog box.

Sorting imported files in the Links pane

The next three commands in the Links pane's palette menu let you control how the files in the scroll list are arranged:

✦ **Sort by Status** lists files with missing links first, followed by files that have been modified, and finally files whose status is OK.

✦ **Sort by Name** lists all files in alphabetical order.

✦ **Sort by Page** lists imported files on page 1 first, followed by imported files on page 2, and so on.

New Feature

If you Option+double-click or Alt+double-click a picture, InDesign will open the original in either the program that created it or, if you don't have that program, another program that can edit the picture.

Changing the view

Finally, the Links pane's palette menu has an option called Small Palette Rows that lets you reduce the size of text in the pane and decrease the space between entries so you can see more entries at once. Of course, the reduced rows are also harder to read. To go back to the normal display size, simply select this option again.

Summary

After you import a picture into a document, you have many options for changing its appearance. You can crop it in a rectangular or freeform frame or manipulate it with three transformation tools — the Rotation, Scale, and Shear tools. The Transform pane and Control palette both let you perform the same modifications as the transformation tools and offer other choices for modifying pictures, including moving, scaling, skewing, and flipping. For gray-scale and bitmap pictures only, you have the option to apply a color and a tint to the image.

The Fitting command (Object ➪ Fitting) provides four options for positioning and scaling a picture relative to its frame, while the Links pane displays link-related information about imported pictures and lets you update links for pictures that are missing or have been modified.

✦   ✦   ✦

Special Effects for Pictures

In This Chapter

Creating text runarounds

Masking pictures with clipping paths

Applying transparency

Knowing other cool tricks for pictures

The options offered by the transformation tools and the Control palette and Transform pane let you change the appearance of imported pictures in several ways, as covered in Chapter 24, but that's not all you can do with your graphics.

InDesign provides several other picture-modification features that let you — among other things — wrap text around pictures, show and hide portions of pictures using clipping paths, place pictures within compound shapes, and place pictures within a text thread so that they move along with the surrounding text.

Wrapping Text around Pictures

In the "old" days before personal computers and page-layout software, wrapping text around a picture was a time-consuming and expensive task. Text wraps were rare, found only in the most expensively produced publications.

Not any more. Not only do all page-layout programs let you create text runarounds, most programs — including InDesign — provide several options for controlling how text relates to pictures and other objects that obstruct its flow.

When a graphics frame is positioned in front of a text frame, InDesign provides the following options. You can:

- ✦ Ignore the graphics frame and flow the text behind it.
- ✦ Wrap the text around the frame's rectangular bounding box.
- ✦ Wrap the text around the frame itself.

✦ Jump the text around the frame (that is, jump the text from the top of the graphics frame to the bottom).

✦ Jump the text to the next column or page when the text reaches the top of graphics frame.

✦ Specify the amount of distance between the text and the edge of the obstructing shape.

✦ Flow text within the obstructing shape rather than outside it.

New Feature

InDesign CS now lets you wrap text around frames on hidden layers — as well as remove text wrap for objects on hidden layers. This is handy when you want to hide images or other distracting items but preserve the layout.

Tip

If you want to wrap text around only a portion of a picture — perhaps you need to isolate a face in a crowd — the best solution is to open the graphics file in its original program, create a clipping path around that portion, then resave the file and import it and its clipping path into an InDesign document (clipping paths are explained in the next section). Another option is to use the Pen tool to create a free-form shape within InDesign and then use the shape as both a frame and a clipping path.

The Text Wrap pane

The controls in the Text Wrap pane, shown in Figure 25-1, let you specify how a selected object will affect the flow of text behind it. Remember, the flow of text around an obstructing object is determined by the text wrap settings applied to the obstructing object.

Tip

You can override the text-wrap settings of objects that are in front of a text frame by telling the text frame to ignore them. To do so, click on a text frame, then choose Object ➪ Text Frame Options or press ⌘+B or Ctrl+B. In the Text Frame Options dialog box, check Ignore Text Wrap, then click OK. Text in the frame will now flow behind any obstructing items regardless of the text-wrap settings applied to them.

Note

The Text Wrap pane has only one option in its palette menu: Hide Options/Show Options, which hides or shows the Contour Options and Include Inside Edges sections of the pane. You can more easily hide/show these functions by double-clicking the double-arrow symbol to the right of the Text Wrap label in the pane's tab.

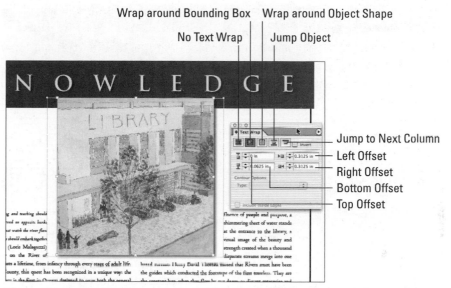

Figure 25-1: The Text Wrap pane and its palette menu. Also, note the preview frame for the wrap area outside the text frame's bounding box.

Here's how to apply text-wrap settings to a frame:

1. **If the Text Wrap pane is not displayed, choose Window ⇨ Type & Tables ⇨ Text Wrap or press Option+⌘+W or Ctrl+Alt+W.**

2. **Click on either of the selection tools.**

   If the Type tool isn't selected, you can press V to select the Selection tool or press A to select the Direct Selection tool.

3. **Click on the graphics or text frame to which you want to apply text-wrap settings.**

   The frame can be anywhere, but you'll probably want to position it on top of a text frame that contains text so you can see the results of the settings you apply.

4. **Click on one of the five text-wrap buttons at the top of the Text Wrap pane.**

   Figure 25-2 shows how each of these options affects a graphics frame.

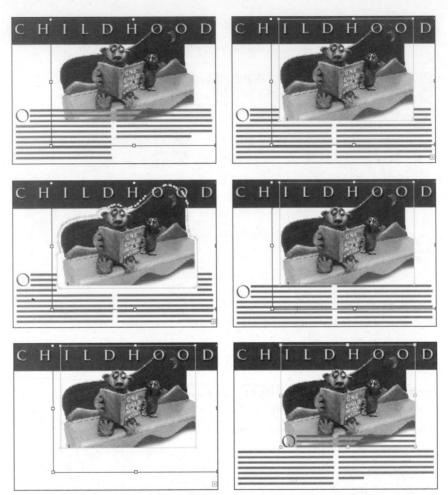

Figure 25-2: The five text-wrap options (top to bottom): No Text Wrap, Wrap around Bounding Box, Wrap around Object Shape, Jump Object, and Jump to Next Column, as well as the Invert option selected for the Wrap around Bounding Box option.

5. **If you want, adjust the space between the surrounding text and the obstructing shape by entering values in the Top Offset, Bottom Offset, Left Offset, and Right Offset fields. (These fields are not available if you click the No Text Wrap button.)**

If the object is a rectangle, all four fields are available if you click the Wrap around Bounding Box button or Wrap around Object Shape. Only the Top

Offset field is available if you click the Wrap around Object Shape button for a free-form shape or the Jump to Next Column button. The Top Offset and Bottom Offset fields are available if you click the Jump Object button.

Note   A bounding box is the dimensions of the picture, whether or not it is wholly contained in its frame. You would use a bounding box if you want to have the wrap follow the picture's dimensions rather than that of the frame containing it.

6. **If you want to flow the text in the obstructing shape, select Invert.**

7. **If you chose the Wrap around Object Shape button, you can also select from the Contour Options.**

   Its Type pop-up menu has six options (Figure 25-3 shows examples of each):

   • Bounding Box, which is the same as having chosen the Wrap around Bounding Box button.

   • Detect Edges, which tries to determine the picture's outside boundary by ignoring white space — you would use this for bitmapped images that have a transparent or white background.

   • Alpha Channel, which uses the image's alpha channel, if any, to create a wrapping boundary.

   • Photoshop Path, which uses the image's Photoshop clipping path, if any, to create a wrapping boundary.

   • Graphic Frame, which uses the frame's boundary rather than the bounding box.

   • Same as Clipping, which uses the clipping path for the graphic created in InDesign.

   By selecting the Include Inside Edges check box, InDesign will let text appear inside any interior "holes" in the picture. You'll rarely use this technique, because in most cases it's hard for the reader to follow text that wraps around an image, then flows inside it, and then continues to flow outside it. But if the interior is large enough and not too distant from the text that flows on the outside, this effect might be readable.

Tip   If you specify text-wrap settings when no objects are selected, the settings are automatically applied to all new objects.

Tip   To apply text-wrap settings to a master item on a document page, hold down Shift+⌘ or Ctrl+Shift to select the item, then use the controls in the Text Wrap pane as described above.

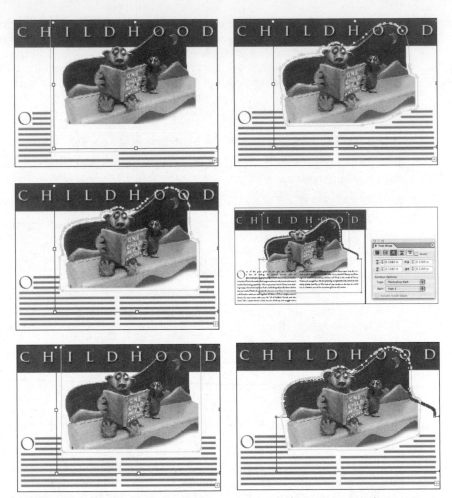

Figure 25-3: The six contour options for text-wrap options (top to bottom): Bounding Box, Detect Edges, Alpha Channel, Photoshop Path, Graphic Frame, and Same as Clipping.

There are several global text-wrap options you should be aware of, all of which are accessed via the Composition pane of the Preferences dialog box (choose InDesign ➪ Preferences on the Mac or Edit ➪ Preferences in Windows, or press ⌘+K or Ctrl+K). Figure 25-4 shows the pane. Here are the options:

✦ The Justify Text Next to an Object option is useful when you have left-aligned text that wraps around an object at the right. (It also works if you have right-aligned text that wraps around an object at the left.) This can lead to an awkward wrap, since InDesign won't try to make the text align precisely to the wrap's contour (because the text isn't justified). Use this option to justify the text just around the wrap, then continue using the text's specified nonjustified alignment.

✦ The Skip by Leading option makes text wrapping below or above an object based on the text's leading, so there's at least a full line space between the text and the object, even if the object's text-wrap settings would allow less space.

New Feature

InDesign CS now lets you select whether text wrap affects all text frames in a stack or just frames behind the text-wrap object.

✦ The new Text Wrap Only Affects Text Beneath option, if checked, prevents text frames placed on top of an object from wrapping, while those behind the picture frame will still be allowed to wrap. This option lets you have some text overlap the picture and other text wrap around it. Note this is a global setting, affecting all objects. To override wrap settings of individual text frames, choose Object ➪ Text Frame Options, or press ⌘+B or Ctrl+B, and check Ignore Text Wrap.

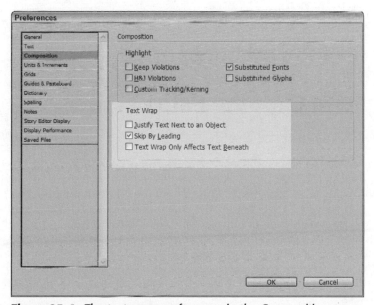

Figure 25-4: The text-wrap preferences in the Composition pane of the Preferences dialog box.

Changing the shape of a text wrap

When you specify text-wrap settings for an object, an editable shape is created. If the text-wrap shape is the same shape as the object, the text-wrap boundary is superimposed on the object. You can modify a text-wrap boundary by clicking on it with the Direct Selection tool then moving, adding, deleting, and changing the direction of anchor points and by moving direction lines. Figure 25-5 shows a text wrap before and after being manually reshaped.

Cross-Reference   For more information about modifying free-form shapes, see Chapter 27.

Figure 25-5: The example on the left shows a text wrap created by using the picture's built-in alpha channel (Wrap around Object Shape). The text wrap was modified — by dragging anchor points — to create the variation on the right.

Working with Clipping Paths

Some graphics file formats — including TIFF, JPEG, and Photoshop EPS, and Photoshop-native (.psd) files — let you embed a clipping path in the file. A clipping path is used to mask certain parts of a picture and reveal other parts. For example, if you want to create a silhouette around a single person in a crowd of people, you could open the file in an image editing program like Photoshop, and then create and save a clipping path that isolates the shape of the person. (You could also erase everything except the person you want to silhouette; not only can this be time-consuming, but if you want to reveal other parts of the picture later, you're out of luck.)

If you want to use a clipping path to mask parts of a picture, InDesign offers three options. You can

✦ Use a graphics file's built-in clipping path. (Be sure to check the Import Options in the Place dialog box when you import the image and check the Apply Photoshop Clipping Path option as described in Chapter 23.)

✦ Create a free-form shape that will act as your mask in InDesign and then place a picture in the shape.

✦ Create a clipping path in InDesign by choosing Object ⇨ Clipping Path or pressing Option+Shift+⌘+K or Ctrl+Alt+Shift+K.

Regardless of the method you use to clip an imported picture, you can modify a clipping path by moving, adding, deleting, and changing the direction of anchor points and by moving direction lines.

Cross-Reference

See Chapter 25 for more information about modifying free-form shapes. See Deke McClelland's *Photoshop 7 Bible* (Wiley Publishing) for more on creating clipping paths in Photoshop.

Creating clipping paths in Photoshop

Creating a clipping path in Photoshop is simple, once you get the hang of the process. A path is essentially a selection, which you can create with any of the Photoshop selection tools, including tracing your own selection to hand-draw a path. Once the selection has been made, here's how you make a path:

1. Open the Paths pane by choosing Window ⇨ Paths.

2. Using the pane's palette menu, choose Make Work Path.

You'll be asked to choose a Tolerance setting in pixels — the smaller the number, the finer the path's shape.

3. Click OK to accept your setting.

A work path will now display in the Paths pane, showing in white the area contained by the path.

4. Convert the work path into a named path by double-clicking the work path in the pane or by choosing Save Path in the palette menu.

5. Give the path a name, then click OK.

6. Now choose Clipping Path from the palette menu.

You'll be asked to choose which path to use as a clipping path (you can have multiple clipping paths in a Photoshop file) and then be asked to choose a Flatness setting. Like the earlier Tolerance setting, the smaller the number of pixels, the finer the path's contours.

7. Click OK.

That's it! The tricky part is creating the selection area to begin with.

Using a free-form shape to clip a picture

If you want to mask a portion of a picture that doesn't include a built-in clipping path, no problem. The easiest way is to simply edit the text-wrap boundary. To do so, set the text wrap to Wrap around Object Shape, then select the picture with the Direct Selection tool. The text-wrap boundary will appear as a blue line — you can make it easier to select by setting offsets in the Text Wrap pane, which will move the boundary away from the frame edge, as Figure 25-6 shows. Now use InDesign's free-form editing tools, as covered in Chapter 27, to edit the text-wrap boundary.

Figure 25-6: To create a custom wrap, just edit the text-wrap boundary after selecting Wrap around Object as if it were any other path. The boundary is the blue path that appears outside the frame; you can more easily see and work with the wrap boundary if you enter offset amounts in the Text Wrap pane.

There are two other methods you can use as well:

✦ You can use the Pen tool to create the shape, and then use the Place command (File ➪ Place, or ⌘+D or Ctrl+D) to place a picture in the shape.

✦ You can import the picture into a rectangular frame (by using the Place command with no object selected), use the Pen tool to create a free-form shape that surrounds the portion of the image you want to show, and then copy and paste the picture into the free-form shape. In this case, you must use the Paste Into command (Edit ➪ Paste Into, or Option+⌘+V or Ctrl+Alt+V) to place the copied picture in the selected free-form shape. When you create the free-form shape, make sure that the default color for the Pen tool is set to None so that the shape you create is transparent. Otherwise, the colored area in the shape will obscure the picture behind it.

You're more likely to use the second method than the first because it's difficult to mask a portion of a picture without seeing it. Figure 25-5 shows a picture in a rectangular frame next to a copy of the same picture in a free-form shape.

The Pen tool lets you create one shape at a time. The Compound Paths command lets you combine multiple shapes to create more complex objects. For example, you could place a small circle on top of a larger circle and then use the Compound Paths command to create a doughnut-shaped object. Figure 25-9, later in this chapter, shows a picture in a compound path. (See Chapter 27 for more information about creating complex shapes with the Compound Paths command.)

Using InDesign's Clipping Path command

If you import a picture that doesn't have a clipping path, you can use the Clipping Path command (Object ➪ Clipping Path, or Option+Shift+⌘+K or Ctrl+Alt+Shift+K) to generate one automatically in InDesign. The clipping paths that InDesign generates are based on a picture's value. For this reason, the Clipping Path command works very well for images that have a white background but no clipping path. It's less useful for pictures whose backgrounds have not been erased and for pictures that contain a broad range of intermingling values.

If you use the Clipping Path command to generate a clipping path for a picture that has a built-in clipping path, the one that InDesign generates replaces the built-in path.

To create a clipping path using the Clipping Path command:

1. **Select either the Selection tool or the Direct Selection tool, and then click on the picture to which you want to add a clipping path.**

   If the Type tool isn't selected, you can press V to select the Selection tool or press A to select the Direct Selection tool.

2. **Choose Object ➪ Clipping Path, or press to display the Clipping Path dialog box, shown in Figure 25-7.**

3. **To have InDesign detect the likely boundary of the image, as opposed to a white or other light background, choose Detect Edges from the Type pop-up menu.**

   You can use the other options to select Alpha Channel or Photoshop Path as the clipping path, for pictures that have one or more of these — InDesign can only use one as the clipping path.

4. **Enter a value in the Threshold field or drag the field's slider to specify the value below which pixels will be placed outside the clipping path shape (that is, pixels that will become transparent).**

   Pixels darker than the Threshold value remain visible and thus are inside the clipping path shape. The lowest possible Threshold value (0) makes only white pixels transparent. As the value gets higher, less of the picture remains visible. The lightest areas are removed first, then midtones, and so on. (Click Preview to see the results of your changes without closing the dialog box.)

Figure 25-7: The Clipping Path dialog box.

5. **The value you enter in the Tolerance field determines how closely InDesign looks at variations in adjacent pixels when building a clipping path.**

   Higher values produce a simpler, smoother path than lower values. Lower values create a more complicated, more exact path with more anchor points.

6. **If you want to enlarge or reduce the size of the clipping path produced by the Threshold and Tolerance values, enter a value in the Inset Frame field.**

   Negative values enlarge the path; positive values shrink it. (The Inset Frame value is also applied to the path's bounding box.)

7. **Click Invert to switch the transparent and visible areas of the clipping path produced by the Threshold and Tolerance values.**

8. **If you want to include light areas in the perimeter shape InDesign generates based on the Threshold and Tolerance values, click Include Inside Edges.**

   For example, if you have a picture of a doughnut and you want to make the hole transparent (as well as the area around the outside of the doughnut), click Include Inside Edges. If you don't click Include Inside Edges, InDesign builds a single shape (in the case of a doughnut, just the outside circle). The portion of the picture in the shape remains visible; the rest of the picture becomes transparent.

9. **Click Restrict to Frame if you want InDesign to generate a clipping path from just the portion of the picture visible in the picture frame, as opposed to the entire picture (such as if you cropped the picture).**

10. **Click Use High Resolution Image if you want InDesign to use the high-resolution information in the original file instead of using the low-resolution proxy image.**

    Even though using the high-resolution image takes longer, the resulting clipping path is more precise than it would be if you didn't check Use High Resolution Image.

11. **When you've finished specifying clipping path settings, click OK to close the dialog box and apply the settings to the selected picture.**

Figure 25-8 shows a picture before and after a clipping path was applied to it using the Clipping Path command.

You can remove a clipping path by choosing None as the Type in the Clipping Path dialog box. You can also select a different path — detectable edges, alpha channel, embedded Photoshop path, or hand-edited path — than was selected previously if you decide to change the current clipping path.

Figure 25-8: At left is a picture of coastal France with a picture of a glider superimposed. At right is the same set of pictures, but with a clipping path applied to the glider so the outside area is masked out, making it transparent.

Using Transparency

One of InDesign's most sophisticated tools is its set of transparency options, which let you make items partially transparent. You apply transparency with the

Transparency pane (Window ➯ Transparency, or Shift+F10). Figure 25-9 shows the pane as well as a brochure that uses transparency to create a vellum effect on a stripe that contains text that overprints a background photo. The artist chose a transparency setting of 74 percent for the white frame's Opacity, as well as the Screen setting for transparency type.

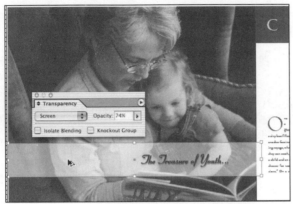

Figure 25-9: The Transparency pane and its pop-up menu, as well as an example of a transparent object overprinting the photograph.

Note   You cannot apply transparency to text selections or to layers, nor can you apply different transparency settings to an object's fill and stroke. Also, if you remove an object from a group that had transparency applied (via cut and paste or copy and paste), that pasted object will not have the group's transparency settings applied to it.

There are 16 different transparency types — called *blending modes* — as shown in Figure 25-10. The differences among them can be subtle or extreme, depending on a variety of issues. (Photoshop and Illustrator users will recognize these options from those programs.) You should experiment with them to see what effect works best in each case. The 16 modes are:

✦ **Normal:** Colors the selection with the blend color, without interaction with the base color. This is the default mode.

✦ **Multiply:** Multiplies the base color by the blend color. The resulting color is always a darker color. Multiplying any color with black produces black. Multiplying any color with white leaves the color unchanged. The effect is similar to drawing on a page with multiple Magic Markers.

✦ **Screen:** Multiplies the inverse of the blend and base colors. The resulting color is always a lighter color. Screening with black leaves the color unchanged. Screening with white produces white. The effect is similar to projecting multiple slide images on top of each other.

Figure 25-10: The 16 transparency blending modes in the Transparency pane.

✦ **Overlay:** Multiplies or screens the colors, depending on the base color. Patterns or colors overlay the existing artwork, preserving the highlights and shadows of the base color while mixing in the blend color to reflect the lightness or darkness of the original color.

✦ **Soft Light:** Darkens or lightens the colors, depending on the blend color. The effect is similar to shining a diffused spotlight on the artwork. If the blend color (light source) is lighter than 50 percent gray, the artwork is lightened, as if it were dodged. If the blend color is darker than 50 percent gray, the artwork is darkened, as if it were burned in. Painting with pure black or white produces a distinctly darker or lighter area but does not result in pure black or white.

✦ **Hard Light:** Multiplies or screens the colors, depending on the blend color. The effect is similar to shining a harsh spotlight on the artwork. If the blend color (light source) is lighter than 50 percent gray, the artwork is lightened, as if it were screened. This is useful for adding highlights to artwork. If the blend color is darker than 50 percent gray, the artwork is darkened, as if it were multiplied. This is useful for adding shadows to artwork. Painting with pure black or white results in pure black or white.

✦ **Color Dodge:** Brightens the base color to reflect the blend color. Blending with black produces no change.

✦ **Color Burn:** Darkens the base color to reflect the blend color. Blending with white produces no change.

✦ **Darken:** Selects the base or blend color — whichever is darker — as the resulting color. Areas lighter than the blend color are replaced, and areas darker than the blend color do not change.

✦ **Lighten:** Selects the base or blend color — whichever is lighter — as the resulting color. Areas darker than the blend color are replaced, and areas lighter than the blend color do not change.

✦ **Difference:** Subtracts either the blend color from the base color or the base color from the blend color, depending on which has the greater brightness value. Blending with white inverts the base color values; blending with black produces no change.

✦ **Exclusion:** Creates an effect similar to, but lower in contrast than, the Difference mode. Blending with white inverts the base color components. Blending with black produces no change.

✦ **Hue:** Creates a color with the luminance and saturation of the base color and the hue of the blend color.

✦ **Saturation:** Creates a color with the luminance and hue of the base color and the saturation of the blend color. Using this mode in an area with no saturation (a gray) produces no change.

✦ **Color:** Creates a color with the luminance of the base color and the hue and saturation of the blend color. This preserves the gray levels in the artwork, and is useful for coloring monochrome artwork and for tinting color artwork.

✦ **Luminosity:** Creates a color with the hue and saturation of the base color and the luminance of the blend color. This mode produces the inverse of the Color mode.

Note

The Difference, Exclusion, Hue, Saturation, Color, and Luminosity modes do not blend spot colors, just process colors.

Note

InDesign's blending calculations differ based on whether the document is to be printed (usually via CMYK) or seen on-screen (as RGB). Be sure to choose the right blending space based on the intended output. To do so, choose Edit ➪ Transparency Blend Space ➪ Document CMYK or Edit ➪ Transparency Blend Space ➪ Document RGB, as appropriate.

You have two other options in the Transparency pane:

✦ **Isolate Blending** restricts the blending modes to the objects in a group, instead of also applying them to objects beneath the group. This can prevent unintended changes to those underlying objects.

✦ **Knockout Group** obscures any objects below the selected group. But those objects beneath the knocked-out group are still affected by any blend mode settings applied to the group, unless Isolate Blending is also checked.

Trying Other Special Effects

When you combine your imagination with InDesign's picture-modification, page-layout, and typographic features, the possibilities for manipulating imported pictures become endless. Here are a few of my favorite tricks for adding pizzazz to your pictures.

Using text characters as graphics frames

InDesign's Pen tool lets you create any kind of shape for use as a graphics frame, but if you want to place a picture in the shape of a text character or in several characters, there's a much easier way than drawing the characters yourself: You can use the Create Outlines command (Type ➪ Create Outlines, or Shift+⌘+O or Ctrl+Shift+O) to convert highlighted text into editable outlines, and then place a picture in the character shapes. Here's how:

1. **Format then highlight the text you want to use as a graphics frame.**

   You can use a single character or a range of text.

2. **Choose Type ➪ Create Outlines or press Shift+⌘+O or Ctrl+Shift+O.**

3. **Choose either of the selection tools, and then click on the highlighted text.**

4. **Choose File ➪ Place, or press ⌘+D or Ctrl+D, and then locate and select the graphics file you want to import.**

   You can also copy and paste a picture you've already imported. In this case, when you're ready to paste the copied picture, make sure you select the outlines and then choose Edit ➪ Paste Into, or press Option+⌘+V or Ctrl+Alt+V.

5. **Click OK or double-click on the filename to place the picture into the selected outlines.**

6. **Adjust the size and position of the imported picture so that it's displayed the way you want it in the character shapes.**

You can modify character outlines created with the Create Outlines command the same as you modify any shape — by adding a stroke and/or fill, by using the transformation tools or Transform pane to apply rotation, scale, or shear, and so on.

When you convert text to outlines using the Create Outlines command, the outlines replace the highlighted text and are embedded in the text. One handy aspect of the Create Outlines command is that the text remains editable. If you want to remove the outlines from the text and place them elsewhere, select the outlines with either of the selection tools, copy them (Edit ➪ Copy, or ⌘+C or Ctrl+C), then click on an empty portion of the page and choose Edit ➪ Paste or press ⌘+V or Ctrl+V. Figure 25-11 shows a picture that's been placed in the outline of a single text character.

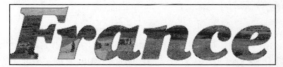

Figure 25-11: Converting the word *France* into an outline with the Create Outlines command and then using the Paste Into command to import the graphics file into the shape created this picture-in-text effect.

Using compound shapes as graphics frames

The Object ➪ Compound Paths command lets you combine several paths into a single object. Once you've created a multishape object, you can use the Place command or the Copy and Paste Into commands to put a picture in. In Figure 25-12, three paths have been placed in front of the cup and saucer picture:

Figure 25-12: Three separate shapes (left) were combined to create the effect on the right. Notice how the areas in the two inner shapes on the left are transparent (that is, the blended background is visible in the shapes) in the example on the right.

1. **A clipping path generated with the Clipping Path command surrounds the cup and saucer.**

2. **A path created with the Pen tool is in the cup handle.**

3. **A third, oval-shaped path — also created with the Pen tool — surrounds the coffee in the cup.**

In the image on the left, the picture — rather than the blended background shape — is visible in all three paths. The image on the right shows the results of creating a compound path out of the three paths. The blended background shows through in the two inner paths — areas that were previously obscured.

Cross-Reference   For more information about working with compound paths and reversing the direction of paths, see Chapter 27.

Creating inline frames

In most cases, you place a picture into a graphics frame and then, if necessary, manually move the frame by clicking and dragging it with the Selection tool or by changing the frame's X Location or Y Location values in the Transform pane or Control palette. If you want to place a picture relative to text in such a way that the picture moves — and thus remains close to its associated text — when editing causes the text to reflow, you can create an inline frame out of the graphics frame. Inline frames are particularly useful for publications like catalogs that contain lengthy text threads that, in turn, contain pictures that must flow with the text.

An inline frame behaves much like a single character, yet it retains all the attributes of a frame, which means you can add a stroke or fill, transform it with the transformation tools, the Transform pane, or Control palette, and so on.

If you want to create an inline frame from an object you've already created, all you have to do is copy or cut the object and then paste it into text as you would a piece of highlighted text.

Tip   If you place an inline frame in text to which automatic leading has been applied, the resulting line spacing can be inconsistent. To fix this problem, you can resize the inline frame.

In addition to using the Paste command to create an inline frame from an existing object, you can use the Place command to create an inline graphic from an external picture file. The key is to use the Type tool to select an insertion point in your text before placing the graphic (using File ⇨ Place, or ⌘+D or Ctrl+D); the graphic will be placed in the text in an inline frame.

Cross-Reference   For more information about working with inline frames, see Chapter 12.

Slicing a picture with the Scissors tool

The Scissors tool is the InDesign equivalent of a utility knife. It lets you slice objects into two parts. Figure 25-13 shows a picture that's been cut into halves with the Scissors tool. To slice a picture:

Figure 25-13: The Scissors tool was used to create the split image (right) from a clone of the original image (right).

1. **Select the Scissors tool.**

   If the Type tool isn't selected, you can press C to select the Scissors tool.

2. **Position the crosshair pointer anywhere over a graphics frame, then click.**

3. **Move the pointer to a different position along the frame edge, then click again.**

After you've clicked twice on the frame edge, you can switch to either of the selection tools and then drag either of the two picture pieces that your scissors cut created.

Note If you use the Scissors tool to split a frame to which a stroke has been applied, the resulting edges will not include the stroke.

Applying Lighting Effects

InDesign offers built-in drop shadow and feathering that let you create dimensional effects based on simulated lighting.

Cross-Reference I covered these features in Chapter 19, showing examples of how to use them with text. But you can also use them with graphics objects such as frames, pictures, and lines as shown here.

QuarkXPress User QuarkXPress does not offer drop shadow or feathering features, although there are third-party plug-ins to add these capabilities.

Drop shadows

The Drop Shadow dialog box, shown in Figure 25-14, is accessed by choosing Object ➪ Drop Shadow or pressing Option+⌘+M or Ctrl+Alt+M. To apply a drop shadow to an object, you select it with a selection tool — you cannot apply the shadow to just highlighted characters. In the dialog box, you set the following options:

Figure 25-14: The Drop Shadow dialog box and an example drop shadow.

✦ Check the Drop Shadow option to turn on the drop shadow function.

✦ Select a lighting type (technically, a blend mode) by choosing one of the 16 options in the Mode pop-up menu. These are the same blending modes used in transparencies and covered earlier in this chapter.

✦ Specify the opacity by entering a value in the Opacity field — 0% is invisible, while 100% is completely solid.

✦ Specify the shadow's position relative to the object using the X Offset and Y Offset fields. A positive X Offset moves the shadow to the right, while a positive Y Offset moves the shadow down. Negative values go in the other direction.

✦ Specify the shadow's size by entering a value in the Blur field — this blurs a copy of the text used in the drop shadow to make it look like it was created by shining light on solid letters.

✦ Choose a color source — Swatches, RGB, CMYK, and LAB — from the Color pop-up menu, then select a color from the sliders or swatches below. You'll get sliders for RGB, CMYK, and LAB with which to mix a color if you selected RGB, CMYK, or LAB in the Color pop-up menu, and a set of previously defined color swatches if you selected Swatches in the Color pop-up menu.

✦ To see the effects to your selected object as you experiment with various settings, check the Preview option.

Tip   Although traditionally associated with text, you can apply drop shadows to any objects, such as frames and shapes.

Feathering

A similar option to drop shadows is feathering, which essentially softens the edges of objects. Like drop shadows, feathering can be applied only to objects, not individual text, paths, or strokes. To feather an object, first select it and then choose Object ⇨ Feather. You'll get the dialog box shown in Figure 25-15.

Figure 25-15: The Feather dialog box and a sample feathering effect.

To apply feathering, check the Feather option. You then enter a value for the degree of feathering—smaller numbers have the least effect, larger numbers have the most effect. The featuring area starts at the outside edge of the object, so a larger number "eats into" the object, making it a wispier version of itself (refer to Figure 25-15). The Corners pop-up menu gives you three options: Sharp, Rounded, and Diffused. The Sharp option retains the original shape as much as possible. The Rounded option rounds the corners of the object; it can distort the shape dramatically at larger Feather Width settings. The Diffused option creates a soft, almost smoky effect by making the object more translucent.

Summary

After you import a picture into an InDesign document, you can use the Text Wrap pane to control how text flows when the picture is in front of a text frame. You can also use this to have one text frame wrap around another, though that is not common.

To mask out certain areas of a picture, you can use a picture's built-in clipping path (if it has one), edit the text-wrap boundary, place the picture in a free-form shape created with the Pen tool, or use the Clipping Path command to have InDesign build a clipping path.

InDesign offers sophisticated transparency tools to let items blend together, create ghost effects, and translucent items, and other such effects. Plus it offers tools to create sophisticated drop shadows and feathered edges, as well as fancy corners.

If you want to get even trickier with your imported pictures, you can place them in complex shapes created with the Compound Path command, paste them into a text thread so that they move along with the surrounding text, or slice them into two pieces with the Scissors tool.

✦   ✦   ✦

Drawing Free-Form Shapes and Curved Paths

In This Chapter

Understanding path basics

Drawing zigzag and wavy lines

Drawing closed shapes

Drawing free-form shapes

InDesign's basic drawing tools let you create basic shapes, such as straight lines, rectangles and squares, circles and ellipses, and equilateral polygons. But what about when you need to create shapes that aren't so basic? An amoeba, perhaps, or a cursive version of your first name? That's where InDesign's Pen tool comes in. You can use the Pen tool to create any kind of line or closed shape. And anything you create with the Pen tool can be used as an independent graphic element or as a frame for text or a picture.

If you've ever used an illustration program like Illustrator, FreeHand, or CorelDraw, or a page-layout program like PageMaker or QuarkXPress, you may already be familiar with Bézier drawing tools. (Bézier tools are named after Pierre Bézier, a French engineer and mathematician, who developed a method of representing curved shapes on a computer in the 1970s.) If you aren't familiar with Bézier tools, you should know in advance that getting the hang of using them takes a little time and patience. Even if you're a virtuoso when drawing with a piece of charcoal or a Number 2 pencil, you'll need to practice with the Pen tool for a while before your drawing skills will kick in. The good news is that, once you get comfortable using the Pen tool, you can draw any shape you can imagine. (Of course, if you can't draw very well in the first place, using the Pen tool won't magically transform you into an illustrator!) If this is new terrain for you, start simply and proceed slowly.

Tip

If you intend to use InDesign extensively as a drawing tool, you might want to purchase a drawing tablet, which can make working with the Pen tool a bit easier than using a mouse or trackball.

Finding Out All about Paths

Every object you create with InDesign's object-creation tools is a path. That includes

✦ Straight lines created with the Line tool

✦ Lines and shapes created with the Pen tool or the Pencil tool

✦ Basic shapes created with the Ellipse, Rectangle, and Polygon tools

✦ Basic frames created with the Ellipse Frame, Rectangle Frame, and Polygon Frame tools

All of InDesign's object-manipulation features are available for all paths. This includes the transformation tools, the Control palette and the Transform pane, the Stroke and Color panes, and the option to place a text file or graphics file either on or within the path. (You can't place text within a straight line, since there is not even a partial enclosure in which to create the bounds of a text frame.)

The properties of a path

Regardless of the tool you use to create a path, you can change its appearance by modifying any of four properties that all paths share: closure, stroke, fill, and contents.

Closure

A path is either *open* or *closed*. Straight lines created with the Line tool and curved and zigzag lines created with the Pen tool are examples of open paths. Basic shapes created with the Ellipse, Rectangle, and Polygon tools and free-form shapes created with the Pen and Pencil tools are examples of closed shapes. A closed free-form shape is an uninterrupted path with no endpoints. Figure 26-1 shows the difference between open and closed paths.

Tip   You can use the Scissors tool to convert a closed path into two (or more) open paths, and you can use the Pen tool to create a closed path from an open path.

Cross-Reference   See Chapter 27 for more information about creating a closed path from an open path and vice versa.

Stroke

If you want to make a path visible, you can apply a *stroke* to it. (An unselected, unstroked path is not visible.) When you stroke a path, you can specify the stroke's width, color, tint, and style. Figure 26-2 shows a path before and after a stroke was added.

Figure 26-1: The five paths on the left are open; the five on the right are closed. A stroke and fill have been added to show how they affect open and closed paths.

Figure 26-2: The original path (left) is selected. At right, a 2-point stroke was added to a clone of the original path.

Fill

A color, color tint, or gradient applied to the background of an open path or a closed path is called a *fill*. Figure 26-3 shows some examples of fills.

Figure 26-3: From left to right: a color fill (black), a color tint fill (50 percent black), and a gradient fill. The paths are selected and displayed in their bounding boxes.

Drawing tools

InDesign uses the same drawing tools as Adobe Illustrator and Adobe Photoshop, so if you're familiar with those, you'll have no trouble using InDesign's tools. If not, it might help to get a refresher on the tools:

✦ **Pen tool:** This draws both segments and Bézier curves. It has several associated tools to add, delete, and convert corner points, which are the handles that you use to change direction and curvature of a curve or line segment.

✦ **Pencil tool:** This is a free-form drawing tool that simply draws out your mouse motions. The result is a Bézier curve. A Pencil tool is great if you have a steady, accurate drawing hand; the Pen tool is better if you want to control each segment and curve as you create it.

✦ **Shape tools:** The shape tools create closed objects that aren't intended to hold text or graphics—they're basically shapes you can color and/or stroke. There is a Rectangle, Polygon, and Oval version, as described in Chapter 10.

✦ **Frame tools:** The frame tools are the same as the shape tools, except they're meant to create shapes that will contain text or graphics, though they can be empty.

✦ **Text and Text Path tools:** The Text and Text Path tools let you add text in an object and on an object's stroke, respectively. You cannot add text into a straight line, but you can add text to an open shape, as well as closed shapes and frames.

Contents

You can place a text file or a graphics file in any path (with the exception of a straight line). When a path is used to hold text or a picture, the path functions as a *frame*. Although InDesign can place text in an open path, placing text and pictures in closed paths is far more common than placing them in open paths. Figure 26-4 shows several examples of pictures imported into paths.

Figure 26-4: Top row: The same picture was imported into three different paths. (A stroke has been added to the paths to make them more visible.) Bottom row: Text has been placed in clones of the paths on the top row.

QuarkXPress User

For QuarkXPress users, the idea of placing text and pictures in lines (that is, in open paths) may seem strange at first. (In QuarkXPress, lines cannot contain text or pictures, although line-like text paths can contain text.)

The anatomy of a path

No matter how simple (a short, straight line) or complicated (a free-form shape with several straight and curved edges) a path is, all paths are made up of the same components. Figures 26-5 through 26-7 show the parts that make up a path:

✦ A path contains one or more straight or curved *segments,* as shown in Figure 26-5.

✦ An anchor point is located at each end of every segment. The anchor points at the ends of a closed path are called *endpoints*. When you create a path of any kind, anchor points are automatically placed at the end of each segment. After you create a path, you can move, add, delete, and change the direction of corner points.

Cross-Reference

See Chapter 27 for more information about modifying paths.

Figure 26-5: From left to right, each path contains one more segment than the previous path. The two rightmost paths each contain three segments.

✦ There are two kinds of anchor points: *smooth points* and *corner points*. A smooth point connects two adjoining curved segments in a continuous, flowing curve. At a corner point, adjoining segments — straight or curved — meet at an angle. The corners of a rectangular path are the most common corner points. Figure 26-6 shows some examples of smooth and corner points.

Figure 26-6: The path on the left has only corner anchor points; the path in the center has only smooth anchor points; and the path on the right has both kinds of anchor points.

✦ A *direction line* runs through each anchor point and has a handle at both ends. You can control the curve that passes through an anchor point by dragging a direction line's handles. Figure 26-7 shows how you can change the shape of a path by dragging a direction line handle.

Note   Anchor points and direction lines do not print.

Reading about riding a bike is one thing; riding a bike is another. If you've read Chapter 10, you already know how to ride with training wheels — you can create basic shapes with the basic object-creation tools. Now that you know more about what paths are made of, you're ready to tackle more-complex shapes. You're ready to wield the Pen tool.

Figure 26-7: Cloning the original path on the left and then dragging the direction handle of the right endpoint created the path on the right.

Drawing Lines with the Pen Tool

The Pen tool is very versatile. With it you can create lines (open paths) and shapes (closed paths).

Straight and zigzag lines

The simplest kind of path is a straight line (that is, an open path) with a single segment, which you can create with either the Line tool or the Pen tool. But the Pen is much mightier than the Line, because it lets you draw zigzag lines with multiple straight segments, curvy lines, and lines that contain straight and curved segments. You can't draw those kinds of shapes with the Line tool, or any of the other object-creation tools, for that matter.

Cross-Reference Chapter 10 covers the Line tool.

To draw lines with straight segments:

1. **Select the Pen tool or press P if the Type tool isn't selected.**

2. **Move the Pen pointer to where you want to place one of your line's endpoints, then click and release the mouse button (make sure you don't drag before you release the mouse button).**

   When you click and release the mouse button while using the Pen tool, you create a corner point. A small, filled-in square indicates the anchor point, which is also an endpoint of the open shape you're creating.

3. **Move the Pen pointer to where you want to place the next anchor point, then click and release the mouse button.**

When you create the second point, a straight line connects it with the first point, the first anchor point changes to a hollow square, and the second anchor point is filled in. (If you want to create a line with a single segment, you can stop drawing at this point by choosing another tool.)

4. **For each additional anchor point, move the Pen pointer, then click and release the mouse button.**

   If you hold down the Shift key as you click, the angles you create are limited to multiples of 45 degrees. To reposition an anchor point after you click the mouse button but before you release it, hold down the spacebar and drag. (Be careful: If you drag before you press the spacebar, you'll create a smooth point and curved segments.)

5. **To complete the path, hold down the ⌘ key or the Ctrl key and click on an empty portion of the page or choose another tool.**

   If you click on the page, the Pen tool remains selected and you can continue creating additional paths. Figure 26-8 shows a path in various stages of being drawn.

Figure 26-8: As each anchor point was created (from left to right), a new, straight segment was added to the path. The finished open path is a zigzag line that contains four straight segments produced by clicking and releasing the mouse a total of five times.

You can also complete the path by clicking on the first point you created, but if you do, you'll create a closed path (closed paths are covered in the next section).

Tip   As you create a path, you can move any anchor point, direction line handle, or the entire path by holding down the ⌘ or Ctrl key, then clicking and dragging whatever element you want to move.

Curved lines

If all you ever need to create are zigzag lines with corner points and straight segments, the click-and-release method in the preceding section is all you need to know. But if you want to create curvy lines, you need to take the next step up the

Bézier ladder and learn to add smooth points. Creating smooth points and curved segments is much like creating corner points and straight segments — with a twist. There are two ways of connecting curved segments when drawing a path: with smooth points and with corner points. Both methods are explained in the steps that follow.

Curved segments connected by smooth points

If you want to draw a continuously curvy path that contains no corner points and no straight segments, you should create only smooth points as you draw. Here's how:

1. **Select the Pen tool or press P if the Type tool isn't selected.**

2. **Move the Pen pointer to where you want to place one of your line's endpoints, then click and hold down the mouse button.**

   The arrowhead pointer is displayed.

3. **Drag the mouse button in the direction of the next point you intend to create.**

   (Adobe suggests dragging about one-third of the way to the next point.) As you drag, the anchor point, its direction line, and the direction line's two handles are displayed, as shown in Figure 26-9. If you hold down the Shift key as you drag, the angle of the direction line is limited to increments of 45 degrees.

Figure 26-9: To create a smooth point when beginning a path, click and hold the mouse and drag in the direction of the next point. Here you see the direction line of a smooth endpoint created by clicking and dragging in the direction of the next anchor point.

4. **Release the mouse button.**

5. **Move the Pen pointer where you want to establish the next anchor point — and end the first segment — then drag the mouse.**

   If you drag in approximately the same direction as the direction line of the previous point, you'll create an S-shaped curve; if you drag in the opposite direction, you'll create a C-shaped curve. Figure 26-10 shows both kinds of curves.

6. **When the curve between the two anchor points looks how you want it to look, release the mouse button.**

7. **Continue moving the Pen pointer, clicking, dragging, then releasing the mouse button to establish additional smooth points and curved segments.**

Figure 26-10: A C-shaped curved segment (left); an S-shaped curved segment (right).

8. **To complete the path, hold down the ⌘ key or the Ctrl key and click on an empty portion of the page or choose another tool.**

   If you click on the page, the Pen tool remains selected and you can continue creating additional paths.

You can also complete the path by clicking on the first point you created, but if you do, you'll create a closed path (closed paths are covered in the next section). Figure 26-11 shows a finished line that contains several curved segments.

Figure 26-11: This line contains five anchor points — all smooth points — and four curved segments. The two segments on the left are both C-shaped curves; the two on the right are S-shaped.

Tip

The two segments that form a smooth point's direction line work together as a single, straight line. When you move a handle, the line acts like a teeter-totter; the opposite handle moves in the opposite direction. If you shorten one of the segments, the length of the other segment doesn't change. The angle and length of direction lines determine the shape of the segments with which they're associated.

Curved segments connected by corner points

Sometimes you may need to create a line with curvy segments that don't adjoin smoothly. Figure 26-12 shows an example of a line that's made up of several C-shaped curves that are connected with corner points. When adjoining segments — curved or straight — meet at a corner point, the transition is abrupt rather than smooth, as it is at a smooth point. To create this kind of shape, you need to be able to connect curved segments using corner points instead of smooth points. Here's how:

1. **Select the Pen tool or press P if the Type tool isn't selected.**

2. **Move the Pen pointer to where you want to place one of your line's end-points, then click and hold down the mouse button.**

   The arrowhead pointer is displayed.

3. **Drag the mouse button in the direction of the next point you intend to create.**

   As you drag, the anchor point, its direction line, and the direction line's two handles are displayed. If you hold down the Shift key as you drag, the angle of the direction line is limited to increments of 45 degrees.

4. **Move the Pen pointer to where you want to establish the next anchor point — and end the first segment — then press Option or Alt and drag the mouse.**

   As you drag, the anchor point's handle moves and the direction line changes from a straight line to two independent segments. The angle of the direction line segment that you create when you drag the handle determines the slope of the next segment.

5. **Release the mouse button.**

6. **Continue moving the Pen pointer and repeat Step 4 and Step 5 to create additional segments joined by corner points.**

7. **To complete the path, hold down the ⌘ key or the Ctrl key and click on an empty portion of the page or choose another tool.**

   If you click on the page, the Pen tool remains selected and you can continue creating additional paths.

Figure 26-12 shows a line with several curved segments joined by corner points.

Figure 26-12: Here, three corner points join four curved segments. The direction handles of the two rightmost segments are visible. The direction handles of a corner point are joined like a hinge; moving one handle doesn't affect the other handle.

Note A corner point that connects two curved segments has two direction lines; a corner point that connects two straight segments has no direction lines; and a corner point that connects a straight and curved segment has one direction line. If you drag a corner point's direction line, the other direction line, if there is one, is not affected. The angle and length of direction lines determine the shape of the segments with which they're associated.

Combining straight and curved segments

By combining the techniques for drawing straight segments and curved segments, you can create lines that contain both. Figure 26-13 shows three lines made up of straight and curved segments, as well as curved segments joined by smooth points and curved segments joined by corner points.

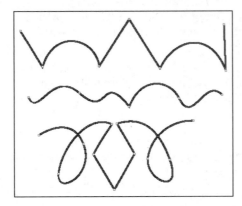

Figure 26-13: Three paths with both curved and straight segments, as well as corner points and smooth points.

Here's how to draw a straight segment followed by a curved segment:

1. **While drawing a path, create a straight segment by clicking and releasing the mouse button, moving the Pen pointer, then clicking and releasing the mouse button again.**

2. **Move the Pen pointer over the last anchor point you created in Step 1.**

   The Convert Point icon (insert icon) is displayed.

3. **Click, drag, and then release the mouse button to create the direction line that determines the slope of the next segment.**

4. **Move the Pen pointer to where you want to establish the next anchor point, then click and drag to complete the curved segment.**

Figure 26-14 shows a step-by-step sequence of a curved segment being added to a straight segment. You can also follow a straight segment with a curved segment by simply clicking and dragging to create a smooth point. However, if you don't use the method explained in the earlier steps, you'll be able to adjust the slope associated with only one of the curved segment's anchor points rather than both.

Move the pointer over the end point, and click and drag to establish the curve of the next segment.

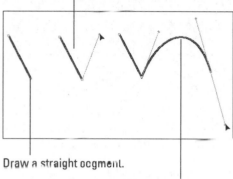

Draw a straight segment.

Move the pointer where you want to place the next anchor point, then click and drag to create a curved segment.

Figure 26-14: At left is a straight segment. In the center, one of the direction lines of the straight segment's endpoint is being dragged. At right, clicking and dragging create a smooth anchor point, and a C-shaped curve is added after the straight segment.

To draw a curved segment followed by a straight segment:

1. **While drawing a path, create a curved segment by clicking, dragging, then releasing the mouse button, and then moving the Pen pointer, clicking, dragging, and releasing the mouse button again.**

2. **Move the Pen pointer over the last anchor point you created in Step 1.**

   The Convert Point icon (insert icon) is displayed.

3. **Click on the anchor point to convert it from a smooth point to a corner point.**

4. **Move the Pen pointer to where you want to establish the next anchor point, then click and release the mouse button to complete the straight segment.**

Figure 26-15 shows a straight segment being added to a curved segment.

Move the pointer over the last anchor
point and click on the anchor point.

Create a curved segment.

Move the pointer where you want to establish the next
anchor point, then click and release the mouse button.

Figure 26-15: At left is a curved segment. In the center, the curved segment's smooth endpoint has been changed to a corner point. At right, clicking and releasing the mouse creates a new corner anchor point, and a straight segment is added to the curved segment.

Tip   When creating paths, you should use as few anchor points as possible. As you become more comfortable creating free-form paths, you should find yourself using fewer anchor points to create paths.

Drawing Free-Form Shapes

A closed path is an uninterrupted enclosure with no endpoints. When you apply a stroke to a closed path, there's no beginning or end. Generally, you'll create closed paths when you want to place text or pictures in free-form frames. Although you can place text or a picture in an open path, the result can look more than a little strange, especially if you add a stroke to the path. Then again, you can achieve some strange effects by using open paths as frames. If strange is your goal, go for it.

Tip   For an easy way to draw free-form shapes, use the Pencil tool. It simply traces the movement of your mouse (or pen tablet) as you move it, much like a pencil works on paper. Although not as exact as the Pen tool, the Pencil tool does create Bézier curves that you can later edit. Do note that the Pencil tool is not meant for creating straight lines — unless you can draw perfectly straight lines by hand, that it.

When it comes to creating closed paths with the Pen tool, the process is exactly the same as for creating open paths, as explained earlier in this chapter, with one difference at the end: If you click on the first endpoint you created, you create a closed path:

✦ To create a straight segment between the endpoint and the last anchor point you created, click and release the mouse button.

✦ To create a curved segment, click and drag the mouse in the direction of the last anchor point you created, and then release the mouse button.

Just like an open path, a closed path can contain straight and/or curved segments and smooth and/or corner points. All the techniques explained earlier in this chapter for drawing lines with curved and straight segments and smooth and corner points apply when you're drawing closed paths. Figure 26-16 shows several closed paths used as graphic shapes, text frames, and graphics frames.

 Cross-Reference If you draw a path and it turns out to be a little (or a lot, for that matter) different than you intended, don't worry. You can always modify it by moving, adding, deleting, and converting anchor points and by adjusting direction lines. You can also use the transformation tools or the Transform pane to rotate, scale, shear, mirror, and change the position of the path.

 Cross-Reference See Chapter 27 for information about modifying lines and shapes. See Chapters 11 and 24 for more information about using InDesign's transformation features.

Figure 26-16: Closed paths of various shapes.

Summary

If you need to create free-form paths — zigzag or curvy lines or complex closed shapes — you must use the Pen tool. All paths are made up of one or more segments, which begin and end in anchor points. Direction lines control the behavior or anchor points, which in turn control the transition between adjoining segments. When you create an open or closed path using the Pen tool, you have the option of creating straight segments or curved segments and corner points or smooth points.

✦   ✦   ✦

Modifying Shapes and Paths

♦   ♦   ♦   ♦

In This Chapter

Working with anchor points

Modifying segments

Manipulating open paths

Manipulating closed paths

Creating compound paths

Applying corner effects to paths

♦   ♦   ♦   ♦

No matter how skillful you become using InDesign's Pen and Pencil tools to create free-form paths, it's difficult to create exactly what you want on your first attempt. For example, after creating a path, you may want to add detail, smooth out a rough spot, or turn a straight segment into a curved one. No problem. InDesign lets you modify the paths you create in several ways. You can

+ Add or delete anchor points.
+ Move anchor points.
+ Change corner points to smooth points and vice versa.
+ Modify direction lines.
+ Extend an open path.
+ Change a closed path to an open path and vice versa.

Note   The path-manipulation techniques explained in this chapter apply to all types of paths, including open and closed paths created with the Pen tool, the Pencil tool, and the object-creation tools; text and picture frames (which are simply paths that act as containers); clipping paths created with the Clipping Path command (Object ⇨ Clipping Path, or Option+Shift+⌘+K or Ctrl+Alt+Shift+K) or built into imported pictures; and text-wrap paths created with the Text Wrap pane (Object ⇨ Text Wrap, or Option+⌘+W or Ctrl+Alt+W).

Generally, when you want to manipulate a path, you'll use one of the three variations of the Pen tool, all of which are displayed in a single pop-up menu in the Tools palette (shown in Figure 27-1):

✦ Both the Add Anchor Point tool and the Delete Anchor Point tool let you add and delete anchor points.

✦ The Convert Direction Point tool lets you change smooth points to corner points and vice versa.

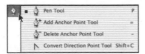

Figure 27-1: The four Pen tools in the Tools palette.

You can also use the Pen tool with keyboard shortcuts to perform all the functions of the Add Anchor Point, Delete Anchor Point, and Convert Direction Point tools.

Tip   If you find that you simply can't create a particular graphic effect within InDesign, you can always resort to your illustration program (assuming you have one). If you're an Illustrator user, you can easily drag and drop objects from Illustrator into InDesign documents.

Cross-Reference   See Chapter 23 for information about dragging and dropping Illustrator objects and files into InDesign documents.

Adding and Deleting Anchor Points

If you want to add detail to an existing path, you'll need to add anchor points that give you more precise control over a portion of the path. Perhaps you've drawn the profile of a face and you want to add detail to the lips. Or maybe you've written your name longhand and you need to add a flourish that your original attempt lacks. In both cases, you could add smooth or corner points and then manipulate the curves associated with those points by moving them or manipulating their direction lines. (The next section explains how to move anchor points and manipulate direction lines.)

On the other hand, maybe you've created a path that's more complicated than necessary. Perhaps you drew a hand with six fingers instead of five or a camel with one too many humps. In these instances, you need to simplify the path by removing anchor points. InDesign lets you add and delete as many anchor points as you want.

Tip   You should always try to use as few anchor points as possible in the paths you create. The fewer points a path has, the less likely it is to cause printing problems.

Note   When you want to modify the shape of a path, you should begin by selecting it with the Direct Selection tool rather than the Selection tool. If you select a path with the Selection tool, the path's bounding box is displayed with eight moveable handles. In this situation, you can modify the bounding box (thereby resizing the path), but you can't modify the path itself.

To add an anchor point:

1. **Select the path by clicking on it with the Direct Selection tool.**

   You can also select multiple paths and then modify them one at a time.

2. **Select the Pen tool, the Add Anchor Point tool, or the Delete Anchor Point tool.**

   You can use any of these tools to add and delete anchor points. If the Type tool is not selected, you can select the Pen tool by pressing P, the Add Anchor Point tool by pressing =, and the Delete Anchor Point tool by pressing - (hyphen).

3. **Move the Pen pointer over the selected path at the point where you want to add an anchor point.**

4. **Click and release the mouse button.**

   A new anchor point is created where you click. If the Delete Anchor Point tool is selected, you must hold down the ⌘ or Ctrl key to add an anchor point. If you click on a straight segment between two corner points, a corner point is created. If you click on a curved segment between two smooth points or between a smooth point and a corner point, a smooth point is created. You can also click, drag, and then release the mouse button if you want to adjust the direction line of the point you create. Figure 27-2 shows a before and after example of a path to which a smooth anchor point is added.

Figure 27-2: The original path (left) is modified by adding a smooth point (second from left). Dragging the smooth point (third from left) produced the final shape (right).

After you add an anchor point, you can hold down the ⌘ or Ctrl key or switch to the Direct Selection tool and drag it or either of its direction handles to adjust the adjoining segments.

Tip

Whenever you're working on a path, you can hold down the ⌘ or Ctrl key and then click and drag any element of the path — an anchor point, a direction line, or the entire path.

To delete an anchor point:

1. **Select the path by clicking on it with the Direct Selection tool.**

   You can also select multiple paths and then modify them one at a time.

2. **Select the Pen tool, the Add Anchor Point tool, or the Delete Anchor Point tool.**

   You can use any of these tools to add and delete anchor points. If the Type tool is not selected, you can select the Pen tool by pressing P, the Add Anchor Point tool by pressing =, and the Delete Anchor Point tool by pressing - (hyphen) on the main keyboard or on the numeric keypad.

3. **Move the pointer over the anchor point that you want to delete, and then click.**

   If the Add Anchor Point tool is selected, you must hold down the ⌘ or Ctrl key to delete an anchor point. Figure 27-3 shows a before and after example of a path from which an anchor point has been deleted.

Figure 27-3: The curved segment of the original path (left) is removed by deleting the smooth anchor point (center) with the Delete Anchor Point tool. The resulting path is shown on the right.

Modifying Segments

In Chapter 26, you learned that a path is made up of one or more segments, and every segment is defined by a pair of anchor points. If you want to modify a segment, you can do so by dragging either or both of its anchor points, dragging the direction handles (if present) of the anchor points, or converting either of the anchor points from smooth to corner or vice versa. For example, you could drag an anchor point on a curvy path to increase or decrease the severity of a particular bump, or you could convert a straight-edged polygon into a curvy shape by converting all its corner points to smooth points.

Moving anchor points

When you select a path with the Direct Selection tool, its anchor points are displayed as small, hollow squares. When you click and drag an anchor point, the two adjoining segments change, but the direction handles, if present, are not affected. If you hold down the Shift key as you drag an anchor point, movement is restricted to increments of 45 degrees. Figure 27-4 shows how moving an anchor point affects adjoining curved and straight segments.

Figure 27-4: Top row: The arc of the curve was reduced (right) by clicking and dragging the smooth anchor point at the top of the curve (left). Bottom row: Dragging a corner point changes the two adjoining segments.

Tip

If all you need to do is resize a path — particularly a simple rectangle — rather than change its shape, you should select it with the Selection tool rather than the Direct Selection tool, and then drag one of its bounding box handles.

Converting anchor points

If you want to change a wavy path that contains only curved segments to a zigzag path that contains only straight segments, you can do so by converting the smooth anchor points of the wavy path into corner points. Similarly, by converting corner points to smooth points, you can smooth out a path that contains straight segments. Figure 27-5 shows how straight and curved paths are affected by converting their anchor points.

To converting an anchor point:

1. **Select the path by clicking on it with the Direct Selection tool.**

2. **Choose the Convert Direction Point tool.**

   You can also perform the functions of this tool by holding down Option+⌘ or Ctrl+Alt when the Direct Selection tool is selected.

Figure 27-5: Top row: The outer corner points of a straight-edged polygon path (left) were converted to smooth points to create the shape on the right. Bottom row: The zigzag path (right) was created by converting all the smooth points in the path on the left into corner points.

3. Move the pointer over the anchor point you want to convert.

Depending on the point you want to convert, do one of the following:

- To convert a corner point to a smooth point, click on the corner point, and then drag (direction lines are created and displayed as you drag).

- To convert a smooth point to a corner point without direction lines, click and release the mouse on the smooth point.

- To convert a smooth point to a corner point with independent direction lines, click and drag either of the smooth point's direction handles.

- To convert a corner point without direction lines to a corner point with direction lines, click and drag the corner point to create a smooth point, then release the mouse button. Then click and drag either of the direction lines.

Tip   When using the Convert Direction Point tool, you can temporarily switch to the most recently used selection tool by pressing the ⌘ or Ctrl key.

QuarkXPress User   QuarkXPress uses a very different approach to changing direction points from smooth to corner: It has iconic buttons in its Measurement palette that let you easily convert segment and corner types. The InDesign approach is more efficient in that it uses one tool and relies on a mouse-based tool (since you're likely using the mouse when you edit a shape), but it does require a bit more getting used to initially.

Manipulating direction handles

In addition to dragging and converting anchor points, you can adjust the shape of a curved segment by dragging any of the direction lines associated with the anchor points at either end of the segment. Figure 27-6 shows how moving direction lines affects a curved segment.

Figure 27-6: The two shapes on the right were created by dragging a direction line of a smooth point.

Note   Remember, corner points between straight segments don't have direction handles. If you want to modify the segments associated with a corner point, simply click and drag the point.

To drag a curved segment's direction handle:

1. **Use the Direct Selection tool to select the path.**

2. **Click on either of the two endpoints that define the curved segment.**

    Handles are displayed at the ends of the two lines that make up the selected point's direction line (and the lines make up what appears to be a single, straight line). The direction lines of the two adjoining segments (if present) are also displayed.

3. **Click and drag any available handle.**

    Hold down the Shift key as you drag to constrain movement to multiples of 45 degrees. As you drag, the handle at the opposite end of the direction line moves in the opposite direction like a teeter-totter. However, if you lengthen or shorten one side of a direction line, the other side is not affected.

4. **Release the mouse button when the shape is the way you want it.**

Note   If you use the Convert Direction Point tool to click and drag a smooth point's direction-line handle, the opposite portion of the direction line remains unchanged. This lets you adjust the segment on one side of a smooth point without affecting the segment on the other side.

Working with Open and Closed Paths

If you've created an open path and subsequently decide that you want to extend the path at either or both ends, you can do so using the Pen tool. Along the same lines, you can use the Pen tool to connect two open paths and to close an open path. For example, if you've placed text or a picture into an open path, you may decide that the path would work better in a closed frame. And if you want to get even trickier, you can use the Scissors tool to split an open or closed path into two separate paths.

Extending an open path and connecting open paths

The steps required to extend an open path and to connect two open paths are very similar. Here's how you extend an open path:

1. **Use the Direct Selection tool to select the path you want to extend.**

2. **Move the Pen pointer over one of the path's endpoints.**

   When the Pen pointer is over an endpoint, a small, angled line is displayed below and to the right of the Pen.

3. **Click and release the mouse button.**

4. **Move the pointer to where you want to place the next anchor point.**

   If you want to create a corner point, click and release the mouse button. If you want to create a smooth point, click and drag, and then release the mouse button.

5. **Continue adding smooth and corner points until you're done extending the path.**

6. **Finish the path by holding down the ⌘ or Ctrl key and clicking on an empty portion of the page or choosing another tool.**

To connect two open paths, follow Steps 1 through 3 above, and then click on the endpoint of another path (the other path doesn't have to be selected). Figure 27-7 shows a path before and after being extended; Figure 27-8 shows an open path produced by connecting two open paths.

Figure 27-7: The original path (left) was cloned to create the path on the right. The cloned path was then extended by clicking on its right endpoint with the Pen tool and then clicking four more times to create four additional corner points.

Figure 27-8: Connecting the two open paths on the left with the Pen tool produced the single path on the right.

Tip

If you hold down the Shift key when you click an endpoint with the Pen tool, an endpoint for a new path is created (that is, the selected path remains unchanged). In this situation, a small *x* is displayed below and to the right of the Pen pointer. This is useful if you want to create two paths that touch at a particular point. For example, you could draw a path and apply a 4-point black stroke to it and then create another path that shares an endpoint with the first path. By adding a different kind of stroke to the second path, the two paths would look like a single path to which two kinds of kinds of stroke have been applied.

Closing an open path

Closing an open path is much the same as extending an open path. The only difference is that you *complete* the path—that is, you close it—by clicking on the other endpoint. For example, if you slice a graphics frame into two pieces using the Scissors tool (this is explained in the next section of this chapter), two open paths are created. If you add a stroke to these open frames, a portion of the picture edge (the nonexistent segment between the endpoints) will not be stroked. If you close the path, the stroke will completely enclose the picture within. Figure 27-9 shows an open path that's been converted into a closed path.

Figure 27-9: The closed path on the right was created from a clone of the open path on the left.

Using the Scissors tool

The Scissors tool does precisely what its icon suggests: It lets you slice things. Specifically, it lets you split paths — open and closed — into two pieces. There are a few things you should know about using the Scissors tool:

✦ It only takes one click with the Scissors tool to split an open path, but it takes two clicks to completely split a closed path.

✦ You can split graphics frames, but you can't split text frames that contain text. If you want to split a text frame that contains text, you must first cut the text and paste it elsewhere.

✦ If you split a graphics frame, a copy of the picture is placed within both frames.

✦ When you split a path, all stroke and fill attributes of the original path are inherited by the two offspring. After you split a path, it looks the same as before you split it until you move or modify one of the resulting paths.

To split an open path, use the Scissors tool and move the crosshair pointer over a path, and then click and release the mouse button. You can click on an open portion of a segment (that is, between anchor points) or on an anchor point. In both cases, two anchor points — endpoints of the two resulting paths — are created.

To split a closed path, use the Scissors tool and move the crosshair pointer over a path, then click and release the mouse button. You can click on an open portion of a segment or on an anchor point. In both cases, two anchor points — endpoints of the two resulting paths — are created. Move the crosshair pointer to a different position along the same path, then click and release the mouse button.

After you split a path, you can switch to either of the selection tools and then select, move, or modify either of the two resulting paths as you wish. If you've split a closed path, you may want to close the two open paths (as described in the previous section). Figure 27-10 shows a pair of open paths that were created using the Scissors tool on an open path. Figure 27-11 shows a closed picture frame that's been split into two open frames.

Figure 27-10: The original path (left) was split into two pieces by clicking on it with the Scissors tool (center). On the right, you see the two resulting paths after the one on the right has been moved.

Figure 27-11: The closed path on the left was cut twice with the Scissors tool (center). On the right, one of the resulting open paths has been moved with the Selection tool.

Working with Compound Paths

When more than one path is selected, you can use the Make (Compound Path) command (Object ⇨ Compound Paths ⇨ Make, or ⌘+8 or Ctrl+8) to convert the paths into a single object. A compound path is similar to a group (Object ⇨ Group, or Ctrl+G or ⌘+G), except that when you create a group out of several objects, each object in the group retains its original attributes, such as stroke color and width, fill color or gradient, and so on. By contrast, when you create a compound path, the attributes of the backmost path are applied to all the other paths (that is, the attributes of the backmost path replace the attributes of the other paths).

You can use a compound path to do such things as:

✦ **Create transparent areas within a path.** For example, by drawing a circular path in front of a picture, you could then use the Make (Compound Paths) command to poke a hole in the picture and reveal the objects or the empty page behind the picture. Figure 27-12 shows a compound path used as a picture frame.

Figure 27-12: Designer John Cruise created the picture with the hole in it (right) by drawing a circular path (center) in front of a clone of the original picture frame (left), and then creating a compound path from the picture frame and the circular path. The background shape shows within the transparent hole.

✦ **Apply a single background color or place a single picture within several shapes.** For example, you could use the Create Outlines command (Type ➪ Create Outlines, or Shift+⌘+O or Ctrl+Shift+O) to convert text characters into a compound path, and then place a blend behind the path so that it extends across all characters. (The Create Outlines command is explained in Chapter 28.) Figure 27-13 shows an example of this.

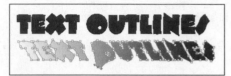

Figure 27-13: Designer John Cruise converted the text on the top into the editable outlines on the bottom. He then skewed the character outlines — which make up a compound path — by –30 degrees via the Skew field in the Transform pane or Control palette and applied a gradient fill.

✦ **Quickly create complex shapes that would be difficult to create with the Pen tool.** For example, you could create the complex shape in Figure 27-14 by drawing each of the shaded areas as a separate, closed path. Or you could simply create a square, place four circles in front of it so that they overlap the edges of the square, and then choosing the Make (Compound Paths) command — a process that takes only a few seconds.

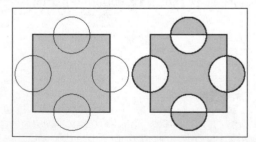

Figure 27-14: Designer John Cruise converted the five closed paths on the left into a compound path via the Make (Compound Path) command to create the shape on the right. InDesign automatically applied the attributes of the original square path, which is the backmost path, to the resulting compound path. Notice that the four semicircular areas where the original shapes overlapped became holes after converting the shapes to a compound path.

That's only the beginning of what you can do with the Make (Compound Paths) command. Mix in a little bit of your imagination and InDesign's other path-, picture-, and text-manipulation features, and the possibilities become endless.

Creating compound paths

You can create a compound path out of any kind of path, including open and closed paths as well as text and graphics frames. When you create a compound path, all the original paths become subpaths of the compound shape and inherit the stroke and fill settings of the path that's farthest back in the stacking order. After you create a compound path, you can modify or remove any of the subpaths.

Tip   If the results of choosing Make (Compound Path) are not what you expected or want, you can undo the operation (Edit ⇨ Undo). In this case, try changing the stacking order and then choose Make (Compound Path) again.

Note   The direction of each subpath determines whether the subpath is filled or transparent. If a particular subpath is transparent instead of filled, or vice versa, you can use the Reverse Path command (Object ⇨ Reverse Path) to switch the behavior of a subpath. (The Reverse Path command is explained more fully later in this chapter.)

If frames that contain text and/or pictures are selected when you choose Make (Compound Path), the resulting compound path will retain the content of the frame that's closest to the bottom of the stacking order. If the bottommost frame doesn't have any content, the content — text or picture — of the next highest nonempty frame is retained in the compound path. The content of all frames above the frame whose content is retained is removed.

Tip   To change an object's stacking order (to determine which path's attributes are used for the compound path), use Object ⇨ Arrange ⇨ Send to Back, or Shift+⌘+[or Ctrl+Shift+[.

Editing compound paths

After you create a compound path, you can change the shape of any of the subpaths by clicking on one with the Direct Selection tool, and then clicking and dragging any of its anchor points or direction handles. The Pen, Add Anchor Point, Delete Anchor Point, and Change Direction Line tools work the same for subpaths as for other paths, which means that you can reshape them however you want.

The Stroke pane (Window ⇨ Stroke, or F10), Swatches (Window ⇨ Swatches, or F5), and Color pane (Window ⇨ Color, or F6) — as well as the transformation tools, the Control palette (Window ⇨ Control), and the Transform pane (Window ⇨ Transform, or F9) also let you change the appearance of a compound path. When you change the appearance of a compound path, the changes are applied uniformly to all subpaths.

Moving a subpath is a little tricky because you can't drag just that subpath. If you try, all the subpaths move. If you want to move an entire subpath, you must move each of the subpath's anchor points individually. In this case, it's probably easier to release the compound path, as described next, move the path as needed, then re-create the compound path by choosing Make (Object ⇨ Compound Path ⇨ Make, or ⌘+8 or Ctrl+8).

If you want to delete a subpath, you must use the Delete Anchor Point tool to delete all its anchor points. If you delete an anchor point of a closed subpath, it becomes an open subpath.

Note   You can't delete anchor points using the Cut command (Edit ⇨ Cut, or ⌘+X or Ctrl+X), the Clear command (or Edit ⇨ Clear, or Delete or Backspace), nor the Del or Delete key. All of these keyboard commands remove the entire path.

Changing a subpath's direction

When you create a path, it has a built-in direction — clockwise or counterclockwise — that is generally not noticeable but affects a compound path. Generally, you can't determine the direction of a path by looking at it. However, you can tell if subpaths' directions differ by how subpaths interact:

✦ If a subpath in a compound path has the same direction as the backmost path, the area within the subpath is transparent.

✦ Conversely, if a subpath's direction is different than the backmost path, the area within the subpath will be filled.

If a subpath is filled in and you want it to be transparent, or vice versa, click on the compound path with the Direct Selection tool, then click on one of the anchor points of the subpath whose direction you want to change and choose Object ⇨ Compound Path ⇨ Release, or Option+⌘+8 or Ctrl+Alt+8. Figure 27-15 shows how changing the direction of a subpath changes it from filled to transparent.

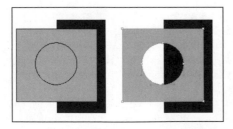

Figure 27-15: The gray square and circle on the left have been combined into a compound path, but the direction of the circular subpath causes it to be filled in instead of transparent. Changing the subpath's direction produced the results on the right: a transparent hole in the square shape.

Splitting a compound path

If you decide you want to "deconstruct" a compound path, you can do so by clicking anywhere within the compound path and then choosing Object ➪ Compound Paths ➪ Release, or Option+⌘+8 or Ctrl+Alt+8. The resulting paths retain the attributes of the compound path.

Note   The Release command is not available if the selected compound path contains text or if it's nested within a frame.

Using the Pathfinder

Sometimes, you want to combine multiple paths. You could join them, as described earlier, or you could use the new Pathfinder tool, accessed by selecting the objects and then choosing Object ➪ Pathfinder. You'll see five options in the resulting submenu: Add, Subtract, Intersect, Exclude Overlap, and Minus Back. Figure 27-16 shows how they affect a group of paths (two open and one closed).

Figure 27-16: Three paths and the five Pathfinder options. Top row: The three original paths, after applying Add, and after applying Subtract. Bottom row: After applying Intersect, Exclude Overlap, and Minus Back.

New Feature   InDesign CS offers a new feature to combine paths, called the Pathfinder.

Here's what they do:

✦ **Add** adds all objects' shapes together.

✦ **Subtract** subtracts all objects from the bottommost object in the stack.

✦ **Intersect** creates an object where objects overlap — this works only on closed paths.

✦ **Exclude Overlap** removes overlapping paths and keeps the nonoverlapping paths of all objects.

✦ **Minus Back** subtracts all objects from the top object in the stack.

QuarkXPress User   The Pathfinder options are similar to QuarkXPress's Merge options.

Adding Corner Effects to Paths

When a path is selected, the Corner Effects command (Object ➪ Corner Effects) lets you apply any of several graphic embellishments to its corner points (if the path has any corner points). For example, you could use a corner effect to add pizzazz to the border of a coupon or a certificate. Generally, corner effects work best with rectangular shapes, but they can also produce interesting results when applied to free-form shapes, as shown in Figure 27-17.

Figure 27-17: The original shapes are on the top row. The bottom row shows the same shapes after applying (from left to right) the Fancy, Rounded, and Inverse Rounded corner effects.

To apply a corner effect to a path:

1. **Use either of the selection tools to select the path to which you want to apply corner effects.**

2. **Choose Object Corner Effects.**

   The Corner Effects dialog box, shown in Figure 27-18, is displayed.

Figure 27-18: The Effect menu in the Corner Effects dialog box displays the names of five built-in corner effects. A standard corner plus the five effects are shown above the dialog box.

3. **Choose a Corner Effect from the Effect pop-up menu.**

   If you want to see the effect as you create it, click Preview and, if necessary, move the dialog box out of the way so you can see the selected path.

4. **In the Size field, enter the distance away from the corner point that the effect will extend.**

5. **After you've finished specifying the appearance of the corner effect, click OK to close the dialog box.**

InDesign doesn't let you modify the built-in corner effects or add your own to the list of choices. Nor can you use the Direct Selection tool to modify the corner of a path to which a corner effect has been applied (anchor points are not displayed for the additional segments that are added when a corner effect is applied to a corner point). The only control you have over a corner effect is the value you specify in the Radius field of the Corner Effects dialog box.

Summary

When it comes to drawing with the Pen or Pencil tool, close is plenty good enough. That's because InDesign lets you modify paths in many ways — by moving, adding, and deleting anchor points; by switching smooth points to corner points and vice versa; and by dragging direction lines. You also have the option to extend either or both ends of an open path and to close open paths.

If a path requires more drastic surgery, you can use the Scissors tool, which lets you split any kind of path into two pieces.

Because InDesign is primarily a page-layout program, it doesn't contain the breadth of illustration-specific features that you would find in a dedicated vector-based drawing program. Although you may decide that you need a dedicated illustration program to handle your industrial-strength drawing tasks, InDesign does have several features for creating complex shapes.

For example, the Compound Path command lets you combine several paths into a single object. If you want to add a graphic flourish to the corners of a path, the Corner Effects command lets you apply any of several built-in corner styles and specify the size of the corner effect.

✦   ✦   ✦

Treating Text as Artwork

In This Chapter

Understanding and using strokes with text

Using colors and gradients with strokes and text

Converting text to graphics

Text can be beautiful, thanks to some of the innovative, engaging letterforms that type designers have created. So it makes sense to think of type as an art element, not just a medium with which to convey information. For centuries designers have used type as a design element, using beautiful letterforms to embellish the appearance of their layouts.

Desktop publishing quickly gave users much more control over typography, blurring the distinction between type and art. On a computer, type is represented mathematically as a series of curves, just as an illustration is. But it has taken almost 15 years for page-layout programs to manipulate those curves, whether for type or illustrations. InDesign takes this to a whole new level.

Although InDesign will not replace programs like Illustrator, FreeHand, and CorelDraw, it gives you many tools to handle illustration (see Chapters 25 though 27). How does this relate to type? You can use many of those tools to transform letterforms — from the actual shapes to their use of color.

Applying Strokes to Type

Text is made up of a series of *outlines* — curves that form the shape — as Figure 28-1 shows. When printed or displayed, those outlines are filled in, giving the appearance of a solid shape. When you resize text, programs like InDesign stretch those curves automatically, which is how InDesign lets you use almost any size imaginable for your text. Most programs keep those outlines hidden from you, using them only for their internal calculations.

But InDesign lets you work with those outlines to create special effects called *strokes*. A stroke is an outline of the character that is made visible and given a thickness (called a *weight*) and often a color. The thicker the stroke, the fatter the character will appear. Figure 28-2 shows some examples of what you can do with strokes.

Figure 28-1: Text is made up of invisible outlines that InDesign can then manipulate to change size and create special effects.

 Note

As you increase stroke size, the stroke grows outward from the letter. That can cause overlapping into adjacent text, as you see in the *"o"* in Figure 28-2.

A 1-point colored gray, with
the character made white, to
create an outline effect

A 2-point light-colored stroke
with a colored character inside

Normal text

A 6-point light-colored
stroke with a regular
(black) character inside

A 1-point stroke the
same color as the text

A 1-point medium-colored stroke
with a gradient-filled character inside

A 1-point stroke using a gradient,
with a colored character inside

Figure 28-2: Examples of how you can apply strokes — a process that makes the outlines visible and lets you change their size and coloration — to text.

At first, using strokes with text can be a little confusing. There are several palettes and panes involved, and you'll also need to have defined the colors, tints, and gradient fills you want to use before you apply them. Figure 28-3 shows the palettes and panes involved:

Figure 28-3: The palettes and panes used to apply strokes to text. Note that all panes are showing all options (use the palette menu and Show Options to display all options).

✦ **In the same floating palette are usually four panes related to strokes: Stroke, Color, Gradient, and Attributes.** Use these to apply the stroke's attributes. Note that the Color and Gradient panes display only existing color, tint, and gradient definitions — you cannot create them from here.

Note Because InDesign lets you move panes to new palettes or to other existing palettes, these panes may not appear together on your system, but you can always access them through the Window menu. Note that the Stroke pane also has the keyboard shortcut F10 and the Color pane has the shortcut F6.

✦ **The Tools palette lets you switch between the stroke and the fill for text.** (By default, the stroke is the active control in this palette.) It also lets you apply the last-used color and gradient to either the stroke or fill, saving you the hassle of switching to the Color pane.

✦ **You'll also need the Swatches pane open if you intend to define or use new colors, tints, or gradients for your strokes.** Chapter 8 covers this in detail; choose Window ➪ Swatches or F5 to access this pane. You can open this pane at any time; new colors, tints, and gradients defined here will appear in the Color and Gradients pane immediately.

If question marks (?) display on the Fill or Stroke icons in either the Color pane or the Tools palette, that means there are several colors and/or gradients used in the selected text.

See Chapter 8 for information on defining colors, swatches, tints, and gradient fills.

To create a stroke:

1. **Highlight the text with the Type tool that you want to apply a stroke to.**

   It can be as little as one character or as much as your entire story.

2. **Go to the Stroke pane (use Window ➪ Stroke or F10 if it is not on your screen).**

   I suggest you move the pane so the text you're applying the stroke to remains visible on-screen and you can see the effects of your actions.

3. **Use the Weight pop-up menu to select a thickness for the stroke, or just enter a value in increments as fine as 0.001 point.**

   Note that the other controls in this pane do not apply to strokes on text and, thus, are grayed out.

Once you've selected a weight, you can adjust it with the arrow icons—up to increase and down to decrease—but you cannot use these icons to increase the weight if the weight is empty or 0.

4. **Here's where you get choices that may initially be confusing. If you want to change the stroke color, you have several options:**

   • If you want to use the most recently used color, select the Stroke icon on the bottom of the Tools palette and then click the Apply Color button (refer to Figure 28-3).

   • If you want to pick a different color, select the Stroke icon on the bottom of the Tools palette and then click an existing color from, or create a new color in, the Swatches pane.

- You can also select the stroke icon in either the Tools palette or Color pane, then drag the color onto either location's stroke icon or directly onto selected text.

- Or you can use the Color pane. The small form of the pane shows just the None color and a range of *tints* (shades) for the last color used — select a tint by clicking on the tint range at the location of the tint you want. The full version of the pane shown here (use its palette menu and its Show Options) lets you create colors by showing a range of colors (pick the color model — LAB, RGB, or CMYK — from the palette menu) and letting you define the color with sliders or by specifying exact percentages of each color. Select the Stroke icon on the pane, then select the color you want to apply.

Note

The Color pane shows an additional item — the Last Color button, as shown in Figure 28-3 — only when the current stroke is set to either None or to a gradient. If you click the Last Color button, the last color selected (the button will be in this color) is applied to the stroke in place of None or of the gradient. You cannot use this to undo a color change — it works only if the stroke did not have a solid color applied to it.

5. **If you want to use a gradient fill, you also have some choices:**

- If you want to use the most recently used gradient, select the Stroke icon on the bottom of the Tool palette and then click the Apply Gradient button (refer to Figure 28-3).

- Go to the Gradient pane and click the gradient — it will be the last-used color. (If there are no gradients defined in your document, you will need to create one via the Swatches pane.) When you click the gradient, you will see gradient controls (refer to Figure 28-3). The bottom ones (squares) display the colors used in the gradient, while the top ones (diamonds) show the gradation slope. You can slide the colors to change how the gradient looks. You can also add color controls by double-clicking in the gradient bar; the color at that point will appear as a control that you can then slide. You can also change the gradient slope — how quickly one color changes to the next by dragging the diamonds. Note that you cannot apply an angle to a gradient used on text.

- If you want to pick a different gradient, select the Stroke icon on the bottom of the Tools palette and then click an existing gradient for, or create a new gradient in, the Swatches pane.

Note

If you use the full Gradients pane (use the palette menu's Show Options item to display this, as shown in Figure 28-3), you can change the gradient type from radial (circular) to linear, or vice versa, as well as add exact percentages for the gradient controls (click a control then change its location percentage; that percentage starts at 0 at the far left and ends at 100% at the far right of the gradient bar).

6. In the Attributes pane, decide whether to enable Overprint Stroke.

Normally, this should not be checked. If checked, InDesign will have the stroke's color print on top of any object underneath them if you're making color separations for output to a printing press, which can make them appear wrong. For example, if you overprint blue on a yellow object, you get green where they overlap.

Tip You may want to overprint black strokes, since doing so ensures that there are no registration issues in four-color printing — no gap between the black stroke and the underlying color.

When you apply gradient to text, you'll find that InDesign makes some assumptions that you may not like. The gradient is centered in the text frame, so as your text moves, the gradient appears to move as well (see Figure 28-4 for examples). The same gradient is applied to any text, so you cannot have a gradient reset for each center. (For example, if you use a radial gradient, you might want an effect where each letter appears to have a circular halo created from a gradient. You can't do that if you apply a gradient to the stroke, as the center of the radial gradient will be the center of the text frame, not of each character. You'll have to convert each letter to a graphic, as described later in this chapter, and apply the stroke to achieve this halo effect.)

Figure 28-4: InDesign keeps the gradient centrally located in your text frame, which affects how the gradient will appear in your text as the text moves within the frame. Here, you see three examples of how changes to the text frame's size — and thus to the text's relative position — affects the gradient for the 5-point strokes on this text.

The order in which you use the Color, Gradient, and Attributes panes doesn't matter, and you may find yourself jumping back and forth among those, the Stroke pane, and the Swatches pane as you experiment with various settings. In fact, expect to spend time experimenting—it's a crucial part of defining and applying special effects that enhance rather than disrupt.

 Note You can also apply these settings in character and paragraph styles via the Character Color pane in the New Character Style dialog box when creating or editing a style. Chapters 17 and 18 cover style creation in depth.

Applying Color to Type

Applying color and gradients is almost exactly the same as applying color to strokes, except you choose the Fill icon in the Tools palette or Color pane. Follow the steps for creating a stroke in the previous section, substituting *fill* for *stroke*. The same tips, notes, and caveats apply for fills as for strokes.

 Note If you want to color text consistently—such as having all subheads be green—do so using style sheets, as covered in Chapter 20.

Although I recommended earlier a case where it makes sense, via the Attributes pane, to overprint black strokes rather than have them print cleanly, that case doesn't apply for black fills. The only time you want to overprint black on a color is to get a richer, deeper black, but in that case, it makes more sense to not use the Overprint option and instead create a "superblack" color from 100 percent black and either 100 percent magenta or 100 percent cyan, and use that as the fill color.

 Tip For gray text, use a tint of black.

You can mix the use of colors and gradients for strokes and text to get some unusual typography. Figure 28-3 showed some examples; Figure 28-5 shows some more exotic ones, using 30-point text in all cases. Here are the techniques used:

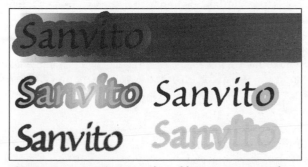

Figure 28-5: Exotic examples of how you can apply strokes and fills to text.

✦ The top text frame uses a linear gradient for the 6-point text stroke and the same gradient — with the colors in the opposite order — as the fill for the text frame.

✦ The first frame in the second row uses a light-gray fill with a radial gradient from white to black for the 2-point strokes. An optical illusion makes the gray fill appear to be a gradient as well, since the progression of white to black next to gray makes the eye think the gray is changing as well.

✦ The second frame in the second row uses a 3-point gray stroke on just one letter to accentuate it.

✦ The first frame in the third row uses a 0.5-point, radial white-to-black gradient to soften the edges of the letters.

✦ The second frame in the third row uses a thicker gray stroke for each subsequent character, starting at 0.5 point and ending at 3.5 points.

Converting Text into Graphics

If you want to use the shape of a letter, or the combined shapes of several letters, as a frame for text or a picture, you could test your skill with the Pen tool and create the letter shape(s) yourself. But getting hand-drawn characters to look just the way you want them can take lots of time. A quicker solution is to use the Create Outlines command (Type ➪ Create Outlines, or Shift+⌘+O or Ctrl+Shift+O) to convert text characters into editable outlines. The Create Outlines command is particularly useful if you want to hand-tweak the shapes of characters, particularly at display font sizes, or place text or a picture within character shapes.

You can create outlines from TrueType, OpenType, and PostScript (Type 1) format fonts. When you create outlines of highlighted characters, any hinting information in the font is removed. (Hinting information is used to adjust the space between characters, especially at small font sizes.) Therefore, you should adjust the appearance of any characters before you choose Create Outlines.

Note   The character shape information required to create outlines is not available in all fonts. If such information is not available when you choose Create Outlines, InDesign will alert you to this fact.

Tip   If all you need to do is apply a stroke or fill to characters within text, you don't have to convert the characters into outlines. Instead, simply highlight the characters and use the Stroke pane (Window ➪ Stroke, or F10) and Swatches pane (Window ➪ Swatches, or F5) to change their appearance. This way you'll still be able to edit the text.

When you use the Create Outlines command, you have the choice of creating an inline compound path that replaces the original text or an independent compound path that's placed directly on top of the original letters. If you want the text outlines to flow with the surrounding text, create an inline compound path. If you want to use the outlines elsewhere, create an independent compound path.

To convert text into outlines:

1. **Use the Type tool to highlight the characters you want to convert into outlines.**

   Generally, this feature works best with large font sizes.

2. **Choose Type ⇨ Create Outlines or press Shift+⌘+O or Ctrl+Shft+O.**

   If you hold down the Option or Alt key when you choose Create Outlines, or if you press Shift+Option+⌘+O or Ctrl+Alt+Shift+O, a compound path is created and placed in front of the text. In this case, you can use either of the selection tools to move the resulting compound path. If you don't hold down Option or Alt when you choose Create Outlines, an inline compound path is created. This object replaces the original text and flows with the surrounding text.

Tip   If you hold the Option or Alt keys when creating text outlines, the text in the resulting inline compound path will be editable.

Figure 28-6 shows text outlines created with the Create Outlines command, then modified using the Control palette.

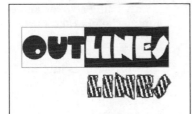

Figure 28-6: Top: Designer John Cruise converted the highlighted characters into an independent compound path by holding down Option or Alt when applying the Make (Compound Path) command. Bottom: After moving the compound path with a selection tool, he placed the angled-line image in the path and added a 2-point stroke.

After you create text outlines, you can modify the paths the same as you can modify hand-drawn paths — by selecting them with the Direct Selection tool and then adding, deleting, or moving anchor points; dragging direction handles; and converting smooth points to corner points and vice versa. You can also use the transformation tools, the Control palette (Window ⇨ Control), and the Transform pane (Window ⇨ Transform, or F9) to change the appearance of text outlines. You cannot, however, edit text after converting it to outlines. (See Chapters 11 and 24 for more information about InDesign's transformation features.)

Additionally, you can use the Place command (File ⇨ Place, or ⌘+D or Ctrl+D) to import text or a picture into text outlines. Figure 28-7 shows character outlines used as text and graphics frames.

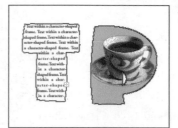

Figure 28-7: Both character shapes were created with the Create Outlines command. Designer John Cruise placed text into the shape on the left, and he placed a picture with a clipping path into the shape on the right and then filled the path with a tint.

Tip

When you create outlines out of a range of highlighted characters, a compound path is created; and each of the characters becomes a subpath. You can use the Release (Compound Path) command (Object ⇨ Compound Path ⇨ Release, or Option+⌘+8 or Ctrl+Alt+8) to turn each of the subpaths into independent paths.

Cross-Reference

Chapter 27 covers editing paths and subpaths in more detail.

Summary

You can do more with text than adjust its font and size. In InDesign, you can color text and add *strokes* (outlines) that can also be colored. By using strokes and colors, you can create all sorts of text effects, from thickening the characters to creating a neon-glow effect.

You can convert text to a graphic, letting you import text or pictures into the frame, as well as apply colors, strokes, and other effects in InDesign.

✦   ✦   ✦

Output Fundamentals

There are few thrills as exciting as seeing the results of countless hours of publication design. You labor over everything from text creation to layout to graphics, until you wonder what you got yourself into. Then you send it off for printing, and sometime later get your printed copies. All of a sudden, you feel great — memories of those long days and nights evaporate as you see all that work made real. You lovingly hold the copy, and remember why you love publishing so much.

Ironically, the output step of publishing is often the last thing on people's minds when they begin a project, even though it's such a vital step. Decisions you make early in the process will affect what you can output (such as color models used in graphics, which you learned about in Chapter 8). For example, the whole issue of color prepress, covered in Chapter 29, relies on the decisions you made when creating your colors and graphics.

So, even though you may be buried eye-deep in the tasks of creating your publication, find a way to step back and consider the production implications of your decisions. The chapters in this part will show you what you need to be aware of as well as show you how to output your documents for printing or for use in the Adobe Portable Document Format (PDF) format often used for network- and CD-based documents, as well as for Web-based documents.

The first — and most tricky — step in document output is setting up your printer and the related driver files on your computer. This varies considerably from platform to platform, and InDesign has expectations that will vary from the other programs you use, so be sure to pay close attention to the setup details in Chapter 30.

Chapter 29
Preparing for Color Prepress

Chapter 30
Preparing for Printing

Chapter 31
Printing Techniques

Chapter 32
Creating Output Files

Once printing is set up, you should check the document to ensure that it will be output correctly. This process is known as *preflighting,* and Chapter 30 also shows you how to use InDesign's preflighting tool. Finally, if you're not doing the actual outputting yourself but will pass the document and its elements on to someone else, be sure to use the Package feature also described in this chapter.

With your document preflighted, you're ready to actually print it. There are dozens of output decisions to make in doing so, and Chapter 31 walks you through each one.

In some cases, you won't actually print a document but instead will deliver a version in electronic form with all printing settings embedded. That's where InDesign's several file-output options come in handy, as Chapter 32 shows.

Preparing for Color Prepress

✦ ✦ ✦ ✦

In This Chapter

Setting color
calibration defaults

Setting up a monitor's
color profile

Applying color
profiles to imported
images

Altering color profiles
for objects and
documents

Applying color
profiles during
printing

Understanding
color traps

Defining and
applying trapping
presets

✦ ✦ ✦ ✦

Since their invention in the mid-1980s, desktop publishing programs have broadened their features to cover more and more color publishing needs. Many of the color-oriented features have caused consternation among professional color separators and printers who have seen amateurs make a tough job worse or ruin an acceptable piece of work. This situation is familiar to anyone in desktop-publishing in the early years when the typographic profession looked on in horror at amateurs publishing documents without understanding tracking, hyphenation, and many other fundamental areas.

Some programs have added more and more high-end color prepress features. InDesign is one of those, offering two types of trapping engines, the ability to control trapping of individual objects and pages, the ability to apply color models to imported pictures to help the printer adjust the output to match the original picture's color intent, and support for composite workflow, which creates files that have a version for output on a proofing printer such as a color inkjet and a version for output on an imagesetter as film negatives or directly to plate.

The perfect scenario for InDesign color output is that you're using all Adobe software in their latest versions: Photoshop 5.0 or later, Illustrator 8.0 or later, and a PostScript Level 3 output device or PDF/X export file. But most people won't have that perfect scenario, especially the PostScript Level 3 part, because it's new and the output devices that commercial printers use are expensive and not replaced often. And not everyone uses Illustrator: FreeHand is very popular among professional artists, and CorelDraw has established a toehold among that group as well, especially on Windows.

Having said that, don't panic if you're not using cutting-edge equipment and software. After years of user education and efforts by software developers like Adobe to build in some of the more basic color-handling assumptions into their programs, most desktop publishers now produce decent color output by simply using the default settings, perhaps augmented by a little tweaking in Photoshop or an illustration program. To really use the color-management and trapping tools in InDesign effectively, you should understand color printing. But if you don't, you can be assured that the default settings in InDesign will produce decent-quality color output.

Please note that the illustrations and figures in this chapter are in black and white. You'll need to look at your color monitor to see the effects of what's described here, or download the image files from the companion Web site (www. INDDcentral.com). Also take a look at the full-color examples in this book's special eight-page insert "Color Techniques."

Calibrating Color

InDesign comes with several color management system (CMS) options. A CMS helps you ensure accurate printing of your colors, both those in imported images and those defined in InDesign. What a CMS does is track the colors in the source image, the colors displayable by your monitor, and the colors printable by your printer. If the monitor or printer does not support a color in your document, the CMS alters (recalibrates) the color to its closest possible equivalent.

To activate a CMS, make sure color management is enabled in your document. Do so by using Edit ➪ Color Settings to get the dialog box shown in Figure 29-1. Be sure Enable Color Management is checked. (I'll get to the other options a bit later in this chapter.)

Don't confuse InDesign's CMS capabilities with color *matching*. It is impossible to match colors produced in an illustration or paint program, or via a scanner, with what a printer or other output device can produce. The underlying differences in color models (which actually determine how a color is defined) and the physics of the media (screen phosphors that emit light versus different types of papers with different types of inks that reflect light) make color matching impossible. But a calibration tool like a CMS can *minimize* differences.

Figure 29-1: The Color Settings dialog box lets you activate color calibration and set document defaults.

Setting up your system

To achieve the best reproduction of printed colors on-screen, you need a closely controlled environment for your computer. Most people don't bother, relying instead on their brain's ability to mentally substitute the print color for what they see on-screen after they've had experience seeing what happens in actual printed documents. But the more you do to control the color viewing environment, the closer the match between what you see on-screen and what you see on the page.

These tips on setting up your system are in order from simplest to most complex:

✦ **Dim the lights.** Most people turn the brightness of their monitors too high, which distorts colors by overdoing the blues and underdelivering on the reds. Turn the brightness lower, to between 60 and 75 percent maximum. To make sure you can still see the screen, lower the amount of light in your workspace by using lower-wattage bulbs, turning off overhead lighting right above your monitor, and/or using translucent shades in nearby windows.

✦ **Change the color temperature of your monitor to 7,200 degrees on the Kelvin scale.** Most monitors have on-screen controls to do so.

✦ **If your monitor came with a color profile, use it.** On the Mac, the Displays control panel has an option in the Color pane for setting color to a profile (stored in the `System\Library\ColorSync\Profiles` folder), or you can use the ColorSync control panel to set profiles for several devices. In Windows, use the Display control panel; the Settings pane has an option called Advanced that will open a dialog box that has a Color Management pane. The profiles are stored in the `Windows\System\Color` folder. Some monitors or video cards come with their own color-setup software.

✦ **Use a calibration tool.** Tools such as Monaco Systems' Monaco Sensor or X-Rite's Monitor Optimizer calibrate your monitor and create a color profile specifically for it. These calibrators cost $375 to $600, so they're typically purchased by graphics departments, not individual designers. Note that color calibration software without a hardware calibrator device is worthless — without being able to measure what colors actually come from your monitor, there's no way they can meaningfully adjust the colors your display shows. Also note that monitors vary their color display over their lifetime (they get dimmer), so you should recalibrate every six months. For most users, the variances in monitor brightness, color balance, and contrast — coupled with the varying types of lighting used in their workspace — mean that true calibration is impossible for images created on-screen and displayed on-screen. Still, using the calibration feature will make the on-screen color closer to what you'll print, even if it's not an exact match.

✦ **Work in a color-controlled room.** In such a room, the lighting is at 5,000 degrees Kelvin, so the light reflecting off your color proofs matches that of a professional prepress operation. (There's long been a standard, the latest version of which is called ISO 3664, that has set 5,000 degrees Kelvin as the industry standard for proofing color printing. Basically, 5,000 degrees is filtered daylight where the red, green, and blue components are equal. The International Prepress Association [`www.ipa.org`] has a lot of standards information and resources related to color accuracy.) Monitors should also be set with a white point of D65 (something done with calibration hardware and software). Also try to buy monitors with a neutral, light gray shade — or paint them that way — so your brain doesn't darken what you see on-screen to compensate for the off-white monitor frame right next to the screen image. Similarly, all furnishings should be neutral, preferably a light gray. Avoid having anything with a strong color in the room — even clothes.

Defining color models

Whether you define colors in InDesign or in your illustration or paint program, the method you use to define them is critical to ensuring the best possible output. Defining all colors in the same model as the target output device is best. Use the following guidelines:

✦ If your printer is RGB (this is rare), use the RGB model to define colors.

✦ If your printer is CMYK (like an offset printer or most ink-jets), use CMYK to define colors.

✦ If you're using Pantone colors for traditional offset printing, pick one of the Pantone solid models if using Pantone inks. Pick the Pantone Process Coated model if your printer is using inks from companies other than Pantone.

✦ If you're using Pantone colors for traditional offset printing, pick the Pantone Process Coated model if you will color-separate those colors into CMYK.

✦ Trumatch and Focoltone colors were designed to reproduce accurately whether output as spot colors or color-separated into CMYK. Other models (such as Toyo and DIC) may or may not separate accurately for all colors, so check with your printer or the ink manufacturer.

✦ If you're using any Pantone, Focoltone, Trumatch, Toyo, or DIC color and outputting to a desktop color printer (whether RGB or CMYK), watch to ensure that the color definition doesn't lie outside the printer's gamut, as explained in the next section.

✦ Never rely on the screen display to gauge any non-RGB color. Even with the InDesign CMS's monitor calibration, RGB monitors simply cannot match most non-RGB colors. Use the on-screen colors only as a guide, and rely instead on a color swatchbook from your printer or the color ink's manufacturer.

✦ InDesign's CMS does *not* calibrate color in EPS or PDF files. If you use EPS, I strongly recommend that you use the DCS (pre-separated CMYK) variant. If you use PDF files, embed the correct color profile in the application that you created the PDF file from or by using Adobe Acrobat Distiller's options to set color profiles.

Adjusting on-screen display

Here's how InDesign's CMS works in practice:

✦ **To have color calibration in effect for a monitor, you must be displaying thousands of colors (16-bit color depth) or more colors (or a higher color depth, such as 24-bit).** On the Mac, use the Displays control panel to change your monitor's bit depth. In Windows, use the Display control panel.

✦ **Select the monitor or color space in the RGB pop-up menu in the Working Spaces section of the Color Setting pane (refer to Figure 29-1).** The monitor or color space that you select will tell InDesign how to display imported images and colors defined within InDesign. The first four options — Adobe RGB (1998), Apple RGB, ColorMatch RGB, and sRGB IEC61966-2.1 — are all "neutral" color spaces, meaning that they aren't adjusted for specific monitors. Adobe program typically save their images with the sRGB profile, which works well if you define colors based on swatches and use exact RGB settings or existing swatches. The other options are monitor-specific profiles, which make sense to use if you choose your colors based on what you see on-screen.

✦ **Select the output devices in the CMK pop-up menu in the Working Space section.** This is only for the imaging device used at your prepress bureau to create the actual color separations (covered in more detail later in this chapter). If you're outputting to PDF files for on-screen display, choose a neutral option in the RGB pop-up menu instead of a monitor-specific option.

✦ **Set the color management of imported images in the Color Management Policies section of the dialog box.** In the RGB and CMYK pop-up menus, you can select a color profile to apply to each imported or pasted picture — these will override any embedded profiles in the pictures. The default option in both cases is Preserve Embedded Profiles, which is the best option if your graphics sources have already had color models applied intentionally to help calibrate the output. If your pictures are not usually color-managed at the source, it's best to override them and choose either Convert to Working Space, which uses the color profiles selected in the Working Space section of the dialog box, or Off, which strips out any color profiles. There are also two options on when to notify you of profile mismatches — Ask When Opening and Ask When Pasting — as well as one to alert you to pictures without a profile (Ask When Opening). You should check all three; one exception is that if you have chosen Convert to Working Space in the RGB and CMYK pop-up menus, you can uncheck Ask When Opening for Missing Profiles, since you won't be using any embedded profiles from the original picture.

✦ **Use the Conversion Options section to control the display and printing of bitmapped images.** (Make sure the Advanced check box option is selected to display this section.) The Engine pop-up menu lets you choose the CMS technology to use, while Intent determines how colors are adjusted by the selected engine. You have four options in the Intent pop-up menu, as well as a related check box:

In the Engine pop-up menu, the list of available CMSs depends on what platform you're using: The Adobe ACE CMS is available for all platforms, while the Apple ColorSync and Apple CMM CMSs are available just for Macintosh, and Microsoft ICM CMS is available just for Windows. Choose a CMS that is compatible with your output equipment; if in doubt, choose Adobe ACE.

- **Perceptual** tries to balance the colors in an image when translating from the original color range to the output device's color range under the assumption that it's a photograph and, thus, needs to look natural. This is appropriate for photographs.

- **Saturation** tries to create vivid colors when translating from the original color range to the output device's color range—even if doing so means some colors are printed inaccurately. This is appropriate for charts and other slide-like graphics whose colors are intended for impact rather than naturalness.

- **Relative Colorimetric** is the same as Absolute Colorimetric except that it will shift all the colors to compensate for the white point of the monitor as set in the Monitor profile (essentially, adjusting the brightness of the output to compensate for any dimness or excess brightness in the monitor).

- **Absolute Colorimetric** makes no adjustments to the colors during output. So it allows, for example, an image that uses two similar colors to end up being output as the same color because of the printer's limited color range.

- **Use Black Point Compensation** adjusts the color range for maximum range, permitting truer colors in most cases and a more natural look to converted photographs. You should leave this checked, unless you know your source image has a small range (such as being mostly midtones), in which case black-point compensation can distort shadows and subtle colors in an effect similar to a moiré pattern.

Tip Depending on what kinds of documents you produce, you'll likely want Perceptual or Saturation as your setting.

QuarkXPress User InDesign and QuarkXPress have comparable color-calibration features, but there are some differences: QuarkXPress does not let you apply black-point compensation. And InDesign lets you save your color-management preferences for use in other documents.

Using calibrations from other programs

Other programs may have similar settings for calibrating their display against your type of monitor. For example, Adobe Photoshop offers such an option (via Photoshop ⇨ Color Settings on the Mac and Edit ⇨ Color Settings in Windows); it's similar to the InDesign Color Settings dialog box. If you're creating colors in a program and importing those colors into InDesign, it's important to have them calibrated the same way, or at least as closely as the different programs will allow.

Understanding profiles

The mechanism that a color management system (CMS) uses to do its calibration is the profile that contains the information on color models and ranges supported by a particular creator (such as an illustration program or scanner), display, and printer. InDesign includes dozens of such predefined profiles.

A CMS uses a device-independent color space to match these profiles against each other. A color space is a mathematical way of describing the relationships among colors. By using a device-independent color model (the CIE XYZ standard defined by the Commission Internationale de l'Éclairage, the International Commission on Illumination), a CMS can compare gamuts from other device-dependent models (like RGB and the others). What this means is that a CMS can examine the colors in your imported images and defined colors, compare them against the capabilities of your monitor and printer, and adjust the colors for the closest possible display and printing.

Calibrating imported colors

When you load an image into InDesign, the active CMS applies the default settings defined in the Color Settings dialog box. But you can change those settings for specific images as follows:

✦ As you import each file, check Show Import Options when you place a graphic into InDesign in the Place dialog box (File ➪ Place, or ⌘+D or Ctrl+D). In the resulting dialog box, go to the Color pane and select the appropriate profile from the Profile menu, as well as the appropriate rendering intent from the Intent pop-up menu. Figure 29-2 shows the dialog box.

Figure 29-2: You can apply color profiles when importing pictures.

✦ Any time after you place a graphic, select it with a selection tool and choose Object ➪ Image Color Settings to set a new profile and/or rendering intent. You can also turn off color management for this object. Figure 29-3 shows the dialog box.

Figure 29-3: You can apply color profiles to an object after it's placed in your document.

Only profiles appropriate for the image type will appear in these pop-up menus — for example, only CMYK profiles (generally, these are output devices) will appear for a CMYK TIFF file, even though the image may have been scanned in from an RGB scanner and later converted to CMYK with Photoshop. This limitation exists because InDesign assumes that the image is designed for output to that specific printer and, thus, will calibrate it with that target in mind. For RGB files, InDesign lets you apply monitor-oriented profiles and scanner-oriented profiles.

Saving color-management preferences

You can save and use color-management settings in other documents. The process is simple: Use the Save button in the Color Settings dialog box to save the current dialog box's settings to a file. If you want to use that saved color-settings information in another document, open that document and click the Load button in the Color Settings dialog box, then browse for and select the color-settings file. That's it! This is a handy way to ensure consistency in a workgroup.

Changing document color settings

If you put together a document with specific color settings, as described earlier, but then decide you want to apply a new profile across your pictures or replace a specific profile globally in your document, you can.

Choose Edit ➪ Assign Profiles to replace the color management settings globally, as Figure 29-4 shows. You can set the RGB profile and CMYK profiles separately, as well as set the color intent for solid colors, bitmap images, and gradient blends using the Solid Color Intent, Default Image Intent, and After-Blending Intent pop-up menus.

Figure 29-4: InDesign provides two dialog boxes —
Assign Profiles (top) and Convert to Profile — to change
color-management preferences throughout a document.
While their functions overlap, each has unique settings.

Similarly, you can change the document's color workspace by choosing Edit ➪
Convert to Profile, which opens the Convert to Profile dialog box also shown in
Figure 29-4. It also lets you change the CMS engine, rendering intent, and black-
point compensation settings.

There's real overlap in these two dialog boxes. Using the Assign Profiles dialog box
to replace the document profile does the same as the Convert to Profile dialog box
when it comes to replacing the profiles. The only difference there is that the Assign
Profiles dialog box can also remove profiles from the document. Both dialog boxes
let you change the rendering intents for colors, though the Assign Profile dialog box
gives you several levels of control not available in the Convert to Profile dialog box.
But the Convert to Profile dialog box lets you change the black-point compensation
and the CMS engine. These really could be combined into one dialog box.

Calibrating output

When you're ready to output your document to a printer or other device, you set the profile and rendering intent for that destination device in the Color Management pane of the Print dialog box (File ➪ Print, or ⌘+P or Ctrl+P), which has a Print Space section with a Profile pop-up menu and an Intent pop-up menu. Here you select the appropriate options for your output device. Chapter 31 cover printing in more detail.

Working with Color Traps

Color trapping controls how colors overlap and abut when printed. InDesign offers moderate controls over trapping — enough to set the basics document-wide without getting into the expertise level of a commercial printer. It's also a feature that novice users can abuse terribly, which is one reason InDesign hides these options. If you don't know much about trapping, leave the features of the program at the default settings. Before you use InDesign trapping tools, study some books on color publishing, talk to your printer, and experiment with test files that you don't want to publish. If you're experienced with color trapping — or after you become experienced — you'll find InDesign trapping tools easy to use.

You'll still want to use the trapping tools within the illustration product with which you create your EPS and PDF graphics, because these tools will help you to finely control the settings for each image's specific needs. Also, if you're using a service bureau that does high-resolution scanning for you and strips these files into your layout before output, check to make sure that the bureau is not also handling trapping for you with a Scitex or other high-end system. If it is, make sure you ask whether and when you should be doing trapping yourself.

Note   If you're printing to a color laser, dye-sublimation, ink-jet, or thermal wax printer, don't worry about trapping. You're not getting the kind of output resolution at which this level of image fine-tuning is relevant. But if you're outputting to an imagesetter (particularly if you're outputting to negatives) for eventual printing on a standard web offset press (SWOP) or other printing press, read on.

Using choking versus spreading

So what is trapping, anyway? Trapping adjusts the boundaries of colored objects to prevent gaps between abutting colors. Gaps can occur because of misalignment of the negatives, plates, or printing press — all of which are impossible to avoid.

Colors are trapped by processes known as *choking* and *spreading*. Both make an object slightly larger — usually a fraction of a point — so that it overprints the abutting object slightly. The process is called choking when one object surrounds a second object, and the first object is enlarged to overlap the second. The process is known as spreading when you enlarge the surrounded object so that it leaks (bleeds) into the surrounding object.

The difference between choking and spreading is the relative position of the two objects. Think of choking as making the hole for the inside object smaller (which in effect makes the object on the outside larger), and think of spreading as making the object in the hole larger.

Tip   The object made larger depends on the image, but you generally bleed the color of a lighter object into a darker one. If you did the opposite, you'd make objects seem ungainly larger. Thus, choke a dark object inside a light one, and spread a light object inside a dark one. If the objects are adjacent, spread the light object.

Figure 29-5 shows the three types of trapping techniques. Spreading (at upper-right) makes the interior object's color bleed out; choking (at lower-left) makes the outside color bleed in, in effect making the area of the choked element smaller. The dashed lines show the size of the interior object; as you can see in the image at right, when you choke a darker object into a lighter one, the effect is to change its size (here, the interior object gets smaller). At upper-left is an untrapped image whose negatives shifted slightly during printing, causing a gap.

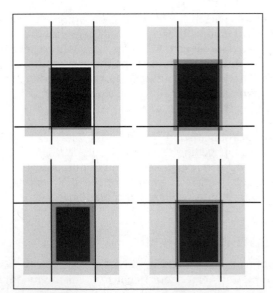

Figure 29-5: Three kinds of traps: spreading (upper-right), choking (lower-left), and centering (lower-right), with an untrapped image in the upper-left that was misregistered during printing.

There's a third type of trapping technique supported by InDesign: Called *centering,* it both chokes and spreads, splitting the difference between the two objects. This makes traps look nicer, especially between light and dark colors where regular choking and spreading can encroach on the light object, as shown in Figure 29-5 at lower-right.

Finally, InDesign offers a fourth trapping method—neutral density—that adjusts the trap as color hues and tints shift to minimize the possibility of darker lines where colors trap. But this can be dangerous—for a bitmap image, it will most likely create an uneven edge as the trapping changes from pixel to pixel.

In practice, trapping also involves controlling whether colors *knock out* or *overprint.* The default is to knock out—cut out—any overlap when one element is placed on top of another. If, for example, you place two rectangles on top of each other, they print like the two rectangles on the right side of Figure 29-6. If you set the darker rectangle in this figure to overprint, the rectangles print as shown on the left side of the figure. Setting colors to overprint results in mixed colors, as on the left, while setting colors to knock out results in discrete colors, as on the right.

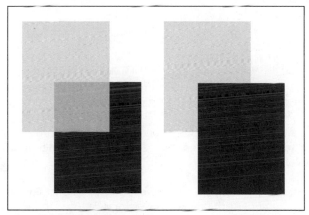

Figure 29-6: The two kinds of untrapped options:
overprint (left) and knockout.

In InDesign, you use the Attributes pane (Window ➪ Attributes) for individual objects—text, frames, shapes, and lines—to pick from the pane's four trapping options: Overprint Fill, Overprint Stroke, Overprint Gap, and Nonprinting. Most objects won't have all four settings available, since not all objects have fills, gaps, and strokes, but all objects have Nonprinting available, which prevents the object from printing. All four options are normally unchecked, since you usually want objects' fills, gaps, and strokes to knock out (and you want the object to print). Figure 29-7 shows the pane.

Figure 29-7: The Attributes pane lets you set whether objects overprint or knock out (the default, or unchecked, status).

Specifying trapping presets

In InDesign, document-wide trapping settings are handled as part of the printing process (see Chapter 31). But you specify them like you do colors or other document attributes, via a pane. In this case, you use the Trap Presets pane (Window ⇨ Trap Presets), shown in Figure 29-8. Choose New Preset from the pane's palette menu to create a new preset, or select an existing preset and choose Preset Options to modify it. (Figure 29-9 shows the New Preset dialog box.) You can also delete and duplicate trap presets from the palette menu, as well as import them from other documents (via the Load Trap Presets option).

Figure 29-8: The Trap Presets pane.

Note   Consult your service bureau or commercial printer before changing the default settings. They'll know what setting you should used based on the paper, inks, printing press, and image types you're using.

New Feature   Trap Presets is the new name for the Trap Styles pane, but they're functionally the same otherwise. InDesign is adopting the name *presets* for what used to be called styles, to distinguish saved groups of attributes from text styles such as boldface and italics, which are often called just *styles.*

Figure 29-9: The New Preset dialog box.

Here are the settings you can change when creating or modifying a trap preset:

✦ **Name:** Give the trap style a name in the Name field—make sure it's a meaningful name, like Choke, rather than New Preset 1, so you'll know what it's for.

✦ **Trap Width:** Set your *trap width* (the amount of overlap you want between adjacent colors). The default is 0.25 point, a common setting. The Default field is for all colors except black and white. You set the trap width separately for black, using the Black Width field; this value is usually one and a half to two times as much as the regular trap settings because it controls how colors spread into black objects. The value is higher because you have more leeway with black—spreading a color into it won't change it from being black, while, for example, spreading yellow into blue makes a green, so you want to minimize that spreading.

✦ **Trap Appearance:** You can choose the type of end for traps, just as you do for strokes, with options of Miter, Round, and Bevel for both Join Style and End Style. In almost every case, you want to select Miter, since this keeps the trap confined to the abutting images. If you choose another option, the choke or spread will extend past the trapped objects a tad. If you think of the boundary of the trap as a line, then choosing Bevel or Round would extend that line slightly past the objects. If the objects have white or a light color on either side, readers might notice that slight extension.

✦ **Images:** InDesign lets you control how trapping is applied with several options: Trap Placement plus four picture-specific settings, Trap Objects to Images, Trap Images to Images, Trap Inside Images, and Trap 1-Bit Images.

- **Image Trap Placement** determines how to handle trapping between an image and an abutting solid color. Your choices are Center, which has the trap straddle the edge between the image and the abutting color object; Choke, which has the abutting color object overprint the image by the Trap Width amount; Spread, which has the image overprint the abutting color object by the Trap Width amount; Neutral Density, defined earlier; and Normal, which traps each pixel in the image individually and thus can result in an uneven edge between the image and the abutting object.

- **Trap Objects to Images** turns on trapping for images and any abutting objects such as text or graphics created in InDesign.

- **Trap Images to Images** turns on trapping for images and any abutting images.

- **Internal Image** actually will trap colors within the bitmap image. Use this only for high-contrast bitmaps, such as cartoons and computer screenshots, where the color has fewer gradations and more broad, consistent swaths.

- **Trap 1-Bit Images** will trap black-and-white bitmaps to any abutting objects (including those underneath). This prevents the black portions from having a white ghost area around them if there is any misregistration when printing.

✦ **Trap Thresholds:** These guide InDesign in how to apply your trapping settings:

- **Step** gives InDesign the color-difference threshold before trapping is implemented. The default is 10%, a value that will trap most objects. A higher value will trap fewer objects. The way this works is that the value represents the difference in color variance between adjacent objects, and you're telling InDesign not to worry about colors that are within the percentage difference. This is usually a low setting because that means you don't care if there are traps between similar colors, since the human eye will notice misregistration less between them because they are, in fact, similar. In most cases, keep this value between 8% and 20%.

- **Black Color** defines at what point InDesign should treat a dark gray as black for the trap width in Black Width. For coarse paper, which usually absorbs more ink, dark tints and grays often end up looking like a solid color — 85% black will appear as 100% black. Use Black Color Limit in such cases so that an 85% black object traps as if were a 100% black object.

- **Black Density** is similar to Black Color Limit, except that it treats dark colors as black (like navy blues), based on their ink density. You can enter a value of 0 to 10, with 1.6 being the default (0 is full black, while 10 is white).

- **Sliding Trap** adjusts the way a choke or spread works. The normal value is 70%, which tells InDesign — when the difference in ink density (a good measure of color saturation) is 70% or more — not to move the darker color so much into the lighter color. The greater the contrast between two colors, the more the lighter object is distorted as the darker color encroaches on it. At 0%, all traps are adjusted to the centerline between the two objects, while at 100%, the choke or spread is done at the full trap width.

- **Trap Color Reduction** controls over-inking that some traps can create. The default is 100%, which means that the overlapping colors in a trap are produced at 100%, which in some cases can cause the trap to be darker than the two colors being trapped, due to the colors mixing. Choosing a lower value in Trap Color Reduction will lighten the overlapping colors to reduce this darkening. A value of 0% will keep the overlap no darker than the darker of the two colors being trapped.

Specifying trapping to pages

Once you've created trapping presets, you apply them. (The [Default] preset, which you can modify, is applied to all pages by default.) To do so, choose the Assign Trap Presets option in the Trap Presets pane's palette menu. Figure 29-10 shows the dialog box.

Figure 29-10: The Assign Trap Presets dialog box.

The process is simple: Choose the desired trap preset from the Trap Preset pop-up menu, then select the pages to apply it to in the Pages section (click All, or Range; if you click Range, enter the page numbers in the Range field). Click the Assign button to complete the application of the trap preset to the selected pages. You can set multiple presets in a document, to different page ranges, so if you want, select another trap preset and assign it to the desired pages. InDesign will show you what pages have what trap presets applied at the bottom of the dialog box. When done, click Done.

Note   If your document uses sections, you can enter page numbers in the Range field using the section numbering style (such as A-2, D-3, F-5-F-10) or by using absolute page numbers (+1, +5, +10-+15).

Summary

Although it's often impossible to precisely match colors from an electronic image when printing, InDesign can help make the color fidelity as high as possible through its support of color profiles and color management. It can also help make what you see on-screen and print on proofing devices look close to the final output, to help you better gauge your actual colors.

If you use a compatible output device, InDesign also lets you control how adjacent colors print, in a process known as *trapping*, minimizing the chances of gaps appearing between colored objects. Fortunately, most users won't need to worry about fine-tuning trapping settings, since InDesign's default settings handle most objects well.

✦   ✦   ✦

Preparing for Printing

Once your document is created and all elements are perfectly in place, with the right colors, frame strokes, kerning, and so on, it's time to make tangible all that work you've done on-screen. You're ready to print the document.

Well, not quite. You may in fact be ready to just print your document, but if your document is at all complex or will be output at a service bureau or via your company's creative services group or print shop, you should take a few minutes and dot your *i*'s and cross your *t*'s. Little things can go wrong as you or your team work on a document — a font might deactivate, a picture might move or be renamed, or a new output device might be acquired.

That's where InDesign's Preflight and Package tools come into play. The Preflight tool checks your document to make sure that all elements are available, while the Package tool copies all required elements — from fonts to graphics — to a folder so you can give your service bureau all the pieces needed to print your document accurately.

Making Initial Preparations

Before you can do anything, you need to make sure your system is set up with the right printer driver and printer description files — without these, your output will likely not match your needs or expectations. It's important to set these up before you use the Preflight tool because the Preflight tool checks your document against the printer settings you have active (such as color separations), and you can't have selected printer settings until the printer is set up.

In This Chapter

Setting up printers and drivers

Setting general printer options

Using the Preflight tool

Using the Package tool

Working with service bureaus

The Mac and Windows handle printing differently, so in this chapter I've divided all system-specific printing information, such as the coverage of drivers, into platform-specific sections.

Chapter 38 covers the different kinds of printers available.

Setting up Macintosh printers

Although you choose the printer type in the Setup pane of the InDesign Print dialog box, you still need to set up the printer on your Mac before you can use it. To do that, the Mac has a program called the Print Center, which is well hidden (it's in the Utilities folder in the Applications folder). The Print Center will list any installed printers. Make sure the printer you want to set up is connected to your Mac (directly or via the network) and turned on. (If you're using a network printer, make sure the right network protocols, such as IP and AppleTalk, are turned on via the Network control panel in the System Preferences dialog box, which you access by choosing ✦ ➪ System Preferences.)

To install a printer, you typically run a program that comes with the printer. Such programs often add the printer to the Print Center utility's Printer List. If not, click the Add button and locate the printer driver for your printer (again, usually found on a CD that accompanies the printer).

Figure 30-1 shows the Printer List that appears when you open the Print Central application.

Figure 30-1: The Mac's Print Center utility shows which printers are installed, and lets you configure them, as well as add additional printers.

Configuring an installed printer varies based on the software provided with the printer. In some cases, a printer's configuration software is accessible via the Configure button in the Print Center utility. In other cases, you need to run a separate utility that came with the printer or use controls on the printer itself.

Note You may need to install a PostScript Printer Description (PPD) file that contains specific details on your printer; this file should come on a disk or CD with your printer and is often installed with the printer's setup program. Otherwise, download it from the printer manufacturer's Web site. These files should reside in the PPDs folder in the Mac's `System\Library\Printers` folder. Note that Mac OS X pre-installs some for you, particularly those for Apple-branded printers and some Hewlett-Packard printers.

If you're installing a printer not connected to your computer or network, such as the imagesetter used by your service bureau, you'll need to install the PPD files so InDesign knows what its settings are. Installing the printer software isn't necessary.

Mac OS X supports multiple printers, but it also lets you define the default printer — the ones used unless changed via a button or pop-up menu in an application's Print dialog box. (InDesign uses a pop-up menu called Printer to change the printer from the default setting.) In the Print Center utility, choose the printer you want to be the default, and then click Make Default button.

Setting up Windows printers

To set up a Windows 2000 or XP printer, use Start ⇨ Settings ⇨ Printers. (Some XP users will have to choose Start ⇨ Control Panel ⇨ Printers and Other Hardware.) You'll then see a window with a list of existing printers and an icon labeled Add New Printer. Double-click the printer to set up, or double-click Add New Printer (you'll likely need a disk that came with the printer, or the Windows CD-ROM, if you add a new printer because Windows needs information specific to that printer). Note that some printers have their own setup software that you should use instead of the Add Printer utility in Windows.

Note If you're setting up a printer connected via the network, you usually should select the Local Printer option during installation. The Network Printer option is for printers connected to a print server, as opposed to printers connected to a hub or router. (A print server is a special kind of router, but it's typically used only for printers that don't have networking built in, such as many ink-jet printers.) In some cases, even if your printer uses a print server, you'll still install the printer as a local printer and then create a virtual port that maps to a network address (Hewlett-Packard uses this approach, for example, as Figure 30-2 shows).

If you're installing a printer not connected to your computer or network, such as the imagesetter used by your service bureau, you'll need to install the PPD files so InDesign knows what its settings are. You don't need to install the printer software.

When you open an existing printer, use Printer ⇨ Properties to get the dialog box shown in Figure 30-2.

Figure 30-2: The Device Settings pane in Windows set up for PostScript devices. It's the key pane in the Properties dialog box for a Windows printer. (Not all panes appear for all printers, depending on the printer type chosen and the network protocols installed.)

One pane matters greatly: The Device Settings pane is where you specify all the device settings, from paper trays to memory to how fonts are handled. For PostScript printers, this pane has several key options as follows:

✦ The best (and default) setting is to have the printer translate TrueType fonts such as Arial to PostScript fonts such as Helvetica. The Font Substitution Table option opens a list of available fonts and lets you select how any TrueType fonts are translated to PostScript. (The Windows standards of Arial, Times New Roman, Courier New, and Symbol are set by default to translate to the PostScript fonts Helvetica, Times, Courier, and Symbol. PostScript fonts are set by default to Don't Substitute.)

✦ Be sure to select Add Euro Currency Symbol to PostScript Fonts in this pane, so the euro symbol (€) is available in all output.

Tip   I strongly recommend you use Adobe's PostScript driver rather than Microsoft's. The Microsoft driver often doesn't send fonts to the printer, and it often prints extra blank pages at the end of a job. The Adobe Universal PostScript driver doesn't have these issues. You can download the Adobe driver from `www.adobe.com/support/downloads/main.html` in the PostScript Printer Drivers section. When you install the driver, it gives you the option of converting your existing PostScript printers to the Adobe driver. You can also run this program again to install new printers using the Adobe driver—using the Add Printer wizard automatically installs the Microsoft driver for those new printers—or you can use the Drivers pop-up menu in the Advanced pane of the printer's Properties dialog box.

Note   You may need to install a PostScript Printer Description (PPD) file that contains specific details on your printer; this file should come on a disk or CD with your printer and is often installed with the printer's setup program. Otherwise, download it from the printer manufacturer's Web site. (Windows places PPD files in the `Windows\System32\spool\drivers\w32x86` **folder.**)

To set a printer as the default printer, right-click the printer in the Printers window (Start ➪ Settings ➪ Printers), and select Set Default Printer from the context menu that appears. (Some Windows XP users will need to choose Start ➪ Control Panel ➪ Printers and Other Hardware.)

Preflighting Your Document

Now that your printers are set up, you can use InDesign's printing and preprinting checkup tools. The Preflight tool that's part of InDesign will examine your document for any issues of concern and give you a report on what may need to be fixed.

You might wonder why you need a preflight tool to check for things such as missing fonts and images when InDesign will list any missing fonts and graphics when you open a document. The answer is that sometimes fonts and graphics files could be moved after you've opened a file, in which case you wouldn't get the alerts from InDesign. This is more likely to happen if you're working with files and fonts on a network disk, rather than with local fonts and graphics. Preflighting also checks for other problematic issues, such as the use of RGB files and TrueType fonts.

Before you run the preflight tool, you may want to set up your printer output so the tool can accurately check your document's setup in anticipation of, for example, whether you plan to output color separations or spot colors. To do that, you need to go to the Print dialog box, set your output settings, use Save Preset, provide a name in the Save Preset dialog box and click OK, and then click Cancel to put them into effect *without actually printing the document.*

Cross-Reference   Selecting your output settings is covered in detail in Chapter 31.

Tip   If you're working with the InDesign Books feature (see Chapter 9), you can preflight the book's chapters from an open book's pane, using the Preflight Book option in its palette menu. (If one or more documents in the book are selected in the pane, the menu option will change to Preflight Selected Documents.) The options are the same as for preflighting individual documents.

Running the Preflight tool is easy. Choose File ➪ Preflight, or press Shift+Option+⌘+F or Ctrl+Alt+Shift+F. In a few seconds, you'll get a dialog box that shows the status of your document. Here's a walkthrough of what the six panes in the Preflight dialog box do:

✦ **The Summary pane** (shown in Figure 30-3) shows you a summary of alerts. If your document has layers, you can select or deselect the Show Data for Hidden Layers option. If selected, layers that won't print will be analyzed for font, image, and other issues — check this option only if the person receiving your document plans on printing hidden layers (for example, in a French-and-English document, you may have hidden the French layer for proofing but still want it checked, since the service bureau will be instructed to print the document twice — once with the English layer on and the French layer off, and once with the English layer off and the French layer on).

Tip

In a complex document with lots of graphics and fonts, you may want to select the Show Problems Only option in the Fonts pane and in the Links and Images pane. If selected, this option will display only elements flagged by the preflight tool in that pane.

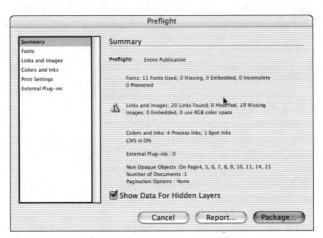

Figure 30-3: The Summary pane.

✦ **The Fonts pane** (shown in Figure 30-4) shows the type (Type 1 PostScript, OpenType, or TrueType) of each font, so you can spot any TrueType fonts before they go to your service bureau. (TrueType fonts usually don't print easily on imagesetters, so use a program like Pyrus FontLab or Macromedia Fontographer to translate them to PostScript instead.) It will also show if any fonts are missing from your system.

Figure 30-4: The Fonts pane.

✦ **The Links and Images pane** (shown in Figure 30-5) shows whether any graphics files are missing or if the original image has been modified since you placed it in your layout. You can use the Relink button to correct any such bad links one at a time, or Repair All to have InDesign prompt you in turn for each missing or modified file. The pane also shows whether a color profile is embedded in your graphics, in case files that should have them don't or in case a file that should not have an embedded profile does. It also shows an alert if you use RGB images; although such images will print or color-separate, InDesign provides the warning because it's usually better to convert such images to CMYK in an image editor or Illustration program so you control the final appearance, rather than rely on InDesign or the output device to do the translation.

Figure 30-5: The Links and Images pane.

✦ **The Colors and Inks pane** (shown in Figure 30-6) shows what color inks will be used in the output (if you are printing color separations, these correspond to the color plates that will eventually be used to print the document on a printing press). You can't modify anything here; it's simply for informational purposes.

Figure 30-6: The Colors and Inks pane.

✦ **The Print Settings pane** (shown in Figure 30-7) shows how the document is configured to print in the Print dialog box. That's why configuring the output settings, as described earlier, before preflighting your document is key.

Figure 30-7: The Print Settings pane.

✦ **The External Plug-ins pane** (shown in Figure 30-8) shows any plug-in programs required to output the file. Some third-party plug-ins make changes to the InDesign document that require the same plug-in to be installed at each computer that opens the file. This dialog box alerts you if you have such a dependency.

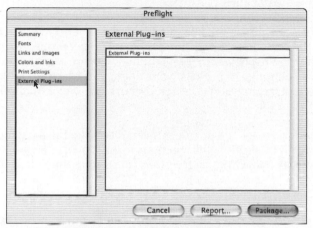

Figure 30-8: The External Plug-Ins pane.

You can create a report of the preflight information by clicking the Report button. It generates a text file containing the information from the Preflight dialog box's panes, which you can give to your service bureau to check its settings and files against.

You can also click the Package button to gather all related fonts and files into one folder for delivery to a service bureau or other outside printing agency. The next section describes this option in more detail.

Click Cancel to exit the Preflight dialog box and go back to your document.

Creating a Document Package

If you've ever had the experience of giving a page-layout document to a service bureau, only to be called several hours later by the person who is outputting your document because some of the files necessary to output it are missing, you'll love the Package feature in InDesign.

This command, which you access by choosing File ➪ Package, or Option+Shift+⌘+P or Ctrl+Alt+Shift+P, copies all the font, color-output, and picture files necessary to output your document into a folder. It also generates a report that contains all the information about your document that a service bureau is ever likely to need, including the document's fonts, dimensions, and trapping information. You can also create an instructions file that has your contact information and any particulars you want to say about the document.

When you run the Package command, InDesign preflights your document automatically and gives you the option of viewing any problems it encounters. If you elect to view that information, you're shown the Preflight dialog box (refer to Figures 30-3 through 30-8). You can continue to package your document from that dialog box by clicking the Package button once you've assured yourself none of the problems will affect the document's output.

Before you can actually package the document, you'll be asked to save the current document and then fill in the Printing Instructions form shown in Figure 30-9. You can change the default filename from Instructions.txt to something more like the name of your job.

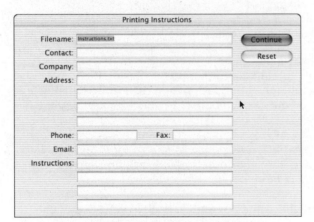

Figure 30-9: The Printing Instructions dialog box.

Caution   If you *don't* want to create an instructions form, don't click Cancel — that cancels the entire package operation. Just click Continue, leaving the form blank. Similarly, you must click Save at the request to save the document; clicking Cancel stops the package operation as well.

The next step is to create the package folder, which you do in the dialog box that follows, called Create Package Folder on the Mac and Package Publication in Windows. Figure 30-10 shows both versions.

Figure 30-10: The Create Package Folder (Mac, left) and equivalent Package Publication (Windows, right) dialog boxes.

The Create Package Folder and Package Publication dialog boxes – different names for the same function – look substantively different between the Mac and Windows versions of InDesign. Both use their operating systems' standard Save dialog box formats, so even though they offer the same features, they're arranged differently on-screen.

In the dialog box, you can select what is copied: the fonts, color output profiles, and *linked graphics* (graphics pasted into an InDesign document rather than imported are automatically included). You can also have InDesign update the graphics links for those that were modified or moved; if this option is not selected, any missing or modified graphics files will not be copied with the document.

You can tell InDesign to include fonts and links from hidden layers (which you would do only if you wanted the service bureau to print those hidden layers or if you were giving the document's files to a colleague to do further work on).

You also can specify whether the document should use only the hyphenation exceptions defined within it. This often makes sense, since it ensures that the printer's hyphenation dictionary—which may differ from yours—doesn't cause text to flow differently.

See Chapter 15 for more details on these dictionaries. Chapter 31 explains which files you should send to others using your documents.

You can also modify the instructions text file by clicking the Instructions button.

Finally, you can view the report after the package is created—on the Mac, InDesign will launch TextEdit and display the report file, while on Windows it will launch the Notepad and display the report file.

Click the Package button when everything is ready to go. Your document will be placed in the folder you specified, as will the instructions file (the report). There will also be a folder called Fonts that includes the fonts, a folder called Links that has the graphics files, and a folder called Output Profiles that has the color output profiles.

We strongly recommend using the Package feature. It ensures that your service bureau has all the necessary files and information to output your document correctly.

Dealing with Service Bureaus

Service bureaus are great: They keep and maintain all the equipment, know the ins and outs of both your software and your printing press requirements, and turn jobs around quickly—at least most of the time. Working with a service bureau involves commitment and communication between both parties. They need your business; you need their expertise and equipment.

To ensure that you get what you want (fast, accurate service) and that the service bureau gets what it wants (no-hassle clients and printing jobs), make sure that you both understand your standards and needs. Keep in mind that the service bureau has many customers, all of whom do things differently. Service bureaus likewise must not impose unreasonable requirements just for the sake of consistency, because customers can have good reasons for doing things differently.

Paying attention to a few basic issues can help you establish a productive relationship with your service bureau.

Sending documents versus output files

Since you have the Package feature, do you give the service bureau your actual InDesign documents or do you send an EPS, PostScript, or PDF output file?

Cross-Reference   Chapter 32 shows you how to create output files.

The answer depends on several things:

✦ **A document file, even if the graphics files are copied with it, takes less space than an output file created from your document, which means fewer disks or cartridges to sort through and less time copying files from your media to theirs.**

✦ **A document file can be changed accidentally, resulting in incorrect output.** For example, a color might be changed accidentally when the service bureau checks your color definitions to make sure that spot colors are translated to process colors. Or document preferences might be lost, resulting in text reflow.

✦ **The service bureau cannot always edit an output file.** So the service bureau may not be able to come to your rescue if you make a mistake such as forgetting to print registration marks when creating the output file or specifying landscape printing mode for a portrait document.

Basically, the question is "Whom do you trust more—yourself or the service bureau?" Only you can answer that question. But in either case, there are two things that you can do to help prevent miscommunication: Provide the report file to the service bureau and also provide a proof copy of your document. The service bureau uses these tools to see if its output matches your expectations—regardless of whether you provided a document file or output file.

Determining output settings

A common area of miscommunication between designers and service bureaus is determining who sets controls over line screens, registration marks, and other output controls. Whoever has the expertise to make the right choices should handle these options. And it should be clear to both parties who is responsible for what aspect of output controls—you don't want to use conflicting settings or accidentally override the desired settings:

✦ **Assuming you're sending InDesign documents to the service bureau, for output controls such as line screens and angles, the layout artist should determine these settings and specify them on the proof copy provided to the service bureau.** That way the service bureau can use its own PPD files rather than take the chance you had incorrect or outdated ones.

✦ **If the publication has established production standards for special effects or special printing needs or if the job is unusual, I recommend that the layout artist determine the settings for such general printing controls as the registration marks and the printer resolution.**

Cross-Reference   InDesign print-control setup is described in Chapter 31.

✦ **For issues related to the service bureau's internal needs and standards, such as how much gap to have between pages and what trapping settings should be, I recommend that the service bureau determine its own settings.** If you're sending the service bureau output files instead of InDesign documents, you'll have to enter such settings in the Print dialog box pane before creating the file, so be sure to coordinate these issues with the service bureau in advance.

✦ **Issues related to the printing press (such as which side of the negative the emulsion should be on), should be coordinated with the printer and service bureau.** Again, let the service bureau enter this data unless you send output files.

In all cases, determine who is responsible for every aspect of output controls to ensure that someone does not specify a setting outside his or her area of responsibility without first checking with the other parties.

Note   Smart service bureaus do know how to edit an output file to change some settings, such as dpi and line-screen, that are encoded in those files, but don't count on their doing that work for you except in emergencies. And then they should let you know what they did and why. And remember: not all output files can be edited (such as EPS and PostScript files created as binary files), or they can be edited only in a limited way (such as PDF files).

Ensuring correct bleeds

When you create an image that bleeds, it must actually print beyond the crop marks. There must be enough of the bleeding image that if the paper moves slightly in the press, the image still bleeds. (Most printers expect ⅛ inch, or about a pica, of *trim* area for a bleed.) In most cases, the document page is smaller than both the page size (specified in InDesign through the File ➪ Document Setup option) and the paper size, so that the margin between pages is sufficient to allow for a bleed. If your document page is the same size as your paper size, the paper size limits how much of your bleed actually prints: Any part of the bleed that extends beyond the paper size specified is cut off. (This problem derives from the way PostScript controls printing; it has nothing to do with InDesign.)

Note   This paper-size limit applied even if you set bleed and slug space in the Document Setup dialog box. These tell the printer how much of material outside the page boundaries to output, so they're not cropped out automatically. But the paper, film negatives, or plates they are output to still has to be large enough to physically accommodate them.

Make sure that your service bureau knows that you're using bleeds and whether you specified a special paper or page size because that may be a factor in the way the operator outputs your job.

Sending oversized pages

If you use a paper size larger than U.S. letter size (8.5 by 11 inches), tell the service bureau in advance, because the paper size might affect how the operator sends your job to the imagesetter. Many service bureaus use a utility program that automatically rotates pages to save film, because pages rotated 90 degrees still fit along the width of typesetting paper and film rolls. But if you specify a larger paper size to make room for bleeds or because your document will be printed at tabloid size, this rotation might cause the tops and/or bottoms of your document pages to be cut off.

I've worked with service bureaus that forgot that they loaded this page-rotation utility, so the operator didn't think to unload it for our oversized pages. It took a while to figure out what was going on because my publication's layout staff were certain that we weren't doing the rotation (the service bureau assumed we had), and the service bureau had forgotten that it was using the rotation utility.

Summary

After you've installed the printer drivers for the various printers you'll use — both those on site for proofing and those at a service bureau or prepress house — you should turn your attention to setting global printing defaults, the ones that affect all printing jobs, such as the use of paper trays and the handling of TrueType fonts.

Before you actually print, InDesign will check your document for possible output problems using its preflight tools. You also have the chance to create a print package — which collects all graphics, fonts, and a copy of the document file — to send to your service bureau or other output service.

✦   ✦   ✦

Printing Techniques

In This Chapter

Understanding the many print options

Saving printer settings for reuse

Specifying options used in imagesetters

Printing to file

Working with process and spot colors

Working with transparency

Your document is done. You've set up your printers and printer options and preflighted your document, as described in Chapter 30. You're ready to see all that effort become reality by printing a proof copy or an actual version on a high-resolution imagesetter or printer.

The good news is that your hard work is over. Printing from InDesign is straightforward once everything has been set up. Just use File ⇨ Print, or ⌘+P or Ctrl+P, to go to the Print dialog box.

Selecting InDesign Printing Options

The Print dialog box has many panes — eight, to be precise — as well as several options common to all the panes. Change any options and choose Print, and InDesign sends your document to the printer. Figure 31-1 shows the dialog box.

Tip If you're working with the InDesign Books feature (see Chapter 9), you can print the book's chapters from an open book's pane, using the Print Book option in its palette menu. (If one or more documents in the book are selected in the pane, the menu option will change to Print Selected Documents.) The setup options are the same as for printing individual documents.

Figure 31-1: The default view for the Print dialog box.

General options

The general options available in the dialog box, no matter what pane is selected, are as follows:

✦ The Print Preset pop-up menu lets you save a group of printer settings, which makes it easy to switch between, say, a proofing printer and a final output device.

✦ The Printer pop-up menu let you select the printer to use.

✦ The PPD pop-up menu lets you select PostScript Printer Descriptions, files that contain configuration and feature information specific to a brand and model of printer. These are installed into your operating system using software that comes from your printer manufacturer. If it finds no compatible PPDs, InDesign will use generic options if there is no compatible PPD. If it finds just one compatible PPD, it will use that automatically; otherwise, it will let you select a PPD.

✦ The Save Preset button saves any settings you changed in the Print dialog box, letting you choose a name for those saved settings for reuse. If you change the dialog box's settings but don't save these changes as a print preset, InDesign will change the name of the current settings in the Print Preset pop-up menu to [Custom] to remind you the settings are changed and unsaved.

Tip

You can also create print presets by choosing File ⇨ Print Presets ⇨ Define, or edit an existing preset by choosing File ⇨ Print Presets ⇨ [preset name]. When you click New or Edit in the resulting dialog box, you'll get a dialog box identical to the Print dialog box, except that the Print button becomes the OK button.

✦ The Setup button in Windows and the Page Setup and Printer buttons on the Mac give you access to printer-specific controls. Figure 31-2 shows the three resulting dialog boxes. You would use these dialog boxes to specify options such as printing to file, paper sources, and printer resolution.

Windows and Mac OS X provide access to printer controls in different ways. In Windows, the Setup button gives you access to these, while on the Mac, you use both the Page Setup and Printer buttons to access these controls.

✦ The Cancel button closes the Print dialog box without printing. Use this if you've clicked Save Preset but don't want to print, as well as when you have any reason not to print.

✦ The Print button prints the document based on the current settings.

✦ The page preview panel at lower-left shows the current settings graphically. In Figure 31-1, the page is indicated by the blue rectangle, while the direction of the large *P* indicates the printing orientation; in this case, rotated 90 degrees. The panel shows that the paper itself is smaller than the page (the paper is shown in white, the overflow in gray). This preview will change as you adjust settings in the dialog box.

New Feature

The Save Preset button used to be called Save Style in previous versions of InDesign, but it's the same feature.

Figure 31-2: Mac OS X's Page Setup and Printer dialog boxes (top) and Windows' Setup dialog box.

The General pane

The General pane (refer to Figure 31-1) contains the basic settings for your print job:

✦ The Copies text field is where you tell InDesign how many copies of the document you want to print. You can also check the Collate option to have InDesign print the pages in sequence. This is useful when printing multiple copies, so you get, for example, pages 1 through 16 printed in sequence, then printed again in sequence if you're making two copies. Otherwise, InDesign would print two copies of page 1, two copies of page 2, and so on, forcing you to manually collate them. If you check Reverse Order, InDesign will print from the last page to the first page, which is meant for printers that stack pages face up rather than the usual face down.

✦ The Pages radio buttons let you choose to print all pages or a range, in which case you enter a range in the Range field. When specifying a range of pages, you can enter nonconsecutive ranges, such as **1-4, 7, 10-13, 15, 18, 20**.

Tip   If you want to print from a specific page to the end of the document, just enter the hyphen after the initial page number, such as **4-**. InDesign will figure out what the last page is. Similarly, to start from the first page and end on a specified page, just start with the hyphen as in **-11**.

New Feature   InDesign CS now lets you enter absolute page numbers in the Range field. For example, entering **+6-+12** would print the document's sixth through twelfth pages, no matter what their page numbers are.

✦ The Sequence pop up menu lets you choose from All Pages, Odd Pages Only, and Even Pages Only.

✦ The Spreads option, if checked, prints facing pages on the same sheet of paper — this is handy when showing clients comps, but make sure you have a printer that can handle that large paper size or that you scale the output down to fit (via the Setup pane, covered in the next section).

Tip   You may not want to use the Spreads option when outputting to an imagesetter if you have bleeds because there will be no bleed between the spreads. If you use traditional *perfect-binding* (square spines) or *saddle-stitching* (stapled spines) printing methods, in which facing pages are not printed contiguously, do not use this option.

✦ The Print Master Pages option will print your master pages, which is handy for having reference copies available to page designers.

✦ There are three check boxes in the Options section that are self-explanatory: Print Non-Printing Objects, Print Blank Pages, and Print Visible Guides and Baseline Grids. Print Blank Pages is usually used for collation, such as when you have blank pages dividing sections of a manual. The other two are used typically by page designers to display hidden designer notes or wrap objects, as well as to ensure that objects really do align to the standard grids.

The Setup pane

The Setup pane, shown in Figure 31-3, is where you tell InDesign how to work with the paper (or other media, such as film negatives) that you're printing to. The options are straightforward.

Figure 31-3: The Setup pane.

Paper size and orientation

In the Paper Size section, choose the paper size using the Paper Size pop-up menu. You can also check the page orientation using any of the four buttons, which rotate the image as follows from left to right: 0 degrees (standard portrait), –90 degrees, 180 degrees, and 90 degrees (standard landscape).

Choosing some printer models will in turn let you choose a Custom option in the Page Size pop-up menu, in which case you enter the dimensions in the Width and Height fields, as well as position the output via the Offset and Gap fields. These latter two options are usually used when printing to a roll, such as in an imagesetter using photo paper (called *RC paper,* a resin-coated paper that keeps details extremely sharp), so you can make sure there is space between the left edge of the roll and the page boundary (the *Offset*), as well as between pages (the *Gap*). Most printers can't print right to the edge, thus the Offset setting; you also want a Gap between pages for crop and registration marks, as well as to have room to physically cut the pages.

The Transverse check box, if checked, will rotate the output 90 degrees. This is done mainly for imagesetters, whose paper and film negatives are usually about 12 inches wide. At that width, it's cheaper for the service bureau to rotate the pages 90 degrees in most cases (since most publications are usually no taller than 11 inches), packing more pages onto the RC paper or film.

Caution Many service bureaus use a utility program that automatically rotates pages to save film, so check with your service bureau to make sure that checking the Transverse option won't conflict with any rotation they might do. Also, if you specify a larger paper size to make room for bleeds or because your document will be printed at tabloid size, this rotation might cause the tops and/or bottoms of your document pages to be cut off. The basic rule: Discuss all output settings with your service bureau or prepress department first.

Scaling, positioning, and tiling options

The Setup pane also lets you set scaling, positioning, and tiling settings.

The Scale settings are straightforward. You can choose separate Width and Height scalings to reduce or enlarge the page image. If Constrain Proportions is checked, then a change in the Width field is applied to the Height field, and vice versa. To make a page fit the paper size, choose the Scale to Fit radio button. InDesign will then display the actual percentage it will use. Note that Scale to Fit takes into account bleeds and crop marks, so even if the document page size is the same as the output device's paper size, Scale to Fit will reduce it to make room for those elements.

The Page Position pop-up menu lets you choose how the page image is positioned on the paper you're printing to. The default is Centered, which centers the page image vertically and horizontally. You can also choose Center Horizontally, which aligns the top of the page image to the top of the paper and centers the page horizontally; Center Vertically, which aligns the left side of the page to the left side of the paper and centers the page vertically; and Upper Left, which places the page image's upper-left corner at the paper's upper-left corner.

Caution These three positioning options — Center Horizontally, Center Vertically, and Top Left — run the risk of putting part of the page outside the printer's imaging margin — a strip of a pica or so from the paper edge in which the printer cannot print. That's why it's best to use the default Page Position setting of Centered when printing to paper, such as from an ink-jet, laser, or thermal wax printer. This option also makes room available on all sides where possible for crop marks and bleeds.

Caution But when you print to an imagesetter or platesetter, Centered may not be the best option. Your service bureau may not want the pages centered, because they may be spacing them or rotating them to minimize wastage of paper or film negatives. Imagesetters output to rolls of paper or film, so the service bureau has some control over the page's size. Always check first. On a local laser printer or other proofing device that outputs discrete pages, go ahead and use this option to make room available on all sides where possible for crop marks and bleeds.

A very nice option is InDesign's Thumbnails check box and its adjoining pop-up menu. Here, you can have InDesign print *thumbnails* — miniature versions of pages, several to a sheet — for use in presenting comps, seeing whole articles at a glance, and so on. If you check the Thumbnails option, you then select how many thumbnails you want per page from the adjoining pop-up menu. Your choices are 1×2, 2×2, 3×3, 4×4, 5×5, 6×6, and 7×7. InDesign will size the pages based on what it takes to make them fit at the number of thumbnails chosen per page, the page size, and the paper size.

QuarkXPress User

InDesign's Thumbnails option is more flexible than QuarkXPress's, letting you choose the umber of thumbnails per page.

Use the Tile options to print oversized documents. InDesign will break the document into separate pages — called *tiles* — that you later can assemble together. To enable tiling, check the Tile option. Then choose the appropriate option from the adjoining pop-up menu:

✦ **Manual** lets you specify the tiles yourself. To specify a tile, you change the origin point on the document ruler; that becomes the upper-left corner of the current tile. To print multiple tiles this way, you need to adjust the origin point, print, adjust the origin point to the next location, print, and so on, until you're done.

Cross-Reference

Chapter 2 covers the origin point in more detail.

✦ **Auto** lets InDesign figure out where to divide the pages into tiles. You can change its default amount of overlap between tiles of 1.5 inches using the Overlap field. The overlap lets you easily align tiles by having enough overlap for you to see where each should be placed relative to the others.

✦ **Auto Justified** is similar to Auto except that it makes each tile the same size, adjusting the overlap if needed to do that. (The Auto option, by contrast, simply starts at the origin point and then does as much of the page as will fit in the tile, which means the last tile may be a different width than the others. You can see the difference between the two by watching how the page preview window at left changes as you select each option.

The Marks and Bleeds pane

The Marks and Bleeds pane, shown in Figure 31-4, lets you specify which printer marks are output with your pages, as well as areas to reserve for items that bleed off the page. The printer's marks are set in the Marks section, while the bleeds are set in the Bleed and Slug section.

Figure 31-4: The Marks and Bleeds pane.

Printer's marks

In most cases, you'd select All Printer's Marks and have all print on each sheet or negative. But you can select which ones you want to print. Here's what each option means:

✦ **Crop Marks** are lines at the corners of the page that tell a commercial printer where the page boundaries are, and thus where the paper will be trimmed to.

✦ **Bleed Marks** add a very thin box around your page that shows the bleed area — where you expect items to print into, even though they're past the page boundary. (A *bleed* is an object that you want to be cut at the page boundary; you need to have the object overshoot that boundary in case, during printing, the page is not trimmed exactly where it should be. Normally, 0p9, or 0.125 inches, is sufficient area for a bleed. You set the bleed area in the Marks and Bleeds pane, covered later in this chapter.)

✦ **Registration Marks** are crosshair symbols that are used to ensure that the color negatives are properly aligned on top of each other when combined to create a color proof and when lined up on a printing press to make sure the final pages will not have the colors misregistered.

✦ **Color Bars** print the CMYK colors and tints so a commercial printer can quickly check during printing whether ink is under- or oversaturated — the shades could be too light or dark. The CMYK colors also help a commercial printer know which color a particular negative is for (after all, negatives are produced using transparent film with black images).

✦ **Page Information** lists the filename and page number.

Note

If a printer has options for printer's marks, they will display in the Type pop-up menu, but most will simply have one option: Default. You can also adjust the thickness of the printer's marks, using the Weight pop-up menu to 0.125, 0.25, and 0.5 points; the default is 0.25 points (a hairline rule). You can also control the offset of crop marks from the page corners by adjusting the Offset value; the default of 0.833 inches (6 points) usually suffices. For all of these, check with your service bureau.

Tip

Using any printer's marks will automatically increase the page size in PDF files exported from InDesign to add room for the printer's marks. This is handy, since when you output EPS or other PostScript files, the page size selected determines the page boundary, and printer's marks often get eliminated because they fall outside that boundary. One solution is to use a larger page size than your final output will be, so there's naturally enough room for printer's marks. The preview window at right in the dialog box will show you if printer's marks will fall outside the page's boundaries.

Bleeds and slugs

The Bleed and Slug area of the Setup pane controls how materials print past the page boundary.

A bleed is used when you want a picture, color, or text to go right to the edge of the paper. Because there is slight variation on positioning when you print, since the paper moves mechanically through rollers and might move slightly during transit, publishers have any to-the-edge materials actually print beyond the edge, so there are never any gaps. It's essentially a safety margin. A normal bleed margin would be 0p9 (0.75 inch), though you can make it larger if you want.

A *slug* is an area beyond the bleed area in which you want printer's marks to appear. The reader will never see this, but the staff at the commercial printer will, to help them make sure they have the right pages, colors, and so on. Like the bleed, the slug area is trimmed off when the pages are bound into a magazine, newspaper, or whatever. (The word *slug* is an old newspaper term for this identifying information, based on the lead slug once used for this purpose on old printing presses.)

The purpose is to ensure there is enough room for all the printer's marks to appear between the bleed area and the edges of the page. Otherwise, InDesign will do the best it can.

It's best to define your bleed and slug areas in your document itself when you create the document in the New Document dialog box (File ➪ New, or ⌘+N or Ctrl+N), as covered in Chapter 4. You can also use the Document Setup dialog box (File ➪ Document Setup, or Option+⌘+P or Ctrl+Alt+P). The two dialog boxes have the same options; if they don't show the Bleed and Slug section, click the More Options button to see them.

But if you didn't define your bleeds previously, you can do so in the Print dialog box's Marks and Bleed pane. You can also override those document settings here. To use the document settings, check the Use Document Bleed Settings option. Otherwise, enter in a bleed area using the Top, Bottom, Left, and Right fields. If you want them to be the same, click the broken-chain icon to the right of the Top field; it will become a solid chain, indicating that all four fields will have the same value if any is modified. Any bleed area will be indicated in red in the preview pane at the bottom-left.

If you want to set the slug area, check the Include Slug Area option. InDesign will then reserve any slug area defined in the New Document or Document Setup dialog box. You cannot set up the slug area in the Print dialog box.

New Feature
The Include Slug Area option is new to InDesign CS, since slugs are new to this version.

The Output pane

The next pane is the Output pane, which controls the processing of colors and inks on imagesetters, platesetters, and commercial printing equipment. You'll definitely want to check these settings with your service bureau. For proof printing, such as to a laser printer or ink-jet printer, the only option that you'll need to worry about is the Color pop-up menu. Figure 31-5 shows the pane.

Caution
These options should be specified in coordination with your service bureau and commercial printer—they can really mess up your printing if set incorrectly.

Figure 31-5: The Output pane.

Here's what the options do:

✦ **In the Color pop-up menu, choose how you want the document to print.**
Your options are Composite Leave Unchanged, Composite Gray, Composite
RGB, Composite CMYK, Separations, and In-RIP Separations. (*RIP* stands for
"raster image processor," the device in a printer or imagesetter that converts
lines, curves, colors, and pictures into the tiny dots that make up printed
output.)

The Composite options are meant for proofing devices such as ink-jets and
laser printers. Most such printers are black-and-white or CMYK, so you'll usually pick Composite Gray or Composite CMYK. Pick Composite RGB for documents output to PDF format for display on-screen. Composite Leave
Unchanged is meant for proofing printers that support specialty ink swatches
such as Pantone; very few do. (If your document uses colors like Pantone colors, you typically would pick Composite CMYK, and your printer will approxi-
mate the Pantone colors. You would use Composite Leave Unchanged only if
your proofing printer had actual Pantone inks.) If you check the Text as Black
option, text will appear in pure black, rather than be converted to gray or be
printed in a color (even if you applied a color to the text). This can make text
more readable in a proof copy.

New Feature InDesign CS now offers the Composite Leave Unchanged option for all color printers, rather than just for PDF output. Also, InDesign CS now correctly prints Photoshop DCS 1.2 files with transparency when you use the In-RIP Separations option.

Select Separations if you're printing to an imagesetter to create film negatives or to a platesetter to create color plates. If your output device supports in-RIP separations — where the device creates the separate color plates, rather than having InDesign do it — choose In-RIP Separations. (Note that only a few printers' PPDs support this option.)

✦ **In the Trapping pop-up menu, select how color trapping is handled.** (This will be grayed out if Separations or In-RIP Separations are not selected in the Color pop-up menu.) The choices are Off, Application Built-In (meaning, as set in InDesign), and Adobe In-RIP (available only for printers that have Adobe's in-RIP separations technology).

Note Adobe would like the publishing world to standardize on its PostScript Level 3 printing language and its default trapping and color technologies, which is what the Adobe In-RIP option uses. Adobe may get its wish one day, but the reality is that most companies use a variety of technologies, so you'll likely use the standard Separations option that uses whatever settings you created in InDesign, or you'll select the Off option and let your service bureau manage trapping directly. Check with your service bureau.

✦ **Use the Flip pop-up menu and the associated Negative check box to determine how the file prints to film negatives or plates.** Commercial printers have different requirements based on the technology they use. They tend to use language such as "right reading, emulsion side up," which can be hard to translate to InDesign's Flip settings. Type on the page is *right reading* when the photosensitive layer is facing you and you can read the text. Horizontally flipping the page would make it *wrong reading* (type is readable when the photosensitive layer is facing away from you). Check with your service bureau as to whether and how you should flip the output. Pages printed on film are often printed using the Horizontal & Vertical option in the Flip pop-up menu.

✦ **The Negative check box, if checked, creates a photographic negative of the page, which some commercial printers may request.** This option is available only if Composite Gray, Separations, or In-RIP Separations is selected in the Color pop-up menu.

✦ **The Screening pop-up menu works differently depending on whether you have chosen Composite Gray or one of the separations options in the Color pop-up menu:**

- If you select Composite Gray in the Color pop-up menu, your Screen pop-up menu choices are Default and Custom. If you choose Custom, you can select the preferred line screen frequency and angle at the bottom of the pane using the Frequency and Angle fields.

- If you select Separations or In-RIP Separations in the Color pop-up menu, you get a series of options that will vary based on the selected printer and PPD. But all will show an lpi setting and a dpi setting. (See the sidebar "What 'lpi' and 'dpi' mean" for more on these.) And the Frequency and Angle fields at the bottom of the pane will display very precise angles optimized for the selected output device based on the chosen lpi/dpi settings. Although you can change the Frequency and Angle fields, you shouldn't.

Note   The Inks section of the pane lets you see the frequency and angle settings for selected colors; you change a specific color plate's settings by first selecting the color and then altering the Frequency and Angle fields. You can also disable output of specific color plates by clicking the printer icons to the left of the colors — a red line will be drawn through the icon for disabled plates — as well as control color plate output by clicking the Ink Manager button. Color output is covered in more detail later in this chapter.

✦ **Finally, the Simulate Overprint check box at the bottom of the Output pane lets InDesign overprint colors for printers that normally don't support this.** (You would set an object to overprint another by checking one of the Overprint options in the Attributes pane.) This option is available only if the Color pop-up menu is set to Composite Gray, Composite CMYK, or Composite RGB.

What "lpi" and "dpi" mean

Lines per inch (lpi) and dots per inch (dpi) are not related because the spots in a line screen are variable-sized, while dots in a laser printer or imagesetter are often fixed-sized. (Because newer printers using techniques like Hewlett-Packard's Resolution Enhancement Technology or Apple Computer's FinePrint and PhotoGrade use variable-sized dots, the distinction may disappear one day.)

Lines per inch specifies, in essence, the grid through which an image is filtered, not the size of the spots that make it up. Dots per inch specifies the number of ink dots per inch produced by the laser printer; these dots are typically the same size. A 100-lpi image with variable sized dots will, therefore, appear finer than a 100-dpi image. The figure shows an example, with a fixed-dot arrow at left and a variable-size-dot arrow at right.

Depending upon the size of the line-screen spot, several of a printer's fixed-sized dots may be required to simulate one line-screen spot. For this reason, a printer's or imagesetter's lpi is far less than its dpi. For example, a 300-dpi laser printer can achieve about 60-lpi resolution; a 1,270-dpi imagesetter can achieve about 120-lpi resolution; a 2,540-dpi imagesetter about 200-lpi resolution. Resolutions of less than 100 lpi are considered coarse, and resolutions of more than 120 lpi are considered fine.

But there's more to choosing an lpi setting than knowing your output device's top resolution. An often overlooked issue is the type of paper the material is printed on. Smoother paper (such as *glossy-coated* or *super-calendared*) can handle finer halftone spots because the paper's coating (also called its *finish*) minimizes ink bleeding. Standard office paper, such as that used in photocopiers and laser printers, is rougher and has some bleed that is usually noticeable only if you write on it with markers. Newsprint is very rough and has a heavy bleed. Typically, newspaper images are printed at 85 to 90 lpi; newsletter images on standard office paper print at 100 to 110 lpi; magazine images are printed at 120 to 150 lpi; calendars and coffee-table art books are printed at 150 to 200 lpi.

Other factors affecting lpi include the type of printing press and the type of ink used. Your printer representative should advise you on preferred settings.

If you output your document from your computer directly to film negatives (rather than to photographic paper that is then shot to create negatives), inform your printer representative. Outputting to negatives allows a higher lpi than outputting to paper because negatives created photographically cannot accurately reproduce the fine resolution that negatives that output directly on an imagesetter have. (If, for example, you output to 120 lpi on paper and then create a photographic negative, even the slightest change in the camera's focus will make the fine dots blurry. Outputting straight to negatives avoids this problem.) Printer representatives often assume that you're outputting to paper and base their advised lpi settings on this assumption.

The Graphics pane

The Graphics pane, shown in Figure 31-6, controls how graphics are printed, as well as how fonts are downloaded. The options here are meant for professional printing, such as to imagesetters, in situations where you're working with a service bureau or in-house printing department.

Figure 31-6: The Graphics pane.

Your first option is the Send Data pop-up menu, in the Images section. It has three additional options: All, Optimized Subsampling, and Proxy (a low-resolution, 72-dpi version), and None. Typically, use All. The other two options are meant to increase speed of proof prints, with Proxy being the fastest. The None option is handy for quick proofs meant to focus on the layout and the text.

The Download options in the Font section require that you understand how your output device is configured to handle fonts. Be sure to ask your service bureau what options it prefers:

✦ **Normally, when printing to a local printer, keep the Font Downloading option set to Subset, which sends font data to the printer as fonts are used.** This means that if you use just one character of a font on a page, only that character is sent for that page, and if more characters are used on later pages, they are sent at that time. This is an efficient way to send font data to printers that don't have lots of memory or hard drives to store complete font information for many typefaces.

✦ **If you're printing to a device that has a lot of font memory — or if your document has many pages and uses a font in bits and pieces throughout — use the Complete option.** This sends the entire font to the printer's memory, where it resides for the entire print job. In cases such as those described, this is more efficient than the standard Subset method.

✦ **Use the None option if you're certain all the fonts you use reside in the printer's memory or in a hard disk attached to the printer.** Many service bureaus will load all the fonts for a job into the printer memory, then print the job. They'll then clear out the printer memory for the next job and load just the fonts that job needs. This is efficient when a service bureau has lots of clients who use all sorts of fonts. Alternatively, some service bureaus attach a hard drive loaded with fonts to their imagesetters, saving the font-loading time for them and for InDesign.

✦ **If checked, the Download PPD Fonts will download any fonts specified as resident in the printer's PPD file.** PPD files include lists of fonts that should reside in printer memory and thus don't need to be downloaded with each print job. Checking this option overrides this, downloading those fonts from your computer even if they should reside in the printer's memory. You'll rarely need to check this — it's more of a safety when creating output files for printing by someone else.

Finally, you can specify what PostScript language is used and how PostScript data is transmitted. Although you set these up in the Mac OS and Windows printer settings (refer to Figure 31-2), InDesign gives you the opportunity to override any defaults here, which can be handy when creating output files for printing elsewhere. From the PostScript pop-up menu, you can choose Level 2 or Level 3; use whichever the output device supports. (Most still use Level 2.) The Data Format pop-up menu is grayed out unless you chose PostScript File in the Printer pop-up menu; your choices are ASCII and Binary. If you choose ASCII, the PostScript file is more likely to be editable in programs like Adobe Illustrator, but the file will be larger. Ask your service bureau which it prefers.

The Color Management pane

The Color Management pane, shown in Figure 31-7, is where you manage color output (apply color calibration). The options are straightforward:

✦ **Choose the Source Space — either Document, which uses the document's color space, or Proof, which selects a color space automatically based on the selected printer.**

✦ **Select a Profile for the print space, meaning the space of the device the document will ultimately be printed to.** InDesign compares the source and print space to makes its color adjustments. If you choose PostScript Color Management for the Print Space Profile — this is used only on newer PostScript Level 3 devices that have built-in color calibration — you choose the profile using the CRD pop-up menu. A CRD (color reference dictionary) is essentially the same as a color profile; it's just in the format that the PostScript color-calibration tool uses. Choose default to use the CRD in the output device, or override it by choosing another CRD.

✦ **If you had selected Proof as the Source Space, you can also choose the rendering intent using the Intent pop-up menu.** Its options are Perceptual, Saturation, Relative Colorimetic, and Absolute Colorimetric.

Cross-Reference   Chapter 29 covers color calibration in detail.

Figure 31-7: The Color Management pane.

The Advanced pane

The options in the Advanced pane, shown in Figure 31-8, control graphics file substitutions in an Open Prepress Interface (OPI) workflow and also set transparency flattening, which controls how transparent and semitransparent objects are handled during output.

If graphics files exist in high-resolution versions at your service bureau — typically, this occurs when the bureau scans in photographs at very high resolutions and sends you a lower-resolution version for layout placement — check the OPI Image Replacement option. This will ensure that InDesign uses the high-resolution scans instead of the low-resolution layout versions.

Figure 31-8: The Advanced pane.

A related graphics-file-handling option are the three check boxes in the Omit for OPI section: You can have InDesign *not* send EPS, PDF, and bitmap images (such as TIFF files) by checking the appropriate options. You would do so either to speed printing of proof copies, or when the service bureau will have such files in higher-resolution or color-corrected versions and will substitute their graphics for yours. InDesign will keep any OPI links, so the graphics at the service bureau will relink to your document during output.

There are just two Transparency Flattener options:

✦ The Preset pop-up menu lets you select a transparency preset, or saved set of options. At the least, InDesign will provide the three default options: [Low Resolution], [Medium Resolution], and [High Resolution].

✦ The Ignore Spread Overrides check box, if checked, ignores any transparency settings you manually applied to document spreads, instead using the selected preset in all cases.

Cross-Reference
Transparency settings and setup are covered later in this chapter.

The Summary pane

The final Print dialog box pane is the Summary pane, shown in Figure 31-9. It simply lists your settings all in one place for easy review. The only option — Save Summary — saves the settings to a file so you can include it with your files when delivering them to a service bureau, or for distribution to other staff members so they know the preferred settings.

Figure 31-9: The Summary pane.

Printing to File

You won't see an option to print to file in InDesign. If you choose PostScript File or Adobe PDF as your "printers," InDesign will create a file in the chosen format. But if you want to print a document to file with specific printer settings embedded, you need to use the operating system's printer options. As mentioned earlier, you access those using the Printer and Page Setup buttons on Mac OS X and using the Setup button in Windows (see Figure 31-2).

The process differs between Mac OS X and Windows.

In Windows, click the Setup button and then check the Print to File option in the resulting dialog box and click Print.

On the Mac, click the Printer button, choose the Output Options menu item from the pop-up menu in the resulting dialog box, then check the Save as File Option, choose the file format (PDF or PostScript) from the Format pop-up menu, and click Save.

Note You should make all other Print dialog box changes in InDesign *before* taking this step, since at this point you're actually creating the output file.

Working with Spot Colors and Separations

Accidentally using spot colors such as red and Pantone 111 (say, for picture and text box frames) in a document that contains four-color TIFF and EPS files is very easy. The result is that InDesign outputs as many as six plates: one each for the four process colors, plus one for red and one for Pantone 111.

The Ink Manager dialog box

That's where the Ink Manager dialog box comes in. Accessed via the Output pane's Ink manager button, this dialog box gives you finer controls over how color negatives output. Figure 31-10 shows the dialog box.

Figure 31-10: The Ink Manager dialog box.

Most users will use the All Spots to Process check box at the bottom of the dialog box. Checking this box converts all colors to CMYK, reducing the print job to four plates (cyan, yellow, magenta, and black). Obviously, if you want to print a spot color on its own plate — perhaps a neon, metallic, or hard-to-simulate color like green or orange — you should not use this option. Instead, make sure that only the colors you do want to output to separate negatives are listed in the Ink Manager dialog box or in the Output pane.

If any colors should have been converted to process color but weren't, you have two choices:

✦ **Override the spot color in the Ink Manager dialog box by clicking the spot color (circle) icon to the left of the color's name.** That will convert it to a process color. (Clicking the process color icon, a four-color box, converts a color back to a spot color.) This is the way to go for a quick fix.

✦ **Close the Ink Manager and Print dialog boxes, and edit the color incorrectly set as a spot color in the Swatches pane (Window ➪ Swatches, or F5), as covered in Chapter 8, to make it a process color instead.** This will ensure that the color is permanently changed to a process color for future print jobs.

The other Ink Manager options are for experts and should be changed only in consultation with your service bureau and commercial printer:

✦ **You can change the ink type, in the Type pop-up menu.** Most inks — including the process inks — should be left at Normal. Use Transparent for varnishes and other finishes that let color through — you don't want InDesign to trap to such "colors"; if they did, no color would print under the varnish or finish. (A varnish is often used to highlight part of a page, such as making the text reflective in contrast to the rest of the page.) Use Opaque for metallics, pastels, and other thick colors; this setting will let adjacent colors trap to the edge of opaque objects, but it prevents trapping of underlying colors (since they will be totally covered over). Finally, use OpaqueIgnore for inks that don't trap well with any other color — your service bureau or commercial printer will tell you when you need to do this.

✦ **For each ink, you can change the neutral density, which tells InDesign how to handle the trapping of differently saturated inks.** For example, a dark color (highly saturated) will need to be trapped more conservatively against a light color to prevent excess intrusion. In coordination with your commercial printer, you might want to override the default neutral density settings if you're finding that the defaults don't properly handle some trapping combinations. It's possible that your commercial printer is using a different brand of ink than is assumed in the settings, for example, and that could require a density adjustment.

✦ **Some commercial printers let you arrange the order in which color negatives print.** This affects the trapping, because InDesign presumes that the colors are printed in the standard order — cyan, then magenta, then yellow, then black, then any spot colors — and factors that into its trapping adjustments. In some cases, changing the printing order can improve a publication's color balance, because it happens to favor a range of tones that the standard order might not treat properly. For example, if there's a lot of black in the background, you might want to print black first, so other colors overprint it, giving it a warmer feel than if black were printed on top of the other colors as is normal. To change the order of output used by InDesign's trapping calculations, select a color, and change its ink sequence number in the Trapping Sequence field; all other colors' sequences will be automatically adjusted.

✦ **Use the Ink Alias pop-up menu to apply a process color's settings to a spot color.** I don't recommend you do this very often, as it will make the spot color print each dot over the dots of the selected process color, rather than be offset slightly so the color remains visible. You'd set an ink alias only if you were using a spot color in place of a standard process color — such as substituting a yolk color for standard yellow to create a special effect. In this case, the yolk color would overprint the yellow color, replacing the yellow where both colors happened to be used.

Process colors

By default, each color defined in InDesign is set as a spot process color. And each spot color gets its own negative (plate), unless you specifically tell InDesign to translate the color into process colors. You do so when defining a new color by selecting the Process option in the Color Type pop-up menu in the Swatch Options dialog box, described in Chapter 8, when you create or edit a color in the Swatches pane (Window ➪ Swatches, or F5). No matter whether a color was defined as a process or spot color, you can also choose the All to Process option in the Print dialog box's Output pane's Ink Manager dialog box when printing to convert all spot colors to process colors.

If your work is primarily four-color work, edit the spot colors in the Swatches pane to make them process colors. If you make these changes with no document open, they become the defaults for all new documents.

If you do some spot-color work and some four-color work, duplicate the spot colors and translate the duplicates into process colors. Make sure that you use some clear color-naming convention, such as Blue P for the process-color version of blue (which is created by using 100 percent each of magenta and cyan).

The same is true when you use Pantone colors (and Trumatch, Focoltone, Toyo, and DIC colors). If you do not select the Process option in the Swatch Options dialog box, these colors are output as spot colors. Again, you can define a Pantone color twice, making one of the copies a process color and giving it a name to indicate what it is. Then all you have to do is make sure that you pick the right color for the kind of output you want.

Tip   You still can mix process and spot colors if you want. For example, if you want a gold border on your pages, you have to use a Pantone ink because metallic colors cannot be produced via process colors. So use the appropriate Pantone color, and *don't* select the Process option when you define the color. When you make color separations, you get five negatives: one each for the four process colors and one for gold. That's fine because you specifically want the five negatives.

Color and separations preview

One thing to be careful of in computer-based layout is that on-screen colors interact differently than they do when printed. When inks overlap, the colors mix to produce a new color — cyan on yellow makes a green, for example. On-screen, cyan on yellow shows cyan where the two overlap. To compensate for that, InDesign can simulate color overprinting. To do so, choose View ➪ Overprint Preview, or type Option+Shift+⌘+Y or Ctrl+Alt+Shift+Y. You should have this on as your default so what you see on-screen better represents what will print.

New Feature   InDesign CS now lets you preview color separations in your document with the new Separations Preview pane.

You can preview your color separations, as well as overprinting any other output, using the new Separations Preview pane (Window ➪ Output Preview ➪ Separations, or Shift+F6). Figure 31-11 shows the pane and its palette menu. By clicking each color and then the eye icon, you can turn on or off specific color plates; InDesign will adjust what appears on-screen accordingly. To see just the CMYK plates, you can click the CMYK color (instead of turning on the cyan, yellow, magenta, and black plates individually). You can also hide all process colors the same way, so only spot colors are visible.

Figure 31-11: The Separations Preview pane.

If you select Show Single Plates in Black in the palette menu and have the eye icon selected for only one plate, InDesign will show that plate in black on-screen. That's because it's often hard to see colors like magenta, yellow, and cyan clearly when they're by themselves.

And if color management is turned off, you can choose the Desaturate Black option in the Separations Preview pane's palette menu. This will convert any black objects overprinting other color objects to 80 percent black so the other objects are more visible during the preview.

The Separations Preview pane also lets you open the Ink Manager dialog box, covered earlier in this chapter.

QuarkXPress User InDesign and QuarkXPress offer similar levels of color output controls, but InDesign does have several options QuarkXPress does not. One is setting ink density, another is automatic calculation of screen angles for spot colors. A third is the ability to more accurately preview documents with overprinting colors.

Screen angles

Normally, you'd probably never worry about the screening angles for your color plates. After all, the service bureau makes those decisions, right? Maybe.

If you have your own imagesetter, or even if you're just using a proofing device, you should know how to change screen angles for the best output. If you're working with spot colors that have shades applied to them, you'll want to know what the screen angles are so that you can determine how to set the screening angles for those spot colors.

Screening angles determine how the dots comprising each of the four process colors — cyan, magenta, yellow, and black, or any spot colors — are aligned so they don't overprint each other. The rule of thumb is that dark colors should be at least 30 degrees apart, while lighter colors (for example, yellow) should be at least 15 degrees apart from other colors. That rule of thumb translates into a 105-degree angle (also called –15 degrees — it's the same angle) for cyan, 75 degrees for magenta, 90 degrees for yellow, and 45 degrees for black.

But those defaults sometimes result in *moiré patterns,* which are distortions in the image's light and dark areas caused when the dots making up the colors don't arrange themselves evenly. With traditional color-separation technology, a service bureau would have to adjust the angles manually to avoid such moirés — an expensive and time-consuming process. With the advent of computer technology, modern output devices, such as imagesetters, can calculate angles based on the output's lpi settings to avoid most moiré patterns. (Each image's balance of colors can cause a different moiré, which is why there is no magic formula.) Every major imagesetter vendor uses its own proprietary algorithm to make these calculations.

InDesign automatically uses the printer's PPD values to calculate the recommended halftoning, lpi, and frequency settings shown in the Output pane of the Print dialog box. But for spot colors, it's basically a guess as to what screening angle a color should get. The traditional default is to give it the same angle as yellow, since if a spot color's dots overprint yellow dots, the effect will be less noticeable than if it overprinted, say, black dots. But if you have multiple spot colors, that approach doesn't work. In that case, choose a screening angle for the color whose hue is closest to the spot colors. Fortunately, InDesign will calculate a recommended angle for you, so you don't have to make any guesses. As always, don't forget to consult your service bureau or printing manager.

Working with Transparency

InDesign CS lets you import objects with transparent portions, as well as create transparent objects using the Color and Swatches panes. Using features such as the Drop Shadow and Feather options in the Object menu also might create transparency. But working with transparency can create unintended side effects in how overlapping objects actually appear when printed or viewed on-screen in a PDF file. To address that, InDesign offers the ability to both control transparency on selected objects and groups, as well as to control how transparency is handled during output.

To apply transparency to objects in InDesign, you use the Transparency pane (Window ➪ Transparency, or Shift+F10), as Chapter 25 explains. The more objects you have overlapping each other with transparency settings applied, the more complex the output calculations will be to print those effects. This can prevent a document from printing, as it overwhelms the printer or other output device. That's where transparency *flattening* comes into play. This feature breaks up the overlapping areas into distinct graphics during output—creating a mosaic of pieces that will produce the intended effect.

QuarkXPress User   QuarkXPress has no equivalent to InDesign's transparency settings. QuarkXPress users instead must rely on such settings in Adobe Photoshop and Illustrator for imported pictures and do without them for objects created in QuarkXPress.

InDesign comes with three transparency flattening settings—[Low Resolution], [Medium Resolution], and [High Resolution]—which you can edit in the Transparency Flattener Presets dialog box. To open this dialog box, shown in Figure 31-12, choose Edit ➪ Transparency Flattener Presets. The dialog box shows the settings for each preset as you select them. Use this dialog box to create, modify, delete, export (Save), and import (Load) presets. (You cannot modify or delete the three default presets.)

Figure 31-12: The Transparency Flattener
Presets dialog box.

Figure 31-13 shows the Transparency Flattener Preset Options dialog box, which you get when you create or modify a preset. There's a lot of trial and error in developing transparency flattener presets, since the complexity of your documents and the capacity of your output devices will vary widely. But here are some guidelines:

Figure 31-13: The Transparency Flattener Preset
Options dialog box.

✦ The most accurate transparency blends are achieved with a Raster/Vector Balance set to 100, which means use all vectors rather than convert blends to bitmap images. The [Low Resolution] preset is set at 75, which means that three-quarters of the blends are vectors and one-quarter is converted to bitmaps. The other options have higher vector proportions.

✦ Flattener resolution should be set to a value that corresponds with your output device's dpi. For Line Art and Text Resolution, 600 ppi or higher is fine, while 150 ppi is fine for gradients and meshes (overlapping transparencies). But the higher the output resolution of your output device, the higher you would make these values.

✦ If you have applied transparency to objects that overprint or underprint text, you likely will check Convert All Text to Outlines; otherwise, InDesign may make the text that interacts with transparent objects thicker than text that doesn't.

✦ Convert Strokes to Outlines has the same effect on lines and strokes for InDesign objects that overlap or underlap objects with transparency.

✦ The Clip Complex Regions options apply only if the Raster/Vector Balance is less than 100. It corrects for a phenomenon called *stitching,* in which a transparent area has both vectors and bitmaps that create a blocky feel. This option isolates those areas and forces them to be all-vector.

Note You can apply transparency settings directly to a spread by selecting a spread in the Pages pane (Window ➪ Pages, or F12), then choosing Spread Flattening ➪ Custom from the palette menu. You'll get a dialog box like the Transparency Flattener Presets dialog box (refer to Figure 31-12), except that any settings created here are applied only to the selected spread and are not saved as a preset for use elsewhere.

Once set up, you can apply transparency presets to your document via the Advanced pane of the Print dialog box, as described earlier in this chapter.

InDesign also lets you preview flattening settings, using the new Flattener Preview pane. Shown in Figure 31-14, this pane lets you preview transparent objects and their flattening. To open the pane, choose Window ➪ Output Preview ➪ Flattener.

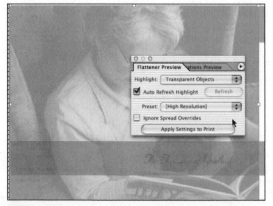

Figure 31-14: The Flattener Preview pane.

New Feature The Flattener Preview pane is new to InDesign CS.

In the pane, you can select what to preview via the Highlight pop-up menu. Your options are None, Rasterized Complex Regions, Transparent Objects, Affected Objects, Affected Graphics, Outlined Strokes, Outlined Text, Raster-Fill Text and Strokes, and All Rasterized Regions. (Note that the rasterized options display overlapping transparent objects that InDesign would need to convert to bitmaps during flattening—not simply any bitmap images in your document.) Select the area you're concerned may not output at sufficient quality. If you check the Auto Refresh Highlight option, InDesign will update the preview if you change any settings; if not, you can update the preview by clicking the Refresh button.

You can also check the flattening of different presets—just choose a preset from the Preset pop-up menu. Likewise, you can see what would happen to a spread that has a custom flattening applied if you were to override those custom settings—just check the Ignore Spread Overrides option.

If you like how the flattening looks, you can pre-apply them to the Print dialog box by clicking the Apply Settings to Print button.

Summary

When printing from InDesign, you have many options to choose from to control exactly how your document prints. The right options will depend on the document's contents and the output device you're using.

Be sure to define your colors as process colors unless you want them to print on their own plates. Although InDesign will let you convert all colors to process colors when you print, there are times when you want some colors to print on their own plate (these are called *spot colors*) and others to be converted to process, and the only way to make that happen is to define colors as process or as spot in the first place.

InDesign's transparency options let you control how overlapping objects print, as well as how those overlapping areas are handled during output to ensure both quality reproduction and speedy processing.

✦   ✦   ✦

Creating Output Files

✦ ✦ ✦ ✦

In This Chapter

Evaluating output options

Understanding printing forms

Creating Portable Document Format (PDF) files

Creating Encapsulated PostScript (EPS) files

Creating PostScript prepress files

✦ ✦ ✦ ✦

In this electronic age, there are many reasons not to print a document, at least not directly. You may want to deliver the document to readers in electronic format, such as in HTML or Adobe Acrobat. Or you may want to generate a file that your service bureau can output for you at an imagesetter — a file that you may send over a network, through the Internet, on a high-capacity disk, or even as an electronic-mail attachment to a device that could be down the hall or in another state.

Selecting the Best Output Option

InDesign has several options for creating output files: You can export to two variants of the PostScript printing language: Adobe Portable Document Format (PDF) or Encapsulated PostScript (EPS). You can print to file using all the settings described in Chapter 31 but save to a file — either in EPS or plain PostScript format — rather than output directly to a printer, creating a file tuned specifically to the printer driver chosen.

New Feature InDesign CS no longer supports export to HTML, the language of the Web. You can no longer use InDesign to create documents intended for Web distribution. However, you can create PDF documents that can be opened as a link from a Web document.

The option you pick has several advantages and consequences; let's look at each choice separately.

Exporting to PDF

This option creates a file that can be linked to from a Web page, whether on the Internet or on a corporate intranet. It can also be accessed from a CD or other disk medium, as long as the recipient has the free Adobe Acrobat Reader program (available for download from www.adobe.com/acrobat). Finally, a PDF file can be used by a commercial printer or service bureau as the master file from which to print your documents.

This file can include some or all of the fonts, or expect the ultimate output device to have them. You also have control over the resolution of the graphics, letting you, for example, create a high-resolution file for output on an imagesetter or a low-resolution version for display on the Web.

The PDF file won't have information on the specific printer, so a service bureau or printing department could use it on any available output devices. But not all service bureaus and printing departments are geared to print from PDF files; while this is an increasingly popular option, it is by no means ubiquitous. To print a PDF file directly, the output device must be a PostScript 3 device; otherwise, the service bureau must print the PDF file from Adobe Acrobat or use a PDF-oriented workflow publishing system such as those offered by Creo (go to www.creo.com for more information on this product).

Exporting to EPS

This option creates a file that can be sent to many output devices or edited by a PostScript-savvy graphics program like Illustrator, FreeHand, or CorelDraw. With InDesign, you can add a margin for bleeds — but you can't include printer's marks.

Most service bureaus can print directly from EPS files. But note that each page or spread in your document is sent to a separate file, so a service bureau may prefer a prepress-oriented PostScript file or a PDF file that combines all pages into one file — which simplifies their output effort.

The lack of printer's marks might also bother your commercial printer, since they need them to properly combine film negatives. Using a system such as Creo's, the service bureau can add printer's marks and integrate high-resolution and color-corrected images — so EPS could remain a solid output option depending on your service bureau's capabilities.

Tip Exported PDF or EPS files can be imported back into InDesign (or other programs, including QuarkXPress, PageMaker, FreeHand, Illustrator, CorelDraw, Photoshop, and Photo-Paint) as a graphic. This is handy if you want, for example, to run a small version of the cover on your contents page to give the artist credit, or if you want to show a page from a previous issue in a letters section where readers are commenting on a story. If you're creating PDF files, be sure in these cases just to export the page or spread you want to use — even though only one page or spread will display when imported into a page-layout program, the file will contain the data for all other pages, possibly and unnecessarily making its size unwieldy. (When exporting to EPS, a separate file is created for each page or spread, so this is not an issue.)

Exporting to PostScript prepress

If you know exactly what device your service bureau will use to output your document, and you know all the settings, you can create a PostScript prepress file. All your printer settings are embedded, making the file printable reliably only by the target printer.

Note

Remember to work with your service bureau, commercial printer, or printing department — whoever will get the output file — to understand what their needs and expectations are. Although some output files are fully or partially editable, it's usually not easy to know what might be incorrect in a document until the expensive step of actually printing pages or negatives.

Understanding imposition

Layout artists may work on single pages or spreads, but printing presses rarely do. Sure, for short-run jobs, your printer may actually work with one page at a time, but typically, they work with forms.

Forms are groups of pages aligned so that when they are folded, cut, and trimmed, they end up in proper numerical sequence. This arrangement of pages on a form is called *imposition.*

One popular printing method takes a huge sheet of anywhere from 4 to 64 pages, folds them, cuts them, and trims them. This results in a stack of pages in the right order — a process known as *perfect binding* — the technique used for square-backed publications like books, many magazines, and many catalogs.

The other popular printing method also uses forms, but aligned in a different way. Here, the form is broken into two-page spreads that are cut and trimmed, then stacked separately. A page from each stack is added to a pile, and the pile is then folded to create the right page sequence — this is called a *booklet.* These folded spreads are stapled in the center, in a process known as *saddle-stitching.* Many magazines and catalogs use this approach.

Both approaches usually use large sheets of paper, called a *web,* which is why such commercial printing is known as SWOP, or standard web offset printing. (*Offset* refers to the way the ink is delivered to the page, with the ink offset to an intermediate roller between the color plate and the paper. This ensures that just the right amount of ink is placed on each sheet, sort of how an ink stamp works.)

Continued

Continued

Understanding how forms are configured will show why what InDesign calls a *reader's spread*—the two adjacent pages that a reader sees when reading (and that a layout artist sees when designing on-screen) — is usually not how you want to output pages for use at a commercial printer. Printing reader's spreads makes more sense if you are, for example, wanting to show a client a mockup of the document, so you print spreads together on large paper (such as printing two 8½-by-11-inch pages on an 11-by-17-inch sheet of paper).

The figure shows how a perfect-bound publication form is numbered, as well as a saddle-stitched form. Note that a form can have a number of pages other than 16 but must be in multiples of 4 pages.

To figure out the page sequence for a perfect-bound form, take a sheet of paper, and fold it as often as needed to create the number of pages on the form. You now have a booklet. Number the pages (front and back) with a pencil, then unfold the paper to see how the form is put together. The front sides are one form, and the back sides another.

To figure out the page sequence for a saddle-stitched form, you can take a sheet of paper for each spread, stack them, fold them once, and then number the pages (front and back) with a pencil, then separate the sheets to see how the form is put together. The front sides are one form, and the back sides another. Another way to do it is to realize that the bottom sheet contains page 1 and the final page on the back, and page 2 and the next-to-final page on the front. The sheet on top would have pages 3 and FP–2 (where FP is the final page number) on the back and pages 4 and FP–3 on the back, and so on until the middle sheet.

Creating PDF Files

Typically, you'll want to directly export your InDesign files to PDF format rather than create a PostScript file and translate to PDF using the separate Adobe Acrobat Distiller product. First, I'll show how to export, then I'll explain how to print to PDF on those occasions when that's the better option.

Exporting PDF files

An easy way to create a PDF file from InDesign is to export it by choosing File ⇨ Export, or pressing ⌘+E or Ctrl+E. You'll get the Export dialog box, which like any standard Save dialog box lets you name the file and determine what disk and folder the file is to be saved in. The key control in the Export dialog box is the Formats pop-up menu, where you choose the format (in this case, Adobe PDF).

Tip   The fastest way to create a PDF file is to choose File ⇨ PDF Export Presets and then select a preset from the submenu. There are seven presets optimized for different output needs. You can also add your own, as explained a bit later in this chapter. When you select a preset from the submenu, you then see the Export dialog box. Choosing a preset defaults the Formats pop-up menu to Adobe PDF and preconfigures the PDF export settings covered in the following sections.

Tip   If you're working with the InDesign Books feature (see Chapter 9), you can export the book's chapters to PDF files from an open book's pane, using the Export Book to PDF option in its palette menu. (If one or more documents in the book are selected in the pane, the menu option will change to Export Selected Documents to PDF.) The setup options are the same as for exporting individual documents.

After you've selected Adobe PDF in the Export dialog box's Formats pop-up menu, and given the file a name and location, click the Save button to get the Export PDF dialog box, shown in Figure 32-1. The dialog box has six panes, with General being the one displayed when you open the dialog box. There are several options that are accessible from all six panes:

✦ The Preset pop-up menu lets you select from both predefined sets of PDF-export settings (similar to the printer presets covered in Chapter 31), as well as any presets you may have created.

✦ The Save Preset button lets you save any settings made in the Export PDF dialog box as a new preset. (You can also define new PDF presets by choosing File ⇨ PDF Export Presets.)

✦ The Cancel button cancels PDF export.

✦ The Export button creates the PDF file based on the settings chosen in the various panes.

Figure 32-1: The Export PDF dialog box's General pane.

InDesign does not import Acrobat Distiller job option files (called Adobe PDF settings in Acrobat Distiller 6), which are essentially the same as PDF export presets.
If you're used to creating PDF files using Acrobat Distiller (covered later in this
chapter), you'll either want to stick with that approach or create InDesign presets
that match your Distiller job options.

The General pane

Use the General pane to determine what is exported. The pane has three sections:
Pages, Options, and Include.

In the Pages section, you can set the following options:

✦ The Pages radio buttons let you choose to print all pages or a range, in which
case you enter a range in the Range field. When specifying a range of pages,
you can enter nonconsecutive ranges, such as **1-4, 7, 10-13, 15, 18, 20**.

If you want to print from a specific page to the end of the document, just enter the
hyphen after the initial page number, such as **4-**. InDesign will figure out what the
last page is. Similarly, to start from the first page to a specified page, just start with
the hyphen as in **-11**.

InDesign CS now lets you enter absolute page numbers in the Range field. For
example, entering **+6-+12** would print the document's sixth through twelfth
pages, no matter what their page numbers are.

✦ The Spreads option, if checked, prints facing pages on the same sheet of paper — this is handy when showing clients comps, but make sure you have a printer that can handle that large paper size.

Tip

You may not want to use the Spreads option when outputting a PDF file for eventual printing on an imagesetter if you have bleeds, because there will be no bleed between the spreads. If you use traditional *perfect-binding* (square spines) or *saddle-stitching* (stapled spines) printing methods in which facing pages are not printed contiguously, do not use this option.

In the Options section, you can set the following options:

✦ Use the Compatibility pop-up menu to choose the PDF version you want to export the file as. Your options are Acrobat 4 (PDF 1.3), Acrobat 5 (PDF 1.4), and Acrobat 6 (PDF 1.5). Choosing Acrobat 4 (PDF1.3) is the best option for documents to be distributed on CD or via the Web, because it ensures the broadest number of people will be able to view the file. Choose a later version only if you're certain your intended recipients use that version of Acrobat or Acrobat Reader. For example, if your company has standardized on Acrobat 5 and the document will be used only internally, it's fine to pick the Acrobat 5 (PDF 1.4) option. Likewise, if you're sending the PDF file to a service bureau, use the version of Acrobat they have, since later version of Acrobat support more features, especially for commercial printing.

✦ For prepress workflow, you might choose the PDF/X-1a or PDF/X-3 options in the Standard pop-up menu. PDF/X is a standard version of the PDF format, sanctioned by the International Standards Organization (ISO), meant to ensure consistent reproduction across a range of equipment. Irrelevant for on-screen viewing, PDF/X should be used if your service bureau is using compatible equipment. Otherwise, leave this pop-up menu at the default setting of None.

New Feature

PDF/X support and Acrobat 6 (PDF 1.5) format support are new to InDesign CS. Also new are support for layers (in Acrobat 6 format only), for JPEG 2000 compression (also just in Acrobat 6 format), and for OPI 1.3 comments, which are now preserved during export.

✦ Check the Embed Page Thumbnails option if you're creating a PDF file to be viewed on-screen — these thumbnails will help people using the Acrobat Reader program navigate your document more easily. But if the PDF files are being sent to a service bureau or commercial printer for printing, there's no need to generate the thumbnails.

✦ Always check the Optimize for Fast Web View option — this minimizes the file size without compromising the output.

✦ If you want to see the results of the PDF export as soon as the export is complete, check the View PDF after Exporting option. Typically, you should not select this option, since you likely will have other things you want to do before launching Acrobat Reader (or the full Acrobat program, if you own it) to proof your files.

✦ If you select Acrobat 6 (PDF 1.5) in the Compatibility pop-up menu, you can check the Create Acrobat Layers option, which outputs any InDesign layers to separate layers in Acrobat. (Acrobat 6 is the first version of Acrobat to support layers.) If you choose a different Compatibility option, Create Acrobat Layers is grayed out.

In the Include section, you can set the following options:

✦ Bookmarks, which takes InDesign table-of-contents (TOC) information and preserves them as bookmarks in the exported PDF file.

✦ Hyperlinks, which preserves any hyperlinks added in InDesign. Otherwise, the hyperlinks are converted to standard text.

✦ Non-Printing Objects, which includes any objects marked as Nonprinting via the Attributes pane (Window ➪ Attributes).

✦ Visible Guides and Baseline Grids, which includes the on-screen guides and grids in the output version — an option you'd use only when creating PDF files meant to be used as designer examples, not for readers or for prepress.

✦ eBook Tags, which helps eBook viewers distinguish different document components readily. InDesign creates the tags automatically during export.

✦ Interactive Elements, which preserves interactive objects such as buttons rather than convert them to static graphics.

✦ Multimedia, which lets you control how embedded sound and video are handled. This option is available only if you choose Acrobat 6 (PDF 1.5) in the Compatibility pop-up menu. The options are Use Object Settings, Link All, or Embed All. In InDesign, you can embed a sound or movie file, or link to one. This option lets you override the individual settings and make all such objects embedded or linked.

Chapter 33 covers interactive documents and eBooks, including the use of buttons and multimedia elements.

The Compression pane

All the options in this pane, as shown in Figure 32-2, compress your document's graphics. For documents you're intending to print professionally, make sure that for all three image types, No Sampling Change is selected and that Compression is set to None. You don't want to do anything that affects the resolution or quality of your bitmap images if you're outputting to a high-resolution device.

Figure 32-2: The Export PDF dialog box's Compression pane.

But it's fine to check the Crop Image Date to Frames option, since this discards portions of pictures not visible on-screen, reducing file size and reducing processing time during output (imagesetters and other devices usually have to process the entire image, even if only part of it is actually printed).

It's also fine to check the Compress Text and Line Art option. It compresses vector graphics (both imported and those created in InDesign) as well as text, but does so without affecting output quality.

The compression settings are more appropriate for documents meant to be viewed online, as the sidebar "Settings for on-screen usage" explains later in this chapter. You usually leave the image downsampling at 150 pixels per inch (ppi) for color and gray-scale images, and at 300 ppi for black-and-white images. Even though a computer monitor's resolution is 72 ppi, you want enough resolution so when a reader zooms in that the images are still clear. A good rule of thumb for documents to be printed is that the downsampling or subsampling ppi for color and gray-scale images should be at least double the printer's lpi.

For the Image Quality setting for images, Medium quality is fine for on-screen documents, but not for documents you intend to let readers print or that will be output at a service bureau. A rule of thumb is to choose High if the documents will be printed on an ink-jet or laser printer, and Maximum if they will be printed at an imagesetter or other high-end output device.

Note that JPEG compression is *lossy,* meaning it discards data to save space. That's why its Image Quality settings are characterized with subjective terms like Low, Medium, and High. Zip compression is lossless, so no image detail data is discarded. Instead, you limit the color depth by choosing between 4-bit (16 colors) and 8-bit (256 colors).

The Tile Size check box and field determine the size of the tiles for progressive display. For large images, this option will show subsequent pieces, or tiles, of the image, until the full image has been displayed, so the reader has a visual indication that the page is in fact loading. This option is only available when Compatibility is set to Acrobat 6 (format version 1.5) and Compression is set to JPEG2000. You can change the size of the tile from the default of 256 pixels.

Understanding compression methods

The act of choosing a compression method for the color, grayscale, and monochrome images in a PDF is simple — you just pick something from a menu in the Compression pane of the Export PDF dialog box. The challenge is in knowing what to pick. Take a look at the type of images the compression methods work best for, and then choose the one that represents the bulk of the images in your layout.

✦ Zip compression is appropriate for black-and-white or color images with repeating patterns (usually screenshots or simple images created in paint programs).

✦ JPEG compression works well for continuous-tone photographs in gray-scale or color. JPEG results in smaller files than Zip compression, because it throws out some image data, possibly reducing image accuracy.

✦ Use CCITT compression for black-and-white images or 1-bit images. Group 4 works well for most monochrome images, while Group 3 is good for PDFs that will be faxed electronically.

Downsampling and subsampling accomplish similar goals, but use different mathematic techniques to do so. When you reduce the dpi, you're essentially throwing away image data to make it smaller — for example, replacing a 100-by-100-pixel image with a 25-by-25-pixel version reduces the file size to $\frac{1}{16}$. Downsampling averages adjacent pixels' colors and replaces the cluster of adjacent pixels with one averaged pixel as it reduces the image size. (There are two methods for downsampling: bicubic and average. Bicubic usually, but not always, results in a truer image. Average downsampling tends to work better in nonphotographic images, with less-minute detail.) Subsampling does no averaging; it simply throws away pixels in between the ones it retains. Downsampling looks better for photographic images with lots of detail and color; subsampling looks better for images with clear color differences and few intricate details.

For prepress purposes, the resolution should be one and a half to two times the line screen ruling used to print the file. For on-screen purposes, keep in mind that higher resolutions are better when users need to increase the view scale in the PDF (for example, if they need to see detail in a map). In the Acrobat support section of www.adobe.com, you can find more details about specific image resolutions that work well with printer resolutions.

Marks and Bleeds pane

Use this pane, shown in Figure 32-3, to set the page bleed and printer's marks.

Figure 32-3: The Export PDF dialog box's Marks and Bleeds pane.

You typically set printer's marks only for files meant to be output on an imagesetter or other prepress device. Typically, you should select All Page Marks. Your Offset amount should be the same as or more than the bleed amount — if your Offset is less than the bleed, it's possible the marks could appear in your page's margins.

If you have elements bleeding off the page, you'll want a Bleed setting of at least 0p9 (0.125 inch) — that builds in enough forgiveness so that, when the pages are folded and trimmed, any elements that bleed off the page will, in fact, do so even if there's a slip in the page alignment.

If you specified a slug area (which specifies space for the printing of printer's marks) in the New Document (File ➪ New ➪ Document, or ⌘+N or Ctrl+N) or Document Setup (File ➪ Document Setup, or Option+⌘+P or Ctrl+Alt+P) dialog boxes, check Include Slug Area to reserve that space in your PDF file.

Likewise, if you specified bleed settings in the New Document or Document Setup dialog boxes, you can have InDesign use those settings by checking the Use Document Bleed Settings option.

Cross-Reference These marks, bleed, and slug options are the same as for direct printing and are covered in detail in Chapter 31.

The Advanced pane

Use the Advanced pane, shown in Figure 32-4, to manage color calibration, font embedding, Open Prepress Interface (OPI) image substitution, and transparency flattening.

Figure 32-4: The Export PDF dialog box's Advanced pane.

The Color and PDF/X sections are where you control color calibration, as follows:

✦ The Color pop-up menu lets you choose from Leave Unchanged, which keeps the colors in whatever model they were defined in; RGB, which converts them all to RGB (use this for online documents), and CMYK, which converts them all to CMYK (use this if you're using no spot colors and you're creating color negatives).

✦ Check the Include ICC Profiles option if your output device includes a color calibration feature that uses such profiles.

✦ Check the Simulate Overprint option if you're exporting to Acrobat 4 (PDF 1.3) format and have objects overprinting each other (via the Attributes pane). This option is grayed out if you're exporting to Acrobat 5 or 6 format, because these formats support actual overprinting.

✦ Click the Ink Manager button to change which color plates print, adjust ink density, and alter trapping sequence.

✦ If you're exporting to a PDF/X format, you can apply a rendering intent to the document using the Output Intent Profile pop-up menu in the PDF/X section. The PDF/X format uses PostScript color reference dictionary (CRD) files for managing rendering intent rather than the more common ICC profiles.

Cross-Reference See Chapter 29 for more on color calibration, rendering intent, and color trapping settings. See Chapter 31 for more on working with color plates, the Ink Manager, and ink density.

The Fonts section lets you control which fonts are included in the PDF file. Including fonts increases the file size but ensures that the document will display or print correctly, no matter if the recipient has the same fonts the document uses. The Subset Fonts When Percent of Characters Used Is Less Than field tells InDesign how to embed fonts in the exported PDF file. The default value of 100% tells it to include the entire font for each typeface used. This is the best option because it ensures that if your service bureau needs to edit the file later, the file will include all font information. If you choose a lower value and the service bureau changes some text, there's a chance that some characters used in the editing won't be in the file.

The value is a threshold, telling InDesign that if the file uses less than that percentage of the font's characters, to embed just the characters used; or, if the file uses more than that percentage, to embed them all. If your document uses many fonts but just a few characters in each, you might want to pick a value like 35%, since chances are less that you have typos in such documents (they tend to be ads and posters that are heavily proofed beforehand).

You can use a lower threshold for documents intended to be viewed solely on-screen, since you don't expect readers to edit the files. In fact, you may lock the file to prevent such modification.

 Note Some fonts can be locked, preventing their inclusion in PDF files. To avoid that problem, simply don't use them.

In the OPI section, use the three options in the Omit section to strip out EPS, PDF, and/or bitmap images — you would use this only if you had high-resolution or color-corrected versions of these files at a service bureau and wanted them to substitute those files for the lower-resolution placeholder files you used during layout.

In the Transparency Flattener section, you can select a transparency preset, as well as override any transparency settings applied to individual spreads. Transparency flattening reduces the complexity of documents that have lots of transparent and semitransparent objects overlapping each other, which can dramatically increase output time and even prevent printing.

 Cross-Reference See Chapter 31 for more on OPI and transparency flattening.

Security pane

The Security pane, shown in Figure 32-5, has no relevance to documents intended to be output at a service bureau or commercial printer, so make sure the Require a Password to Open the Document and Use a Password to Restrict Printing, Editing, and Other Tasks options are unchecked.

Figure 32-5: The Export PDF dialog box's Security pane.

These settings are useful if you're publishing the document electronically, since they control who can access the document and what they can do with the document once open. Here's how they work:

✦ The encryption level is adjustable only by choosing a preset in the Preset pop-up menu. All presets but the [eBook] and [Acrobat 6 Layered] presets use Low (40-Bit RC4) encryption, which is compatible with Acrobat 3 (PDF 1.2) format and later. [eBook] and [Acrobat 6 Layered] use High (12-Bit RC4) encryption, which is compatible with Acrobat 5 (PDF 1.4) and later. If you want to use 128-bit encryption for a custom export, choose [eBook] or [Acrobat 6 Layered], then make other changes in the PDF Export dialog box.

 New Feature   Support for 128-bit encryption is new to InDesign CS.

✦ You can require a password to open the exported PDF file by checking the option in the Document Open Password section and providing a password in the associated text field. If no password is entered here, you'll be forced to enter one via a dialog box that pops up later. To access protected content, recipients must use the Security pane in Acrobat (File ➪ Document Settings).

✦ You can restrict recipients' actions by checking the option in the Permissions section, then specifying permissible actions using the Printing Allowed and Changes Allowed pop-up menus, as well as with the check boxes that follow (the number of check boxes displayed varies based on the preset chosen). You can also require a password to allow editing of the file in another application. Your management options include the following:

- For Printing Allowed, you can select None, Low-Resolution (150 dpi), and High Resolution.

- For Changes Allowed, you can select None; Inserting, Deleting and Rotating Pages; Filling in Form Fields and Signing; Commenting, Filling in Forms Fields, and Signing; and Any Except Extract Pages. (*Signing* means using digital signatures to verify sender and recipient identities.)

- If it's okay for recipients to use the ODF file's objects, check the Enable Copying of Text, Images, and Other Content option.

- If you want the file to be accessible to visually impaired recipients that read text aloud, check the Enable Text Access of Screen Reader Devices for the Visually Impaired option.

- For documents with *metadata* — authoring information associated with XML documents and Web pages — you can make that metadata visible to Web-based search engines and similar applications by checking the Enable Plaintext Metadata option.

Using the Summary pane

The final Export PDF dialog box pane is the Summary pane, shown in Figure 32-6. It simply lists your settings all in one place for easy review. The only option — Save Summary — saves the settings to a file so you can include it with your files when delivering them to a service bureau, or for distribution to other staff members so they know the preferred settings.

Figure 32-6: The Export PDF dialog box's Summary pane.

Settings for on-screen usage

If your output is destined for use on a monitor — such as via CD, on the Web, or in a corporate intranet, the settings you choose will differ from the print-oriented ones described in the "Exporting PDF files" section. Here's what you need to do:

✦ In the PDF Options pane, change the Color pop-up menu to RGB, change the Images pop-up menu to Low Resolution, and check Generate Thumbnails. This will optimize the color and file size for on-screen display.

✦ In the Compression pane, choose Downsample to or Subsample to in all three image types' sections. The DPI value should be either 72 (if you intend people just to view the images on screen) or 300 or 600 (if you expect people to print the documents to a local ink-jet or laser printer — pick the dpi value that best matches most users' printers' capabilities). For the Compression pop-up menus, choose Automatic for the color and gray-scale bitmaps, and CCITT Group 3 (the standard method for fax compression) for black-and-white bitmaps. Set Quality to Maximum for color and gray-scale bitmaps. Finally, check Compress Text and Line Art.

✦ In the Pages and Page Marks pane, make sure no printer's marks are checked. Check Reader's Spreads if your facing pages are designed as one visual unit.

✦ In the Security pane, check User Security features and the options for which you want to add security. Use the Printing and Copying Text and Graphics options to prevent readers from copying and pasting your content, or to prevent printing — this is particularly aimed at Web-based readers or publicly distributed documents. The Changing the Document and Adding or Changing Notes and Form Fields options are meant for internally distributed documents, where you don't want a recipient who has the Acrobat program to modify the PDF file and then pass it on to someone else who might not realize it was altered. Similarly, you typically would use the passwords only for documents distributed internally, where you don't want all employees to have access to all documents. For Web-based documents, the presumption is that a page and its content are meant for public consumption unless the whole page has a password required, so these settings are usually irrelevant.

Printing to PDF format

Sometimes, you may want to create a PDF file when printing, such as to save printer-specific options in the file. Note that, using this method, you'll need the $449 Adobe Acrobat Professional software to create a PDF file for prepress output, or the $299 Acrobat Standard for documents meant for display on-screen and printing on ink-jet, laser, and other medium-resolution printers. Both include the Acrobat Distiller program that creates PDF files. (The free Acrobat Reader is only for viewing PDF files.)

Set up your Print dialog box settings as described in Chapter 31. But don't click the Print button. Instead, follow these steps:

1. **Whether you use a Macintosh or a Windows PC, open the Acrobat Distiller program.**

   For Acrobat Distiller 4 and 5, choose Settings ⇨ Job Options to set the output options. For Acrobat Distiller 6, choose a setting from the Default Settings pop-up menu in the Acrobat Distiller dialog box. Then go back to the InDesign Print dialog box.

2. **On the Mac, click the Printer button, choose the Output Options menu item from the pop-up menu in the resulting dialog box, then check the Save as File Option, choose the file format (PDF) from the Format pop-up menu, and click Save. You'll get the Save to File dialog box, where you choose the file-name and location, then click the Save button to save the file. In Windows, select Acrobat Distiller from the Printer pop-up menu. Then click the Print button. In a few seconds, a new window will open up asking for a filename and file location. After choosing those, click the Save button.**

Note   You can also create PDF files by exporting to an EPS or PostScript file, then using the Acrobat Distiller program to convert the file to PDF format. There's no need to do this if you have InDesign unless you happen to have EPS or PostScript files you've previously generated that you'd rather convert to PDF via Distiller than find the InDesign originals and export PDFs from InDesign. You can, of course, use Distiller to create PDFs from any PostScript or EPS file, no matter what program created it.

Creating EPS Files

To create an Encapsulated PostScript (EPS) file from InDesign, choose File ⇨ Export, or press ⌘+E or Ctrl+E. You'll get the Export dialog box, which like any standard Save dialog box lets you name the file and determine what disk and folder the file is to be saved in. The key control in the Export dialog box is the Formats pop-up menu, where you choose the format (EPS, in this case).

After you've selected EPS in the Export dialog box's Formats pop-up menu, and given the file a name and location, click the Save button to get the Export EPS dialog box, shown in Figure 32-7. The dialog box has two panes, with General being the one displayed when you open the dialog box.

The General pane

Most export options are in the General pane, shown in Figure 32-7.

Figure 32-7: The Export EPS dialog box's General pane.

In the Pages section, you can set the following options:

✦ The Pages radio buttons let you choose to print All pages or a Range, in which case you enter a range in the Range field. When specifying a range of pages, you can enter nonconsecutive ranges, such as **1-4, 7, 10-13, 15, 18, 20**.

Tip   If you want to print from a specific page to the end of the document, just enter the hyphen after the initial page number, such as **4-**. InDesign will figure out what the last page is. Similarly, to start from the first page to a specified page, just start with the hyphen as in **-11**.

New Feature   InDesign CS now lets you enter absolute page numbers in the Range field. For example, entering **+6-+12** would print the document's sixth through twelfth pages, no matter what their page numbers are.

✦ The Spreads option, if checked, prints facing pages on the same sheet of paper — this is handy when showing clients comps, but make sure you have a printer that can handle that large paper size.

Tip   You may not want to use the Spreads option when outputting an EPS file for eventual printing on an imagesetter if you have bleeds because there will be no bleed between the spreads. If you use traditional *perfect-binding* (square spines) or *saddle-stitching* (stapled spines) printing methods in which facing pages are not printed contiguously, do not use this option.

The unnamed, middle section of the pane controls the handling of fundamental elements: PostScript version, graphics, and fonts. Here are what the options do:

✦ In the PostScript pop-up menu, choose the version of the PostScript language to use in creating the EPS file: The Level 2 option will work on a PostScript Level 2 or later printer (the majority in professional environments), while Level 3 will work only on the newer PostScript 3 devices, which can include built-in color calibration, color separation and trapping. Be sure to ask whoever is outputting your files which version to use.

✦ The Color pop-up menu determines what happens to colors; your options are CMYK (for commercial printing), RGB (for online display), Gray (for black-and-white printing), or Leave Unchanged (which lets the output device figure out what to do with the colors). For commercial printing, choose either CMYK or Leave Unchanged, depending on your service bureau's recommendations and the capabilities of their output devices. If your file uses spot colors, you'll want to use Leave Unchanged so they aren't converted to process colors, but the service bureau will need to have a printer that can handle that format.

New Feature InDesign CS adds the Leave Unchanged option to the Color pop-up menu in the Export EPS dialog box's General pane.

✦ The Preview pop-up menu lets you choose the format for the EPS file's on-screen preview, which is what you see on screen when you place an EPS file in a program like InDesign, Adobe Illustrator, QuarkXPress, or Macromedia FreeHand. Your options are None, TIFF, and — on the Mac only — PICT. TIFF is a safe option if you're using recent versions of image editing, desktop publishing, and illustration programs. Older Mac programs may require you to select PICT.

✦ Use the Embed Fonts pop-up menu to determine whether all fonts, no fonts, or just the characters used will be embedded into the documents; the corresponding menu options are Complete, None, and Subset. Complete is the best option because it ensures that if your service bureau needs to edit the file later, the file will include all font information. If you choose Subset and the service bureau changes some text when editing the EPS file (such as to fix a typo), there's a chance that some characters used in the editing won't be in the file. Use None only if the service bureau has all the fonts you use and knows to load them into the printer before outputting this file.

✦ In the Data Format pop-up menu, select ASCII or Binary. The ASCII option creates a larger file but can be edited by someone who understands the PostScript language; the Binary option creates a smaller file that is not editable. The one you choose depends on whether you want or expect your service bureau or commercial printer to try to fix any problems in your file encountered during output. Be sure to talk to those people up front, so you and they are agreed on whether such efforts should be made.

In the Bleed section, you can set the bleed area for the Top, Bottom, Left, and Right sides of the page. If you have element bleeding off the page, you'll want a bleed setting of at least 0p9 (0.125 inch) — that builds in enough forgiveness so that, when the pages are folded and trimmed, any elements that bleed off the page will in fact do so, even if there's a slip in the page alignment.

Note   The Export EPS option does not let you use any bleed settings you may have set in the New Document (File ➪ New ➪ Document, or ⌘+N or Ctrl+N) or Document Setup (File ➪ Document Setup, or Option+⌘+P or Ctrl+Alt+P) dialog boxes. That's odd, since the Export PDF (File ➪ Export, or ⌘+E or Ctrl+E) and Print (File ➪ Print, or ⌘+P or Ctrl+P) dialog boxes let you use those document settings. Nor can you have all four bleed automatically use the same settings, as you can in those other dialog boxes.

The Advanced pane

The Advanced pane contains specialty settings affecting image substitution, transparency flattening, and color plates. Figure 32-8 shows the pane.

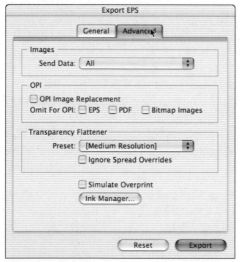

Figure 32-8: The Export EPS dialog box's Advanced pane.

The options are:

✦ In the Images section's Send Data pop-up menu, you can select from All and Proxy. Use the All option (the default) for all documents that will be printed, even if you're publishing the file electronically (on a CD or via the Web). Use Proxy (which sends a low-resolution on-screen preview version of the document's images) only for documents that will be viewed on-screen and won't be printed (or where you don't care that the printouts will have low-quality graphics).

✦ In the OPI section, check the OPI Image Replacement option if you're using Open Prepress Interface (OPI) image substitution, in which the high-resolution files are stored elsewhere and the layout uses for-position-only versions to save disk space and save screen redraw time. You can also use the three options in the Omit section to specify which images should be stripped out: EPS, PDF, and/or bitmap images. You would use this only if you have high-resolution or color-corrected versions of these files at a service bureau and want them to substitute those files for the lower-resolution placeholder files you used during layout. By omitting these graphics files from the EPS file, you make the EPS file much smaller.

✦ In the Transparency Flattener section, you can select a transparency preset, as well as override any transparency settings applied to individual spreads. Transparency flattening reduces the complexity of documents that have lots of transparent and semitransparent objects overlapping each other, which can dramatically increase output time and even prevent printing.

✦ At the bottom of the pane, check the Simulate Overprint option if you're exporting to Acrobat 4 (PDF 1.3) format and have objects overprinting each other (via the Attributes pane). This option is grayed out if you're exporting to Acrobat 5 or 6 format, because these formats support actual overprinting.

✦ Click the Ink Manager button to change which color plates print, adjust ink density, and alter trapping sequence.

See Chapter 31 for more on OPI and transparency flattening. See Chapter 29 for more on overprint simulation and the Ink Manager.

Creating PostScript Prepress Files

You'll use this option the least, since it generates a file that almost always gets sent directly to a printer. In most cases, generating an EPS or PDF file is a better option; since it gives the service bureau or commercial printer a more structured document they can usually troubleshoot or print more easily. But sometimes, this option is what the service bureau will want, based on their equipment and expertise.

To create a PostScript prepress file, you have two options. The simplest is to choose PostScript File from the Printer pop-up menu in the Print dialog box, as well as the appropriate PostScript Printer Description using the PPD pop-up menu (this should be the PPD for the ultimate output device). Then set the various options in the Print dialog's panes and click Save when done (the Print button becomes Save when you choose PostScript File in the Printer pop-up menu).

The other method is to print to file. *After* setting all the appropriate attributes in the Print dialog box (File ➪ Print, or ⌘+P or Ctrl+P), do the following, as appropriate for your platform:

✦ On the Mac, click the Printer button, choose the Output Options menu item from the pop-up menu in the resulting dialog box, then check the Save as File Option, choose the file format (PostScript, in this case) from the Format pop-up menu, and click Save.

✦ In Windows, click the Setup button and then check the Print to File option in the resulting dialog box and click Print.

Summary

In many cases, you'll want to generate an output file that ensures that your service bureau prints your document exactly as you want it, with no chance to accidentally make a change to your InDesign document. The service bureau's equipment will dictate in most cases what format these output files are in: EPS, PostScript, or PDF. Each option has pros and cons, and varying levels of controls, so be sure to use the option that gives you the most control and works with your service bureau's equipment.

✦   ✦   ✦

Cross-Media Fundamentals

Chapter 33
Interactive Document Setup

Chapter 34
Working with XML

Although primarily a tool for creating print documents, InDesign has several features to aid the creation of electronic documents. Even though the program no longer creates HTML files for use on the Web, it does let you create PDF and XML files. PDF files are commonly used to distribute documents electronically for on-screen display and optional printing by the recipient via CD, an intranet, or the Web. PDF files can contain page actions, movies, and sounds, as well as hyperlinks. XML files are structured versions of a document designed for Web-oriented database and Web content engines.

Chapter 33 explains how to set up interactive elements in an InDesign document for use in a PDF file created from the InDesign document, while Chapter 34 explains how to import and create the tags that XML uses to define the structure and purpose of a document's objects, as well as how to export an InDesign document with such tags for use in an XML system.

Interactive Document Setup

In This Chapter

Working with hyperlinks

Creating bookmarks

Adding page actions

Working with audio and video objects

In most respects, a document is a document is a document. But in today's electronic world, documents have evolved to include more than text and graphics that for centuries have comprised documents. Not only can you print documents the traditional way, you can deliver them electronically as Adobe Portable Document Format (PDF) files. And that electronic delivery format permits a degree of interactivity never possible in printed documents, including hyperlinks, automated page actions, and the use of audio and video objects.

You create interactive documents just as you create a print document. InDesign's interactive functions work with those traditional capabilities — there's no special "interactive" mode to work under.

Note

InDesign CS no longer lets you export documents to HTML format, the standard format for the Web. (This may be because Adobe has a separate product meant to create Web pages.) That's too bad for publishers who wanted to convert their print layouts to a Web format, but because few publishers actually create their Web content directly from their print files, it will have limited effect. Instead, most publishers will do what they've long done — export or copy text from the final print document, then import that text and associated graphics (converted from print standards such as TIFF and EPS to Web standards such as GIF and JPEG) into a Web-creation program like Macromedia Dreamweaver or Adobe GoLive, using Web-specific templates and formatting. Publishers typically haven't directly converted their print documents to Web formats, even in programs like QuarkXPress that have had plug-in software to do so, because the horizontally oriented, single-column, typographically plain Web page didn't allow for easy adaptation of print publications' vertically oriented, multicolumn, typographically sophisticated content. For many publishers, it was easier to start the Web layout from scratch than convert from print layouts.

Chapter 32 covers how to export InDesign documents to PDF format.

Using Hyperlinks in PDF and eBook Files

The most common attribute you'll add to a print document to make it more useful when distributed electronically is the inclusion of hyperlinks. Just like Web pages, PDF files can include these "hot spots" that, when clicked, direct a browser to open a new file or page. It's a whole new way to deliver related contents through an active cross-reference.

InDesign uses its Hyperlinks pane (Window ➪ Interactive ➪ Hyperlinks) to add, edit, and delete hyperlinks. In a sense, a hyperlink is a character attribute — it's applied to selected text. Figure 33-1 shows the Hyperlinks pane.

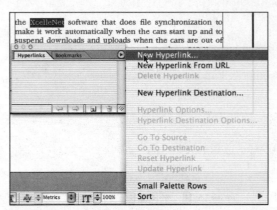

Figure 33-1: The Hyperlinks pane.

Creating hyperlinks

Although the process is straightforward, InDesign's terminology can make it a bit confusing on how to start. You first create a hyperlink destination — the place a hyperlinks goes to, or its *target* — by choosing New Hyperlink Destination from the Hyperlinks pane's palette menu. You give the destination a name in the Name field and then choose from one of the three options in the Type menu:

✦ **Page,** which lets you specify a specific page in a selected document. If you select this option, InDesign provides a Page field in which you specify the page number to open in the selected document, as well as the Zoom Setting pop-up menu, which lets you select how the page will be displayed. (Options are Fixed, meaning at the default size in Acrobat Reader; Fit View; Fit in Window; Fit Width; Fit Height; Fit Visible; and Inherit Zoom, which uses the current zoom setting in Acrobat.)

✦ **Text Anchor,** which lets you specify a specific piece of text in the selected document. This would be the selected text.

✦ **URL,** a Web page address (the official name is Uniform Resource Locator), as shown in the dialog box. If you select this option, InDesign will display the URL field in which you enter the Web address.

With the destinations defined, you can now create the hyperlinks to them (the hyperlink *sources*).

Note To create a hyperlink to another PDF file, you can't use the New Hyperlink Destination method. You must use the New Hyperlink method described next.

To create a hyperlink source:

1. **Select the text or frame you want to be a hyperlink's source, then choose New Hyperlink from the Hyperlinks pane's palette menu.**

   That opens the New Hyperlink dialog box, as shown in Figure 33-2.

Figure 33-2: The New Hyperlink dialog box.

2. **Enter a name for the hyperlink source.**

   This lets you apply the same link to more than one location in your document — sort of a character style sheet for hyperlinks.

3. **If the hyperlink is to another InDesign document, you can select that document by choosing Browse from the Document pop-up menu.**

4. **Use the Type pop-up menu to determine what you're hyperlinking to:**

   • Page, which lets you specify a specific page in a selected document. If you select this option, InDesign provides a Page field in which you specify the page number to open in the selected document, as well as the

Zoom Setting pop-up menu, which lets you select how the page will be displayed. (Options are Fixed, meaning at the default size in Acrobat Reader; Fit View; Fit in Window; Fit Width; Fit Height; Fit Visible; and Inherit Zoom, which uses the current zoom setting in Acrobat.)

Note   If you want to create a hyperlink to another document, you must do so here, using the Page option. You cannot first create a destination hyperlink. Also, unintuitively, you must browse for the actual InDesign file you want to link to. But the link will be to the PDF version of that file, which means you must be sure to create the PDF of that other document and use the same filename, except for the filename extension. For example, if you link to ITWForm.indd, the link will actually be to ITWForm.pdf. This approach requires that you have all the target files in InDesign format—you cannot link to a specific PDF file created in another program or by someone whose source files you don't have access to.

- Text Anchor, which lets you specify a specific piece of text in the selected document.

- URL, a Web page address (the official name is Uniform Resource Locator), as shown in the dialog box. (You can also use mailto, ftp, and other standard URLs.) If you select this option, InDesign will display the URL field in which you enter the Web address.

- All Types, which displays previously defined hyperlinks in the document.

5. **Use the Name pop-up menu to select a previously defined hyperlink destination (target) or an anchor.**

You can also create a hyperlink to an Unnamed destination by leaving the Name pop-up menu set to [None]. I advise against this, however, since that hyperlink destination won't appear in the menu for future hyperlink sources, making it hard to modify later.

6. **In the Appearance section, you can control how the hyperlink appears on-screen:**

- Use the Type pop-up menu to choose Invisible Rectangle or Visible Rectangle. The Invisible Rectangle option gives no visual indication that the text contains a hyperlink, except that the mouse pointer would turn to a hand icon when the reader maneuvers through the document. (You would typically pick this option when you've used blue underline as a character attribute for the hyperlink text to mirror the standard Web way of indicating a hyperlink.) The Visible Rectangle puts a box around the text using the four settings below (they are grayed out if Invisible Rectangle is selected).

- The Highlight pop-up menu lets you choose how the source text or frame is highlighted: None, Invert (reserve the foreground and background colors), Outline (places a line around the source), and Inset (places a line around the source, but inside any frame stroke; for text, it's the same as Outline).

- The Color pop-up menu displays Web-safe colors, as well as any colors you defined in the document.

- The Width pop-up menu lets you choose the thickness of the line used in the Outline and Inset options from the Highlight pop-up menu. The choices are Thin, Medium, and Think.

- You can choose the type of line in the Style pop-up menu: Solid or Dashed.

Tip If your text includes a valid hyperlink, such as `www.INDDcentral.com`, you can select it and create a URL hyperlink automatically by choosing New Hyperlink from URL in the Hyperlinks pane's palette menu.

Once your hyperlink sources are defined, you can easily apply them by selecting text and clicking an existing hyperlink source from the Hyperlinks pane.

Modifying and deleting hyperlinks

It's also easy to modify hyperlinks: Choose Hyperlink Options from the Hyperlinks pane's palette menu, which has the same options as the New Hyperlinks dialog box, to modify the source. Choose Modify Destination Options from the palette menu, then select the target from the Name pop-up menu. You can change the source text or frame by selecting it, then clicking the hyperlink name in the Hyperlinks pane, and finally choosing Reset Hyperlink from the pane's palette menu. To change the target for a hyperlink to an InDesign document, choose Update Hyperlink from the palette menu (hold Option or Alt to select a file that is not open).

To delete a hyperlink target, choose it in the Hyperlink Destination Options dialog box, then click the Delete button. (Click Delete All to delete all targets defined in the document.) To delete a hypertext source, select it in the Hyperlinks pane and then choose Delete Hyperlink from the palette menu.

Note When you export your InDesign files to PDF files (as described in Chapter 32), be sure to check the Hyperlinks option in the Include section of the General pane in the Export PDF dialog box (File ➪ Export, or ⌘+E or Ctrl+E), then choose Adobe PDF in the Format pop-up menu.

What are eBooks?

InDesign lets you create eBook files. An eBook is a form of PDF meant for digital book readers, electronic devices that you can download book files to and read on-screen. Think of it as a read-only computer, or as a browser that only displays PDF files.

The big difference between a PDF file and an eBook file is that an eBook file includes a bunch of tags to help the reader device display it properly no matter what the screen dimensions are. These tags are added automatically by InDesign when you export to a PDF file, as long as you select the eBook Tags option in the General page of the Export PDF dialog box. Chapter 32 covers PDF export in detail.

Creating Bookmarks

Bookmarks are an indexing mechanism used in Acrobat PDF files. They typically act like tables of contents, letting you view the organization of a document through a set of clickable headings. Figure 33-3 shows an example file viewed in Acrobat.

Figure 33-3: An example PDF document with bookmarks (at left).

InDesign has two ways to create bookmark entries. One is simply to create a table of contents using the standard InDesign Table of Contents tool. (Be sure that the Create PDF Bookmarks option is checked in the Table of Contents dialog box.) The other is to specify bookmarks to specific pages, objects, and/or text using the Bookmarks pane. Figure 33-4 shows the Bookmarks pane (Window ⇨ Interactive ⇨ Bookmarks).

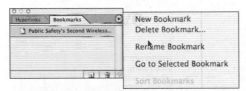

Figure 33-4: The Bookmarks pane.

 The Bookmarks pane is new to InDesign CS. Previous versions could only create bookmarks from InDesign tables of contents.

 Chapter 9 covers the table-of-contents feature.

To create your own bookmark entries — either instead of or in addition to having InDesign use the table of contents — choose what you want the bookmark to refer to (what will appear on-screen in the PDF file when a user clicks the bookmark in Acrobat or Acrobat Reader). This can be a text selection or an object (frame or line); then choose New Bookmark from the Bookmarks pane's palette menu. If nothing is selected, the bookmark will be to the current page. After you create the bookmark, use the Rename Bookmark menu option to give it a name — this is the name that will appear in the Bookmarks pane in Acrobat.

 If you want a bookmark to be a subentry of another bookmark — the equivalent to a second-level or third-level headline in a table of contents — make sure that, before you create the bookmark, you've selected a bookmark in the Bookmarks pane. Any new bookmark is made a child of the selected bookmark.

The other Bookmarks palette options are straightforward:

✦ Choose Delete Bookmark to delete any bookmarks selected in the pane.

✦ Choose Go to Selected Bookmark to jump to that page in your InDesign document. An easier way is to simply double-click the bookmark entry in the pane.

✦ Choose Sort Benchmarks to sort benchmark subentries — this alphabetizes second-level, third-level, and other page-based subentries, and it sorts in order of appearance on the page any text- and/or object-based entries. It will not sort the top-level bookmarks, which appear in sequential order from the beginning of the document.

However you create your bookmarks, you have InDesign place them into your PDF file during PDF export. In the General pane of the PDF Export dialog box (choose File ➪ Export, or press ⌘+E or Ctrl+E, and choose Acrobat PDF in the Format pop-up menu), make sure the Bookmarks section is checked in the pane's Include section.

Creating Page Actions

One underused feature of the PDF format is the ability to set page actions. Most people simply create PDF files that are on-screen versions of the print document—static representations—but PDF files can include forms, buttons, and other interactive elements. One reason for the underuse of page actions is that few tools let you create the placeholder items for them, and adding them in Acrobat Standard or Acrobat Professional is awkward—they really work best when created in the program that creates the whole document. InDesign CS addresses this reality with its enhanced support for interactive features.

In InDesign, you use the States pane to create buttons and other objects that have actions associated with them.

The first thing you do is draw a button, using the Button tool. A button is essentially a rectangular frame. Once created, you can resize it like any other object, though you cannot create nonrectangular shapes.

New Feature   The Button tool and the ability to create rollovers (covered later in this section) are new to InDesign CS.

 Tip   You can convert an existing frame to a button by choosing Object ➪ Interactive ➪ Convert to Button.

After you create the button shape, you should immediately choose its appearance, using the Appearance pop-up menu in the States pane (Windows ➪ Interactive ➪ States). It's imperative that you choose the appearance now, because if you later change the appearance, any actions you associate to the button are wiped out. If you want a transparent button (perhaps to make part of an existing graphic a hot spot), choose None from the pop-up menu. The other options are Drop Shadow, Glow, Bevel, and Custom. Figure 33-5 shows the States pane, the three standard states (Up, Rollover, and Down), and an example button (at lower-left).

Then you create the states for the button by choosing New State from the States pane's palette menu. You always have an Up state when you create a button. You'll get a Rollover state the first time you choose New States and a Down state the second time. You can have only these three states for any button.

Figure 33-5: The States pane and an example button.

The states correspond to mouse actions:

✦ Up is what is displayed and occurs when the mouse is not over the button — the default appearance and action.

✦ Rollover is what displays and occurs when the mouse passes over the button but the mouse is not clicked onto the button.

✦ Down is what displays and occurs when the mouse clicks the button.

You can disable or enable any state by unchecking or checking the check box to its left in the pane. You can also select a state in the pane and choose State Options from the palette menu to disable or enable the state.

If you want to create a custom appearance for any state, select the state and choose Place Content into State from the palette menu. You will then be provided a Place dialog box from which to choose a picture file. You can crop, resize, and otherwise manipulate the picture as you would any picture in a frame. (Note how the Appearance pop-up menu changes to Custom when you do this.) To remove placed content, choose Delete Content from State.

Now comes the fun part: associating the action with the button. To do so, choose Button Options from the palette menu. You'll get the Button Options dialog box shown in Figure 33-6, which defaults to the General pane. In this pane, you provide a name for the button and set the button's visibility in the PDF file you'll later export. The options are self-explanatory: Visible, Hidden, Visible But Doesn't Print, and Hidden But Printable.

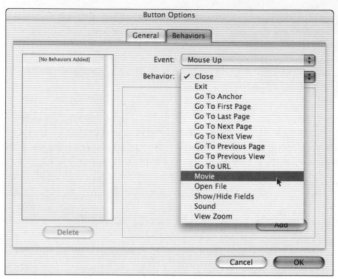

Figure 33-6: The Button Options dialog box and its Behaviors pane.

The real action association happens in the Behaviors pane, shown in Figure 33-6. Here, you first select the event that triggers the action, using the Events pop-up menu:

✦ Mouse Up is when you release the mouse after clicking the button.

✦ Mouse Down is when you click the mouse button.

✦ Mouse Enter is when you move the mouse pointer over the button.

✦ Mouse Exit is when you move the mouse pointer away from the button after first passing over it.

✦ On Focus is when you tab into a form field (since a form field is simply a button, this is similar to Mouse Enter except that it detects keyboard access to the button).

✦ On Blur is when you tab out of a form field (since a form field is simply a button, this is similar to Mouse Exit except that it detects keyboard departure from the button).

Note   You may wonder what happens if you've selected a specific state before opening the Button Options dialog box. Nothing. It doesn't matter which state is selected in the pane — these are simply previews of the button's appearance based on the mouse status — since the behaviors selected in the Button Options menu affect the button as a whole.

You then choose the action in the Behavior pop-up menu. Most are self-explanatory: Close, Exit, Go to First Page, Go to Last Page, Go to Next Page, Go to Preview Page, Go to Preview View, Go to Anchor, Go to URL, Move, Open File, Sound, and View Zoom. Some of these — Go to Anchor, Go to URL, Movie, Sound, Open File, and View Zoom will cause other pop-up menus and fields to display in the palette to select a file to open or a hyperlink or anchor to jump to.

The Show/Hide Fields option is meant for Acrobat forms. InDesign will consider every button to be a form field and will provide a list of all buttons if you select this option. You can then decide which buttons (form entry fields in this case) display on the mouse action — you would have only those display that you want to be used as form-entry fields. (To specify the order in which a reader tabs through form fields [buttons], select the fields in the form, then choose Object ⇨ Interactive ⇨ Set Tab Order, which opens a dialog box in which you can sort the buttons in the order that you want the reader to move through as he or she press the Tab key.)

Click Add to add a behavior to this state. You can add multiple behaviors to each state. And each Event can have multiple behaviors — just select a new Behavior then click Add for each one.

Playing Movies and Sound

In addition to having a button that opens a movie or sound, you can simply place a movie or sound file in your InDesign document. (Once placed, you can size a movie file like any other placed graphic.)

New Feature   The ability to add movies and sounds to documents is new to InDesign CS.

Note   InDesign can open QuickTime and Microsoft .AVI movies only, so be sure to have a version in that format. For sounds, it supports the Apple AIFF and Microsoft .WAV formats.

To control how a movie behaves and what control the reader has, choose Object ⇨ Interactive ⇨ Movie Options, shown in Figure 33-7.

New Feature   A new, faster way to set movie and sound settings is to double-click the frame containing the movie or sound; you'll get the Movie Options dialog box or Sound Options dialog box, as appropriate.

Move Options

The options in the Movie Options dialog box are straightforward:

✦ In the Source section, select whether the movie file is copied into your document or simply linked to a URL on the Web or on a CD. If you're embedding the movie file and plan to export the InDesign document to PDF format, be sure to check Embed Movie in PDF — otherwise the PDF file won't have the movie available.

✦ In the Options section, you can change the Poster — the on-screen image inside the frame containing the movie. The default, Default Poster, lets Acrobat choose what displays (usually, it's the first frame of the move). You could also select None (for a blank frame), Standard (for the Adobe logo), Choose Image as Poster (in which case you would select an image using the Browse button, such as perhaps the QuickTime logo), or Frame from Movie (to select a specific frame from the movie; not all movies will let you select this option).

✦ You also set the Mode — Play Once Then Stop, Play Once Stay Open, and Repeat Play — to determine the movie's playback action. Note that the Play Once Stay Open option lets the user choose to play the movie again.

✦ The Play on Page Turn option, if checked, plays the movie when a reader moves to the page containing it (as opposed to going directly to the page through a hyperlink).

✦ The Show Controller During Play option displays the QuickTime movie controller to adjust sound volume, pause and resume play, and rewind and fast-forward the movie.

✦ The Floating Window option puts the movie in a window that the reader can move. If selected, the dialog box also makes two pop-up menus accessible: Size, which determines the size of the window relative to the move frame size, and Position, which places the floating window on the page.

Figure 33-7: The Movie Options dialog box.

Sound Options

The options in the Sound Options dialog box (shown in Figure 33-8) are likewise straightforward:

✦ You can change the sound by clicking the Browse button to the right of the filename and then selecting a new sound.

✦ Using the Poster pop-up menu, you can change the placeholder image that appears on the page where you placed the sound. Your options are None to have no placeholder image, Standard to have the Adobe logo, and Choose Image as Poster to use an image of your own choice (use the Browse button to the right of the Poster pop-up menu to select the image file).

✦ If checked, the Play on Page Turn option automatically plays the sound when someone moves to this page in the exported PDF file.

✦ If checked, the Do Not Print Poster option hides the poster icon when someone prints the PDF page containing the sound.

✦ If checked, the Embed Sound in PDF option ensures that the PDF file exported from the InDesign document includes the sound file.

Figure 33-8: The Sound Options dialog box.

Summary

InDesign lets you create hyperlinks and anchors within your documents — to Web addresses, pages, and text in your InDesign document, and to pages and text in other InDesign documents — that are then clickable from a PDF file created from your InDesign file.

You can also create buttons that have associated actions — such as opening a movie file, closing a page, changing the zoom level, or moving to a new page — when exported to PDF format. InDesign also lets you import movie and sound files that likewise play in exported PDF files.

✦   ✦   ✦

Working with XML

In This Chapter

Understanding XML

Creating XML tags
in InDesign

Importing XML tags
Into InDesign

Exporting InDesign
documents for use in
XML documents

One of the most complex features in InDesign is its set of XML features. XML is a structured language that essentially treats document components as data, so you can manage them through a database. The XML tools in InDesign let you treat InDesign documents as sources for XML databases, which are then linked into Web pages, PDF files, CD-ROMs, and so forth. They also let you create InDesign templates into which you flow data from XML files, all formatted and in the proper frames.

The key to XML is the fact that it's extensible. You create the tags, or labels, for various kinds of content (these are called *data type descriptions, or DTDs*) based on what makes sense for your content. Then you specify what happens to each of the types of labeled content in terms of what's published, how it's presented, and so forth. Compare that to the more rigid HTML and PDF formats, where there are only certain tags available that cannot be changed, and the presentation is fixed based on the label chosen.

XML code is similar to HTML in the sense that there are tags surrounded by angle brackets (< and >) and that commands and labels are turned on and off (such as `<standardHeader>` at the beginning of a header item and `</standardHeader>` at the end of it. Comments begin with `<!--` and end with `>`, while custom commands and declarations (called *processing instructions*) begin with `<?` and end with `?>`. You don't have to understand this level of detail—just keep in mind that there are different codes to look for in examining XML code, If the need arises.

Note

A DTD may define several types of content that have their own subcontent types and rules. These are called *branches*. For example, there could be an AuthorInformation branch and a CustomerList branch that both contain tags named Name. You'll need to know which branch text tagged Name should go into, because XML won't know the context.

The use of XML will likely involve assistance from a Webmaster, content engineer, or other programming-savvy person. Page designers might also want to read *XML For Dummies,* 3rd Edition, by Ed Tittel (Wiley Publishing, Inc.). The *InDesign CS Bible* limits itself to an overview of InDesign XML functions and is no substitute for a thorough understanding of XML.

Importing and Creating XML Tags

Chances are that most of the time, you'll be exporting InDesign documents for use in XML databases, such as converting a publication's articles into a structured format used by a Web site's content management system. To export content properly, you need to apply tags to it. In InDesign, you can do that directly or by having InDesign translate style tags into XML tags. You'll use both methods, since some content (such as images) wouldn't have style tags associated to them but need XML tags for proper processing in an XML database.

Those tags come from two sources: They're imported from a file provided by the Web site's content engineer, or they're created in InDesign by the page designer. Most of the time, you should use tags created by the content engineer, since that engineer is creating a standard set of tags for multiple page designers (both print- and Web-based). You might create your own tags when helping develop the initial tags in concert with that content engineer — or if you also are the content engineer, as well as page designer.

Importing tags

There are two places where you import tags: the Tags pane (Window ✦ Tags) and the Import XML dialog box (File ✦ Import XML). In the Tags pane, shown in Figure 34-1, you use the Load Tags option in the pane's palette menu to import tags from an XML file or an InDesign document that has tags defined in it. All tags are imported when you choose Load Tags.

Figure 34-1: The Tags pane.

The other way to import XML tags is to choose File ➾ Import XML, which imports not only XML tags but also XML content from an XML file. This process works two ways, depending on how your document is set up:

✦ If your document has no content, importing an XML file adds the XML tags to the Tags pane and into the document's Structure window (covered later in this chapter). It also adds the content to the Structure pane, where you can drag it into InDesign frames in your layout.

✦ If your document has content, importing an XML file brings in the content to your document and places it in frames in your document that have the same tags already applied. This is a way to automatically populate a layout in InDesign.

Caution

Be careful: The order of the tags in the XML file's tags definitions is important. If the XML file has three tags — defined in the order of Body, Head, and Caption — but the Structure pane in InDesign lists them in the order Head, Body, and Caption, InDesign will import only Body and Caption content. That's because it imports Body first and then looks for the first occurrence of the Body tag in the InDesign file. It then begins matching style tags at that point. Since Head was listed in InDesign before Body, Head is ignored. (All the tags will be in the Structure pane, so you can manually place the imported Head content.)

Creating tags

You also create XML tags in the Tags pane using the New Tag palette menu. A tag simply consists of the tag name and the tag color — its formatting is defined in the XML database or in a DTD file.

Mapping tags and styles

In the Tags pane's palette menu, you can also map style tags to XML tags and vice versa using the Map Tags to Styles menu option and the Map Styles to Tags menu option, respectively. (They're also available in the Structure pane's palette menu.) Figure 34-2 shows the Map Tags to Styles dialog box; the Map Styles to Tags dialog box is nearly identical, except the two columns are switched. Here's what they do:

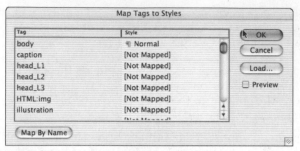

Figure 34-2: The Map Tags to Styles dialog box.

✦ Map Tags to Styles tells InDesign what XML tag to substitute for a specified character or paragraph style during XML export. The text retains its original InDesign style tags.

✦ Map Styles to Tags tells InDesign to immediately replace the specified style sheets with the XML tags. You'll see colored brackets around each string of text (paragraphs for paragraph styles and text selections for character styles) to indicate the text has an XML tag applied to it. The color corresponds to the tag color in the Tags pane. (You can change tag colors, as well as the tag name, using the Tag Options menu in the pane's palette menu or simply by double-clicking the tag name in the pane.)

New Feature The ability to map character styles to tags and to map tags to character styles is new in InDesign CS.

Note InDesign checks to make sure that you include valid XML tag names according to XML standards. If you include a space or an illegal character in the tag name, an alert message appears when you click OK.

Applying Tags

It's easy to apply tags to text: Simply select the text and click on the tag name in the Tags pane. If you want to replace the tag for selected text, be sure to check the Retag radio button in the Tags pane—otherwise, the original tag will remain and the new tag applied as well. Unless they're style tags, multiple XML tags can be applied to the same object or text. If you choose View ➪ Structure ➪ View Tag Markers, tagged text will display brackets around it in the color of the tag in the Tags pane. Similarly, if you choose View ➪ Structure ➪ Show Tagged Frames, tagged frames and lines will also show a color indicator.

You can remove a tag by selecting the tagged text or object and then clicking the Untag button in the Tags pane.

It gets slightly more complex if you're using the Structure pane to place tagged content imported from an XML file into InDesign objects. Figure 34-3 shows the Structure pane, which opens automatically as you begin using XML tags. (You can hide this pane by choosing View ⇨ Structure ⇨ Hide Structure, or pressing Option+⌘+1 or Ctrl+Alt+1.) The pane shows the document's tagged content, as well as the tags associated with it. The content displays in a hierarchy, reflecting any nesting in the tags (similar to how a character style can be thought of as a subset of a paragraph tag, since it applies to a component of a paragraph).

Figure 34-3: The Structure pane.

To apply XML content to a frame, simply drag the appropriate content (indicated with the Text Content icon) onto a frame. As you apply tags from the Tags pane to selected objects, you'll see icons for text and objects appear along with the name of the applied tags.

You can reorder the tags in the Structure pane to reflect the hierarchy of elements. Do this in coordination with your content engineer, since the hierarchy in the InDesign file needs to match the hierarchy expectations in the XML database or content system.

Taking Advantage of Other XML Options

For the more XML-savvy, InDesign offers several controls in the Structure pane and its palette menu.

In the pane:

✦ The **Validate Structure button** checks the current XML structure in the Structure pane and compares it against the DTD file imported with the XML data or imported later using the Import DTD option in the pane's palette menu. There's a copy of the button at the bottom of the pane, along with the View Errors List button that shows any errors found.

✦ The **Add an Attribute button** lets you add an XML attribute, which is essentially a comment such as the revision date. It has no effect on the flow of information or the appearance or role of an element.

✦ The **Add an Element button** lets you add an XML element, which is a tag applied to text or an object.

✦ The **Remove Selected Elements button** removes any selected elements.

In the palette menu:

✦ The **New Element, New Attribute, New Comment, and New Processing Instruction menu items** let you add those items.

✦ **Delete** deletes items.

✦ **Edit** edits items.

✦ **Untag Element** removes an elements XML tag.

✦ **Validate from Root Element** verifies the structure starting at the *root* (top-most) object against the DTD information.

✦ **Validate from Selected Element** starts the validation at the selected item.

✦ **View List of Errors** shows a dialog box with any validation errors found.

✦ **Import DTD** imports a data type description file, which defines the "role" of tags (such as indicating that the Head tag begins a section of a story).

New Feature   The ability to specify and validate DTDs is new to InDesign CS.

✦ **Delete DTD** removes the DTD file from the InDesign document but leaves the structure untouched.

✦ **View DTD** shows a dialog box with the actual DTD information (similar to a code preview in an HTML editor).

✦ The **Hide Attributes, Hide Comments, and Hide Processing Instructions menu options** remove these non-content markers from view in the Structure pane so you can concentrate on just the elements.

✦ **Show/Hide Text Snippets** shows or hides the first few words of text for each Text Content icon in the pane. Seeing these snippets is very helpful in knowing what each element actually contains.

✦ **Add Untagged Items** adds to the Structure pane all objects in the InDesign document that aren't already tagged with an XML tag. This helps ensure that you don't miss any object when reviewing the document structure.

✦ The **Map Tags to Styles and Map Styles to Tags menu options** match InDesign styles to XML tags, as covered earlier in this chapter.

Exporting XML Files

When the InDesign document has the proper elements properly tagged to the document's content, you're ready to export it to an XML file for use by a Web site's content-management system or other XML database. Choose File ➪ Export, or press ⌘+E or Ctrl+E, to open the Export dialog box. In this dialog box, give the XML file a name in the Save As dialog box (InDesign automatically adds the filename extensions .xml), select a folder in which to place the file, and — most important — choose XML from the Format pop-up menu. Then click Save.

You now will have the Export XML dialog box, which opens with the General pane. This pane is simple:

✦ **Check the Include DTD Declaration option to include the DTD information in the exported file.** Otherwise, the XML database will need to import the DTD file separately.

✦ **Check the View XML Using option and select a Web browser in the adjacent pop-up menu to preview the XML file in that browser.**

✦ **If an element was selected in the Structure pane, the Export from Selected Element option will be available; it exports the XML file only from that element on.**

✦ **Use the Encoding pop-up menu to choose the text encoding mechanism — a way of representing international characters across different computer systems.** Your content engineer or Web master will tell you whether to select UTF-8, UTF-16, or Shift-JIS.

In the Graphics pane, you tell InDesign how to handle the output of any tagged pictures. Figure 34-4 shows the pane. Your options are:

Figure 34-4: The Export XML dialog box and its Images pane.

✦ **In the Image Options section, indicate which images to copy to the Images subfolder that InDesign will create.** Your choices are Original Images, Optimized Original Images, and Optimized Formatted Images. You can select any or all of these. The optimized images are converted to GIF or JPEG for use on the Web unless you specify GIF or JPEG in the Image Conversion pop-up menu rather than leave the default setting of Automatic; the formatted images crop the images to reduce file size.

✦ **In the GIF Options section, you can choose the color palette in the Palette pop-up menu, with choices of Adaptive (No Dither), Web, System (Mac), and System (Win).** Ask your Web master what to use; usually, you select Adaptive (No Dither). For very large images, interlacing can make on-screen display via the Web seem faster (by building the image line by line rather than waiting until the whole image has been transferred to the browser before anything is displayed); if you want to have such interlaced display of GIF files, check the Interlace option.

✦ **In the JPEG Options section, there are similar options for JPEG files.** In the Image Quality pop-up menu, choose the desired image quality (Low, Medium, High, and Maximum). In the Format Method, choose Progressive to have the file displayed progressively (similar to the interlace option for GIF files) or Baseline to display it all at once. Unless your images are very large, keep the default Baseline.

New Feature
When you export an XML file with pictures, InDesign automatically embeds XMP media management properties with the pictures' tags. You can view those properties by choosing File ➪ File Info and then choosing the Advanced pane. This information may be of interest to your content engineer but has no real meaning for the page designer. However, the content engineer may want to fill out the information in the File Info dialog box's other panes — Description and Origin — into which you can add comments, creator information and contact details, copyright information, credit and source information, keywords, and copyright URLs.

New Feature
InDesign CS provides another way to generate XML files: Choose File ➪ Package For GoLive. This option creates an XML file preformatted for Adobe GoLive 7.0 or later. You'll make adjustments to the XML file and choose image settings such as those in the Export XML dialog box in GoLive rather than in InDesign.

Summary

InDesign lets you tag content within documents with XML tags, transferring that content to an XML database or Web content engine from which it can be used in a variety of media, formatted as appropriate for each. You can also import XML content into InDesign, automatically placing content into the appropriate frames if you've created an appropriate template and tagged it with the right XML tags. But InDesign's XML tools are only the beginning — you'll need an XML database and content-creation and -presentation tools to use the XML data derived from InDesign documents.

✦   ✦   ✦

Going Beyond the Program

Working with others in a workgroup adds a whole level of complexity to using a program like InDesign, and that complexity grows even more if you're working in a cross-platform environment. Chapter 35 explains how to share preferences and other InDesign components with others in your workgroup, as well as how to integrate Macs and PCs.

As Adobe and other companies continue to develop plug-ins for InDesign, you'll have the option to make InDesign do even more. That too adds to the complexity of using InDesign, but for a worthwhile reason. Chapter 36 explains how to work with plug-ins.

Finally, you can make InDesign work on autopilot by using its scripting capability. Although scripting is essentially a form of programming that requires strong technical skill, organizations that have the ability to develop scripts in any of the three supporting scripting languages — JavaScript, AppleScript, and Visual Basic for Applications — will be able to save much repetitive labor in the layout and production process. Chapter 37 introduces InDesign's scripting capabilities.

P A R T

VIII

◆　◆　◆　◆

Chapter 35
Working with Others

Chapter 36
Using Plug-Ins

Chapter 37
Using Scripts

Working with Others

✦ ✦ ✦ ✦

In This Chapter

Sharing common
elements with
multiple users

Sharing document
and general
preferences with
other documents

Creating common
libraries and
graphics

Transferring files
safely between
Macintosh and
Windows versions
of InDesign

Using file-transfer
tools

✦ ✦ ✦ ✦

Publishing is rarely a one-person enterprise. Chances are that the creators of your text and graphics are not the same people who do your layout. And in many environments, the chances are high that many people are involved in layout and production.

By its very nature, publishing is a group activity, so publishing programs must support workgroups. Yet a Mac or a PC is a *personal* computer, so it's easy to work on a Mac or PC without worrying about how your setup and work style might affect others. InDesign lets you create your own balance between the individual and the workgroup.

The key to working effectively in a workgroup environment is to establish standards and make sure they're easy to stick to. A basic way to accomplish this task is to place all common elements in one place so that people always know where to get the standard elements. This practice also makes it easy to maintain (add, modify, and delete) these elements over time, which is essential because no environment is static. How you do this depends on your computing environment:

  ✦ If you don't use a network, keep a master set of disks and copy elements from the master set in a folder with the same name on each person's computer. Update these folders every time a standard element changes on the master disk.

  ✦ If you do use a network, keep a master set of disks (networks do go down, so you'll want your files accessible when that happens) and create a folder for your standard elements on a network drive accessible to all users. Update this folder whenever a standard element changes on the master disk.

Sharing with Other Users

Some standard elements can be accessed easily from a common folder because InDesign can import certain elements that are stored outside InDesign documents. These elements include graphics files, libraries, keyboard shortcut sets, and spelling dictionaries.

Other elements reside within documents and templates and cannot be saved in separate files. These elements include style sheets and master pages. But style sheets can be exported/imported from one document to another.

Where InDesign stores what

The Presets folder in the InDesign application folder contains folders for several kinds of preference-related elements: InDesign Shortcut Sets, InDesign Workspaces, Scripts, and Swatch Libraries. The Presets folder also includes any document preset files.

The spelling and hyphenation exception dictionaries that come with InDesign are stored in the `Plug-ins\Dictionaries\Proximity` folder inside the InDesign application folder. But the exception dictionaries you create when adding words and hyphenation breakpoints in InDesign's spell checker and dictionary tools are stored elsewhere: On the Mac, they're stored in the path `Users\[user name]\Library\Preferences\Adobe InDesign\Version 3.0\Dictionaries\Proximity`. In Windows, they're stored in `Documents and Settings\[user name]\Application Data\Adobe\InDesign\Version 3.0\Dictioaries\Proximity`.

Note   The Application Data folder in Windows is hidden by default. To see it, open any folder in Windows, then choose Tools ➪ Folder Options to open the Folder Options dialog box. Go to the View pane and click the Show Hidden Files and Folders radio button. Then click OK.

Plug-ins — both those that come with InDesign and those you buy from other companies — are stored in the Plug-ins folder, often in subfolders within it.

But the actual InDesign preferences file — called InDesign Defaults — is stored in a different location on the Mac and in Windows.

On the Mac, InDesign Defaults is stored in the path `Users\[user name]\Library\Preferences\Adobe InDesign\Version 3.0`. In Windows, it is stored in `Documents and Settings\[user name]\Application Data\Adobe\InDesign\Version 3.0`.

Preference files

When no document is open and you change the preferences, add swatches and styles, modify tool settings (such as change the number of sides on the polygon tool by double-clicking it), and modify some dialog box's default settings (such as Text Wrap and Text Frame Options), these changes are saved in the InDesign Defaults file.

Tip

You can use the Mac's alias feature or the Windows shortcut feature to use an InDesign Defaults file stored in a folder other than the one in which InDesign resides. On a network, being able to use this technique means that everyone can share the same InDesign Defaults file. You can also set keyboard shortcuts sets, spelling and hyphenation dictionaries, libraries, and swatch libraries to be shared this way. Note that if you're sharing these across platforms, you'll need to create a Windows shortcut from Windows to these files as well as a Mac alias from the Mac.

The InDesign Defaults file cannot be shared across platforms, so if you want to have a master copy on a network server, you'll need to maintain two masters — one for Macintosh and one for Windows. Because the files have the same name on both platforms (there is no filename extension for this file in Windows), you'll need to store them in separate directories or add something to the name such as "Mac" and "Windows." If you do change the name, note that the alias and shortcut on each user's system must simply be named InDesign Defaults.

Color definitions

Wanting to keep color, tint, and gradient definitions consistent across documents isn't unusual. This consistency helps you ensure, for example, that corporate-identity colors, if you have them, are used instead of someone's approximations.

You can import swatches created in other documents (and templates) by having both documents open, then dragging the swatch from the source document's Swatches pane (Window ⇨ Swatches) to anywhere in the other document's window. By creating a file that contains nothing but swatches, you can, in effect, create a color library for users.

You can't add swatches to a library, but any swatch used in a library element will be copied to a document along with that element. So you could use a library that has a series of rectangles each with a different swatch applied as another way of creating a color library.

InDesign also lets you share swatch libraries, even across platforms (just give the library the file extension .ai if you're transferring a swatch library from the Mac to Windows).

Cross-Reference   See Chapter 8 for more on creating swatches.

Note   On the Mac, color profiles are stored in the path `Users\[user name]\Library\ColorSync\Profiles`. In Windows, they're stored in the `System32\Color` folder inside the folder that contains Windows (usually called Windows or WinNT).

Style sheets

The Character Styles pane (Type ➪ Character Styles, or Shift+F11) and the Paragraph Styles pane (Type ➪ Paragraph Styles, or F11) include an option in the palette menu to import styles from other InDesign documents and templates. Use Load Character Styles or Load Paragraph Styles to import just character or paragraph styles, respectively; use Load All Styles to load both from a document or template.

Tip   By importing styles with no document open, you copy all new styles into your global defaults (those stored in the InDesign Defaults file covered earlier). This technique is a handy way of bringing new styles into your default settings without affecting existing styles.

Cross-Reference   See Chapter 20 for more on style sheets.

Spelling dictionaries

InDesign saves any spelling or hyphenation exceptions you add via Edit ➪ Dictionary or when spell-checking via Edit ➪ Check Spelling, or ⌘+I or Ctrl+I. These exception dictionaries can be copied from one computer to another (regardless of platform), or you can use an alias or shortcut from each computer to a central location on a server.

On both Mac and Windows, hyphenation exception files have the filename extension .not, while the spelling exception dictionaries have the extension .udc. The files will have the same name as the language dictionaries (but different filename extensions) to which they are associated, such as FREN.not for French hyphenation exceptions and USA.udc for U.S. English spelling exceptions.

Cross-Reference   See Chapter 15 for more on hyphenation and spelling dictionaries.

Graphics and text files

Perhaps the most obvious elements to standardize are the *source elements* — the text and graphics that you use in your documents — especially if you have common elements like logos that are used in multiple documents.

The simplest method of ensuring that the latest versions of these common elements are used is to keep them all in a standard folder (either on each computer or on a network drive). This method works well when you first use a text or graphic element, but it does not ensure that these elements are updated in InDesign documents if the elements are changed after being imported.

For both text and graphics files, using InDesign's links feature — when you keep common elements in a common location — can ensure consistency across documents. You can also use libraries to store commonly used graphics and text blocks (including any formatting for the text and its frame).

Libraries

InDesign libraries are a great aid to keeping documents consistent. Because libraries are stored in their own files, common libraries can be put in common folders. You can even access them across the network. If you want, you can keep an alias to a library elsewhere on the network on your computer's local drive.

For many people, libraries offer more flexibility than just linking to graphics files because all attributes applied to graphics and their picture boxes are also stored in the library.

Libraries can be shared across platform, and although Windows InDesign libraries have the filename extension .indl, that extension is not required for Windows InDesign to open and use Mac libraries.

Cross-Reference   See Chapter 7 for more information on libraries.

Templates

In the course of creating documents, you're likely to evolve templates (also called *stationery*) that you want to use over and over. InDesign can save a document as a template. The only difference between a template and a document is that a template forces you to use Save As rather than Save in the File menu so that you don't overwrite the template but instead create new documents based on it.

Although the optimum approach is to design a template before creating actual documents, the truth is that no one can foresee all possibilities. Even if you create a template (and you should) with a style sheet, swatches, and master pages intended for use in all new documents, you can expect to modify your template, because working on real documents brings up the need for modifications and additions.

Whether or not you use templates, you'll still need to transfer basic layout elements like styles and master pages from one document to another, as described earlier in this chapter.

Templates can be shared across platforms, and although Windows InDesign templates have the filename extension .indt, that extension is not required for Windows InDesign to open and use Mac templates.

See Chapter 4 for more on templates.

Master pages

Moving master pages between documents is tricky because InDesign offers no feature that explicitly performs this task. But you can use InDesign libraries as way stations for master pages that you want to move from one document to another. Here are the steps:

1. **Open a library by choosing File ⇨ Open, or pressing ⌘+O or Ctrl+O, or create a library by choosing File ⇨ New ⇨ Library.**

2. **Open the document with the master page that you want to copy, and display that master page (by double-clicking the master page in the Pages pane, which you open by choosing Window ⇨ Pages, or pressing F12).**

   I recommend that you change the view to something small, like 25 percent, so you can see the full page.

3. **Select the Selection tool and then select all items (via Edit ⇨ Select All, or ⌘+A or Ctrl+A).**

4. **Drag (or use copy and paste) the items into an open library and release the mouse.**

   All the elements on the master page will appear in their own library box.

5. **Open the document that you want to copy the master page into.**

   You don't need to close the other document, but unless you intend to get other elements from it or work on it later, go ahead and close it to reduce clutter both on the screen and in the computer's memory.

Tip

Choose Window ⇨ Arrange ⇨ Cascade or Window ⇨ Arrange ⇨ Tile to manage how documents display if you have several open. Tile creates non-overlapping windows — either side by side or one at the top and one at the bottom, if you have two documents open — while Cascade overlaps the windows. The names of all open documents also appear in the Window menu so that you can switch among them. You can also resize windows manually by clicking and holding the mouse on the window's resize box on the Mac, or by clicking and holding any of its sides or corners in Windows.

6. **Insert a new blank master page in the second document, using the Pages pane.**

7. **Drag (or copy and paste) the library item containing the first document's master-page elements into the new master page.**

8. **Rename the new master page (using the Master Options option in the Pages pane's palette menu) so that you can remember what it is.**

Now you're done.

Cross-Reference

See Chapter 7 for more on master pages.

Mixing Mac/Windows Environments

As a cross-platform application, InDesign appeals strongly to all sorts of users who find that they deal with "the other side." This includes corporate users whose various divisions have standardized on different platforms, service bureaus whose clients use different machines, and independent publishers or layout artists who deal with a range of clients.

InDesign differences

InDesign can read document files from either platform. However, the Windows version may not recognize a Mac-generated file as an InDesign file unless you do one of two things:

✦ **Add the file extension .indd for documents or .indt for templates to the Mac-generated file's name.** InDesign does this automatically, so unless a Mac user removed the filename extension, most files will have it.

✦ **For cases when the document does not have its identifying filename extension, select the All Files in the File of Type pop-up menu in the Open dialog box (File ⇨ Open, or Ctrl+O).**

On the Mac, you'll typically not be able to double-click a PC-generated InDesign document (it'll have the PC icon rather than the InDesign icon); instead, you'll need to open it from the InDesign Open dialog box (File ⇨ Open, or ⌘+O).

Which elements transfer

The following elements may be transferred across platforms, with any limits noted:

✦ **Color, tint, and gradient swatches are retained.** They may also be imported across platforms. For swatch libraries copied from the Mac to Windows, be sure to add the filename extension .ai.

✦ **Although color profile files cannot be exchanged across the two platforms, both the Mac and Windows InDesign versions retain color-profile information from the other platform's files.** And if both platforms have color profiles for the same device (monitor, scanner, printer, and so on), InDesign will apply the correct color profiles. If a color profile is not available on the new platform, you can apply a new profile or ignore the issue. (If you ignore this issue, the correct profile will be in place when you bring the document back to the original platform.) If you print with a missing profile, InDesign will substitute the default profile based on the type of color model used (RGB or CMYK).

✦ **Style sheets are retained.** They may also be imported across platforms.

✦ **Hyphenation and spelling exceptions are retained.** These files use a filename extension on both the Mac and in Windows: .not for hyphenation additions, .udc for spelling additions.

✦ **Document preferences are retained, but the InDesign Defaults file cannot be shared across platforms.**

✦ **Plug-ins must be present on both platforms if you're moving documents that use specific plug-ins' features.** You'll need versions specific to each platform, because these are essentially miniprograms that must be written to work on the Mac or Windows; these files are not interchangeable across platforms.

Which elements don't transfer

Adobe has removed most barriers between Mac and Windows in InDesign. Only the following elements cannot be moved across platforms:

✦ Shortcut sets

✦ Color profiles

✦ The InDesign Defaults preferences file

✦ Scripts other than those using JavaScript

Platform differences

There are also some general differences between Windows and Macintosh themselves that will add a few bumps along the road to cross-platform exchange.

Filenames

The most noticeable difference between Windows and Macintosh is the file-naming convention, which has diminished since the advent of Mac OS X.

Macintosh files follow these rules:

✦ **Names are limited to 255 characters (to 31 characters for Mac OS 9 applications).**

✦ **Any character may be used except for colons (:).** Colons are used by the Macintosh system software internally to separate the folder name (which is not visible on-screen) from the filename.

✦ **Filenames typically have a file extension of up to four characters, which is often added by newer programs such as InDesign CS to identify the file type.** A period separates the filename from the extension: Filename.ext. Mac OS X hides these file extensions from view, unless you select the Always Show File Extensions in the Finder Preferences pane (choose Finder ➪ Preferences) to make Mac OS X display them. Mac OS 9 files typically did not have file extensions, so documents, graphics, and other materials created under Mac OS 9 programs usually won't have file extensions.

✦ **Case does not matter.** "FILE," "file," and "File" are all considered to be the same name. If you have a file named "FILE" and create or copy a file named "file," "FILE" will be overwritten.

Windows files follow these rules:

✦ **Names are limited to 250 characters.**

✦ **Names must also have a file extension of up to four characters, which is almost always added automatically by programs to identify the file type.** A period separates the filename from the extension: Filename.ext. Windows hides these file extensions from view, unless you use the View option in View ➪ Options in a drive or folder window to make Windows display them.

✦ **Names may use any characters except for most punctuation.** Pipes (|), colons (:), periods (.), asterisks (*), double quotes ("), less-than symbols (<), greater-than symbols (>), question marks (?), slashes (/), and backslashes (\) are all used by Windows to separate parts of paths (file locations, such as drives and folders) or to structure commands. A period may be used as the separator between a filename and an extension.

✦ **Case does not matter.** "FILE," "file," and "File" are all considered to be the same name. If you have a file named "FILE" and create or copy a file named "file," "FILE" will be overwritten.

When you bring Mac InDesign files and any associated graphics to Windows, you'll have to translate the Mac names into names that are legal on Windows. Similarly, you'll need to make Windows filenames Mac-legal when going the other direction. This rule applies not only to the InDesign document but also to any associated files, such as graphics.

If you rename these files, either before transferring or while transferring, you'll find that, within the InDesign document itself, the original names are still used. When InDesign tries to open these files, it will look for them by their original names.

The simplest way to ensure that you won't have problems with transferred files looking for incompatible names is to use a naming convention that satisfies both Windows and Mac standards. That means you should:

✦ **Keep file names to 250 characters.**

✦ **Always include the file extension.** Use .indd for documents, .indt for templates, .indl for libraries, .ai for swatch libraries, .not for hyphenation exceptions, and .udc for spelling exceptions. Typical extensions for cross-platform graphics are .tif or .tiff for TIFF, .jpg for JPEG, .eps for Encapsulated PostScript, .ai for Adobe Illustrator, .pct for PICT, .pcx for PC Paintbrush, .bmp and .rle for Microsoft bitmap, .gif for Graphics Interchange Format, .wmf for Windows metafile, and .psd for Adobe Photoshop. Microsoft Word files typically have the file extensions .doc, text-only (ASCII) files the extension .txt, and Microsoft Excel files the extension .xls.

✦ **Don't use the pipe (|), colon (:), period (.), asterisk (*), double quote ("), less-than symbol (<), greater-than symbol (>), question mark (?), slash (/), or backslash (\) characters.**

Font differences

Although the major typeface vendors like Adobe Systems and Bitstream offer their typefaces for both Windows and Macintosh users, these typefaces are not always the same on both platforms. Cross-platform differences are especially common among typefaces created a few years ago, when multiplatform compatibility was not a goal for most users or vendors.

Differences occur in four areas:

✦ **The internal font name — the one used by the printer and type scalers like Extensis Suitcase, DiamondSoft FontReserve, and Adobe Type Manager — is not quite the same for the Mac and Windows version of a typeface.** This discrepancy will result in an alert box listing the fonts used in the document that are not on your computer. The solution is to use the Find/Replace dialog box (covered in Chapter 15) to replace all instances of the unrecognized font name with the correct one for the current platform.

✦ **Even if typefaces use the same internal names, the font files' tracking, kerning, and other character-width information may be different on the two platforms, possibly resulting in text reflow.** The solution is to check the ends of all your stories to make sure text did not get shorter or longer.

✦ **Symbols do not always translate properly.** Even when created by the same vendors, the character maps for each font file differ across platforms because Windows and the Macintosh use different character maps. This problem is complicated by the fact that some vendors didn't stick to the standard character maps for any platform or didn't implement all symbols in all their typefaces. The solution is to proofread your documents, note the symbols that are incorrect, and then use the Find/Change dialog box to replace them with the correct symbol. (Highlight the incorrect symbol and use the copy and paste commands to put it in the Text field of the Find/Change dialog box rather than trying to figure out the right keypad code in Windows or the right keyboard shortcut on the Mac.) If you use OpenType fonts, you'll find far fewer issues with symbol translation than with PostScript Type 1 and TrueType fonts.

✦ **Ligatures are supported only on the Mac (Windows doesn't support ligatures at all).** Windows InDesign will use just the regular fi, fl, ffi, and ffl letter combinations, and Mac InDesign will substitute the ligatures (fi, fl, ffi, and ffl) if you bring the file back to the Mac.

Tip   To minimize font problems, use a program like Macromedia's Fontographer or Pyrus FontLab to translate your TrueType and PostScript files from Mac to Windows format or vice versa. (Fontographer and FontLab are available in both Mac and Windows versions.) This will ensure that the internal font names, width information, and symbols are the same on both platforms. The companion Web site (www.INDDcentral.com) includes links to these and other utilities.

Cross-Reference   See Chapters 38 and 40 for more information on fonts, and Chapter 41 for more information on special characters.

Transfer methods

Moving files between Macs and Windows PCs is easier now than ever before, thanks to built-in support of Windows formats and networking in Mac OS X, the use of TCP/IP networking by both the Mac and Windows, and a selection of products on both platforms that let each machine read the other's disks (floppies, removable disks like Zip disks, and even hard drives).

Cross-Reference   Chapter 38 covers these disk-reading products in detail.

Summary

When working with other users, you can share preferences by copying or making aliases to just one InDesign Defaults file, ensuring that all users have the same preferences. But the InDesign Defaults file is not cross-platform-compatible, so Windows users cannot use a Mac user's file or vice versa.

Except for shortcut sets, color profiles, the InDesign Defaults preferences file, plug-ins, and scripts, cross-platform users can share InDesign support documents. Otherwise, sharing file between PC and Mac users is very simple, thanks to a variety of disk- and network-based utilities now available for both platforms.

✦   ✦   ✦

Using Plug-Ins

In This Chapter

Using the default plug-ins

Purchasing special-purpose plug-ins

How plug-ins work within InDesign

Setting plug-in preferences

The InDesign team engineered the software to be *extensible* — meaning you can extend its capabilities by adding more software. To do this, you use *plug-ins,* which are small software modules, often developed by third parties. If you're a Photoshop user, you might be familiar with plug-ins such as Kai's Power Tools; or if you're a QuarkXPress user, you're probably familiar with the concept of add-on software through XTensions. Even if you're new to publishing, you may have purchased add-on software for your operating system, such as a custom screen saver or virus-protection software.

Extensible programs solve the one-size-fits-all nature of most software, letting you customize your tools to your workflow. If InDesign doesn't meet a need of yours — say, indexing, table editing, or imposition — you can look for a plug-in that does.

Using the Default Plug-Ins

Many core features in InDesign are actually implemented through plug-ins. When you launch the application, you may notice the words *Caching plug-ins* on the InDesign startup screen — this is when the plug-ins load. Structuring the software this way lets Adobe update or modify a finite area of the software, then distribute a new plug-in, instead of updating and distributing the entire application. Go to the Adobe Web site (www.adobe.com) periodically to look for both fixes and new plug-ins. There's also a directory of plug-ins at this book's companion Web site (www.INDDcentral.com).

The default plug-ins are stored in a folder called Plug-Ins inside your InDesign application folder. If you open the Plug-Ins folder, as shown in Figure 36-1, you'll notice the plug-ins have been consolidated into special-purpose folders such as Filters and Text. You should leave the default plug-ins alone, for the most part.

Figure 36-1: The InDesign Plug-Ins folder stores the default plug-ins, as well as additional plug-ins you may install.

QuarkXPress User

QuarkXPress users might be accustomed to removing XTensions to reduce launch time and consume less RAM. Don't use this technique with InDesign. Many core features of the application — such as the text handling — are implemented through plug-ins, and the program may not work at all if you remove required plug-ins.

Purchasing Special-Purpose Plug-ins

With the backing of a software and publishing giant like Adobe, InDesign has enticed a variety of proven developers to create special-purpose plug-ins.

Many plug-in developers provide a free evaluation copy so you can try before you buy. This is important, so you can figure out if the plug-in really solves your problem, whether everyone in your workgroup will need it, and whether your service bureau will need it as well. One place to start looking for plug-ins is www. pluginsource.com, which sells Adobe plug-ins from many developers. Or check the individual Web sites of the current plug-in developers.

Cross-Reference

To quickly find available InDesign plug-ins, go to the Plug-Ins page of this book's companion Web site (www.INDDcentral.com).

Knowing How Plug-Ins Work within InDesign

To use a new plug-in, the first thing you need to do is install it. Many plug-ins include their own installers that search out your copy of InDesign and plant themselves in the Plug-Ins folder. If a plug-in doesn't include an installer or installation instructions, try dragging it into the Plug-Ins folder. Once a plug-in is in the correct location, you need to restart InDesign so the plug-in is recognized and its code is loaded. You cannot use a new plug-in installed while InDesign is running — you should always quit the application before changing anything in the Plug-Ins folder and then restarting.

If a plug-in cannot load with InDesign, an alert will display while the application is starting up. Usually, loading errors result from incompatible versions of InDesign and the plug-in. Check the plug-in's ReadMe file or contact the developer for assistance. To remove a plug-in, simply drag it out of the subfolder of the Plug-Ins folder and store it someplace else. (You might create a folder called Disabled Plug-Ins, in which to store plug-ins that you're not using — just be sure it's not stored in the Plug-Ins folder!)

When a plug-in is loaded with InDesign, new controls appear in the interface. You might see entire menus, menu commands, dialog boxes, panes, palettes, and tools added to the application by a plug-in. No matter the combination of interface elements, when you're using the features of a plug-in, it should look and feel as if you're using InDesign. Some plug-ins will meet this criteria, and others will not.

For example, the PMPack set of plug-ins from Adobe adds its own toolbar plus the Template Browser and Data Merge panes, to bring in PageMaker features not otherwise available in InDesign. Figure 36-2 shows the added interface elements.

Caution

In some cases, plug-ins may add objects or information to documents that can be recognized only when the plug-in is loaded. If the plug-in is missing, you may not be able to open the document, or the document may look differently. If it turns out that a plug-in is required to open a document or preserve information, you'll need to ensure that each member of a workgroup and your service bureau owns the same plug-in.

Figure 36-2: The two panes and one toolbar added by the PMPack set of plug-ins.

Setting Plug-In Preferences

After acquiring several plug-ins, you may have trouble managing all the features in InDesign, since you'll have new panes, toolbars, and menu options throughout the program. Fortunately, InDesign has a tool to let you manage your plug-ins, so you can turn them on and off as needed, as well as save sets of plug-ins so you can turn on and off related plug-ins simultaneously.

To manage plug-ins, use the Configure Plug-Ins dialog box, shown in Figure 36-3. To open this dialog box, choose InDesign ➪ Configure Plug-Ins on the Mac and Help ➪ Configure Plug-Ins in Windows.

The default list of plug-ins will be very long, since so many basic InDesign features are implemented via plug-ins. To help manage the display, you have six check boxes at the bottom of the dialog box that filter what appears: Enabled, Adobe, Required, Disabled, Third Party, and Optional. Unchecking any of these options does *not* disable the plug-ins themselves; it simply removes them from the dialog box's list.

Figure 36-3: The Configure Plug-Ins dialog box.

To manage plug-ins, you'll want to enable Third Party to see non-Adobe plug-ins, Optional to see plug-ins that can be turned off safely. Be sure that Enabled is also checked to see what is enabled, or that Disabled is checked to see what plug-ins have been previously turned off. If neither Enabled nor Disabled is checked, you won't see any plug-ins in the list — you have to use these check boxes in combination with each other. For example, checking Enabled, Adobe, and Required shows only required Adobe plug-ins that are enabled.

Note   Required plug-ins will have a lock icon to their left, while other plug-ins will have a check mark to their left if enabled and nothing if disabled.

To enable and disable plug-ins, simply click to the left of the plug-in name — if checked, a plug-in will be enabled when you relaunch InDesign. If unchecked, it will be disabled. If you're not sure what a plug-in does, you can get more information (the name of the developer, the version, and a brief description) by clicking the plug-in name and then clicking the Show Info button.

When you first disable plug-ins, InDesign will force you to create a new *set* of plug-ins — sets are essentially a list of which plug-ins should be enabled and which should be disabled. You can copy, edit the name of, and delete sets using the Duplicate Set, Rename Set, and Delete Set buttons. You choose a set of plug-ins to put in use by using the Set pop-up menu at the top of the dialog box. You can also import and export plug-in sets using the Import and Export buttons. Click OK when done, or Cancel to leave the plug-ins as they were when you first opened the Configure Plug-Ins dialog box.

Note   You must quit and relaunch InDesign for any changes to plug-ins to take effect.

Summary

Plug-ins are software modules that serve two purposes in InDesign: incorporating core features into the application and adding special functions. Plug-ins are stored in the Plug-Ins folder within the InDesign application folder. Many established developers of QuarkXPress XTensions and Photoshop plug-ins have developed InDesign plug-ins to provide additional features such as table editing and imposition. When purchasing and using plug-ins, consider whether other users of your workgroup and your service bureau will need the plug-in as well. Finally, you can manage which plug-ins are in use through the Configure Plug-Ins dialog box.

✦   ✦   ✦

Using Scripts

Scripting automates many features in InDesign—it's essentially a way to program InDesign to do specific actions. Because InDesign uses standard script languages, you can also run scripts that work with multiple programs in concert, including InDesign. (All the applications must support the same scripting language, of course.) For example, you might use scripts to automate database publishing, such as to run a database search, export data to a text file, import that file into InDesign, and then apply the appropriate formatting.

InDesign supports three scripting languages:

+ On both Mac and Windows, it supports JavaScript.
+ On the Mac only, it supports AppleScript.
+ On Windows only, it supports Visual Basic for Applications (VBA).

Because of this, I recommend you use JavaScript wherever possible, so your scripts can work in cross-platform environments. InDesign doesn't force you to choose just one scripting language, so you could keep using old AppleScript or VBA scripts created for previous versions of InDesign, as well as new scripts written in JavaScript.

New Feature   JavaScript support is new to InDesign CS.

As you become comfortable with scriptwriting, you're also likely to discover that virtually everything you do with InDesign is a repetitive task. The more you can free yourself of this kind of work by using scripts, the more time you have to be creative. The possibilities are endless. But before you get too excited, remember that scripting *is* programming, so most layout artists stay clear, using scripts only if they have a programmer available to write them.

In This Chapter

Installing and accessing scripts

Exploring JavaScript

Exploring AppleScript

Exploring VBA

Writing scripts

Learning more about scripting

Using Scripts

Accessing scripts is easy — they show up in the Scripts pane (Window ⇨ Scripting ⇨ Scripts) if you've placed scripts in the Scripts folder inside the folder that contains the InDesign CS application, as shown in Figure 37-1. Scripts don't have to be in the Scripts folder — they can be anywhere on your computer — but to use a script outside this folder means you have to double-click the script from your desktop rather than access it in InDesign.

New Feature   If you create many scripts, you can control how their names sort in the scripts list. Also, you can now assign keyboard shortcuts to scripts.

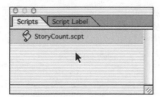

Figure 37-1: The Scripts pane in InDesign.

No matter what scripting language you use, there are several basic principles to observe. These fall into four basic categories:

✦ **Grammar.** All languages — including programming languages such as Pascal and C++, as well as scripting languages — include grammatical components that are used in standardized sequences. In English, we combine nouns, verbs, adjectives, adverbs, and so on to create sentences. Everybody knows the meaning of "The weather is especially nice today," because it uses common words in a sequence that makes sense. The sentence "Nice is the especially today weather," has the right components, but it's arranged in the wrong sequence, so the meaning is lost.

✦ **Statements and syntax rules.** In JavaScript, AppleScript, and VBA, verbs, nouns, adjectives, and prepositions are combined to create statements; statements are combined to form scripts. Verbs are also called *commands* and *methods;* nouns are called *objects;* and adjectives are called *properties.* Syntax rules specify how statements and scripts must be constructed so that they can be understood by a computer.

✦ **The object hierarchy.** All three scripting languages use a structural element called an *object hierarchy.* It's a fancy term for a simple concept. An object hierarchy works like a set of boxes within boxes. A large box contains a smaller box, which contains a smaller box, which contains a smaller box, and so on, until you reach the smallest box, which contains nothing and is the final level in the hierarchy of boxes.

✦ **The InDesign hierarchy.** InDesign contains its own hierarchy, which lends itself nicely to scripting. A project contains layouts, a layout contains pages, pages contain boxes, and boxes contain text and pictures. You can create scripts that perform actions at any of these levels. In other words, with scripts you can create documents, add pages, add items to pages, and modify the contents of boxes — right down to a particular character in a text box. You can think of this hierarchy in InDesign as a chain of command. You can't talk directly to an item that's at the bottom of the chain. Rather, you must first address the top level, then the next, and so on, until you've reached the item at the bottom of the chain. This is analogous to the way you use InDesign: You create new layouts, add pages, place text and graphics on the pages, and, finally, modify the contents of the frames containing those items.

New Feature

Scripts can now address individual graphics in a layout as objects, create dialog boxes, access object labels (which you can set in InDesign, as well as have InDesign automatically extract from converted QuarkXPress files), set object properties, and identify the file path on which the script resides.

If you're thinking about dabbling with any of the scripting languages supported by InDesign, the following words of both caution and encouragement are in order. First the encouragement: You don't necessarily need programming experience, scripting experience, or a pocket protector to begin creating scripts. A bit of curiosity and a touch of patience will suffice. Now the caution: Scripting is essentially a euphemism for programming (that is, figuring out the right commands and then typing them in for the application to execute). Writing scripts isn't a matter of choosing commands from menus, clicking and dragging, or entering values into fields; nor is it like writing a limerick. If you're starting from scratch, know in advance that you'll have to learn some new skills.

Learning to create scripts is like learning to swim: You can read books, documentation, and articles until your head spins, but eventually you have to get a little wet. The best way to learn about scripting is to write a script. So put on your swimsuit and dive in.

Be forewarned: There's something almost narcotic about creating scripts, and it's not uncommon for novice scriptwriters to get hooked. Don't be surprised if what starts out to be a 15-minute look-see turns into a multi-hour, late-night programming episode.

Note

Because scripting languages differ, you can't always duplicate the functionality of a specific script in one language into a script written in a different language.

Exploring JavaScript

JavaScript is a scripting language developed by Sun Microsystems and initially meant to let Web browsers manage resources on far-flung servers by running scripts to control the servers from a desktop. It soon became a popular scripting language because it runs on so many types of computers, including Windows, Macintosh, and Unix. Now, JavaScript is used for both server and desktop programs. Because it is based largely on the object-oriented approach taken by professional computer languages such as C and C++, it can be difficult for nonprogrammers to use.

Cross-Reference   The JavaScript functionality in InDesign CS was not available before this book went to press. For updated information on how to use JavaScript with InDesign, go to this book's companion Web site, `www.INDDcentral.com`.

Tip   There are lots of JavaScript editor programs available. Most of these are developed by individuals and small firms, so the list is always changing. I recommend you use the Google search engine (`www.google.com`) and search for *JavaScript editor* to find the most current programs.

Getting more information on JavaScript

Before you venture too far into scripting, you should review the JavaScript-related information provided with InDesign:

✦ **JavaScript documentation and tools.** Sun places the very technical JavaScript documentation on its Web site at `http://devedge.netscape.com/central/javascript/`. A good independent source is the O'Reilly & Associates Web site's scripting section (`http://scripting.oreilly.com`).

✦ **InDesign scripting documentation.** The InDesign CD contains a 600-plus-page PDF file that explains JavaScript programming for InDesign. This document, although a bit on the technical side, is a valuable resource. It includes an overview of JavaScript scripting and the object model, as well as a list of InDesign-specific scripting terms and scripting examples.

If you want still more information about JavaScript, several books are available, including *JavaScript: The Definitive Guide,* by David Flanagan; *Beginning JavaScript,* by Paul Wilton; and *JavaScript Bible,* 4th Edition, by Danny Goodman.

Exploring AppleScript

AppleScript is a scripting language developed by Apple and initially released with System 7.5 that can be used to control Macs, networks, and scriptable applications, including InDesign. The AppleScript language was designed to be as close to normal English as possible so that average Mac users—specifically, those who aren't familiar with programming languages—can understand and use it.

 New Feature InDesign can now run text-only AppleScripts in addition to compiled (binary) ones.

Learning the language

Many of the actions specified in AppleScripts read like sentences you might use in everyday conversation, such as:

```
set color of myFrame to "Black"
```

or

```
set applied font of myCharacterStyle to "Times"
```

Getting more information on AppleScript

Before you venture too far into scripting, you should review the AppleScript related information provided with the Mac OS and with InDesign:

✦ **Mac scripting documentation and tools.** Apple places the AppleScript documentation on its Web site at `www.apple.com/applescript`. In your hard drive's Applications folder, you should have a folder called AppleScript that contains the Script Editor program, along with a folder of example scripts and the AppleScript Script Menu that adds the Script menu to the Finder. Apple also offers a professional AppleScript editor called AppleScript Studio for download at its developer Web site, `http://developers.apple.com/tools.macosxtools.html`.

✦ **InDesign scripting documentation.** The InDesign CD contains a 600-plus-page PDF file that explains scripting, including AppleScript programming, for InDesign. This document, although a bit on the technical side, is a valuable resource. It includes an overview of Apple events scripting and the object model, as well as a list of InDesign-specific scripting terms and scripting examples.

If you want still more information about AppleScript, several books are available, including *AppleScript in a Nutshell: A Desktop Quick Reference,* by Bruce W. Perry; *Danny Goodman's AppleScript Handbook,* 2nd Edition; and *AppleScript 1-2-3,* by Sal Soghoian.

What you need to write and run scripts

The Script Editor, provided with the Mac OS, lets you write scripts. You'll find the Script Editor inside the AppleScript folder inside your Applications folder (at the root level of your hard drive). An uncompiled script is essentially a text file, so you can actually write scripts with any word processor. The Script Editor, however, was created for writing AppleScripts and includes several handy features for scriptwriters.

Checking for syntax errors

The next step is to determine if the statements are correctly constructed. Click the Check Syntax button. If the Script Editor encounters a syntax error, it alerts you and highlights the cause of the error. If the script's syntax is correct, all statements except the first and last are indented, and a number of words are displayed in bold, as illustrated in Figure 37-2. Your script has been compiled and is ready to test.

Figure 37-2: The Script Editor window containing sample AppleScript text. When you check the syntax of a script, the Script Editor applies formatting and indents.

Running your script

Click the Run button and then sit back and watch. If you've done everything correctly, you'll see InDesign become the active program, and then the actions you put in your script will take place. Voilà — and congratulations! You can now call yourself a scripter without blushing. That's all there is to creating and running a script.

If you have trouble getting a script to run, double-check the name that InDesign uses for itself. It might use InDesign® CS or simply InDesign® (yes, the name may include the registered trademark symbol). If you run a script from AppleScript (rather than just double-clicking it) and AppleScript can't find InDesign, it will give you a dialog box with which you find the InDesign program. When you've found and selected the InDesign application, AppleScript will find out what InDesign's filename is and use that in your script.

Saving your script

When you're finished writing and testing a script, choose Save from the Script Editor's File menu. Name your script, choose its storage location, and choose Compiled Script from the Format pop-up menu. It's best to save the script in the Scripts folder inside the InDesign folder, so it will show up in the Scripts menu (after you restart InDesign).

Note   If you save the script in Application format and want to edit your script later, you must open it by dragging and dropping It on the Script Editor application. This is because Application-format scripts are designed to immediately run when double-clicked. You would choose the Application format when creating scripts for use by others, since chances are you don't want them to open the script in Script Editor but instead simply want them to use the script by double-clicking it like any other application.

Locating more AppleScript tools

A few software utilities are also available for AppleScripters. The most widely used is Script Debugger, from Late Night Software ($189, www.latenightsw.com); it's an interface development tool to quickly create AppleScript-based applications that have the standard Mac look and feel. Apple also offers its AppleScript Studio as a free download to developers who register at the Apple site; this is more capable than the basic Script Editor that comes with Mac OS X.

Exploring VBA

Visual Basic for Applications (VBA), and its subset version VBScript, is Microsoft's technology for writing your own programs, both those that run in other programs (scripts) and those that run by themselves (custom applications). InDesign works with both VBA and VBScript. The Visual Basic language that underlies both VBA and VBScript is not meant for everyday computer users — a knowledge of programming is very useful in taking advantage of this technology. Although based on the Basic language developed in the 1970s to help new users write their own programs, it has evolved a lot since then and is no longer so simple.

Learning the language

Many of the actions specified in VBA have some degree of "Englishness," such as:

```
set myTextFrame =
InDesign.Documents.Item(1).Spreads.Item(1).TextFrames.Add
```

or

```
mySelection.RotationAngle = 30
```

But as you can see, VBA has moved far from English. The first code segment, for example, means to add a text frame to the first spread in the first document. The second means to rotate the selected object by 30 degrees.

Getting more information on VBA

Before you venture too far into scripting, you should review the VBA-related information provided by Microsoft and with InDesign:

✦ **Microsoft scripting documentation and tools.** Microsoft has a lot of information on VBA, Visual Basic, and VBScript on its Web site. Unfortunately, it's not well organized and is hard to find and understand. There's no tutorial that simply explains how a new scripter needs to get started. However, you can search on the Microsoft site for VBA, Visual Basic, and VBScript to get links to documents that may prove useful.

✦ **InDesign scripting documentation.** The InDesign CD contains a 600-plus-page PDF file that explains VBA programming for InDesign. This document, although a bit on the technical side, is a valuable resource. It includes an overview of VBA scripting and the object model, as well as a list of InDesign-specific scripting terms and scripting examples.

If you want still more information about VBA and its two "sister" technologies, several books are available, including *Programming Microsoft Visual Basic 6.0,* by Francesco Balena; *Visual Basic 6 For Dummies,* by Wallace Wang; and *VBScript in a Nutshell by* Paul Lomax and Ron Petrusha.

What you need to write and run scripts

To use InDesign scripting in Windows, you'll need Microsoft Visual Basic or an application that contains Visual Basic for Applications (VBA); these include Microsoft Office, Microsoft Visio, and AutoCAD. In Microsoft Office, you can run the Microsoft Script Editor by choosing Tools ➪ Macros ➪ Microsoft Script Editor, which lets you create scripts, edit them, test your code, and fix errors. Figure 37-3 shows the editor with a sample script.

You can also write scripts in VBScript, a VBA subset, in a text editor such as WordPad. You'll need Microsoft's free Windows Scripting Host (WSCRIPT.EXE), which is usually installed with Windows and can be downloaded from Microsoft's Web site.

There's a third choice for your scriptwriting: You can also use the full Microsoft Visual Basic product from Microsoft.

Note To use InDesign scripting in Windows, your user profile must have Administrator privileges.

Figure 37-3: The Microsoft Script Editor window containing sample VBA text. When you work on a script, the Microsoft Script Editor applies indents automatically.

Running your script

To run a VBA, Visual Basic, or VBScript program, simply double-click the script. You can also run the script directly from the application that you create a VBA or Visual Basic script in, such as the Microsoft Script Editor. (For VBScripts, you can run them from the Scripting Host application.) If you've done everything correctly, you'll see InDesign become the active program, and then the actions you put in your script will take place. Voilà — and congratulations! You can now call yourself a scripter without blushing. That's all there is to creating and running a script.

Saving your script

When you're finished writing and testing a script, choose Save from the script editor's File menu. Name your script and choose its storage location. It's best to save the script in the Scripts folder inside the InDesign folder (usually `C:\Program Files\Adobe\InDesign CS`), so it will show up in the Scripts menu (after you restart InDesign).

Creating and Running Scripts

At this point, I'm assuming that the appropriate scripting software is installed on your computer. If this is the case, you're ready to begin. For your first trick, you're going to make InDesign roll over — sort of. Actually, you're going to rotate an EPS graphic. First, you'll prepare InDesign for its role. Launch the program, and then create a new document (do not check Automatic Text Box). In the middle of the first page, place an EPS graphic. Make sure that it remains active after you place it.

Writing simple scripts

The following three scripts, taken from Adobe's InDesign script examples, do the same thing in AppleScript and VBA: Rotate an EPS graphic and its frame. (For JavaScript versions, go to the companion Web site at www.INDDcentral.com.)

Cross-Reference   You can get the example scripts shown in this chapter, as well as other samples, from the PDF scripting manual that comes on the InDesign CS CD. Just cut and paste them from the PDF file into the appropriate scripting editor. Adobe's user forums are also a good place to go for scripting help.

Enter the lines that follow this paragraph exactly as they're written for the scripting language you've chosen. Enter a return character at the end of each line. Note also the use of straight quotation marks instead of curly typesetter's quotes (the script editor does this for you). Be very careful when you enter the text: Typos are script killers.

AppleScript

```
tell application "InDesign CS"
  set myPageItems to {EPS, oval, rectangle, polygon}
  set mySelection to selection
  if class of item 1 of mySelection is in myPageItems and
(count mySelection) > 0 then
    if class of item 1 of mySelection is EPS then
      set myFrame to parent of mySelection
    else
      set myFrame to item 1 of mySelection
    end if
    set rotation angle of myFrame to 30
  end if
end tell
```

Note

Make sure to enter the name of your InDesign program exactly as it appears on the desktop. Because you're free to rename your program, the name may not match the name in the first line of the script.

If you're in an adventurous mood, try substituting the statement `set rotation angle of myFrame to 30` in the preceding script with each of the following statements:

```
set text wrap of myFrame to off
set shear angle of myFrame to 30
set vertical scale of myFrame to 200
```

If you want to get really fancy, combine all the `set` statements into a single script, so you can use the script to make all the changes at once.

VBA

```
Dim myInDesign As InDesign.Application
Set myInDesign = CreateObject("InDesign.Application.CS")
Set mySelection = myInDesign.Selection
If TypeName(mySelection.Item(1)) = "EPS" Then
  mySelection.Parent.RotationAngle = 30
Else
  mySelection.RotationAngle = 30
End If
```

If you're in an adventurous mood, try substituting the statement `mySelection.RotationAngle = 30` in the preceding script with each of the following statements:

```
set the color of the current box to "Blue"
set the shade of the current box to 50
set the width of the frame of the current box to 10
set the box shape of the current box to ovular
```

If you want to get really fancy, combine all the set statements into a single script, so you can use the script to make all the changes at once.

Note   Perhaps you noticed the chain of command used in the preceding scripts. First, the script addresses InDesign, then the active document (layout), and finally the active frame. If you understand this concept, you'll be scripting like a pro in no time.

Labeling items

As you can see from the examples in the previous section, scripts often refer to items by their type and location in the document. But there's another way to refer to objects that makes sure you can select an item precisely: You can label, or name, an item. You do so in the Script Label pane (Window ➪ Scripting ➪ Script Label). The process is easy: Select the object, then enter a name in the pane. That's it!

When writing scripts, you refer to the labeled object as follows. In these examples, the label is *TargetFrame,* and don't worry that the samples seem to do different things — they in fact are unrelated examples, not variations of the same command.

AppleScript
```
select (page item 1 of page 1 of myTargetDocument whose label
is "TargetFrame")
```

VBA
```
Set myAsset = myLibrary.Assets.Item("TargetFrame")
```

Writing conditional scripts

Some scripts simply automate a set of tasks in documents whose content is predictable. But more often than not, documents differ, and so you need conditional statements to evaluate if certain things are true before applying a script's actions. Otherwise, you'll get an error message when something turns out not to be true. As a simple example, a script that does a search and replace needs to have a document open and a frame selected. If no frame is selected, the script won't know what to search, and the user will get an error message.

The same issue arises for repeated series of actions, where you want the script to do something for all occurrences. The script will need to know what to do when it can't find any more such occurrences. As an example, look at the following script, which counts all open documents. For it to work, at least one document has to be open, so the script checks first to see if in fact any documents are open, and delivers an error message that the user can understand if none are open. The rotate-EPS-graphic script earlier also used a conditional to make sure there was an EPS graphic in the document. Notice that in all three scripting languages, it is the command If that you use to set up such conditionals.

AppleScript

```
tell application "InDesign CS"
set myNumberOfDocuments to (count documents)
if myNumberOfDocuments = 0 then
display dialog "No InDesign publications are open!"
end if
end tell
```

VBA

```
Dim myInDesign as InDesign.Application
  Set myInDesign = CreateObject ("InDesign.Application.CS")
  If myInDesign.Documents.Count
    MsgBox "No InDesign publications are open!"
  End If
End Sub
```

Another form of conditional is what's called a *control loop,* in which an action occurs either for a specified number of iterations or until a condition is met. The following scripts show an example of each for each language. Note the use of comments in the scripts — a handy way to document what you're doing for later reference. In JavaScript, a comment begins with /* and ends with */. In AppleScript, a comment begins with -- and continues until you press Enter or Return. In VBA, it begins with Rem followed by a space, and it continues until you press Enter or Return.

AppleScript

```
repeat with counter from 1 to 20
  --do something
end repeat

set myStop to false
repeat while myStop = false
  --do something, at some point setting myStop to true to leave
the loop.
end repeat
```

VBA

```
For counter = 1 to 20
  Rem do something
Next counter

Do While myStop = false
  Rem do something, at some point setting myStop to true to
leave the loop.
loop
```

Summary

If your workflow goes beyond original designs for each client and reaches into repetitive production, scripting is for you. Scripts are ideal for automating repetitive tasks — from importing pictures to creating and formatting entire documents. You can even link InDesign to other scriptable applications.

Because InDesign supports JavaScript on the Mac and Windows, as well as AppleScript on the Mac only and VBA on Windows only, you can choose the script language you're most familiar with and/or that is compatible with your other applications. Even better, you can use more than one scripting language with InDesign (though any individual script can use only one language).

✦   ✦   ✦

Introduction to Publishing

I t may seem strange to put the chapters that explain fundamental publishing theory and practice at the end of a book on publishing, but this lets experienced publishing users — whether experienced with InDesign or not — jump right into the program while letting new publishing users get all the background they need collected in one place.

In this part, I cover the fundamentals of publishing as an art and as a practice: what tools you need on your desktop, how to put together layouts, how to use typography and work with fonts, how to use and apply special symbols and international characters, and how to understand color theory so you can work with publishing's specific color specifications and tools.

Although aimed at those not highly experienced in desktop publishing, the five chapters in this part are also great refreshers for experienced designers for whom a refresher on some of the underlying principles may stimulate new ideas.

Chapter 38
The Publishing
Environment

Chapter 39
Layout Theory
and Practice

Chapter 40
Typography Theory
and Practice

Chapter 41
Using Special
Characters

Chapter 42
Color Fundamentals

The Publishing Environment

In This Chapter

Choosing the
right hardware

Getting the
essential software

Working with fonts

InDesign by itself doesn't do anything. You need to work with it in the context of a computer, add-on hardware, other software, and of course the operating system of your Mac or PC. And once you have the equipment and platform that's right for you, you need to learn to make the most of it. This chapter gives you the basic information you need to get the right equipment and to get started on your platform of choice. However, I do recommend that you pick up more detailed books on Mac OS or Windows; the publisher of this book, Wiley Publishing, has many good books for beginners (the *For Dummies* series) and for more experienced users (the Bible series).

Choosing the Right Hardware

You don't need the fastest computer available to use InDesign, but factors such as processor (CPU) speed, RAM, hard disks, removable media, connectivity, and input/output devices can make a difference. The following sections take you on a tour of what works best in a full spectrum of publishing situations.

The computer

Adobe provides system requirements for InDesign, but this is just the bare minimum you need to run the software. They're not concerned about whether you can run InDesign and, say, Photoshop at the same time or whether your font manager will run on the operating system it supports. But since you need to be concerned about your entire publishing system—not just InDesign—let me provide a realistic minimum system for Mac OS and Windows. Then I'll give you a wish list for the ideal publishing system.

The minimum system

For Adobe's official system requirements, see Appendix A, "Installing or Upgrading InDesign." But for best results, I recommend the following minimum publishing system:

✦ **Mac OS:** Any non-beige G3 or higher Macintosh computer running Mac OS X 10.2 or higher, with a minimum of 256MB of RAM and a 20GB hard drive. Note that InDesign CS will not run on Mac OS 8 or 9.

✦ **Windows:** An Intel Pentium III, AMD Athlon, or newer processor running at least at 400MHz, running Windows 2000 or Windows XP, with 256MB of RAM and a 20GB hard drive. Note that InDesign will not run on Windows 95, 98, Millennium (Me), NT 3, or NT 4.

The ideal system

In any kind of graphic-arts environment, you typically need to run at least Adobe InDesign, Photoshop, and Illustrator — not to mention an e-mail program and a Web browser — at the same time. Photoshop in particular runs faster and more reliably with plenty of RAM. Plus, images, EPS files, and the like eat up disk space fast. As a rule, buy as much RAM and the largest hard disk you can afford. If you're just getting started or have just come into some money, set yourself up right with the following system:

✦ **Mac OS:** A 400 MHz or faster Power Mac G4 running Mac OS X 10.2 with 512MB to 1GB of memory (online sources such as `www.ramseeker.com` have Mac memory available at very affordable prices), a 60GB or greater hard drive, and a CD-RW (read/write) or DVD R/W drive.

✦ **Windows:** A Pentium III, Pentium 4, or AMD Athlon computer running Windows 2000 or XP with 512MB to 1GB of RAM, a 60GB or greater hard drive, and a CD-RW or DVD R/W drive. Note that although Windows typically requires less operational overhead than Mac OS; the RAM requirement for applications is usually the same.

Storage capacity

Today, computers usually come with plenty of RAM (memory) and storage capacity (hard-drive space). But if you have an older computer, or you're taxing your current system, upgrading RAM and storage can speed up your work significantly. Here are my recommendations for storage:

✦ **RAM:** Adding RAM lets the computer work more efficiently, and you'll want 128MB as a bare minimum, which you can get by with if you work with just one program at a time. Better for publishers is 256MB to 1GB, and more than that if you're doing complex work on large files in Adobe Photoshop as well (512MB is typical for such users). Be sure to check the maximum amount of RAM your system can accommodate before making an upgrade purchase.

Computer acronyms explained

If you're not a techie, here are the acronyms explained:

✦ **MHz, or megahertz,** is the speed of the chip that does all the calculation in a computer.

✦ **MB, or megabyte,** is a unit of storage capacity equal to 1,024 kilobytes, or about 1 million characters. (A kilobyte is 1,024 bytes, and a byte is essentially one character.)

✦ **GB, or gigabyte,** is a unit of storage capacity equal to 1,024MB, or about 1 billion characters.

✦ **bps, or bits per second,** is the speed at which data travels over a wired or wireless connection. These speeds are typically shown as Kbps (1Kbps equals 1,024 bits per second) and Mbps (1Mbps equals 1,024Kbps). There are 8 bits in a byte, so to calculate transmission time, multiply the number of bytes of file size by 8 to get the number of seconds of transmission time. For example, a 2MB file transmitted at 1Mbps will take 16 seconds: $2048 \div 1024 \times 8 = 16$.

✦ **Hard disks:** Programs and files eat through disk space, so these days, a 10GB to 20GB drive (which holds about 10 to 20 billion characters) is considered small. Look for 30GB to 100GB or higher. And remember that you can usually add hard drives to your Mac or PC. You don't have to replace your existing one in most cases. Be sure to check the largest capacity of hard drive that your system can fully utilize. Due to upper limitations of the internal ATA hard connection, many Mac and PC systems more than a few years old can only use hard drives of 120GB or less. Buying a drive larger than 120GB may just be a waste of money, because an older Mac or PC will only be able to use the first 128GB of the drive. External FireWire and USB hard drives are generally not subject to this 128GB limitation.

✦ **CD-RW or DVD R/W:** Using a read/write CD drive (also called a *CD burner* or *DVD burner*) as part of your storage solutions is your best choice for long-term archiving. CDs and DVDs also work well for delivering large projects — including documents, graphics, and fonts — to service bureaus and printers. CD-RW drives are cheap ($100 to $300) depending on the speed, and the CD-R discs themselves are very inexpensive. (You can also use the more expensive CD-RW discs, which let you erase and modify the CD's contents, but for delivering, say, an issue of a magazine to a printer, there's no reason to use such a rewritable disc, because you're not expecting the CD back. CD-RWs are great, though, for storing templates that might be adapted over time and as a backup device.) Be aware that CD-RW media can only be rewritten a relatively few number of times, depending on the quality of the media. Each CD can hold 650MB of data and it's easy to store, permanent, and universal. DVD R/W drives cost more — the drives and media cost about four times as much as

CD-RW drives and media—but they hold seven times as much per disc. Early competition between formats is winding down, as are the compatibility issues this competition introduced, but do note that older DVD, DVD-R, and DVD R/W drives may not be able to read all DVD R/W discs.

✦ **Zip drives:** If your computer didn't come with a Zip drive, don't worry. While previously the standard way to exchange files, the 100MB and 250MB Zip drives have fallen into disuse because CD and DVD drives and media offer much more storage capacity at cheaper prices for the media. The new 750MB drives may help change that, but very few service bureaus will have them, while almost any computer can read a CD and most can read a DVD.

✦ **Tape drives:** If you don't have a CD-RW drive and don't work on a network that automatically backs up files to a server, you can use a tape drive for back-ups. Prices range from $100 to $1,000 depending on the capacity, with the majority under $400. These drives back up your system on inexpensive tapes, saving your work in case your hard drive gets damaged. If you're making a living from your computer, don't put that living at risk. Macintosh users will find a much more limited selection of tape drives than Windows users, though the newer external USB and FireWire drives are increasingly available in Mac versions.

✦ **Extra hard drives:** An increasingly popular alternative to tape—which can be slow and is subject to physical damage—is second hard drives—internal or external—on which you make mirror copies of your data and from which you can easily start up in case of failure. A consistent backup method using a second hard disk, tape drive, CD-R, or DVD-R can mean the difference between tearing every last hair out or staying sane even under the tightest of deadlines. You'll appreciate the nearly incalculable value of a complete daily or weekly backup the first time you lose everything on a 100GB hard drive in your Mac or PC. I promise.

Connectivity

Another essential component in workgroup environments is a network. At the very least, you want peer-to-peer networks, in which your Macs and PCs are connected to one another so they can share files. Both the Mac OS and Windows have this capability built in.

The Mac/PC connection

The following list describes programs that Macs and PCs use to connect to each other and read each other's disks:

✦ Mac OS X includes both Apple and Windows file-sharing support, so you can connect a Mac OS X system out of the box to Windows PCs. It also lets Windows computers connect to it without additional software.

✦ Miramar Systems' PC MacLAN lets PCs join Mac-based networks, whether AppleTalk- or IP-based. It provides better control over what items are accessed and shared than Mac OS X does, and unlike Mac OS X, it allows PCs to use Mac-connected printers. It costs about $200 per person but only needs to be installed on PCs.

✦ DataViz's MacOpener and Media4's MacDrive let PCs read Mac disks (floppies, CDs, Zips, SyQuests, external hard drives, and so on). They cost about $50 per user. Access Systems's TransMac does the same for about $65.

✦ DataViz's MacLinkPlus lets Macs read PC disks and also offers file translation. Most people don't need file-translation capability because most programs now use the same file format on Mac and Windows, but if you tend to use older or specialty programs, MacLinkPlus is a necessity. It costs about $100 per person. Apple's Mac OS X supports PC disks natively as well, although with less control than MacLinkPlus allows.

The network connection

Ethernet has become the standard means of networking computers together. Ethernet is a kind of wiring that lots of different transmission protocols, like TCP/IP or AppleTalk, can run and it's pretty fast yet inexpensive. All Macs built since late 1998 have Ethernet connectors built in, and so do most PCs. For those that don't, the cost is $10 to $50 per computer for the needed card or adapter box.

Older Macs have both AppleTalk and Ethernet, so you need to tell the Mac which you want to use; you can switch back and forth. I recommend you stick with Ethernet, using AppleTalk only if you have a printer that is not Ethernet-compatible (such as an older color ink-jet printer). Similarly, on a PC, getting an Ethernet version of your printers is better than relying on the slow, single-user parallel port or USB connection. Of course, if you're a one-person design firm, that's not a big issue.

Finally, consider wireless networks in small offices. The 802.11g wireless standard supports wireless connections of up to 54 Mbps (more typically, 20 Mbps to 24 Mbps), as well as the previous 802.11b 11 Mbps technology, and costs about $100. 802.11a is a third, 54 Mbps wireless technology that has been slow to catch on, since it suffers from a smaller typical coverage area and is not compatible with the widely installed 802.11b devices, such as the Apple AirPort wireless networking products; 802.11a is not a suggested general-use wireless technology at this time.

At the center of a wireless network is a wireless access point, which contains a radio transmitter and can serve a half-dozen connected systems and printers in a typical 150- to 300-foot radius, depending on whether there are major obstructions and interference from other wireless devices such as cordless phones and microwave ovens. (No matter which kind of wireless networking you use, there is a significant gap between the advertised rate and the real rate that your data can be moved. The wireless network's bandwidth must accommodate the overhead of interference and its transmission protocol. 802.11b is commonly rated at 11 Mbps but rarely achieves a real-world data-transfer rate of more than 6 Mbps.) If your Mac or PC doesn't have 802.11b or 802.11g wireless networking built in, an internal PCI card or external USB box costs typically about $50 to $75. Just be sure to turn on encryption if you use wireless networks so no one can snoop into your network.

You should be aware that even using the built-in encryption methods will not keep determined snoops out of your wireless network. There are alternative methods for improving the security of a wireless network, but they typically require a corporate network be in place, so they are not really an option for small businesses and individual users. The surest way to secure a wireless network is to place the access point or wireless router so its transmission range does not extend beyond the walls, floor, and ceiling of the space that you can physically control access to. If someone can get physical access into your space, then the security of your wireless network is a fairly minor concern by comparison.

The Internet connection

Even if you're working just on print projects, you'll need to be on the Internet. You need to be able to send and receive files — from e-mail to text files to entire InDesign documents and graphics — download program updates, and use your computer as a fax. Basically, you should get the fastest Internet connection available to you. Unfortunately, the availability is often limited by the phone lines and other factors in your area.

If you can get a cable, ISDN, or DSL connection from your cable or phone company, that's ideal. Cable modem and DSL are quickly becoming the connections of choice based on cost, availability, and ease of use. They let you access and download data at 384 kilobits per second (Kbps) or higher. Most often, the provider will send you the equipment you need or tell you what to buy. Make sure you carefully research all the types of cable modem and DSL services available in your area. Price, speed, and flexibility vary a lot from company to company. The best service is one that is not shared — where that 384 Kbps is always yours only. Some companies offer dedicated DSL service, while others offer shared DSL high-speed Internet; all cable-modem lines are shared with other users in your neighborhood. (Not only can this slow performance, it also means someone else on the connection could access your computers unless you have enabled the Mac OS X or Windows security software and, better, are using a hardware firewall.)

If you're stuck with a dial-up account — because DSL or other services are not available where you live — you need some type of modem. Most newer computers, such as iMacs or any PC, have an internal 56 Kbps modem, so all you do is plug a phone line into the computer. If you need an external modem, be sure to buy one that supports speeds of 56 Kbps.

Input and output devices

The following sections cover some of the things you'll need to consider in the input/output realm: printers, scanners, digital cameras, CD-ROM drives, multibutton mice, trackballs, and pen-based tablets.

Printers

Invest in a good printer. You'll want a black-and-white laser printer capable of 600 dots per inch (dpi) output or better. Older printers support 300-dpi output, which is acceptable but not as sharp when it comes to printing text and images. Get a printer with PostScript language built in, since you'll get better output, more functionality, and a more accurate preview of what you'll get on your imagesetter (these are PostScript-based). That pretty much means a Hewlett-Packard printer, because most other manufacturers don't provide PostScript options.

Fast network printers

If you work in an office and need only black-and-white or gray-scale output, you can buy one or two fast network printers (16 to 25 pages per minute [ppm] or faster) and share them. Such printers — such as the Hewlett-Packard 2200dn, 4100, or 5100 series — cost between $800 and $2,000 each. They typically have PostScript, the printing language standard for desktop publishing, already installed and can hold lots of paper, often in several sizes.

Personal laser printers

If you work alone and need only black-and-white or gray-scale output, you can consider an affordable laser printer such as the HP 1200 or 2200 series. Look for one that prints between 9 and 15 ppm. Consider getting a refurbished printer, especially if it has Ethernet built in (Ethernet is an expensive option for personal laser printers). A better choice for personal printing is one of the newer color ink-jets.

PostScript printers

If you're producing final output, as opposed to proofs, you'll want a PostScript-capable printer, because that's the language that all professional output devices, such as imagesetters, use. Printers aimed at Mac owners almost always have PostScript, while printers aimed at PC owners usually do not. Mac-oriented printers almost always work with PCs, so PC owners will find it easier to get PostScript by looking at Mac-oriented printers than by looking at PC-oriented printers. You can have Macs and PCs plugged into them and using them simultaneously.

Note If you use Windows 2000 or XP, be sure to go to Adobe's Web site (www.adobe.com) and download its free PostScript printer driver rather than use the one that comes with Windows — the Windows PostScript driver is less capable and can result in output errors. On a Mac, the Apple PostScript driver that comes with the Mac OS is fine, though Adobe also offers its own version.

Color ink-jet printers

For graphic-arts applications, the inexpensive color ink-jet printers, such as a Hewlett-Packard Photosmart, Epson Color Stylus, or Canon S series, are a great choice. These printers are essential if you're doing color work and want to get color proofs occasionally. And for low-volume color printing, they're a great deal and very convenient. Color ink-jets cost between $100 and $500. Although they're slower than most laser printers, they provide glorious color and gray-scale output.

While most of these do not support PostScript, you can purchase Strydent Software's PowerPrint PostScript rendering software for many models for about $100 (for serial and USB printers) or $250 (for network printers) — just be sure it works with your ink-jet printer. Epson also sells PostScript software ($145 to $200, depending on the model) for many of its ink-jet printers.

Multifunction printers

Multifunction printers — which include copy and scanner functions — from Brother, Canon, Epson, and Hewlett-Packard can be great printers for simple proofing. They come in both color ink-jet and black-and-white laser models, but they almost never include PostScript support.

Color scanners

One device that has recently become very affordable is a color scanner. Epson, Umax Technologies, Agfa, and Canon are all excellent and are inexpensive ($150 to $500) yet have color quality that approaches that of a professional scanner costing several thousand dollars. (Other brands tend to rate unevenly in reviews, but because manufacturers' quality changes over time, be sure to check out reviews at places such as *Macworld, PC World, PC Magazine,* and Cnet to see who's got the best current models.) These scanners work with both Macs and PCs, feature USB connectivity, and at these low prices and great quality, are almost a requirement to own. They also can double as copy machines or fax machines. You scan in a paper document and then print it to your printer or fax it from your Internet connection.

Digital cameras

These are becoming popular, and their image quality is presentable, however, you'll need to spend $600 or more for the 4- to 5-megapixel versions. This resolution is adequate for print publishing if your final output is under 8 by 10 inches and you're doing super-high-quality printing. The less-expensive 3- to 4-megapixel cameras, which cost $200 to $600, are fine for images that are printed at no larger than 5 by 7 inches.

The biggest problem with using a digital camera for print publishing is that most of the cameras use JPEG image compression, so you're not necessarily dealing with optimum quality no matter how high the resolution of the camera is. The best solution is to experiment — some image subjects work better than others. For Web publishing, however, digital cameras are fine, and using them is more convenient than having your 35mm film processed and scanned.

Mice, trackballs, and tablets

Also consider getting a multibutton mouse. The extra buttons can save you strain on your hands and arms by being used for common operations such as dragging and double-clicking. I advise both Mac and Windows users to get a three- or four-button mouse (or trackball, if that's your fancy); Kensington Microware and Logitech both offer good models for both platforms. A pen-based tablet makes sense if you're also doing illustration work, but consider that a secondary input device, not a primary one. However many buttons you get on your mouse, I strongly recommend the new optical mice, which don't require a mousepad, don't get gunk in their gears that can interfere with scrolling, and generally are easier to operate on most surfaces. You may find a mouse pad is necessary for use with an optical mouse if your desk or work surface is highly reflective or made of glass (optical mice need to "see" a slight variation in the texture of surface they're placed on).

Tip   If your optical mouse skips or jumps, try taping a piece of plain copier paper for use as a mouse pad.

Getting the Essential Software

A flurry of utility programs, specialized software, fonts, and plug-ins can help you complete your specific publishing environment. The following items detail some of the more outstanding ones:

✦ **An image editor:** Almost all publishers need an image editor, and the standard is really Adobe Photoshop (for both Macintosh and Windows). Even if you're more of an editor, you'll be surprised at how often you'll need to open a graphic file in Photoshop to simply crop or edit a photograph. For professional work, get the full version. If you really just need to resize and crop photos and other images, you can get by with the much cheaper LE version.

✦ **An illustration program:** If you draw, or you need to edit EPS files, you need an illustration program such as CorelDraw, Adobe Illustrator, or Macromedia FreeHand. They're all good cross-platform programs, so try them out first to see what feels best to you. All three companies let you download demo versions from their Web sites.

Go to `www.INDDcentral.com` for easy links to these and other software demos.

✦ **A word processor:** A word processing program is a must. Microsoft Word is the standard, but many still use WordPerfect — it's up to you. If you use WordPerfect, I recommend you save your InDesign-destined files in Word format.

✦ **A font manager:** See the next section, "Working with Fonts," for more information.

✦ **A compression utility:** Files are always too big, so compression utilities are a must. Here are two of the more common ones:

• **StuffIt Deluxe:** On the Mac, there's no substitute for Aladdin Systems's StuffIt Deluxe, a $50 utility package that reads both Mac .sit files and PC .zip files, as well as several Internet compression formats. Aladdin also has a Windows version of StuffIt.

• **WinZip:** On Windows, the equivalent program to StuffIt Deluxe is the $30 shareware program WinZip, from Niko Mac Computing.

✦ **Plug-ins:** You'll probably want add-on programs, known as *plug-ins,* for InDesign that extend its capabilities.

See Chapter 36 and this book's companion Web site `www.INDDcentral.com` for comprehensive coverage of plug-ins.

Working with Fonts

Fonts, traditionally known as *typefaces,* are a collection of characters that share a similar look. Fonts usually include several variations such as bold and italic. The electronic files that make up fonts are managed by your operating system or other utilities, not by InDesign. InDesign doesn't come with fonts and it doesn't manage fonts. So when you're talking about fonts, you're talking about *foundries* (companies that design and distribute fonts), Mac OS and Windows features, and third-party utilities and applications that manage fonts.

Procuring fonts

No matter what type of design or publishing you're doing, you'll need — or you'll eventually acquire — lots of fonts. You can never have enough, and there are so many interesting yet useful ones. There are five ways to get fonts: You can create your own, get them free with applications, acquire them through colleagues, purchase them, or translate them from one platform to another.

✦ **Created fonts:** The FontLab program for Windows and Macs lets you create fonts in all popular font formats, for both Windows and Mac users. And although it hasn't been updated in years, Macromedia Fontographer was long the premier tool for creating fonts, as well as for adding or modifying characters in existing fonts (such as adding the euro currency symbol [€] to older fonts). If you happen to still own a copy, note that Fontographer hasn't been updated for Windows 2000, Windows XP, or Mac OS X, but it will run under those operating systems (Windows 2000 and XP users should read the technical notes at `www.macromedia.com/software/fontographer`; Mac OS X users should note that Fontographer will run under Classic mode).

✦ **Free fonts:** More and more programs come with free fonts (all the image-editing and illustration programs mentioned earlier do, for example). In addition, you can download free fonts from many Web sites. I list some popular sources at `www.INDDcentral.com`. Or just type **free fonts** into a search engine such as Google (`www.google.com`) and it's a free-for-all. Although this is an inexpensive way to build a font collection, it may not provide all the fonts you need. The quality can vary, and service bureaus may balk at using some of these fonts, because they don't come from a source they know. For a variety of technical and aesthetic reasons, it is generally prudent to avoid substituting free fonts for their similar-looking, more costly, and usually more carefully created cousins from Adobe, Bitstream, or Agfa Monotype and the like. Your files may have bad reflow or even fail to output at all.

✦ **Acquired fonts:** Often, people will e-mail fonts with a file they want you to edit. And most people will send you fonts upon request, because the files are small and easily portable. In most cases, this is in violation of the font's license agreement, so it isn't a good way to build a font library. Providing fonts to a service bureau for one-time output is usually okay, but "acquiring" fonts is generally a poor — even illegal — way to build a font collection.

✦ **Purchased fonts:** Although you can go into a computer store and purchase font CDs, the most convenient method is to buy them online. You can do everything from purchasing base collections of fonts to get you started to buying a single font you need to work on a client's document. Good sites include `www.adobe.com`, `www.fonts.com`, `www.fontsite.com`, `www.itcfonts.com`, and `www.myfonts.com`. All five sites are worth visiting to learn about and explore typography.

✦ **Translated fonts:** Although major font houses offer Mac and Windows versions of their fonts, many free and low-price fonts come only in one version of the other. Cross-platform publishers need to have the same fonts on both platforms, and to do so, Acute Systems offers the $45 CrossFont, a Windows program that translates TrueType and PostScript fonts bidirectionally between Mac and Windows. FontLab offers TransType, a $97 Mac program that converts fonts across platforms, as well as from TrueType to PostScript or vice versa. And UniDoc Systems offers the $50 Truekeys to convert East Asian TrueType fonts between Mac and Windows.

TrueType, OpenType, or PostScript?

The most basic question about fonts usually is whether you should use TrueType, OpenType, or PostScript fonts. The answer depends on the work you do. If you produce newsletters, magazines, ads, or brochures that you output on a typesetter or imagesetter, use PostScript, because PostScript is the standard format on these devices. If your final output is to a laser or ink-jet printer, TrueType is probably the better bet, because it prints faster in most cases, especially if you print to a non-PostScript printer. However, you don't have to use one font format exclusively: OpenType is increasingly popular, since it is a merger of PostScript and TrueType. But make sure your service bureau can work with OpenType fonts before using them. Follow these guidelines when choosing which font formats to use:

✦ If you see a TrueType typeface that you want to use in your typeset document, use it. The Mac and Windows operating systems automatically convert TrueType fonts into PostScript format when printing to a PostScript device (or to a file designated for use by a PostScript device). The drawback is that this conversion process may make your files larger because the computer must download the converted TrueType font file into your document.

✦ But if you're sending files to a service bureau for output, don't use TrueType fonts. Stay all-PostScript. Similarly, if you're outputting to the Acrobat portable document format (PDF), either for prepress or electronic distribution, avoid using TrueType fonts. You cannot reliably embed TrueType fonts in PDF files.

✦ Conversely, if you have PostScript typefaces, there's no reason to give them up if you switch to TrueType. On a PostScript printer, you can use both formats. On other printers, all you need is a program such as the free Adobe Type Manager Light for Windows to make the outlines of the letters appear smooth when they print. Mac OS X does this conversion automatically.

Don't base decisions about whether to use TrueType or PostScript fonts on assumptions about quality. Both technologies provide excellent results, so any quality differences are due to the font manufacturer's standards. If you purchase typefaces from recognized companies, you don't need to worry. (Many smaller companies produce high-quality fonts as well.)

There's a new format slowly coming into use called OpenType, which essentially is a merger of the TrueType and PostScript standards. Before using these fonts, make sure your service bureau or imagesetter can handle them. Mac OS X, Windows 2000, and Windows XP all support them, as do current versions of font managers. In a few years, they'll be normal and supported by newer equipment, but it generally takes several years for new technologies to be widely deployed, so check first. InDesign supports these fonts, including their special capabilities such as access to more special characters and international characters.

A book such as the *Adobe Type Library Reference Book,* available from www.adobe.com, shows printed samples of hundreds of typefaces. You can use this kind of book to select a typeface for a specific job, then you can purchase the font. This can save you hours in sifting through your fonts and poring over Web pages to find the typeface you want to use.

Go to www.INDDcentral.com for quick links to font sources and other font resources.

Installing fonts through the operating system

When you get a font on your computer, you need to install it so applications such as InDesign can recognize it — and let you use it. The procedures are different depending on your operating system and whether you're using a font manager.

Macintosh fonts

In Mac OS X, fonts can exist in several places:

✦ **Fonts folder in the Library folder (/Library/Fonts/):** This is where you should place fonts that you want all users to have access to. Just drag them in, whether PostScript, TrueType, or Open Type.

✦ **Fonts folder in the user's Home folder's Library folder (/Users/[your user name]/Library/Fonts/):** Any fonts dragged here will be available only to that user.

✦ **Fonts folder in the System folder's Library folder (/System/Library/Fonts/):** This is where Apple places the default fonts for Mac OS X applications. You can add fonts here as well by dragging them, but I recommend you leave this folder alone.

Any fonts installed in the Mac OS X folders will not be available to Mac OS 9 applications. You need to also maintain fonts in the System Folder's Fonts folder — note that the Mac OS 9 folder name is System Folder while the Mac OS X folder name is simply System — or use a Mac OS 9 font manager such as Adobe Type Manager.

If you use a third-party font manager such as DiamondSoft's Font Reserve or Extensis's Suitcase, your fonts can be installed anywhere as long as you have told the font manager where they are stored. These programs can autoactivate fonts as needed for both Mac OS X and Mac OS 9 applications, and I strongly recommend you invest in one. (Note that Adobe has no plans to release a Mac OS X version of Adobe Type Manager or Adobe Type Reunion.)

Another source of confusion for new Mac OS X users is its nonsupport of Multiple Masters PostScript fonts. The Multiple Masters format lets programs modify fonts on the fly, such as creating a semibold version from a bold typeface. But the format never took off or got widespread adoption. So Mac OS X is essentially killing off the format. That means that Mac OS 9 applications running under Mac OS X can use Multiple Masters fonts, but native Mac OS X applications like InDesign CS cannot. That can cause problems when opening older InDesign documents with Multiple Masters fonts in InDesign CS. So, you'll need to replace the Multiple Masters fonts with PostScript or OpenType fonts. If you created instances of Multiple Masters fonts — such as a semibold — don't worry: When those instances are saved or exported as their own font files, they're no longer Multiple Masters fonts and should work just fine under Mac OS X.

Note

When you install Mac fonts, make sure you install both the screen fonts and the printer fonts for each PostScript font. You may have a *font suitcase* — a special font file — with several screen fonts for your PostScript font, or you may have separate files for each screen font, depending on which option the company decided to use. OpenType and TrueType fonts don't come in several files — all variants are in one suitcase. Also, the same single OpenType suitcase file will work for both Mac OS X and Windows 2000 and XP, so there is no need to purchase separate Mac and PC versions of an OpenType font.

Windows fonts

You can add TrueType fonts to Windows through the Fonts control panel. PostScript fonts, however, require a font manager such as Font Reserve, ATM Light or Deluxe, or Suitcase.

To add TrueType fonts to Windows:

1. **Choose Start ➪ Settings ➪ Control Panel to open the Control Panel folder, and then double-click the Fonts folder.**

2. **Choose File ➪ Install New Font to get the Add Fonts dialog box shown in Figure 38-1.**

3. **Navigate the dialog box using the Folders and Drives scroll lists to get to the folder or disk that has the TrueType fonts you want to install.**

   A list of fonts will appear in the dialog box.

4. **Select the fonts to install and click OK.**

Figure 38-1: The Fonts window for adding TrueType fonts in Windows.

Using a font manager and font utilities

Although you can manage fonts to a certain extent through the operating system, I highly recommend that you use a font manager. With a font manager, you can control precisely which fonts are active at any one time. This is important because many different versions and kinds (PostScript, TrueType, and OpenType) of fonts exist with the same name — and simply using any font with the same name is not okay. For example, if you use TrueType Helvetica instead of PostScript Helvetica, the text in the document may reflow, altering the design and even cutting off text. In addition to a font manager, most Windows users will need the free Adobe ATM Light for viewing PostScript fonts on-screen and most Mac users will want a font menu manager.

Using font managers

With a font manager such as DiamondSoft Font Reserve, Extensis Suitcase, or Adobe ATM Deluxe (Windows-only), you can see more information about fonts and activate fonts on the fly without restarting programs. My favorite, in terms of compatibility and features, is Font Reserve. On the Mac, the drag-and-drop interface makes it easy to install and export fonts; on Windows, you can easily create a library of all the TrueType, PostScript, and OpenType fonts on your system. On both platforms, Font Reserve provides features such as on-screen previews, sample printing, character maps, and sets for grouping fonts for projects (see Figure 38-2).

Figure 38-2: Font Reserve provides an intuitive interface for installing fonts, activating fonts on the fly, previewing fonts, and creating font sets.

Because Extensis Suitcase was the first popular font manager, many Mac OS and Windows users are accustomed to using it and prefer to stick with it. That's fine, too.

Using ATM Light in Windows

A potentially confusing issue with Windows font managers is that a necessary control panel—ATM Light—often masquerades as the font manager ATM Deluxe. That's not a problem if you're using ATM Deluxe in Windows, but it is if you use another font manager. The reason is that no matter what font manager you use, you need the ATM Light control panel to render PostScript fonts on-screen for Windows. ATM Light comes with many programs and is available from www.adobe.com.

Although ATM Deluxe incorporates ATM Light, you don't need it—and in fact, you can't use it—if you're using another font manager or are installing fonts through the operating system. If you're using Suitcase or Font Reserve, you can't simply disable the Deluxe features of ATM Deluxe. To prevent conflicts, you need to remove ATM Deluxe and replace it with ATM Light.

Summary

Modern computers are typically well-equipped for publishers. Boosting memory and hard drive size are typically the only changes users need to make.

Publishers will want several peripherals, either attached to their computer or available on the network, including a PostScript printer for high-volume output, a low-cost ink-jet printer for basic color proofing, and a scanner for image capture — as well as a fast Internet connection.

Font management software is a must for Mac and Windows users. Both Extensis Suitcase and DiamondSoft Font Reserve can do the job. On Windows, Adobe Type Manager also fits the need.

✦　　✦　　✦

Layout Theory and Practice

✦　✦　✦　✦

In This Chapter

Understanding layout terms

Knowing the seven basic rules of good design

Getting started

Imitating and creating good designs

✦　✦　✦　✦

Many InDesign users are not trained graphic designers — they're administrators, hobbyists, entrepreneurs, or volunteers who have something to say. Armed with the best layout and typography tool in the world, they sometimes forget that they're not, in fact, armed with the training (and sometimes the talent) that producing clear, interesting publications requires. That's okay. A quick review of standard layout terminology and design rules helps any user get started in the right direction. Then, by dissecting other people's designs and messages, you can learn to plan and create publications that clarify and reinforce your message. Armed with this background in layout and design, you can step into the world of InDesign and have at it.

Layout Terms

Document layout — the placement of text, images, and other items on a page — involves many elements. To communicate effectively with your peers and service providers, it helps to understand layout terminology, much of which is rooted in printing and production history. A brief primer on layout terms follows.

Layout tools

When a graphic designer creates a layout, she uses the following tools — either on paper or through software such as InDesign:

　✦ **Grid:** The basic layout design of a publication. It includes standard positions of folios, text, graphics, bylines, and headlines as shown in Figure 39-1. A layout artist modifies the grid when necessary. Grids also are called *templates*.

Figure 39-1: This master-page template contains placeholders
for the logos, headlines, and artwork for the first pages
(whether starting on the left or right) of its reports articles.
A similar master page exists for the interior reports pages.

✦ **Dummy:** A rough sketch of the layout of a particular story.

✦ **Guidelines:** Lines that show the standard placement of columns and margins in the grid. In most layout programs, guidelines are nonprinting lines that you can use to ensure that elements align.

✦ **Overlay:** A piece of transparent paper or film laid over a layout board. On the overlay, the artist can indicate screens in a different color or overprinted material such as text or graphics. InDesign has the electronic equivalents of overlays: layers (Window ➪ Layers or F7).

✦ **Knockout:** When one element cuts out the part of another element that it overlaps, a designer would say that one element *knocks out* the other or that one element is *knocked out of* the other. In either phrasing, it means the first element covers up the part of the other element under it. This differs from overlaying the other element, because in an overlay, both elements are visible (as in a superimposed image).

✦ **Galleys:** Single columns of type that are not laid out in any sort of printed-page format. In the past, publishers used galleys to check for proper hyphen-ation and to proof for errors. Galleys also were sent to authors for proofreading so that corrections could be made before the text was laid out. Galleys have all but disappeared from publishing, because most people now proofread on the first draft of page layouts, instead of making the intermedi-ate step of proofreading on galleys.

Design elements

Most publications, regardless of size and style, consist of the same basic design elements: columns, margins, frames, and so on. Take a look at what you'll be dealing with:

✦ **Column:** A block of text.

✦ **Gutter:** The space between columns that are placed side by side. (In newspapers and magazines, gutter space is usually 1 or 2 picas.)

✦ **Margin:** The space between the edge of a page and the nearest standard block of text. Some designers allow text or graphics to intrude into the margin for visual effect.

✦ **Bleed:** A graphic element or block of color that extends to the trimmed edge of the page.

✦ **Wrap:** When text follows the contours of an obstructing element such as a graphic or other text. The column margins are altered so that the column text wraps around the intruding graphic or text instead of being overprinted by the intruding element. Depending on what the text wraps around and the capabilities of the layout program, a wrap can be rectangular, polygonal, curved, or irregular. InDesign can wrap text around any shape, including a picture's clipping path, as shown in Figure 39-2.

Figure 39-2: InDesign lets you easily wrap text around the contours of images.

✦ **Folio:** The page number and identifying material (such as the publication name or month) that appears at the bottom or top of every page.

✦ **White space:** The part of the page left empty to create contrast with the text and graphics. White space provides visual relief and emphasizes the text and graphics.

✦ **Boxes:** The frames that hold layout elements (text, graphics, and blocks of color) on a page. Using a mouse, you can delete, copy, resize, reshape, or otherwise manipulate boxes in your layout.

✦ **Strokes:** The ruling lines around boxes that hold layout elements.

✦ **Template:** By filling a project with empty boxes and defining style tags in advance, you can use the resulting template repeatedly to create projects that use the same boxes and styles.

Image manipulation

Page-layout programs make it easy for you to decide which parts of an image to display and at what size. Although InDesign doesn't provide the power of a dedicated illustration program such as Adobe Illustrator, you can perform some special effects as well:

✦ **Cropping:** Selecting a part of an image for use on the page.

✦ **Sizing (scaling):** Determining how much to reduce or enlarge the image (or part of the image). With layout programs, you often can distort an image by sizing it differently horizontally and vertically, which creates special effects such as compressing or stretching an image.

✦ **Reversing:** Also called *inverting* in some programs, reversing exchanges the black and white portions of an image. This effect is similar to creating a photographic negative.

✦ **Special effects:** *Flipping* (mirroring) and *skewing* (slanting) are other popular design effects. InDesign even lets you apply color to some types of grayscale images.

Seven Basic Rules of Good Design

Think about it: Many documents are offputting. What makes them that way, and how do you build a layout that is inviting? Figure 39-3 shows two pages that contain the same information but use different layouts. The page on the left has body text set close to the headline. The leading is tight, and except for a spot around the illustration, the white space is in short supply. Notice how the page on the right has a lighter, more vibrant look. Also note the variety of sizes, the use of generous margins, and a few strategic elements that don't quite align with the others (providing something for the eye to follow). Which page are you more inclined to read?

Figure 39-3: The page on the left is clean but dull—even the image adds little visual interest. The page on the right uses different typefaces, alignment, color, and text wraps to create interest and reinforce the subject matter without getting too busy.

If you're a trained graphic designer, you already know the basics. You can immediately put InDesign to use, creating effective layouts. But if you're new to the field of graphic design, try keeping the following seven basic rules in mind as you begin learning about layout.

Rule #1: Keep an idea file

As you read magazines, books, newspapers, annual reports, ads, and brochures, save page layouts you like and dislike. Keep these layouts—good and bad—in a file, along with notes to yourself about which aspects of the layout work well and which work poorly. As you build your layout file, you educate yourself about layout basics.

Rule #2: Plan your document

It sounds corny, but it's true: Laying out a document is a lot like taking a journey. If you know where you're headed, it's much easier to find your way. Because InDesign makes it easy to experiment as you design a document, it's also easy to end up with a messy conglomeration of text and images. You can avoid this pitfall by knowing ahead of time what you're trying to accomplish with the document's layout. Don't be afraid of those old low-tech tools—pencil and paper.

Rule #3: Keep it simple

When it comes to page layout, simple is better. Even the most experienced, trained graphic designers can tell you that this rule applies at least 99 percent of the time. If you're just beginning to learn how to lay out pages, you'll make far fewer design mistakes if you follow this rule. Regardless of the application, simple layouts are appealing in their crispness, their readability, and their straightforward, no-gimmicks approach.

Rule #4: Leave some white space

Pages that are crammed full of text and pictures tend to be unappealing—meaning that the average, busy reader is likely to skip them. Keep some space between text columns and headlines and between page edges and layout elements. This white space is refreshing and encourages the reader to spend some time on the page. Regardless of the particular document type, readers always appreciate having a place on every page to rest their eyes, a place that offers an oasis in a sea of ink.

Rule #5: Don't use every bell and whistle

InDesign is powerful, yes, but that doesn't mean that it's necessarily a good idea to push the program to its limits at all times. You can, for example, lay out a page with 30 columns of text, but would you want to try reading such a page? With InDesign, you can achieve an amazing number of special effects:

✦ Stretch, condense, and scale type

✦ Create boxes of almost any shape, and then fill and frame them

✦ Add graphics and lines (with custom dash or stripe patterns)

✦ Bleed photos and artwork off the edge of the page

✦ Flow text along a path, wrap text around all sides of any shape

✦ Add colors and create a variety of vignettes (called *blends* and *gradients*)

✦ Rotate and skew text and graphics

Using all these effects at once, however, can overwhelm readers and cause them to miss any message you're trying to convey Conveying a message with words and images is usually the most important task of the design and typography. A good rule: Use no more than three special typographic or design effects per two-page spread.

Rule #6: Make it look like what it is

Lay out the document so that someone looking at it can get an idea of what it is. This sounds like a common-sense rule, but you'd be surprised at how often this rule is broken. If you're laying out an ad for a product, make sure the layout *looks* like an ad, not like a technical brochure. See Figure 39-4 for a sidebar that ended up looking like an ad.

Figure 39-4: There's nothing wrong with this design — except that it's supposed to be a sidebar, not an ad. Placed on a crowded page, its intent was lost on readers.

Rule #7: Don't break Rule #6

Creativity is okay — and InDesign helps you express your layout ideas creatively — but unless you know what you're doing, don't get carried away. If you *are* laying out a technical brochure, for example, don't make it look like a display ad unless you understand that this may confuse readers, and you're doing it for a compelling reason.

Getting Started

After you come up with a design, expect it to evolve over time. Styles change, and so does your content. So don't be afraid to try different techniques over the months and years — just make sure that you're not making changes willy-nilly, for change's sake.

The key to a successful layout is planning, a rule that matches the InDesign approach to design. You don't just start doing a layout in InDesign. Instead, you start building the foundation of your document — the page size and columns, the paragraph and character styles, the standard elements such as page numbers and logos — to serve as a receptacle for the content. The idea is that most content you create is a variation on a theme. For example, if you produce a magazine, each issue is different, but the basic design structure is the same from month to month. Rather than start each month from scratch, you start with a template and modify it each month as necessary. The same approach works for newspapers, catalogs, brochures, newsletters, and books.

Visualizing your layout

Even before you build your basic structure, you need a mental image of what your document will be. Have no fear — nothing is cast in stone. If you change your mind as you work on your first document, you can modify your structure. Having an initial structure in mind before starting, however, helps immensely.

Sketching your layout on paper

How do you start to develop a layout plan? If you're still thinking about what the pages should look like, you can develop some more-specific ideas by spending a few minutes sketching out the layout before you sit down to produce the document on the computer.

Using the dummy approach

Let's say you want to create an eight-page newsletter that has standard, 8½-by-11-inch pages. One way to do this is to create a dummy document, a valuable layout-planning aid. Figure 39-5 shows a sample dummy — the cover and the first two pages.

Here's how to create a dummy:

1. **Take two sheets of blank, 8½-by-11-inch paper, aligning one on top of the other, and folding them in half across the width of the paper.**

   This technique gives you a miniature version of your eight-page newsletter.

2. **Use a pencil to sketch the dummy's masthead, the cover art and/or stories, and the running headers or footers for each page.**

3. **Form an idea about how wide you want the top, side, and bottom margins to be, and mark them on the pages.**

4. **Indicate which pictures and stories go on each page.**

   Of course, because you will be using InDesign to format the document, you can make changes right up to the point when you produce camera-ready pages.

Figure 39-5: A pencil-sketch dummy lets you think through the basic structure quickly and easily.

Here are some conventions to remember as you make your sketches:

✦ A down arrow means the story continues on another page, while a # symbol means the story ends.

✦ Horizontal lines usually indicate titles, bylines, and other such specific text elements, while vertical lines indicate a column of text.

✦ A box with an *X* through it indicates a picture or photo.

✦ The abbreviation *pq* means a pull-quote — text that is taken from the article and put in a box or other shape to draw attention, similar to a photo.

✦ A *screen* is a background of color or gray ink.

You can see from Figure 39-5 that the basic layout structure is three columns, with a self-contained front page that has a small table of contents and interior pages that put the *masthead* (the list of staff) and a viewpoint column on the second page. The third page has two stories, which of course may not start exactly where indicated on the sketch. The point is, merely, that multiple stories can appear on a page.

Taking the next step

You should find all this planning—which actually doesn't take that much time in relation to the other publishing tasks involved—to be time well spent. The process of sketching out the layout helps clarify your thoughts about the basic layout of your document. You can make preliminary decisions about such things as where to put each illustration and section of text on a page, how many columns of text to use, and whether to use any repeating elements (such as headers and footers).

Sketching your layout in InDesign

If you're already comfortable using InDesign, you may decide to forgo the paper-and-pencil sketching of a new document and use InDesign to do the rough design instead. The obvious advantages to this approach are as follows:

✦ **You can experiment with different approaches.** When a document has a set number of text and graphic elements, you can use InDesign to make a series of sketches of the document. If you like, you can save each sketch as a separate file with a distinct filename. In each sketch, you can use different element positioning, type styles, masthead placement, and so on. Then you can print a copy of each file and use the copies to assist you in finalizing the look of the layout.

✦ **You can print thumbnail views.** If you're considering many different layout possibilities, you can develop them quickly in InDesign and then print the series in *thumbnail* (miniature) size (select File ➪ Print, and then check the Thumbnails box in the Setup pane's Options section, as shown in Figure 39-6). You can also set the number of thumbnails per page using the Per Page pop-up menu. Seeing the pages in thumbnail view makes it easier to evaluate the overall balance between page elements, because you aren't distracted by the text or the graphics in such a reduced view.

✦ **You can get your client's approval.** Printed InDesign copies of rough sketches have a cleaner look, which is especially helpful if you're designing a layout for a client. The advantage to presenting rough sketches that look more "final" is that it tends to make the client approval process go more smoothly, and it can make it easier for you to sell the client on your design. At the same time, slick-looking rough drafts do have a disadvantage: They make it more difficult for clients to understand that what they're seeing is just a rough draft and not a final copy.

Figure 39-6: Checking Thumbnails in the Setup pane of the Print dialog box lets you print miniature versions of your pages.

Imitating and Creating Good Designs

Imitation is the sincerest form of flattery, and as long as you don't cross the line into blatant copying, go ahead and flatter as many people as you can. Go to the newsstand and thumb through a bunch of magazines. (But buy just the ones you really like.) Get a couple of colleagues — or just consult the other coffee lovers in line with you — and look through designs together. Talk about what you like, what you don't like, and — most important — *why* you react the way you do.

You can call this flower-power consciousness-raising. Or you can call it being a copycat. The point is, it's the best way to learn good design. As with any good design ideas, the ones here are based on years of experience and, of course, honest-to-goodness pilfering of other people's good work.

Avoiding formulas

Although I say to steal ideas and follow the rules, I don't mean for you to flat-out copy other designs, making yours look *exactly* like someone else's. Your designs should elucidate *your* message — not somebody else's.

Stealing from great artists

A couple more clichés to drive home the point: Good writers read good writers. (I'm sure someone has said, "Good designers study good designers," but this hasn't gotten enough buzz to become a cliché yet.) Good artists imitate; great artists steal.

Avoiding design recipes

Don't confuse examples of good design with recipes. I don't pretend to be Picasso or even Haring. My designs (and my colleagues' designs) might make no sense for your documents. After all, you need to make sure the designs you produce meet several needs:

✦ Your sense of aesthetics

✦ The requirements of the content being presented

✦ The image you or your organization wants to convey

✦ The financial limitations you're working under (We'd all love to do everything in full, glorious color, but until money comes out of printers without resulting in jail terms, most people do have some concerns about costs.)

The design of the ad mockup in Figure 39-7 works well for the company because the simple black-and-white graphic communicates a 3-D stage. Plus, the company can rotate out the center text each month to sell whatever is hot that month. But if a new drugstore came to town and asked a designer to adapt the design of this ad for its grand opening, the designer would have to refuse — it's just the wrong approach for a grand opening.

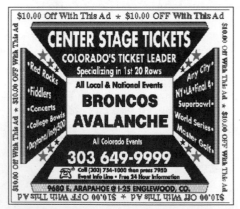

Figure 39-7: The design of this ad works well for its original content, but it is not likely to adapt well to another type of business.

Learning to improvise

Use design samples as starting points, and don't confuse the techniques and fundamental principles they illustrate with the implementation I happened to choose for this particular example. You could use those same techniques and fundamental principles and come up with completely different designs for your projects. Great artists may steal, but they also improvise.

Laying out ads and circulars

The elements of ads, circulars (fliers), and other such sales- and marketing-oriented materials are a critical type of publication, because they must work the first time. You may be willing to put up with a design you don't care for in a newsletter that contains information you find valuable. But an ad has the burden of needing to attract your attention, holding you long enough to deliver its message, and letting you go with a favorable impression. In the following sections, I show you three ads to identify the techniques they use to accomplish these goals. Whether it's an ad, a report cover, a prospectus, a pamphlet, or another such publication, these techniques apply.

An airline ad mockup

Figure 39-8 shows an ad mockup for a fictitious airline. Notice the following about its design:

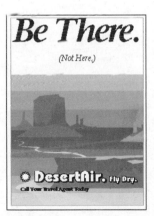

Figure 39-8: A simple ad with a simple message deserves a simple treatment to attract attention. But notice that simple does not mean simplistic — every element has a character of its own.

✦ **The large type:** This is kerned so that the spacing between each pair of characters is the same — just at the point of touching.

✦ **The small type:** This forces the eye to take a look, because of the contrast with the big type above and all the space on either side. This use of contrast is a good way to get attention. Never underestimate the power of type. It is as important as graphics in garnering attention and conveying both the substance and the nuances of the message.

✦ **The airline logo:** This uses reverse-video and shadow effects on a fairly common font (Bauhaus). Notice the sun symbol to the logo's left: That's a symbol in the Zapf Dingbats font. The use of symbols really helps establish a logo as a logo, rather than just a bunch of letters. Also notice the use of a catchphrase (also called a *tag line*) in the same font as the logo. You would do this for a catchphrase that you plan to use in several places. It becomes an extension of the logo. (The desert tableau is a color image, and in color the text is very striking against the colors; in black-and-white, it loses a little of that zing.)

✦ **White space:** Blank areas provide a visually calm port in a storm of images and text. Be sure to provide these resting spots in all your work.

A restaurant ad mockup

The ad mockup in Figure 39-9, for a seafood restaurant, shows a tighter interplay of text and graphics. It also shows, although not at first glance, the power of InDesign's graphics-manipulation tools. Here's what to look for:

Figure 39-9: The interplay between the text and graphics in this ad reinforces the message.

✦ **The schools of fish:** They're in glorious color, although you can't see that in black and white, and there are really only three fish in the ad. I used the copy function in InDesign to create the schools. And to make sure that they didn't look like clones, I used the rotate and skew tools to make each cloned fish slightly different from the others. I used only a very slight skew, less than 5 percent; the rotation accounts for most of the difference in the fishes' appearance. The lesson: Don't forget to use basic tools such as rotation and copying.

✦ **The descriptive text:** The text describing all the sumptuous seafood options ("Atlantic cod. Alaska salmon.") is wrapped around the pictures of fish, using InDesign's Bézier picture box to hold the pictures, combined with the ability to have text wrap around both sides of an image.

✦ **The headlines:** Can you tell what this ad is selling? Why, fresh fish, of course! The repetitive use of the text reinforces the message. Placing the repeating text in different positions among the fish makes sure it doesn't look repetitive. (Predictability is a major reason that repetition is boring, so this design finds a way to repeat without being boring.)

✦ **The tag line:** This added repetition of the words *Fresh Fish* reinforces the primary message. In the case of this ad, there's no large text identifying the restaurant (it's in the body text), but this tag line is one the restaurant uses a lot, so the ad can get away with the low-key treatment of the restaurant's name — just as if an ad said only "Have it your way," you'd probably think of Burger King, while "Just do it!" would evoke Nike.

✦ **Italics:** All the text here, except the list of locations at the bottom, is in italic, which is unusual. But the fluidity of italics works well with the fish theme (underwater, get it?), and by making the text large enough and the layout uncluttered, it works.

✦ **Going beyond the margins:** The fish swim past the margins on the page, which makes the page feel less boxed-in. Overstepping margins to provide a feeling of flexibility and give the eye something unusual to notice is often a good idea.

A public service announcement

Let's take a look at one more ad. This one is not a full page. It's the kind of ad you'd probably run in an in-house publication: what magazines call a PSA (short for *public service announcement*). It's the type of thing you can easily put together using clip art and basic typefaces when you have a hole to fill or need to make an announcement or advertisement for your organization (see Figure 39-10). Notice the following:

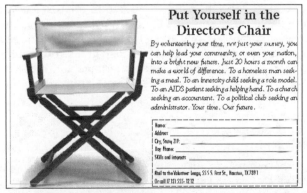

Figure 39-10: A public service announcement designed for black-and-white reproduction.

✦ **The simple graphic:** This simple graphic works well in black-and-white. Photos can be very effective in catching attention — they scream "real!" The simple composition is also pleasing. You'll find many such images in clip-art libraries.

✦ **The message:** Simple text with a simple message that ties into the image — that's the ticket.

✦ **The headline:** A loud, bold title would have competed with the photo. This one's easy to read, but it doesn't fight for attention. If you see the photo and stop, you'll see the headline, and that's all that's required. The centering makes sure that it's clear the headline goes with the text below. It also follows the centered shape of the chair.

✦ **The alignment:** The more ways things line up, the more distracting a layout can be, so try to use only one or two alignments. A left alignment might have worked here, but then the symmetry of the chair would not have been picked up in the rest of the ad — and such reuse of basic visual themes is a hallmark of pleasing design. People just get all warm and fuzzy with such continuity.

✦ **The justified text:** The text is short, readable, and justified. Although having justified text may seem to violate the minimal-alignment rule, the fact is that centered text is rarely easy to read if there're more than a few lines of it. Having the text justified keeps the symmetry of the centered text, because the right and left margins in justified text are symmetrical.

✦ **The dashed lines:** We all know what a dashed line means. The ad practically screams, "Cut me out!" To get a dashed box, just use one of InDesign's box tools and change the frame style to a dashed one. To reinforce the "Cut me out!" message, you could add a pair of scissors (from a symbols font or from clip art) along a top corner of the dashed box.

✦ **The coupon:** In the box is the coupon you're hoping people will fill out. The font here is different (a condensed sans serif, compared to the text's normal serif). The font reinforces that it is a separate element. You want the readers to think of the coupon as separate, so they know that it's okay to remove it from the rest of the ad. The use of a condensed font also gives you more room for the information you want people to fill in. The underlines are right-aligned tabs using an underline leader. That's the simplest way to create fill-in-the-blank lines.

Creating newsletters

Quintessentially, publishing newsletters and magazines represents the focus of page-layout programs, even though InDesign is also great for a whole range of documents, including ads, reports, and catalogs. But when you think publishing, you think newsletters and magazines. So, let's spend a little time going over ways of making top-notch newsletters and magazines, without hiring a huge crew of designers.

Intentional evolution

Newsletters and magazines generally redesign themselves every couple years. The redesign might be subtle, or it might be extreme. But it happens. Why? Because the new art director or publisher wants to put his imprint on the publication, you might say.

Well, that's partially true, but the real reason is more basic: If you don't revisit your look every once in a while, you appear stale, and people will think you're lazy or don't care about them. People do it for their personal appearance, too. (Want proof? Take a look at a snapshot of yourself from five years ago.)

The opposite can also happen: The content changes over time but the design and "image" goals do not. When the content changes but the image goals don't, the situation is a little trickier, because you need to update the design to accommodate the new content (such as increased use of profiles, short stories, gossip and rumors, question-and-answer interviews, and so on) while still reflecting the feel of the old design. For examples of what I mean, take a look at current issues of *The New York Times, The Wall Street Journal, Business Week, Time,* or *Newsweek.* Then compare them with issues from five years ago. You'll find a different look and mix of content, but the same overall feel.

Understanding newsletter basics

A newsletter's main goal is to provide information. So, the focus should be on text: how to make it readable, how to call attention to it, and how to make sure the reader knows where all relevant content is. Here are some basic newsletter design issues to consider:

✦ **Column width:** Most newsletters are two or three columns wide. A three-column format gives you more flexibility, because you can have graphics of three different sizes (one, two, and three columns wide), plus you can add sidebars and separate stories fairly easily to a page, because again there are multiple sizes to choose from. A two-column format is more straightforward, but it gives you fewer options. It's best for newsletters that are essentially sequential — without multiple stories and sidebars on a page or spread.

✦ **Page numbers and folios:** As always, make sure you add page numbers and an identifier of the publication (called a *folio*). Some include a corporate symbol after the page number, to add visual interest and reinforce the identity.

✦ **Body text:** The body text should use a very readable, straightforward font; examples include Caslon, Cheltenham, Concorde, Garamond, Janson Text, Minion, New Baskerville, and Stone Serif. Avoid Times and Times New Roman because they're so overused (consider instead variations such as Times Ten and Times Europa). A typical size for newsletters and magazines is 10 points with 13 points leading. Generally speaking, point size should range from 9 to 10 points (you can use half-point sizes), and leading from 10.5 to 13 points, with the most typical being 2 points more than the font size. Justified text is often used for an authoritative look and left-aligned text for a friendlier look.

✦ **Drop caps:** Using a drop cap is an effective way to alert the reader to the beginning of a new story—you can also use it for the beginning of the conclusion—as well as to provide a visual contrast on the page. Often, drop caps are in a different typeface (sometimes picking up the headline font) and color from the body text. Generally, you should boldface the drop cap, to make it more readable. (Otherwise, the drop cap looks wimpy, which is not what you want for such a big element.)

✦ **Headlines, kickers, and bylines:** The headline, the *kicker* (the type above it, also called a *slug line* for reasons that have nothing to do with gardening), and the byline are usually related. For example, the headline may reflect the body text (Minion Condensed Bold and Minion, respectively) and the kicker and byline may be from the same typeface (Helvetica Condensed Medium and Helvetica Light, respectively). The use of related typefaces provides consistency while still producing a subtle difference from the rest of the text.

Be careful when combining multiple fonts. If they don't work together, it can be a disaster. A rule of thumb is to restrict the number of fonts (not including variants such as boldface and small caps) to two per page. You can break this rule occasionally by using a font that has similarities to one of the other two.

✦ **Dingbats:** A nice touch is to end a story with a *dingbat* (publishing speak for a symbol). The dingbat might be as simple as a single character or the corporate logo—anything that reinforces the identity. Making a dingbat is easy: Just add the symbol after the last paragraph, either by putting a tab before it (and defining the tab in your text style to be flush right against the right margin, or using Shift+Tab to create a right-aligned tab) or an em space (Shift+ ⌘+M or Ctrl+Shift+M). Either way is fine for justified text. Pick one based on your preferences. But use only the em space if your text is not justified.

✦ **Sidebars:** You can make a sidebar or separate, minor story distinct by putting a shaded background behind it. Make sure you have a margin between the edge of the background and the text. You can also box a sidebar, with or without the background, using frames. Or you could just put a line above and below the background. Making sidebars have a different number of columns from the main text—for example, a two-column sidebar that is the width of one column of main text—also helps make the sidebar distinct from the surrounding text. (Obviously, you don't want column widths that are too narrow for easy readability, so if your sidebar column widths need to be the same as the main text's column widths, so be it.)

✦ **Pull quotes:** A pull quote is a great way to call out some interesting material in a story to attract readers' attention. Often, the style reflects the sidebars, including a shaded background or lines above and below. Any embellishments, such as dingbats, should help the text stand out while still providing continuity with the overall design. Pull quotes also help to break up long passages of text when you don't have an image to do so.

Working with magazines

Magazines are very similar to newsletters, except that they generally have color images, more graphics, a cover that has no stories on it, and a full-page (or larger) table of contents. Note that magazines usually are highly designed, so they often look very different from one another.

Creating tables of contents

Let's look first at a sample contents page from a magazine. So take the following techniques as starting points:

✦ **The logo:** This should be distinct and readable. Typically, the name is large and clear.

✦ **The banner:** The issue date and number is called a *banner*. There should usually be a generous amount of space so it isn't lost. Also, when you use a banner, make sure the text is bold; otherwise, it is can be hard to read.

✦ **Feature and column entries:** Magazines generally have *features* (longer articles that appear only once), along with *columns* (regular, short articles that appear in each issue, usually covering a certain topic). Label the content accordingly (for example, the columns might be called *Departments*).

✦ **Page numbers:** The use of large page numbers for the features reinforces that this is a table of contents. You might even use a different font for these page numbers. For departments, the page numbers might use the same font as the story titles, or use the same font that feature page numbers do if you use a different font for them. Either way, set them off from the text with an em space or by making them two-line drop caps.

✦ **Photo and graphic listings:** Putting a page number near any photo or graphic you have in your contents page is a good idea. If people are interested in the photo, they should be able to know where to find the associated article.

Formatting feature articles

An eye-catching design is critical to entice readers to sample a publication's contents. Most publications use a variety of tools — for example, InDesign, Adobe Illustrator, Macromedia FreeHand, and Adobe Photoshop, among others — to create visually rich pages. Feature articles showcase a magazine's many design approaches, because articles of that length give the designers the opportunity to use multiple techniques within the overall design framework.

Working with flexible grids

The magazine's design offers a flexible grid that allows different numbers of columns and column widths from feature to feature. By having a standard grid, the magazine's design director can be assured that the entire package will be cohesive.

By allowing individual designers options within that structure, appropriate creative flexibility is available to keep the reader engaged. Every standard element — body text, sidebars, screen images, diagrams, tables, and captions — must take up an integral number of columns, but the number per element is up to the designer.

You can also mix grids on a page. For example, the main text might follow a two-column grid. But the sidebar on the left-facing page might span all the columns in the grid, allowing for wider columns. Staying within the geometry of the grid, the designer can easily connect sidebars and graphics to related text while creating enough visual distinction. That's the beauty of having multiple grids to use in a layout.

Working with gatefolds

Every once in a while, you see a magazine that has an article with a foldout page. Called a *gatefold,* this kind of page requires some special work in your layout. To create a gatefold, you just add a page to the right of an existing right-hand page, making sure to add an extra page to the left of the next spread's existing left-hand page. (Chapter 5 covers how to use the Pages pane to create gatefolds.) That's the easy part. But there are three possible hazards:

✦ Although it appears on-screen as if the three pages are one long sheet of paper, in the actual magazine the far left page is a separate sheet of paper, while the two right pages are indeed one sheet of paper (folded where the line numbers are).

Tip   Be sure to leave sufficient space between the two sheets so text and images don't get swallowed up in the gutter.

✦ The folded-over page in a gatefold needs to be a bit narrower than the other pages. That's so when it's folded, it doesn't actually get so far into the gutter that it's bound shut into the magazine. Typically, keep an extra pica (⅙") on the outside edge of a gatefold's folded page.

✦ A gatefold must be at the beginning or end of a *form* (the sequence of pages printed and bound at a time on a printing press). That's because the extra-wide sheet must be the first or last sheet in the stack. (Magazines are composed of multiple forms, usually of 8, 16, 24, or 32 pages in length.)

Note   Check with your printer before using a gatefold. Also tell your service bureau you're outputting a gatefold, so the staff can ensure that the extra width doesn't inadvertently get cut off during output to film.

Doing other cool stuff

By combining various techniques, you can create some cool-looking stuff, for any of a variety of documents. Figure 39-11 shows some examples, which are described as follows:

Figure 39-11: Various special effects (from top to bottom, left to right).

✦ **Embossed text:** You can create various embossed-text effects by duplicating a text frame and making one slightly overlap the other. Then make the one on top white (or the paper color).

✦ **Textual graphics:** By duplicating a text frame several times and rotating each copy at a different angle, then applying different shades of gray to each, you can create a textual graphic. Here, each subsequent copy (moving from the bottom to the top of the arc) is rotated 10 degrees more than the previous and is 10 percent darker.

✦ **Stretched text:** Each letter in the word *Stretch* is set 10 percent wider than the previous letter, which gives it the effect of being stretched.

✦ **Spaced-out text:** By increasing the space between letters, you can space out text — an effect lots of designers use. You could put spaces (whether regular spaces, en spaces, or em spaces) between the letters, but by using the inter-character spacing controls (tracking), you ensure that the text is treated as one word and you make it easy to change your spacing settings. (It's easier to adjust the tracking than, say, to replace em spaces with en spaces between every character.)

✦ **Combining skew and shadow:** By combining the skew feature with the shadow feature for text, you can alter how a font looks to create logos. Here, I went a step further and mirrored the text block and changed its color to a shade of gray (by defining a tint of 39 percent black).

✦ **Tinting gray-scale images:** For gray-scale images, you can apply a color or tint to make them ghostly or subtle. It's a great way to mute a photo enough so that you can place text over it.

✦ **Cameo effects:** By using an oval or Bézier frame (with a very thick frame), you can create a cameo effect. It's a way to create a different type of shape or frame.

✦ **Altered opening-page text:** In some publications, the text on the opening page has a radically different style from the rest of the pages. Often, there is little text on the opening page, because the title and graphics usually take up much of the space. The text that's on the page is also treated graphically. One method is to have no paragraph breaks but to use a symbol instead to indicate paragraph breaks.

✦ **Embedded graphics:** Although drop caps are popular, you can also use an embedded graphic to accomplish the same purpose, or if you want the graphic to be dropped down into the text, you can place the graphic at the appropriate location and turn text wrap on.

✦ **Copying and flipping graphics:** By making a copy of the "Skew!" graphic and flipping it vertically, I made the text feel even more like a graphic.

Looking at common threads

Creative design means taking some risks, trying out new ideas. Because you can easily use InDesign to try out ideas — and to abandon those that just don't cut it — you should set aside some time in every project to play around with your design. Save a copy of your original, of course, and then see if you can discover some new approach that adds that special edge. While you're doing that, keep the following principles in mind:

✦ **Look intentional.** A former boss gave me some advice I'll never forget: Make sure you look intentional. Everything in your design should look like you wanted it to be there. If something looks odd, it should look as it were meant to look odd. If it looks intentional — whether or not it actually was! — the reader will think you put a lot of care and attention into your work, which enhances your credibility.

✦ **Have enough white space.** People need a visual resting place as they thumb through a publication. Give it to them. If you don't, they'll start to fall asleep, and they'll stop reading. If it's too *gray* (where everything looks like everything else) or too *busy* (where there are so many things to look at that readers don't know where to start), people will stop making the effort.

✦ **Make the text readable.** Remember that the basic point of publishing is to convey information. So don't make it difficult for the reader to get the information you're providing. Make sure the text is readable. Captions and headlines should be both informative and interesting. Make sure people can tell where a story continues and which stories are related to each other.

✦ **Use type creatively.** Fonts are neat and fun. Invest in several fonts, and use them creatively by applying effects such as small caps, colors, banner backgrounds, rotation, skewing, and mixed sizes (but not all at once, of course).

✦ **Use graphics effectively.** They should be fairly large—lots of small images are hard to look at—and should complement the rest of the layout.

✦ **Use visual themes.** Use a core set of fonts. If you use lines in one place, they may be effective in another. If you use boxes to separate some elements, don't use colored backgrounds to separate others. Instead, pick one approach and stick with it. There can be variances within the approaches, but by picking up variations of the same core approach, you keep your reader from getting distracted by visual chaos—yet you can still be creative.

✦ **Use color judiciously.** Color is expensive and can overwhelm the content. Used well, grays can provide as much visual interest as color. In fact, in something laden with color, a gray image will stand out as distinct and gain more attention than the surrounding color images.

Summary

As much as you might love the hands-on approach—getting in the software and creating those neat-looking columns and boldface type—you need to do your homework first. You need to understand the terminology and the tenets of good design, then you need to think through a project before you jump in and start laying it out. The more you know about design, the more quickly you can produce them with InDesign.

Sketches or rough proofs produced in InDesign help designers get buy-in on their approach. Whether you're showing ideas to a client, a board of directors, or a supervisor—or even reviewing them yourself—getting your different ideas on paper helps you decide on a direction. Then, when you get into InDesign, you can focus on perfecting the final look that speaks to *your* content—not someone else's.

✦   ✦   ✦

Typography
Theory and
Practice

In This Chapter

Understanding
typography terms

Learning about
typefaces

Identifying
typographic color
and typefaces

Selecting the right
typefaces

Desktop publishing has changed typography forever. In the old, old days, typefaces were available in a limited number, and those were available only in a limited number of sizes. You couldn't condense or expand them. And you certainly couldn't add drop shadows or make them print as outlines without hours of work in a darkroom. Desktop publishing has changed all that. By rendering type into a series of mathematical equations — curves and lines and angles — and manipulating that math with today's fast computers, type can be almost anything. In the early days of desktop publishing, that led to experimentation, often without the understanding of several hundred years of typographic traditions and that led to a lot of bad results. That was more than a decade ago, however, and good taste has prevailed. InDesign has very good typographic tools that can dramatically reduce typographic awkwardness. This chapter is your guide to typographic good taste.

While typography can be decorative, at its core it is the art of *not* calling attention to the typeface, but to the content itself, letting the shapes of the letters on a page serve as a carefully constructed, yet transparent guide for the reader's eye to follow.

Identifying Terms

Typography terms include words that describe the appearance of text in a document or on a computer screen. These terms refer to such aspects of typography as the size and style of the typeface used and the amount of space between lines, characters, and paragraphs.

Characters

✦ **Font:** This is a set of characters of a certain size, weight, and style (for example, 10-point Palatino Bold). This term is used often as a synonym for *typeface,* which is a set of characters of a certain style in all sizes, weights, and stylings (for example, Palatino).

✦ **Face:** A face is a combination of a weight and styling in all sizes of a font (for example, Palatino Bold Italic).

✦ **Font family:** This is a group of related typefaces (for example, the Franklin family includes Franklin Gothic, Franklin Heavy, and Franklin Compressed).

✦ **Weight:** This describes typeface thickness. Typical weights, from thinnest to thickest, are ultralight, light, book, medium, demibold, bold, heavy, ultrabold, and ultraheavy.

✦ **Style:** Type can have one of three basic stylings: Roman type is upright type; oblique type is the Roman type that has been mathematically slanted to give the appearance of italic type; and italic type is both slanted and curved (to appear more like calligraphy than Roman type). Type also may be expanded (widened), condensed (narrowed), or compressed (severely narrowed). See Figure 40-1 for examples of some of these stylings.

Syntax Medium

Syntax Medium Italic

Syntax Bold

Syntax Bold Italic

Syntax Black

Syntax Black Italic

Syntax Ultrablack

Syntax Ultrablack Italic

Figure 40-1: A sample sans serif typeface with different stylings.

Tip

Keep in mind that some of these type-style variations are created mathematically, while other fonts are created to appear a certain way. For example, you can compress a Roman font, but it won't be the same as the official, compressed version of the face and will most likely appear squished rather than compressed.

✦ **X-height:** This refers to the height of the average lowercase letter (this is based on the letter *x*). The greater the height, the bigger the letter looks when compared to letters in other typefaces that are the same point size but have a smaller X-height (see Figure 40-2).

Figure 40-2: The elements of a typeface.

✦ **Cap height:** Cap height is similar to X-height. It refers to the height dimension of the average uppercase letter (based on the letter *C*). (Refer to Figure 40-2.)

✦ **Descender:** In a letter such as *q,* the part of the letter that drops below the baseline is called a *descender*. (Refer to Figure 40-2.)

✦ **Ascender:** The part of a letter that extends above the X-height (as in the letter **b**) is called an ascender. (Refer to Figure 40-2.)

✦ **Serif:** This is a horizontal stroke used to give letters visual character. The strokes on the upper-left and bottom of the letter *p* in a typeface such as Times are serifs. The serif is usually designed to improve the horizontal flow of letters and words, making serif typefaces easier to read at small sizes and in long paragraphs. (Refer to Figure 40-2.)

✦ **Sans serif:** This means that a typeface does not use serifs. Helvetica is an example of a sans serif typeface.

✦ **Ligature:** A ligature is a set of joined characters, such as fi, fl, ffi, or ffl. The characters are joined because the characters' shapes almost blend together by default, so typographers of yore decided to make them blend together naturally.

Note

Automatic ligatures are available only for fonts that support them. OpenType fonts do, as do most PostScript and TrueType fonts created by professional type foundries. For InDesign to set ligatures for such fonts, make sure that Ligatures is checked in the Character pane's palette menu or that it is checked in the Basic Character Formats pane of the New Character Styles or Character Styles Options dialog boxes.

Typographic measurement units

✦ **Pica:** A pica is a measurement unit that specifies the width and depth of columns and pages. A pica is just a little less than ⅙ of an inch (most people round it up to an even ⅙ inch). All major desktop publishing applications — including QuarkXPress and InDesign — use the 6-picas-per-inch conversion ratio.

✦ **Point:** A point is a measurement used to specify type size and the space between lines. There are 12 points in a pica, so there are about 72.27 points to an inch. Although this is the historically accurate measurement, desktop publishing software generally drops the extra $^{27}\!/_{100}$ of a point per inch. As with picas, the conversion ratio of points to inches is simplified so that there are only 72 points per inch in all major desktop publishing applications, including InDesign.

✦ **Cicero:** A cicero is a unit of measure used in many parts of Europe. One inch equals about 5.62 ciceros.

✦ **Agate:** An agate is used for measuring vertical column length in classified ads. One agate equals about 5.5 points. An agate inch is one column wide and ¼₄ of an inch deep.

✦ **Em, en, and punctuation spaces:** The terms em, en, and punctuation space (also called a thin space) are units of measurement that reflect, respectively, the horizontal space taken up by a capital *M*, capital *N*, and lowercase *t*.

Note

Typically, an em space is the same width as the current point size; an en space is ½ of the current point size, and a punctuation (thin) space is ¼ of the current point size. In other words, for 12-point type, an em is 12 points wide, an en space is 6 points wide, and a punctuation or thin space is 3 points wide.

✦ **Figure space:** This refers to the width of a numeral, which usually is the same as an en. (In most typefaces, all numerals are the same width so that tables align naturally.)

Spacing

✦ **Leading:** This term, also called line spacing, refers to the space from the base of one line (the baseline) to another. (Leading is named after the pieces of lead once used to space out lines.) See Figure 40-3 for examples of leading.

> This is 14-point type set to +1 point of leading in the QuarkXPress Measurements palette. As you can see, the lines are simply too close to each other. See how the text almost overlaps between the first two lines?
>
> This is 14-point type with the leading set to Auto in the QuarkXPress Measurements palette—the normal setting for leading. Notice how the space in between lines is more than enough to avoid text overrunning other text, but not so much that there are large gaps between lines. Note that Auto sets the leading to be 20 percent more than the point size, which usually results in the correct 1.5 to 3 points of extra space between lines (for 14-point text, that means leading of 16.8 points, or 2.8 points extra space). As text gets larger than about 18 points, you'll want to avoid Auto and use a specific leading amount (usually 2 points more than the text size). You can specify your own Auto value in the Document Preferences dialog box's Paragraph pane (⌘ + Y).
>
> This is 14-point type with the leading set to 20 points in the QuarkXPress Measurements palette—the normal setting for leading. Notice how the space in between lines is far more than enough to avoid text overrunning other text,; in fact, it's an unusually large amount that probably looks a little strange. You might find such large leading in a kid's book, since young children need help distinguishing characters and the extra space does that. It also makes sense in very wide columns, so people can keep the long lines separated visually. You'll also find it in some layouts for parts of an introduction or other special elements that you want to call attention to. But you rarely find this amount of leading in regular body text.

Figure 40-3: The same type with different leading has a very different appearance.

✦ **Tracking:** *Tracking* determines the overall space between letters within a word.

✦ **Word spacing:** This defines the preferred, minimum, and maximum spacing between words.

✦ **Letter spacing:** Letter spacing (sometimes called character spacing) defines the preferred, minimum, and maximum spacing between letters.

Note InDesign uses your preferred spacing specifications unless you justify the text or apply manual spacing adjustments; if you justify text, the program spaces letters and words within the limits you set for maximum and minimum spacing.

✦ **Kerning:** This refers to an adjustment of the space between two letters. You kern letters to accommodate their specific shapes. For example, you probably would use tighter kerning in the letter pair *to* than in *oo* because *to* looks better if the *o* fits partly under the cross of the *t*.

✦ **Pair kerning:** This is a table of characters, built into the font itself, that indicates the letter pairs you want the publishing program to kern automatically. InDesign lets you adjust the kerning on a case-by-case basis or for all highlighted text. Kerning is used most frequently in headlines where the letter spacing is more noticeable. See Figure 40-4 for an example of kerning.

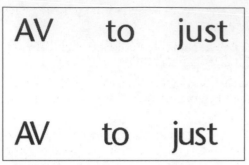

Figure 40-4: An example of unkerned (top) and kerned letter pairs.

✦ **Justification:** Justification adds space between words (and sometimes between letters) so that each line of text aligns at both the left and right margin of a column or page. Justification also is used to refer to the type of spacing used for optimum letter and word spacing: justified, ragged right, centered, or ragged left (see the following definitions).

- **Ragged right and flush left:** Both these terms refer to text that aligns with a column's left margin but not its right margin.

- **Ragged left and flush right:** This refers to text that aligns with the right margin but not the left margin.

- **Centered:** This refers to text that aligns so that there is equal space on both margins.

- **Vertical justification:** This adds space between paragraphs (and sometimes between lines) so that the tops and bottoms of each column on a page align. (This term is often confused with column balancing, which ensures that each column has the same number of lines.)

- **Carding:** Carding is a vertical-justification method that adds space between paragraphs in one-line increments.

- **Feathering:** This is another vertical-justification method that uses fractional-line spaces between paragraphs.

Paragraphs

✦ **Indent:** You typically indicate a new paragraph with an indent, which inserts a space (often an em space in newspapers and magazines) in front of the paragraph's first letter.

✦ **Outdent:** An outdent (also called an exdent) shifts the first character past the left margin and places the other lines at the left margin. This paragraph alignment is typically used in lists.

✦ **Block indent:** A block indent, a style often used for long quotes, moves an entire paragraph in from the left margin.

✦ **Hanging indent:** A hanging indent is like an outdent except that the first line begins at the left margin and all subsequent lines are indented.

✦ **Bullet:** This is a character (often a filled circle) used to indicate that a paragraph is one element in a list of elements. Bullets can be indented, outdented, or kept at the left margin.

✦ **Drop cap:** A drop cap is a large capital letter that extends down several lines into the surrounding text (the rest of the text wraps around it). Drop caps are used at the beginning of a section or story.

✦ **Raised cap:** A raised cap is the same as a drop cap except that it does not extend down into the text. Instead, it rests on the baseline of the first line and extends several lines above the baseline.

✦ **Style sheets:** These contain named sets of such attributes as spacing, typeface, indent, leading, and justification.

✦ **Style or style tag:** A set of attributes is known as a style or style tag.

Note

Essentially, styles are formatting macros. You *tag* each paragraph or character with the name of the style that you want to apply. Any formatting changes made to one paragraph or character are automatically reflected in all other paragraphs or characters tagged with the same style.

Hyphenation

✦ **Hyphen:** A hyphen is used to indicate the division of a word at the end of a line and to join words that combine to modify another word.

✦ **Hyphenation:** This determines where to place the hyphen in words that need to be split.

✦ **Consecutive hyphenation:** This determines how many lines in a row can end with a hyphen (more than three hyphens in a row is considered bad typographic practice).

✦ **Hyphenation zone:** The hyphenation zone determines how far from the right margin a hyphen can be inserted to split a word.

✦ **Exception dictionary:** An exception dictionary lists words with nonstandard hyphenations. You can add words that the publishing program's default dictionary does not recognize and override the default hyphenations for a word such as *project,* which is hyphenated one way as a noun ("proj-ect") and another as a verb ("pro-ject").

✦ **Discretionary hyphen:** Placing a discretionary hyphen (also called a *soft hyphe*n) in a word tells the program to hyphenate the word at that place if the word must be split. A discretionary hyphen affects only the word in which it is placed.

Using Typographic Color and Typefaces

Throughout the history of publishing, professional typographers have enhanced the look of documents by selecting from a variety of fonts to produce a desired look, and by increasing or decreasing character spacing. When done correctly, character spacing gives a finished look. Words set in characters that are surrounded by generous amounts of space have a light, airy feel; words set in characters that are close together feel heavier and more serious.

Typographic color

As a group, four aspects (kerning, tracking, scale, and hyphenation) determine what typographers call *color,* simply another way of describing the overall quality or appearance of text on a page. If you want to see a document's typographic color, make your eyes go slightly out of focus. Here's a good way to understand the concept of typographic color: Find a magazine page that has a good amount of text on it. Stare at the page for two minutes or so. Then focus on something halfway between you and the page. You'll see the text blur. The resulting gray level and consistency is *color.* Why is a document's color so important? Because it affects both the document's mood and readability. For most publishing applications, a light to medium color is preferable because it is easier on the eye.

The influence of typeface

Factors in addition to character spacing influence color. The most fundamental factor is the typeface. An airy, light typeface such as Baskerville Old Face has a light color, while a solid, heavy typeface such as Franklin Gothic Heavy has a dark color. Figure 40-5 shows the same text in these two typefaces. Notice how the text on the right, in Baskerville, looks lighter than the Caslon 224 text on the left. The example shown in the figure clearly demonstrates that type fonts are major contributors to typographic color. Some typefaces are light, some are heavy. Regardless of a typeface's intrinsic weight, InDesign includes character spacing controls that let you modify a font's effect on typographic color.

Two decades ago, when they first began buying homes, the Donegans decided that creating a beautiful garden would be a weekend pastime they could share. "I hated boring yards!" Lorene, a writer who specializes in 19th century New York history, recalls. "Even though the yard was nearly two acres, we knew it could be a magic place."

Lorene and Joe shared a vision of natural foliage mixed with fragrant native flowers, with a border of wild raspberries. Together, the couple created a tranquil, comfortable garden that includes both annuals – many in raised beds – and perennials. Roses in many vivid colors add the final touch.

A major task for the retired couple each spring is the raking and removal of more than 100 garbage bags full of leaves, applied as a winter compost cover the previous fall to the many rose bushes. Eventually, the decomposing leaves become mulch used on perennials, except in winter, when the soil at the base of some bushes is kept bare.

Two decades ago, when they first began buying homes, the Donegans decided that creating a beautiful garden would be a weekend pastime they could share. "I hated boring yards!" Lorene, a writer who specializes in 19th century New York history, recalls. "Even though the yard was nearly two acres, we knew it could be a magic place."

Lorene and Joe shared a vision of natural foliage mixed with fragrant native flowers, with a border of wild raspberries. Together, the couple created a tranquil, comfortable garden that includes both annuals — many in raised beds — and perennials. Roses in many vivid colors add the final touch.

A major task for the retired couple each spring is the raking and removal of more than 100 garbage bags full of leaves, applied as a winter compost cover the previous fall to the many rose bushes. Eventually, the decomposing leaves become mulch used on perennials, except in winter, when the soil at the base of some bushes is kept bare.

Figure 40-5: Different typefaces produce different shades of typographic color.

Learning about Typefaces

The two basic types of typefaces are serif and sans serif. A serif typeface has horizontal lines (called *serifs*) extending from the edges of the character, such as at the bottom of a *p* or at the top of an *I*. A sans serif typeface does not have these lines (*sans* is French for without). There are more types of typefaces than just serif and sans serif, but these are all in the minority. Calligraphic, block, and other nonserif/non–sans serif typefaces usually have other elements that serve the purpose of serifs — extensions to the characters that add a distinctive character to the typeface. Another distinct type of typeface is the pi font, which is a font made up of themed symbols (anything from math to Christmas ornaments). The name pi font comes from the Greek letter pi (π), a common mathematical symbol.

 Cross-Reference For more on special characters such as symbols, see Chapter 41.

Typeface variations

A typeface usually has several variations, the most common of which are Roman, italic, boldface, and boldface italic for serif typefaces; and medium, oblique, boldface, and boldface oblique for sans serif typefaces. Italic and oblique differ in that italics are a curved variant of the typeface, with the serifs usually heavily curved, while an oblique is simply a slanted version of the typeface. Other variations that involve type weight include thin, light, book, demibold, heavy, ultrabold, and black. Compressed, condensed, expanded, and wide describe type scale.

InDesign will show all variations available for a font, as long as those variations are stored in the font file, not as a series of separate files. For example, if you have a font file named Big Bold and a separate font file named Big Semibold, those will appear as two separate fonts in InDesign's menus and dialog boxes. But if you have a font file called Big that contains Big Normal, Big Light, Big Semibold, Big Bold, Big Ultra, and Big Compressed, all will appear as options for the font Big.

Understanding typeface formats

Typefaces come in several formats, with two predominating. InDesign supports them all, as long as your operating system or font-management utility does.

✦ **PostScript Type 1:** This is the publishing industry's standard for fonts. Anyone outputting to an imagesetter or other prepress device must use these fonts. PostScript Type 1 font support is native to Mac OS X. Windows does not support PostScript natively and so requires a font-management utility like Adobe Type Manager, DiamondSoft Font Reserve, or Extensis Suitcase to work with PostScript fonts. Note that Adobe has ATM Light available for free download from its Web site at www.adobe.com.

✦ **TrueType:** Codeveloped by Microsoft and Apple Computer, this is the standard font format of Windows, and it also is supported natively on the Mac OS. However, TrueType fonts are not supported by most imagesetters and prepress devices, and their use in your layouts can cause output problems. Do not use them in any professionally published document.

✦ **OpenType:** This new version of PostScript, codeveloped by Adobe and Microsoft, combines some TrueType technology and is meant to eventually replace both Type 1 and TrueType. Its biggest asset is that it supports a wide range of international characters, symbols, and character variations within the same font, such as true small caps and ligatures — called *glyphs* as a group. Mac OS X, Windows 2000, and Windows XP support it natively, but you'll need to make sure that your imagesetter or other prepress device can handle them — at the time of this writing, many cannot. InDesign has strong support for OpenType, making all character and glyph attributes available in character formatting.

Note that Windows will display an icon letting you know what format a font is in, as the figure here shows. The code T1 stands for PostScript Type 1, TT for TrueType, and O for Open Type.

Syntax UltraBlack
Tahoma
Tempus Sans ITC

What's in a face?

Each of these variants, as well as each available combination of variants (for example, compressed light oblique), is called a *face*. Some typefaces have no variants; these are typically calligraphic typefaces, such as Park Avenue and Zapf Chancery, and symbol typefaces (pi fonts), such as Zapf Dingbats and Sonata. In Figure 40-6, you see samples of several typefaces and some of their variants. By using typeface variants wisely, you can create more-attractive and more-readable documents.

Figure 40-6: A variety of typefaces and their variants.

A font is a typeface by any other name

Desktop publishing programs popularized the use of the term *font* to describe what traditionally was called a typeface. In traditional terms, a typeface refers to a set of variants for one style of text, such as Times Roman. A face is one of those variants, such as Times Roman Italic. A font, in traditional terms, is a face at a specific point size, such as 12-point Times Roman Italic. (Until electronic typesetting was developed, printers set type using metal blocks that were available only in a limited range of sizes.) The word *font* today means what *typeface* used to mean, and almost no one uses *font* any more for its original meaning.

The heart of a document is its typography. Everything else can be well laid out and illustrated, but if the text is not legible and appealing, all that other work is for naught. If you don't believe type is central, then consider this: You've surely seen engaging documents with no artwork, but have you ever seen artwork carry the day if the type is ugly or scrunched? I didn't think so.

Selecting the Right Typefaces

If you've ever seen a type chart, you already know that thousands of typefaces are available, each with a different feel. Matching the typeface's feel to the effect that you want for your document is a trial-and-error process. Until you are experienced at using a wide variety of typefaces (and even then), experiment with different typefaces on a mock-up of your document to see what works best.

Defining a standard set

We recommend that you take the time necessary to define a standard set of typefaces for each group of publications. You may want all employee newsletters in your company to have a similar feel, which you can achieve by using common body text and headline typefaces, even if layout and paragraph settings differ. The key to working with a standard set of typefaces is to avoid limiting the set to only a few typefaces. Selecting more typefaces than any one document might use gives you enough flexibility to be creative, while providing an obviously standard appearance. You also can use the same typeface for different purposes. For example, you might use a newsletter's headline typeface as a kicker in a brochure. A consistent — but not constrained — appearance is a good way to establish an identity for your company.

Some basic guidelines

If you're feeling confused about which typeface is right for you, here are some basic guidelines:

✦ **Use a Roman medium or book weight typeface for body text.** In some cases, a light weight works well, especially for typefaces such as Bookman and Souvenir, which tend to be heavy in the medium weights.

Understanding typeface names

The many variants of typefaces confuse many users, especially because most programs use only the terms *normal* (or plain), *italic* (or oblique), *bold,* and *bold italic* (or bold oblique) to describe available variations. When a typeface has more than these basic variations, programs usually split the typeface into several typefaces.

For example, in some programs, Helvetica comes as Helvetica, with medium, oblique, boldface, and boldface oblique faces; Helvetica Light/Black, with light, light oblique, black, and black oblique faces; Helvetica Light/Black Condensed, with condensed light, condensed light oblique, condensed black, and condensed black oblique faces; Helvetica Condensed, with condensed medium, condensed oblique, condensed boldface, and condensed boldface oblique faces; and Helvetica Compressed, with compressed medium and condensed oblique faces. When there are this many variations, you have to choose from among several Helvetica typefaces, and you have to know that, for example, selecting bold for Helvetica Condensed results in Helvetica Condensed Bold type.

For some typefaces, the variants are even more confusing. For example, in text, Bookman is usually printed in light face, which is lighter than the medium face. So when you select plain, you really select Bookman Light. And when you select bold, you really select Bookman Demibold. Bookman Medium and Bookman Bold are too heavy for use as body text, which is why the typeface comes in the light/demi combination of faces. Fortunately, the issue of what face a program designates as plain, italic, and the rest rarely comes into play. You usually encounter a problem only in one of the following situations:

✦ When you are exchanging files between PCs and Macs — because some vendors use slightly different names for their typefaces on different platforms. The Type ➪ Find Font option lets you correct this problem by replacing one typeface name with another in your document.

✦ When you are working with a service bureau that has typeface names that are different, or whose staff uses the traditional names rather than the desktop-publishing names.

✦ When you are working with artists or typesetters to match a typeface. Typically, the problem is a lack of familiarity with the different names for a typeface. The best way to reach a common understanding is to look at a sample of the typefaces being discussed.

You may have noticed that many people use serif typefaces for body copy and sans serif typefaces for headlines, pull-quotes, and other elements. But there is no rule you should worry about following. You can easily create engaging documents that use serif typefaces for every element. All-sans-serif documents are possible, but they are rare because sans serif typefaces tend to be hard to read when used in many pages of text. (Exceptions include typefaces such as News Gothic and Franklin Gothic, which were designed for use as body text.) No matter which typefaces you use, the key is to ensure that each element calls an appropriate amount of attention to itself.

✦ **Output some samples before deciding on a light typeface for body text because many light typefaces are hard to read when used extensively.** Also, if you intend to output publications on an imagesetter (at 1,270 dpi or finer resolution), make sure that you output samples on that imagesetter because a light font may be readable on a 300- or 600-dpi laser printer but too light on a higher-resolution printer that can reproduce thin characters more faithfully than a laser printer. (The laser printer may actually print a light typeface as something a bit heavier: Because the width of the text's stroke is not an even multiple of the laser printer's dots, the printer has no choice but to make the stroke thicker than it should be.) Although 1,200-dpi laser printers are increasingly common, and make more accurate proofs than a 300- or 600-dpi model, note that imagesetters are still more accurate, since they use smooth paper, which allows less distortion than the standard bond paper used in laser printers.

✦ **Use a heavier typeface for headlines and subheads.** A demibold or bold usually works well. Avoid using the same typeface for headlines and body text, even if it is a bolder variant. On the other hand, using the same typeface for subheads and headlines, even if in a different variant, helps ensure a common identity. (And if you mix typefaces, use those that have similar appearances. For example, use round typefaces with other round typefaces and squared-off typefaces with other squared-off typefaces.)

✦ **If captions are long (more than three lines), use a typeface with the same weight as body text.** If you use the same typeface as body text, differentiate the caption visually from body text. Using a boldface caption lead-in (the first words are boldface and act as a title for the caption) or putting the caption in italics distinguishes the caption from body text without being distracting. If captions are short (three lines or fewer), consider using a heavier face than body text or a typeface that is readily distinguished from your body text.

✦ **As a general rule, avoid using more than three typefaces (not including variants) in the main document elements (headlines, body text, captions, pull-quotes, and other elements that appear on most pages).** However, some typefaces are very similar, so you can use them as a group as if they were one. Examples include Helvetica, Univers, and Arial; Futura, Bauhaus, and Avant Garde; Times and its many relatives (including Times New Roman and Times Ten); Galliard and New Baskerville; Souvenir and Korinna; Benguiat, Americana, Garamond, Stone Serif, and Cheltenham; New Baskerville and Esprit; and Goudy Old Style and Century Old Style. You can treat the individual typefaces within these groups almost as variants of one another, especially if you use one of the individual typefaces in limited-length elements such as kickers, pull-quotes, and bylines.

✦ **Use italics for kickers, bylines, sidebar headlines, and pull-quotes.**

Summary

Typography is an often unappreciated component of a layout's visual style and character. Typefaces have distinct looks that can support or even create the publication's fundamental tone. The spacing of characters can also play a key role in the visual tone, or "color," of typography.

Because fonts come in several formats, it's key to coordinate font usage with service bureaus and internal production departments. Generally speaking, only PostScript fonts should be used for files that will be output at a service bureau or production department. The common TrueType format should be reserved for personal and local documents printed from your own computer, because most professional-class printers and typesetters do not support this format.

✦   ✦   ✦

Using Special Characters

◆ ◆ ◆ ◆

In This Chapter

Recognizing shortcuts for symbols

Identifying shortcuts for foreign characters

Using foreign characters

◆ ◆ ◆ ◆

InDesign has 18 different language versions available, covering American English, Brazilian Portuguese, British English, Castilian Spanish, central and eastern European (Czech, Greek, and Polish in one edition), Czech, Danish, Dutch, Finnish, French, German, Greek, Italian, Japanese, Middle Eastern Arabic and Hebrew (in one edition), Norwegian, Polish, and Swedish. For North American users who want to use special characters — foreign letters and accents, as well special symbols like ¢, £, ©, and • — InDesign takes advantage of the Mac and Windows font standards to provide access to those glyphs as well. Typically, there are shortcuts to access such common glyphs, but for uncommon or specialty glyphs, you'll need to use specialized fonts, whether foreign-language or pi (symbol) fonts.

Tip   InDesign lets you insert glyphs from the current font via Type ➪ Insert Glyphs. But if you deal with such characters, you probably need to access them in other programs. In that case, a great tool for accessing special characters on the Macintosh is PopChar, which adds a spot next to the Apple logo that, when clicked, opens a palette of all available characters for the current font. (Go to www.INDDcentral.com for a link to this software.) Windows comes with a similar utility, Character Map, that is available by choosing Start ➪ Accessories ➪ Character Map.

For quick access to frequently used glyphs (from multiple fonts), InDesign CS lets you create glyph sets.

New
Feature   The ability to create glyph sets is new to InDesign CS.

To create glyph sets:

1. **Choose New Glyph Set from the Glyphs pane's palette menu, as shown in Figure 41-1. (Choose Window ➭ Type & Tables ➭ Glyphs to open the pane.)**

Figure 41-1: The Glyph pane's palette menu.

2. **Enter a name in the New Glyph Set dialog box, and click OK.**

3. **In the Glyphs pane, select the special character you want to add to your new set.**

   You may need to change the font and style using the pop-up menus at the bottom of the pane.

4. **In the pane's palette menu, choose Add to Glyph Set ➭ *set name* to add the symbol to the chosen set.**

5. **Repeat Steps 3 and 4 for each glyph you want to add.**

6. **When done adding glyphs, choose Edit Glyph Set ➭ *set name* to edit the glyph set.**

   This will open the Edit Glyph Set dialog box shown in Figure 41-2.

Figure 41-2: The Edit Glyph Set dialog box.

7. **If you want a specific font to be used for a glyph (which you'll need to do for symbols chosen from pi fonts, as opposed to common symbols like (tm) available in most fonts), make sure that Remember Font with Glyph is checked.**

   You can also choose or change the font using the Font and Style pop-up menus in the dialog box.

8. **To delete a glyph, select it in the dialog box then click the Delete from Set button.**

9. **Click OK when you're done.**

To access a glyph set, simply choose the desired glyph set from the Show pop-up menu in the Glyph pane. Make sure the Text tool is active and that the text cursor is active in a text frame or path. Now double-click the desired glyph in the Glyphs pane; InDesign will insert it at the text cursor location.

Shortcuts for Symbols

Symbols are commonly used in all sorts of documents, from legal symbols to scientific ones. That's why most fonts have a selection of popular symbols built in. Table 41-1 shows the common symbols for Windows and Macintosh fonts.

Table 41-1 Shortcuts for Symbols		
Character	**Mac Shortcut**	**Windows Shortcut**
Legal		
Copyright (©)	Option+G	Shift+Alt+C *or* Ctrl+Alt+C *or* Alt+0169
Registered trademark (®)	Option+R	Shift+Alt+R *or* Alt+0174
Trademark (™)	Option+2	Shift+Alt+2 *or* Alt+0153
Paragraph (¶)	Option+7	Shift+Alt+7 *or* Ctrl+Alt+; *or* Alt+0182
Section (§)	Option+6	Shift+Alt+6 *or* Alt+0167
Dagger (†)	Option+T	Shift+Alt+T *or* Alt+0134
Double dagger (‡)	Option+Shift+T	Alt+0135

Continued

Table 41-1 *(continued)*

Character	Mac Shortcut	Windows Shortcut
Currency		
Cent (¢)	Option+4	Alt+0162
Euro (€)	Option+Shift+2	Alt+Ctrl+5
Pound sterling (£)	Option+3	Alt+0163
Yen (¥)	Option+Y	Ctrl+Alt+- (hyphen) *or* Alt+0165
Punctuation		
En bullet (•)	Option+8	Alt+8 *or* Alt+0149
Thin bullet (·)	*not supported**	Alt+0183
Ellipsis (…)	Option+; (semicolon)	Alt+0133
Measurement		
Foot (')	Control+"	Ctrl+"
Inch (")	Control+Shift+"	Ctrl+Alt+"
Mathematics		
One-half fraction (½)	*not supported*	Ctrl+Alt+6 *or* Alt+0189
One-quarter fraction (¼)	*not supported*	Ctrl+Alt+7 *or* Alt+0188
Three-quarters fraction (¾)	*not supported*	Ctrl+Alt+8 *or* Alt+0190
Infinity (∞)	Option+5	*not supported*
Multiplication (×)	*not supported*	Ctrl+Alt+= *or* Alt+0215
Division (÷)	Option+/	Alt+0247
Root (√)	Option+V	*not supported*
Greater than or equal to (≥)	Option+>	*not supported*
Less than or equal to (≤)	Option+<	*not supported*
Inequality (≠)	Option+=	*not supported*
Rough equivalence (≈)	Option+X	*not supported*
Plus or minus (±)	Option+Shift+=	Alt+0177
Logical not (¬)	Option+L	Ctrl+Alt+\ *or* Alt+0172
Per mil (‰)	Option+Shift+R	Alt+0137
Degree (°)	Option+Shift+8	Alt+0176

Character	Mac Shortcut	Windows Shortcut
Mathematics		
Function (*f*)	Option+F	Alt+0131
Integral (∫)	Option+B	*not supported*
Variation (∂)	Option+D	*not supported*
Greek beta (ß)	Option+S	*not supported*
Greek mu (µ)	Option+M	Alt+0181
Greek Pi (Π)	Option+Shift+P	*not supported*
Greek pi (π)	Option+P	*not supported*
Greek Sigma (Σ)	Option+W	*not supported*
Greek Omega (Ω)	Option+Z	*not supported*
Miscellaneous		
Apple logo ()	Option+Shift+K	*not supported*
Light (¤)	*not supported*	Ctrl+Alt+4 *or* Alt+0164
Open diamond (◊)	Option+Shift+V	*not supported*

Shortcuts for Foreign Characters

Although most American publishers don't produce work in other languages, they may still use accents in their work. And, of course, many publishers do publish in other languages, such as Spanish, French, German, and Portuguese, because they do business with customers in multiple countries. Even all-English publishers may choose to use accents in foreign words like *café* to help pronunciation and show a bit of international flair.

See Table 41-2 for foreign-language characters. Note that Windows shortcuts involving four numerals (such as Alt+0157) should be entered from the numeric keypad while holding the Alt key.

Tip

If your font doesn't have the accented characters you need, you may be able to create them by kerning accent marks over the letters. See Chapter 17 for detailed information on kerning.

Table 41-2
Shortcuts for Accents and Foreign Characters

Character	Mac Shortcut	Windows Shortcut
acute (´)*	Option+E *letter*	´ *letter*
cedilla (¸)*	*see Ç and ç*	´ *letter*
circumflex (ˆ)*	Option+I *letter*	^ *letter*
grave (`)*	Option+` *letter*	` *letter*
tilde (˜)*	Option+N *letter*	~ *letter*
trema (¨)*	Option+U *letter*	" *letter*
umlaut (¨)*	Option+U *letter*	" *letter*
Á	Option+E A	´ A *or* Alt+0193
á	Option+E a	´ a *or* Alt+0225
À	Option+` A	` A *or* Alt+0192
à	Option+` a	` a *or* Alt+0224
Ä	Option+U A	" A *or* Alt+0196
ä	Option+U a	" a *or* Alt+0228
Ã	Option+N A	~ A *or* Alt+0195
ã	Option+N a	~ a *or* Alt+0227
Â	Option+I A	^ A *or* Alt+0194
â	Option+I a	^ a *or* Alt+0226
Å	Option+Shift+A	Alt+0197
å	Option+A	Alt+0229
Æ	Option+Shift+´	Alt+0198
æ	Option+´	Alt+0230 *or* Ctrl+Alt+Z
Ç	Option+Shift+C	´ C *or* Alt+0199
ç	Option+C	´ c *or* Alt+0231 *or* Ctrl+Alt+,
Ð	*not supported*	Alt+0208
đ	*not supported*	Alt+0240
É	Option+E E	´ E *or* Alt+0201
é	Option+E e	´ e *or* Alt+0233
È	Option+` E	` E *or* Alt+0200
è	Option+` e	` e *or* Alt+0232

Character	Mac Shortcut	Windows Shortcut
Ë	Option+U E	" E *or* Alt+0203
ë	Option+U e	" e *or* Alt+0235
Ê	Option+I E	^ E *or* Alt+0202
ê	Option+I e	^ e *or* Alt+0234
Í	Option+E I	' I *or* Alt+-205
í	Option+E i	' i *or* Alt+0237
Ì	Option+ ` I	` I *or* Alt+0204
ì	Option+` i	` i *or* Alt+0236
Ï	Option+U I	" I *or* Alt+0207
ï	Option+U i	" I *or* Alt+0239
Î	Option+I I	^ I *or* Alt+0206
î	Option+I i	^ I *or* Alt+0238
Ñ	Option+N N	~ N *or* Alt+0209
ñ	Option+N n	~ n *or* Alt+0241
Ó	Option+E O	' O *or* Alt+0211
ó	Option+E o	' o *or* Alt+0243 *or* Ctrl+Alt+O
Ò	Option+` O	` O *or* Alt+0210
ò	Option+` o	` o *or* Alt+0242
Ö	Option+U O	" O *or* Alt+0214
ö	Option+U o	" o *or* Alt+0246
Õ	Option+N O	~ O *or* Alt+0213
õ	Option+N o	~ o *or* Alt+0245
Ô	Option+I O	^ O *or* Alt+0212
ô	Option+I o	^ o *or* Alt+0244
Ø	Option+Shift+O	Alt+0216
ø	Option+O	Alt+0248 *or* Ctrl+Alt+L
Œ	Option+Shift+Q	Alt+0140
œ	Option+Q	Alt+0156
Þ	*not supported*	Alt+0222
þ	*not supported*	Alt+0254
ß	not supported	Ctrl+Alt+S *or* Alt+0223

Continued

Table 41-2 *(continued)*

Character	Mac Shortcut	Windows Shortcut
Š	*not supported*	Alt+0138
š	*not supported*	Alt+0154
Ú	Option+E U	' U or Alt+0218
ú	Option+E u	' u or Alt+0250 *or* Ctrl+Alt+U
Ù	Option+` U	` U or Alt+0217
ù	Option+` u	` u or Alt+0249
Ü	Option+U U	" U or Alt+0220
ü	Option+U u	" u or Alt+0252
Û	Option+I U	^ U or Alt+0219
û	Option+I u	^ u or Alt+0251
Ý	*not supported*	' Y or Alt+0221
ý	*not supported*	' y or Alt+0253
Ÿ	Option+U Y	" Y *or* Alt+0159
ÿ	Option+U y	" y *or* Alt+0255
Ž	*not supported*	Alt+0142
ž	*not supported*	Alt+0158
Spanish open exclamation (¡)	Option+1	Ctrl+Alt+1 *or* Alt+-0161
Spanish open question (¿)	Option+Shift+/	Ctrl+Alt+/ *or* Alt+0191
French open double quote («)	Option+\	Ctrl+Alt+[*or* Alt+0171
French close double quote (»)	Option+Shift+\	Ctrl+Alt+] *or* Alt+0187

* On the Mac, enter the shortcut for the accent and then type the letter to be accented. For example, to get é, type Option+E and then the letter e. In Windows, if the keyboard layout is set to United States-International — via the Keyboard icon in the Windows Control Panel — you can enter the accent signifier and then type the letter (for example, type ` and then the letter e to get è). To avoid an accent (for example, if you want the begin a quote — such as "A man" rather than have Ä man — type a space after the accent character — for example, " then space, then A, rather than " then A.

European languages and accented characters

Using accents in foreign words is great, but many Americans use them incorrectly, which is embarrassing. Although I can't tell you how to properly spell and accent every foreign word (a good dictionary for that language can!), I can tell you which accented characters are used in European languages. If you're using a word from one of the languages here and that word uses an accented character not shown for the language, you either have the wrong accent or that word is actually from a different language. I've also indicated which countries use the euro currency symbol (€) by including that symbol in their lists, and special currency symbols for other nations.

Many of the characters shown here are not available in standard PostScript and TrueType fonts. Most are available in OpenType fonts, though not in every case. You may need a special font for the specific language to get all the characters.

Albanian: ç, ë

Basque (Euskara): ñ

Breton: â, ê, è, ñ, ô, ù, ü, €

Catalan: à, ç, è, é, í, ï, ŀ, ò, ó, ú, ü, €

Croatian: c, č, đ, š, ž

Czech: á, č, d', é, ě, í, ň, ř, š, t', ú, ů, ý, ž

Danish: å, æ, é, ø, ú

Dutch: á, â, è, é, ê, ë, í, ï, ij, ó, ô, ö, ú, û, €

English, American and Canadian: $, ¢

English, British: ö, £

English, Old: ð, þ

Estonian: ä, õ, ö, s, ž

Faroese: á, æ, ð, í, ó, ø, ú, ý

Finnish: ä, ö, €

French: à, â, æ, è, é, ê, ë, ç, î, ï, ô, ö, œ, ù, û, ü, ÿ, «, », €

Frisian: â, ê, î, ô, ú, û

Gaelic (Scots): à, á, è, é, ì, ò, ó, ù, £

German: ä, ö, ß, ü, €

Hungarian: á, é, i', ó, ö, ő, ú, ü, ű

Icelandic: á, æ, é, ð, í, ó, ö, þ, ú, ý

Continued

Continued

Irish: á, é, í, ó, ú, €

Italian: à, è, ì, í, ò, ó, ù, €

Latvian: a, č, ē, ģ, ī, ļ, ņ, š, ū, ž

Lithuanian: a, č, ę, ė, į, š, ų, ū, ž

Luxembourgean: ä, ë, é, ï, ö, ü, €

Maltese: à, ċ, è, ġ, ħ, î, ì, ò, ù, ż

Norwegian: å, ø, æ

Occitan (Provençal): á, à, ç, é, è, í, ó, ò, ú, €

Polish: ą, ć, ę, ł, ń, ó, ś, ź, ż

Portuguese: à, á, â, ã, é, ê, ç, í, ñ, ó, ô, ö, õ, Ú, ü, €

Rhaeto-Roman: à, è, é, ì, î, ò, ù

Romanian: â, ă, î, ş, ţ

Slovak: á, ä, č, ď, é, í, Í, ľ, ń, ó, ô, ŕ, š, ť, ú, ý, ž

Slovenian: c, š, ž

Spanish (Castilian, Galician): á, é, í, ñ, ó, ú, ü, ¿, ¡, €

Swedish: å, ä, é, ö

Turkish: â, ç, _, î, ı, ö, _, û, ü

Welsh: à, á, â, ä, è, é, ê, ë, ì, í, î, ï, ò, ó, ô, ö, ù, ú, û, ü, ŷ, ý, ŷ, ÿ

A great source for information on foreign characters and fonts is the Yamada Language Center, accessible on the Web at `http://babel.uoregon.edu/yamada/fonts.html`.

Summary

Windows and Macintosh fonts come with a wealth of special characters called glyphs, but they are usually accessible only with special codes or shortcuts. Plus, not all fonts support all glyphs. Similarly, the Mac OS and Windows support different glyphs. This makes it important to use the same symbol fonts on both platforms and to be sure that you know the glyphs you use are available in all the fonts you use.

✦   ✦   ✦

Color Fundamentals

In This Chapter

Getting acquainted with color terminology

Making sense of process and spot colors

Working with color models in InDesign

You see color every day, so it probably seems like working with it should come naturally. But color is a complex issue in printing, involving both physics and chemistry. The inks that produce color are designed chemically to retain those colors and to produce them evenly, so your images don't look mottled or fade. How light reflects off of ink and paper to your eye determines the color you see, and many factors (particularly different textures of paper) can affect the physics of how the light carries the color.

You also have implementation issues to consider: How many colors can your printing press produce, and how much will it cost? When do you decide to go for the exact pure color, and when do you decide to go with a close-enough version that's cheaper to print?

This chapter explains the basic theory behind color and InDesign's use of it. Although color is part of your everyday life, in order to get it to look the way you want in your printed pieces you need a solid understanding of how it works.

Defining Color Terms

Color is an expansive (and sometimes confusing and esoteric) concept in the world of publishing. The following definitions, however, should start you on your way to a clear understanding of the subject.

Chapter 8 covers defining and using color in InDesign.

✦ **Build:** Attempts to simulate a color-model color by overprinting the appropriate percentages of the four process colors.

✦ **CIE LAB:** A standard that specifies colors by one lightness coordinate and two color coordinates — green-red and blue-yellow. The first part of the name means Comité International d'Éclairage, an international standards group, and the second part refers to the mathematical approach used to describe the colors in a cubic arrangement: luminance, *a*-axis, and *b*-axis.

✦ **CMYK:** A standard that specifies colors as combinations of cyan, magenta, yellow, and black. These four colors are known as *process colors.*

✦ **Color gamut:** The range of colors that a device, such as a monitor or a color printer, can produce. Each color model has a different color gamut.

✦ **Color model:** An industry standard for specifying a color, such as CMYK or Pantone.

✦ **Color separation:** A set of four photographic negatives — one filtered for each process color — shot from a color photograph or image. When overprinted, the four negatives reproduce that original image.

✦ **Color space:** A method of representing color in terms of measurable values, such as the amount of red, yellow, and blue in a color image. The color space RGB represents the red, green, and blue colors on video screens.

✦ **Four-color printing:** The use of the four process colors in combination to produce most other colors.

✦ **Hexachrome:** Pantone's six-color alternative to CMYK. It adds green and orange inks for more accurate color reproduction in those hues, as well as enhanced versions of black, magenta, cyan, and yellow inks. (InDesign does not support Hexachrome unless you use a third-party utility.)

✦ **Process color:** Any of the four primary colors in publishing — cyan, magenta, yellow, and black (known collectively as CMYK). A six-color, high-fidelity variant produced by Pantone is called Hexachrome.

✦ **RGB:** The standard used by monitors, and the abbreviation from the three colors in it: red, green, and blue. One of the biggest hurdles to producing color documents that look as you'd expect is that computers use RGB while printers use CMYK, and the two don't always produce colors at the same hue.

✦ **Spot color:** A single color applied at one or more places on a page, such as for a screen or as part of an illustration. You can use more than one spot color per page. Spot colors can also be process colors.

✦ **Swatchbook:** A table of colors collected together as a series of color samples. The printer uses a premixed ink based on the color model identifier you specify; you look up the numbers for various colors in the table of colors in a swatchbook.

Understanding Process and Spot Color

Let's briefly explore the differences between spot and process colors, the two primary ways of indicating color in print documents.

Identifying methods of color printing

Several forms of color are used in printing, but the two most-used ones are process color and spot color.

Process color is the use of four basic colors — cyan, magenta, yellow, and black (known collectively as CMYK) — that are mixed to reproduce most color tones the human eye can see. A separate negative is produced for each of the four process colors. This method, often called *four-color printing,* is used for most color publishing.

Spot color is any color ink — whether one of the process colors or some other hue — used for specific elements in a document. For example, if you print a document in black ink but print the company logo in red, the red is a spot color. A spot color is often called a *second color* even though you can use several spot colors in a document. Each spot color is output to its own negative (and not color-separated into CMYK). Using spot color gives you access to special inks that are truer to the desired color than any mix of process colors can be. These inks come in several standards. Basically, spot-color inks can produce some colors that are impossible to achieve with process colors, such as metallics, neons, and milky pastels. You even can use varnishes as spot colors to give layout elements a different gleam from the rest of the page. Although experienced designers sometimes mix spot colors to produce special shades not otherwise available, you probably won't need to do so.

There are several advantages to spot colors. You can use colors like metallic inks that are impossible to create with CMYK. Also, your printed results will be more consistent than with CMYK separations, which can suffer from *color shift* (variation in the hue produced) over the length of a long printed piece. But spot colors work only in objects that have distinct, continuous hue — such as a solid brick red — that can be printed with just one ink. To produce any image with multiple colors, such as a photograph, you need to use multiple inks, and since printing presses can traditionally print only four to eight colors on a page, you have to mix colors to create the range of hues in such multicolor objects.

Mixing spot and process colors

Some designers use both process and spot colors in a document — known as using a *fifth color.* Typically, the normal color images are color-separated and printed using the four process colors, while a special element (such as a logo in metallic ink) is printed in a spot color. The process colors are output on the usual four negatives; the spot color is output on a separate, fifth negative and printed using a fifth plate, a fifth ink roller, and a fifth inkwell. You can use more than five colors, however; you're limited only by your budget and the capabilities of your printing plant. (Most commercial printers can handle six colors for each run through the press, and larger ones often can handle as many as eight colors.)

Converting spot color to process color

InDesign can convert spot colors to process colors. This handy capability lets designers specify the colors they want through a system they're familiar with, such as Pantone, without the added expense of special spot-color inks and extra negatives. Conversions are never an exact match, but guidebooks are available that can show you in advance the color that will be created. And with Pantone Process variation, which InDesign supports, designers can pick a Pantone color that will color-separate predictably.

You can set InDesign to convert some spot colors in a document to process colors while leaving others alone. (For example, you would keep a metallic silver as a spot color so it prints with a metallic ink, rather than be converted to a grayish color that is the closest the CMYK colors can produce to simulate a silver. But you would convert common colors like deep blue, purple, and green to process colors, since the CMYK inks can combine fairly accurately to reproduce them.) Or you can leave all spot colors as spot colors, or convert all spot colors to process colors.

Working with Color Models

Once you understand color terminology—and the difference between process and spot colors—you can start thinking about the type of colors you create in InDesign. You will define colors in the Swatches palette. The color models fall into two broad classes:

✦ Those that let you define a color by selecting a color from a *color wheel* (which represents a spectrum of available colors) or by entering specific values for the color's *constituent colors* (the colors that the color is made up of), which include CMYK, RGB, LAB, and Multi-Ink.

✦ Those that have a predefined set of colors, which you select from a palette of swatches. These swatches include seven variants of Pantone, Focoltone, Trumatch, DIC (Dainippon Ink & Chemical), Toyo, four variants of HKS, and seven variants of Pantone. There are also two sets of colors meant for use on the Web.

Note   Most North American publishers use Pantone color models. Focoltone, HKS, and Trumatch tend to be used in Europe. DIC, Focoltone, and Toyo tend to be used in Asia. And everyone uses CMYK.

Keep in mind that the colors displayed are only on-screen representations; the actual color may be different. The difference will be particularly noticeable if your monitor is running in 8-bit (256 hues) color mode. Check the actual color in a color swatchbook for the model you are using. (Art and printing supply stores usually carry these swatchbooks. See the "Using color swatchbooks" sidebar for lists of other sources.)

Tip   InDesign uses the same swatch format as Illustrator, so you can add color models to InDesign created in or for Illustrator. Use the Other Library option in the New Swatch dialog box to select these other color models (from the Swatches pane, select New Swatch from the palette menu to get the New Swatch dialog box).

Using color swatchbooks

Anyone who uses a lot of color should have a color swatchbook handy. You probably can get one at your local art supply store or from your commercial printer (prices typically range from $50 to $100, depending on the color model and the type of swatchbook). But if you can't find a swatchbook, here's where to order the most popular ones:

✦ **Pantone:** Several Pantone swatchbooks are available, including ones for coated and uncoated paper, and for spot-color output and process-color output. If you are converting (called *building* in publishing parlance) Pantone colors to CMYK for four-color printing, I particularly recommend the *Pantone Process Color Imaging Guide: CMYK Edition* or the *Pantone Process Color System Guide* swatchbooks. Pantone, 590 Commerce Blvd., Carlstadt, NJ 07072-3098; phone: 201-935-5500; fax: 201-935-3338; Internet: www.pantone.com.

✦ **Hexachrome:** Pantone also created the Hexachrome standard and sells Hexachrome swatchbooks, as well as the $299 HexWare software that adds Hexachrome output capability to Adobe Photoshop and Illustrator. Because InDesign uses Illustrator color swatch files, you can add Hexachrome support to InDesign via HexWare. (See the contact information for Pantone in the preceding bullet.)

✦ **Trumatch:** Based on a CMYK color space, Trumatch suffers almost no matching problems when converted to CMYK. Variants of the swatchbooks for coated and uncoated paper are available. Trumatch, 50 E. 72nd St. #15B, New York, NY 10021; phone: 800-878-9100; fax: 212-517-2237; Internet: www.trumatch.com.

✦ **ANPA:** Designed for reproduction on newsprint, these colors also are designed in the CMYK color space. Although InDesign doesn't have an ANPA color library predefined, you can create these colors using the swatchbook's definitions. Newspaper Association of America, 1921 Gallows Rd., Suite 600, Vienna, VA 22182-3900; phone: 703-902-1600; fax: 703-917-0636; Internet: www.naa.org.

Continued

Continued

✦ **Focoltone:** Like Trumatch, this color model is based on the CMYK color space. A & P Publishing Network, No. 6 Aljunied Ave. 3 #01-02, Singapore 389932; phone: +65-6746-0188; fax: +65-6746-1890; Internet: www.apmedia.com.

✦ **HKS:** This new-to-InDesign color model is used mainly in Germany and other European countries, with variants for industrial printing such as on plastics. It uses various combinations of cyan, magenta, and yellow with black overlays to achieve different shades. Hostmann-Steinberg, Bremer Weg 125, D-29223 Celle, Germany; phone: +49-5141-591-0; fax: +49-5141-591-202; Internet: www.hks-colour.de.

✦ **Dainippon Ink & Chemical:** Like Pantone, the DIC color set is a spot-color-based system. Dainippon Ink & Chemical Americas, 222 Bridge Plaza South, Fort Lee, NJ 07024; phone: 201-592-5100; fax: 201-592-8232; Internet: http://dicwww01.dic.co.jp/eng/index.html.

✦ **Toyo:** Similar to Pantone in that it is based on spot-color inks, this model is popular in Japan. Toyo Ink America, 710 W. Belden, Addison, IL 60101; phone: 630-930-5100; Internet: www.toyoink.com.

Paper Variation Models

Both the Pantone and HKS color models recognize that the type of paper you print on affects how a color appears, so they have variations based on popular paper types. Here's how they work:

✦ **Pantone Process Coated:** Use this variant when you color-separate Pantone colors and your printer uses the standard Pantone-brand process-color inks on coated paper. Colors in this variant have the code DS added *before* the numerals in their names and the code C *after* the numerals.

✦ **Pantone Solid Coated:** Use this variant when your printer uses actual Pantone-brand inks (as spot colors) when printing to coated paper stock. Colors in this variant have the code C appended to their names.

✦ **Pantone Solid Matte:** This is the same as Pantone Coated but for paper with a matte finish. Colors in this variant have the code M appended to their names.

✦ **Pantone Solid Uncoated:** This is the same as Pantone Solid Coated but for uncoated paper. Colors in this variant have the code U appended to their names.

✦ **Pantone Coated:** This is the generic Pantone coated color model, for use on any kind of paper. Colors in this variant have the code CVC appended to their names.

✦ **Pantone Process:** This is the generic Pantone process color model, for use on any kind of paper. Colors in this variant have the code CVS appended to their names.

✦ **Pantone Uncoated:** This is the generic Pantone uncoated color model, for use on any kind of paper. Colors in this variant have the code CVU appended to their names.

✦ **HKS E:** Use this HKS variant for continuous-form stationery. Colors in this variant have the code E appended to their names.

✦ **HKS K:** Use this HKS variant for glossy art paper (highly coated). Colors in this variant have the code K appended to their names.

✦ **HKS N:** Use this HKS variant for natural paper (uncoated). Colors in this variant have the code N appended to their names.

✦ **HKS Z:** Use this HKS variant for newsprint. Colors in this variant have the code Z appended to their names.

When printing on uncoated stock with any colors designed for use on coated stock, you will usually get weaker, less-saturated color reproduction.

Summary

Using color in publishing involves complex decisions. There are many ways to define colors, but they don't all result in the same colors when you finally print your documents. That's why choosing the color models for your documents up front is important.

Color can also be expensive to print, so you may need to weigh when you use color and how you apply it. A spot color — a single ink — is cheaper to print than full color (produced by combining four or six process colors) but of course gives you less visual flexibility. You can also mix spot colors with process colors to add special colors such as pastels and metallics that process colors cannot produce.

✦　　✦　　✦

Appendixes

Odds and ends. When you're working with a program as complex, capable, and extensible as InDesign, you're going to have odds and ends. The eight appendixes to this book collect such odds and ends.

Several appendixes provide more context related to InDesign itself. One appendix walks you through the installation of InDesign, while another walks you through the companion Web site for this book. Yet another appendix brings together all the keyboard shortcuts mentioned throughout the book in one handy place. Another gives you one-stop shopping to see what's new in InDesign CS compared to the previous version.

Several appendixes cover issues for users making a major software change: One covers the move to Mac OS X, since InDesign CS doesn't run on previous versions of the Macintosh operating system. There are also two appendixes for users switching to InDesign from other layout programs: one for QuarkXPress users and one for PageMaker users.

Finally, I've provided a tour of the companion program InCopy, which larger publishers should consider so they can manage the flow of files during the layout and production process and provide editors and copy editors the ability to edit and copyfit stories in production, as well as write headlines that fit the layout space, without needing a full copy of InDesign.

Make no mistake: These appendixes cover key issues about InDesign. But the book is organized around publishing workflow and the discrete segments in that workflow. The topics in the appendixes either transcend that workflow breakdown or live outside it.

◆   ◆   ◆   ◆

Appendix A
Installing or
Upgrading InDesign

Appendix B
What's New in
InDesign CS

Appendix C
Switching from
QuarkXPress

Appendix D
Switching from
PageMaker

Appendix E
Switching to
Mac OS X

Appendix F
Using Adobe InCopy

Appendix G
The InDesign Central
Web Site

Appendix H
Shortcuts Cheat Sheet

Installing or Upgrading InDesign

APPENDIX

◆ ◆ ◆ ◆

In This Appendix

Identifying InDesign
CS system
requirements

Installing InDesign CS

Upgrading from prior
versions of InDesign

◆ ◆ ◆ ◆

Installing InDesign CS is surprisingly easy. Before installing or upgrading, make sure your system meets the InDesign CS system requirements. Then use the steps in this appendix to make quick work of the installation process. If you're upgrading from an earlier version, you'll actually perform a new installation. But read the section on upgrading at the end of this appendix for information about making the transition to InDesign CS.

InDesign CS System Requirements

InDesign CS does not require extraordinary resources — if you have a Mac or PC that runs one of the required operating systems, you can run InDesign CS. Just be sure to have enough hard-drive space and memory to be able to work with large images, many fonts, and multiple projects, as well as to have multiple applications like Adobe Photoshop open at the same time.

Here are the official requirements:

✦ For Macintosh systems, a PowerPC G3 or G4 processor running Mac OS X version 10.2 (Jaguar) or later

✦ For Windows systems, an Intel Pentium II, III, or 4, or equivalent AMD processor running Windows 2000 Service Pack 2 or later, or running Windows XP or later

✦ At least 220MB of free hard-disk space on the Mac and 245MB of free hard-disk space in Windows for installation (installation also requires free disk space on the startup drive, even if you install InDesign CS software on a different drive)

✦ 128MB of RAM

✦ Eight-bit color depth (256 monitors) at 1024-by-768 monitor resolution

✦ For PostScript printing, Adobe PostScript Language Level 2 or Adobe PostScript 3

✦ For the eBook features, QuickTime 6

Note   InDesign CS runs only on Mac OS X 10.2 and later (and only in native mode, not in Classic mode), Windows 2000, and Windows XP. You must use InDesign 2 for earlier versions of Mac and Windows.

Cross-Reference   See Chapter 38 for my advice on the computer, operating system, and amount of RAM you need to run InDesign, as well as advice on hardware peripherals and software options.

Installing InDesign CS

Both the Mac OS and Windows installers for InDesign CS provide easy-to-follow on-screen instructions. Before beginning the installation process, make sure you have your serial number provided by Adobe.

Tip   Both installers provide a Custom Install option that lets you decide what to install with InDesign. Even if you're not sure whether you want all the InDesign plug-ins, filters, and the other items, you may want to install them anyway. Installing more than you absolutely need is better than not having a feature or information available when you need it. (You can always disable plug-ins and filters via InDesign ➪ Configure Plug-ins on the Mac or Help ➪ Configure Plug-ins in Windows, as covered in Chapter 36.)

STEPS: Installing InDesign

1. Insert the CD in the CD-ROM drive or access the CD over the network.

If necessary, double-click the CD icon to open the CD.

2. Double-click the Installer program.

On the Mac, you may be asked for a system password to allow the installation of new software.

3. The InDesign installer will ask you what language to install, US English or International English; choose one and click Continue.

International English is British English, used in Canada, the United Kingdom, Australia, and most former British colonies.

4. **Read the License Agreement, and click Accept to continue.**

   If you want to file this information, click Print to create a hard copy.

5. **In the next dialog box, type your name, company (leave blank if you're an individual, such as a self-employed designer), and your serial number, then click Continue.**

   You'll be shown a new dialog box to confirm your name, company, and serial number. If correct, click Continue; if incorrect, click Back.

6. **The next dialog box gives you the opportunity to decide where to install InDesign; choose the location and click Next.**

   - By default, the installer places InDesign in the Applications folder (Mac) or Program Files folder (Windows) on your startup hard drive. If you want to change the location (for example, to your Applications folder), choose Select Folder from the Install Location menu. Select or create another folder, and click Select.

   - If you're short on hard-drive space — or you're very confident that the installation includes items you don't need — choose Custom Install from the menu at the top of the dialog box. Click the arrow next to "InDesign 3.0" to see all the options. Uncheck any items that you don't want to install. If you need more information about an item to make this decision, click the **i** button next to the item.

7. **When you've decided what to install and where to install it, click Install.**

   The installation should only take a few minutes.

8. **When the installation is complete, an alert asks if you want to register online. If you have an Internet connection and are ready to register, click Yes.**

   This launches your default browser and takes you through the registration process. After you register online, an alert may prompt you to restart your computer, depending on whether system-level files were installed.

Upgrading from Prior Versions of InDesign

Actually, all installations of InDesign CS are new installations. The installer creates a new folder and places your new copy of InDesign in it — regardless of whether you were using a previous version of InDesign. The only difference between purchasing a new product and upgrading is the price you pay for the software.

Installing new software has its good points and bad points. On the plus side, your existing, earlier-version copy of InDesign is available for future use. You never know when you'll need it — for example, for that new client who has no intention of upgrading to InDesign CS yet — so it's worth keeping on your machine or at least storing on a CD or Zip disk. The drawback is, of course, that you need space in which to store this old software.

For Mac-based organizations that have Mac OS 9–based systems, or that want to run Mac Classic mode from Mac OS X for compatibility with other software (including plug-ins), having both InDesign CS and an earlier version is a good idea. After all, InDesign CS does not run on Mac OS 9 or earlier.

A bigger drawback to the fact that InDesign CS requires a new installation is that InDesign CS won't have any of the custom settings you've selected in your earlier version of InDesign — you often don't realize how many preferences you've set over time until you switch to a new version of the software.

If you did put some effort into customizing InDesign, when you start using InDesign CS, do the following:

✦ Reset your preferences in the Preferences dialog box (InDesign ➪ Preferences on the Mac and Edit ➪ Preferences in Windows, or ⌘+K or Ctrl+K).

✦ Copy any color swatch libraries from the previous version of InDesign (as well as from Adobe Illustrator) to the Swatch Libraries folder in the Presets folder in your InDesign application folder.

✦ With no document open, set any preferences such as style sheets and color definitions that you want to be used in all future documents. You can also load such settings from other documents using the Load menu option in the various panes' palette menus.

Although the customizing process can be tedious, it's definitely preferable to performing repetitive tasks such as creating the same style sheet for each document.

✦   ✦   ✦

What's New in InDesign CS

✦ ✦ ✦ ✦

In This Appendix

New interface
features

New document and
object features

New text features

New color and
gradient features

New graphics
features

New output features

Other new InDesign
features

✦ ✦ ✦ ✦

In its fourth major version (after 1.0, 1.5, and 2.0), InDesign 3.0—known formally as InDesign CS—has become a very strong page-layout program, offering a broad range of flexible, powerful tools.

Most InDesign users discovered the program in its 2.0 version. You'll find a host of new features and updated features in this latest release. Although the chapters in this book identify new features as they come up in discussing publishing techniques, this appendix brings the whole list to you in one place for easy browsing. The new features are arranged in the same order as this book, since that reflects the basic workflow of publishing and the major functional divisions.

InDesign Interface

Operating-system interaction

InDesign now runs only under Mac OS X, Windows 2000, and Windows XP.

You can drag and drop layout objects to the Mac Trash Can or Windows Recycle Bin to delete the object.

Presets and shortcuts

InDesign is adopting the name *presets* for what used to be called styles, to distinguish saved groups of attributes from text styles such as boldface and italics, which are often called just *styles*. There are print presets, trap presets, transparency flattener presets, PDF export presets, and workspace presets.

The Option+spacebar and Alt+spacebar shortcuts for temporary Hand tool access replace the shortcuts previously used: spacebar when not using the Text tool and Shift+Spacebar when using the Text tool.

Hyperlink and hyperlink destinations are now accessible via InDesign's contextual menus.

Palettes and panes

The InDesign CS Tool palette (also called the Toolbox) adds the Measure and Push Button tools, as well as the Bleed Mode and Slug Mode buttons in the Preview Mode button's new pop-up menu. Also, the Scissors tool now occupies its own place in the Toolbox, no longer stored in the Gradient tool's pop-up menu (that pop-up menu no longer exists in the CS version).

You can now use percentages in dialog box and pane fields, such as 50%, which adjust the current value by that percentage.

InDesign CS adds many new panes. The most useful is the Control palette, which combines many attributes into one location. Other new panes include the Bookmarks, Flattener Preview, Info, Pathfinder, Separations Preview, States, and Story Editor panes. It also has grouped the text- and table-oriented panes under a new submenu accessed by choosing Window ⇨ Type & Tables.

InDesign adds the Control palette in version CS, taken from PageMaker (which took it from QuarkXPress). It provides the basic controls for objects all in one place; the options change based on what is selected, which reduces on-screen palette clutter. Among the most commonly used options in the Control palette are the ones to move and resize objects.

The new Info palette provides positioning and size information on selected objects.

To try to gain some control over InDesign's palette profligacy, you can create workspaces, which are essentially memorized palette collections and locations. Display the palettes you want, where you want them, and create a new workspace by choosing Window ⇨ Workspace ⇨ Save Workspace. Give it a name that makes sense, such as Text Palettes. That workspace is now available via Window ⇨ Workspace ⇨ [workspace name], automatically displaying just those saved palettes in their saved locations. By having several such workspaces, you can quickly switch among collections of palettes based on the tasks you're focused on.

You can collapse panes to tabs on the side of the screen and open them by clicking the pane's tab. To collapse a pane into a side tab, click on the palette's tab and drag it to the left or right side of your screen. To open the pane, click on its tab. To collapse the pane, double-click on its tab. To separate a pane from the screen edge, drag the tab out from the side of your screen or move it into a palette.

You can dock panes to the top or bottom of the screen using the Dock to Top and Dock to Bottom options in the panes' palette menu—this works like Microsoft Office's docked formatting toolbars. To undock docked panes, use the Float menu in the palette menu or simply drag the pane away from the screen edge.

The Navigator pane now has a scroll bar to make it easier to navigate pages when View All Spreads is selected in the palette menu.

Preferences

InDesign CS adds two new preview options via a pop-up menu in the Preview Mode button: Bleed Mode and Slug Mode. Bleed Mode shows any objects that bleed beyond the page boundaries, while Slug Mode shows the space reserved for information such as crop marks and color separation names used in final output. You set these up when you create new documents or by choosing File ➪ Document Setup.

InDesign CS adds the option of deleting the InDesign Defaults preference files when opening InDesign: Press Control+Option+Shift+⌘ or Ctrl+Alt+Shift when launching InDesign.

InDesign CS adds the ability to create keyboard shortcuts for the Align and Distribute buttons. Although there are no default shortcuts, these buttons are now listed in the Object Editing commands in the Keyboard Shortcuts dialog box (Edit ➪ Keyboard Shortcuts) so you can create shortcuts for them.

The Guides pane in the Preferences dialog box has been renamed the Guides & Pasteboard pane. The new Pasteboard Options section controls the pasteboard dimensions. The Guide section adds more guides to which you can select the colors; you can also apply a color now to the pasteboard itself.

The Workgroup preferences pane no longer exists in InDesign CS. Its functions — which involve managing documents in a workgroup environment—are now part of the Open and Save dialog boxes. Likewise, the Online Settings pane is gone, replaced by the Updates pane; InDesign now automatically connects to Adobe's servers to get product updates, and the Updates pane controls that behavior. Finally, the Spelling and Story Editor Display preference panes are new.

Document and Object Functions

Document settings

InDesign CS lets you create predefined document types, called *document styles,* to supplement the standard ones such as Letter in the New Document dialog box. You can also create these by editing the New Doc Sizes.txt file, which you can also use to share these document styles with others.

InDesign CS documents can now have bleed and slug areas. Bleed areas ensure that objects that run past the page boundaries have sufficient imaging area to print to, while slug areas ensure that there is room in the output for the printer's marks.

If you select a reference point in the Transform pane or Control palette with no object selected, that reference point is retained. When you next create a new document, that new reference will be used. Earlier versions of InDesign always reverted to the center point as the default reference point.

Page actions

In previous versions of InDesign, if you added or removed an odd number of pages from a facing-pages document, all pages after the new or deleted pages changed sides: Even pages got bumped to become odd pages, and odd pages got bumped to become even pages. This wreaked havoc with page designs. For example, a two-page opening spread for a magazine article could get split so that the original left-hand page is on the right and the original right-hand page gets bumped to the next (left-hand) page. But InDesign CS fixes that — pages are automatically changed from left-hand pages to right-hand pages, and vice versa, as needed when individual pages are added and removed in a facing-pages document.

The ability to drag-copy pages or spreads from one document to another is new to InDesign CS. Any associated master pages are copied as well.

The Override All Master Pages function in the Pages pane's palette menu is new to InDesign CS. It moves all master items to the document page on the selected pages, so any local changes to the selected pages override the master page settings.

Libraries and books

When you close a palette containing library panes, all libraries in the palette are now closed. Similarly, when you close a palette containing book panes, all books in the palette are now closed.

Multiple users may now open a library as long as the file is locked via Mac OS X's Show Info feature's Locked option or via the Windows Properties feature's read-only option.

File exchange

The new InDesign Interchange format lets users of InDesign 2 read InDesign CS (version 3) files — if they acquire the Interchange plug-in for InDesign 2. You cannot otherwise downsave to earlier versions of InDesign.

Object selection

InDesign CS adds the Select submenu, which provides new controls for object selection, to the Object menu. You can select the contents, the frame, the next object in a group, or the previous object in a group.

Text Functions

Text editing and import

New to InDesign CS is the Story Editor (Edit ➪ Edit in Story Editor, or ⌘+Y or Ctrl+Y), a mini word processor that Adobe has long had in its PageMaker product. You set its preferences in the new Story Editor pane in the Preferences dialog box.

InDesign CS now lets you import word processor and spreadsheet text as unformatted; select Remove Text and Table Formatting or Remove Text Formatting (depending on what kind of file is selected) in the Import Options dialog box, accessed from the Place dialog box by checking the Show Import Options option.

Text frame modifications

InDesign CS fixes a flaw in earlier versions. Before, if you changed the size of a text frame via the Transform pane, InDesign adjusted the text size accordingly on-screen but still reported the original text size in the Character pane, Control palette, and other character formatting tools. Now, InDesign changes the reported text size to match its new, actual size after the text frame has been resized.

If you resize a text frame, you can preview the text reflow by holding the mouse button down for a second, then see the text reflow as you resize the frame.

InDesign CS lets you resize text as you resize a text frame (or group of text frames). Hold the ⌘ or Ctrl key when resizing a frame edge to do so.

Double-clicking a text frame with any tool selects the frame and brings up the Text tool.

You can now resize a text frame with the Text tool.

Text wrap

The Suppress Text Wrap When Layer Is Hidden check box is new to InDesign CS's Text Wrap pane. This lets you keep text wrap on hidden layers in case you're hiding the layer to speed screen preview, while also giving you the option to stop wrapping around a hidden object, in case you've hidden it because you don't want it to appear in the final output.

You can now wrap text around frames on hidden layers — as well as remove text wrap for objects on hidden layers. This is handy when you want to hide images or other distracting items but preserve the layout.

Paragraph and character formatting

InDesign CS adds two new options to the Paragraph pane's palette menu and Control palette's palette menu. One is Only Align First Line to Grid. The other is Balance Ragged Lines. The first option helps "reset" text alignment to the baseline grid without overriding the leading on every single line. The second option makes the rag flow more nicely, in an undulating pattern; this effect is typically used for large text, such as multiline headlines, subheads/decks, and pull-quotes.

Nested styles are new to InDesign CS. They let you apply a character style to a specified range of text in the first sentence, or the first three words, or all text until a tab character. You can have multiple nested styles in a paragraph style, applying a sequence of character styles based on different parameters. Nested styles are handy for items such as numbered lists that may have the numeral and its period in one font and the rest of the text in another.

The ability to create custom underlines and strikethroughs is new to InDesign CS. These are applied locally only, and cannot be saved as styles or presets for reuse. You create them via the palette menu in the Character and Character Styles panes, as well as in the Control palette.

The Preserve Text Attributes When Pasting option is new to InDesign CS's Preferences dialog box's General pane. It lets you control whether text formatting is preserved during paste operations.

Tables

InDesign CS adds the ability to specify whether tables' row lines overprint column lines or vice versa.

InDesign CS can now convert regular (body) rows in tables to header and footer rows, or vice versa. Select the row(s) you want to convert, then choose Table ➪ Convert Rows and then choose To Header, To Body, or To Footer as appropriate.

The ability to unmerge table cells is new to InDesign CS.

The ability to apply stroke types, such as dashed and dotted lines, to cell edges is new to InDesign CS. You apply these strokes via the Stroke pane (Window ➪ Stroke, or F10). Use the palette menu to select the Stroke Styles menu option, which provides a list of styles and the ability to create your own.

You can now preview color swatches in the Table Options dialog box, instead of seeing just their names.

You can now preview frame edges in tables whose cell are set at 0 points; this helps identify cell boundaries. To see them, choose View ➪ Show Frame Edges.

Glyphs and fonts

Choosing Type ➪ Glyphs is a revised menu option for what had been Type ➪ Insert Glyphs in previous version of InDesign.

You can create sets of frequently used *glyphs* (symbols and special characters) by selecting New Glyph set from the Glyph pane's palette menu

If you have several active fonts of the same name but based on different fonts standards, all will be available in InDesign. The program will append a code indicating the font format, such as *Helvetica (T1)* for PostScript Type 1, *Helvetica (T1')* for TrueType, and *Helvetica (OTF)* for OpenType.

The Inline Input check box in the Text pane of the Preferences dialog box enables input method editors (IMEs) from Microsoft, Apple, or other companies, if installed on your computer, for entering Asian language characters on a non-Asian operating system. It's meant for the occasional use of Chinese, Japanese, or Korean characters. If you publish regularly in these languages, you should use the appropriate Asian version of InDesign instead.

Color and Gradient Functions

Colors

Mixed-ink colors are new to InDesign CS. They are swatches composed of user-defined percentages of one or more process colors and of one spot color. A related feature, called *mixed-ink groups*, lets you create a set of mixed-ink colors at one time by specifying the range of source colors and the increments of each to mix for each subsequent swatch in the group.

Spot colors (called *spot inks* in Photoshop) are now imported into InDesign CS when you place Photoshop images into InDesign. They'll appear in the Swatches pane.

The Add button in the New Color Swatch and New Tint Swatch dialog boxes is new to InDesign CS. It lets you add several items in turn without having to leave the panes.

Gradients

If you paste or drag and drop Illustrator objects into InDesign, any gradients are now editable in InDesign CS.

In InDesign CS, you can now select the [Paper] swatch — essentially, transparency or no color — as a stop point in a gradient.

You can now drag swatches from the Swatches pane to the gradient ramp to set a stop point.

The Add button in the New Gradient Swatch dialog box is new to InDesign CS. It lets you add several items in turn without having to leave the pane.

Graphics Functions

Image editing

InDesign CS lets you easily open a graphics program to edit placed images from within InDesign. Hold Option or Alt and then double-click the image. InDesign will then launch the program that created the graphic; if you don't own that program, InDesign will launch a compatible program if you have one. For example, if you Option+double-click or Alt+double-click an EPS file in your layout that was created in Adobe Illustrator, but you use Macromedia FreeHand instead, InDesign will launch FreeHand on your system.

Strokes and paths

Several Stroke pane options are new to InDesign CS: the Gap Color and Gap Tint fields and the Align Stroke options.

New to InDesign CS is the ability to create your own custom dashes, dotted lines, and stripes. You do so in the Strokes pane, by choosing Stroke Styles from the palette menu.

Adding arrowheads to a line no longer increases its length to make room for the arrowhead.

InDesign CS offers a new feature to combine paths, called the Pathfinder.

InDesign CS now lets you select whether text wrap affects all text frames in a stack or just frames behind the text-wrap object.

Output Functions

Presets

Trap Presets is the new name for the Trap Styles pane, but they are functionally the same otherwise.

The Save Preset button in the Print dialog box used to be called Save Style in previous versions of InDesign, but it's the same feature.

Page options

InDesign CS now lets you enter absolute page numbers in the Range field. For example, entering **+6-+12** would print the document's sixth through twelfth pages, no matter what their page numbers are.

The Print dialog box's Include Slug Area option is new to InDesign CS, since slugs are new to this version.

PDF export

PDF/X export support and Acrobat 6 (PDF 1.5) format export support are new to InDesign CS. Also new are support for layers (in Acrobat 6 format only) and for JPEG 2000 compression (also just in Acrobat 6 format).

Support for 128-bit encryption (used when exporting to Acrobat 6's PDF 1.5 format) is new to InDesign CS.

Color and image handling

InDesign CS now offers the Composite Leave Unchanged option for all color printers, as well as for EPS export, rather than just for PDF output.

The software now correctly prints Photoshop DCS 1.2 files with transparency when you use the In-RIP Separations option.

InDesign CS now lets you preview color separations in your document with the new Separations Preview pane.

The Flattener Preview pane is new to InDesign CS. It shows the effects of the flattening settings applied during output on transparent and semitransparent objects.

InDesign now preserves OPI 1.3 comments during PDF export.

Font handling

The Complete Font Download Glyph Limit text field is new to InDesign CS's Preferences dialog box. It is used for OpenType fonts that have many special characters, such as accented letters, symbols, and diacritical marks. To prevent output files from getting clogged up with very large font files, this option lets you set the maximum number of characters (glyphs) that can be downloaded from a font file into an output file. Any characters actually used are always downloaded; the reason you might want to download an entire font is so someone could edit the file as a PDF or EPS file and have access to all characters in the proper fonts for such editing.

Other Functions

PDF and eBooks creation

InDesign CS no longer supports export to HTML, the language of the Web. You can no longer use InDesign to create documents intended for Web distribution. However, you can create PDF documents that can be opened as a link from a Web document.

InDesign has a new Bookmarks pane that lets you create bookmarks — a table-of-contents-like list — for PDF files. InDesign can use a table of contents to create the PDF bookmarks during export, or it can use user-selected text and page items that are tagged as bookmarks in the Bookmarks pane.

When creating eBooks, you can place QuickTime movies in a frame from either the Place dialog box or the Movie Options dialog box. That Movie Options dialog box (Object ➪ Interactive ➪ Movie Options) also specifies the behavior of the movie in an exported PDF file.

Similarly, the Sound Options dialog box, accessed by choosing Object ⇨ Interactive ⇨ Sound Options, lets you import sound files and control how they play in exported PDF files.

The new Push Button tool lets you create push buttons for PDF forms.

InDesign CS now lets you assign rollovers to push buttons in PDF files.

Double-clicking eBook page items (push button, movie, or sound) now opens the associated options dialog box.

XML files

In creating XML files, you can now map character styles to XML tags (and vice versa).

You can now specify XML data type description (DTD) files, as well as validate XML file structures against them.

The new Package for GoLive feature (in the File menu) lets you export XML files for use in Adobe GoLive 7 or later. If you drag page items from the exported InDesign files onto GoLive HTML pages, the InDesign file's underlying XML structure will be applied to the GoLive HTML page.

InDesign now supports the XMP standard for placed images in XML files.

Scripting

InDesign CS adds JavaScript support for cross-platform application scripting, in addition to Visual Basic for Windows and AppleScript for Mac OS X.

Scripts can now address individual graphics in a layout as objects, create dialog boxes, access object labels (which you can set in InDesign, as well as have InDesign automatically extract from converted QuarkXPress files), set object properties, and identify the file path on which the script resides.

InDesign can now run text-only AppleScripts in addition to compiled (binary) ones.

You can now assign keyboard shortcuts to scripts.

If you create many scripts, you can control how their names sort in the scripts list.

✦ ✦ ✦

Switching from QuarkXPress

◆ ◆ ◆ ◆

In This Appendix

Opening
QuarkXPress
documents

Recognizing the
differences between
InDesign and
QuarkXPress

◆ ◆ ◆ ◆

Learning to use new software, or even learning to use an upgrade of a familiar application, can be so intimidating that many users resist passionately. Even if an application is woefully out-of-date and lacking in functionality, you cling to it knowing you can accomplish your mission—even with workarounds—with less frustration than the untried, but powerful, new application. Users are particularly passionate about their choice of page-layout software—which is usually QuarkXPress—probably because they're involved with it for 8 to 12 hours a day. (A QuarkXPress user once said he spent more time with QuarkXPress than with his wife, so you can see where the dedication is coming from.)

But times, circumstances, and jobs change. Eventually, your old software won't run on your zippy new machine or you switch jobs or you simply prefer another vendor. No matter what circumstances lead you to choosing InDesign, this appendix is designed to help you let go and move forward, showing you the differences between your old layout application and InDesign, and pointing out a few benefits of InDesign as well. InDesign lets you open documents from both QuarkXPress and PageMaker so you can continue working with existing designs, and you can apply much of your page-layout knowledge to InDesign.

Opening QuarkXPress Documents

The Open command (File ➪ Open, or ⌘+O or Ctrl+O) lets you select and open documents and templates saved in QuarkXPress versions 3.3 through 4.11 on Macintosh or Windows. (You can't open libraries or books, though, nor version 5 or 6 files.) All the text, graphics, items, master pages, style sheets, and more in the QuarkXPress document are converted to their InDesign equivalents. If the document contains items, content, or formatting that can't be converted, an alert notifies you of the issues. Once the document is converted, it displays as a new, untitled document.

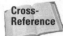

Cross-Reference   See Chapter 4 for complete information about opening files.

Now that you know what InDesign is supposed to do, take a look at how well it actually does it. Yes, you can open QuarkXPress documents, save them as InDesign documents, and continue working with them. But the documents don't convert perfectly: You're likely to lose some formatting because InDesign doesn't have equivalent formatting or its options work differently. In general, you can expect to use a QuarkXPress document as a starting point for a design — usually with a little repair work — but you should not expect to simply open a QuarkXPress document and have it look and print exactly the same way.

Tip   After realizing which QuarkXPress features are not supported or converted well, and considering how your own QuarkXPress documents are created, you can decide on a document-by-document basis whether conversion is worth the effort. In some cases, it might be easier to simply reconstruct a document, while in other cases you might be able to start working almost immediately.

When you convert QuarkXPress documents to InDesign, you can expect the following:

✦ Master pages are converted, including all items, content, and guides.

✦ All line and frame styles are converted to dashed or plain strokes.

✦ Text boxes are converted to text frames; picture boxes are converted to graphics frames.

✦ Text paths are converted.

✦ All paragraph and character style sheets are converted to InDesign styles.

✦ Incremental auto leading (such as +4, which adds 4 points to the largest font size on the line) is converted to InDesign's standard auto leading.

✦ The Next Column (keypad Enter) or Next Box (Shift+keypad Enter) characters (which you use to bump text to the next column or next text box rather than resizing the box) are retained.

✦ The Bold and Italic type styles are converted to the appropriate typeface (if available), and Underline, Strike Thru, Superscript, Subscript, All Caps, and Small Caps are converted. Superior, Word Underline, Outline, and Shadow revert to plain text.

✦ Index tags are not maintained, and you may have difficulty opening chapters of a book.

✦ If a picture is missing or modified in QuarkXPress, it won't display in the InDesign document. If you want to retain the picture, you'll need to update the links in QuarkXPress (Utilities ➪ Usage ➪ Pictures) before converting it.

✦ Pasted (embedded) pictures, pictures imported using OLE or Publish and Subscribe, and pictures created with third-party XTensions will not convert.

✦ The customizable dashes in QuarkXPress are converted to solid and dashed lines — note that stripes do convert properly.

✦ Clipping paths created in QuarkXPress or imported with an image into QuarkXPress are not converted, so the image's display will change.

✦ The Same as Clipping Runaround feature in QuarkXPress leaves a runaround shape based on the clipping path in InDesign — but if you've resized the image in QuarkXPress, the runaround path stays at 100 percent in InDesign.

✦ Items for which Suppress Printout is checked are placed on a separate layer called ""Nonprinting layer." To view these objects in InDesign, view the layer.

✦ If a group contains an item for which Suppress Printout is checked, all the items are ungrouped and the suppressed items are placed on the nonprinting layer.

✦ ICC-compliant color profiles (used in QuarkXPress 4.0 and greater) are retained; other profiles (the EfiColor profiles used in QuarkXPress 3.3x) are not retained.

✦ Colors in QuarkXPress 3.3x documents are converted to InDesign swatches according to their CMYK values (except for HSB colors, which are converted to RGB swatches).

✦ Colors in QuarkXPress 4.x documents are converted to InDesign swatches according to their RGB values (except for HSB and LAB colors, which are converted to RGB swatches). Hexachrome colors are not converted.

✦ Blends are converted to linear or circular blends.

Switching from QuarkXPress

For the QuarkXPress veteran, the toughest thing about switching to InDesign is the set of tools. In your world, you've been using the Item tool (which you might call the pointer) and the Content tool (the little hand) for almost everything. Not only did you use them all the time, but the Item tool or Content tool was selected automatically for you most of the time (since object-creation tools snap back to the last-used selection tool). Over time, the two tools have evolved into almost one, so you might have been using the Content tool all the time, pressing ⌘ or Ctrl when you needed to manipulate an entire item.

You need to forget about this way of working entirely. In InDesign, you'll be switching tools constantly. When you create an object, its tool remains selected so you can't move or resize the objects immediately after creation. The Selection tool only lets you move and resize objects, while the Direct Selection tool lets you reshape objects and work with graphics.

The difference between the Selection tool and Direct Selection tool takes some getting used to for QuarkXPress users. In terms of working with content, the Direct Selection tool is much like QuarkXPress's Content tool, but it also lets you edit the frame as if it were a Bézier object. For example, if the Direct Selection tool is selected and you drag a point on the frame, you'll move that point and thus change the shape of the object — a rectangle would be converted into a polygon, since the lines immediately adjacent to the moved point will move with the point, while the rest of the frame will not be affected. In QuarkXPress, if the Content tool is selected and you drag a point on the frame, you'll resize the frame (perhaps nonproportionally) but the entire side(s) adjacent to the point will move with the point, so a rectangle would still be a rectangle. To change a frame in the way that QuarkXPress does with both the Content and Item tools, use the Selection tool in InDesign.

Think of the Type tool as a combination of the Rectangle Text Box tool and the Content tool for text. You must have the Type tool to work with text, but there's no moving or resizing of text frames while you're using it.

This will seem restrictive to you at first — but the key is to embrace InDesign's single-letter shortcuts for selecting tools. (InDesign also provides QuarkXPress-like keyboard commands for temporarily activating tools, but it's easier to press a single letter to switch tools.)

As long as the Type tool isn't selected, you can activate any tool by pressing the letter displayed next to it in the tool's Tool Tip. In particular, you'll want to memorize the following:

✦ Press V for the Selection tool.

✦ Press A for the Direct Selection tool.

✦ Press T for the Type tool.

✦ Press H for the Hand tool (you can also press the spacebar; when editing text, you can press Option or Alt).

✦ Press Z for the Zoom tool (you can also press ⌘+spacebar or Ctrl+spacebar then click the mouse to zoom in, and Option+⌘+spacebar or Ctrl+Alt+spacebar then click the mouse to zoom out).

If you're also a Photoshop user, the single-letter shortcuts might be familiar to you, but it's an odd concept for a QuarkXPress-only user. Once you get the hang of it, however, you'll appreciate how fast and easy it is to switch tools.

A few overall interface differences between QuarkXPress and InDesign might hang you up initially. Keep in mind that many menu commands simply display a pane (which may already be open) rather than showing a dialog box. Get used to deciphering icons or using tool tips on the panes because there are few dialog boxes containing named fields as you're used to in QuarkXPress's Character Attributes, Paragraph Attributes, and Modify dialog boxes. Contextual menus are implemented on a much broader scale than in QuarkXPress, so you can Control+click or right+click on objects, rulers, and more to make changes quickly.

InDesign CS also offers docking panes, whose tabs can be aligned to the screen edges so they're not in the way, as well as docked to the top of the screen like Microsoft Word's formatting palettes. You can drag these docked panes to your document to make them floating panes à la QuarkXPress. Note that InDesign's panes can be rearranged and combined into multipane palettes by dragging them on top of each other — QuarkXPress's palettes are fixed and cannot be combined. Because InDesign has so many panes, it needs a way to manage them. Unlike QuarkXPress, InDesign lets you save these interface settings using its Workspaces feature (Window ➪ Workspace, whose submenu lets you select, create, and delete these workspaces).

InDesign uses all of QuarkXPress's measurement abbreviations, as well as its own. For example, InDesign accepts QuarkXPress's use of " to indicate inches, as well as InDesign's own standard of *in* and *inch*. Likewise, it accepts QuarkXPress's *mm* for millimeter as well as InDesign's own standard of *m*.

 Tip InDesign offers a set of keyboard commands similar to those in QuarkXPress (Edit ➪ Keyboard Shortcuts). I recommend that you avoid this set and learn the commands in InDesign. This will help you in communicating about InDesign and working with other Adobe software. If you do choose to use the QuarkXPress set of keyboard commands, see Chapter 3 for more information.

Converting Keyboard Shortcuts

If you're switching from QuarkXPress and committed to learning InDesign's keyboard shortcuts, skim Table C-1 to see the primary differences.

Table C-1
Keyboard Shortcuts Translated from QuarkXPress to InDesign

QuarkXPress Shortcut	Result	InDesign Equivalent
Control or Ctrl	Zoom in	⌘+spacebar or Ctrl+spacebar
Control+Option or Ctrl+Alt	Zoom out	Option+⌘+spacebar or Ctrl+Alt+spacebar
Option or Alt	Page grabber hand	H, or Option or Alt
Option+Shift+⌘+Y or Ctrl+Alt+Shift+Y	Preferences	⌘+K or Ctrl+K
⌘+E or Ctrl+E	Get Text/Picture	⌘+D or Ctrl+D for Place
⌘+Shift+F or Ctrl+Shift+F	Paragraph formats	Option+⌘+T or Ctrl+Alt+T
⌘+Shift+D or Ctrl+Shift+D	Character formats	⌘+T or Ctrl+T
F11	Style Sheets palette	F11 (Character Styles), Shift+F11 (Paragraph Styles)
⌘+L or Ctrl+W	Spelling (word)	⌘+I or Ctrl+I
⌘+M or Ctrl+M	Modify dialog box	*No equivalent*
⌘+K or Ctrl+K	Delete selection	Delete
⌘+D or Ctrl+D	Duplicate	Option+Shift+⌘+D or Ctrl+Alt+Shift+D
Option+⌘+D or Ctrl+Alt+D	Step and Repeat	Shift+⌘+V or Ctrl+Shift+V
F6	Lock/Unlock	⌘+L or Ctrl+L (lock), Option+⌘+L or Ctrl+Alt+L (unlock)
⌘+U or Ctrl+U	Ungroup	Shift+⌘+G or Ctrl+Shift+G
⌘+, or Ctrl+,	Space Align	F8
Shift+F5	Send to Back	Shift+⌘+[or Ctrl+Shift+[
Option+Shift+F5 or Ctrl+Shift+F5	Send Backward	⌘+[or Ctrl+[
F5	Bring to Front	Shift+⌘+] or Ctrl+Shift+]
Option+F5 or Ctrl+F5	Bring Forward	⌘+] or Ctrl+]

Document differences

By and large, documents in InDesign and QuarkXPress are the same. You have master pages, layers, and pages. You can also set bleeds for objects that go beyond the page boundary. But there are some differences:

✦ InDesign lets you specify a slug area, which reserves space during printing for the printer's marks.

✦ QuarkXPress 6 permits several layouts in one document file, called a *project,* so you can mix layouts with different page sizes. InDesign does not permit that.

✦ The InDesign master text frame is not the same as QuarkXPress's automatic text box on a master page. You cannot flow text into a QuarkXPress automatic text box while you're working on a master page — instead, an empty text box is placed on each of your layout pages for you automatically. Although you can have QuarkXPress flow text into automatic text boxes across pages as you add pages to your layout, you can also place text in these boxes individually, without them being linked. An InDesign master text frame is linked automatically from page to page and is not meant for holding text that does not flow from page to page.

✦ QuarkXPress 5 and 6 also support Web documents, which InDesign does not.

✦ InDesign can generate TOCs only based on paragraph style sheets, not on character style sheets. This means you can't create other kinds of lists, such as a list of companies in a magazine article or research report, based on the use of character style sheets. InDesign doesn't have a flexible Lists feature as QuarkXPress does, just the Table of Contents feature that is essentially a subset of QuarkXPress's Lists feature. However, you can use the InDesign Table of Contents feature to create some lists besides TOCs. Also, the level of formatting you can achieve over TOC entries in InDesign is greater than in QuarkXPress.

✦ The InDesign index features are similar to those in QuarkXPress, though the InDesign Index pane and QuarkXPress Index palette have very different interfaces.

✦ The corner-style feature in InDesign (Object ➪ Corner Effects) is similar to the text-box and picture-box variants in QuarkXPress, which offer the same selection of corners except for the Fancy option. In QuarkXPress, you create, or convert, a box to a variant that has one of these corner effects, while in InDesign, you apply the corner effect to a frame.

✦ InDesign's nested frames are similar to QuarkXPress's constrained boxes — the biggest difference is that, to nest a frame in InDesign, you paste a frame into another (Edit ➪ Paste Into, or Option+⌘+V or Ctrl+Alt+V). In QuarkXPress, you choose Item ➪ Constrain.

Working with objects rather than items

In QuarkXPress, you're used to items such as text boxes, picture boxes, lines, and maybe text paths. In InDesign, you have paths and frames, with the only difference being that frames contain graphics or text. You can therefore, make a one-to-one relationship between text boxes and text frames, and picture boxes and picture frames. Just keep in mind that, with InDesign, you're not restricted to using boxes for content — you can fill any path, even an open one, with text or graphics and have it become a frame. And if you don't make a box (or the right kind of box) up front, you can still import graphics and text in InDesign (unlike in QuarkXPress, which requires you to change the box type first).

While selecting and manipulating objects with tools, remember the following:

✦ Use the Selection tool to move objects or resize frames. It's kind of like QuarkXPress's Item tool.

✦ Use the Direct Selection tool to reshape objects, work with graphics, and change the endpoints of lines (it's kind of like QuarkXPress's Content tool).

✦ When reshaping objects, you can use the Pen tool, Anchor Point tool, and Remove Anchor Point tool in addition to the Direct Selection tool.

✦ You can't just click on master-page objects to select them on the document pages: Instead, use Shift+⌘+click or Ctrl+Shift+click to select them.

When modifying objects, remember the following:

✦ Users of QuarkXPress may find InDesign's object-location approach to be a little strange. In QuarkXPress, a picture's X+ and Y+ coordinates are relative to the box that contains it; in InDesign, the X+ and Y+ coordinates are relative to the upper-left corner of the page. (I'm assuming here that you haven't moved the document's ruler origin, which by default is in the upper-left corner of a page or spread.)

✦ InDesign CS adds a clone of QuarkXPress's Measurements palette, called the Control palette in InDesign (Window ➪ Control, or Option+⌘+6 or Ctrl+Alt+6). You can also use the Transform pane in InDesign (Window ➪ Transform, or F9). Use these tools for the equivalent of QuarkXPress's Modify dialog box's Box and Line panes.

✦ To specify runaround, choose Window ➪ Types & Tables ➪ Text Wrap, or press Option+⌘+W or Ctrl+Alt+W, to open the Text Wrap pane.

✦ To specify attributes of text frames, choose Object ➪ Text Frame Options, or press ⌘+B or Ctrl+B, to open the Text Frame Options dialog box.

✦ The InDesign Shear tool is not the same as the QuarkXPress Skew tool — Shear both slants and rotates an object, while Skew just slants it. To simulate the QuarkXPress Skew tool, hold the Shift key while you move the mouse horizontally when using the InDesign Shear tool — this ensures that there is no rotation. You can also use the Shear fields in the Control palette or Transform pane to only slant an object.

Flowing text

Once you learn how to flow text in InDesign, you'll find it's easier and more flexible than QuarkXPress. It's easy to get stuck and to restrict yourself to QuarkXPress techniques. To prevent that, keep these differences in mind:

✦ To import a text file, use File ➪ Place, or ⌘+D or Ctrl+D. You can also drag files and text from the desktop or any application that supports drag and drop.

✦ You do not need to create or select a text frame before you import text; you'll be able to create or select a text frame after choosing the file to import.

✦ InDesign does not have linking tools. To flow text from frame to frame, use a selection tool to click the out ports and in ports on text frames. (Make sure View ➪ Show Text Threads is checked.)

✦ To flow text and add pages automatically, check Master Text Frame in the New Document dialog box (File ➪ New Document, or ⌘+N or Ctrl+N). Then, you'll need to Shift+⌘+click or Ctrl+Shift+click the master text frame on a document page. Finally, Option+click or Alt+click the loaded text icon. See Chapter 16 for complete information about flowing text.

Editing text

A few minor differences exist when it comes to editing and selecting text:

✦ InDesign doesn't support "smart space" the way QuarkXPress 4.0 and later do, so when you double-click to select, then cut and paste a word, you won't also select the trailing space.

✦ In QuarkXPress, clicking three times in text selects the line, and clicking four times selects the entire paragraph. In InDesign, clicking three times selects the paragraph.

✦ To type special characters such as ñ, •, or ¶, you can use Type ➪ Glyphs rather than system utilities or key combinations.

✦ The control for showing invisible characters such as spaces, tabs, and paragraph returns is Type ➪ Show Hidden Characters, or press Option+⌘+I or Ctrl+Alt+I.

✦ InDesign lets you select from various Western European languages for spell checking and hyphenation — you first apply a Language to text selections via the Character or Character Styles panes. The Passport edition of QuarkXPress has a similar feature to specify the hyphenation and spelling language, but not the standard version of QuarkXPress.

Formatting text

In general, formatting text in InDesign will feel comfortable to QuarkXPress users. You'll miss those nice, big Character and Paragraph Attributes dialog boxes (featuring real words, not icons!), but you have most of the same power. Review these differences, and keep them in mind while formatting text:

✦ Use the Character pane (Type ➪ Character, or ⌘+T or Ctrl+T) to format highlighted characters. You'll notice there are no type style buttons — InDesign requires you to choose the appropriate version of a typeface rather than attributes such as bold and italic, while other type styles are listed in the Character pane's palette menu.

✦ Leading is a character-level format in InDesign, therefore the controls are in the Character pane rather than the Paragraph pane as you might have come to expect. Fortunately, you can change the leading behavior by selecting the Text pane of the Preferences dialog box and checking Apply Leading to Entire Paragraphs. Checking this box will make InDesign match the behavior of leading in QuarkXPress. Leading is always measured from baseline to baseline in InDesign.

✦ Unlike QuarkXPress, you can stroke and fill characters in InDesign.

✦ Use the Paragraph pane (Type ➪ Paragraph, or Option+⌘+T or Ctrl+Alt+T) to format selected paragraphs; the palette menu includes additional commands for adding rules and controlling hyphenation.

✦ InDesign lets you apply OpenType settings to OpenType fonts, using the palette menu of the Character pane or the OpenType Features pane of the Character Styles pane. QuarkXPress can use OpenType fonts but apply only standard formatting to them.

✦ InDesign does not have H&J sets, so set up your hyphenation using the Paragraph pane and save your settings in paragraph style sheets.

✦ Use the Tabs pane (Type ➪ Tabs, or Shift+⌘+T or Ctrl+Shift+T) to set tabs for selected paragraphs.

✦ To create style sheets, use the new commands in the palette menus on the Character pane (Type ➪ Character Styles, or Shift+F11) and the Paragraph pane (Type ➪ Paragraph Styles, or F11). To share style sheets with other documents, use the Load commands in the same menus.

✦ Applying style sheets to text with local formatting has the opposite effect as it has in QuarkXPress. Style sheets always wipe out local formatting when first applied — *unless* you hold the Option or Alt key when applying the style sheet. If you add local formatting later and want to revert the text to the style sheet's formats, click the style sheet twice. (Note that applying No Style then the style sheet does not work, as it does in QuarkXPress.)

✦ InDesign imports all style sheets when you use one of the Load commands. It does not let you select specific style sheets for import, as QuarkXPress does. That can add a lot of irrelevant style sheets to your InDesign document, unfortunately.

✦ Unlike Windows QuarkXPress, InDesign for Windows supports automatic ligatures in Windows fonts that have them.

✦ InDesign has no equivalent to QuarkXPress's fraction-building tool.

✦ InDesign has no equivalent to QuarkXPress's Underline Styles. Instead, specify custom underlines and strikethroughs as part of a character style sheet. To add stripes and dashed lines, open the Strokes pane (Window ➪ Stroke, or F10) and select the Stroke Styles option from the palette menu.

✦ QuarkXPress converts may be surprised at the seemingly large kerning and tracking values produced by all of the program's kerning and tracking methods. Keep in mind that InDesign lets you adjust space in 0.001-em units ($\frac{1}{1,000}$ of an em). In QuarkXPress, for example, the kerning unit is 0.005 em ($\frac{1}{200}$ of an em). So QuarkXPress users should not be surprised to see kerning and tracking values that are 10 to 20 times greater than you're used to — you're working with multiples of finer increments.

Working with tables

Recent editions of QuarkXPress and InDesign have added significant table formatting capabilities. Among the differences:

✦ InDesign does a good job of importing Word tables and Excel spreadsheets as tables, unlike QuarkXPress, which does not support tables during import without extra-cost add-on software.

✦ InDesign tables and QuarkXPress tables have several differences. Although both treat tables as collections of cells, InDesign offers more formatting options for cell strokes than QuarkXPress does. InDesign has more controls for text and row placement than QuarkXPress offers. InDesign also imports Word, Excel, and RTF tables, while QuarkXPress does not. But QuarkXPress offers more control over the flow of text among cells in a table — InDesign doesn't let you flow text from one cell to another, for example, much less control the order of that flow.

✦ In one way, InDesign is more savvy about text-to-table conversion than QuarkXPress is, since InDesign lets you choose any string as the column or row separator during conversion (just enter that string in the appropriate field). But in another way, InDesign is less savvy: QuarkXPress lets you "pivot" data during conversion, so you can swap columns and rows for a better fit.

Working with graphics

Importing and manipulating graphics in InDesign is very similar to QuarkXPress. As long as you remember to use the Direct Selection tool to select a graphic rather than its frame, you and the InDesign graphics features will get along fine. Differences between the programs include the following:

✦ To import a graphics file in InDesign, use File ➪ Place, or ⌘+D or Ctrl+D. You can also drag files in from the desktop or other programs if InDesign supports their file formats.

✦ You do not need to create or select a graphics frame before you import a graphic; you'll be able to create or select a graphics frame after choosing the file to import.

✦ Use the Control palette (Window ➪ Control, or Option+⌘+6 or Ctrl+Alt+6) or the Transform pane (Window ➪ Transform, or F9) to rotate, scale, and skew graphics. You can create clipping paths by choosing Object ➪ Clipping Paths or pressing Option+Shift+⌘+K or Ctrl+Alt+Shift+K.

✦ To automatically scale a graphic to fit within its frame — proportionally or not — use the Fitting commands in the Object menu or their keyboard commands. As a bonus, you get a Fit Frame to Picture command, a task you have to perform manually in QuarkXPress.

✦ The InDesign Stroke Styles feature (accessed via the Strokes pane's palette menu) looks and works very much like the QuarkXPress Dashes & Stripes feature. The major difference is that InDesign has a separate option for dotted lines.

✦ Although InDesign doesn't have background, frame, and contents icons in its Swatches pane to let you select where color is applied, as QuarkXPress does, InDesign lets you determine what component of the image gets the color based on how you apply the color: Drag a color swatch onto an object to change the foreground color. Click a picture frame and then the Fill or Stroke icon in the Tool palette, then select a color from the Swatches pane to change the background or frame color, respectively. Furthermore, you can use the Control palette's Select Container and Select Contents icons to choose whether the image background or contents, respectively, are colored when you click a swatch.

✦ InDesign offers a customizable drop-shadow tool (Object ➪ Drop Shadow, or Option+⌘+M or Ctrl+Alt+M) that lets you determine the shadow angle, distance, and lighting effects. QuarkXPress's drop shadow is fixed to one setting. Although InDesign's drop shadow can be applied to any object, not just a text frame, it cannot be applied to selected text. By contrast, QuarkXPress's drop shadow can be applied only to selected text as a character attribute.

✦ InDesign lets you feather the edges of objects, to create soft outlines and other lighting-oriented effects by choosing Object ➪ Feather. QuarkXPress has no equivalent.

✦ QuarkXPress has no equivalent to InDesign's transparency settings, which let you make objects transparent or semitransparent, allowing a wide variety of special effects. QuarkXPress users instead must rely on such settings in Adobe Photoshop and Illustrator for imported pictures and do without them for objects created in QuarkXPress. InDesign also provides controls for how overlapping transparent objects are output, since they can sometimes interfere with printing.

✦ To track the location of graphic files, use the Links pane (File ➪ Links, Shift+⌘+D or Ctrl+Shift+D).

✦ InDesign's relink function is not as smart as QuarkXPress's equivalent Picture Usage. If you have multiple broken links to the same file in an InDesign document, you must relink each one manually from the Links pane. QuarkXPress will automatically fix all links to the same file as soon as you correct any link to it. That's another reason to use InDesign's automatic fix when you open a document and InDesign identifies that links are broken or out of date.

✦ QuarkXPress uses a very different approach to changing direction points from smooth to corner: It has iconic buttons in its Measurement palette that let you easily convert segment and corner types. The InDesign approach is more efficient in that it uses one tool and relies on a mouse-based tool (since you're likely using the mouse when you edit a shape), but it does require a bit more getting used to initially.

✦ The Pathfinder in InDesign options to connect paths are similar to QuarkXPress's Merge options for paths.

Manipulating pages

You'll find the controls for working with document pages and master pages to be quite similar to QuarkXPress — if not slightly better. Once you realize the differences and start working, you can take advantage of InDesign's improvements. The differences mostly relate to guides and using the InDesign Pages pane rather than the QuarkXPress Document Layout palette:

✦ InDesign provides three methods for creating guides: Drag them off the ruler as you do in QuarkXPress, double-click the ruler where you want a guide, or choose Layout ➪ Create Guides.

✦ To delete guides, you need to select them and click Delete. (To select all guides on a page, press Option+⌘+G or Ctrl+Alt+G.)

✦ Use the Pages pane (Window ➪ Pages, or F12) as you would the QuarkXPress Document Layout palette (called the Page Layout palette in QuarkXPress 6). To place more than two pages side-by-side, you'll need to use the Keep Spreads Together command in the pane's palette menu.

✦ If you're missing the QuarkXPress Page menu, look for your favorite commands in the InDesign Layout menu and in the Pages pane's palette menu. There's a bonus in the Layout menu: an Insert Page Number command (Option+⌘+N or Ctrl+Alt+N) so you don't have to remember that odd ⌘+3 or Ctrl+3 that QuarkXPress requires.

✦ You can base one master page on another, the same way you can base style sheets on each other.

✦ To share master pages among documents, you can drag a master page icon into another document window.

Working with color

Not to intimidate you, but color will confound you (although Photoshop users will have an easier transition). Basically, try to forget everything you know about creating and applying colors in QuarkXPress. Here's what you need to know to work with colors in InDesign:

✦ Most of your work with colors happens through the Swatches pane (Window ➪ Swatches, or F5) — not through the Colors pane as QuarkXPress users might think.

✦ To create colors, use the New Swatches command in the Swatches pane's palette menu. You cannot create Hexachrome colors in InDesign.

✦ To apply colors, first click the Stroke or Fill button on the Toolbox to specify where the color goes on the selected object. Then click a color in the Swatches pane.

✦ Use the Colors pane (Window ➪ Colors, or F6) to specify a shade (tint) of a color.

✦ InDesign's Paper color is equal to the QuarkXPress White color. Both programs use the color None for transparency, but InDesign provides None in both the Swatches pane and as a button on the Toolbox.

✦ To share colors among documents, drag a colored object into another document window.

Printing and output

InDesign and QuarkXPress offer many of the same output capabilities — such as print styles (called *print presets* in InDesign), PDF export, color calibration, and color separation support. But there are some notable differences beyond the different organization of their Print dialog boxes:

✦ You cannot print hidden layers in InDesign CS as you can in QuarkXPress 6. You must make them visible before printing.

✦ To suppress printout of individual objects, use the Attributes pane (Window ⇨ Attributes) and choose Nonprinting. You can also hide layers using the Layers pane (Window ⇨ Layers, or F7), which works pretty much like QuarkXPress's Layers feature.

✦ InDesign's Thumbnails option is more flexible than QuarkXPress's, letting you choose the number of thumbnails per page.

✦ Note that InDesign does not have any options to change image contrast or line-screen element for gray-scale and black-and-white images, as QuarkXPress does. You'll need to apply such effects in an image editor.

✦ InDesign and QuarkXPress offer similar levels of color output controls, but InDesign does have several options QuarkXPress does not. One is setting ink density, another is automatic calculation of screen angles for spot colors. A third is the ability to more accurately preview documents with overprinting colors. InDesign also can apply black-point compensation as part of its color calibration during output. And InDesign lets you save your color-management preferences for use in other documents.

✦　　✦　　✦

Switching from PageMaker

In This Appendix

Opening PageMaker
documents

Recognizing the
differences between
InDesign and
PageMaker

Because Adobe hasn't given PageMaker even a minor update since version 7.0 came out in 2001 — and there are no plans to make it Mac OS X–native — it's clear that PageMaker is an all-but-dead product. So PageMaker users need to move to either InDesign or long-time rival QuarkXPress. However, most PageMaker users who would have switched to QuarkXPress have already done so. Most of the remaining users simply don't like the QuarkXPress structured approach to layouts, preferring PageMaker's more freeform style.

InDesign knows the PageMaker mentality, having adopted much of the PageMaker freeform approach since its very first version. (As InDesign has been updated, it has also taken on more of the structured QuarkXPress approach — but without removing its PageMaker-like roots.) So InDesign is a natural upgrade for PageMaker users.

Opening PageMaker Documents

The Open command (File ➭ Open, or ⌘+O or Ctrl+O) lets you select and open documents and templates saved in PageMaker 6.5 or 7.0 on Macintosh or Windows. (You can't open libraries, though.) All the text, graphics, elements, layers, master pages, style sheets, and more in the PageMaker document are converted to their InDesign equivalents. If formatting can't be converted, an alert notifies you of the issues. After the document is converted, it displays as a new, untitled document.

Cross-Reference See Chapter 4 for complete information about opening files.

Since InDesign and PageMaker are similar, documents from PageMaker usually convert reliably. However, you still shouldn't count on PageMaker documents displaying and printing exactly the same way once they're converted in InDesign. You may need to do a little repair work, depending on the type of formatting you use.

When you convert PageMaker documents to InDesign, you can expect the following:

✦ Master pages are converted, including all elements and content.

✦ Guides on master pages are placed on a separate layer called "Guides."

✦ All line and stroke styles are converted to dashed or plain strokes.

✦ All style sheets are converted to InDesign styles.

✦ The Bold and Italic type styles are converted to the appropriate typeface (if available), Underline and Strikethrough are converted, while Outline, Shadow, and Reverse revert to plain text.

✦ Index tags are not maintained.

✦ If an imported graphic's link is not intact, it won't display in the InDesign document. If you want to retain the graphic, you'll need to update the links in PageMaker (File ➪ Links Manager) before converting it.

✦ Pasted (embedded) graphics and graphics imported using OLE or Publish and Subscribe will not convert.

✦ Items for which Suppress Printout is checked are placed on a separate layer called "Non-printing layer." To view these objects in InDesign, view the layer.

✦ If a group contains an item for which Suppress Printout is checked, all the items are ungrouped and the suppressed items are placed on the non-printing layer.

✦ PageMaker fill patterns are not supported.

✦ Tracking values will be modified to InDesign's settings.

✦ Color profiles are converted.

✦ Colors are converted to InDesign swatches according to their CMYK values (except for HLS colors, which are converted to RGB swatches).

Differences from PageMaker

As you might expect, because both come from the Adobe world, the transition from PageMaker to InDesign isn't that tough. The basic methods for working with frames, lines, and pages are the same in both programs. What you will get with InDesign is more control, with improved tools for drawing, formatting text, and manipulating objects. And there's not much to miss about PageMaker, either.

The biggest change will be that you're using Mac OS X—required by InDesign. If you're switching from PageMaker on Mac OS 9 to InDesign CS on Mac OS X, you should also get a good Mac OS X reference. A good start is Appendix E.

Using tools and setting preferences

The basic selection, object-creation, and navigation tools in InDesign are similar to those in PageMaker. You do have to remember that InDesign has two selection tools: the Selection tool for moving and resizing objects, and the Direct Selection tool for reshaping objects and working with graphics.

Because you'll be switching tools often, as you did in PageMaker, get in the habit of using the keyboard shortcuts. (Table D-1, later in this chapter, shows InDesign keyboard shortcuts that differ from PageMaker shortcuts. It's not a long list since the two programs share many shortcuts as part of Adobe's strategy to have a common interface across its creative programs, with the exception of Adobe Acrobat.) As long as the Type tool isn't selected, you can hop from tool to tool by simply pressing a letter on the keyboard. In particular, you'll want to memorize the following:

✦ Press V for the Selection tool.

✦ Press A for the Direct Selection tool.

✦ Press T for the Type tool.

✦ Press H for the Hand tool. (You can also press the spacebar; when editing text, you can press Option or Alt.)

✦ Press Z for the Zoom tool (you can also press ⌘+spacebar or Ctrl+spacebar to zoom in and Option+⌘+spacebar or Ctrl+Alt+spacebar to zoom out). Remember you can zoom to 1600% in InDesign!

InDesign includes significantly more preferences than PageMaker. You'll definitely want to explore all the panes in the Preferences dialog box (choose InDesign ➪ Preferences on the Mac or Edit ➪ Preferences in Windows, or press ⌘+K or Ctrl+K). You might find some power you've never had before (although you will be disappointed to see values for Superscript, Subscript, and Small Cap relegated to a document-wide preference rather than a character attribute as they were in PageMaker).

Working with objects rather than elements

As with other aspects of InDesign, when you work with objects, you gain more than you lose. The types of objects are similar: text frames, graphics frames, and lines. PageMaker is limited to creating closed frames and straight lines.

While selecting and manipulating objects with tools, remember the following:

✦ Use the Selection tool to move objects or resize frames.

✦ Use the Direct Selection tool to reshape objects, change the endpoints of lines, and work with objects in groups. The Direct Selection tool also works like PageMaker's Crop tool, letting you move graphics within a frame.

✦ You get Bézier curves in InDesign! Using the Pen tool, Anchor Point tool, and Remove Anchor Point tool, you can draw and manipulate curves to your heart's content.

✦ You can't just click on master page objects: Use Shift+⌘+click or Ctrl+Shift+click to select them.

When modifying objects, remember the following:

✦ Look in the Object menu for familiar Elements menu commands.

✦ InDesign CS now uses a more powerful version of the PageMaker Control palette.

✦ To specify runaround, choose Window ➪ Text Wrap or press Option+⌘+W or Ctrl+Alt+W to display the Text Wrap pane.

✦ To specify attributes of text frames, use the Object ➪ Text Frame Options command, or ⌘+B or Ctrl+B.

✦ To suppress printout of objects, put them on a different layer and hide the layer.

Working with text

When it comes to working with text, PageMaker users will feel comfortable, now that InDesign CS has added the Edit Story mode (choose Type ➪ Edit Story, or press ⌘+Y or Ctrl+Y) that PageMaker users have long enjoyed.

If the display of graphics make it difficult for you to edit text, go to the Display Preferences pane of the Preferences dialog box (choose InDesign ➪ Preferences on the Mac or Edit ➪ Preferences in Windows, or press ⌘+K or Ctrl+K). Chapter 3 covers this pane.

Other differences between PageMaker and InDesign include

✦ To type special characters such as ñ, •, or ¶, you can choose Type ➪ Glyphs or Type ➪ Insert Special Character rather than system utilities or key combinations.

Tip   Use the Keyboard Shortcuts feature (Edit ➪ Keyboard Shortcuts) to assign a keyboard command to the Insert Character command if you find yourself using it often.

✦ In PageMaker's Edit Story mode, you can only see invisible characters such as spaces and tabs. But you can see them all the time in InDesign by choosing Type ➪ Show Hidden Characters.

✦ Use the Character pane (Window ➪ Type & Tables ➪ Character, or ⌘+T or Ctrl+T) to format highlighted characters. You'll notice there are no type-style buttons — InDesign requires you to choose the appropriate version of a typeface rather than bold and italic, while other type styles are listed in the Character pane's palette menu.

✦ Unlike PageMaker, you can stroke and fill characters in InDesign.

✦ Use the Paragraph pane (Window ➪ Type & Tables ➪ Paragraph, or Option+⌘+T or Ctrl+Alt+T) to format selected paragraphs; the palette menu includes additional commands for adding rules and controlling hyphenation.

✦ Use the Tabs pane (Window ➪ Type & Tables ➪ Tabs, or Shift+⌘+T or Ctrl+Shift+T) to set tabs for selected paragraphs.

✦ To create style sheets, use the new commands in the palette menus on the Character pane (Window ➪ Type & Tables ➪ Character Styles, or Shift+F11) and the Paragraph pane (Window ➪ Type & Tables ➪ Paragraph Styles, or F11). To share style sheets with other documents, use the load commands in the same menus.

✦ When you apply style sheets in PageMaker, local formatting is retained. InDesign style sheets have the opposite effect — they wipe out all local formatting when applied.

Table D-1
Keyboard Shortcuts Translated from PageMaker to InDesign

PageMaker Shortcut	Result	InDesign Equivalent
F10 or Shift+F7	Page grabber hand	H, or Option or Alt
⌘+M or Ctrl+M	Paragraph Specifications dialog box	Option+⌘+T or Ctrl+Alt+T
⌘+B or Ctrl+B	Styles pane	F11 (Character Styles), Shift+F11 (Paragraph Styles)
⌘+I or Ctrl+I	Indents/tabs dialog box	Shift+⌘+T or Ctrl+Shift+T
⌘+E or Ctrl+E	Edit in Story Editor	⌘+Y or Ctrl+Y
⌘+L	Spell-check	⌘+I or Ctrl+I
⌘+' (apostrophe) or Ctrl+' (apostrophe)	Control palette	Option+⌘+6 or Ctrl+Alt+6

Continued

Table D-1 *(continued)*

PageMaker Shortcut	Result	InDesign Equivalent
⌘+J or Ctrl+J	Colors pane	F12 (Swatches pane)
⌘+8 or Ctrl+8	Layers pane	F7
Option+⌘+8 or Ctrl+Alt+8	Master Pages pane	F12 (Pages pane)
⌘+9 or Ctrl+(	Hyperlinks pane	none
⌘+U or Ctrl+U	Fill and Stroke dialog box	F10 (Stroke pane)
Shift+⌘+E	Align dialog box	none
Option+⌘+E	Text Wrap dialog box	Option+⌘+W or Ctrl+Alt+W

Working with graphics

InDesign and PageMaker are very much alike when it comes to importing and manipulating graphics. There's no Crop tool in InDesign, but the Direct Selection tool functions pretty much the same way for graphics.

Other differences include the following:

✦ You can drag graphics files into a layout in addition to using the Place command (File ➪ Place, or ⌘+D or Ctrl+D).

✦ You now get to create clipping paths — use the Object ➪ Clipping Path command.

✦ InDesign can automatically scale pictures or frames for you. Use the Object ➪ Fitting commands: Fit Content to Frame, Fit Frame to Content, Center Content, and Fit Content Proportionally.

✦ To track the location of graphic files, use the Links pane (File ➪ Links, or Shift+⌘+D or Ctrl+Shift+D).

Manipulating pages

The one thing you'll miss about PageMaker is those neat little page icons in the lower-left corner of the document window. In shorter documents especially, the icons provided a quick, easy method for jumping to pages. Get used to using the Page Number text field and arrows at the bottom of the document window or the icons in the Pages pane instead.

Other differences between InDesign and PageMaker's page handling include the following:

- ✦ InDesign provides three methods for creating guides: dragging them off the ruler as you do in PageMaker, double-clicking the ruler where you want a guide, or choosing Layout ➩ Create Guides.

- ✦ To delete guides, you need to select them and click Delete. (To select all guides on a page, press Option+⌘+G or Ctrl+Alt+G.) Make sure that guides are not locked (View ➩ Lock Guides, or Option+⌘+; [semicolon] or Ctrl+Alt+; [semicolon]).

- ✦ Use the Pages pane (Window ➩ Pages, or F12) to create and apply master pages; to add, move, and delete document pages; and to display different pages.

- ✦ You can now place more than two pages side-by-side. Choose the Keep Spread Together command in the Pages pane's palette menu to ensure they stay together if you add more pages later before them.

- ✦ Some of your favorite commands from the Layout menu seem to be missing (such as Insert Pages), but you can access similar commands from the Pages pane's palette menu.

- ✦ You can base one master page on another, the same way you can base style sheets on each other.

- ✦ To share master pages among documents, you can drag a master page icon into another document window.

Working with color

Although creating colors is somewhat different in InDesign, applying colors is fairly similar. You can create colors in the same color models, and you can manage colors in a similar way. Differences between PageMaker and InDesign include the following:

- ✦ Most of your work with colors happens through the Swatches pane (Window ➩ Swatches, or F5) — not through the Colors pane as PageMaker users might think.

- ✦ To create colors, use the New Swatches command in the Swatches pane's palette menu.

- ✦ To apply colors, first click the Stroke or Fill button on the Toolbox to specify where the color goes on the selected object. Then click a color in the Swatches pane.

✦ Use the Colors pane (Window ➪ Colors, or F6) to specify a shade (tint) of a color.

✦ Apply the color None to strokes and fills for transparency; you can also click the None button on the Toolbox.

✦ To share colors among documents, drag a colored object into another document window.

✦   ✦   ✦

Switching to Mac OS X

✦ ✦ ✦ ✦

In This Appendix

Understanding
interface issues

Knowing where
everything is

Running Mac OS 9
applications

Customizing
Mac OS X

✦ ✦ ✦ ✦

Although Mac OS X has now been around for several
years, the Jaguar 10.2 version released in fall 2002 is the
first real one—the first that works reliably and truly unlocks
the promise of an advanced Mac OS that is stable, powerful,
and flexible. InDesign 2 supported Mac OS X as well as Mac OS
9, so experienced InDesign users will likely already be familiar
with Mac OS X.

However, because both QuarkXPress 5 (and earlier versions)
and PageMaker 7 (and earlier versions) could run only in Mac
OS 9 compatibility mode under Mac OS X, most PageMaker
and QuarkXPress users stuck with Mac OS 9 so they'd have a
consistent operating system and not have to worry about
managing fonts and other tools in two environments. But now,
PageMaker and QuarkXPress users switching to InDesign CS
have to switch to Mac OS X and leave Mac OS 9 behind, since
InDesign CS does not run on older versions of the Mac OS.

Very quickly, you'll find that Mac OS X is *not* Mac OS 9.
Although there are some similarities in terms of icons, the two
operating systems are very different, and former PageMaker
and QuarkXPress users steeped in Mac OS 9 will experience
some culture shock. If you're one of those getting used to Mac
OS X for the first time, I've put together a quick guide to
adjusting to Mac OS X, so you can master the essentials and
then unlock the new features in InDesign CS.

Interface Issues

Mac OS X at first presents a very simple screen, as Figure E-1
shows. At upper-right are any disk drives and network connections, while at bottom is the Dock, which contains a selection of programs (any that are running have a triangle beneath
them). At top is the menu for the currently active application
(the Finder is considered an application).

Figure E-1: The initial Mac OS X interface.

Dock

The Dock combines the Mac OS 9 Application menu and the Mac OS 9 Apple (✿) menu's Favorites folder. You can drag application icons or files onto the Dock so they're accessible at any time—similar to the Favorites folder. And any applications that are running—whether or not you launched them from the Dock—will display as well. So will minimized windows. The Dock is preloaded with a variety of Apple applications, as well as Microsoft Internet Explorer, the Systems Preferences control panel (which replaces the Mac OS 9 Apple menu's Control Panels folder), and the trash can.

Tip   As in Mac OS 9, you can drag icons into the trash can to delete them, but Mac OS X uses contextual menus more widely than Mac OS 9 did, and you'll find it easier in many cases to simply right-click (if you have a two-button mouse) or Control+click (if you don't) icons that you want to delete and select the Move to Trash option in the menu that pops up.

When you launch an application, you'll see its icon on the Dock bounce. After it has launched, a triangle appears below it so you know it is active.

Finally, if you click and hold the mouse down over a Dock's icon, you'll get a pop-up menu that lets you quit the program, force-quit it if it is frozen, keep it in the dock from now on, and show the actual application's folder location.

Common menus

There are three other key interface issues you'll need to know to start using Mac OS X. Apple has redefined the Apple menu's purpose and added two new standard menus, the application menu and the Go menu.

✦ The Apple menu (shown in Figure E-2) contains basic system functionality: System Preferences, Force Quit, Sleep, Restart, Shut Down, and Log Out — as well as Dock settings, a list of recent items, a link to Apple's OS X software Web page, and Location settings (for those who travel and have different network settings for work, home, remote office, and so on).

Figure E-2: The Apple menu.

✦ The new application menu (shown in Figure E-3) — which is always the name of the current application, such as Finder or InDesign — is where application preferences are accessed, as well as where you quit the application, hide it or other applications, and access basic Mac OS X system services such as mail, speech, the basic TextEdit text editor, and so on.

Figure E-3: The application menu for the Finder; all applications have a similar menu in which preference-oriented settings may be added in addition to the options shown here.

✦ The new Go menu (shown in Figure E-4) provides shortcuts to standard locations on your Mac — Computer, which shows the drives and network connections; Home, which is the home folder for the currently logged-on user (you can have multiple user accounts, and each has its own folder for files and settings); iDisk, which is an Internet-based storage site for subscribers to Apple's .Mac Internet and e-mail service; Applications, which is the default folder for installed applications; Favorites, which contains aliases placed by the user for quick access; and Recent Folders. This is also where the Mac OS 9 Chooser functionality has been placed: You use the Connect to Server menu item to connect to Apple or Windows servers.

Figure E-4: The Go menu.

Folder views and navigation

Mac OS X provides three ways to look at folder contents: the Icon view, the List view, and the new Column view. Figure E-5 shows all three. The Column view is similar to the List view in that it can display subfolders. The difference is that subfolders are always opened for the currently selected folder or drive, and you can scroll the folder hierarchy using the scroll bar at the bottom.

Note that Open dialog boxes in programs use the new Column view. That can be a problem—if your filenames tend to be long (more than 20 characters), the view skips over the middle part of the filename and displays an ellipsis (...) instead. That can make it hard to know which file is which, especially if you keep copies of file revisions. Unfortunately, there's no way to know what the file actually is until you open it.

Figure E-5: The three folder views (from top to bottom): Icon, List, and Column.

Windows have several options as well:

✦ There are three icons at the upper-left: Close, Minimize, and Restore. These work like the Mac OS 9 equivalents, except for the Minimize icon, which places a thumbnail of the window in the Dock. As in Mac OS 9, you can also double-click the title bar to minimize the window.

✦ Windows have a toolbar that contains a series of icons at top, such as Back and Forward to navigate, View to choose the view type, shortcuts for standard Mac OS X locations such as Home, and Search. You can hide the toolbar by clicking the oblong icon at the window's upper-right.

✦ In addition to using the Back and Forward navigation buttons, you can navigate via a folder hierarchy. Just ⌘+click the folder name to get a list of folders containing the current one, as Figure E-6 shows.

✦ You can resize windows by dragging the resize corner at the bottom-right.

Tip   You can customize the toolbar's contents by Control+clicking it. (Multibutton mice should let you right-click instead of Control+click.) You can also choose View ⇨ Customize Toolbar from the Finder.

Figure E-6: Mac OS X displays this folder hierarchy when you ⌘+click the folder name.

Where Is Everything?

Mac OS X places many items in new locations, so new users can easily get lost. Here are where some of the common items are.

Network connections and file sharing

Access AppleTalk and Windows TCP/IP servers via Go ⇨ Connect to Server or via the shortcut ⌘+K. You'll get a list of server domains that, in turn, contain available servers. Click the server you want to access, and you'll then be prompted for the user name and password, and finally for the specific drive to open.

Set up access to users on other computers — Mac and Windows — via the Accounts and the Sharing control panels. Accounts sets up the users who have access, and Sharing sets up the allowable connections (such as AppleShare, now called Personal File Sharing, and Windows File Sharing) and security settings. Note that anyone set up as a user via the Accounts control panel has both network access rights and login rights to the Mac itself — the user can log on to the Mac at startup — because Mac OS X doesn't care whether the connection is over the network or physically from the Mac. (This is similar to how Windows XP handles user access.)

Printers

Apple has buried its printer controls in the Utilities folder in the Applications folder, which is on the drive on which you installed Mac OS X. The Print Center utility is shown in Figure E-7. Here, you choose active printers and install new ones. Mac OS X comes with drivers for some popular printers, but you'll likely need an installation program from your printer vendor (either on a CD that came with it or via download from the manufacturer's Web site.)

Figure E-7: The Print Center utility.

When you add a printer, you'll get a Printer List dialog box that has a pop-up menu of connection types (such as USB, Firewire, and IP). Choose the appropriate connection, and after a few seconds, Mac OS X will show a list of printers. Figure E-8 shows an example.

Figure E-8: The Printer List dialog box displays when you add printers.

Applications

Applications are typically installed in the Applications folder, but they can also be installed in any folder (however, doing so can confuse product updaters, so leave applications in the Applications folder). Typically, Mac OS X applications will be in the Applications folder, but your Mac OS 9 applications will remain wherever you installed them — and you can continue to run them from those locations.

Startup applications — ones you want to run every time you launch Mac OS X, such as the Palm handheld synchronization software or a font manager — are managed through the Login Items control panel. Note that some applications automatically install as startup applications, while others do not.

Fonts

Fonts can exist in several places, which is sure to confuse many new Mac OS X users. Here are the key locations for Mac OS X applications:

✦ **Fonts folder in the Library folder.** You should place fonts here that you want all users to have access to. Just drag them in, whether PostScript, TrueType, or Open Type.

✦ **Fonts folder in the user's Home folder's Library folder.** Any fonts dragged here will be available only to that user.

✦ **Fonts folder in the System folder's Library folder.** Apple places the default fonts for Mac OS X applications here. You can add fonts here as well by dragging them, but I recommend you leave this folder alone.

Any fonts installed in the Mac OS X folders will not be available to Mac OS 9 applications. You need to also maintain fonts in the System Folder's Fonts folder—note that the Mac OS 9 folder name is System Folder while the Mac OS X folder name is simply System—or use a Mac OS 9 font manager such as Adobe Type Manager.

It can be confusing enough to have both a Mac OS X and a Mac OS 9 environment on the same system, but it can get even more confusing if you also keep your old Mac OS 9 setup (which I recommend in case something goes horribly wrong when you install Mac OS X). In that case, you'll have your original Mac OS 9 System Folder, the Mac OS X System folder for Mac OS X, and a separate System Folder containing the version of Mac OS 9 that Mac OS X runs Mac OS 9 applications in. Make sure all fonts used are placed in all Fonts folders that you might use—Mac OS X, the Mac OS 9 used by Mac OS X, and the original Mac OS 9 that you may occasionally start up from instead of Mac OS X.

Tip

If you use a third-party font manager such as DiamondSoft's Font Reserve or Extensis's Suitcase, your fonts can be installed anywhere as long as you have told the Font Manager where they are stored. These programs can autoactivate fonts as needed for both Mac OS X and Mac OS 9 applications, and I strongly recommend you invest in one. (Adobe has no plans to release a Mac OS X version of Adobe Type Manager or Adobe Type Reunion.)

Another source of confusion for new Mac OS X users is the operating system's non-support of Multiple Master PostScript fonts. The Multiple Master format lets programs modify fonts on the fly, such as creating a semibold version from a bold typeface. But the format never took off or got widespread adoption, so Mac OS X is essentially killing off the format. That means that Mac OS 9 applications running under Mac OS X can use Multiple Master fonts, but native Mac OS X applications such as InDesign CS cannot. That can cause problems when opening older InDesign, PageMaker, or QuarkXPress documents with Multiple Master fonts in InDesign CS. So, you'll need to replace the Multiple Master fonts with PostScript or OpenType fonts. If you created instances of Multiple Master fonts—such as a semibold— don't worry: When those instances are saved or exported as their own font files, they're no longer Multiple Master fonts and should work just fine under Mac OS X.

Running Mac OS 9 Applications

It's easy to use the "Classic" Mac OS 9 applications in Mac OS X: Just double-click their icons or run them from the Dock (if you've dragged them there). The first time you run a Mac OS 9 application in Mac OS X, you'll see a window of the Mac OS 9 environment, as Figure E-9 shows. That window disappears after Mac OS 9 has fully loaded.

Figure E-9: This launch window appears when first running Mac OS 9 applications.

The Mac OS 9 applications themselves look and run like they always have—you'll get the standard Mac OS 9 menu bar, as Figure E-10 shows. A nice touch, the menu bar's Applications menu shows Mac OS X programs that are running (they all will have a generic icon) as well as any Mac OS 9 applications that are running. Thus, when running a Mac OS 9 application, you can switch to other Mac OS 9 or Mac OS X applications through either the Mac OS 9 Application menu or the Mac OS X Dock. (When running a Mac OS X application, you must use the Dock to switch to other running applications.)

Note   If you shut down or restart Mac OS X and a Mac OS 9 application is running, Mac OS X may not restart or shut down until you manually quit the Mac OS 9 application.

Note that almost all Mac OS 9 functions are available, including the Chooser, when Classic mode is running. If you want Mac OS 9 to run automatically at Mac OS X startup, you can do so via the System Preferences' Classic control panel.

Figure E-10: Mac OS 9 applications have the standard menu bar, but also display Mac OS X applications in the Application menu.

Customizing Mac OS X

After you figure out where the key components are, you'll want to customize Mac OS X to your liking. You do so primarily through the System Preferences control panels. The set of System Preferences control panels is available through both the Dock and the Apple menu. Figure E-11 shows the System Preferences window and the standard control panels. (At bottom are user-installed control panels for specific devices they may have installed.)

Tip

You can't close a control panel after you've opened it. Instead, you either close the System Preferences window or click Show All or one of the control panel group icons at the top of the window. Doing so essentially closes the control panel and saves any changes. Note that there is no option to leave a control panel without canceling any settings changed—you'll have to reopen the control panel and change back any undesired or mistaken changes yourself.

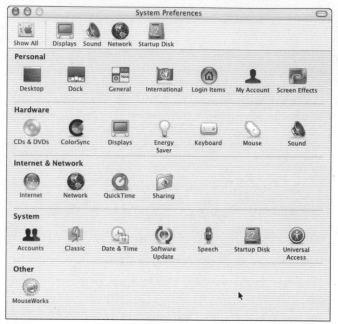

Figure E-11: The System Preferences control panels.

You should explore all the control panels. What follows is my advice for initial setup.

Classic

Use the Classic control panel to determine whether Mac OS 9 launches automatically when you start Mac OS X or only when you first launch a Mac OS 9 application. It's usually best to have Mac OS 9 launch only when a Mac OS 9 application is launched, so you're not reserving all that memory for Mac OS 9 until you need it.

You can change which Mac OS 9 System Folder Mac OS X uses — but be careful. If you kept your original Mac OS 9 System Folder, Mac OS X created a new, separate System Folder for it to run Mac OS 9 from, because there are some added files it needs to do so. If you run an older copy of Mac OS 9 (it must be at least version 9.2), Mac OS X will copy those needed files to that older version, but then you may have trouble if you later decide to start up in your old Mac OS 9. The downside to using the Mac OS X's Mac OS 9 files rather than your original ones is that all your preferences, fonts, and so forth won't be in the Mac OS 9 System Folder that Mac OS X created. I recommend that if you decide to have Mac OS X use your old Mac OS 9 System Folder, you first make a copy as a backup.

Dock

The Dock is pretty big by default, so you'll want to make it smaller. You can do that in the Dock control panel, or you can drag the vertical line in the Dock itself, which appears to the left of the Mac OS X Web site icon at the Dock's right side — up increases the Dock size and down decreases it. I also recommend you set the Dock to auto-hide, so it disappears entirely unless you move your mouse to the bottom of the screen, and that you set up magnification, which makes individual Dock icons grow in size as the mouse passes over them. This way you can have a small dock height but still be able to see icons and minimized windows clearly.

Login Items

The Login Items control panel lets you select (and deselect) which programs start up when you launch Mac OS X. Click the Add button to select applications, and the Remove button to remove them. You can also hide startup items so they aren't visible on-screen (they will be in the Dock).

My Account and Accounts

The My Account control panel is where you set your password, while Accounts is where the system administrator (main user) sets up accounts for other users, including those who may connect over the network for file sharing.

Network and Sharing

The Network control panel sets up the network connections to the Internet. Typically, you'll have DHCP as the connection mechanism for the Internet, but in some circumstances, your network may be set up differently and so you'll want to change these settings. The Sharing control panel sets what kinds of connections others can make to your Mac and what kind of security is enabled. Be sure to enable firewall protection if you're working on an unsecured network, as with many locations that use cable modems and DSL lines to connect to the Internet.

Figure E-12 shows a customized Mac OS X environment.

Figure E-12: A customized Mac OS X environment.

✦   ✦   ✦

Using Adobe InCopy

♦   ♦   ♦   ♦

In This Appendix

Knowing what InCopy does

Seeing how InCopy works within InDesign

Figuring out how to use InCopy alone

Tracking changes in InCopy

♦   ♦   ♦   ♦

Publishing is almost always a workgroup activity, involving writers, editors, copy editors, layout artists, and production editors. Even when a person has multiple roles, most publications still involve multiple people. And that means that files go back and forth as edits are made, layouts are created, and text and other elements are adjusted to fit the available space. Like rival QuarkXPress, InDesign has a companion product called InCopy to facilitate this back and forth. InCopy is not as powerful as InDesign — it's not a layout tool — but it does let copy editors, editors, and other wordsmiths work on InDesign layouts to make sure headlines fit, stories fit, and captions can be written in context without needing a full copy of InDesign.

InCopy works best in a networked environment, where everyone shares files from a common folder. That way, a copy editor can work on a layout without worrying that the designer might be working on a local copy at the same time, for example.

InCopy is both a separate program that runs by itself for text editing of stories in an InDesign layout, and a plug-in that works with InDesign to provide shared-editing capabilities.

Using InCopy in InDesign

InCopy does more than install on a user's system. It changes how InDesign works, adding a new menu and pane, both called Notes, and several new menu options in the File and Edit menus.

Working with notes

The Notes feature inserts comments into text. To use it, click the Text tool inside a text box. You can now choose New Note to add a note, which will be indicated in the file with a green dual-triangle character called a *note anchor* (see Figure F-1). (The Notes menu duplicates options in the Notes pane's palette menu, shown in Figure F-1.)

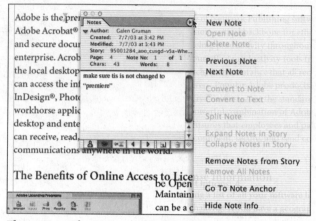

Figure F-1: The Notes pane, its palette menu, and (at upper left) the note anchor icon indicating a note in text.

Caution   If you select a string of text, InDesign won't display the New Note menu option; instead, it will display the Convert to Note option to make that text into a note. That's great if someone typed a note directly into text, but it can be dangerous if you're trying to highlight an entire word, as you would do when adding notes in Adobe Acrobat. You can convert a note back to text by choosing Convert to Text from the palette menu or from the Notes menu.

You can use the Notes pane's palette menu or the Notes menu in InDesign to navigate through notes (choose Previous Note or Next Note), control notes' display (Expand Notes in Story and Collapse Notes in Story), remove notes (choose Delete Note, Remove Notes from Story, or Remove All Notes), move to the note's anchor (choose Go to Note Anchor), or split a note into multiple notes (choose Split Note).

The InCopy plug-in also adds a Notes pane to the Preferences dialog box (choose InDesign ➪ Preferences on the Mac or Edit ➪ Preferences in Windows, or press ⌘+K or Ctrl+K). Figure F-2 shows the pane. In addition to changing the note anchor's color, you can also tell InDesign whether to spell-check notes, search notes in find/change operations, and display a user color behind notes in text. (Each user who edits a file gets assigned a unique color for easy identification, à la Microsoft Word's Track Changes feature.)

Figure F-2: The Notes preferences pane.

Working with other users

Before an InCopy user can work on a layout, an InDesign user has to InCopy-enable that layout. That means exporting the layout's stories to InCopy format (InCopy files have a filename extension of .incd), which you do by choosing Edit ⇨ InCopy Stories ⇨ Export Story; this exports the currently selected story. (A *story* is all text in a text frame or path and any frames and/or paths linked to it.) You could also choose Export Layer Stories to export all stories on the current layer or Export All Stories to export all stories in the document.

After navigating to the folder that you want to store the InCopy file to, click Export. As Figure F-3 shows, you'll be asked to select what is exported; you generally want all attributes to export. Then click OK.

If you have not done so already, you'll be asked to provide a user name, which InCopy uses to track the author of every change. Enter a name, then click OK. (You can set up your user name in InDesign by choosing File ⇨ User.)

Figure F-3: The three dialog boxes that appear after you choose the folder in which to place an exported story for use by others in InCopy. The User dialog box only displays the first time you export, and not at all if you choose File ➪ User before exporting that first time.

Creating an InCopy file also makes the stories unavailable in the InDesign layout for further work. But you can keep working on the layout, such as resizing frames, adding graphics, and even changing text's color. If you want to work on the text, you need to *check out* the story, making it available to you but to no one else. To do so, click on the frame containing the story you want to edit, then choose Edit ➪ InCopy Stories ➪ Check Out Story. When done, choose either Check In Story or Check In All to return the stories to use by others. (Or choose Cancel Check to undo all your changes and leave the story unchanged.)

If someone else is working on a story, you can have InDesign apply the current changes to the layout on your screen by choosing Edit ➪ InCopy Stories ➪ Update Story.

Tip   If you're making textual changes, you'd normally have an editor do so in InCopy. But because InCopy doesn't show the text as actually laid out, editors can't use InCopy to write or edit headlines to fit or do fine-level copy fitting such as getting rid of widows. In those cases, they'll need to use a copy of InDesign and check out the story as described earlier.

Caution   When you choose Export All Stories, InDesign will export every story it finds. And by *story*, InDesign means any text in any text frame. So, if your headlines are in separate frames and not linked to their body copy frames, the headlines will each be a separate story. Ditto for any captions, or text in figures. This can create dozens of files in your project folder. So it's usually better not to choose Export All Stories and instead individually export each story that you want to be editable.

Using InCopy Alone

The standalone InCopy application looks and works very much like the new InDesign Story Editor. You'll also find a bevy of familiar panes — Notes, Scripts, Swatches, Tags, Tools, and the various text editing panes — in the Window menu. You'll also find the standard Edit and Type menu options to change text attributes and do spell checking. Plus you'll find many of the standard InDesign preferences panes.

What's different? Plenty.

Story views

First, there are three panes in which to view the story. The Story pane is the plainest view, essentially the same as the InDesign Story Editor. Here, you work on text as if you were in a word processor, with applied styles shown at left. Figure F-4 shows this pane. The Layout pane shows the story as it appears in InDesign. The Galley pane is like the Story pane, except that each line breaks as it does in InDesign, so you can see where lines end and whether the last lines in paragraphs have room for more text or whether small text deletions could easily eliminate a short last line during copy fitting.

Note   Although this seems counterintuitive, you don't actually work on InCopy story files. You need to open the InDesign file in InCopy. InCopy will then load the InCopy files as needed. The reason that InCopy has all these separate story files is so multiple users can work on the same layout, but on different stories, at the same time. You can open and edit InCopy story files in InCopy, but you won't see the layout or line breaks properly.

Note   Note the bars that indicate different InCopy stories — you can display and hide stories by clicking the triangles to the left of the story name.

Note tool

Type tool

Commandbar pane

Info Column

Change Tracking pane

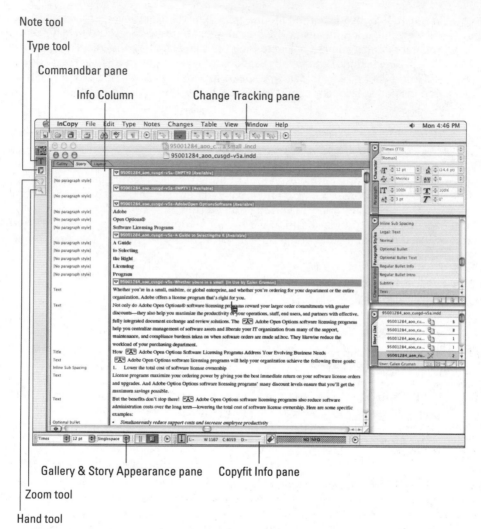

Gallery & Story Appearance pane   Copyfit Info pane

Zoom tool

Hand tool

Figure F-4: Adobe InCopy, with a layout viewed in the Story pane.

Story checkout, check in, and saving

When you open an InDesign file in InCopy, you need to check out stories to edit them, and check them in to make them available to others, as described in the previous section. To check out stories, go to the story in any of the panes, then choose File ➪ Check Out Story, or press ⌘+Y or Ctrl+Y. You check stories back in by choosing File ➪ Check In Story, or pressing Option+⌘+W or Ctrl+Alt+W, or by choosing File ➪ Check In All, or pressing Option+Shift+⌘+W or Ctrl+Alt+Shift+W. The Story List pane (Window ➪ Story List) shows which stories are already checked out.

You can also choose File ➪ Cancel Checkout to make a story available to others without saving any changes you made. Choose File ➪ Revert Story instead to undo changes made since the last save but keep the story checked out for your use.

To save a story, you have four options in the File menu:

✦ Save Story, or ⌘+S or Ctrl+S, to save the current story.

✦ Save Story As, or Shift+⌘+S or Ctrl+Shift+S, to save the current story with a new name or in a new location. Such a story will have to be imported into the InDesign layout.

✦ Save Story Copy, or Option+⌘+S or Ctrl+Alt+S, to save a copy of the current story, such as for archiving story versions.

✦ Save All Stories, or Option+Shift+⌘+S or Ctrl+Alt+Shift+S, to save all stories — this helps ensure all changes are made to the InDesign document, no matter what stories the changes occurred in.

Revisions tracking

InCopy can track who made what changes to InDesign files. To enable such revisions tracking, choose Changes ➪ Track Changes in Current Story, or press Shift+⌘+H or Ctrl+Shift+H. If multiple stories are open, you can choose Changes ➪ Enable Tracking in All Stories.

When reviewing changes, you can move from change to change by choosing Changes ➪ Next Change, or pressing Option+Shift+⌘+right arrow or Ctrl+Alt+Shift+ right arrow. You can move backward by choosing Changes ➪ Previous Change, or pressing Option+Shift+⌘+left arrow or Ctrl+Alt+Shift+left arrow. You can accept individual changes by choosing Changes ➪ Accept Change, or pressing Option+⌘+=, and you can accept all changes by choosing Changes ➪ Accept All Changes, or Option+Shift+⌘+=. Likewise, you can reject changes individually by choosing Changes ➪ Reject Change, or pressing Option+⌘+- (hyphen) or Ctrl+Alt+- (hyphen), or globally by choosing Changes ➪ Reject All Changes, or pressing Option+Shift+⌘+- (hyphen) or Ctrl+Alt+Shift+- (hyphen). When reviewing changes, you can get information on who made the change and when by having the Change Info pane open (Window ➪ Change Info, or Shift+⌘+F3 or Ctrl+Shift+F3).

Tip You can hide changes as you make them by choosing View ➪ Hide Changes, or pressing ⌘+7 or Ctrl+7. To review changes, you'll need to make changes visible.

Note You can also use the Change Tracking pane to move among revisions and accept or reject changes. The iconic palette offers the following buttons from left to right: Track Changes in Current Story, Show/Hide Changes, Previous Change, Next Change, Accept Change, Reject Change, Accept All Changes, and Reject All Changes.

Special features

The editing and formatting features are the same as in InDesign, so this appendix does not cover them. Likewise, the Notes features are the same as described earlier in this appendix. But there are some specific InCopy features you should know about:

✦ The awkwardly named Commandbar pane provides iconic button access for, from left to right, New Document, Open Document, Save, Print, Find, Check Spelling, Show/Hide Hidden Characters.

✦ The Galley & Story Appearance pane likewise provides Font, Size, and text preview Spacing pop-up menus to change the Story and Galley panes' text display, plus iconic controls to Show/Hide Line Numbers and Show/Hide Paragraph Styles. You can also change these settings, plus the text cursor display, via the Galley & Story Display pane in the Preferences dialog box (choose InCopy ➪ Preferences on the Mac or Edit ➪ Preferences in Windows, or press ⌘+K or Ctrl+K). The pane is identical to the Story Editor preferences pane covered in Chapter 15. The show/hide options in the Galley & Story Appearance pane are also available in the View menu.

✦ The Copyfit Info pane shows how many lines a story is over what fits in its text frame(s) and/or path(s), using the bar at its far right. As you delete text, the progress bar will get smaller and smaller until there is no runover. The pane also tracks the number of lines, words, characters, and column depth. The Update Copyfit Info button checks the current InDesign layout to see if changes to the layout have solved or created copy fitting problems, in which text overflows its text frame(s). The pane also has the Update Story Info button at far left that updates the Story Info pane (File ➪ Story Info) with the name of the current reviser.

Refer to Figure F-4 for an illustration of these three panes, as well as the Change Tracking pane.

✦   ✦   ✦

The InDesign Central Web Site

Technology doesn't stand still, especially not in an area as dynamic as publishing, where multiple products work together. That's why I've created the InDesign Central Web site, available at www.INDDcentral.com. At this site, you'll find the following resources:

- ✦ **Tools:** Links to plug-ins, scripts, utilities, and Adobe downloads
- ✦ **Tips:** More of my favorite tips, as well as reader tips
- ✦ **Resources:** Print publishing links, Web publishing links, Mac OS X links, and Windows 2000/XP links
- ✦ *InDesign CS Bible:* Excerpts from the book, including color versions of the screenshots from Chapter 8, as well as purchase links to the *InDesign CS Bible* and related books

Figure G-1 shows the site's home page.

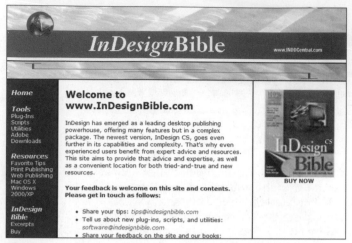

Figure G-1: The home page for the InDesign Central Web site at `www.INDDcentral.com`.

✦   ✦   ✦

Shortcuts Cheat Sheet

Shortcuts are essential to making the most of InDesign. Sure, you can access everything from a menu or pane, but shortcuts make the work much faster. This appendix covers InDesign's keyboard shortcuts and working with contextual menus, which lets you use the mouse to find out what options are available for specific objects.

Because there are so many keyboard shortcuts, I've broken them into functional areas to help you find them more easily in the following table.

Action or command	Macintosh	Windows
Opening/closing/saving		
New document	⌘+N	Ctrl+N
New default document	Option+⌘+N	Ctrl+Alt+N
Open document	⌘+O	Ctrl+O
Open library	Shift+Option+⌘+L	Ctrl+Alt+Shift+L
Close document	⌘+W	Ctrl+W or Ctrl+F4
Close all documents	Option+Shift+⌘+W	Ctrl+Alt+Shift+W
Quit program	⌘+Q	Ctrl+Q or Alt+F4
Save document	⌘+S	Ctrl+S
Save document as	Shift+⌘+S	Ctrl+Shift+S
Save copy of document	Option+⌘+S	Ctrl+Alt+D
Export document to PDF or FPS	⌘+E	Ctrl+E
Place text and graphics	⌘+D	Ctrl+D

Continued

Action or command	Macintosh	Windows
Viewing		
Hide/show panes	Tab	Tab
Hide/show all panes but toolbox	Shift+Tab	Shift+Tab
Zoom in	⌘+plus	Ctrl+plus
Zoom out	⌘+hyphen	Ctrl+hyphen
Fit page/spread in window	⌘+0	Ctrl+Alt+plus
Fit spread in window	Shift+⌘+0	Ctrl+Alt+0
Fit entire pasteboard in window	Option+Shift+⌘+0	Ctrl+Alt+Shift+0
Display actual size	⌘+1	Ctrl+1
Display at 50%	⌘+5	Ctrl+5
Display at 200%	⌘+2	Ctrl+2
Display at 400%	⌘+4	Ctrl+4
Overprint preview	Option+Shift+⌘+Y	Ctrl+Alt+Shift+Y
Switch between current and previous view	Option⌘+2	Ctrl+Alt+2
Set magnification	Option⌘+5	Ctrl+Alt+5
Set all pages to same view	⌘+percent in view percent menu	Ctrl+percent in view percent menu
Switch to previous document window	Shift+⌘+F6	Ctrl+Shift+F6
Switch to next document window	⌘+Y	Ctrl+F6
Show/hide text threads	Option+⌘+Y	Ctrl+Alt+Y
Show/hide frame edges	⌘+H	Ctrl+H
Show/hide rulers	⌘+R	Ctrl+R
Show hidden characters	Option+⌘+I	Ctrl+Alt+I
Preference/setup		
Preferences dialog box	⌘+K	Ctrl+K
Document setup	Option+⌘+P	Ctrl+Alt+P

Action or command	Macintosh	Windows
Tools		
Selection tool	V	V
Direct Selection tool	A	A
Type tool	T	T
Text Path tool	Shift+T	Shift+T
Pen tool	P	P
Ellipse tool	L	L
Rectangle tool	M	M
Rectangle Frame tool	F	F
Rotate tool	R	R
Scale tool	S	S
Shear tool	O	O
Scissors tool	C	C
Hand tool	H	H
Temporary Hand tool	Shift+spacebar	Shift+spacebar
Zoom tool	Z	Z
Temporary zoom-in tool	⌘+spacebar	Ctrl+spacebar
Temporary zoom-out tool	Option+⌘+spacebar	Ctrl+Alt+spacebar
Gradient tool	G	G
Fill box	X	X
Stroke box	X	X
Swap Fill/Stroke box	Shift+X	Shift+X
Default Fill/Stroke box	D	D
Apply Color box	, (comma)	, (comma)
Apply Gradient box	. (period)	. (period)
Apply None box	/	/
Panes		
Apply value in field	Option+Enter	Shift+Return
Show Control palette	Option+⌘+6	Ctrl+Alt+6
Show Links pane	Shift+⌘+D	Ctrl+Shift+D

Continued

Action or command	Macintosh	Windows
Show Layers pane	F7	F7
Show Pages pane	F12	F12
Show Swatches pane	F5	F5
Show Color pane	F6	F6
Show Transform pane	F9	F9
Show Character pane	⌘+T	Ctrl+T
Select Font Name field	NA	Ctrl+Alt+Shift+M
Show Paragraph pane	Option+⌘+T	Ctrl+Alt+T
Show Character Styles pane	Shift+F11	Shift+F11
Show Paragraph Styles pane	F11	F11
Show Text Wrap pane	Option+⌘+W	Ctrl+Alt+W
Show Text Frame Options pane	⌘+B	Ctrl+B
Show Index pane	Shift+F8	Shift+F8
Show Table pane	Shift+F9	Shift+F9
Show Tabs pane	Shift⌘+T	Ctrl+Shift+T
Show Align pane	Shift+F7	Shift+F7
Show Stroke pane	F10	F10
Show Transparency pane	Shift+F10	Shift+F10
Show Info pane	F8	F8

Guides

Show/hide guides	⌘+; (semicolon)	Ctrl+; (semicolon)
Lock/unlock guides	Option+⌘+; (semicolon)	Ctrl+Alt+; (semicolon)
Snap to guides on/off	Shift+⌘+; (semicolon)	Ctrl+Shift+; (semicolon)
Show/hide baseline grid	Option+⌘+' (apostrophe)	Ctrl+Alt+' (apostrophe)
Show/hide document grid	⌘+' (apostrophe)	Ctrl+' (apostrophe)
Snap to document grid on/off	Shift+⌘+' (apostrophe)	Ctrl+Shift+' (apostrophe)
Select all guides	Option+⌘+G	Ctrl+Alt+G
Create zero-point guidelines	⌘+click zero point when dragging guides	Ctrl+click zero point when dragging guides

Action or command	Macintosh	Windows
Adding and navigating pages		
Add new page	Shift+⌘+P	Ctrl+Shift+P
Go to first page	Ctrl+Shift+Page Up	Shift+⌘+PgUp
Go back one page	Ctrl+Page Up	⌘+PgUp
Go forward one page	Ctrl+Page Down	⌘+PgDn
Go to last page	Ctrl+Shift+Page Down	Shift+⌘+PgDn
Object selection		
Select master page	Shift+⌘+click	Ctrl+Shift+click
Select topmost object	Option+Shift+⌘+]	Ctrl+Alt+Shift+]
Select object above current object	Option+⌘+]	Ctrl+Alt+]
Select bottommost object	Shift+Option+⌘+[	Ctrl+Alt+Shift+[
Select object below current object	Option+⌘+[	Ctrl+Alt+[
Go to last frame in thread	Shift+Option+⌘+PgDn	Ctrl+Alt+Shift+Page Down
Go to next frame in thread	Option+⌘+PgDn	Ctrl+Alt+Page Down
Go to first frame in thread	Shift+Option+⌘+PgUp	Ctrl+Alt+Shift Page Up
Go to previous frame in thread	Option+⌘+PgUp	Ctrl+Alt+Page Up
Moving objects		
Move selection 1 point	left, right, up, and down cursors	left, right, up, and down cursors
Move selection 10 points	Shift+left, right, up, and down cursors	Shift+left, right, up, and down cursors
Bring object to front	Shift+⌘+]	Ctrl+Shift+]
Bring object forward	⌘+]	Ctrl+]
Send object to back	Shift+⌘+[	Ctrl+Shift+[
Send object backward	⌘+[	Ctrl+[
Object commands		
Cut	⌘+X	Ctrl+X
Copy	⌘+V	Ctrl+V
Paste	⌘+P	Ctrl+P

Continued

Action or command	Macintosh	Windows
Paste into	Option+⌘+V	Ctrl+Alt+V
Paste in place	Option+Shift+⌘+V	Ctrl+Alt+Shift+V
Clear	Backspace	Backspace or Del
Duplicate object	Option+⌘+D	Ctrl+Alt+D
Step and repeat	Shift+⌘+V	Ctrl+Shift+V
Resize proportionately	Shift+drag	Shift+drag
Resize frame and content	⌘+drag	Ctrl+drag
Center content	Shift+⌘+E	Ctrl+Shift+E
Fit content proportionally	Option+Shift+⌘+E	Ctrl+Alt+Shift+E
Fit content to frame	Option+⌘+E	Ctrl+Alt+E
Fit frame to content	Option+⌘+C	Ctrl+Alt+C
Decrease size/scale by 1%	⌘+comma	Ctrl+comma
Decrease size/scale by 5%	Option+⌘+comma	Ctrl+Alt+comma
Increase size/scale by 5%	Option+⌘+period	Ctrl+Alt+period
Duplicate	Option+drag, or Option+left, right, up, and down cursors	Alt+drag, or Alt+left, right, up, and down cursors
Group	⌘+G	Ctrl+G
Ungroup	Shift+⌘+G	Ctrl+Shift+G
Lock	⌘+L	Ctrl+L
Unlock	Option+⌘+L	Ctrl+Alt+L
Drop shadow	Option+⌘+M	Ctrl+Alt+M
Graphics handling		
Convert text to outlines	Shift+⌘+O	Ctrl+Alt+O
Create outlines without deleting text	Option+Shift+⌘+O	Ctrl+Alt+Shift+O
Image color settings	Option+Shift+⌘+D	Ctrl+Alt+Shift+D
Make compound path	⌘+8	Ctrl+8
Release compound path	Option+⌘+8	Ctrl+Alt+8

Action or command	Macintosh	Windows
Text selection		
Select all	⌘+A	Ctrl+A
Deselect all	Shift+⌘+A	Ctrl+Shift+A
Select word	double-click	double-click
Select one word to left	Shift+⌘+left cursor	Ctrl+Shift+left cursor
Select one word to right	Shift+⌘+right cursor	Ctrl+Shift+right cursor
Select range	Shift+left, right, up, and down cursors	Shift+left, right, up, and down cursors
Select paragraph	triple-click	triple-click
Select one paragraph before	Shift+⌘+up cursor	Ctrl+Shift+up cursor
Select one paragraph after	Shift+⌘+down cursor	Ctrl+Shift+down cursor
Select to start of story	Shift+⌘+Home	Ctrl+Shift+Home
Select to end of story	Shift+⌘+End	Ctrl+Shift+End
Moving within text		
Move left one word	⌘+left cursor	Ctrl+left cursor
Move right one word	⌘+right cursor	Ctrl+right cursor
Move to start of line	Home	Home
Move to end of line	End	End
Move to previous paragraph	⌘+up cursor	Ctrl+up cursor
Move to next paragraph	⌘+down cursor	Ctrl+down cursor
Move to start of story	⌘+Home	Ctrl+Home
Move to end of story	⌘+End	Ctrl+End
Text/paragraph formats		
Bold	Shift+⌘+B	Ctrl+Shift+B
Italic	Shift+⌘+I	Ctrl+Shift+I
Normal	Shift+⌘+Y	Ctrl+Shift+Y
Underline	Shift+⌘+U	Ctrl+Shift+U
Strikethrough	Shift+⌘+/	Ctrl+Shift+/
All caps on/off	Shift+⌘+K	Ctrl+Shift+K
Small caps	Shift+⌘+H	Ctrl+Shift+H

Continued

Action or command	Macintosh	Windows
Superscript	Shift+⌘+plus	Ctrl+Shift+plus
Subscript	Option+Shift+⌘+plus	Ctrl+Alt+Shift+plus
Update character style based on selection	Option+Shift+⌘+C	Ctrl+Alt+Shift+C
Update paragraph style based on selection	Option+Shift+⌘+R	Ctrl+Alt+Shift+R
Drop caps and nested styles	Option+⌘+R	Ctrl+Alt+R
Paragraph rules	Option+⌘+J	Ctrl+Alt+J
Set horizontal scale to 100%	Shift+⌘+X	Ctrl+Shift+X
Set vertical scale to 100%	Option+Shift+⌘+X	Ctrl+Alt+Shift+X
Increase point size by 1 point	Shift+⌘+>	Ctrl+Shift+>
Increase point size by 10 points	Option+Shift+⌘+>	Ctrl+Alt+Shift+>
Decrease point size by 1 point	Shift+⌘+<	Ctrl+Shift+<
Decrease point size by 10 points	Option+Shift+⌘+<	Ctrl+Alt+Shift+<

Text alignment and spacing

Action or command	Macintosh	Windows
Align left	Shift+⌘+L	Ctrl+Shift+L
Align right	Shift+⌘+R	Ctrl+Shift+R
Align center	Shift+⌘+C	Ctrl+Shift+C
Justify full	Shift+⌘+F	Ctrl+Shift+F
Justify left	Shift+⌘+J	Ctrl+Shift+J
Justify right	Option+Shift+⌘+R	Ctrl+Alt+Shift+R
Justify center	Option+Shift+⌘+C	Ctrl+Alt+Shift+C
Autohyphenation on/off	Option+Shift+⌘+H	Ctrl+Alt+Shift+H
Hyphenation on/off (selected text)	Option+⌘+H	Ctrl+Alt+H
Set spacing and justification	Option+Shift+⌘+J	Ctrl+Alt+Shift+J
Set keep options	Option+⌘+K	Ctrl+Alt+K
Increase leading by 2 points	Option+up cursor	Alt+up cursor
Decrease leading by 2 points	Option+down cursor	Alt+down cursor

Action or command	Macintosh	Windows
Increase leading by 10 points	Option+⌘+up cursor	Ctrl+Alt+up cursor
Decrease leading by 10 points	Option+⌘+down cursor	Ctrl+Alt+down cursor
Use autoleading	Option+Shift+⌘+A	Ctrl+Alt+Shift+A
Increase kerning/ tracking by 20 units	Option+right cursor	Alt+right cursor
Increase kerning/ tracking by 100 units	Option+⌘+right cursor	Ctrl+Alt+right cursor
Decrease kerning/ tracking by 20 units	Option+left cursor	Alt+left cursor
Decrease kerning/ tracking by 100 units	Option+⌘+left cursor	Ctrl+Alt+left cursor
Clear all kerning/ tracking (set to 0)	Shift+⌘+Q	Ctrl+Shift+Q
Increase baseline shift by 2 points	Option+Shift+up arrow	Alt+Shift+up arrow
Increase baseline shift by 10 points	Option+Shift+⌘+up arrow	Ctrl+Alt+Shift+up arrow
Decrease baseline shift by 2 points	Option+Shift+down cursor	Alt+Shift+down arrow
Decrease baseline shift by 10 points	Option+Shift+⌘+ down arrow	Ctrl+Alt+Shift+ down arrow
Align to grid on/off	Option+Shift+⌘+G	Ctrl+Alt+Shift+G
Table editing		
Insert table	Option+Shift+⌘+T	Ctrl+Alt+Shift+T
Insert column	Option+⌘+9	Ctrl+Alt+9
Insert row	⌘+9	Ctrl+9
Select table	Option+⌘+A	Ctrl+Alt+A
Select column	Option+⌘+3	Ctrl+Alt+3
Select row	⌘+3	Ctrl+3
Select cell	⌘+/	Ctrl+/
Delete column	Shift+Delete	Shift+Backspace
Delete row	⌘+Delete	Ctrl+Backspace
Table setup	Option+Shift+⌘+B	Ctrl+Alt+Shift+B
Set cell text options	Option+⌘+B	Ctrl+Alt+B

Continued

Action or command	Macintosh	Windows
Find/change text, spelling, and indexing		
Edit in Story Editor	⌘+Y	Ctrl+Y
Find/change	⌘+F	Ctrl+F
Find next	Option+⌘+F	Ctrl+Alt+F
Search for selected text	Shift+F1	Shift+F1
Add selected text to Find What field	⌘+F1	Ctrl+F1
Add selected text to Change To field	⌘+F2	Ctrl+F2
Change current selection	⌘+F3	Ctrl+F3
Change current selection and search forward	Shift+⌘+F3	Ctrl+Shift+F3
Check spelling	⌘+I	Ctrl+I
Add new index entry	Option+⌘+U	Ctrl+Alt+U
Add new index entry (reversed)	Shift+⌘+F8	Ctrl+Shift+F8
New index/open index entry dialog box	⌘+U	Ctrl+U
Special characters		
Bullet (•)	Option+8	Alt+8
Ellipsis (...)	Option+; (semicolon)	Alt+; (semicolon)
Copyright (©)	Option+G	Alt+G
Registered trademark (®)	Option+R	Alt+R
Trademark (™)	Option+2	Alt+2
Paragraph (¶)	Option+7	Alt+7
Section (§)	Option+6	Alt+6
Switch between keyboard and typographic quotes	Option+Shift+⌘+' (apostrophe)	Ctrl+Alt+Shift+' (apostrophe)
Em dash (—)	Option+Shift+- (hyphen)	Alt+Shift+- (hyphen)
En dash (–)	Option+- (hyphen)	Alt+- (hyphen)
Nonbreaking hyphen	Option+⌘+- (hyphen)	Ctrl+Alt+- (hyphen)

Action or command	Macintosh	Windows
Discretionary hyphen	Shift+⌘+- (hyphen)	Ctrl+Shift+- (hyphen)
Em space	Shift+⌘+M	Ctrl+Shift+M
En space	Shift+⌘+N	Ctrl+Shift+N
Thin space	Option+Shift+⌘+M	Ctrl+Alt+Shift+M
Hair space	Option+Shift+⌘+I	Ctrl+Alt+Shift+I
Nonbreaking space	Option+⌘+X	Ctrl+Alt+X
Soft return	Shift+Enter	Shift+Return
Column break	Keypad Enter	Keypad Enter
Frame break	Shift+keypad Enter	Shift+keypad Enter
Page break	⌘+keypad Enter	Ctrl+keypad Enter
Indent to here	⌘+\	Ctrl+\
Right-indent tab	Shift+Tab	Shift+Tab
Insert current page number	Option+Shift+⌘+N	Ctrl+Alt+Shift+N
Insert next page number	Option+Shift+⌘+]	Ctrl+Alt+Shift+]
Insert previous page number	Option+Shift+⌘+[	Ctrl+Alt+Shift+[
Printing and output		
Print document	⌘+P	Ctrl+P
Preflight document	Option+Shift+⌘+F	Ctrl+Alt+Shift+F
Package document	Option+Shift+⌘+P	Ctrl+Alt+Shift+P
Miscellaneous		
Help	Help	F1
Undo	⌘+Z	Ctrl+Z
Redo	Shift+⌘+Z	Ctrl+Shift+Z

✦   ✦   ✦

Index

SYMBOLS

 (Apple) menu, 861
 (Apple) ⇨ System Preferences, 612
* (asterisk) multiplication operator, 58
< > (brackets) XML tag delimiter, 695
^$ (caret, dollar sign) wild card character, 340
^9 (caret, nine) wild card character, 340
^? (caret, question mark) wild card character, 340
-- (dashes) AppleScript comment delimiter, 737
– (minus sign) subtraction operator, 58
¶ (paragraph return symbol), 416
+ (plus sign)
   addition operator, 58
   style sheet name prefix, 445
/* */ (slash, asterisks, slash) JavaScript comment
      delimiter, 737
/ (slash) division operator, 58
~ (tilde) dictionary hyphenation point marker, 348–349

A

A & P Publishing Network Web site, 814
Acrobat software, 658, 672
Acute Systems CrossFont software, 751
Add Anchor Point tool, 47, 565
Add Chapter dialog box, 224
addition (arithmetic), 58, 463
Adobe
   ACE, 598
   Acrobat, 658, 672
   ATM, 754, 755, 756
   Composer, 403, 406, 407
   Distiller, 673
   font resources, 751, 753
   Illustrator
      illustration editor, using as, 749
      importing from, 485, 487, 488, 505–506
   plug-in download, 719
   PostScript printer driver, 614
   tool, 44
   Type Manager, 753
   Type Reunion, 753
   Web site, accessing from InDesign, 44
Adobe Type Library Reference Book (Adobe), 753
Advanced Character Formats pane, 83
Advanced pane
   Export EPS dialog box, 676–677
   Export PDF dialog box, 668–669
   Print dialog box, 644–645
advertisement layout, 771–773

agate (measurement unit), 786
AIFF files, 691
AirPort wireless connectivity, 745
alias feature (Macintosh), 709
aligning
   Align pane, using, 61, 302–304
   arrow key, using, 306
   design considerations, 774
   graphic, 252
   guide, to, 152
   ruler guide, using, 190
   spacing objects evenly, 303–304
   stroke, 270
   table content, 467, 472
   text
      baseline grid, to, 305, 399
      column text, 327, 396
      default alignment, setting, 107
      Paragraph pane, using, 10, 60, 396–397
      tab stop, using, 460, 463, 464
      table text, 467
      text frame, 247
   undoing alignment operation, 304
alpha channel, 501–502, 529
American Newspaper Publishers Association color.
      See ANPA color
anchor
   hyperlink, 683, 684, 691
   InCopy note anchor, 874
   point
      adding, 47, 564–565
      converting type, 567–568
      corner, 552, 556–558, 569
      deleting, 47, 564, 566, 576
      path, of, 551–552, 560, 564–568
      smooth, 552, 555
ANPA (American Newspaper Publishers Association)
      color, 813
anti-aliasing, text, 99
Apple () menu, 861
Apple () ⇨ System Preferences, 612
AppleScript
   condition, testing, 737
   debugger software, 731
   described, 729
   documentation, 729
   editor, 729, 730
   labeling item, 736

Continued

AppleScript *(continued)*
  running, 731
  saving, 731
  support, 725
  syntax error, checking for, 730
AppleScript Handbook, 2nd Edition (Goodman), 729
AppleScript in a Nutshell: A Desktop Quick Reference
        (Perry), 729
AppleScript 1-2-3 (Soghoian), 729
AppleScript Studio utility, 729
AppleScript Web site, 729
AppleTalk, 745, 865
application
  folder, 31–33
  menu (Macintosh), 861–862
Application Data folder, 708
Apply Master dialog box, 180
arithmetic calculation, 58, 463, 515
Arrange command, 286–287, 288
arrowhead, adding to line, 254
ascender, 785
Asian language character, inputting, 84
Assign Profiles dialog box, 602
Assign Trap Presets dialog box, 609
asterisk (*) multiplication operator, 58
ATM software, 754, 755, 756
audio, 70, 691, 693–694
AutoCAD document, importing, 486
autorecovery feature, 100, 132–133
AVI files, 691

B

background
  color
    applying using Tools palette color button, 53
    frame background, 18, 248, 253, 266, 426–427
    path background, 574
    text background, 248, 426–427
  sketch screen, 767
  type, reversing against, 275, 426–427
backup, 743, 744
Balena, Francesco (*Programming Microsoft Visual
        Basic 6.0*), 732
baseline
  grid
    aligning text to, 305, 399
    color, 90–91, 195
    default, 195
    described, 191
    displaying/hiding, 90, 110, 195, 305
    increment value, 91, 195, 305, 398
    locking text to, 305, 398–399
    printing, 631
    snapping to, 305

    spacing, 91, 195, 305
    view threshold, 91, 195
  shift, 90, 380, 381, 382
  table cell, of, 473
  text frame, of, 351–352
Beginning JavaScript (Wilton), 728
Bézier
  curve, 547, 550
  frame, 780
binding, perfect, 631, 659, 660, 663
bitmap
  color, 495, 518–519, 598
  display quality default, setting, 99
  importing, 484, 489–492, 494, 501–502
  scaling, 508
  tint, 519
  vector graphic, rasterizing, 487, 504
bits per second. *See* bps
bleed
  color, 604, 761
  mark, 635, 667
  mode, 53
  page area, 125, 624, 634–635, 636–637, 676
  paper, 641
  service bureau considerations, 624–625, 633
blending mode, 538–540, 545
BMP file, importing, 484, 485, 494, 501
book. *See also* index; TOC (Table of Contents)
  advantages/disadvantages, 223
  chapter
    adding, 224
    editing, 225
    file display as, 221
    opening, 225
    printing, 227
    removing, 225
    synchronizing, 224, 226–227
    TOC, dedicating to, 233
  color swatchbook, 810, 813–814
  creating, 222, 224
  described, 221
  opening, 222
  page
    numbering, 228
    section, working with, 228
  pane, 225–226
  PDF, exporting to, 227, 661
  planning, 222
  Preflight tool, applying to, 615
  printing, 227, 615
  saving, 223
  status, 225–226
  storage location, 223
  style, formatting using, 224, 226

synchronizing, 224, 226–227
template, using in, 222, 227
booklet, 659
bookmark
creating, 65, 686–688
deleting, 687
naming, 687
PDF, exporting to, 232, 664, 688
sorting, 687
subentry, 687
TOC, 232, 664, 687
Bookmarks pane, 65, 686–688
border
frame, of, 248, 266
table, of, 468
bounding box
Direct Selection tool, manipulating using, 258
frame, of, 251–252, 259
graphic, of, 251–252, 529
group of objects, of, 290
line, of, 254–255
moving object, displaying when, 116, 276
Selection tool, manipulating using, 251–252, 258, 259, 264
text wrap around, 15, 528–529
box (frame holding layout element), 762
bps (bits per second), 743
brackets (< >) XML tag delimitor, 695
Bring Forward command, 288
Bring to Front command, 288
brochure, 143
build, color, 810
bullet, 414, 416–420, 789
button, creating interactive, 51, 688–691
byline, 776, 796

C
cameo effect, creating using frame, 780
camera, digital, 748–749
Canon S series printer, 748
carding, 788
caret, dollar sign (^$) wild card character, 340
caret, nine (^9) wild card character, 340
caret, question mark (^?) wild card character, 340
CCITT compression, 666, 672
CD-RW drive, 743
centering color, 605
CGM (Computer Graphics Metafile) file, importing, 486
Change Info pane (InCopy), 879
Change Tracking pane (InCopy), 879
Changes ⇨ Accept All Changes, 879
Changes ⇨ Accept Change, 879
Changes ⇨ Enable Tracking in All Stories, 879
Changes ⇨ Next Change, 879

Changes ⇨ Previous Change, 879
Changes ⇨ Reject All Changes, 879
Changes ⇨ eject Change, 879
Changes ⇨ Track Changes in Current Story, 879
character
Asian language character, inputting, 84
dingbat, 417, 418, 419, 431, 776
palette, 345
pane
baseline shift, adjusting using, 382
bullet, formatting using, 417
font, formatting using, 10–11, 377–378, 379, 422
hyphenation, controlling using, 404
kerning, adjusting using, 59, 381, 390
leading, adjusting using, 59
palette menu, 83
Paragraph pane, combining with, 394
scaling using, 59, 382
sizing text using, 59, 83, 382
tracking, adjusting using, 59, 381, 391
Type tool, working with Character pane while open, 375
underlining using, 435–436
special character
accent, 803–808
Character Map utility, entering using, 316, 464, 799
deleting glyph, 801
font, assigning to glyph, 801
font, availability in, 317
glyph set, creating, 799–801
Glyphs pane, entering using, 61, 464
highlighting substituted glyph, 86
Insert Glyphs command, entering using, 104, 799
Key Caps software, entering using, 315
keyboard shortcut list, 801–803
Macintosh environment, 315–316, 801–806
PopChar X software, entering using, 316, 464, 799
search and replace operation, finding in, 337–340
Windows environment, 316–317, 801–806
style
Advanced Character Formats pane, adjusting using, 83
applying, 447–449
creating, 12, 447–449
default, changing, 110–111
described, 441, 447
editing, 452
fraction formatting, saving as, 430
list, formatting using, 229
manual formatting, combining with, 453
naming, 448–449
nesting, 425

Continued

character, style *(continued)*
  unapplying, 453–454
  updating, 375
  XML tag mapping, 698
  wingding, 417, 419, 431
Character Map utility, 316, 464, 799
Character Styles pane, 12–13, 60, 442, 447–448, 710
Check Spelling dialog box, 343–344
The Chicago Manual of Style, 235
choking color, 603–605
cicero (measurement unit), 29, 89, 786
CIE (Commission Internationale d'Éclairage),
      201, 600, 810
circular (flier) layout, 771–773
Clear command, 68
client approval, 768
Clipboard preference, setting, 81–82
clipping path
  command, 535–537
  creating, 533
  default setup, changing, 108
  dialog box, 108
  free-form, 534–535
  generating, 508
  importing graphic, adding when, 501–502, 503, 508
  JPEG file, setting in, 492, 532
  overriding built-in, 535
  Photoshop, 529, 533
  QuarkXPress, 837
  text wrap around, 526, 529, 534
  threshold value, 535, 536
  TIFF file, setting in, 490, 532
  tolerance value, 536
cloning
  Control palette, using, 300, 514
  described, 263
  moving object, when, 263
  path, 553, 570
  Transform pane, using, 300, 514
Close command, 133
CMS (color management system), 594, 598, 601
CMYK (cyan, yellow, magenta, black) color
  converting other color model to, 208, 495
  creating, 17, 200–201
  described, 810
  gradient, 215, 216
  importing, 495
  introduced, 198
  mixed-ink, 206
  naming, 200–201
  Pantone, converting to CMYK, 494, 495
  printing, 211–212, 597, 636, 647–650
  profile, 598, 601
  screen display, 212

separation, 203, 212, 494
spot color
  CMYK versus, 210–212
  converting to/from, 211, 647–649, 812
  mixing with in same document, 211, 811–812
color
  alpha channel, 501–502, 529
  ANPA, 813
  background
    applying using Tools palette color button, 53
    frame, of, 18, 248, 253, 266, 426–427
    path, of, 574
    text, of, 248, 426–427
  baseline grid, 90–91, 195
  bitmap, 495, 518–519, 598
  bleed, 604, 761
  blending mode, 538–540, 545
  build, 810
  calibrating
    bit depth, adjusting in preparation for, 597
    bitmap handling, 598
    black point compensation, 599
    CMS, enabling, 594
    color space, specifying, 598
    Colorimetric options, 599
    described, 495
    ICC profile, 496, 668
    imported color, 598, 600–601
    monitor, 596, 597–599
    non-RGB color, 597
    output, 598, 603
    PDF export, in, 668
    photograph, for, 599
    printing, applying calibration in, 643–644
    profile, 596, 598, 600
    room color, adjusting in preparation for, 596
    saturation, 599
    temperature, adjusting in preparation for, 596
    tool, using third party, 596, 599
  centering, 605
  choking, 603–605
  CIE standard, 201, 600, 810
  CMS, 594, 598, 601
  CMYK
    converting other color model to, 208, 495
    creating, 17, 200–201
    described, 810
    gradient, 215, 216
    importing, 495
    introduced, 198
    mixed-ink, 206
    naming, 200–201
    Pantone, converting to CMYK, 494, 495
    printing, 211–212, 597, 636, 647–650

profile, 598, 601
screen display, 212
separation, 203, 212, 494
spot color, converting to/from, 211, 647–649, 812
spot color, mixing with in same document, 211, 811–812
spot color versus, 210–212
constituent color, 812
copying, 209, 212
CRD, 643
creating
   CMYK, 17, 200–201
   LAB, 201
   mixed color, 204–207
   RGB, 201
   spot color, 201
   swatch, 199–201
   tint, 203–204
default setup, changing, 110
deleting, 208–209
density, neutral, 605
DIC, 203, 210, 211, 597, 814
document grid, 92, 195
drop shadow, 437, 545
duotone, 204
editing, 207–208
EPS, 212–213, 487, 494, 675
fifth color, 211
fill
   frame, applying to, 18
   list bullet, applying to, 417
   path, applying to, 549
   stroke, adding to, 275
   Swatches pane, applying using, 62
   table, applying to, 470, 474
   text, applying to, 19, 432–433, 587, 588
   Tools palette color button, applying using, 53
Focoltone, 203, 210, 212, 597, 814
folder, 710
gamma value, 502
gamut, 502, 810
GIF, 491, 702
gradient, 53, 62, 214–218, 268, 433
guide, of, 37, 92, 106, 191, 193
Hexachrome, 213, 810, 813
HKS, 203, 206, 814, 815
hyperlink, 685
ICC profile, 496, 668
imagesetter, outputting for, 603
importing, 209–210, 494–496, 501–502, 598, 600–601
knockout, 605
LAB, 200, 201, 215, 810
layer, identifying using, 160, 287–288
layout, using in, 781

line, of, 283
list bullet, of, 417
luminosity, 201
Macintosh environment, 502, 596, 598, 710, 714
management, enabling, 594
matching, 594
mixed color, 204–207, 210
model, 495, 810, 812–813
monitor
   calibrating, 596, 597–599
   Macintosh monitor, 502
   profile, 596, 598, 599
   temperature, 596
   white point, 596
naming, 200–201, 205, 209, 211, 216–217
Navigator pane options, 150
none-colored, 266
overlapping, 205
PageMaker, 857–858
pane, 56, 62, 63, 205
Pantone
   building, 813
   CMYK, converting to, 494, 495
   PageMaker support, 202
   paper used with, 202, 814–815
   PMS, 202
   printing, 211, 597
   QuarkXPress support, 202
   separation, 203, 212
   swatch library, 202
   swatchbook, 813
path, 549, 574
PDF, 213, 668
PNG, 492
predefined, 198
printing
   calibration, applying, 643–644
   CMYK, 211–212, 597, 636, 647–650
   color bar, 636
   composite, 19–20, 638, 639, 640
   DIC, 211, 597
   Focoltone, 597
   four-color, 210, 810, 811
   imagesetter, outputting for, 603, 639
   ink used, displaying, 618
   overlapping color, 205, 603–610
   overprint, 605
   Package tool, preparing using, 620
   Pantone, 211, 597
   Preflight tool, preparing using, 618
   prepress feature overview, 593–594
   printer color space, specifying, 643–644
   RGB, 212, 213, 597

Continued

color, printing *(continued)*
 separation, 638, 650–651
 spot color, 205
 Toyo, 211, 597
 trapping for, 603, 639, 648
 Trumatch, 597
 profile, 596, 598, 600–602, 668
 QuarkXPress, 202, 837, 848
 RGB
  creating, 201
  described, 810
  gradient, 215
  importing, 495
  naming, 200
  printing, 212, 213, 597
  profile, 598, 601
 rule (horizontal line), of, 410, 411
 sampling using Eyedropper tool, 17, 51
 second color, 210
 separation
  DCS, 487
  described, 810
  EPS file, color in, 487, 494
  Focoltone, 203
  In-RIP, 639, 640
  Pantone, 203, 212
  previewing, 64, 65, 650–651
  printing, 638, 650–651
  Trumatch, 203
 sharing, 216, 708, 709–710
 space, 598, 643, 810
 spot color
  CMYK, converting to/from, 211, 647–649, 812
  CMYK, mixing with in same document,
   211, 811–812
  CMYK versus, 210–212
  creating, 201
  described, 811
  gradient, 216
  naming, 211
  printing, 205
 spreading, 603–605
 Story Editor options, 97
 stroke, 219, 267–268, 271–272, 432–433, 584–585
 swatch
  book, 810, 813–814
  copying, 209
  deleting, 208–209
  library, 32, 78, 202–203, 709, 822
  merging swatches, 208
  selecting, 208
 System color, 203

 table
  border, of, 468
  cell, of, 474, 477
  fill, 470, 474
  line, of, 468, 469
 temperature, 596
 text
  background, 248, 426–427
  design considerations, 432
  drop shadow, 437
  fill, 19, 432–433, 587, 588
  reversed text, 275, 426–427
  stroke, 432–433, 584–585
  Swatches pane, applying using, 62, 219, 410
  underline, 436
 TIFF, 212, 213, 490
 tint
  bitmap, 519
  creating, 203–204
  deleting, 209
  editing, 207–208
  grayscale, tinting, 780
  stroke, of, 268, 271–272
 Tools palette color buttons, 52–53
 Toyo, 203, 210, 211, 597, 814
 trapping, 603–610, 639, 648
 Trumatch, 203, 210, 212, 597, 813
 unnamed, 205, 209, 216–217
 Web color library, 203
 wheel, 812
 XML tag, of, 698
Color Management pane, 643–644
color management system. *See* CMS
color reference dictionary. *See* CRD
Color Settings dialog box, 594–595, 598
Colors and Inks pane, 618
ColorSync calibrator, 596, 598
Column Strokes pane, 469–470
column, table. *See* table, column
column, text. *See* text, column
Column view (Macintosh), 862–863
Commandbar pane (InCopy), 880
comment
 OPI, 503, 663
 script, commenting, 737
 XML, 695, 700, 701
Commission Internationale d'Éclairage. *See* CIE
Composer, 403, 406, 407
composite, printing, 19–20, 638, 639, 640
Composition pane, 85–87, 531
Compound Paths command, 535, 542
compression
 CCITT, 666, 672
 downsampling, 666

JPEG, 492, 666
lossy, 666
pane, 664–666
PDF export options, 664–666, 672
PNG, 492
subsampling, 666
TIFF, 490
utility, 750
Zip, 666
Computer Graphics Metafile file, importing. *See* CGM
file, importing
Configure Plug-Ins dialog box, 722–723
Content tool
InDesign, 7
QuarkXPress, 253, 258
contextual menu feature, 75
continued on/from page reference, creating, 146
contrast, adjusting, 519
control, global versus local, 27–28, 394, 445, 453
Control palette
accessing, 59
baseline shift, adjusting using, 382
cloning using, 300, 514
context sensitivity, 57, 258
dimension of object, displaying in, 50
Drop Cap Number option, 400
flipping using, 516–517
floating, 59
font, adjusting using, 378–379, 422
frame, adjusting using, 4–5, 282
graphic, formatting using, 15, 513–514
grid, 263, 265, 514
hyphenation, controlling using, 402, 404
indent, adjusting using, 415–416
justification, adjusting using, 11
keep options, 408–409
kerning, adjusting using, 380, 390
leading, adjusting using, 282
line, formatting using, 14, 48
paragraph, formatting using, 394–395, 399,
408–409, 410
positioning using, 49, 263–264, 358
rotating using, 253, 434, 515–516
scaling using, 382, 515
shearing using, 266, 513
sizing using, 5–6, 247, 250, 282, 379
skewing using, 516
stroke weight, adjusting using, 14, 268, 282
table, formatting using, 477
tracking, adjusting using, 380
Transform pane compared, 282, 364, 513–514
transformation, applying using, 282
underlining using, 435–436
zero point, 36

Convert Direction Point tool, 564, 567–568
Convert Text to Table dialog box, 478
Convert to Profile dialog box, 602
Copyfit Info pane (InCopy), 880
copying
blend, preserving, 81
cloning
Control palette, using, 300, 514
described, 263
moving object, when, 263
path, 553, 570
Transform pane, using, 300, 514
color, 209, 212
Copy/Paste commands, using, 68, 163, 294, 299, 505
Cut command, using, 68, 249, 266
document
object to another, 142, 301
opening as copy, 129
page to another, 142
saving copy of, 133–134, 135, 153
drag and drop, using, 327–328, 362, 505, 506
Duplicate command, using, 300
graphic, 505, 509
index topic/entry, 239
layer
object on, 162–163
remembering in copy operation, 162
library object, 186, 188, 190, 300
master page, 177, 178, 712–713
Paste in Place command, using, 299
pattern, preserving, 81
PDF, 81
Step and Repeat command, using, 300–301
style, 446
text, 82, 188, 326, 327–328, 333
CorelDraw
illustration editor, using as, 749
importing from, 486, 487
corner
effect, 108, 266, 275–276, 578–579
point, 552, 556–558, 569
coupon layout, 774
CRD (color reference dictionary), 643
Create Guides dialog box, 192
Create Outlines command, 541, 574, 588–589
Create Package Folder dialog box, 620–621
Creo software, 658
crop mark, 632, 635, 636
cropping, 508–510, 762
CrossFont software, 751
CS Tools palette, 43
CT file, importing, 484, 486, 489

curve
    Bézier curve, 547, 550
    drawing, 47, 554–558, 560
Cut command, 68, 249, 266, 576
cyan, yellow, magenta, black color. *See* CMYK color

D

Dainippon Ink & Chemical color. *See* DIC color
dashes (—) AppleScript comment delimiter, 737
data type description. *See* DTD
database, publishing, 321–322
DataViz Mac/PC connectivity, 745
DCS (Document Color Separation) file, 487, 639
Delete Anchor Point tool, 47, 566, 576
Delete Swatch dialog box, 209
deleting
    anchor point, 47, 564, 566, 576
    Backspace key, using, 266
    bookmark, 687
    color, 208–209
    Cut command, using, 68, 249, 266, 576
    Delete key, using, 266
    dictionary, word from, 347
    glyph, 801
    hyperlink, 685
    InDesign Defaults file, 825
    index topic/entry, 239, 241
    keyboard shortcut, using, 249
    layer, 164, 166–167
    library
        entire library, 187
        file associated with library, 188
        object from library, 186, 187
    master page, 173, 177
    menu command, using, 249
    page, 62, 142, 173
    Recycle Bin, via dragging object to, 249
    ruler guide, 193
    style, 446
    table column/row, 471–472
    text, 334
    Trash Can, via dragging object to, 249
    XML DTD, 701
descender, 785
design
    advertisement, 771–773
    alignment, 774
    circular (flier), 771–773
    client approval, 768
    colleague input, 769
    consistency, 765–766
    content, matching to, 765, 770, 783
    coupon, 774
    dummy, mockup using, 235, 766–767

element overview, 761–762
    formula, avoiding, 769–771
    headline, 774, 776, 796
    idea file, documenting in, 763
    imitating, 769–770
    intentional, 780
    magazine, 777–778
    masthead, 767
    newsletter, 774–776
    PSA, 773–774
    simplicity, 764, 774
    sketching, 768–769
    tag line, 773
    text design considerations, 381–382, 424, 432,
        771–774, 775–776
    thumbnail, using to visualize, 768, 769
    tool overview, 759–760
    transformation design considerations, 764
    white space, 389, 762, 764, 772, 781
Device Settings pane (Windows), 614
Diagonal Lines pane, 475–476
DiamondSoft Font Reserve software, 753, 755–756
DIC (Dainippon Ink & Chemical) color, 203, 210,
        211, 597, 814
Dictionaries folder, 32
dictionary
    adding word to, 346–347
    CRD, 643
    deleting word from, 347
    hyphenation dictionary, 94, 95, 347–349, 621, 789
    language, specifying, 94–95, 349
    pane, 94–96, 349–350
    replacing, 349–350
    sharing, 708, 710
    spell check dictionary, 94–96, 107, 344, 345–350,
        383–384
    storage location, 708
digital camera, 748–749
dingbat, 417, 418, 419, 431, 776
Direct Selection tool
    anchor point display, 251–252, 265
    bounding box, manipulating using, 258
    described, 45–46
    frame, selecting using, 509–510
    graphic, selecting using, 509
    handle display, 252
    line, selecting using, 254–255
    objects, selecting multiple simultaneously using,
        46, 261, 291
    Selection tool compared, 253, 258
    threading, using in, 46
disk, hard. *See* hard drive
Display Performance pane, 98–99
distance across multiple objects, determining, 50

Distiller software, 673
division (arithmetic), 58, 463
Dock (Macintosh), 860–861, 864, 871
document
    closing, 133
    copying
        object to another document, 142, 301
        opening document as copy, 129
        page to another document, 142
        saving copy of document, 133–134, 135, 153
    creating, 2–4, 33, 37, 122–127
    grid
        color, 92, 195
        described, 92, 305
        displaying/hiding, 90, 110, 196
        distance between lines, specifying, 195
        positioning, 89, 92
        snapping to, 72, 93, 110
        subdividing, 92, 196
    navigating, 148–150
    opening, 122, 127–130
    planning, 121–122, 763
    preset, 3, 125–127
    QuarkXPress difference, 841
    recovering, 100, 132–133
    reverting to previous version, 134, 135
    saving, 99–100, 133–136
    style, 126–127, 825
    tiling display, 713
    variant, creating using layer, 160, 162, 616
    window
        fitting to, 33, 91, 112, 114, 149
        guide display, 37
        Macintosh/Windows differences, 33
        multiple document windows, opening, 116–117
        page area, 37
        page buttons, 39–40
        ruler, 35
        scroll bar, 36, 114–115
        Show/Hide Structure button, 38
        title bar, 33–36
        View Percentage field, 38
        zero point, 36
        Zoom box, 114, 115
Document Color Separation file. *See* DCS file
Document Exchange Format file, importing. *See* DXF
        file, importing
Document Presets dialog box, 127
Document Setup dialog box, 105–107, 151
downsampling compression, 666
dpi (dots per inch), 640–641, 747
drag and drop, copying object using, 327–328,
        362, 505, 506
drawing. *See specific tool and object*

drawing tablet, 547, 749
drop
    cap
        automatic, 420–422
        character style, applying to, 13
        creating, 11, 400–401, 420–422
        depth, 400
        described, 789
        kerning, 421
        newsletter, using in, 776
        quotation mark in, 422
        sizing, 11, 421
        style, as nested, 451
        shadow, 377, 437–438, 544–545, 688
Drop Cap & Nested Styles dialog box, 11, 401, 449–450
DTD (data type description), 695, 700–701. *See also*
        XML (Extensible Markup Language)
dummy
    index mockup using, 235
    layout mockup using, 766–767
duotone color, 204
Duplicate command, 300
DVD R/W drive, 743–744
DXF (Document Exchange Format) file, importing, 486

E

eBook, 664, 686, 820, 832–833
Edit ➪ Assign Profiles, 601
Edit ➪ Color Settings, 110
Edit ➪ Convert to Profile, 602
Edit ➪ Deselect, 262
Edit ➪ Deselect All, 333
Edit ➪ Duplicate, 300
Edit ➪ Edit Dictionary, 346
Edit ➪ Edit in Story Editor, 334
Edit ➪ Export, 331
Edit ➪ Find/Change, 335
Edit Glyph Set dialog box, 800
Edit ➪ InCopy Stories ➪ Check Out Story, 876
Edit ➪ InCopy Stories ➪ Export Story, 875
Edit ➪ InCopy Stories ➪ Update Story, 876
Edit ➪ Keyboard Shortcuts, 103
Edit menu, 66, 68
Edit ➪ Paste, 163
Edit ➪ Paste in Place, 299
Edit ➪ Preferences, 36
Edit ➪ Preferences ➪ Grids, 194
Edit ➪ Preferences ➪ Guides & Pasteboard, 194
Edit ➪ Redo, 135
Edit ➪ Select All, 47
Edit ➪ Step and Repeat, 300–301
Edit TOC Style Sheet dialog box, 233
Edit ➪ Transparency Blend Space ➪ Document
        CMYK, 540

Edit ➪ Transparency Blend Space ➪ Document RGB, 540

Edit ➪ Undo, 79

Ellipse Frame tool, 48, 250–251

Ellipse tool, 49, 360

em space (measurement unit), 389, 786

emboss effect, applying to text, 779

EMF (Enhanced Metafile), importing, 484, 486

en space (measurement unit), 786

encryption
>   PDF output, 670
>   wireless network, 746

endpoint, path, 551, 571

Enhanced Metafile, importing. *See* EMF, importing

EPS (Encapsulated PostScript)
>   bleed area, 676
>   color, 212–213, 487, 494, 675
>   editing, 749
>   encapsulation, 508
>   exporting, 136, 658–659, 673–677
>   font, embedding, 675
>   importing, 484, 485, 487, 503–504
>   OPI information, 487, 503, 522, 677
>   page spread, exporting to, 674
>   PDF, creating from, 673
>   preview, 487, 503, 504, 677
>   service bureau, providing to, 658, 675, 677
>   transformation, applying to, 508
>   transparency, 677

EPS Import Options dialog box, 503–504

Epson Color Stylus printer, 748

Excel, importing from, 132, 314, 331

Export dialog box, 661

Export EPS dialog box, 673–677

Export PDF dialog box
>   Advanced pane, 668–669
>   Compression pane, 664–666
>   General pane, 662–664, 688
>   Marks and Bleeds pane, 667
>   Security pane, 669–671
>   Summary pane, 671

Export XML dialog box, 702

exporting
>   EPS, 136, 658–659, 673–677
>   font, 659, 677–678, 755
>   graphic
>>   OPI replacement information, 668
>>   XML, to, 702–703
>   HTML, 491, 681
>   hyperlink, 664, 685
>   JPEG, 136, 702
>   page spread, 662–663, 674
>   PDF
>>   bleed mark, including, 667
>>   book, 227, 661

>   bookmark, 232, 664, 688
>   color, calibrating, 668
>   compression, 664–666, 672
>   eBook tag, including, 664
>   encrypting output file, 670
>   font, embedding, 661, 669
>   grid, including, 664
>   guide, including, 664
>   hyperlink, preserving, 664, 685
>   layer, preserving, 664
>   metadata, including, 671
>   multimedia, including, 664
>   on-screen usage, for, 672
>   OPI graphic replacement information, 668
>   optimizing, 663
>   overprint, simulating, 668
>   page spread, 662–663
>   password protecting output file, 670
>   PDF Export Presets command, using, 661
>   PDF/X format, to, 663, 668
>   permission to output file, specifying, 670–671
>   printing, for, 658, 667
>   printing to PDF file, via, 672–673
>   saving to PDF file, via, 136
>   security, 669–671, 672
>   signing output file digitally, 671
>   slug area, including, 667
>   thumbnail, embedding, 663
>   transparency flattening, 668
>   version, specifying, 663

PostScript prepress file, 659, 677–678

RTF, 135, 364, 457

story to InCopy, 875–877

style sheet, 364, 457

SVG, 136

text, 135, 136, 319–321, 331–332

XML, 136, 698, 701–703

extensibility, 719

Extensible Markup Language. *See* XML

eXtensible Metadata Platform. *See* XMP

Extensis Suitcase software, 753, 755–756

External Plug-ins pane, 619

Eyedropper tool, 17, 51

F

feathering
>   graphic, 545–546
>   QuarkXPress, 544, 847
>   text, 438, 788

field
>   arithmetic calculation, performing in, 58, 463
>   value, entering, 57–58

fifth color, 211

figure space (measurement unit), 786

file
  book chapter, display as, 221
  button link, assigning to, 691
  displaying hidden, 708
  graphic file location, 500
  layout, documenting in idea file, 763
  naming convention, 715–716
  opening, 122, 127–130, 714
  print output, including filename with, 636
  printing to, 646–647, 672–673, 678
  recovering, 100, 132–133
  saving, 99–100, 133–136
  text file, importing, 132, 311–315, 317–319, 331, 361
  thumbnail view of first page, saving with, 100
File ⇨ Cancel Checkout, 879
File ⇨ Check In All, 878
File ⇨ Check In Story, 878
File ⇨ Close, 133
File ⇨ Document Presets ⇨ Define, 126
File ⇨ Document Setup, 53
File ⇨ Get Info, 187
File ⇨ Import XML, 697
File ⇨ Links, 505
File menu, 66, 67
File ⇨ New, 33
File ⇨ New ⇨ Book, 222
File ⇨ New ⇨ Document, 2
File ⇨ New ⇨ Library, 184
File ⇨ Open, 122
File ⇨ Package, 135
File ⇨ Package For GoLive, 703
File ⇨ PDF Export Presets, 661
File ⇨ Place, 48
File ⇨ Preferences ⇨ Composition, 79
File ⇨ Preflight, 615
File ⇨ Print, 19
File ⇨ Print Presets ⇨ Define, 629
File ⇨ Revert Story, 879
File ⇨ User (InCopy), 875
fill
  frame, applying to, 18
  list bullet, applying to, 417
  path, applying to, 549
  stroke, adding to, 275
  Swatches pane, applying using, 62
  table, applying to, 470, 474
  text, applying to, 432–433, 587, 588
  Tools palette color button, applying using, 53
Fills pane, 470
film, printing to, 632, 633, 639, 641
Find/Change dialog box, 335–336, 341
first-line indentation, 398, 414, 415
Flanagan, David (JavaScript: The Definitive Guide), 728
Flattener Preview pane, 64

flattening
  layer, 166
  transparency, 64, 645, 652–655, 668, 677
flier (circular) layout, 771–773
flip chart, 140
flipping
  Control palette, using, 516–517
  graphic, 516–517
  Transform pane, using, 281, 516–517
FobtLab software, 751
Focoltone color, 203, 210, 212, 597, 814
folder, displaying hidden, 708
Folder Options dialog box, 708
foldout page, 143, 778
folio (publication identifier), 762, 775
font. See also text
  agate, 786
  ascender, 785
  assigning, 10
  boldface, 11, 424, 791–792
  character, availability of special in, 317
  Character pane, formatting using, 10–11, 377–378, 379, 422
  consistency, 781, 794
  Control palette, formatting using, 378–379, 422
  creating, 751
  default, specifying, 107
  descender, 785
  described, 376, 784, 793–794
  downloading, 81, 642, 643
  em space, 389, 786
  e-mailing, 751
  embedded, 81, 486–487, 661, 669, 675
  en space, 786
  expert, 387
  exporting, 659, 677–678, 755
  face, 784
  figure space, 786
  graphic, converting to, 419
  height, 785
  importing embedded, 486–487
  installing, 753–755
  italic, 382–383, 424, 773, 791, 796
  kerning table, 389
  leading, adjusting in function of font size, 391
  library, considerations when copying from, 188
  licensing, 751
  ligature, 385–386, 785–786
  list bullet, of, 417–419
  locked, 669
  Macintosh
    installing, 754, 755
    manager, 753

Continued

font, Macintosh *(continued)*
    OpenType support, 752, 792
    OS X, 752, 753, 754, 792, 866–867
    PostScript support, 752, 754, 792, 867
    storage location, 753, 866–867
    suitcase, 754
    Windows/Macintosh mixed environment, 716–717, 751, 795
  manager, 753, 755–756
  measurement unit, 88, 89, 786
  missing, checking for, 615
  name display, 377
  number used, restricting, 776
  OpenType, 386–388, 752, 754, 792
  point, 88, 786
  PostScript
    importing PostScript file, 487–488
    Level 2, 643, 820
    Level 3, 593, 639, 643, 820
    Macintosh support, 752, 754, 792, 867
    Multiple Masters format, 754, 867
    OpenType versus, 752
    PDF, creating from PostScript file, 673
    PPD file, 613, 623, 628, 643, 678
    prepress file, exporting to, 659, 677–678
    printer, 613, 614–615, 628, 643, 747–748
    TrueType versus, 752
  printing
    device memory considerations, 642–643
    download option, 642, 643
    missing font, checking for, 615
    Preflight tool, preparing using, 615, 616–617
    translation by printer, 614
    TrueType, 614, 615, 616, 792
  Roman, 784, 794
  sans serif, 784, 785, 791
  serif, 785, 791
  service bureau considerations, 619, 642–643, 669, 675, 751–752
  setting, 59
  size, 379–380, 391, 421
  sources, 750–751
  storage location, 753
  style, 784
  substitution, 86, 486, 614
  translation, 614, 751
  TrueType
    PostScript versus, 752
    printing, 614, 615, 616, 792
    support, 754, 792
    translating, 751
  typeface, 376, 377–379, 424, 429, 790–796
  typestyle, 376, 377–379

  visual theme, representing in, 781
  weight, 784, 791, 796
  Windows font, 754–755
Font Reserve software, 753, 755–756
FontLab software, 419, 432
Fontographer software, 419, 432, 751
Fonts
  folder, 753, 866
  pane, 616–617
FontSite Web site, 751
form, printing, 659–660
formatting, global versus local, 27–28, 394, 445, 453
four-color printing, 210, 810, 811
fraction, formatting, 428–430
frame. *See also* threading
  background color, 18, 248, 253, 266, 426–427
  Bézier frame, 780
  border, 248, 266
  bounding box, 251–252, 259
  box (frame holding layout element), 762
  button, converting frame to, 51, 688
  cameo effect, creating using, 780
  Control palette, adjusting using, 4–5, 282
  corner effect, 108, 266, 275–276
  creating, 4–6
  cutting, 51
  described, 43, 245
  edge, displaying/hiding, 72, 110, 116
  ellipse, 48, 250–251, 259, 360
  empty, 43, 266
  graphics frame
    active, 251
    aligning, 252
    anchor point, 251–252
    bounding box, 251–252
    creating, 14, 249
    described, 246
    ellipse, 48, 250–251
    fitting graphic to, 517–518
    handle, 251
    importing graphic into, 246, 250, 499–500, 508
    importing text into, 330
    inserting graphic in, 48, 252
    moving frame leaving graphic in place, 46
    moving graphic in, 46, 509, 514–515
    polygon, 48, 250–251, 252–253
    rectangle, 14, 48, 250–251
    shape, irregular, 509–510
    sizing, 14, 250–251, 508
    splitting, 572
    text frame, converting to graphics frame, 249
  handle, 251, 252
  inline, 293–296, 317–318, 542–543

metaphor, frame-based, 26–27
nesting, 291–293
node, 259
object compared, 245
path, creating from, 47
polygon, 48, 250–251, 252–253, 360
QuarkXPress, 48, 276, 293, 515, 841
rotating, 253, 266, 277, 734–736
scaling, 253, 265, 278–279, 435
selecting
    content of frame, 261, 265
    entire frame, 259, 261, 509–510
shape, converting to frame, 249
shearing, 266, 279, 280
splitting, 544, 572
stroke, applying to, 48, 248, 267–268, 518
table row, breaking across multiple frames, 472
text frame
    aligning, 247
    background color, 248, 426–427
    baseline, 351–352
    border, 248
    bounding box, 259
    column, adjusting in, 369–370
    creating, 4–5, 246–249, 325–326, 356–360
    default setup, changing, 108
    described, 245–246
    ellipse, 360
    entering text in, 7–9, 47–48, 246, 247–248, 333
    graphics frame, converting text frame to, 249
    import operation, overflowing during, 330
    inset, 351, 413, 430, 463, 464
    introduced, 43
    justifying text in, 352–353
    library, copying from, 188
    margin, 351
    master text frame, 124, 177, 247, 326, 357–360
    moving, 5–6, 248
    polygon, 360
    port, 366–367
    rectangular, 47, 360
    rotating, 779
    scaling, 435
    sizing, 4–5, 245, 247, 279, 333
    stroke, applying to, 248
    table row, breaking across multiple frames, 472
    TOC inserting in, 233–234
    wrap, ignoring in, 352, 358, 531
text wrap
    frame, around, 526, 527–529, 531
    text frame, ignoring in, 352, 358, 531
TOC inserting in, 233–234
tool overview, 48–49

transformation, applying to, 276–282
    XML, applying to, 700
Free Transform tool, 50, 512
FreeHand software, 749

G

galley, 760
Galley & Story Appearance pane (InCopy), 880
gamut, color, 502, 810
gatefold, 778
GB (gigabyte), 743
General pane
    Export EPS dialog box, 673–676
    Export PDF dialog box, 662–664, 688
    Preferences dialog box, 79, 80–82
    Print dialog box, 631–632
Generate Index dialog box, 240
GIF (Graphics Interchange Format)
    color, 491, 702
    converting graphic to, 491
    exporting, 702
    importing, 484, 485, 491, 501
gigabyte. See GB
glyph. See character, special character
Glyphs pane, 61, 164, 800
Go ⇨ Connect to Server (Macintosh), 865
Go menu (Macintosh), 862
GoLive, packaging for, 135, 703
Goodman, Danny
    AppleScript Handbook, 2nd Edition, 729
    JavaScript Bible, 4th Edition, 728
gradient
    CMYK, 215, 216
    color, 53, 62, 214–218, 268, 433
    direction, changing, 51
    halo effect, creating using, 586
    importing, 131, 506
    linear, 214, 218
    pane, 62, 217, 585
    path, applying to, 549
    pattern, 53
    QuarkXPress, importing from, 131
    radial, 214, 218
    RGB, 215
    spot color, 216
    stroke, applying to, 62, 268–269, 433, 585
    Swatches pane, applying using, 214–216
    table cell, of, 477
    text, applying to, 219, 432–433, 585, 586, 587–588
    tool, 51, 218
Gradient Options dialog box, 217
graduated fill. See gradient

graphic
  aligning, 252
  bitmap
    color, 495, 518–519, 598
    display quality default, setting, 99
    importing, 484, 489–492, 494, 501–502
    scaling, 508
    tint, 519
    vector graphic, rasterizing, 487, 504
  bounding box, 251–252, 529
  button graphic, 689
  color trapping, 608
  compression
    JPEG, 492, 666
    PNG, 492
    TIFF, 490
  contrast, adjusting, 519
  Control palette, formatting using, 15, 513–514
  copying, 505, 509
  cropping, 508–510, 762
  display preference, setting, 98–99
  editor
    InDesign, using, 483–484, 507–508
    third-party, 484, 749
  embedding, 523
  exporting
    GIF, 702
    JPEG, 136, 702
  feathering, 545–546
  file location, 500
  flipping, 516–517
  font, converting graphic to, 419
  format, converting, 489, 491
  frame
    active, 251
    aligning, 252
    anchor point, 251–252
    bounding box, 251–252
    creating, 14, 249
    described, 246
    ellipse, 48, 250–251
    fitting graphic to, 517–518
    handle, 251
    importing graphic into, 246, 250, 499–500, 508
    importing text into, 330
    inserting graphic in, 48, 252
    moving frame leaving graphic in place, 46
    moving graphic in, 46, 509, 514–515
    polygon, 48, 250–251, 252–253
    rectangle, 14, 48, 250–251
    shape, irregular, 509–510
    sizing, 14, 250–251, 508
    splitting, 572
    text frame, converting to graphics frame, 249

importing
  alpha channel, adding, 501–502
  bitmap, 484, 489–492, 494, 501–502
  BMP, 484, 485, 494, 501
  CGM, 486
  clipping path, adding, 501–502, 503, 508
  copying between applications, via, 505
  CorelDraw, from, 486, 487
  DCS, 487
  dragging and dropping between applications,
    via, 505, 506
  DXF, 486
  embedding imported graphic, 523
  EMF, 484, 486
  EPS, 484, 485, 487, 503–504
  frame, into, 246, 250, 499–500, 508
  GIF, 484, 485, 491, 501
  Illustrator, from, 485, 487, 488, 505–506
  inline graphic, 317–318, 484–486
  JPEG, 484, 492, 501
  line art, 484
  link with source file, 497, 498, 505, 519–524
  OPI information, 487, 503, 522
  PCX, 484, 485, 494, 501
  Photo CD, from, 486
  Photoshop, from, 485, 489–490, 501, 503
  PICT, 484, 486, 489, 494, 501
  Place command, using, 14, 249, 498–500, 518, 590
  PNG, 484, 486, 492, 502
  PostScript file, 487–488
  preparing graphic for, 484
  preview, 497
  publication, customizing for, 500
  resolution considerations, 485, 520
  SCT, 484, 486, 489, 501
  text outline, into, 590
  TIFF, 484, 486, 489, 490–491, 501–502
  vector graphic, 484, 486–489, 503–504
  WMF, 484, 486, 489, 503
inline, 293–296, 317–318, 484–486
link with source file
  imported graphic, 497, 498, 505, 519–524
  pasted graphic, 505, 617, 621
Macintosh/Windows mixed environment, 490, 493
missing, checking for, 615
PageMaker, 856
path
  clipping path, adding when importing,
    501–502, 503, 508
  placing graphic in, 551
PDF treatment as, 488
point of origin, 514
printing, 616, 617, 620, 641–643
QuarkXPress, 846–847

rotating, 510–512, 515–516, 734–736
runaround, 15
scaling, 15, 508, 510–512, 515
script
    referencing in, 727
    rotating using, 734–736
selecting, 509
sharing, 711
shearing, 510–512
simplicity, 774
sizing, 151, 250–251, 508, 517–518
skewing, 516
slicing, 543
source element, 711
table, inserting in, 467
text
    converting text to graphic, 588–590
    font, converting graphic to, 419
    frame, using text character as, 541
    importing text into graphics frame, 330
    letter, using graphic as capital, 420, 423, 780
    wrapping text around graphic, 15, 525–532
tinting grayscale, 780
TOC page, including on, 777
tool overview, 49
transformation, applying to, 510–514
vector graphic
    display quality default, setting, 99
    importing, 484, 486–489, 503–504
    rasterizing, 487, 504
XMP information, embedding, 703
Graphics Interchange Format. *See* GIF
Graphics pane, 641–643
Greek display, 99
grid (object placement aid)
    baseline grid
        aligning text to, 305, 399
        color, 90–91, 195
        default, 195
        described, 191
        displaying/hiding, 90, 110, 195, 305
        increment value, 91, 195, 305, 398
        locking text to, 305, 398–399
        printing, 631
        snapping to, 305
        spacing, 91, 195, 305
        view threshold, 91, 195
    Control palette grid, 263, 265, 514
    document grid
        color, 92, 195
        described, 92
        displaying/hiding, 90, 110, 196
        distance between lines, specifying, 195
        positioning, 89, 92

    snapping to, 72, 93, 110
    subdividing, 92, 196
    PDF export, including in, 664
    preference, setting, 90–92
    snapping to, 72
    Transform pane grid, 263, 265, 514
grid (template). *See* template (grid)
Grids pane, 90–92, 194–195, 398–399
group
    bounding box, 290
    combining objects into, 45, 289–290
    compound path compared, 573
    locking considerations, 290
    nesting, 290
    selecting
        entire group, 290
        object in group, 261, 289, 291
    subgroup, 290
    transformation, applying to, 280
    ungrouping, 291
guide
    aligning to, 152
    color, 37, 92, 106, 191, 193
    column guide, 152
    described, 304–306
    displaying/hiding, 37, 72, 92, 110, 160–161
    locking, 110, 161, 193
    margin, 37, 93
    master page guideline, 178
    PDF export, including in, 664
    preference, setting, 92–93, 825
    printing, 631
    ruler guide, 106, 151, 190–194
    snapping to, 93, 110, 151, 194, 305
Guides in Back feature, 93
Guides pane, 37
Guides & Pasteboard pane, 92–93, 194
gutter
    columns, between, 125, 369, 761
    ruler guides, between, 192

H
halo effect, creating using gradient, 586
Hand tool, 52, 114–115
hanging punctuation, 60, 430–431
hard drive
    backup, dedicating second hard drive to, 744
    space needed for InDesign, 742, 743, 819
hardware requirement, 741–744
Headers and Footers pane, 470–471
headline layout, 774, 776, 796
Help ➪ Configure Plug-Ins, 722
Help menu, 66, 74
Hewlett-Packard printer, 747, 748

Hexachrome color, 213, 810, 813
Hide ➪ Show Frame Edges, 160
HKS (Hostmann-Steinberg) color, 203, 206, 814, 815
HTML (Hypertext Markup Language)
    exporting, 491, 681
    XML compared, 695
hyperlink
    anchor, 683, 684, 691
    button, assigning to, 691
    character attribute, as, 682
    color, 685
    creating, 65, 682–684
    deleting, 685
    destination, 682–683, 685
    exporting, 664, 685
    highlighting, 685
    importing, 315
    naming, 684
    resetting, 685
    source, 683
    target, 682–683, 685
    underlining, 684, 685
    URL, assigning to, 683, 685
    zoom setting, 684
Hyperlink Destination Options dialog box, 685
Hyperlinks pane, 65, 66, 682–684
Hypertext Markup Language. See HTML
hyphenation
    automatic, 402–404
    breakpoint calculation, 403–404, 407
    Character pane, controlling using, 404
    consecutive, 789
    Control palette, controlling using, 402, 404
    dash, conversion of double hyphen to, 318, 330
    described, 401–402, 789
    dialog box, 402–403
    dictionary, 94, 95, 347–349, 621, 789
    discretionary, 339, 388, 402, 789
    Macintosh/Windows mixed environment, 714
    manual, 402
    nonbreaking, 339, 388
    Paragraph pane, adjusting using, 10, 402
    preference, setting, 349–350
    printing, 621
    soft, 789
    spell checking, handling in, 94, 95
    zone, 789

I

ICC (International Color Committee), 496, 668
Icon view (Macintosh), 862–863
idea file, documenting layout in, 763

Illustrator
    illustration editor, using as, 749
    importing from, 485, 487, 488, 505–506
image. See bitmap
Image Import Options dialog box, 491, 492
Image pane, 501–502, 702
imagesetter, outputting for, 603, 616, 633, 639
IME (input method editor), 84
Import Options dialog box, 330
Import XML dialog box, 696
importing
    AutoCAD document, 486
    color, 209–210, 494–496, 501–502, 598, 600–601
    Excel, from, 132, 314, 331
    font, embedded, 486–487
    gradient, 131, 506
    graphic
        alpha channel, adding, 501–502
        bitmap, 484, 489–492, 494, 501–502
        BMP, 484, 485, 494, 501
        CGM, 486
        clipping path, adding, 501–502, 503, 508
        copying between applications, via, 505
        CorelDraw, from, 486, 487
        DCS, 487
        dragging and dropping between applications,
            via, 505, 506
        DXF, 486
        embedding imported graphic, 523
        EMF, 484, 486
        EPS, 484, 485, 487, 503–504
        frame, into, 246, 250, 499–500, 508
        GIF, 484, 485, 491, 501
        Illustrator, from, 485, 487, 488, 505–506
        inline graphic, 317–318, 484–486
        JPEG, 484, 492, 501
        line art, 484
        link with source file, 497, 498, 505, 519–524
        OPI information, 487, 503, 522
        PCX, 484, 485, 494, 501
        Photo CD, from, 486
        Photoshop, from, 485, 489–490, 501, 503
        PICT, 484, 486, 489, 494, 501
        Place command, using, 14, 249, 498–500, 518, 590
        PNG, 484, 486, 492, 502
        PostScript file, 487–488
        preparing graphic for, 484
        preview, 497
        publication, customizing for, 500
        resolution considerations, 485, 520
        SCT, 484, 486, 489, 501
        text outline, into, 590
        TIFF, 484, 486, 489, 490–491, 501–502

vector graphic, 484, 486–489, 503–504
WMF, 484, 486, 489, 503
hyperlink, 315
InCopy file, 312
index topic, 239
location of imported file, displaying, 59
MOV file, 486
PageMaker, from, 127, 128, 130, 131, 851–852
PDF file, 130, 485, 488, 503
PostScript file, 487–488
QuarkXPress, from, 127, 128, 130–131, 835–837
QuickTime movie, 486, 501
RTF file, 132, 312, 331
spreadsheet, 132, 314, 331
story, 365
style sheet, 329, 362–364, 446, 454–457, 710
tab stop, 461
table, 309, 314, 466
text
    autoflowing, 329
    canceling, 330
    dash conversion, 330
    endnote, 314
    file, text, 132, 311–315, 317–319, 331, 361
    footer, 314
    formatting, preserving, 309, 312–314, 329
    graphics frame, into, 330
    header, 314
    InCopy file, 312
    list, 417
    Macintosh into Windows, 310–311
    outline, importing into, 590
    overset, 330, 361
    Place command, using, 8–9, 46, 132, 361, 590
    positioning imported text, 328–329
    quotation mark conversion, 329, 331
    spreadsheet, 132, 314, 331
    style sheet, 329, 362–364, 446, 454–457, 710
    tab stop, 461
    Tagged Text, 331
    threaded text frame, into, 361
    Windows into Macintosh, 310–311
    word processor, from, 247–248, 311–314,
        318–319, 362–364, 417
    updating when source file changes, 84
    XML, 696–697, 700
imposition, 659–660
.incd files, 875
InCopy
    Change Info pane, 879
    Change Tracking pane, 879
    Commandbar pane, 880
    Copyfit Info pane, 880

described, 873
Galley & Story Appearance pane, 880
importing from, 312
Layout pane, 877
Notes feature, 874–875
revision, tracking, 879
standalone, 877–880
story, working with, 875–879, 880
user name, 875–876
indentation
    block, 415–416, 789
    Control palette, using, 415–416
    default, 107
    described, 788
    first-line, 398, 414, 415
    hanging, 398, 414, 415, 416, 789
    list item, 414
    organizing content using, 414
    Paragraph pane, using, 12, 60, 398, 415–416
    tab, using, 327, 339, 398, 464
    text frame inset, 351, 413, 430, 463, 464
InDesign Central Web site
    color resources, 202, 495
    font resources, 419, 751
    graphic resources, 489, 594
    overview, 881–882
    plug-in directory, 719
    scripting resources, 728, 734
InDesign ➪ Configure Plug-Ins, 722
InDesign Defaults file, 77–78, 111, 708–709, 714, 825
InDesign menu, 66–67
InDesign ➪ Preferences, 36
InDesign ➪ Preferences ➪ Grids, 194
InDesign ➪ Preferences ➪ Guides & Pasteboard, 194
index
    browsing, 238
    capitalization, 235, 240, 241
    cross-reference, 235, 236, 237, 238
    dummy, mockup using, 235
    entry
        adding, 236–238
        copying, 239
        deleting, 239
        editing, 238
        topic, relation to, 236
    generating, 240
    layer, specifying for inclusion, 240
    level, 237
    marker, jumping to, 239
    nesting, 239, 240
    page reference, entering, 238
    pane, 62, 235–236
    QuarkXPress, 241, 836, 841

Continued

index *(continued)*
   run-in, 239, 240
   searching, 240
   section, referencing, 238
   separator character, 240
   sorting, 237, 240
   style guide, editorial, 235, 239
   style sheet, formatting using, 235, 240
   topic
      copying, 239
      deleting, 239, 241
      described, 236
      displaying unused, 241
      entry, relation to, 236
      importing, 239
      list, 236
   updating, 240, 241
   workflow, incorporating into, 241
InDex Pro software, 235
.indl files, 185
.indt files, 713
Info pane, 56, 65
Ink Manager, 647–649, 668
input method editor. *See* IME
In-RIP color separation, 639, 640
Insert Glyphs command, 104, 799
Insert Pages dialog box, 141
Insert Table dialog box, 467
.inst files, 272
installing
   font, 753–755
   InDesign, 820–822
   plug-in, 32, 721
Interchange plug-in, 128, 132, 826
International Color Committee. *See* ICC
Internet connectivity, 746–747
inverting. *See* reversing
IPA (International Prepress Association), 596
island page spread, 143–144
ITC (International Typeface Corporation) Web site, 751
Item ▷ Duplicate, 5
Item Information dialog box, 185–186, 187, 189

J

JavaScript, 725, 728, 737
JavaScript Bible, 4th Edition (Goodman), 728
JavaScript Central Web site, 728
JavaScript: The Definitive Guide (Flanagan), 728
JPEG (Joint Photographers Expert Group) file
   clipping path, setting in, 492, 532
   compression, 492, 666
   converting graphic to, 491
   exporting, 136, 702
   importing, 484, 492, 501

Justification dialog box, 405–406
justifying text
   carding, 788
   centered, 788
   Control palette, using, 11
   described, 402, 788
   design considerations, 774
   feathering, 788
   flush, 788
   frame, in, 352–353
   glyph scaling option, 405–406
   horizontal, 352–353
   leading, using, 406
   letter spacing option, 405–406
   object, next to, 86
   Paragraph pane, using, 11, 397
   ragged, 788
   vertical, 352–353, 788
   word spacing option, 405–406
   wrapping text, in, 86, 530–531

K

Keep Options dialog box, 408–409
kerning
   arrow key, adjusting using, 89, 90, 390
   Character pane, adjusting using, 59, 381, 390
   Control palette, adjusting using, 380, 390
   described, 389, 787
   drop caps, between, 421
   font kerning table, 389
   fraction formatting, in, 429
   highlighting, 86
   legibility considerations, 390
   manual, 390
   Metrics, 390
   Optical, 24, 390
   pair, 787–788
   QuarkXPress, 131, 389
   tracking compared, 391
Key Caps utility, 315
keyboard shortcut
   character, entering special using, 801–803
   cheat sheet, 883
   consistency, 102
   default set, 111
   deleting object using, 249
   displaying shortcut set, 105
   PageMaker shortcut set, 853, 855–856
   printing shortcut set, 105
   QuarkXPress shortcut set, 100, 104, 266, 334, 839–840
   saving object using, 103–104
   script, assigning to, 726
   sharing shortcut set, 708, 714

style, assigning using, 445
Tools palette shortcut set, 41–42
Windows shortcut feature, 709
zooming using, 332
Keyboard Shortcuts dialog box, 101
kicker, 426, 776, 796
knockout, 540, 605, 760

L

LAB color, 200, 201, 215, 810
language
    accent, entering, 803–808
    Asian language character, inputting, 84
    dictionary language, specifying, 94–95, 349
    English, specifying US or International during
        installation, 820
    IME, 84
    layer, creating language variant of document using,
        160, 162, 616
    QuarkXPress, 384
    quotation mark preference, setting, 83, 95
    text, assigning to, 344–345, 381, 383–384
    versions available, 799
Late Night Software Script Debugger, 731
layer
    active, 161, 164
    annotation layer, 183
    color, identifying using, 160, 287–288
    copying
        object on, 162–163
        remembering layer in copy operation, 162
    creating, 158–159
    deleting, 164, 166–167
    described, 155–156
    displaying/hiding, 160, 164
    document variant, creating using, 157–158,
        160, 162, 616
    flattening, 166
    guide, displaying when active, 160–161
    index, specifying for inclusion in, 240
    locking
        entire layer, 158, 160
        object on layer, 164–165
    master page layer, 159, 162
    merging layers, 164, 165–166
    moving object to another layer, 163
    naming, 160
    number of layers, maximum, 158
    packaging, 164
    PDF export, preserving in, 664
    placing object on, 162
    printing, 160, 164, 616
    ruler guide, associating with, 191
    selecting
        entire layer, 161, 164
        object on layer, 161–162
    source layer, 166
    stacking order, 70, 155–156, 164, 165, 286–289
    target layer, 166
    text wrap
        frame on hidden layer, around, 526
        suppressing around object on hidden layer, 160
    TOC, including hidden layer in, 232–233
    transparency, 538
Layer Options dialog box, 159–160, 161, 164, 165
Layers pane, 56, 62, 156–157, 159, 166
layout. *See also specific tool and operation*
    advertisement, 771–773
    circular (flier), 771–773
    client approval, 768
    colleague input, 769
    color, using, 781
    consistency, 765–766
    content, matching to, 765, 770
    coupon, 774
    dummy, mockup using, 235, 766–767
    element overview, 761–762
    formula, avoiding, 769–771
    headline, 774, 776, 796
    idea file, documenting in, 763
    imitating, 769–770
    intentional, 780
    magazine, 777–778
    masthead, 767
    menu, 69–70
    newsletter, 774–776
    pane (InCopy), 877
    PSA, 773–774
    simplicity, 764, 774
    sketching, 768–769
    tag line, 773
    thumbnail, using to visualize, 768, 769
    TOC, 777
    tool overview, 759–760
    white space, 389, 762, 764, 772, 781
Layout Adjustment dialog box, 107, 151–152
Layout ➪ Create Guides, 92
Layout ➪ Layout Adjustment, 107, 151
Layout ➪ Margins and Columns, 37, 151
Layout ➪ Numbering & Section Options, 146
Layout ➪ Ruler Guides, 106
Layout ➪ Table of Contents, 233
Layout ➪ Table of Contents Styles, 230
Layout ➪ Update Table of Contents, 233
leader character, 60, 463–464

leading
    arrow key, adjusting using, 89, 90
    automatic, 391, 392, 406, 543
    Character pane, adjusting using, 59
    character-by-character, 389
    default, specifying, 107
    described, 389, 391, 786
    font size, adjusting in function of, 391
    justification, using in, 406
    paragraph, applying to entire, 84, 389, 392, 396
    QuarkXPress, 84, 131, 391, 392
    set solid, 391
    text frame baseline, 352
    text wrap, judging in, 86, 531
letter spacing, 405–406, 787
library
    adding object to, 185, 186, 187–188
    closing, 186
    color swatch library, 32, 78, 202–203, 709, 822
    copying object from, 186, 188, 190, 300
    creating, 184
    deleting
        entire library, 187
        file associated with object in, 188
        object from library, 186, 187
    described, 170
    displaying all objects in, 186–187
    editing file associated with object in, 188
    filename extension, 185
    folder, 78, 753
    font considerations, 188
    information about object in, assigning,
            185, 187, 188–189
    locking, 187
    master page copy operation, using in, 712–713
    moving file associated with object in, 188
    naming, 184
    number of objects in, displaying, 185
    opening, 187
    pane, 185–186
    platform independence, 185
    searching, 185, 187, 189–190
    sharing, 184, 187, 709, 711
    sorting, 187, 190
    storage location, 78, 184, 753
    subset of objects in, working with, 186, 189
    thumbnail view, 187
licensing
    font, 751
    InDesign, 821
ligature, 385–386, 785–786
line. See also stroke
    angle, constraining to, 48, 254
    arrowhead, adding, 254
    bounding box, 254–255
    color, 283
    Control palette, formatting using, 14, 48
    curve, 554–558
    dashed, 271, 272–274, 774
    dotted, 272, 274
    freestanding, 48
    importing line art, 484
    lpi, 640–641
    Orthogonal Line tool, drawing using, 254
    segments, combining straight and curved, 558–560
    selecting, 254–255, 259
    sizing, 254–255
    straight, 47, 254–255, 553–554, 558–560
    table cell, placing diagonal line in, 475–476
    tool, 13–14, 48, 254–255
    Transform pane, formatting using, 48
    weight, 255
    zigzag, 553–554
lines per inch. See lpi
Links and Images pane, 617
Links pane, 59, 505, 520–524
list
    bulleted, 414, 416–420, 789
    importing from word processor, 417
    indenting, 414
    numbered, 414, 416–420
    QuarkXPress, 841
    style, 229, 419–420
    TOC, creating using, 229
List view (Macintosh), 862–863
locking
    baseline grid, text to, 305, 398–399
    font, 669
    grouping objects, considerations when, 290
    guide, 110, 161, 193
    layer
        entire layer, 158, 160
        object on layer, 164–165
    library, 187
    Lock Position command, using, 296, 303
    page, object on, 70, 151, 296
    unlocking, 296
    zero point, 36
Login Items control panel (Macintosh), 871
Lomax, Paul (VBScript in a Nutshell), 732
lpi (lines per inch), 640–641

M
MacDrive system, 745
Macintosh
    AirPort, 745
    alias feature, 709
    AppleScript, 725, 729–731, 735, 736, 737

AppleTalk, 745, 865
character, entering special in, 315–316, 801–806
color, 502, 596, 598, 710, 714
document window, 33
Ethernet connectivity, 745
font
    installing, 754, 755
    manager, 753
    OS X, 752, 753, 754, 792, 866–867
    PostScript support, 752, 754, 792, 867
    storage location, 753, 866–867
    suitcase, 754
Key Caps utility, 315
memory, 742
network connectivity, 745, 865, 871
opening PC-generated file in, 714
OS X
    Apple (✿) menu, 861
    application menu, 861–862
    Column view, 862–863
    Dock, 860–861, 864, 871
    filename extension, 310, 493, 715
    folder environment, 862–864
    font, 752, 753, 754, 792, 866–867
    Fontographer, running under, 751
    Go menu, 862
    Icon view, 862–863
    interface, customizing, 860–872
    List view, 862–863
    Login Items control panel, 871
    menu option specific to, 66
    My Account control panel, 871
    network connection, 865
    Network control panel, 871
    OpenType font support, 752, 792
    OS 9 application, running under, 867–869
    PostScript font support, 752, 754, 792
    printer support, 613, 629, 865–866
    System Preferences dialog box, 869–870
    toolbar, 864
    window environment, 864
    Windows/Macintosh mixed environment,
       717, 745, 865
PageMaker, 853
printing, 612–613, 629, 630, 747–748, 865–866
System Preferences dialog box, 612, 869–870
system requirement, 742, 819, 820
Trash Can, 249
Windows/Macintosh mixed environment
    color, 714
    file naming, 715–716
    filename extension, 493, 713, 715
    font, 716–717, 751, 795
    graphic, 490, 493

hyphenation, 714
InDesign Defaults file, sharing, 709, 714
medium used for data transfer, 717, 743–745
network connectivity, 745
opening PC-generated file in Macintosh, 714
OS X, 717, 745, 865
plug-in, 714
printer, 747–748
script, sharing, 714
service bureau, 713
shortcut set, sharing, 714
spell checking, 714
style, 714
template, 712
text, transferring, 310–311
MacLAN network, 745
MacLinkPlus system, 745
MacOpener system, 745
Macromedia software
    Fontographer, 419, 432, 751
    FreeHand, 749
magazine layout, 777–778
magnification. *See* zooming
Make command, 573
Map Styles to Tags dialog box, 697–698
Map Tags to Styles dialog box, 697–698
margin
    alignment, optical, 24, 60, 107, 430–431
    default setup, changing, 105
    described, 125, 761
    displaying/hiding, 37, 93
    guide, 37, 93
    master page margin, 178
    overstepping, 773
    ragged, 396, 399
    sizing
       automatic, 151, 152
       manual, 3, 105–106, 125
    table cell, of, 467
    text frame, of, 351
Margins and Columns dialog box, 151, 178
Marks and Bleeds pane, 634–637, 667
masking
    alpha channel, adding during import, 501–502
    clipping path
       command, 535–537
       creating, 533
       default setup, changing, 108
       dialog box, 108
       free-form, 534–535
       generating, 508
       importing graphic, adding when,
          501–502, 503, 508

Continued

masking, clipping path *(continued)*
    JPEG file, setting in, 492, 532
    overriding built-in, 535
    Photoshop, 529, 533
    QuarkXPress, 837
    text wrap around, 526, 529, 534
    threshold value, 535, 536
    TIFF file, setting in, 490, 532
    tolerance value, 536
master page
    accessing, 39, 360
    adding, 173
    applying, 173, 179–180
    column layout, specifying in, 178, 179, 357, 369
    copying, 177, 178, 712–713
    creating, 62, 174–176
    deleting, 173, 177
    described, 169, 170–171
    displaying, 116, 117, 172, 175, 181
    document page
        creating from master page, 173
        detaching from master page, 173
        facing page document, 177
        modifying master item on, 181–182
        spread, applying master page to, 179–180
        spread, basing master page on, 176
    guideline, placing on, 178
    layer, 159, 162
    locking object on, 296
    margin, 178
    naming, 175
    numbering, 177
    overriding, 173, 181–182
    prefix, 175, 176
    printing, 631
    QuarkXPress, 176, 178, 359, 841
    ruler guide, associating with, 191
    selecting
        object on master page, 45, 46
        unused master page, 173
    sharing, 712–713
    style, using in, 359
    text frame on, 124, 177, 247, 326, 357–360
    text wrap, 529
master spread. *See* master page
masthead, 767
MB (megabyte), 743
McClelland, Deke *(Photoshop 7 Bible)*, 533
Measure tool, 50
measurement unit
    entry code support, 29
    font, of, 88, 89, 786
    ruler, of, 36, 87–88, 123
Media4 MacDrive system, 745

megabyte. *See* MB
megahertz. *See* MHz
memory
    InDesign, needed for, 742, 820
    printer, 642–643
menu system overview, 66–75
metaphor, software, 26–27
method (scripting element), 726
MHz (megahertz), 743
Microsoft Script Editor, 733
minus sign (–) subtraction operator, 58
Miramar Systems' PC MacLAN network, 745
miter limit, 269
Modify Paragraph Style Options dialog box, 443, 452
moiré pattern, 508, 651
Monaco Sensor color calibrator, 596
monitor color
    calibrating, 596, 597–599
    Macintosh monitor, 502
    profile, 596, 598, 599
    temperature, 596
    white point, 596
Monitor Optimizer color calibrator, 596
mouse
    multibutton, 749
    optical, 749
    scaling using, 353
MOV file, importing, 486
movie
    button link, assigning to, 691
    format support, 691
    PDF, inserting in, 70, 692
    playing, 692
    poster, 692
    QuickTime movie, importing, 486, 501
Movie Options dialog box, 691
Multiple Masters font format, 754, 867
multiplication (arithmetic), 58, 463, 515
My Account control panel (Macintosh), 871
MyFonts.COM Web site, 751

N

NAA (Newspaper Association of America) Web site, 813
naming
    bookmark, 687
    character style, 448–449
    color, 200–201, 205, 209, 211, 216–217
    color trap, 607
    file, 715–716
    gradient, 214
    hyperlink, 684
    layer, 160
    library, 184
    master page, 175

page section, 147
paragraph style, 444
style sheet, 444, 448–449, 454
template, 182
workspace, 55
Navigator pane, 62, 115–116, 149–150
negative, printing photographic, 633, 635–636, 639, 641, 648
nesting
frame, 291–293
group, 290
index, 239, 240
style, 401, 419, 425, 449–452
network connectivity, 744–746, 747, 865
New Book dialog box, 222, 224
New Character Style dialog box, 12, 448
New Color Swatch dialog box, 199–200
New Doc Sizes.txt file, 126
New Document dialog box, 2, 37, 123–126, 358
New Glyph Set dialog box, 800
New Gradient Swatch dialog box, 214
New Hyperlink dialog box, 683
New Layer dialog box, 159, 160
New Master dialog box, 174–175, 176
New Mixed Ink Group dialog box, 207
New Mixed Ink Swatch dialog box, 206
New Page Reference dialog box, 237, 238
New Paragraph Style dialog box, 443–444
New Preset dialog box, 606, 607–609
New Section dialog box, 146
New Set dialog box, 103
New Stroke Style dialog box, 272–273, 274
New Table of Contents Style dialog box, 231
New Tint Swatch dialog box, 203–204
newsletter layout, 774–776
Newspaper Association of America Web site. *See* NAA Web site
none-colored, 266
Normal view, 53
.not files, 714
Notes feature (InCopy), 874–875
Notes pane, 874
Numbering & Section Options palette, 144, 146, 174

O

Object ⇨ Arrange, 286–287
Object ⇨ Arrange ⇨ Bring Forward, 288
Object ⇨ Arrange ⇨ Bring to Front, 288
Object ⇨ Arrange ⇨ Send Backward, 288
Object ⇨ Arrange ⇨ Send to Back, 288
Object ⇨ Clipping Path, 108
Object ⇨ Compound Paths, 542
Object ⇨ Compound Paths ⇨ Make, 573

Object ⇨ Compound Paths ⇨ Release, 576
Object ⇨ Content ⇨ Text, 360
Object ⇨ Corner Effects, 108, 276
Object ⇨ Display Performance, 98
Object ⇨ Drop Shadow, 437
Object ⇨ Feather, 438
Object ⇨ Fitting ⇨ Fit Content Proportionally, 517
Object ⇨ Fitting ⇨ Fit Content to Frame, 517
Object ⇨ Group, 45, 289
Object ⇨ Interactive ⇨ Convert to Button, 688
Object ⇨ Interactive ⇨ Movie Options, 691
Object ⇨ Interactive ⇨ Set Tab Order, 691
Object ⇨ Lock Position, 151, 296, 303
Object ⇨ Pathfinder, 577
Object ⇨ Select ⇨ Next Item, 261
Object ⇨ Select ⇨ Previous Item, 261
Object ⇨ Select ⇨ Select Container, 261
Object ⇨ Select ⇨ Select Content, 261
Object ⇨ Text Frame Options, 108
Object ⇨ Text Wrap, 108
Object ⇨ Ungroup, 45, 201
Object ⇨ Unlock Position, 296
Open a File dialog box, 128–129, 454–455
Open command, 122
OpenType font, 386–388, 752, 754, 792
OPI (Open Prepress Interface)
comment, 503, 663
EPS file, OPI information in, 487, 503, 522, 677
graphic replacement, 644–645, 668
PDF file, OPI information in, 663, 668, 669
TIFF file, OPI information in, 503
Optical Margin Alignment feature, 24, 60, 107, 430–431
O'Reilly & Associates Web site, 728
origin, point of, 514
Orthogonal Line tool, 254
Output pane, 19, 637–640
overlay, 760

P

Package Publication dialog box, 620–621
Package tool, 135, 164, 520, 619–622, 703
page. *See also* master page
action, 688–691
adding, 140–142, 173
bleed area, 125, 624, 634–635, 636–637, 676
break
paragraph widow/orphan control, 408–409
table row, keeping together across, 472
copying to another document, 142
creating, 62, 173
default setup, changing, 80, 105–106
deleting, 62, 142, 173

Continued

page *(continued)*
  displaying
    magnifications, multiple simultaneously, 117
    margin, 37, 93
    multiple pages simultaneously, 116
    spread, 116, 150
  dragging using Hand tool, 52, 114–115
  EPS, exporting page spread to, 674
  facing page options, 124, 139–140, 177, 631, 826
  foldout, 143, 778
  gatefold, 778
  imposition, 659–660
  index page reference, 238
  jumping to specific, 39
  locking object on, 70, 151, 296
  margin
    alignment, optical, 24, 60, 107, 430–431
    default setup, changing, 105
    described, 125, 761
    displaying/hiding, 37, 93
    guide, 37, 93
    master page margin, 178
    overstepping, 773
    ragged, 396, 399
    sizing, automatic, 151, 152
    sizing, manual, 3, 105–106, 125
    table cell, of, 467
    text frame, of, 351
  moving, 142–143
  navigating, 38–39, 62, 69, 148–150
  number of pages
    maximum possible, 140
    specifying total, 124
  numbering
    absolute, 40, 80, 148, 631
    alphabet, using, 144, 146
    automatic, 69, 144, 147, 177
    book, 228
    continued on/from reference, 146
    folio, 762, 775
    index, referencing in, 238
    master page, 177
    printing, 636
    referencing, 144–145, 146
    Roman numeral, using, 144, 146
    section, 39, 62, 80, 146, 174
    starting at specific number, 144, 147
    style, 144
    TOC, formatting in, 232, 777
    type default, specifying, 80
  objects on, keeping to minimum, 286
  orientation, 151, 632
  oversize, 625
  PageMaker difference, 856–857

Pages pane, dragging to/from, 142
PDF, exporting page spread to, 662
printing
  blank, 631
  facing pages, 631
  gap between pages, specifying, 632
  information about page, including in output, 636
  master page, 631
  number, 636
  order, in reverse, 631
  oversize, 625
  positioning, 633
  sizing, 37, 124, 151, 152, 632
  spread, 631
QuarkXPress difference, 847–848
section
  book, in, 228
  breaking large document into sections,
    140, 146–148
  color trapping, assigning to, 609–610
  creating, 146–147
  described, 146
  index, referencing in, 238
  island spread, creating from, 143
  marker, 147
  naming, 147
  numbering, 39, 62, 80, 146, 174
  removing, 148
sizing, 37, 124, 151, 152, 632
slug area, 43, 53, 125, 636–637, 667
spread
  adding, 141
  deleting, 142, 173
  displaying, 116, 150
  exporting, 662–663, 674
  island spread, 143–144
  keeping together, 174
  master page, applying to, 179–180
  master page, basing on, 176
  reader's spread, 660
  selecting, 145
  targeting, 145
turning, 39, 69
window, fitting to, 112, 114, 149
Page Setup dialog box (Macintosh), 630
PageMaker
  color, 857–858
  graphic, 856
  importing from, 127, 128, 130, 131, 851–852
  keyboard shortcut set, 853, 855–856
  Macintosh environment, 853
  page difference, 856–857
  Pantone color support, 202

style, 855
text, 854–855
Pages pane
accessing, 62
Create New Page option, 141, 173
described, 62
dragging page to/from, 142
Insert Pages option, 141, 173
Keep Spreads Together option, 143
master-page options, 171–174, 360
Numbering & Section Options palette, 144, 146, 174
palette menu, 140
section display in, 147–148
Spread Flattening option, 654
spread icon, 145, 148
Trash button, 142
palette
pane compared, 54
using, 54–57, 824–825
pane
palette compared, 54
using, 57–58, 824–825
Pantone color
building, 813
CMYK, converting to, 494, 495
PageMaker support, 202
paper used with, 202, 814–815
PMS, 202
printing, 211, 597
QuarkXPress support, 202
separation, 203, 212
swatch library, 202
swatchbook, 813
Pantone Matching System. *See* PMS
Pantone Process Color Imaging Guide: CMYK Edition
(Pantone), 212, 813
Pantone Process Color System Guide (Pantone), 813
paper
bleed, 641
gloss, 641
newsprint, 641
Pantone color, used with, 202, 814–815
printing setup, 632–633
RC, 632, 633
paragraph
baseline grid, locking to, 398–399
Control palette, formatting using, 394–395, 399, 408–409, 410
default setup, changing, 107
described, 393
exdenting, 788
indenting
block, 415–416, 789
Control palette, using, 415–416

default, 107
described, 788
first-line, 398, 414, 415
hanging, 398, 414, 415, 416, 789
list item, 414
organizing content using, 414
Paragraph pane, using, 12, 60, 398, 415–416
tab, using, 327, 339, 398, 464
text frame inset, 351, 413, 430, 463, 464
keep options, 408–409
labeling, 423–426
leading, applying to entire, 84, 389, 392, 396
outdenting, 398, 788
pane
accessing, 60
alignment, adjusting using, 10, 60, 396–397
Character pane, combining with, 394
described, 60
Drop Cap & Nested Styles option, 11, 401, 449–450
Drop Cap Number option, 400, 421
field, spacing using, 400
Hide Options feature, 394
hyphenation, adjusting using, 10, 402
indentation, adjusting using, 12, 60, 398, 415–416
justification, adjusting using, 11, 397
keep options, 408–409
leading, adjusting using, 392
Paragraph Rules option, 410
Tabs pane, combining with, 461
return symbol (¶), displaying, 416
rule, placing between paragraphs, 409–411
selecting, 393
spacing, 60, 399–400, 473
style
applying, 445–446
copying, 446
creating, 12, 443–445, 446
default, changing, 110–111
deleting, 446
described, 441
editing, 363, 446, 452, 456
manual formatting, combining with, 394, 445, 453
naming, 444
nesting, 450–451
overriding imported, 363–364, 456–457
removing local formatting, 445
TOC, in, 229–230, 231–232
unapplying, 453–454
widow/orphan control, 408–409
Paragraph Rules dialog box, 410, 427
Paragraph Styles pane, 60, 110–111, 363, 442–446, 710
Paste command, 68, 163, 294, 299, 505
Paste in Place command, 299

pasteboard, 27, 37, 92, 93, 114
paste-up board, 171
path
    anchor point, 551–552, 560, 564–568
    clipping path
        command, 535–537
        creating, 533
        default setup, changing, 108
        dialog box, 108
        free-form, 534–535
        generating, 508
        importing graphic, adding when,
            501–502, 503, 508
        JPEG file, setting in, 492, 532
        overriding built-in, 535
        Photoshop, 529, 533
        QuarkXPress, 837
        text wrap around, 526, 529, 534
        threshold value, 535, 536
        TIFF file, setting in, 490, 532
        tolerance value, 536
    cloning, 553, 570
    closed, 51, 548, 560–561, 571
    color, 549, 574
    combining, 64, 558–560, 577–578
    compound, 535, 542, 573–578, 589
    connecting two paths, 570–571
    corner effect, 578–579
    direction
        dragging, 554, 555
        handle, 552–553, 557, 569
        line, 552, 555, 556, 558
        point, converting, 564, 567–568, 847
        subpath, of, 575, 576
    endpoint, 551, 571
    extending, 570
    frame, creating from, 47
    free-form, 534–535, 560–561
    gradient, applying to, 549
    graphic
        clipping path, adding when importing,
            501–502, 503, 508
        placing graphic in path, 551
    open, 47, 51, 548, 549, 570–571
    QuarkXPress, 551, 568, 578, 837
    segment, 551, 552, 558–560
    shaping, 564–565
    splitting, 51, 64, 548, 572–573, 577
    stroke, applying to, 548–549
    subpath, 575, 576, 590
    text
        converting to path, 377, 541, 574
        placing on path, 47, 48, 550–551

    transformation, applying to, 560
    transparency, 573
Pathfinder tool, 64, 577–578
pattern
    copying, preserving during, 81
    gradient, 53
    stroke, 62
PC MacLAN network, 745
PCX file, importing, 484, 485, 494, 501
PDF Export Presets command, 661
PDF (Portable Document Format)
    bookmark
        creating, 65, 686–688
        deleting, 687
        exporting, 232, 664, 688
        naming, 687
        sorting, 687
        subentry, 687
        TOC, 232, 664, 687
    button, creating interactive, 51, 688–691
    color, 213, 668
    copying PDF file, 81
    eBook, 664, 686, 820, 832–833
    EPS file, creating from, 673
    exporting
        bleed mark, including, 667
        book, 227, 661
        bookmark, 232, 664, 688
        color, calibrating, 668
        compression, 664–666, 672
        eBook tag, including, 664
        encrypting output file, 670
        font, embedding, 661, 669
        grid, including, 664
        guide, including, 664
        hyperlink, preserving, 664, 685
        layer, preserving, 664
        metadata, including, 671
        multimedia, including, 664
        on-screen usage, for, 672
        OPI graphic replacement information, 668
        optimizing, 663
        overprint, simulating, 668
        page spread, 662–663
        password protecting output file, 670
        PDF/X format, to, 663, 668
        permission to output file, specifying, 670–671
        preset, 661, 670
        printing, for, 658, 667
        printing to PDF file, via, 672–673
        saving to PDF file, via, 136
        security, 669–671, 672
        signing output file digitally, 671
        slug area, including, 667

thumbnail, embedding, 663
transparency flattening, 668
version, specifying, 663
graphic, treatment as, 488
hyperlink
anchor, 683, 684, 691
button, assigning to, 691
character attribute, as, 682
color, 685
creating, 65, 682–684
deleting, 685
exporting, 664, 685
highlighting, 685
importing, 315
naming, 684
PDF file, in, 664, 682–685
resetting, 685
source, 683
target (destination), 682–683, 685
underlining, 684, 685
URL, assigning to, 683, 685
zoom setting, 684
importing, 130, 485, 488, 503
movie, inserting, 70, 692
opening PDF file, 127
OPI information, 663, 668, 669
password protection, 504
PDF/X support, 663, 668
PostScript file, creating from, 673
printing
file, to, 672–673
paper, on, 636, 658, 667
reader software, 658
service bureau, providing to, 658, 663
sound, inserting in, 70, 693
transparency, 81, 504, 668
Pen tool
anchor point, working with using, 47, 564
described, 46–47, 550
drawing tablet, using with, 547
path
closing using, 47, 548
connecting using, 570–571
drawing curved using, 47, 555–557
drawing straight using, 47, 553–554
extending using, 570
Pencil tool compared, 550
Pencil tool, 550, 560
Perry, Bruce W. (*AppleScript in a Nutshell: A Desktop Quick Reference*), 729
Petrusha, Ron (*VBScript in a Nutshell*), 732
Photo CD graphic, importing, 486

Photoshop
clipping path, 529, 533
importing from, 485, 489–490, 501, 503
Photoshop ➪ Color Settings, 599
Photoshop 7 Bible (McClelland), 533
Photosmart printer, 748
pica (measurement unit), 29, 30, 88, 786
PICT file, importing, 484, 486, 489, 494, 501
picture. *See* graphic
Picture Usage feature (QuarkXPress), 522
Place command
copy and paste versus, 362
drag and drop versus, 328, 362
graphic, importing using, 14, 249, 498–500, 518, 590
inline frame, creating using, 294, 295–296
text, importing using, 8–9, 46, 132, 361, 590
Place dialog box, 8, 328, 488, 498–499
Place PDF dialog box, 488, 503
planning
book, 222
document, 121–122, 763
TOC, 229–230
platesetter, outputting for, 633
plug-in
caching, 719
default set, 719–720
directory, online, 719
disabling, 721, 723
downloading, 719
installing, 32, 721
interface, 721–722
launching, 719, 721
listing installed, 722
optional, 32
preference, setting, 722–723
QuarkXPress, 720
removing, 721
service bureau, providing to, 720
sharing, 708, 714
sources, 720–721
storage location, 32, 708, 719–720
plus sign (+)
addition operator, 58
style sheet name prefix, 445
PMS (Pantone Matching System), 202
PNG (Portable Network Graphics) format
color, 492
compression, 492
importing, 484, 486, 492, 502
transparency, 502
point (measurement unit), 29, 88, 786
point of origin, 514
Polygon Frame tool, 48, 250–251, 252
Polygon Settings dialog box, 49, 109, 252–253

Polygon tool, 48, 49, 109, 252, 360
PopChar X software, 316, 464, 799
pop-out tool display, 42, 44
port (threading entry point), 366–367
Portable Document Format. *See* PDF
Portable Network Graphics format. *See* PNG format
PostScript. *See also* EPS (Encapsulated PostScript)
    importing PostScript file, 487–488
    Level 2, 643, 820
    Level 3, 593, 639, 643, 820
    Macintosh support, 752, 754, 792, 867
    Multiple Masters format, 754, 867
    OpenType versus, 752
    PDF, creating from PostScript file, 673
    PPD file, 613, 623, 628, 643, 678
    prepress file, exporting to, 659, 677–678
    printer, 613, 614–615, 628, 643, 747–748
    TrueType versus, 752
    Type 1, 792
PowerPrint software, 748
PPD (PostScript Printer Description) file, 613, 623,
       628, 643, 678
preference files, 708–709
Preferences
    folder, 78
    menu, 66
Preferences dialog box
    accessing, 78
    Composition pane, 85–87, 531
    Dictionary pane, 94–96, 349–350
    Display Performance pane, 98–99
    General pane, 79, 80–82
    Grids pane, 90–92, 194–195, 398–399
    Guides pane, 37
    Guides & Pasteboard pane, 92–93, 194
    Notes pane, 874
    resetting, 82, 822
    Saved Files pane, 99–100
    Spelling pane, 96
    Story Editor Display pane, 96–98, 334
    Text pane, 82–84, 384, 389, 472–473
    undoing change made in, 79
    Units & Increments pane, 36, 87–90
    Updates pane, 100
    using, 78–79
    Workgroup preferences pane, 79
Preflight tool, 520, 611, 615–619, 620
preset
    described, 823–824
    document preset, 3, 125–127
    leading, automatic, 392
    PDF export preset, 661, 670
    print preset, 615, 628, 629

    sharing, 708
    transparency, 645, 652–653, 654, 655, 669
    trap preset, 64, 65, 606–609
    view percentage, 38
    zoom, 112, 114
Presets folder, 32, 78, 708
Preview Mode view, 53
Print dialog box
    accessing, 19
    Advanced pane, 644–645
    Cancel button, 628
    Color Management pane, 643–644
    General pane, 631–632
    Graphics pane, 641–643
    Marks and Bleeds pane, 634–637
    Output pane, 19, 637–640
    page preview panel, 628
    PPD pop-up menu, 628
    Print button, 628
    Print Preset pop-up menu, 628
    Printer pop-up menu, 628
    Save Preset button, 628
    Setup button, 628
    Setup pane, 632–634
    Summary pane, 646
Print Settings pane, 618
Printer dialog box (Macintosh), 630
Printer ➪ Properties (Windows), 613
printing. *See also* paper; service bureau, working with
    baseline grid, 631
    binding, perfect, 631, 659, 660, 663
    black, overprinting, 81
    bleed area, 125, 624, 634–635, 636–637, 676
    book, 227, 615
    color
        calibration, applying, 643–644
        CMYK, 211–212, 597, 636, 647–650
        color bar, 636
        composite, 19–20, 638, 639, 640
        DIC, 211, 597
        Focoltone, 597
        four-color, 210, 810, 811
        imagesetter, outputting for, 603, 639
        ink used, displaying, 618
        overlapping, 205, 603–610
        overprint, 605
        Package tool, preparing using, 620
        Pantone, 211, 597
        Preflight tool, preparing using, 618
        prepress feature overview, 593–594
        printer color space, specifying, 643–644
        RGB, 212, 213, 597
        separation, 638, 650–651

spot color, 205
Toyo, 211, 597
trapping for, 603, 639, 648
Trumatch, 597
composite, 19–20, 638, 639, 640
copies, specifying number of, 631
crop mark, 632, 635, 636
DCS file, 639
file, to, 646–647, 672–673, 678
filename, 636
film, to, 632, 633, 639
font
device memory considerations, 642–643
download option, 642, 643
missing font, checking for, 615
Preflight tool, preparing using, 615, 616–617
translation by printer, 614
TrueType, 614, 615, 616, 792
form, 659–660
frequency setting, 640
graphic, 616, 617, 620, 641–643
guide, 631
hyphenation, 621
Imagesetter, outputting for, 603, 616, 633, 639
Ink Manager, 647–649, 668
ink used, displaying, 618
instruction form, creating using Package tool, 620
layer, 160, 164, 616
Macintosh, 612–613, 629, 630, 747–748, 865–866
master page, 631
moiré pattern, 651
negative, photographic, 633, 635–636, 639, 641, 648
non-printing object, 631
offset, 659
overprinting, 586, 605, 640, 650–651, 668
Package tool, preparing for using, 619–622
page
blank, 631
facing pages, 631
gap, specifying, 632
information about page, including in output, 636
master page, 631
number, 636
order, in reverse, 631
oversize, 625
positioning, 633
sizing, 37, 124, 151, 152, 632
spread, 631
paper setup, 632–633
PDF
file, to, 672–673
paper, on, 636, 658, 667
platesetter, outputting for, 633

PostScript prepress file, to, 678
preference, setting, 81
Preflight tool, preparing for using, 520, 611, 615–619, 620
preset, 615, 628, 629
preview, 629
printer
color space, specifying, 643–644
dpi, 640–641, 747
font translation by, 614
ink-jet, 748
laser, 747
lpi, 640–641
Macintosh, 612–613, 629, 630, 747–748, 865–866
memory, 642–643
multifunction, 748
networking, 747
PostScript, 613, 614–615, 628, 643, 747–748
preset, creating, 628, 629
quality needed, 747
selecting, 628
Windows, 613–615, 629
Windows/Macintosh mixed environment, 747–748
proof, 637, 638, 642, 644
QuarkXPress, 634, 651, 652, 837, 849
reader's spread, 660
registration mark, 632, 635, 636
rotating output, 633
saddle-stitching, 631, 659, 663
scaling output, 633
screen angle, 640, 651–652
service bureau, working with, 616, 622–625, 633, 641–643, 659
shortcut set, 105
slug area, 43, 53, 125, 636–637, 667
stroke, overprinting, 586
SWOP, 603, 659
thumbnail, 634, 768, 769
tiling output, 634
transparency, 64, 639, 644–645, 652–655
web offset printing, 603, 659
Printing Instructions dialog box, 620
process color. *See* CMYK color
Profiles folder, 710
Programming Microsoft Visual Basic 6.0 (Balena), 732
project, QuarkXPress, 841
property (scripting element), 726
Proximity
dictionary set, 349
folder, 708
PSA (public service announcement) layout, 773–774
.psd files, 532. *See also* Photoshop

pull quote, 428, 776, 796
punctuation, hanging, 60, 430–431
push button, creating interactive, 51, 688–691
Pyrus FontLab software, 419, 432

Q

QuarkXPress
    baseline grid, 91
    clipping path, 837
    color, 202, 837, 848
    constrained box feature, 293
    Content tool, 253, 258
    contrast, adjusting, 519
    Control palette, floating to mimic, 59
    document difference, 841
    drop shadow, 544, 846
    feathering, 544, 847
    fraction, formatting, 428
    frame, 48, 276, 293, 515, 841
    gradient, importing, 131
    graphic, 846–847
    Guides in Back feature, 93
    importing from, 127, 128, 130–131, 835–837
    index, 241, 836, 841
    keyboard shortcut set, 100, 104, 266, 334, 839–840
    language, 384
    list, 841
    menu equivalency, 66
    object environment, 266, 842–843
    page
        difference, 847–848
        master page, 176, 178, 359, 841
    Pantone color support, 202
    Passport edition, 384
    path, 551, 568, 578, 837
    Picture Usage feature, 522
    plug-in, 720
    printing, 634, 651, 652, 837, 849
    project, 841
    ruler, 88
    selection, 45, 253, 258, 838, 842
    skewing, 279
    stroke, 272, 846
    Swatches pane, 519
    table, 479, 845
    text
        box, 359, 836
        editing, 843
        entry, 47
        flow, 843
        formatting, 436, 836, 844–845
        kerning, 131, 389
        leading, 84, 131, 391, 392
        ligature, 386
        tracking, 389
        wrap, 842
    TOC, 230, 233
    tool environment, 40, 47, 48
    transparency, 652, 847
    workspace, 839
    XTension, 131, 720
QuickTime
    eBook requirement, 820
    importing QuickTime movie, 486, 501
quotation mark
    drop cap, in initial, 422
    import operation, conversion during, 329, 331
    preference, setting, 83, 95

R

raised cap, 422, 789
RAM (random access memory) requirement, 742, 820
ramseeker Web site, 742
raster graphic. See bitmap
RC (resin-coated) paper, 632, 633
reader's spread, 660
recovering document, 100, 132–133
Rectangle Frame tool, 4, 14, 48, 250–251
Rectangle tool, 49
red, green, blue color. See RGB color
registration mark, 632, 635, 636
Release command, 576–577, 590
Rem VBA statement, 737
Required folder, 33
resin-coated paper. See RC paper
reversing
    described, 762
    text, 275, 426–427
reverting to previous document version, 134, 135
revision, tracking, 879
RGB (red, green, blue) color
    creating, 201
    described, 810
    gradient, 215
    importing, 495
    naming, 200
    printing, 212, 213, 597
    profile, 598, 601
Rich Text Format. See RTF
rollover effect, creating, 688, 689
Roman
    font, 784, 794
    numeral, using in page numbering, 144, 146
rotating
    Control palette, using, 253, 434, 515–516
    frame, 253, 266, 277, 734–736

Free Transform tool, using, 50, 512
graphic, 510–512, 515–516, 734–736
print output, 633
Rotation tool, using, 49, 277, 280, 434, 511
service bureau, done by, 633
text, 433–434, 467, 472
Transform pane, using, 61, 253, 280–282, 434, 515–516
Row Strokes pane, 469–470
Rows and Columns pane, 475, 476
RTF (Rich Text Format)
exporting, 135, 364, 457
importing, 132, 312, 331
rule (horizontal line)
color, 410, 411
columns, placing between, 370–371
paragraphs, placing between, 409–411
ruler
default setup, changing, 106
displaying/hiding, 36, 72, 88, 110
document window, display in, 35
guide
aligning object using, 190
color, 106, 191, 193
creating, 191–193
deleting, 193
displaying/hiding, 191, 193, 194
gutter, 192
ignoring, 151
layer, associating with, 191
locking/unlocking, 193
master page, associating with, 191
measurement unit, changing, 36, 87–88, 123
moving, 193
origin point, 36, 87
selecting, 193
snapping to, 194
view threshold, 193
zero point, 36
QuarkXPress, 88
spine, positioning relative to, 87
tab ruler, 464–465
Ruler Guides dialog box, 106, 151, 190–194

S

sans serif, 784, 785, 791
Save a Copy As command, 134
Save As command, 133, 134, 153
Save command, 133, 134
Save Preset dialog box, 615
Saved Files pane, 99–100

scaling. See also sizing
arithmetic calculation, basing on, 515
Control palette, using, 382, 515
frame, 253, 265, 278–279
graphic, 15, 508, 510–512, 515
print output, 633
Scale tool, using, 49–50, 278–279, 435, 511
selection, 49
text
attribute, adjusting when, 84
Character pane, adjusting using, 59, 382
Control palette, adjusting using, 382
design considerations, 381–382, 424
emphasis, creating via, 424
frame, 435
glyph, 24, 405–406
mouse, adjusting using, 353
proportional, 84
Scale tool, adjusting using, 435
sizing versus, 435
Transform pane, using, 265, 281, 515
scanning, 644, 748
Scissors tool, 51, 543–544, 548, 572–573
Scitex Continuous Tone file, importing. See SCT file, importing
screen
angle, 640, 651–652
sketch background, 767
Script Debugger software, 731
Script Label pane, 736
scripting
AppleScript, 725, 729–731, 735, 736, 737
command, 726
commenting code, 737
conditional script, 736–737
grammar, 726
graphic
referencing, 727
rotating using script, 734–736
JavaScript, 725, 728, 737
keyboard shortcut, assign to script, 726
labeling item, 736
method, 726
object hierarchy, 726–727
privilege needed, 733
property, 726
sharing script, 708, 714
statement, 726
syntax, 726, 730, 734
VBA, 725, 731–734, 735, 736, 737
VBScript, 731–734
Scripts pane, 63, 726

scrolling
    document window scroll bar, 36, 114–115, 150
    Navigator pane, using, 149–150
SCT (Scitex Continuous Tone) file, importing,
    484, 486, 489, 501
searching
    index, 240
    library, 185, 187, 189–190
    story, 336
    text, searching and replacing, 335–342
    wild card, 340
second color, 210
Section dialog box, 228
Security pane, 669–671
selection
    bounding box, manipulating, 251–252, 258, 259, 264
    color swatch, selecting, 208
    deselecting, 262, 333
    frame
        content, selecting, 261, 265
        entire frame, selecting, 259, 261, 509–510
    graphic, selecting, 509
    group
        entire group, selecting, 290
        object in, selecting, 261, 289, 291
    handle display, 252
    layer
        entire layer, selecting, 161, 164
        object on layer, selecting, 161–162
    line, selecting, 254–255, 259
    master page
        object on, selecting, 45, 46
        unused master page, selecting, 173
    moving, 45, 89
    multiple objects, selecting simultaneously,
        46, 261–262, 290–291
    overlapping objects, selecting, 259–261, 288
    page spread, selecting, 145
    QuarkXPress, 45, 253, 258, 838, 842
    ruler guide, selecting, 193
    scaling, 49
    Selection tool, using, 44–45, 253, 258–259, 261
    table, selecting, 471
    text, 47, 84, 333, 375, 393
    threading, selection tool used in, 46, 365
    Type tool, switching to/from selection tool, 45, 365
Send to Back command, 288
Separations Preview pane, 64, 65, 650–651
serif, 785, 791
service bureau, working with. See also printing
    bleed, 624–625, 633
    coordination, 623–624, 637, 659

    crop mark, 636
    editing done by service bureau, 624, 669, 675
    EPS file, providing, 658, 675, 677
    file format, choosing, 622–623, 643
    flipping output, 639
    font, 619, 642–643, 669, 675, 751–752
    gatefold, 778
    ink, 648
    layer not printed, hiding, 164, 616
    output control, 624
    packaging, 619–622
    page, oversize, 625
    PDF file, providing, 658, 663
    plug-in, 720
    PPD file, providing, 623
    Preflight information, providing, 619
    proof copy, 623
    responsibility, clarifying, 624
    rotating output, 633
    scanning, 644
    screen angle, 651
    storage medium, 743–744
    summary information, providing, 646, 671
    trapping, 603, 606, 639
    Windows/Macintosh mixed environment, 713
Setup pane, 632–634
shadow
    backlit, 382
    button, applying to, 688
    drop shadow, 377, 437–438, 544–545, 688, 846
    QuarkXPress, 544, 846
    text, applying to, 377, 382, 437–438, 780
shape, converting to frame, 249
shearing
    Control palette, using, 266, 513
    described, 276
    frame, 266, 279, 280
    graphic, 510–512
    Shear tool, using, 50, 279, 280, 383, 511–512
    text, 279, 383
    Transform pane, using, 266, 279, 513
shortcut. See keyboard shortcut
Shortcut Sets folder, 78
sidebar, 428, 765, 776, 796
sizing. See also scaling
    Control palette, using, 5–6, 247, 250, 282, 379
    frame
        graphics frame, 14, 250–251, 508
        text frame, 4–5, 245, 247, 279, 333
    graphic, 151, 250–251, 508, 517–518
    line, 254–255
    page, 37, 124, 151, 152, 632

table column/row, 467, 472, 475
text
    Character pane, using, 59, 83, 382
    default size, specifying, 107
    drop cap, 11
    emphasis, creating via, 424
    font size, using, 379–380, 421
    optimal size, finding automatically, 83
    scaling versus, 435
    Transform pane, using, 247, 250, 380
skewing
    Control palette, using, 516
    graphic, 516
    QuarkXPress, 279
    text, 382–383, 779, 780
    Transform pane, using, 516
slash, asterisks, slash (/* */) JavaScript comment
        delimiter, 737
slash (/) division operator, 58
slug area, 43, 53, 125, 636–637, 667
small cap, 83, 380, 384, 387, 424
Soghoian, Sal (*AppleScript 1-3-3*), 729
Sonar Bookends InDex Pro software, 235
sorting
    index, 237, 240
    library, 187, 190
    TOC, 232
sound, 70, 691, 693–694
source element, 711
spaceband, 404
spell checking
    accessing spell checker, 68
    capitalization, handling, 96, 342
    dictionary, 94–96, 107, 344, 345–350, 383–384
    hyphenation, handling, 94, 95
    language, specifying, 94–95, 344–345, 349, 383–384
    Macintosh/Windows mixed environment, 714
    note, 874–875
    preference, setting, 96, 349–350
    skipping text, 345
    specifying text to check, 342–343
    word repetition, handling, 343–344
    workgroup environment, 346, 708, 710
Spelling pane, 96
spot color
    CMYK
        converting to/from, 211, 647–649, 812
        mixing with in same document, 211, 811–812
        spot color versus, 210–212
    creating, 201
    described, 811
    gradient, 216

naming, 211
printing, 205
spreadsheet, importing, 132, 314, 331
stacking order, 70, 155–156, 164, 165, 286–289
standard web offset press. *See* SWOP
States pane, 65, 66, 688–689
Step and Repeat command, 300–301
stitching
    saddle-stitching, 631, 659, 663
    transparency, 654
story. *See also* threading
    alignment, optical, 60, 107, 430–431
    described, 332, 356
    dictionary, recomposing story when modified, 96
    Editor, 68, 96–98, 334
    end-of-story marker, 431–432
    importing, 365
    InCopy, working with in, 875–879, 880
    navigating, 332
    pane, 60–61, 877
    port, 366–367
    revision, tracking, 879
    searching, 336
    sharing, 875–879
    Tagged Text format, saving to, 136
    view, 877–878
Story Editor Display pane, 96–98, 334
Story List pane (InCopy), 878
Strikethrough Options dialog box, 436
stroke
    aligning, 270
    color, 219, 267–268, 271–272, 432–433, 584–585
    corner, 269–270
    creating, 272–274
    dashed, 271, 272–274, 774
    default setup, changing, 108
    described, 581, 762
    dotted, 272, 274
    end options, 270, 271
    fill, adding, 275
    frame, applying to, 48, 248, 267–268, 518
    gradient, applying to, 62, 268–269, 433, 585
    list bullet, of, 417
    miter limit, 269
    overprinting, 586
    path, applying to, 548–549
    pattern, 62
    QuarkXPress, 272, 846
    style, 272
    table element, applying to, 468–470, 473–474, 477
    text, applying to, 24, 377, 433, 581–587, 588
                                              Continued

stroke *(continued)*
  weight
    Control palette, adjusting using, 14, 268, 282
    described, 581–582
    Stroke pane, adjusting using, 255, 269, 584
    Transform pane, adjusting using, 281
Stroke Styles dialog box, 272
Strokes and Fills pane, 473–474
Structure pane, 698–699
Strydent Software PowerPrint, 748
StuffIt Deluxe software, 750
style
  automation tool, as, 170
  book, formatting using, 224, 226
  character style
    Advanced Character Formats pane, adjusting
      using, 83
    applying, 13, 447–449
    creating, 12, 447–449
    default, changing, 110–111
    described, 441, 447
    drop cap, applying to, 13
    editing, 452
    fraction formatting, saving as, 430
    list, formatting using, 229
    manual formatting, combining with, 453
    naming, 448–449
    nesting, 425
    unapplying, 453–454
    updating, 375
    XML tag mapping, 698
  control, global versus local, 27–28, 394, 445, 453
  cookie cutter analogy, 441
  copying, 446
  default, changing, 110–111
  deleting, 446
  described, 441, 447, 789
  document style, 126–127, 825
  editing, 363, 446, 452, 456
  font style, 784
  formatting macro, as, 789
  index, 235, 240
  keyboard shortcut, assigning using, 445
  list, 229, 419–420
  master page, using in, 359
  naming, 444, 448–449, 454
  nesting, 401, 419, 425, 449–452
  page numbering, 144
  PageMaker, 855
  paragraph style
    applying, 445–446
    copying, 446
    creating, 12, 443–445, 446

    default, changing, 110–111
    deleting, 446
    described, 441
    editing, 363, 446, 452, 456
    manual formatting, combining with, 394, 445, 453
    naming, 444
    nesting, 450–451
    overriding imported, 363–364, 456–457
    removing local formatting, 445
    TOC, in, 229–230, 231–232
    unapplying, 453–454
  sheet
    described, 789
    exporting, 364, 457
    importing, 329, 362–364, 446, 454–457, 710
    sharing, 364, 710, 714
  stroke, 272
  tag, 789
  template versus, 442
  TOC, 229–231, 233
  updating, 375, 441
  XML tag style mapping, 65, 697–698, 701
subsampling compression, 666
Subset dialog box, 189
subtraction (arithmetic), 58, 463, 515
Suitcase software, 753, 755–756
Summary pane
  Export PDF dialog box, 671
  Preflight dialog box, 616
  Print dialog box, 646
SVG file, exporting, 136
Swatch Libraries folder, 32, 78, 822
Swatch Options dialog box, 207–208
Swatches pane
  accessing, 16
  Add Unnamed Colors option, 209
  Color pane versus, 205
  Delete Swatch option, 208
  Hide Options menu, 198
  illustrated, 199
  introduced, 62
  Merge Swatches option, 208
  Name option, 198
  New Color Swatch option, 199
  New Gradient Swatch option, 214
  New Mixed Ink Swatch option, 205
  QuarkXPress, 519
  Select All Unused option, 209
  Small Name option, 198
  Small Swatch option, 198
  text color, applying using, 62, 219, 410
  Unnamed Swatch option, 209

SWOP (standard web offset press), 603, 659
system
    color, 203
    folder, 867
    requirement, 741–744, 819–820
System Preferences dialog box (Macintosh),
        612, 869–870

T

tab
    aligning text using tab stop, 460, 462, 464
    creating tab stop, 60, 463, 465
    deleting tab stop, 464, 465
    displaying, 461, 464, 465
    importing tab stop, 461
    indenting using, 327, 339, 398, 464
    leader character, 60, 463–464
    overriding automatic tab stop, 459
    positioning tab stop, 60, 462–463, 464–465
    ruler, 464–465
    table, converting tabbed text to/from, 478–479
table
    aligning content, 467, 472
    border, 468
    cell
        aligning content, 467, 472
        baseline, 473
        clipping content, 473
        color, 474, 477
        gradient, 477
        line, placing diagonal in, 475–476
        margin, 467
        merging cells, 476
        paragraph spacing, 473
        splitting, 476
        stroke, applying to, 473–474, 477
        text overflow indicator, 477
    color
        border, of, 468
        cell, of, 474, 477
        fill, 470, 474
        line, of, 468, 469
    column
        adding, 471–472
        deleting, 471–472
        described, 761
        line options, 468–470
        magazine layout, in, 775
        number of, specifying, 467
        sizing, 467, 472, 475, 775
        spacing, 71, 472
        stroke, 468–470
    Control palette, formatting using, 477
    creating, 71, 467
    graphic, inserting in, 467
    importing, 309, 314, 466
    menu, 71–72
    pane, 62, 466, 468
    QuarkXPress, 479, 845
    row
        adding, 471–472
        deleting, 471–472
        footer, 467, 470–471, 472
        frames, breaking across multiple, 472
        going to specific, 471
        header, 467, 470–471, 472
        height, 467
        line options, 468–470
        number of, specifying, 467
        page break, keeping together across, 472
        sizing, 472, 475
        spacing, 71, 472
        stroke, applying to, 468–470
    selecting, 471
    stroke, applying to table element, 468–470,
        473–474, 477
    text
        aligning, 467, 472
        cell overflow indicator, 477
        converting to/from, 478–479
        inserting in, 467
Table ⇨ Convert Table to Text, 478
Table ⇨ Convert Text to Table, 478
Table ⇨ Distribute Columns Evenly, 472
Table ⇨ Distribute Rows Evenly, 472
Table ⇨ Edit Footer, 471
Table ⇨ Edit Header, 471
Table ⇨ Go to Row, 471
Table ⇨ Insert Table, 467
Table ⇨ Merge Cells, 476
table of contents. See TOC
Table of Contents Styles dialog box, 230–231
Table Options dialog box, 467
Table ⇨ Select ⇨ Table, 471
Table Setup pane, 468–469
Table ⇨ Split Cell Horizontally, 476
Table ⇨ Split Cell Vertically, 476
Table ⇨ Table Options, 467
Table ⇨ Unmerge Cells, 476
Tabs pane, 60, 61, 394, 459–465
Tagged Image File Format. See TIFF
Tagged Text format, 132, 136, 319–322, 331
Tags pane, 65, 66, 696, 697
tape drive, 744

template (grid)
  book, using in, 222, 227
  creating, 182
  described, 169, 182, 762
  editing, 183
  layer
      annotation layer, including template
          instruction in, 183
      locking layer used in, 158
  layout consistency, as tool in achieving, 766
  Macintosh/Windows mixed environment, 712
  magazine, using in, 777–778
  naming, 182
  opening, 127, 129–130
  saving, 134–135, 182–183
  sharing, 711–712
  storage location, 182
  style versus, 442
text. *See also* font; story
  aligning
      baseline grid, to, 305, 399
      column text, 327, 396
      default alignment, setting, 107
      Paragraph pane, using, 10, 60, 396–397
      tab stop, using, 460, 462, 464
      table text, 467
      text frame, 247
  anti-aliasing, 99
  background, reversing against, 275, 426–427
  baseline
      grid, locking to, 305, 398–399
      shift, 90, 380, 381, 382
  body text, 775, 794, 796
  boldface, 11, 424, 791–792
  box (QuarkXPress), 359, 836
  byline, 776, 796
  cap, drop
      automatic, 420–422
      character style, applying to, 13
      creating, 11, 400–401, 420–422
      depth, 400
      described, 789
      kerning, 421
      newsletter, using in, 776
      quotation mark in, 422
      sizing, 11, 421
      style, as nested, 451
  cap, raised, 422, 789
  cap, small, 83, 380, 384, 387, 424
  character, special
      accent, 803–808
      Character Map utility, entering using,
          316, 464, 799

  deleting glyph, 801
  font, assigning to glyph, 801
  font, availability in, 317
  glyph set, creating, 799–801
  Glyphs pane, entering using, 61, 464
  highlighting substituted glyph, 86
  Insert Glyphs command, entering using, 104, 799
  Key Caps software, entering using, 315
  keyboard shortcut list, 801–803
  Macintosh environment, 315–316, 801–806
  PopChar X software, entering using, 316, 464, 799
  search and replace operation, finding in, 337–340
  Windows environment, 316–317, 801–806
character style
  Advanced Character Formats pane, adjusting
      using, 83
  applying, 13, 447–449
  creating, 12, 447–449
  default, changing, 110–111
  described, 441, 447
  drop cap, applying to, 13
  editing, 452
  fraction formatting, saving as, 430
  list, formatting using, 229
  manual formatting, combining with, 453
  naming, 448–449
  nesting, 425
  unapplying, 453–454
  updating, 375
color
  background, 248, 426–427
  design considerations, 432
  drop shadow, 437
  fill, 19, 432–433, 587, 588
  reversed text, 275, 426–427
  stroke, 432–433, 584–585
  Swatches pane, applying using, 62, 219, 410
  underline, 436
column
  aligning text in, 327, 396
  default setup, changing, 105
  guide, 152
  gutter, 125, 369, 761
  layout, adjusting, 151, 357
  Margin and Columns dialog box, adjusting
      using, 151
  master page, specifying in, 178, 179, 357, 369
  number of columns, specifying, 70, 125,
      282, 357, 358
  paragraph widow/orphan control, 408–409
  rule, intercolumn, 370–371
  text frame, adjusting in, 369–370

TOC, 777
    width, 369–370
composing, 403, 406, 407
copying, 82, 188, 326, 327–328, 333
default setup, changing, 107–108
deleting, 334
design considerations, 381–382, 424, 432,
        771–774, 775–776
dingbat, 417, 418, 419, 431, 776
displaying hidden character, 107, 327
dragging and dropping, 327–328
editing, 332–335
emboss effect, 779
entering, 47–48, 246, 247–248, 325–326, 333
exdenting, 788
exporting, 135, 136, 319–321, 331–332
feathering, 438, 788
fraction, formatting, 428–430
frame
    aligning, 247
    background color, 248, 426–427
    baseline, 351–352
    border, 248
    bounding box, 259
    column, adjusting in, 369–370
    creating, 4–5, 246–249, 325–326, 356–360
    default setup, changing, 108
    described, 245–246
    ellipse, 360
    entering text in, 7–9, 47–48, 246, 247–248, 333
    graphics frame, converting text frame to, 249
    import operation, overflowing during, 330
    inset, 351, 413, 430, 463, 464
    introduced, 43
    justifying text in, 352–353
    library, copying from, 188
    margin, 351
    master text frame, 124, 177, 247, 326, 357–360
    moving, 5–6, 248
    polygon, 360
    port, 366–367
    rectangular, 47, 360
    rotating, 779
    scaling, 435
    sizing, 4–5, 245, 247, 279, 333
    stroke, applying to, 248
    table row, breaking across multiple frames, 472
    TOC inserting in, 233–234
    wrap, ignoring in, 352, 358, 531
gradient, applying to, 219, 432–433, 585, 586, 587–588
graphic
    converting text to, 588–590
    font, converting graphic to, 419

frame, using text character as, 541
    importing text into graphics frame, 330
    letter, using graphic as capital, 420, 423, 780
    wrapping text around, 15, 525–532
Greek display, 99
highlighting, 85–86, 333, 685
hyperlink as character attribute, 682
hyphenation
    automatic, 402–404
    breakpoint calculation, 403–404, 407
    Character pane, controlling using, 404
    consecutive, 789
    Control palette, controlling using, 402, 404
    dash, conversion of double hyphen to, 318, 330
    described, 401–402, 789
    dialog box, 402–403
    dictionary, 94, 95, 347–349, 621, 789
    discretionary, 339, 388, 402, 789
    Macintosh/Windows mixed environment, 714
    manual, 402
    nonbreaking, 339, 388
    Paragraph pane, adjusting using, 10, 402
    preference, setting, 349–350
    printing, 621
    soft, 789
    spell checking, handling in, 94, 95
    zone, 789
importing
    autoflowing, 329
    canceling, 330
    dash conversion, 330
    endnote, 314
    file, text, 132, 311–315, 317–319, 331, 361
    footer, 314
    formatting, preserving, 309, 312–314, 329
    graphics frame, into, 330
    header, 314
    InCopy file, 312
    list, 417
    Macintosh to Windows, 310–311
    outline, importing into, 590
    overset, 330, 361
    Place command, using, 8–9, 46, 132, 361, 590
    positioning imported text, 328–329
    quotation mark conversion, 329, 331
    spreadsheet, 132, 314, 331
    style sheet, 329, 362–364, 446, 454–457, 710
    tab stop, 461
    Tagged Text, 331
    threaded text frame, into, 361
    Windows to Macintosh, 310–311
    word processor, from, 247–248, 311–314,
        318–319, 362–364, 417

Continued

text *(continued)*
  indenting
    block, 415–416, 789
    Control palette, using, 415–416
    default, 107
    described, 788
    first-line, 398, 414, 415
    hanging, 398, 414, 415, 416, 789
    list item, 414
    organizing content using, 414
    Paragraph pane, using, 12, 60, 398, 415–416
    tab, using, 327, 339, 398, 464
    text frame inset, 351, 413, 430, 463, 464
  italic, 382–383, 424, 773, 791, 796
  justifying
    carding, 788
    centered, 788
    Control palette, using, 11
    described, 402, 788
    design considerations, 774
    feathering, 788
    flush, 788
    frame, in, 352–353
    glyph scaling option, 405–406
    horizontal, 352–353
    leading, using, 406
    letter spacing option, 405–406
    object, next to, 86
    Paragraph pane, using, 11, 397
    ragged, 788
    vertical, 352–353, 788
    word spacing option, 405–406
    wrapping text, in, 86, 530–531
  kerning
    arrow key, adjusting using, 89, 90, 390
    Character pane, adjusting using, 59, 381, 390
    Control palette, adjusting using, 380, 390
    described, 389, 787
    drop caps, between, 421
    font kerning table, 389
    fraction formatting, in, 429
    highlighting, 86
    legibility considerations, 390
    manual, 390
    Metrics, 390
    Optical, 24, 390
    pair, 787–788
    QuarkXPress, 131, 389
    tracking compared, 391
  kicker, 426, 776, 796
  language, assigning to, 344–345, 381, 383–384
  leader character, 60, 463–464

leading
  arrow key, adjusting using, 89, 90
  automatic, 391, 392, 406, 543
  Character pane, adjusting using, 59
  character-by-character, 389
  default, specifying, 107
  described, 389, 391, 786
  font size, adjusting in function of, 391
  justification, using in, 406
  paragraph, applying to entire, 84, 389, 392, 396
  QuarkXPress, 84, 131, 391, 392
  set solid, 391
  text frame baseline, 352
  text wrap, judging in, 86, 531
legibility, 390, 420, 781
letter spacing, 405–406, 787
list
  bulleted, 414, 416–420, 789
  importing from word processor, 417
  indenting, 414
  numbered, 414, 416–420
  style, 229, 419–420
  TOC, creating using, 229
navigating, 332–333
outdenting, 398, 788
outlining, 377, 541, 574, 588–590
overset, 233, 330, 361, 366
PageMaker, 854–855
pane, 82–84, 384, 389, 472–473
paragraph
  baseline grid, locking to, 398–399
  Control palette, formatting using, 394–395,
    399, 408–409, 410
  default setup, changing, 107
  described, 393
  exdenting, 788
  keep options, 408–409
  labeling, 423–426
  leading, applying to entire, 84, 389, 392, 396
  outdenting, 398, 788
  return symbol (¶), displaying, 416
  rule, placing between paragraphs, 409–411
  selecting, 393
  spacing, 60, 399–400, 473
  widow/orphan control, 408–409
paragraph style
  applying, 445–446
  copying, 446
  creating, 12, 443–445, 446
  default, changing, 110–111
  deleting, 446
  described, 441
  editing, 363, 446, 452, 456

manual formatting, combining with, 394, 445, 453
naming, 444
nesting, 450–451
overriding imported, 363–364, 456–457
removing local formatting, 445
TOC, in, 229–230, 231–232
unapplying, 453–454
path
converting text to, 377, 541, 574, 588–590
placing text on path, 47, 48, 550–551
preference, setting, 82–84, 384, 389
pull quote, 428, 776, 796
punctuation, hanging, 60, 430–431
QuarkXPress
box, 359, 836
editing, 843
entry, 47
flow, 843
formatting, 436, 836, 844–845
kerning, 131, 389
leading, 84, 131, 391, 392
ligature, 386
tracking, 380
wrap, 842
quotation mark
drop cap, in initial, 422
import operation, conversion during, 329, 331
preference, setting, 83, 95
reversed text, 275, 426–427
rotating, 433–434, 467, 472
saving
JPEG, to, 136
RTF, to, 136
text file, to, 135
scaling
attribute, adjusting when, 84
Character pane, adjusting using, 59, 382
Control palette, adjusting using, 382
design considerations, 381–382, 424
emphasis, creating via, 424
frame, 435
glyph, 24, 405–406
mouse, using, 353
proportional, 84
Scale tool, using, 435
sizing versus, 435
searching and replacing, 335–342
selecting, 47, 84, 333, 375, 393
set solid, 391
shadow effect, applying to, 377, 382, 437–438, 780
sharing text file, 711
shearing, 279, 383

sizing
Character pane, using, 59, 83, 382
default size, specifying, 107
drop cap, 11
emphasis, creating via, 424
font size, using, 379–380, 421
optimal size, finding automatically, 83
scaling versus, 435
skewing, 382–383, 779, 780
source element, 711
spaceband, adjusting, 404
spell checking
accessing spell checker, 68
capitalization, handling, 96, 342
dictionary, 94–96, 107, 344, 345–350, 383–384
hyphenation, handling, 94, 95
language, specifying, 94–95, 344–345,
     349, 383–384
Macintosh/Windows mixed environment, 714
note, 874–875
preference, setting, 96, 349–350
skipping text, 345
specifying text to check, 342–343
word repetition, handling, 343–344
workgroup environment, 346, 708, 710
strikethrough, 380, 385, 435–436
stroke, applying to, 24, 377, 433, 581–587, 588
subscript, 83, 380, 384–385, 430
superscript, 83, 380, 384–385, 430
tab
aligning using tab stop, 460, 462, 464
creating tab stop, 60, 463, 465
deleting tab stop, 464, 465
displaying, 461, 464, 465
importing tab stop, 461
indenting using, 327, 339, 398, 464
leader character, 60, 463–464
overriding automatic tab stop, 459
positioning tab stop, 60, 462–463, 464–465
ruler, 464–465
table, converting tabbed text to/from, 478–479
table
aligning text in, 467, 472
cell overflow indicator, 477
converting to/from, 478–479
inserting in, 467
tag line, 773
Tagged Text format, 132, 136, 319–322, 331
tool, 136, 333
tracking
Character pane, adjusting using, 59, 381, 391
Control palette, adjusting using, 380

Continued

text, tracking *(continued)*
    described, 389, 787
    effect, creating special using, 780
    highlighting, 86
    kerning compared, 391
    legibility considerations, 390
    QuarkXPress, 389
transparency, 538
typestyle, 376, 377–379
underlining, 380, 385, 424, 435–436
undoing text edit, 334, 337
wingding, 417, 419, 431
word spacing, 405–406, 787
wrap
    area below object, restricting to, 86
    boundary, creating using alpha channel, 529
    boundary, shaping, 532
    bounding box, around, 15, 528–529
    clipping path, around, 526, 529, 534
    default, 108
    described, 761
    frame, around, 526, 527–529, 531
    global options, 530–531
    graphic, around, 15, 525–532
    ignoring, 352, 358, 526, 531
    justifying text next to object, 86, 530–531
    layer, suppressing around object on hidden, 160
    leading, judging in, 86, 531
    master page, 529
    preference, setting, 86, 530
    pull quote, around, 428
    QuarkXPress, 842
    sidebar, around, 428
    text frame, ignoring in, 352, 358, 531
    Text Wrap pane, adjusting using, 16, 61,
        108, 526–531
XML
    applying to text, 698
    encoding, 701
    snippet, text, 701
zooming, 332
Text Frame Options dialog box
    accessing, 108
    baseline, adjusting using, 351–352
    column, adjusting using, 358
    described, 108
    Ignore Text Wrap option, 526
    justification, adjusting using, 352
    spacing, adjusting using, 351, 358, 413
    text wrap
        adjusting using, 352, 358, 531
        ignoring, 526
Text Path tool, 550

Text Wrap pane, 16, 61, 108, 526–531
threading
    autoflow, 364, 367–368, 370
    breaking thread, 368
    described, 355
    displaying thread, 72, 110, 365, 366
    icons associated with, 370
    importing text into threaded text frame, 361
    manual, 364–365
    order of text flow, default, 365
    port, 366–367
    rerouting, 368
    selection tool used, 46, 365
    semi-autoflow, 364, 366, 370
    Type tool, using, 48
three-hole-punched publication, 140
thumbnail
    file, saving thumbnail view of first page with, 100
    layout, using to visualize, 768, 769
    library thumbnail view, 187
    printing, 634, 768, 769
TIFF (Tagged Image File Format)
    byte order, 490
    clipping path, setting in TIFF file, 490, 532
    color, 212, 213, 490
    compression, 490
    importing TIFF file, 484, 486, 489, 490–491, 501–502
    Macintosh considerations, 490
    OPI information, 503
tilde (~) dictionary hyphenation point marker, 348–349
tint
    bitmap, 519
    creating, 203–204
    deleting, 209
    editing, 207–208
    grayscale, tinting, 780
    stroke, of, 268, 271–272
title bar, 33–36
Tittel, Ed (*XML For Dummies*, 3rd Edition), 696
TOC (table of contents)
    banner, 777
    bookmark, 232, 664, 687
    chapter, dedicating to, 233
    column, 777
    creating, 230–233
    described, 229
    frame, inserting in, 233–234
    generating, 233–234
    graphic, including on, 777
    layer, including hidden in, 232–233
    layout, 777
    length, checking, 233
    level of entry, changing, 232

list, creating using, 229
logo, 777
magazine, of, 777
overset text option, 233
page number, formatting, 232, 777
planning, 229–230
QuarkXPress, 230, 233
sorting, 232
style, 229–231, 233
title, 231
updating, 233, 234
Tool Tip display, 40–41, 81
tool, using appropriate, 28
toolbar (Macintosh), 864
Toolbox. *See* Tools palette
Tools ➪ Folder Options, 708
Tools ➪ Macros ➪ Microsoft Script Editor, 733
Tools palette. *See also specific tool*
accessing, 42
closing, 42
color buttons, 52–53
described, 40–41
orientation, 42, 43
pop-out tool display, 42, 44
Restore/Maximize check box, 43
selecting tool from, 42
shortcut set, 41–42
view buttons, 53
Zoom check box, 43
Toyo color, 203, 210, 211, 597, 814
trackball, 749
tracking, text
Character pane, adjusting using, 59, 381, 391
Control palette, adjusting using, 380
described, 389, 787
effect, creating special using, 780
highlighting, 86
kerning compared, 391
legibility considerations, 390
QuarkXPress, 389
Transform pane
accessing, 279
cloning using, 300, 514
Control palette compared, 282, 364, 513–514
flipping using, 281, 516–517
graphic, applying transformation to using, 513–514
grid, 263, 265, 514
introduced, 61
line, formatting using, 48
positioning using, 49, 263–264, 358
rotating using, 61, 253, 280–282, 434, 515–516
scaling using, 265, 281, 515
shearing using, 266, 279, 513

Show Content Offset option, 282
sizing using, 247, 250, 380
skewing using, 516
stroke weight, adjusting using, 281
Transform Content option, 281
Transform Group Content option, 282
Transformations Are Totals option, 282
zero point, 36
transformation. *See also specific transformation*
Control palette, applying using, 282
design considerations, 764
EPS file, applying to, 508
frame, applying to, 276–282
Free Transform tool, applying using, 50, 512
graphic, applying to, 510–514
group of objects, applying to, 289
path, applying to, 560
transparency
alpha channel, 501–502, 529
blending mode, 538–540
DCS, 630
drop shadow, 437
EPS format, 677
flattening, 64, 645, 652–655, 668, 677
gradient, 215
knockout group, 540
layer, 538
pane, 56, 64, 538
path, 573
PDF, 81, 504, 668
PNG, 502
preset, 645, 652–653, 654, 655, 669
printing, 64, 639, 644–645, 652–655
QuarkXPress, 652, 847
stitching, 654
text, 538
vellum effect, creating using, 538
Transparency Flattener Preset Options
dialog box, 652–653
Trap Presets pane, 64, 65, 606
Trap Styles pane, 606
trapping, color, 603–610, 639, 648
Truekeys software, 751
TrueType font
PostScript versus, 752
printing, 614, 615, 616, 792
support, 754, 792
translating, 751
Trumatch color, 203, 210, 212, 597, 813
Type ➪ Character Styles, 12
Type ➪ Create Outlines, 541
Type ➪ Font, 378
Type ➪ Glyphs, 417

Type ⇨ Insert Character, 464
Type ⇨ Insert Glyphs, 104
Type ⇨ Insert Special Character, 417
Type ⇨ Insert Special Character ⇨ Auto Page
    Number, 145
Type ⇨ Insert Special Character ⇨ End Nested Style, 452
Type ⇨ Insert Special Character ⇨ Next Page
    Number, 146
Type ⇨ Insert Special Character ⇨ Previous Page
    Number, 146
Type ⇨ Insert Special Character ⇨ Right Indent Tab, 432
Type Manager software, 753
Type menu, 70–71, 374
Type on a Path tool, 48
Type ⇨ Paragraph, 392
Type ⇨ Paragraph Styles, 12
Type Reunion software, 753
Type ⇨ Show Hidden Characters, 107
Type ⇨ Size, 379
Type ⇨ Story, 107
Type tool
    accessing, 41
    Character pane, working with while open, 375
    selecting text using, 47
    selection tool, switching to/from, 45, 365
    text frame, creating using, 247–248, 325–326
    threading using, 48
typeface, 376, 377–379, 424, 429, 790–796. *See also* font
typestyle, 376, 377–379. *See also* font
typographer, 373
typography. *See* font; kerning; leading

U

.udc files, 714
Underline Options dialog box, 436
undoing change
    alignment operation, 304
    layer deletion, 167
    preference change, 79
    redoing undone action, 135
    reverting to previous document version, 134, 135
    search/replace operation, 337
    table cell split, 476
    text edit, 334, 337
UniDoc Systems Truekeys software, 751
Uniform Resource Locator. *See* URL
unit of measurement
    font, of, 88, 89, 786
    ruler, of, 36, 87–88, 123
Units & Increments pane, 36, 87–90
Unlock Zero Point command, 36
Updates pane, 100
upgrading from prior version of InDesign, 821–822

URL (Uniform Resource Locator)
    button, assigning to, 691
    hyperlink, assigning to, 683, 685
User dialog box (InCopy), 876

V

VBA (Visual Basic for Applications)
    condition, testing, 737
    documentation, 732
    editor, 733
    labeling item, 736
    Rem statement, 737
    running, 734
    saving, 734
    support, 725
    VBScript, relation to, 731
    versions available, 733
VBScript, 731–734
VBScript in a Nutshell (Lomax and Petrusha), 732
vector graphic
    display quality default, setting, 99
    importing, 484, 486–489, 503–504
    rasterizing, 487, 504
vellum effect, creating using transparency, 538
view. *See also* zooming
    baseline grid view threshold, 91, 195
    Bleed mode, 53
    default setup, changing, 109–110
    Navigator pane features, 115–116
    Normal, 53
    percentage, presetting, 38
    preference, setting, 98–99
    Preview Mode, 53
    ruler guide view threshold, 193
    Slug mode, 43, 53, 125, 636–637, 667
    story view, 877–878
    Tools palette view buttons, 53
View ⇨ Display Master Items, 116, 181
View ⇨ Fit in Window, 91
View ⇨ Fit Page in Window, 33
View ⇨ Fit Spread in Window, 112
View ⇨ Hide Changes (InCopy), 879
View ⇨ Hide Frame Edges, 110
View ⇨ Hide Guides, 110
View ⇨ Hide Rulers, 36, 110
View ⇨ Lock Guides, 110
View menu, 72–73, 113–114
View ⇨ Overprint Preview, 650
View ⇨ Show Baseline Grid, 90
View ⇨ Show Document Grid, 92
View ⇨ Show Frame Edges, 160
View ⇨ Show Guides, 92
View ⇨ Show Ruler, 88

View ⇨ Show Rulers, 191
View ⇨ Show Text Threads, 110
View ⇨ Show/Hide Baseline Grid, 195
View ⇨ Show/Hide Document Grid, 196
View ⇨ Show/Hide Frame Edges, 116
View ⇨ Snap to Document Grid, 110
View ⇨ Snap to Guides, 110
View ⇨ Structure ⇨ Hide Structure, 699
View ⇨ Structure ⇨ Show Tagged Frames, 698
View ⇨ Structure ⇨ View Tag Markers, 698
virgule, 429
Visual Basic for Applications. *See* VBA
Visual Basic 6 For Dummies (Wang), 732

W

Wang, Wallace (*Visual Basic 6 For Dummies*), 732
warning dialog, resetting, 82
WAV files, 691
Web color library, 203
web offset printing, 603, 659
white
    point, 596
    space, 389, 762, 764, 772, 781
wild card, searching, 340
Wilton, Paul (*Beginning JavaScript*), 728
window
    activating, 117
    cascading, 117
    closing all windows, 117
    fitting to, 33, 91, 112, 114, 149
    Mac OS X window environment, 864
    maximizing/minimizing, 33, 35, 864
    tiling, 117, 301
Window ⇨ Align, 302
Window ⇨ Arrange ⇨ Cascade, 117
Window ⇨ Arrange ⇨ New Window, 117
Window ⇨ Arrange ⇨ Tile, 117
Window ⇨ Attributes, 108
Window ⇨ Change Info (InCopy), 879
Window ⇨ Color, 108
Window ⇨ Gradient, 108
Window ⇨ Interactive ⇨ Bookmarks, 687
Window ⇨ Interactive ⇨ Hyperlinks, 682
Window ⇨ Layers, 156
Window menu, 73–74
Window ⇨ Navigator, 115
Window ⇨ Output Preview ⇨ Flattener, 654
Window ⇨ Output Preview ⇨ Separations, 650
Window ⇨ Pages, 141, 174
Window ⇨ Paths (Photoshop), 533
Window ⇨ Scripting ⇨ Script Label, 736
Window ⇨ Story List (InCopy), 878
Window ⇨ Stroke, 108

Window ⇨ Swatches, 199
Window ⇨ Tools, 42
Window ⇨ Transparency, 538
Window ⇨ Trap Presets, 606
Window ⇨ Type & Tables ⇨ Character, 59
Window ⇨ Type & Tables ⇨ Character Styles, 60
Window ⇨ Type & Tables ⇨ Glyphs, 61
Window ⇨ Type & Tables ⇨ Index, 235
Window ⇨ Type & Tables ⇨ Paragraph, 60
Window ⇨ Type & Tables ⇨ Paragraph Styles, 60
Window ⇨ Type & Tables ⇨ Story, 60
Window ⇨ Type & Tables ⇨ Table, 466
Window ⇨ Type & Tables ⇨ Tabs, 60
Window ⇨ Type & Tables ⇨ Text Wrap, 15
Window ⇨ Workspace ⇨ Save Workspace, 55
Windows
    character, entering special in, 316–317, 801–806
    font, 754–755
    Macintosh/Windows mixed environment
        color, 714
        file naming, 715–716
        filename extension, 493, 713, 715
        font, 716–717, 751, 795
        graphic, 490, 493
        hyphenation, 714
        InDesign Defaults file, sharing, 709, 714
        medium used for data transfer, 717, 743–745
        network connectivity, 745, 865
        opening PC-generated file in Macintosh, 714
        OS X, 717, 745, 865
        plug-in, 714
        printer, 747–748
        script, sharing, 714
        service bureau, 713
        shortcut set, sharing, 714
        spell checking, 714
        style, 714
        template, 712
        text, transferring, 310–311
    Recycle Bin, 249
    system requirement, 742, 819
wingding, 417, 419, 431
WinZip software, 750
wireless connectivity, 745–746
WMF (Windows Metafile), importing, 484, 486, 489, 503
word
    processor
        choosing, 750
        fast-save feature, 318
        importing from, 247–248, 311–314, 318–319,
            331, 362–364
        list format considerations, 417

Continued

word, processor *(continued)*
    style sheet from, handling, 362–364
    version considerations, 319
    Word dash conversion feature, 318, 330
  repetition, handling during spell check, 343–344
  spacing, 405–406, 787
workflow, 136, 157, 170, 241
workgroup environment. *See also* InCopy; Windows, Macintosh/Windows mixed environment
  color, sharing, 216, 708, 709–710
  graphic, sharing, 711
  InDesign Defaults file, sharing, 709, 714
  Internet connectivity, 746–747
  library, sharing, 184, 187, 709, 711
  master disk, 707
  master page, sharing, 712–713
  network connectivity, 744–746, 747
  note functionality, 874–875
  plug-in, sharing, 708, 714
  preference, setting, 79, 825
  Presets folder, sharing, 708
  revision, tracking, 879
  script, sharing, 708, 714
  shortcut set, sharing, 708, 714
  spell checking, 346, 708, 710
  standard, importance of establishing, 707
  story, sharing, 875–879
  style sheet, sharing, 364, 710, 714
  template, sharing, 711–712
  text file, sharing, 711
  workspace, sharing, 708
workspace
  described, 32
  naming, 55
  palette collection, 55
  QuarkXPress, 839
  saving, 55
  sharing, 708
  storage location, 32, 78, 708

X

XML (Extensible Markup Language)
  attribute
    adding/removing, 700
    hiding, 701
  commenting code, 695, 700, 701
  DTD, 695, 700–701
  element
    adding/removing, 700
    root, 700
  exporting, 136, 698, 701–703

  frame, applying to, 700
  GoLive, packaging for, 135, 703
  graphic, outputting to, 702–703
  header, 695
  HTML compared, 695
  importing, 696–697, 700
  processing instruction, 695, 700, 701
  style, mapping to tag, 65, 697–698, 701
  syntax error alert, 698
  tag
    applying, 698–700
    color, 698
    creating, 697
    importing, 696–697
    order, 697
    removing, 699
    style mapping, 65, 697–698, 701
    syntax, 695
  text
    applying to, 698
    encoding, 701
    snippet, 701
  validating, 700
  viewing, 38
  XMP information, embedding, 703
XML For Dummies, 3rd Edition (Tittel), 696
XML Structure window, 38
XMP (eXtensible Metadata Platform), 703
X-Rite Monitor Optimizer color calibrator, 596
XTension, QuarkXPress, 131

Z

zero point, 36, 382
Zip
  compression, 666
  drive, 744
zooming
  displaying multiple magnifications simultaneously, 117
  document window Zoom box, using, 114, 115
  hyperlink zoom setting, 684
  keyboard shortcut, using, 332
  maximum, 112
  Navigator pane zoom control, using, 115, 149
  pasteboard, 114
  preset, 112, 114
  text, 332
  Tools palette Zoom check box, 43
  View menu, using, 72, 113–114
  window, fitting to, 33, 91, 112, 114, 149
  Zoom tool, using, 52, 112–113, 332